**Foundations of
Migration Economics**

IZA Prize in Labor Economics Series

Since 2002, the IZA – Institute of Labor Economics has awarded the IZA Prize in Labor Economics for outstanding contributions to policy-relevant labor market research and methodological progress in this sub-discipline of economic science. The IZA Prize is the only international science prize awarded exclusively to labor economists. This special focus acknowledges the global significance of high-quality basic research in labor economics and sound policy advice based on these research findings. As issues of employment and unemployment are among the most urgent challenges of our time, labor economists have an important task and responsibility. The IZA Prize in Labor Economics is today considered one of the most prestigious international awards in the field. It aims to stimulate further research on topics that have enormous implications for our future. All prize-winners contribute a volume to the IZA Prize in Labor Economics Series published by Oxford University Press, which has been established to provide an overview of the laureates' most significant findings.

The IZA Prize in Labor Economics has become an integral part of the institute's manifold activities to promote progress in labor market research. Based on nominations submitted by the IZA Research Fellows, a high-ranking IZA Prize Committee selects the prize-winner.

It is not by coincidence that the IZA Prize in Labor Economics Series is published by Oxford University Press. This well-reputed publishing house has shown a great interest in the project from the very beginning as this exclusive series perfectly complements their range of publications. We gratefully acknowledge their excellent cooperation.

Winners of the IZA Prize in Labor Economics

2011   George J. Borjas (Harvard University)
           Barry R. Chiswick (George Washington University)
2010   Francine D. Blau (Cornell University)
2009   Richard A. Easterlin (University of Southern California)
2008   Richard Layard (London School of Economics)
           Stephen J. Nickell (Nuffield College)
2007   Richard B. Freeman (Harvard University)
2006   David Card (University of California, Berkeley)
           Alan B. Krueger (Princeton University)
2005   Dale T. Mortensen (Northwestern University)
           Christopher A. Pissarides (London School of Economics)
2004   Edward P. Lazear (Stanford University)
2003   Orley C. Ashenfelter (Princeton University)
2002   Jacob Mincer (Columbia University)

George J. Borjas – Barry R. Chiswick
2011 IZA Prize Laureates

Foundations of Migration Economics

George J. Borjas and Barry R. Chiswick

Edited by
Benjamin Elsner

OXFORD
UNIVERSITY PRESS

OXFORD

UNIVERSITY PRESS

Great Clarendon Street, Oxford, OX2 6DP,
United Kingdom

Oxford University Press is a department of the University of Oxford.
It furthers the University's objective of excellence in research, scholarship,
and education by publishing worldwide. Oxford is a registered trade mark of
Oxford University Press in the UK and in certain other countries

Published in the United States of America by Oxford University Press
198 Madison Avenue, New York, NY 10016, United States of America

British Library Cataloguing in Publication Data
Data available

Library of Congress Control Number: 2018950698

ISBN 978-0-19-878807-2

Printed and bound by
CPI Group (UK) Ltd, Croydon, CR0 4YY

Links to third party websites are provided by Oxford in good faith and
for information only. Oxford disclaims any responsibility for the materials
contained in any third party website referenced in this work.

Award Statement
of the IZA Prize Committee

The IZA Prize in Labor Economics 2011 is awarded to George J. Borjas (Harvard University) and Barry R. Chiswick (George Washington University) for their fundamental contributions to the economic analysis of migration. With their groundbreaking work, Borjas and Chiswick have set the stage for assessing migration flows and immigrant assimilation, as well as the consequences of immigration for the labor markets and welfare systems of host countries. They have been the leading figures in the intense debate about earnings assimilation and the nature of migrant selectivity. In an era in which human mobility has been rapidly increasing, and in which global differences in labor market performance pose important questions for the design of migration policies, Borjas' and Chiswick's work provided researchers and policy-makers with the necessary instruments to study some of the most pressing questions in public policy. Their research is distinguished by a focus on thought-provoking questions, rigorous theoretical and empirical analysis, policy-relevance, and accessibility to a wide audience.

Barry R. Chiswick pioneered the economic analysis of immigration with his seminal 1978 paper in the Journal of Political Economy, "The Effect of Americanization on the Earnings of Foreign-Born Men". Putting human capital in the center of the measurement of immigrant earnings, the paper provided the framework for much of the subsequent research on immigrant adjustment. Chiswick made the migration area a fully-fledged field in labor economics and explained immigrant behavior with simple, intuitive and understandable economics. His 1978 paper constitutes a starting point for profound discussions on how immigrants fare relative to natives in the host country's labor market, and what determines their labor market success. The human capital framework provides a better understanding of the relevance of immigrants' educational attainment, differences in assimilation between ethnic groups, or occupational concentration of migrants. In his fundamental 1985 paper in the Journal of Labor Economics, "Assimilation, Changes in Cohort Quality, and the Earnings of Immigrants," George J. Borjas demonstrated the importance of considering differences in cohort characteristics when gauging the speed of immigrants' earnings adjustment. Comparing the 1970 and 1980 waves of U.S. census data, he showed that the availability of longitudinal data is vital for assessing the speed of earnings assimilation. The results underlined that some groups of immigrants may never attain earnings parity with native-born workers. Borjas found that older immigrant cohorts may catch up to the earnings of natives, but that more recent cohorts faced severe assimilation problems, indicating lower endowments of recently arrived immigrants in terms of education or language ability. The work of Borjas and Chiswick suggests that carefully designed migration policies are paramount for the successful labor market integration of immigrants.

Barry R. Chiswick has also written extensively on language proficiency and its effects on migrant assimilation. He developed a theoretical framework in which the acquisition of language can be analyzed, and has subsequently tested the model using data from labor markets in numerous countries. He has addressed a wide range of essential questions regarding the determinants of language proficiency, and the impact of language ability on migrants' labor market success. Chiswick's 2007 book The Economics of Language (co-authored by Paul W. Miller) provides an encompassing overview of the most important results from their research. The book has contributed to a better understanding of the theory, conditions, and consequences of language acquisition and the processes of migrant integration as a whole. By empirically establishing a link between linguistic capital and economic advancement, Chiswick's analyses underscore the importance of education and language skills for socioeconomic mobility.

George J. Borjas has broadened the scope of migration research to further questions that are central for evaluating the impact of migration and for designing immigration policy. First, Borjas turned the attention to the question how immigration affects the host country's population. His thoughtful empirical analysis has provided a much more nuanced view on whether and why certain subgroups of natives are particularly affected by the inflow of immigrants. Borjas' fundamental contributions provided a coherent theoretical and empirical framework in which the welfare effects and distributional consequences of immigration can be studied. In addition to a continuous stream of innovative research papers on these topics, Borjas has also produced two influential books on immigration and immigration policy, including his 1999 book Heaven's Door: Immigration Policy and the American Economy. These books have helped put migration at the top of the political agenda in many countries.

George J. Borjas and Barry R. Chiswick have stimulated a tremendous amount of research by many academics all over the world. The immense contribution of these scholars also lies in their empirical ingenuity and their deep understanding of data. They raised issues about the inadequacy of existing data and developed new techniques, emphasizing the importance of high-quality micro level data for examining serious public policy questions. Their work has served as a role model for many subsequent researchers, and it has been the basis for the rapid growth of interest in the analysis of immigration during the past three decades.

The IZA Prize in Labor Economics 2011 honors the work of two exceptional scholars who have greatly advanced our understanding of some of the most important questions in modern labor market research.

George J. Borjas is the Robert W. Scrivner Professor of Economics and Social Policy at the John F. Kennedy School of Government at Harvard University. He received his Ph.D. in Economics from Columbia University in 1975. Prior to moving to Harvard in 1995, he was a Professor of Economics at the University of California, San Diego and at the University of California, Santa Barbara. Borjas was elected fellow of the Econometric Society in 1998 and fellow of the Society of Labor Economists in 2004. He is also a Research Associate at the National Bureau of Economic Research. Borjas has served as an editor of the Review of Economics and Statistics, and has been on the editorial boards of the Quarterly Journal of Economics and the International Migration Review. Borjas was a member of the Council of Economic Advisors for the Governor of California and of the National Academy of Sciences Panel on the Demographic and Economic Impact of Immigration. He served as a consultant to the World Bank and various governmental agencies, and he chaired the National Science Foundation's Committee of Visitors for the Economics Program. Borjas is also the author of the widely used textbook, Labor Economics, now in its sixth edition.

Barry R. Chiswick is Professor and Chair of the Department of Economics at the Columbian College of Arts and Sciences at George Washington University. He received his Ph.D. in Economics from Columbia University in 1967. Prior to joining George Washington University in 2011, he was UIC Distinguished Professor at the University of Illinois at Chicago. He also held academic positions at UCLA, Columbia University, the City University of New York, and the U.S. President's Council of Economic Advisers. Chiswick is a former chairman of the American Statistical Association Census Advisory Committee, and past president of the European Society for Population Economics. He serves on the editorial boards of the Journal of Population Economics, Research in Economics of the Household, and four other academic journals. Chiswick has received numerous awards for his research, including a Fulbright Research Fellowship, the Senior University Scholar Award from the University of Illinois, the Carleton C. Qualey Article Award from the Immigration History Society, the Marshall Sklare Award from the Association for the Social Scientific Study of Jewry, and the Milken Institute Award for Distinguished Economic Research. He has also served as a consultant to the World Bank, the United Nations, and several U.S. Government agencies.

George A. Akerlof   University of California, Berkeley; IZA
Marco Caliendo   IZA
Richard Portes   London Business School; President CEPR
Jan Svejnar   University of Michigan, Ann Arbor; IZA
Klaus F. Zimmermann   IZA; University of Bonn

Contents

Contents

Contents

Contents

Part I
Introduction by the Editor

Laying the Foundations of Migration Economics

Benjamin Elsner

The IZA Prize in Labor Economics 2011 was awarded to two exceptional scholars who laid the foundations of migration economics. From the beginning of their research agendas in the mid-1970s, the works of George Borjas and Barry Chiswick have shaped the way economists and policymakers think about migration. Up through the current decade, both remain influential figures in research and policy.

Migration these days is as topical as ever. 3 percent of the world population live outside their country of birth, and this figure is projected to increase dramatically in the future. Climate change, conflicts, but also better education in developing countries will lead to more international migration, and will present new challenges to the societies in the sending and receiving countries.

Given the changes it brings to society, migration has been at the center of the political debate in most Western countries. And while it can benefit the countries of destination – and almost certainly benefits the migrants themselves – many people fear the negative consequences through its impact on labor markets or its cultural impact on society. Recent events underline that migration is a highly controversial issue in the public debate. In Europe, the massive inflow of refugees from Syria, North Africa, and other parts of the world, has triggered a resurgence of fear-mongering right-wing parties, and led to a rift between countries willing to host refugees and those who are not. Moreover, the anti-EU camp in the run-up to the British Brexit referendum actively campaigned for severe migration restrictions, blaming immigration for the country's perceived economic problems, and claiming that immigration drains public finances. Similar arguments were expressed during the 2016 presidential campaign in the U.S.

The public debate on migration is often based on emotions, false perceptions, and an ignorance of basic facts. The expressed opinions tend to be either black or white: either one is completely for migration and only highlights its benefits for society, or one completely opposes migration and only highlights its costs. Economists have an important role here, as their models provide a structured way of thinking about the economic and social impacts of migration, along with a thorough empirical analysis that establishes reliable facts. It is thanks to Barry Chiswick and George Borjas that migration economics managed to provide this theoretical and empirical toolbox, and keeps growing in importance in academic and policy circles.

Both laureates have written numerous articles and books on immigration over the decades. Only a small portion of their research productivity could be included in this volume. The effort was made to include representative samples of this research, including evidence of the interactions between them, even though they never actually co-authored. The choice of papers for inclusion was made by the editor in consultation with the laureates.

Before becoming interested in migration, both scholars acquired a strong background in labor economics. Both received their Ph.D. degrees from Columbia University – Chiswick in 1967, Borjas in 1975 –, where they learned the basics of the profession from some of the most prominent labor economists at the time: Jacob Mincer, Gary Becker and a young James Heckman. Around the start of their careers, migration was becoming an important issue in U.S. policy, but was not yet considered an important research topic among economists. The work of both scholars permanently changed this perception. Migration economics has established itself as an important field of economics, with hundreds of papers having been written in the last 30 years. In these papers it is difficult to find a single one that does not cite the works of both prize winners. While their research often addressed similar aspects, both approached migration from different angles. Chiswick, who had previously studied human capital formation and its impact on the wage distribution, viewed migration through the lens of a human capital model. The key question of his research was, and is, "Why do some immigrants fare better than others, and what can policy do to improve the lives of immigrants, and integrate them better in society?" He pioneered migration economics with his 1978 paper on the wage assimilation of foreign-born men in the U.S. This paper presented the first rigorous analysis of the economic integration of migrants, showing that the wages of immigrants increase with time spent in the U.S., and that the wages of immigrants eventually overtake those of natives. Chiswick explains this finding with the imperfect transferability of human capital. Immigrants initially face a disadvantage in the labor market, but through their investment in country-specific human capital, they eventually catch up with natives. Even today, almost 40 years later, this paper proves very insightful. Chiswick alludes to many topics that have eventually become important strands of the literature, such as self-selection, job mobility, employer learning, discrimination, occupational licensing, and citizenship. One dimension of human capital that particularly interested Chiswick is language skills. In his groundbreaking work on the language skills of immigrants, resulting in numerous articles and a book with Paul Miller in 2007, he highlights the importance of speaking, reading, and writing skills for immigrants' success in the host country.

Borjas' work on immigration was written after his previous research on discrimination and labor turnover. It began with a re-examination of Chiswick's 1978 paper on wage assimilation and Chiswick's concerns about the extent that cross-sectional earnings profiles would be biased estimates of longitudinal (life-cycle) profiles for immigrants, as expressed in his 1980 U.S. Department of Labor Report. In Borjas' 1985 paper, with the availability of the 1980 U.S. census he was able to disentangle age from cohort effects in the wage assimilation of migrants, showing that wage assimilation is much more muted when one takes into account that the newly arrived cohorts were less skilled than previous immigrant cohorts. Three topics are central to his research agenda: the self-selection of immigrants – i.e. the question why some people migrate and others don't –, the impact of the ethnic concentration in neighborhoods on the economic outcomes of migrants and their children, and the impact of migration on labor markets and the broader economy.

Over the last 40 years, the research paths of both scholars crossed many times. As this volume will show, both were not always in agreement on the appropriate theoretical framework and empirical approach through which to analyze and interpret migration data. For the profession, these academic disagreements proved particularly fruitful. Whenever both came to different conclusions on the same topic, one could be sure that this topic was of greatest importance. Exciting work often followed, both by the prize winners themselves and by younger generations of migration scholars who refined the theoretical and empirical methods and tested the original hypotheses in many countries and contexts.

Borjas and Chiswick still play a vital role in research and policy. Chiswick's recent work on managing migration in the 21st century, published in Part VI of this volume, proves highly topical in the current policy discussion in Europe and the U.S. Borjas' recent research on the inflow of Soviet-trained mathematicians to the U.S. demonstrates that even the immigration of some of the smartest people in the world has non-negligible consequences for equally high-skilled natives. Moreover, his forthcoming book, We Wanted Workers, summarizes the most important empirical facts about migration for a non-academic audience, and shows with simple examples how immigration can have benefits for some parts of the population while imposing costs on others.

This volume represents a collection of the most important works of both scholars. It is organized in six parts. After an introductory Part I, Part II is concerned with the work of both scholars on the wage assimilation of migrants. Part III considers the role of ethnic networks and neighborhoods for the success of migrants and their children, to which both scholars contributed substantially in the 1990s. Part IV covers Barry Chiswick's work on the language skills of immigrants, while Part V covers Borjas' work on the impact and the efficiency gains from migration, and the impact of migration on wages and employment. Part VI closes the volume with both scholars' views on migration today.

Part II is centered around the question why some migrants do so much better than others, the question that started the modern economics of migration. The seven articles in this part revolve around two broad topics. The first is the wage assimilation of immigrants, i.e. the question whether and at what rate the wages of immigrants converge to those of natives, and why this is the case. The second topic is the self-selection of immigrants, i.e. why some people migrate while others stay in the sending country, and to what extent this can explain why some immigrant groups are more successful in the U.S. than others. The Prize laureates reached different conclusions about the pattern of immigrant wage assimilation in the U.S. Chiswick, in Chapter 1 in this volume, finds in the 1970 U.S. census that immigrants' earnings increase with time spent in the U.S. and eventually overtake those of natives. Borjas, in Chapter 2, challenged this finding, showing that the duration-earnings profile is partially explained by older cohorts having a higher earnings potential than younger cohorts. Chiswick in turn, in Chapter 3, re-examined the hypothesis that the skill levels of immigrant cohorts has declined over time, and found mixed results. On the one hand, the composition of the source countries shifted from Europe and Canada towards Asia, with Asian immigrants having higher education levels than Europeans and Canadians. On the other hand, the rise of illegal migration and family reunifications lowered the skill levels of more recent immigration cohorts.

Overall, it appears that the duration-earnings profile has shifted. Newer migrants have a lower entry wage, but face a higher return to human capital. When compared at their entry into the U.S., later cohorts are indeed doing worse than earlier ones. But this difference disappears once both are compared ten years after immigration. In a further study (Chapter 5), Chiswick tested alternative hypotheses that can explain his original finding of immigrant wage assimilation. An important alternative hypothesis is selective outmigration; if the least able immigrants return home, the average ability of the immigrant cohort increases mechanically. Using the first available longitudinal data, he finds little support for this hypothesis. Rather, the analysis confirms that immigrants from countries with a low skill transferability invest more in their human capital and experience steeper wage increases over time.

While most of the literature on immigrant wage assimilation focuses on low-skilled immigrants, Chiswick's recent paper with Paul Miller (Chapter 7) shows that different assimilation patterns can be observed for high-skilled immigrants. The chapter is motivated by a fascinating question: if incomes across rich countries are similar, why would anyone migrate between those countries? In a theoretical model he shows that people only move if they receive an exceptionally high draw from the distribution of wage offers abroad. However, the high wage offer leaves little incentive for further investments in human capital, because wages cannot increase much further. As a result, the wages of high-skilled immigrants typically stagnate while those of high-skilled natives increase over time.

A further topic to which both scholars made a substantial contribution is the self-selection of migrants. The central question of this research is why some people leave a country while others stay. Motivated by the observation that some immigrant groups are doing much better in the U.S. than others, both explored to what extent this difference was driven by the self-selection of immigrants from the countries of origin, and what economic and political factors drive the selection pattern. In Chapter 4 Borjas presents a simple theory that views the self-selection of immigrants through the lens of a Roy model. This paper challenges the conventional wisdom that migrants are positively selected from their home country, i.e. the best and brightest migrate while everyone else stays put. In the model, negative selection can occur if the income distribution of the sending country is more unequal than the one in the receiving country, giving low-skilled people a larger incentive to migrate than high-skilled people.

In Chapter 6, Chiswick addresses this question using a human capital model. He identifies two opposing forces that shape the pattern of self-selection. On the one hand, a greater earnings inequality in the sending country encourages more low-skilled migration. On the other hand, low-skilled workers earn less than the high-skilled, but both face the same out-of-pocket costs of migration. This makes migration more beneficial for high-skilled workers and encourages a positive selection. Thus, the observed pattern depends on the relative strength of these two forces. Chiswick concludes that due to the existence of migration costs that do not vary with the value of time, greater inequality in the sending country may not necessarily lead to negative self-selection of migrants, but rather to a less favorable but still positive selection.

Part III of this volume is concerned with the role of ethnic networks and neighborhoods in the economic and social integration of migrants. This research is motivated by the massive socioeconomic differences between U.S.-born whites, blacks and Hispanics, as well as between the U.S.-born and immigrants from Central America. Compared to whites, minority groups lag behind in terms of income, employment, education, health and other socioeconomic measures. Particularly worrying is the fact that U.S.-born children growing up in ethnic neighborhoods often do much worse than comparable children growing up in white neighborhoods. This is at odds with the narrative of the "Melting Pot," which states that while immigrants of the first generation have to work hard for their integration, the second generation is fully integrated in the American society from the start. Motivated by this puzzle, the articles in Chapters 8–13 analyze to what extent the concentration of minorities in certain neighborhoods, often called "ghettos" or "enclaves," is responsible for those gaps. In Chapter 8, Borjas considers self-employment as an important channel for the labor market integration of immigrants. While most of labor economics focuses on the wages and employment of employees, more than 10 percent of the American workforce is actually self-employed, and this share is much higher among immigrants (around 17 percent in the 1980 Census). This chapter shows that the self-employment rates of immigrants increase with the time spent in the U.S., and that this is particularly so among immigrants living in neighborhoods with high concentrations of their own ethnic group, as these offer a larger number of self-employment opportunities.

Ethnic networks and neighborhoods seem to have a particularly large impact on the children growing up in them. Chapters 9–11 analyze the impact of ethnic neighborhoods in a dynamic context, focusing on their role in the transmission of abilities, opportunities, and cultural traits across generations. Both scholars developed important models that explain the apparent gaps between U.S.-born children growing up inside or outside ethnic neighborhoods and the persistence of these gaps over multiple generations. Moreover, with the availability of longitudinal data that link children and parents to the characteristics of their neighborhood, they were able to test the theoretical predictions. In Chapter 9, Chiswick is concerned with the socioeconomic gaps between blacks and whites in the U.S. that have persisted over several generations. In an elegant model, he shows that these gaps can exist if blacks and whites face different marginal costs of having an additional child. If this cost is higher among whites, they will choose to have fewer children but invest more in the human capital of each child. This difference in human capital investment leads to higher earnings for whites, which in turn increases the scope for them to invest in the human capital of the next generation.

Motivated by the persistent socioeconomic gaps between U.S.-born children of immigrants and the children of natives, Borjas explores in Chapter 10 the role of ethnicity in the human capital formation of children, and in the transmission of human capital across multiple generations. In his model, a child's human capital is influenced by parental investments as well as the characteristics of the child's ethnic group, which Borjas calls "ethnic capital." A child who grows up in an environment with less favorable ethnic capital will do worse in life than a native child with similar characteristics. Once set in motion, this process may never converge, and the gaps between immigrants and natives may persist or even worsen across generations. This hypothesis is consistent with patterns of intergenerational transmission of education and earnings found in the GSS and the NLSY, two datasets that link parents and children.

In Chapter 11, Borjas delves deeper into the nature of ethnic capital and its transmission across generations. Using newly available neighborhood data, he shows that ethnic capital is the result of immigrants' locational choices. Immigrants tend to move to places where they find others of the same ethnic group, presumably because the proximity of co-ethnics offers them job opportunities and amenities such as ethnic shops and restaurants, religious communities, and cultural institutions. This leads to segregation of immigrants and natives across neighborhoods. As a result, immigrant children are much more exposed to other immigrants than they would be if all immigrants were randomly distributed geographically. The clustering of immigrants with low human capital in ethnic neighborhoods leads to the persistence in low socioeconomic status described in Chapter 10.

Undoubtedly, the key to successful integration of immigrants is knowledge of the host country language. Chiswick has devoted considerable effort to analyzing the determinants of immigrant language skills, as well as their impact on education, wages, and employment. Four chapters in this volume are devoted to this important topic. One problem Chiswick identified was that ethnic neighborhoods provide little incentive for immigrants to become proficient in the host country's language. While this fact has been established in several earlier studies, in a paper in Chapter 12 (with Paul Miller) he analyzes the mechanisms through which ethnic networks affect immigrant language skills. Is it the mere presence of speakers of the same language, is it the social interactions with one's family, or is it the availability of media in one's own language? Using rich survey data from Australia, he tests the relative importance of each of these factors. Not surprisingly, having a spouse who speaks the same language and having access to television and radio in one's own language is detrimental to a migrant's language proficiency. And while such detailed information is rarely available in surveys, the authors show that the concentration of co-ethnic immigrants performs well as a proxy for these more detailed variables. In Chapter 13, Chiswick explores more broadly the impact of ethnic networks on immigrants' investment in human capital. Enclaves offer ethnic goods and services at lower (money and time) prices than the world outside the enclave, while at the same time offering jobs with a low language requirement. These two forces provide little incentive for migrants to move out of an enclave and to invest in host-country-specific human capital. In light of this, the observed wage gap between migrants inside and outside of ethnic enclaves may simply represent a compensating wage differential for the difference in human capital and the difference in living costs.

While it seems natural that immigrants should be proficient in the host country language if they want to successfully integrate, it is less clear whether better language skills actually pay off in terms of higher earnings. After all, immigrants could be paid higher wages in ethnic enclaves, where foreign language skills are not needed. Chiswick (Chapter 14) provides evidence on this question for a group of immigrants that is rarely studied in the literature: illegal immigrants. He conducted a survey among apprehended illegal migrants in Los Angeles and Chicago that includes retrospective questions on language skills at the time when they entered the U.S.. The results reveal that language fluency increases with time spent in the U.S. and, perhaps surprisingly, that reading skills are more important for immigrant earnings than speaking skills.

No matter how able and qualified immigrants are, after arrival they often work in jobs for which they are over-qualified. Anecdotes abound of doctors working in bars, engineers working in construction, and such. This overeducation is problematic, because the host country wastes the human capital of its immigrants. In a paper with Paul Miller (Chapter 15), Chiswick developed a framework that allows him to quantify the degree of immigrants' overeducation and to study its determinants and consequences. The empirical analysis, based on Australian panel data, reveals that immigrants are initially overeducated, but the degree of overeducation is reduced over time as immigrants acquire more host-country-specific human capital.

While the first four parts of this volume are centered around the skills and labor market outcomes of immigrants, Part V is concerned with the impact of immigration on the broader economy, and in particular on its impact on native labor markets. This topic has been central to George Borjas' research agenda in the last 20 years. In Chapter 16, he assesses the aggregate impact of immigration on economic welfare in the U.S. To this end, he develops a simple and intuitive partial-equilibrium model that clearly predicts a welfare gain from immigration. However, once the model is calibrated to the U.S. economy, it turns out that the welfare gains are dwarfed by the redistribution migration causes between different groups of the population (high- and low-skilled workers, and capital owners).

In Chapter 17 Borjas studies the impact of immigration on the wage distribution of natives. This paper overcomes severe challenges in the identification of a causal effect. Previous studies have tried to tease out this relationship using a so-called "area approach," which compares the wages of workers in cities with high and low inflows of migrants. The fundamental problem is that immigrants go to places with high wages, resulting in a spurious positive correlation between immigration and native wages. Moreover, cities may adjust to immigrant inflows through many channels: natives move out, firms produce with a different technology, or trade flows between cities adjust. Borjas' work eliminates all those biases by shifting the focus to wages at the national level. He divides the workforce into groups with similar skills and estimates the reaction of wages to immigrant inflows within skill groups over time. The analysis yields a significant negative relationship between immigration and the wages of natives. The conclusion of the paper appears in its title: "The Labor Demand Curve IS Downward-sloping." This paper led to an intense academic debate about the appropriate approach to identify the impact of migration on wages. This debate is still ongoing.

At the macro-level, immigrants can benefit the economy if they adjust to economic shocks faster than natives. In Chapter 18, Borjas estimates efficiency gains if immigrants have greater geographic mobility than natives. The idea is simple: natives face very high moving costs and may not move even if the economy in their city is in decline. From a welfare perspective, this situation is inefficient, because people do not move away from places where the economy is doing badly, and they do not move to places where the economy is growing. Immigrants, by contrast, have low moving costs once they arrive and move to places with high economic growth. This reduces the inefficiency in the labor market or, as Borjas puts it in the title, "Immigration Greases the Wheels of the Labor Market." The empirical analysis confirms this mechanism to be at play, but it turns out that its impact is not large enough to be economically important in the U.S. labor market.

One empirical problem of the "area approach" is that natives may choose to leave in response to an immigrant inflow, or they may choose not to move there, whereas they would have moved to that city had there not been an immigrant inflow. In Chapter 19, Borjas quantifies the importance of this channel for the estimation of wage and employment effects of immigration. He finds strong evidence for immigration being a deterrent for natives moving to cities with many immigrants. For every ten immigrants moving to a city, between three and six natives choose not to live there. This response leads to severe under-estimation of the true wage impact of migration.

The volume concludes with both scholars' statements of their views on migration (Part VI). Borjas reflects upon the lessons he learned in over 30 years of migration research. He summarizes the important progress migration economics has made in creating a better understanding of migration. He also cautions economists to let themselves be guided by the best theoretical and empirical approaches, even if they produce results that are at odds with their own opinions or current public opinion on migration. In his closing statement, Chiswick looks to the future of migration policy, highlighting some of the challenges receiving countries will face. On the one hand, they will compete for the brightest minds, including attempting to retain their own high-skilled workers; on the other hand they face growing migration pressure from low-skilled workers who often try to enter illegally. High-skilled and low-skilled immigration present very different challenges to most Western countries, and require different policies. Chiswick outlines some directions for the design of these policies.

From the beginnings of IZA in the late 1990s, Barry Chiswick and George Borjas have been enthusiastic members of the network, and have actively shaped IZA's research agenda on migration. Chiswick founded IZA's Migration Program and served as Program Director from 2004 to 2011. Borjas became Director of the newly established Program Area "Labor Mobility and Migration" following the Institute's restructuring in 2016.

Migration has been at the center of the Institute's activities in research and policy advice. Of the 10,000 discussion papers that have appeared since 1998, more than 600 are on migration, and almost all of them cite the works of both prize winners. In addition, the IZA Policy Paper series, which addresses a broad policy-focused audience, has seen a substantial number of contributions on migration. Chiswick alone contributed four papers to this series. Beginning in 2004, the Annual Migration Meeting brought together some of the brightest minds in the field to discuss the latest research on migration. Both scholars gave keynote lectures at the meeting, Chiswick in 2007 on the economics of language, and Borjas in 2016 on the content of his new book. Moreover, with the IZA Journal of Migration, the Institute created the first economics journal that is purely devoted to migration; and with the IZA World of Labor it created a platform that informs non-economists about the state-of-the-art research knowledge. Migration is among the central topics of this exciting venture. Both laureates have supported the IZA Journal of Migration and the IZA World of Labor as associate editors.

Without the works of both, migration would not have such a central place at IZA. Yet more importantly, it would not play such a central role in the entire field of economics. Once again, congratulations to two outstanding scholars for laying the foundations of migration economics!

Part II
Assimilation

1

The Effect of Americanization on the Earnings of Foreign-born Men

From 1973 to 1977 I was a Senior Staff Economist on the U.S. President's Council of Economic Advisers (CEA). In 1975, Attorney General Levy was chairing the Domestic Council Committee on Illegal Aliens, a committee appointed by President Ford. The concern over illegal immigration was growing, but it was not yet the hot-button issue that it subsequently became. At his first meeting with the representatives sent by the various government agencies, Mr. Levy realized that although immigration – whether legal or illegal – was an economic phenomenon, there were no economists in the group and no one was thinking of the economic issues. He contacted the Council of Economic Advisers and Paul McAvoy, then a member of the Council, asked me to represent the CEA. I was assigned by the Attorney General to write the economics chapter for the Domestic Council report (Chiswick 1976).

I worked on two issues: What is the economic adjustment of immigrants in the U.S.? And what is the impact of immigrants on the rest of the economy? These two questions have continued to define much of my research agenda since then. At that time the literature search on these – and any other – questions about the economics of immigration was quite simple because the research was very sparse. Since then the economics literature on immigration has grown exponentially, not only regarding the United States but internationally as well.

I proceeded to work on both questions for the Domestic Council report. I was already using microdata from the 1970 Census of Population for other purposes at the CEA. By developing a conceptual framework, I was able to use these data to analyze the earnings of immigrants in the U.S. among themselves and in comparison to the native born. After leaving the CEA I was encouraged by Ellen Seghal, of the Department of Labor's Employment and Training Administration, to expand this approach for a major project on the adjustment and impact of immigrants. This resulted in my 1980 Department of Labor (DOL) monograph (Chiswick 1980a) from which several journal articles evolved.

I gave several academic seminars on my paper on the earnings of immigrants. This paper was rejected by the editors of two major journals, not on technical grounds but because they felt the topic was neither interesting nor important. (Paraphrasing the TV show Dragnet, I am not revealing their identity to protect the guilty.) I disagreed with them, since I believed that immigration was both an interesting phenomenon in its own right and an important issue for national policy, not only currently but even more so as immigration to the U.S. (and other advanced economics) was increasing. When I expressed my frustration to Gary Becker after presenting my paper at his seminar, he chided me for not sending it to the Journal of Political Economy. I then did, and it was accepted without major changes. This paper, "The Effect of Americanization on the Earnings of Foreign-Born Men" (JPE, October 1978, reprinted as Chapter 1 in this volume), has often been described as seminal and is frequently cited in the literature. It spawned a large literature on the labor market adjustment of immigrants in numerous immigrant-receiving countries.

The "...Americanization..." journal article was of necessity limited in length. Much of the insight on immigrant earnings in the 1980 DOL report could not be included, although some were published in a subsequent book chapter (reprinted as Chapter 5 in this volume). In particular, the DOL report raised and addressed the question as to whether the cross-sectional profile of earnings with respect to duration in the destination (years since immigration, YSM) was a biased estimate of the longitudinal profile. This could arise if cohort quality changed over time. If the unmeasured quality of new immigrants had risen (or fallen) over time, the cross-section would be a downward (upward) biased estimate of the longitudinal pattern. Alternatively, selective re-migration of immigrants, whether to return to their origin or to a third country, could introduce a bias in the cross-sectional earnings-duration profile. The direction of this bias would depend on whether the unmeasured characteristics of the emigrants were more favorable or less favorable for labor market success than the characteristics of immigrants who remained. These analyses suggested that the cross-sectional analysis was indeed not a biased estimate of the longitudinal profile.

The chapter prepared for the 1976 Domestic Council report, expanded in the 1980 DOL report, also included theoretical analyses of the labor market impact of immigrants. These analyses were expanded further in subsequent published papers (Chiswick 1982c; Chiswick, Chiswick and Karras 1992). These analyses emphasized the importance of considering the heterogeneity of immigrant skills (e.g., high- vs. low-skilled immigrants), heterogeneity of the skills of natives in the destination, and adjustment over time of the human capital of both immigrant and native workers. Thus the impact of immigration on the labor market depends (among other things) on the characteristics of the immigrants, the characteristics of native workers, and how these characteristics change over time after the immigrants arrive.

Barry R. Chiswick (2015)

1.1.   Introduction

In 1970, 9.6 million persons, or 5 percent, of the population of the United States were foreign born. In spite of the increased public interest in ethnicity and discrimination, and more recently the concern with the impact of legal and illegal immigrants and hence with immigration policy, the earnings and labor market behavior of the foreign born in the United States have not been the subject of much systematic research.[1] This chapter examines the effect of foreign birth and length of time in the United States on the earnings of foreign-born white men.[2]

Although foreign-born white men aged 25–64 had approximately the same annual earnings in 1969 as the native born ($9,700), they differ in several important characteristics that are associated with earnings (Table 1.1). Foreign-born men have a lower level of schooling, a mean of nearly 11 years compared with a mean of nearly 12 years for the native born. The foreign born also worked one less week in 1969, an average of 47 weeks for the foreign born compared with 48 weeks for the native born. However, foreign-born men are nearly three years older than are the native born (46 years compared with 43 years) and are less likely to be married. There are also substantial differences in place of residence. Foreign-born men are less likely to reside in rural areas (11 percent compared with 30 percent). They are also less likely to live in the South (13 percent live in the Census Bureau's definition of the South, compared with 29 percent for the native born).

19

Some of these differences in earnings-related characteristics would lower the earnings of the foreign born compared with the native born, such as the schooling and marital status differences.[3] Others would tend to raise the relative earnings of the foreign born, such as the greater proportion living in urban areas and living outside the South, and possibly the longer labor market experience. The effect of the latter depends, in part, on how much training was acquired in the United States and on the international transferability of training acquired in the country of origin. Thus, without multivariate analysis one cannot account for the extent to which factors favorable to earnings have offset any earnings disadvantages that may arise from being of a foreign origin. For this reason, the data are applied to a multiple regression analysis using a basic human capital earnings function that includes some demographic control variables.

The statistical approach and hypotheses are developed in Section 1.2. In Section 1.3 the earnings of foreign-born and native-born white men are compared, while in Section 1.4 differences in earnings among the foreign born by country of origin are examined.[4] Section 1.5 is a summary and conclusion.

1.2. The Hypotheses and Statistical Approach

This section sets out several hypotheses as to how the earnings of the foreign born would differ from that of the native born, and how earnings would vary among the foreign born by country of origin, the number of years in the United States, and citizenship. The statistical framework used for analyzing the data and the data base are also described.

1.2.1. Hypotheses

In labor markets in the United States, earnings are largely related to characteristics associated with productivity, although for some jobs certification of one form or another is important. This certification may be a union card, an occupational license, or a school degree.

Recent immigrants to the United States are likely to have less of the characteristics associated with higher earnings than the native born. Being recent arrivals, they have less knowledge of the customs and language relevant to U.S. jobs, have less information about U.S. job opportunities, and have less firm-specific training (i.e., they are likely to have been at their current U.S. job fewer years than native-born workers).[5] They are also less likely to have acquired the union card or occupational license relevant in the United States to apply the skills acquired in their country of origin.

As time passes, however, the immigrant gains knowledge of the United States, acquires job-specific training, and either acquires the union card or modifies his skills accordingly. Thus, because knowledge and skills are not perfectly mobile across countries, other things the same, immigrants initially would have earnings significantly lower than native-born persons, but the gap would narrow the longer they are in the United States. The initial earnings deficiency, and the steepness of the subsequent rise in earnings, would be smaller the greater the similarity between the country of origin and the United States. The number of years since migrating would be less important for explaining earnings for immigrants from Canada, for example, than for immigrants from Germany. If the foreign and native born have the same level of innate labor market ability and work motivation, the earnings of the foreign born would approach, and might equal, but would not exceed that of the native born, *ceteris paribus*.[6]

Immigrants may have a steeper experience-earnings profile after they arrive than do the native born, even if they receive the same total postschool training, if there is a difference in the nature and financing of their training. Becker (1964) has shown that for the same total investment in training, experience-earnings profiles are steeper the smaller the proportion that is firm specific and the smaller the proportion of firm-specific training financed by the employer. Having less knowledge relevant to U.S. labor markets, immigrants would gain information by "experiencing" a variety of jobs. Even if they do not intentionally change jobs as a means of gaining information, as their knowledge and skills relevant to the United States improve, there would be a tendency to move into jobs in which their productivity is now higher.[7] As with youths just entering the labor force, recent immigrants would tend to have high quit rates. This will discourage job-specific investment financed by the worker and the employer.

Employers are likely to have less information about the productivity of a job applicant who is a recent immigrant compared with a native-born person with similar general characteristics. It is more difficult to check school and previous employment references, and employers may be less familiar with the implications of foreign schooling for a worker's productivity. The greater risk associated with hiring a new immigrant would discourage employer investments in job-specific training.[8]

Economic theory suggests that migration in response to economic incentives is generally more profitable for the more able and more highly motivated.[9] This self-selection in migration implies that for the same schooling, age, and other demographic characteristics immigrants to the United States have more innate ability or motivation relevant to the labor market than native-born persons.[10] If so, holding measured variables constant, as earnings rise with time in the United States, the earnings of immigrants may, but would not necessarily, exceed that of native-born persons. The earnings crossover is less likely to occur if the migration is less selected in favor of the more able or more highly motivated. The self-selection may be weaker, for example, if the migration is induced by political pressure in the country of origin, if it is the mass migration of an entire community, or if it is induced by the availability of more generous welfare benefits in the place of destination than if it is the more conventional economic migration of workers for higher real earnings. The number of years since migration at which this earnings crossover occurs, if it does occur, is a parameter of considerable interest.

The effect of citizenship per se on the earnings of foreign-born persons can be studied. Aliens could earn less than naturalized citizens because of the wage effects of occupational segregation, direct discrimination in wages, or a lower quality of skills not reflected in the other variables in the analysis.[11] As citizenship is not likely to be related to unmeasured skill characteristics and as most employers would not know the citizenship of foreign-born job applicants, holding constant the number of years in the United States, one would not expect aliens to be at a significant earnings disadvantage.

The foreign born are less rural and less southern than the native born. Among white men, reported earnings tend to be lower in rural areas and in the southern states. A variety of explanations can be offered for the lower earnings, including a lower real income due to a lower quality of schooling in rural/southern areas, self-selection in the out-migration of the most able from these areas, and a compensating differential for lower living costs (including a more pleasant environment).

By definition, the foreign born have migrated to the United States. They would tend to migrate to the area or region in which their skills would command the highest real income (see, e.g., Hansen 1940a).

After arriving in the United States the nonmoney cost of migration is likely to be less for the foreign born than the native born, as the latter have stronger ties to the area many of them have lived in since birth. That is, interarea migration is less likely to have been sufficient to equalize urban–rural or North–South differences in real incomes for the native born than for the foreign born. If the coefficient of a dichotomous variable for rural or southern residence is negative for the native born but is zero for the foreign born, it suggests that cost-of-living differences are not relevant for explaining the native-born coefficient. However, if the foreign- and native-born coefficients are the same, it suggests that cost-of-living differences, rather than quality of schooling or self-selection in migration, are the causal factors.

Married men tend to have higher labor force participation rates, invest more in human capital, and have better health than men who are not married. For the same age, schooling, and place of residence, married men have higher earnings. As a somewhat smaller proportion of the foreign-born men are currently married, marital status is included as a variable in the regression analysis.

Variables for the occupation or industry in 1970 of the foreign born are not included in the analysis. Part of the process of change associated with time in the United States is the mobility of the foreign born to occupations and industries where their productivity is higher. It is, therefore, to be expected that the foreign born experience more changes in occupation and industry than native-born persons in the same age group. The occupational mobility of immigrants, including a comparison of the "last" occupation in the country of origin with the "first" occupation in the United States, has been studied elsewhere (Chiswick 1978a).

Some testable hypotheses relevant for an analysis of the earnings of the foreign born can now be specified. (1) As there are aspects of schooling that are country specific, a year of schooling prior to immigration will have a smaller effect on earnings than a year of schooling for the native born. (2) As there are aspects of labor market experience that are country specific, a year of experience prior to immigration has a smaller effect on earnings than a year of experience for a native-born person. (3) As immigrants initially have less human capital specific to the United States than native-born persons of the same schooling and age, just after they arrive their earnings are lower than the native born. (4) After they arrive, as they make investments in postschool training and they informally acquire "experience" living in the United States, the earnings of immigrants rise at a faster rate than the earnings of the native born. (5) As immigrants have the incentive to make their largest adjustment investments just after they arrive, the absolute decline in the "knowledge gap" between immigrants and the native born is sharpest in these years. The rise in earnings with time in the United States is steepest in the first few years. (6) The effect on earnings of time in the United States, holding total labor market experience constant, is weaker for immigrants from countries that more closely resemble the United States. Holding years in the United States constant, the earnings of immigrants would be higher the more similar the country of origin is to the United States. (7) As immigrants tend to be more able, more highly motivated workers, if not for the disadvantages of their foreign origin, they would have higher earnings than the native born. After they have acquired U.S. specific skills, the earnings of the foreign born may, but need not, equal or exceed that of the native born. (8) For the same number of years in the United States, whether a foreign-born person is an alien or a naturalized citizen has no effect on earnings.

1.2.2. Estimating Equation

The empirical analysis of the effect of Americanization on earnings uses the human capital earnings function as the point of departure. This earnings function has been successfully applied to analyses of the determinants of earnings in a wide variety of countries. This is, however, its first application to a comparative analysis of the determinants of earnings of the foreign born in the United States.

Native-born men are assumed to have made all of their investments in human capital in the United States. If rates of return (r) to all levels of schooling (S) are constant, a year of schooling requires an investment of a full year's potential earnings; and, if the men are in the labor force continuously after leaving school, the earnings function for the native born can be written as

$$(1) \qquad \ln \Upsilon_{n,i} = \ln \Upsilon_0 + rS_i + b_1 T_i + b_2 T_i^2 + U_i,$$

where T is years of labor market experience, measured as age minus years of schooling minus 5; $\Upsilon_{n,i}$ is earnings; and U_i is a residual (Mincer 1974). Among the foreign born, however, the total number of years of schooling can be decomposed into the schooling acquired before immigration (S_b) and the schooling after immigration (S_a).

Similarly, years of labor market experience (T) can be decomposed into years of experience before (T_b) and after (T_a) immigration. If there are country-specific aspects of training, the training acquired prior to migration (S_b, T_b) would have a weaker effect on earnings than years of training in the United States (S_a, T_a).

Assuming that the effect of years of training in a country can be described by a quadratic experience variable, the earnings function of the foreign born can be written as

$$(2) \qquad \ln Y_i = \ln Y_0 + r_b S_{b,i} + r_a S_{a,i} + b'_1 T_{b,i} + b'_2 T^2_{b,i}$$
$$+ b'_3 T_{a,i} + b'_4 T^2_{a,i} + U_i.$$

Since $S_i = S_{b,i} + S_{a,i}$ and $T_i = T_{b,i} + T_{a,i}$,

$$\ln Y_i = \ln Y_0 + r_b S_i + (r_a - r_b) S_{a,i} + b'_1 T_i$$
$$(3) \qquad + b'_2 T^2_i + (b'_3 - b'_1) T_{a,i} + (b'_2 + b'_4) T^2_{a,i}$$
$$- 2 b'_2 T_i T_{a,i} + U_i.$$

Empirically, there is little difference between r_a and r_b, and the interaction of total labor market experience with U.S. experience $(T_i T_{a,i})$ is not statistically significant.[12] In most of the analyses that follow, the variables S_a and TT_a are deleted from the earnings function, Equation (3). In addition, the variable T_a, the number of years of postschool training since migration, is replaced by YSM, the number of years since migration, a change that has no substantive effect on the conclusions. The earnings function for the foreign born is then reduced to

$$(4) \qquad \ln Y_i = \ln Y_0 + r S_i + C_1 T_i + C_2 T^2_i$$
$$+ C_3 (YSM_i) + C_4 (YSM_i)^2 + U_i.$$

The basic equation used in the empirical analysis is a linear regression of the natural logarithm of annual earnings (wages, salary, and self-employment income expressed in hundreds of dollars, $\ln E$) on the exogenous variables: EDUC, years of schooling completed; T, labor market experience, measured as age – schooling – 5; 72, experience squared; LN WW, the natural logarithm of weeks worked; RU-RALEQl, dichotomous variable equal to unity for a person living in a rural area otherwise, it is zero; SOUTHEQ1, dichotomous variable equal to unity for a person living in the 17 southern states, including the District of Columbia – otherwise, it is zero; NOTMSP, marital status variable equal to zero for a person who is married, spouse present – otherwise, it is unity; FOR, dichotomous variable equal to unity for a person of foreign birth, zero for a native-born person; YSM, years since migrating to the United States; YSM2, the square of YSM; ALIEN, dichotomous variable equal to unity if the foreign-born person is an alien and equal to zero if he is a naturalized citizen; and a set of dichotomous variables for country of origin.[13]

1.2.3.   Data Base

The foreign born are only 5 percent of the population, and the proportion from subsets of foreign countries is even smaller. An analysis of the earnings of the foreign born requires either a moderate-sized data set which substantially oversamples the foreign born or a very large simple random sample. Although some data sets include information on whether a person was born or grew up outside the United States, data are usually lacking on the specific country or continent of origin and the year of immigration to the United States. The *1970 Census of Population* 5 percent questionnaire appears to be unique in satisfying the very stringent data requirements of this study.[14]

The population under study is white men, aged 25–64 in 1970, residing in the 50 states and the District of Columbia, who worked in at least 1 week in 1969 and who reported earnings from wages, salary, and self-employment.[15] The native born are defined as those born in the 50 states and the District of Columbia. The foreign born are defined as those born in a foreign country and not of American parents.[16] Persons born in an outlying area of the United States (Puerto Rico, the Canal Zone, etc.), born abroad of American parents, or born at sea are excluded from the data.

1.3.   Analysis of Earnings for the Native and Foreign Born

Section 1.3 is primarily a comparative analysis of the earnings of the native and foreign born. Of particular interest are the effects of schooling and postschool training in the United States and abroad and the effects of citizenship. The effect of country of origin among the foreign born is the subject of Section 1.4.

The average earnings of the foreign-born white men, aged 25–64, who worked in 1969 was $9,660, compared with $9,738 for the native born, a difference of 1 percent in favor of the native born. The mean of the natural logarithm of earnings (expressed in hundreds of dollars) was 4.29 for the foreign born and 4.32 for the native born, a difference of about 1 percent in the natural logarithm of the geometric mean of earnings (Table 1.1).

Table 1.1

Means and Standard Deviations, Native- and Foreign-born White Men, Age 25–64, in 1970

	All Men		Native Born		Foreign Born	
	Mean	SD	Mean	SD	Mean	SD
Earnings ($)	9,734.09	7,937.94	9,738.13	7.915.25	9,662.01	8,334.20
Log of earnings						
(hundreds of dollars)	4.32	.85	4.32	.85	4.29	.88
Education	11.84	3.44	11.90	3.37	10.83	4.46
Age	42.93	11.16	42.77	11.11	45.64	11.70
Experience						
(age - education - 5)	26.08	12.43	25.87	12.35	29.81	13.22
Weeks worked	48.16	7.94	48.22	7.86	47.16	9.20
Log of weeks worked	3.85	.29	3.85	.29	3.81	.34
Rural (%)	29.39	45.55	30.39	46.00	11.49	31.89
South (%)	28.03	44.91	28.88	45.32	12.89	33.52
Not "married,						
spouse present" (%)	14.76	35.47	14.66	35.37	16.53	37.15
Foreign born (%)	5.31	22.42	.0	.0	100.00	.0
Years since migration	N.A.	N.A.	N.A.	N.A.	21.69	17.60

Note: N of observations: all, 36,245; native born, 34,321; and foreign born, 1,924.
Source: U.S. Bureau of the Census (1972).

1.3.1. Pooled Sample

Table 1.2 presents the regression analysis of earnings for native-born men (column 1) and for the pooled sample of native- and foreign-born men (columns 2–4). The coefficient of the foreign-birth variable (FOR) in column 2 implies that, *ceteris paribus*, foreign-born men have weekly earnings 3.0 percent higher than native-born men, in contrast to the simple difference of 1 percent lower earnings. However, the variable FOR is just significant at the 8 percent level, two-tailed test. Thus, on the basis of this regression, one would conclude that there is no significant difference between the earnings of native- and foreign-born men.

Table 1.2

Regression Analysis of Earnings for Native- and Foreign-born Adult White Men, 1970

	Native Born	Native and Foreign Born			Foreign Born
	(1)	(2)	(3)	(4)	(5)
EDUC	.07154	.07058	.07004	.07164	.05740
	(53.78)	(55.68)	(55.18)	(54.11)	(12.93)
T	.03167	.03050	.03071	.03097	.02028
	(22.99)	(22.86)	(22.99)	(23.10)	(3.47)
T2	-.00052	-.00049	-.00050	-.00051	-.00031
	(-20.77)	(-20.45)	(-20.78)	(-20.93)	(-3.18)
LN WW	1.10335	1.10326	1.10169	1.10111	1.07151
	(81.75)	(84.78)	(84.70)	(84.67)	(21.97)
RURALEQ1	-.17222	-.16970	-.17080	-.16915	-.05821
	(-20.28)	(-20.25)	(-20.39)	(-20.18)	(-1.13)
SOUTHEQ1	-.12090	-.12620	-.12530	-.12389	-.21587
	(-14.17)	(-15.01)	(-14.91)	(-14.74)	(-4.38)
NOTMSP	-.30647	-.31078	-.30947	-.30874	-.34498
	(-27.76)	(-28.97)	(-28.86)	(-28.79)	(-7.66)
FOR	*	.02951	-.16359	.00990	*
		(1.75)	(-4.32)	(0.18)	
(FOR) (YSM)	*	*	.01461	.01555	.01500
			(3.98)	(4.23)	(3.87)
(FOR) (YSM2)	*	*	-.00016	-.00018	-.00019
			(-2.47)	(-2.79)	(-2.82)
(FOR) (EDUC)	*	*	*	-.01619	*
				(-4.23)	
CONSTANT	-1.03646	-1.01537	-1.00016	-1.02156	-.78891
Observations (N)	34,321	36,245	36,245	36,245	1,924
R	.55423	.55455	.55533	.55564	.58194
R^2	.30717	.30753	.30839	.30873	.33866
Standard error	.70900	.71008	.70966	.70949	.71676

Note: t-ratios in parentheses; dependent variable: natural logarithm of earnings in
hundreds of dollars.
       * Variable not entered.
Source: U.S. Bureau of the Census (1972).

When the variable years since migration (YSM) is included in the regression analysis, a quite different picture emerges. The partial effect of foreign birth (FOR) on earnings, evaluated at the mean levels of years since migration and schooling for the foreign born, is still 3 percent (Table 1.2, columns 3 and 4). However, the sets of foreign-born variables are now highly significant.[17] The rise of earnings with time in the United States, holding constant schooling and total labor market experience, is important for understanding the earnings of the foreign born.[18]

The rise in earnings of the foreign born with time spent in the United States is at a decreasing rate. Other things the same, the earnings of the foreign born are 9.5 percent lower than the native born after five years in the country, equal after about 13 years, and 6.4 percent greater after 20 years.[19]

Since the foreign born are neither predominantly very recent immigrants or predominantly long-term residents (nearly half have been in the United States less than 15 years), a regression analysis shows a lack of statistical significance of foreign birth if no effort is made to control for years since migration. As will be shown below, however, in an analysis comparing Cuban immigrants with native-born white men when YSM is not in the equation, the coefficient of the Cuban-birth variable is negative and highly significant. This occurs because a very large proportion of the Cubans are recent arrivals – in 1970, 80 percent were in the United States less than ten years. The Cuban refugees in the United States 10–15 years have reached earnings parity with the native born. On the other hand, a study of the predominantly long-term immigrants from Russia indicates that they have substantially higher earnings than native- and other foreign-born persons if YSM is not taken into account. If the lower initial earnings and higher subsequent earnings were due solely to larger investments by immigrants in postschool training during their early years in the United States, the internal rate of return on the earnings difference would be competitive. The rate of return on the earnings difference is low, 5 percent.[20] Thus, when they arrive, immigrants have a lower permanent income (i.e., a lower present value of future earnings) than native-born men with similar measurable characteristics, even though they eventually have higher annual earnings.

For the earnings of the foreign born to exceed the native born eventually suggests that the greater ability, work motivation, or investments in training of the foreign born more than offset whatever earnings disadvantages persist from discrimination against them or from their initially having less knowledge and skills relevant in U.S. labor markets.[21] It also indicates that the total gains from migration are greater the younger the immigrant.

The interaction of the foreign born and the education variables is negative and highly significant (Table 1.2, column 4). For the native born, an extra year of schooling, other variables the same, raises earnings by 7.2 percent, but for the foreign born only by 5.5 percent.

1.3.2.   *Comparing Native- and Foreign-born Regression Coefficients*

The explanatory power of the earnings function is somewhat greater for the foreign born (Table 1.2, column 5) than for the native born or the pooled sample. A Chow test indicates that for the same set of human capital and demographic variables there is a significant difference in the coefficients of the native- and foreign-born regressions.

The partial effect of a year of schooling for the foreign born is 5.7 percent when years since migration (YSM) is held constant. This is similar to the estimate for the foreign born in the pooled regression analysis. The coefficients of the experience variables $(T, T2)$ are lower in absolute value for the foreign born, indicating a smaller effect on earnings in the United States of labor market experience prior to immigration. The lower coefficients for schooling and pre-immigration experience would arise if the benefits from training are partly country specific.[22] (The lower coefficient of schooling will be discussed in more detail later.)

Among foreign-born persons earnings rise, although at a decreasing rate, the longer one has been in the country (peak at 39 years). The predicted percent increase in earnings ($\partial \ln E$) at different years since migration (YSM) is 1.5 for one year; 7.0, five years; 13.1, ten years; 22.4, 20 years; 27.9, 30 years; and 29.6, 40 years (source: Table 1.2, column 5). Earnings increase with time in the United States by about the same percentage for all schooling levels. Although the education-years-since-migration interaction variable is negative, the coefficient is small ($-.00019$) and is not significant ($t = -0.79$).

The effect on earnings of labor market experience is more complex for the foreign born than for the native born because some of their experience was acquired prior to migration and some afterward. The percent increase in earnings for an additional year of experience can be evaluated at, for example, ten years of experience ($T = 10$) and five years of residency in the United States (YSM $= 5$). For an additional year of experience in the country of origin ($\partial \ln E / \partial T$), the percent increase in earnings is 1.4 for the foreign born and 2.1 for the native born. For those arriving in the United States one year earlier but with the same total number of years of experience ($\partial \ln E / \partial YSM$), the percent increase in earnings is 1.3. For foreign-born persons with an additional year of experience in the United States [($\partial \ln E / \partial T$) + ($\partial \ln E / \partial YSM$)], the percent increase is 2.7; for the native born, the percent increase is 2.1 (source: coefficients in Table 1.2, columns 2 and 5). Thus, once they have arrived, earnings rise faster with age for immigrants than for the native born because the effect of acquiring U.S.-specific knowledge, contacts, etc., outweighs the weaker effect on their earnings in the United States of experience acquired prior to immigration. Among native-born white men, earnings are lower in rural areas by a statistically significant 17 percent, but for the foreign born there is no significant difference (Table 1.2, column 5). The South–non–South earnings differential appears to be larger for the foreign born than for the native born. Upon controlling for country of origin, however, the effect of living in a southern state is similar in magnitude (coefficient $= -0.141$, t-ratio $= -2.71$) and not significantly different from that for the native born.

The importance of country of origin arises from the disproportionate number of Mexican and Cuban immigrants in Texas and Florida, and, as will be shown in Section 1.4, the Mexican and Cuban immigrants appear to have lower earnings than other foreign-born persons.

Men who are single (never married, divorced, or widowed) tend to have lower earnings than married men. The effect is similar for the native and foreign born. Earnings are about 31 percent lower for native-born men who are not married and about 34 percent lower among the foreign born, but the difference is not significant.

1.3.3. Decomposing the Difference in Earnings

As already noted, the 1969 earnings of the native- and foreign-born men were approximately equal ($9,700); the earnings of the foreign born were only one percent lower. Some variables tend to lower their earnings compared with the native born, while others tend to raise it.

The foreign born have 1 year less of schooling, and this by itself would lower their earnings by about 6 percent. Their lower slope coefficient of schooling would, at the mean, lower earnings by another 8 percent. The fewer number of weeks worked, an average of 47 for the foreign born and 48 for the native born ($\Delta \ln WW = 0.04$), would account for another 4 percent lower earnings for the foreign born. The somewhat smaller percent married among the foreign born has a very small effect; it accounts for about 1 percent lower earnings for the foreign born.

Other variables operate in the opposite direction. The foreign born are older and less concentrated in the South and in rural areas. The effect of the four years' additional experience is about a 1 percent increase in earnings. Assuming no effect on earnings of rural rather than urban residence for the foreign born, the depressing effect of rural residence for the native born would raise the relative earnings of the foreign born by 5 percent. The smaller proportion of immigrants living in the South raises the relative earnings of the foreign born by 2 percent.

An important difference appears in the intercept which is higher for the foreign born. Although a higher intercept and lower slope coefficients of schooling, experience, and urban/rural residence can arise from random measurement error in the explanatory variables, this would also imply a lower R^2. However, for the same set of explanatory variables, the R^2 is higher in the foreign-born analysis.[23]

1.3.4.   The Lower Coefficient of Schooling

Recall that the partial effect on earnings of a year of schooling is lower for the foreign born than for the native born, 5.7 percent compared with 7.2 percent. One issue that this raises is whether the smaller partial effect is due to schooling acquired abroad.

Although the census reports the total number of years of schooling completed, there is no direct information on the division between schooling pre- and post-immigration. The number of years of schooling received before immigration (EDUCPRE) can be estimated indirectly, however, by assuming that an immigrant was in school continuously from age 5 to the lesser of (a) the age at immigration or (b) the age at which schooling was completed (years of schooling plus five years). Schooling after immigration (EDUCPOST) is estimated as a residual, EDUCPOST = EDUC − EDUCPRE. This procedure is likely to underestimate the number of years of schooling after immigration and overestimate schooling prior to immigration.

When years of schooling pre- and post-immigration are treated as separate variables, an extra year of schooling prior to immigration raises earnings by 5.8 percent, while an extra year after immigration raises earnings by 5.0 percent.[24] The difference of about 1 percentage point is small, and it is on the margin of statistical significance (10 percent level, two-tailed test).[25]

The smaller partial effect of schooling for the foreign born may, in part, arise from being raised in a home less familiar with the language and institutions of the United States. Yet if this were an important explanation, the native-born sons of the foreign born would be expected to have a lower coefficient of schooling than the native-born sons of native-born parents. Empirically, however, compared with the sons of native-born parents, the sons of immigrants have about the same level of schooling and an insignificantly higher coefficient of schooling (Chiswick 1977).

The smaller effect of schooling could arise from labor market discrimination against immigrants increasing with the level of schooling, as is hypothesized by Greeley (1976, p. 55). The data, however, do not suggest that the effect of schooling declines with the level of schooling for the foreign born. If anything, there is a slight (barely significant) rise – from 5.6 percent at ten years of schooling to 6.8 percent at 15 years of schooling. On the other hand, analyses for all adult white men suggest that the partial effect of schooling declines slightly with the level of schooling when weeks worked are held constant (Mincer 1974, chap. 5).

The self-selection of immigrants may be the most telling explanation for the weaker measured effect of schooling. Immigrants tend to be high-ability, highly motivated persons. This is also true of persons with higher levels of schooling. Suppose that among those with little schooling only the most able and most highly motivated migrate, while among those with high levels of schooling the immigrants are drawn more widely from the ability distribution. Then, a regression equation which did not include ability or motivation variables would show an upward-biased intercept and a downward-biased slope coefficient of schooling. Unfortunately, it is not possible to include measures of ability or motivation in the data under study, and data sets with these measures are inadequate for a study of immigrants.

1.3.5. Aliens

About two-thirds of the foreign-born adult white men in the United States in 1970 were naturalized citizens, and the remaining one-third were aliens. Holding constant other variables – schooling, total labor market experience, weeks worked, place of residence, and marital status – aliens (ALIEN) earn 15 percent less than naturalized citizens, and the difference is highly significant.[26] When the number of years since migration (YSM and YSM2) is held constant, however, the ALIEN variable is still negative but is not significant. Aliens earn less than naturalized citizens because on average they have been in the United States for fewer years.

1.4.   Country of Origin

To analyze the effect of country of origin on earnings for the foreign born, dichotomous variables for country of birth are entered into the regression equation where the excluded group is those born in the British Isles (Great Britain and Ireland).[27] Except for men from the category Canada, Australia, and New Zealand (primarily Canada), all of the country-specific regression coefficients are negative but generally are not statistically significant. Earnings differ significantly from the British Isles' immigrants only for those from Mexico, Cuba, and Asia/Africa.

1.4.1.   Mexican, Cuban, and Asian/African Immigrants

The significantly lower earnings of immigrants from Mexico appears to be a Mexican ethnic-group effect rather than simply a characteristic of first-generation Mexican-Americans. Other things the same, the earnings of first, second, and "third" (third and higher order) generation Mexican-Americans are lower than the earnings of other white men of the same immigrant status. The ethnic-group differential does not appear to narrow the greater the number of generations that have lived in the United States.[28] Otherwise, the patterns observed among men of Mexican origin by immigrant status are similar to the patterns observed among white men in general.[29] For example, when the earnings of Mexican immigrants are compared with those of native-born men of Mexican origin, other things the same, the immigrants initially have substantially lower earnings, their earnings rise with time in the United States, and equal those of the native born after about 15 years, after which the immigrants have higher earnings (Table 1.3, column 1).

The finding of significantly lower earnings among Cuban immigrants is modified when the data are examined more closely. In an analysis comparing Cuban immigrants with native-born white men, whether limited to urban Florida, the New York area, or the rest of the country, the Cubans in the United States 10 to 15 years (i.e., who came between 1955 and 1959) have reached earnings equality.[30] However, the Cubans in the United States less than five years and more than 15 years in 1970 have low earnings.

Table 1.3

Regression Analysis of Earnings for Adult Foreign-born White Men within Country Categories, 1970

	Born in Mexico or Native Born of Spanish Surname[a]		Born in English-Speaking Developed Countries[b]	Foreign Born Other than English-Speaking Developed Countries[b]	
	(1)	(2)	(3)	(4)	(5)
EDUC	.03573	.04324	.09217	.05211	.05086
	(4.01)	(4.28)	(5.70)	(10.27)	(7.06)
T	.01211	.01373	.06139	.01147	.01070
	(1.15)	(1.30)	(5.11)	(1.67)	(1.42)
T2	-.00028	-.00030	-.00095	-.00018	-.00017
	(-1.62)	(-1.74)	(-4.49)	(-1.59)	(-1.33)
LN WW	1.16436	1.16567	1.06921	1.05887	1.05879
	(12.47)	(12.50)	(11.39)	(18.72)	(18.71)
RURALEQ1	-.14442	-.14008	-.10296	-.05025	-.05122
	(-1.72)	(-1.67)	(-1.30)	(-.77)	(-.79)
SOUTHEQ1	-.24159	-.22760	-.12351	-.24956	-.24896
	(-3.81)	(-3.56)	(-1.31)	(-4.36)	(-4.34)
NOTMSP	-.45087	-.45043	-.41734	-.32680	-.32709
	(-5.91)	(-5.91)	(-5.09)	(-6.16)	(-6.17)
FOR	-.33633	-.18680	c	c	c
	(-2.55)	(-1.15)			
(FOR) (EDUC)	c	-.02402	c	c	c
		(-1.57)			
(FOR) (YSM)	.02715	.03027	.01456	.01877	.01799
	(2.05)	(2.26)	(1.43)	(4.15)	(3.25)
(FOR) (YSM2)	-.00033	-.00038	-.00004	-.00024	-.00024
	(-1.38)	(-1.59)	(-.33)	(-3.09)	(-3.08)
(EDUC) (YSM)	c	c	-.00103	c	.00007
			(-2.06)		(.24)
CONSTANT	-.73694	-.84163	-1.48900	-.62107	-.59879
Observations (N)	804	804	439	1,485	1,485
R	.55229	.55424	.63190	.56761	.56764
R2	.30503	.30718	.39930	.32218	.32221
Standard error	.80627	.80533	.61350	.74032	.74056

Note: *t*-ratios in parentheses: dependent variable: natural logarithm of earnings in hundreds of dollars.

[a] For the five Southwestern states Arizona, California, Colorado, New Mexico, and Texas.

[b] The English-speaking developed countries are Great Britain, Ireland, Canada, Australia, and New Zealand.

[c] Variable not entered.

Source: U.S. Bureau of the Census (1972).

The low earnings of the Cubans in the United States less than five years is partly spurious and partly real. The year-of-immigration data are for 5-year intervals, and most of the Cubans who came between 1965 and 1969 actually arrived between 1967 and 1969, while the other immigrants were more uniformly spread over the interval. Recall that the first few years in the United States have a big impact on earnings. In addition, an analysis of occupational mobility (Chiswick 1978c) suggests that recently arrived refugees experience an initial sharp decline in occupational status and more rapid subsequent upward mobility compared with economic migrants from non-English-speaking countries. The one puzzle in the Cuban analysis is the lower than expected earnings of the small group (10 percent) who came to the United States prior to 1955.

Foreign-born white men from Asia/Africa is a heterogeneous category, and sample sizes become very small when it is split into its regional components. Compared with men from the British Isles, there is no difference in earnings for white men from South Asia (coefficient .043, t-ratio $= 0.26$, $N = 20$), but there are weakly significant lower earnings for those from the rest of the region.

1.4.2. *English-speaking and Non-English-speaking Country of Origin*

The regression analysis was also computed separately for immigrants from the developed English-speaking countries (British Isles, Canada, Australia, and New Zealand) and all other countries (see Table 1.3, columns 3–5).[31] The partial effect of schooling is larger for the immigrants from English-speaking countries, 6.6 percent, compared with 5.2 percent. They also have a much steeper experience-earnings profile, holding years since migration constant. That is, labor market experience acquired in the country of origin is more productive in the United States for immigrants from the English-speaking countries.

There are substantial differences in the effect of years since migration on earnings. Among immigrants from the English-speaking countries, years since migration has no significant separate effect on earnings for those in the middle schooling category (say, 10–14 years). For those who are college graduates, however, earnings tend to decline with YSM, but this may be reflecting the effects of a "job change" rather than adverse effects of Americanization.[32] Essentially, labor market experience in the United States and in the country of origin appears to be equally productive in U.S. labor markets for immigrants with middle and high levels of schooling from the English-speaking developed countries.

The partial effect of schooling declines the longer a cohort of immigrants from English-speaking countries is in the United States; the partial effect is 8.5 percent for YSM $= 10$ and 6.3 percent for YSM $= 30$. This occurs because holding constant total labor market experience, the earnings of those with middle levels of schooling are invariant with years in the United States, while the earnings of those with more schooling tend to be lower the longer they have been here. Among other immigrants the effect of schooling on earnings is invariant with time in the United States.

Among the white male immigrants from the non-English-speaking countries, earnings rise at a decreasing rate with years in the United States, holding constant years of total labor market experience. Compared with the all foreign-born analysis evaluated at $T = 10$ and YSM $= 5$, an additional year of experience in the country of origin has a weaker effect on earnings (only 0.8 percent); an additional year of experience in the United States, total labor market experience held constant, has a larger effect (1.6 percent), and an additional year of post-migration experience raises earnings by 2.4 percent (Table 1.3, column 4).

1.5. Summary and Conclusion

This chapter is an analysis of the economic progress, as measured by earnings, of foreign-born white men in the United States. The analysis involves comparisons with the native born and among the foreign born by country of origin, length of time in the United States, and citizenship. The hypotheses developed in Section 1.2 are supported by the empirical analyses in Section 1.3 and 1.4. The data base is the *1970 Census of Population*, 1/1,000 sample, 5 percent questionnaire.

Overall, foreign-born adult white men have annual earnings 1 percent lower than the native born. Holding other variables constant (schooling, years of total labor market experience, area of residence, and weeks worked) the foreign born have weekly earnings that are on average 3 percent higher, but this is at the margin of statistical significance. However, when the number of years since immigration is held constant and is evaluated at the mean, the 3 percent higher earnings are *highly* significant. In an analysis of the earnings of immigrants, the number of years since migration is an important variable, and ignoring it would mask important differences between the native and the foreign born and among the foreign born.

After they arrive, immigrants gradually acquire knowledge of the language, customs, and nature of labor markets in the United States, and these factors tend to raise their earnings. In addition, immigrants make investments in postschool training that are relevant for jobs in the United States. The investments, which are more profitable if they are made without a long delay, depress earnings initially and raise them later on. Immigrants may finance a greater proportion of the investments in their postschool training. Because of the expectation of greater job mobility for immigrants than for the native born as they gravitate to their most productive (high-wage) job in the United States, and because employers have less knowledge about them, immigrants would receive less firm-specific training than do the native born, and less of it is financed by the employer. Larger worker-financed investments mean a steeper post-immigration experience-earnings profile, a sharper rise of earnings with years in the United States. Earnings rise, although at a decreasing rate, with the number of years in the United States for immigrants from non-English-speaking countries, holding schooling and total labor market experience constant. There is, however, little differential effect of experience in the United States relative to experience in the country of origin for immigrants with middle and high levels of schooling from English-speaking developed countries.

There are aspects of pre-immigration labor market experience and of schooling that appear to have country-specific effects on earnings in the United States. The effect of a year of pre-immigration labor market experience is lower for the foreign born (especially those from non-English-speaking countries) than a year of experience for the native born. An additional year of schooling for the foreign born raises earnings by 5.7 percent, compared with 7.2 percent for the native born. Among the foreign born, the effect is larger for those from English-speaking countries (6.6 percent compared with 5.2 percent for other immigrants).

The smaller partial effect of schooling on earnings in the United States is an important finding. It is not due to returns from schooling declining with the level of schooling, as the foreign born have one year less schooling and among them there is a weak tendency for the effect of schooling to rise with its level. It is not due to a substantially smaller effect on earnings of pre-immigration schooling, as the effects of schooling before and after immigration are about the same. The smaller effect of pre-immigration schooling may be "explained" by country-specific aspects of the knowledge acquired in school, by a lower quality of foreign schooling, or by the poorer information it provides employers who use schooling as a screen. A more complex story would be needed to interpret the smaller effect of post-immigration schooling. The weaker partial effect of schooling may in part reflect self-selection in migration in which only the most able and most highly motivated of those with little schooling migrate, while those with (or who subsequently acquire) higher levels of schooling came from a broader ability and motivation spectrum.

Upon arrival, immigrants earn on the average substantially less than the native born with similar characteristics. As earnings rise more sharply with post-immigration experience, the earnings gap narrows. Other things the same, five years after immigration foreign-born white men have weekly earnings 10 percent lower than the native born, but earnings are approximately equal after 13 years and are 6 percent higher after 20 years. The earnings crossover at 10–15 years appears to be quite robust. Using native-born white men as the base, it emerges for the analysis of all foreign-born white men, foreign-born white men who came at age 18 or older, and the Cuban refugees. An earnings crossover at about 15 years is also found when the Mexican born are compared with native-born men of Mexican origin.

That the foreign born eventually have higher earnings than the native born suggests that they may have more innate ability, are more highly motivated toward labor market success, or self-finance larger investments in postschool training. The higher earnings may therefore be a consequence of a self-selection in migration in favor of high-ability, highly motivated workers, and workers with low discount rates for human capital investments. The ability-motivation hypothesis is consistent with the lower slope coefficient of schooling for immigrants. It is also consistent with the finding that, other things the same, the native-born sons of immigrants (particularly men with a foreign-born father) have higher earnings than the native-born sons of native-born parents.

Some commentators have suggested that aliens are at an earnings disadvantage compared with naturalized citizens. It appears, however, that aliens earn less than naturalized citizens because on average they have been in the United States for fewer years. When the number of years since migration is held constant, there is no significant difference in earnings between the two groups.

Immigrants from Mexico earn significantly less than other immigrants, but this appears to be a characteristic of Mexican-origin men in general, rather than only first-generation (immigrants) Mexican-Americans. The Cuban refugees are experiencing an earnings history similar to that of other immigrants. Overall, the Cubans have low earnings compared with the native born because a large proportion are very recent arrivals (80 percent since 1960) and about half of them live in a low income state, Florida. Those who have been in the United States for 10 to 15 years have reached earnings parity with native-born men living in the same area.

The analysis indicates that white male immigrants are generally successful in U.S. labor markets. Although initially they have low earnings, their earnings rise rapidly, particularly during their first few years in the country. After 10–15 years their earnings equal and then exceed that of the native born.

2

Assimilation, Changes in Cohort Quality, and the Earnings of Immigrants

Sometime in the mid-1970s, while I was finishing up my graduate educa-
tion, Barry Chiswick presented an early version of his work on the assimila-
tion of immigrants at the Columbia University labor seminar. Having mi-
grated from Cuba to the United States when I was a child, I was predisposed
to find the topic interesting. During the seminar, I asked a question that
summarized everything I knew about immigration at the time: Although
nearly a million Cubans had migrated to the United States, the flow was
composed of two distinct waves, prior to and after the interruption caused
by the Cuban missile crisis. It was suspected that the two waves were "differ-
ent," so I inquired into how the analysis took account of such situations.

It was not until the early 1980s, after I had moved to California and
had seen first hand the impact of large-scale immigration, that my aca-
demic interest in immigration issues surfaced. My thoughts, for some rea-
son, kept returning to the question that I had asked at that seminar years
prior. In fact, some version of that question would occasionally surface in
exams in my labor economics courses even before I had begun to actually
examine the data.

The original version of this chapter was published as: Borjas, G. J. (1985). Assimilation, Changes in Cohort Quality, and the Earnings of Immigrants, in: Journal of Labor Economics, 3(4): 463–89. © 1985 by University of Chicago Press on behalf of the Society of Labor Economists and the NORC at the University of Chicago. The author is grateful to Barry Chiswick, Bill Gould, Daniel Hamermesh, Jacob Mincer, and Marta Tienda. This research was supported by grants from the Rockefeller Foundation and the Department of Health and Human Services.

I knew that the answer to my question required "tracking" specific immigrant cohorts over time, and I started working on this issue immediately after the 1980 Census microdata was released. I vividly recall the morning that I replicated the typical Chiswick-style cross-section regression in both the 1970 and 1980 Censuses and at the same time discovered that the tracking of cohorts in the pooled 1970–1980 Censuses led to dramatically different results. I immediately grasped that this discrepancy was very important, and my career studying immigration issues had begun.

George J. Borjas (2015)

2.1. Introduction

The question how immigrants do in the U.S. labor market has again become an important policy issue, mainly because of the rapid increase in immigration rates during the postwar period. The work of Chiswick (1978d, 1980a) has been extremely influential in the development of the current consensus that immigrants adapt quite rapidly and quite well to the U.S. labor market. The two fundamental results in Chiswick's research are that in a *cross section* of immigrant men (1) the earnings of recently arrived immigrants are significantly lower than the earnings of immigrants who have been in this country for longer periods, and (2) the relatively rapid growth of immigrant earnings over time leads to the existence of an overtaking age, at which point the earnings profiles of the native and the foreign-born cross. This creates the remarkable finding that for most immigrant groups at later stages of the life cycle, immigrant earnings exceed the earnings of the U.S.-born persons. In Chiswick's (1978d) study, the overtaking point was estimated to be around 10–15 years after immigration.

These findings appeal to labor economists because the human capital framework can be easily invoked to explain the empirical regularities. In particular, persons immigrating to the United States for "economic" reasons have strong incentives to devote a large fraction of their effort to the process of accumulating U.S.-specific human capital skills.[1] This investment process explains the relatively rapid rates of growth in immigrant earnings observed in cross sections and, combined with assumptions about how the immigration decision leads to a relatively select group of immigrants, also explains the existence of the overtaking age.

A large literature developed after the appearance of Chiswick's study. This literature borrows both the theoretical framework and the empirical methodology of Chiswick's original work. The studies in Carliner (1980), DeFreitas (1980), Long (1980), Borjas (1982), Borjas and Tienda (1985), and others essentially expand the literature by analyzing both male and female immigrants, studying alternative data sets (such as the 1976 Survey of Income and Education), and focusing on specific immigrant populations (e.g., Hispanics or Asians). These various studies tend to confirm the robustness of the results in cross-section analyses of the problem, and their cumulative impact has led to the current conventional wisdom that after 10–15 years immigrants do extremely well in the U.S. labor market.

The analysis presented in this chapter questions the empirical validity of this conclusion. Using the 1970 and 1980 Public Use Samples from the U.S. census, the analysis shows that the cross-section regressions commonly used in the literature confound the true assimilation impact with possible quality differentials among immigrant cohorts. The empirical analysis below shows that the study of earnings within immigrant cohorts leads to a very different picture of the rate of assimilation of immigrants into the U.S. labor market. Instead of the rapid growth found by the cross-section studies, the cohort analysis predicts relatively slow rates of earnings growth for most immigrant groups. The direct comparison of immigrant cohorts in the 1970 and 1980 Census data shows that the strong assimilation rates measured in the cross section may be partly due to a precipitous decline in the "quality" of immigrants admitted to this country since 1950. Thus the positive impact of the years-since-migration variable in cross-section earnings equations captures both the higher quality of earlier immigrant cohorts as well as the increase in U.S.-specific capital hypothesized in the literature. Finally, the cohort analysis indicates that, for most immigrant groups, the overtaking point takes place much later in the life cycle (if at all) than the point predicted by the cross-section regression.[2]

Section 2.2 of the chapter presents the conceptual framework allowing the identification of the assimilation and cohort effects in census data. This methodology is applied in Section 2.3 to the study of immigrant earnings and in Section 2.4 to the study of the earnings of immigrants relative to the earnings of natives. Finally, Section 2.5 summarizes the results of the study.

2.2. Framework

The economic analysis of how immigrant earnings respond to the assimilation process is commonly based on the results obtained from the following cross-section model:

$$(1) \qquad \ln w_i = X_i \lambda + \beta t_i + \varepsilon_i,$$

where w_i is the wage rate of immigrant i; X_i is a vector of his socioeconomic characteristics (e.g., years of completed schooling, years of labor market experience, etc.); and t_i measures how long immigrant i has been in the United States.[3]

Since total labor market experience (i.e., Age – Education – 6) is usually included as one of the regressors in (1), the coefficient measures the differential value placed by the U.S. labor market between U.S. experience and foreign experience. As was noted in the introduction, one of the most important findings of the cross-section literature is that $\hat{\beta}$ is significantly positive. Thus the U.S. labor market rewards U.S. experience at a higher rate than it rewards foreign experience. The economic interpretation of this finding is usually couched in terms of human capital. When immigrants first arrive in the United States they lack U.S.-specific human capital, which results in relatively low earnings on entrance to the labor market. In order for the costs of immigration to be recouped, the immigrant rapidly begins an investment path with high levels of investment costs. These high levels of human capital investment further depress the current earnings of recent immigrants but guarantee high rates of growth in earnings as the immigrants "assimilate" into the U.S. labor market. Thus the positive and significant $\hat{\beta}$ obtained in cross-section estimates of Equation (1) captures how earnings grow with the assimilation process.

The fallacy in this interpretation lies with its use of a cross-section regression model to explain a dynamic series of events. There are (at least) two obvious factors that can bias cross-section estimates of β and raise serious doubts about the conclusion that the earnings of immigrants rise rapidly as they assimilate. The first of these problems (and one about which little can be done with data currently available) arises from the fact that many immigrants eventually return to their country of origin. Piore (1979), for example, estimates that over 30 percent of the immigrants admitted into the United States in the early 1900s emigrated back to their country of origin. Similarly, Warren and Peck (1980), using the

1960 and 1970 Censuses, estimate that 18 percent of immigrants admitted to the United States between 1960 and 1970 had emigrated by 1970. Since the incidence of emigration is not likely to be a random process in the immigrant population, potentially serious selection biases can affect the cross-section estimate of β. For example, if immigrants who do not do well in the United States are more likely to emigrate, the coefficient $\hat{\beta}$ will be biased upward, since earlier cohorts of immigrants will have been self-selected to include only the most successful immigrants, while the recent cohorts contain a more representative selection of the immigrant pool. Unfortunately, despite the potential importance of this problem, the complete lack of emigration data for the United States implies that any analysis of this issue (even the simple counting of how many emigrants there are) requires the making of many unverifiable statistical and institutional assumptions.[4]

The second problem with the dynamic interpretation of the cross-section coefficient β is its implicit assumption that, to abstract from the emigration problem, the average "quality" of successive cohorts of immigrants is not changing over time. This stationarity assumption permits the inference that since the cross-section regression indicates that a recently arrived immigrant earns $(10\beta) \cdot 100\%$ less than one who arrived ten years earlier, it follows that the earnings of recently arrived immigrants will increase by $(10\beta) \cdot 100\%$ in the next decade (net of aging effects).

Note that the direction of the bias if the stationarity assumption is not empirically valid depends on the secular trend in the quality of the immigrant cohorts admitted to the United States. If, for example, institutional changes in immigration policies or political disturbances in sending countries lead to higher quality immigration, the cross-section estimate of β would be downwardly biased. If, on the other hand, the shift from occupational to family preferences mandated by the 1965 Immigration and Nationality Act and the increase in unscreened illegal immigrants has lowered the average quality of immigrant cohorts, the cross-section estimate of β would be upwardly biased and the impact of the assimilation process on the earnings of immigrants would be overestimated.

It is likely that the rapid increase in immigration rates since 1950 has violated the stringent requirements imposed by the stationarity assumption in cross-section studies. Thus the estimates of Equation (1) are likely to suffer from serious biases. To derive a general framework for comparing the cross-section results with the findings obtained from within-cohort analyses, consider the group of immigrants ages 18–54 in 1970. Using the 1970 Census, it is convenient to partition this group into four cohorts: arrivals in 1965–69, arrivals in 1960–64, arrivals in 1950–59, and immigrants who arrived prior to 1950. Consider next the group of immigrants ages 28–64 in the 1980 Census. The 1980 Census data allows the partitioning of this group of immigrants into six cohorts: arrivals in 1975–79, arrivals in 1970–74, arrivals in 1965–69, arrivals in 1960–64, arrivals in 1950–59, and immigrants who arrived prior to 1950. Note that the last four cohorts defined in the 1980 group exactly match the definitions of the cohorts from the 1970 Census. In addition, the age composition of the two samples ensures that (if the census data contained all observations from the population) the same individuals are included in each of these cohort samples.[5] Given these data, two cross-section regressions can be estimated:

$$(2) \qquad \ln w_{70} = X\gamma_{70} + \alpha_{65}D_{65} + \alpha_{60}D_{60} + \alpha_{50}D_{50} + \alpha_{40}D_{40} + \varepsilon_{70},$$

$$(3) \qquad \ln w_{80} = X\gamma_{80} + \beta_{75}D_{75} + \beta_{75}D_{75} + \beta_{65}D_{65} + \beta_{60}D_{60}$$
$$+ \beta_{50}D_{50} + \beta_{40}D_{40} + \varepsilon_{80},$$

where the dummy variables indexing years-since-immigration/cohort are defined by D_{75} = one if immigrated in 1975–79; D_{70} = one if immigrated in 1970–74; D_{65} = one if immigrated in 1965–69; D_{60} = one if immigrated in 1960–64; D_{50} = one if immigrated in 1950–59; and D_{40} = one if immigrated prior to 1950. By definition, the vector X in (2) and (3) does not contain a constant term.

Consider cohort k, where $D_k = 1$ ($k = 40, 50, 60, 65$). Let $\overline{X}_k$ give the mean values of the socioeconomic characteristics for this cohort as of 1980. Define:

$$(4) \qquad \hat{\gamma}_{70,k} = \overline{X}_k\hat{\gamma}_{70} + \hat{\alpha}_k,$$

$$(5) \qquad \hat{\gamma}_{80,k} = \overline{X}_k\hat{\gamma}_{80} + \hat{\beta}_k,$$

$$(6) \qquad \hat{\gamma}_{80,k+10} = \overline{X}_k\hat{\gamma}_{80} + \hat{\beta}_{k+10}.$$

Equations (4) and (5) give the predicted (ln) earnings of the average member of cohort k in 1970 and 1980, respectively. Equation (6) gives the predicted (ln) earnings in 1980 for the cohort who arrived ten years after cohort k. Note that, by definition, as of 1970 cohort k has been in the United States, say, j years. As of 1980, cohort $k + 10$ has also been in the United States j years. Thus the comparison of these two cohorts across censuses holds constant the number of years since immigration.

Using the definitions in (4)-(6), the 1980 regression predicts that over ten years, the cross-section growth for cohort k (net of aging) is given by[6]

(7)
$$\hat{\gamma}_{80,k} - \hat{\gamma}_{80,k+10} = \hat{\beta}_k - \hat{\beta}_{k+10}.$$

The cross-section growth given by (7) can be rewritten as

(8)
$$\hat{\gamma}_{80,k} - \hat{\gamma}_{80,k+10} = (\hat{\gamma}_{80,k} - \hat{\gamma}_{70,k}) + (\hat{\gamma}_{70,k} - \hat{\gamma}_{80,k+10}).$$

Equation (8) decomposes the cross-section growth into two parts. The first term in (8) gives the earnings growth experienced by cohort k over the decade and will be called the "within-cohort" growth. The second term in (8) estimates the difference in earnings that occurred over the decade for individuals with a given number of years since immigration. Thus it compares different cohorts at the same point of their U.S. life cycle and will be called the "across-cohort" earnings growth. If, for example, the quality of cohorts is declining over time, the earnings of immigrants who have been in the United States j years will decline across censuses. Thus the second term in (8) is positive, upwardly biasing the cross-section measure of earnings growth. Equation (8), therefore, illustrates a very useful result: the comparison of immigrant cross sections over time can be used to infer the extent to which the underlying quality of immigrant cohorts is changing.[7]

It is important to note that although, as Equation (8) shows, the cross-section growth is biased by the existence of quality differentials across cohorts, the within-cohort growth can also be biased by the effect of secular changes in aggregate labor market conditions. For example, if economic conditions worsened between 1970 and 1980, the within-cohort growth in (8) will be biased downwards and the decomposition in (8) will exaggerate the extent of quality differences across cohorts. One possible solution to this problem is simply to analyze the behavior of immigrant earnings relative to a base of native workers. Suppose the wage structures for native workers are given by

(9)
$$\ln w_{70,n} = X\delta_{70} + \alpha_n + \varepsilon_{70},$$

(10)
$$\ln w_{80,n} = X\delta_{80} + \beta_n + \varepsilon_{80},$$

where the subscript n indicates native status. Define the earnings a native worker statistically similar to the average immigrant from cohort k would earn by

(11)
$$\hat{\gamma}_{70,n} = \overline{X}_k \hat{\delta}_{70} + \hat{\alpha}_n$$

(12) $$\hat{\gamma}_{80,n} = \overline{X}_k \hat{\delta}_{80} + \hat{\beta}_n.$$

Note that the cross-section growth in the relative earnings of immigrant cohort k is given by

(13) $$(\hat{\gamma}_{80,k} - \hat{\gamma}_{80,n}) - (\hat{\gamma}_{80,k+10} - \hat{\gamma}_{80,n}) = \hat{\beta}_k - \hat{\beta}_{k+10}.$$

Thus the estimate of cross-section growth is unaffected by the introduction of native workers into the analysis.[8] Equation (13) can be decomposed into

(14) $$\hat{\beta}_k - \hat{\beta}_{k+10} = [(\hat{\gamma}_{80,k} - \hat{\gamma}_{80,n}) - (\hat{\gamma}_{70,k} - \hat{\gamma}_{70,n})]$$
$$+ [(\hat{\gamma}_{70,k} - \hat{\gamma}_{70,n}) - (\hat{\gamma}_{80,k+10} - \hat{\gamma}_{80,n})].$$

The first bracketed term in (14) gives the difference in the relative earnings of cohort k between 1980 and 1970. This within-cohort effect measures the rate at which the earnings profiles of immigrants and natives are converging (or diverging). The second bracketed term in (14), as before, gives the across-cohort effect. It estimates the difference in the relative earnings of immigrants who are at the same position in their U.S. life cycle between 1970 and 1980. If this difference is positive, the across-cohort growth indicates that, relative to the native base, the quality of immigrants is falling over time, upwardly biasing the cross-section growth in immigrant earnings.

Finally, it should be noted that the statistical framework leading to Equations (8) and (14) is rather general. By allowing the socioeconomic vector X to have a different effect between the native and the foreign born, and across different time periods, the biases introduced by invalid restrictions on the coefficients are avoided. It turns out that in the census data analyzed below, the large sample sizes used led to the rejection of equality constraints on these coefficients for practically all immigrant and native groups.

2.3.   The Earnings of Immigrants

The data used in the analysis are drawn from the 1970 1/100 Public Use Sample from the U.S. census (5% SMSA and County Group Sample), and the 1980 A Sample from the U.S. census (a 5 percent random sample of the population). Because of the very large sample sizes in these data sets, random samples were drawn for some of the larger groups (e.g., white natives in both 1970 and 1980, black natives in 1980, etc.).[9]

The analysis is restricted to male persons ages 18–54 in 1970 and 28–64 in 1980. The four sample selection rules, used in both censuses, require that (1) the individual was not self-employed or working without pay; (2) the individual was not in the armed forces (as of the census week); (3) the individual did not reside in group quarters; and (4) the individual's record can be used to calculate the 1969 or 1979 wage rate.[10] Since previous research has shown that major differences in economic status exist within the male immigrant (and native) labor force, the study will be conducted separately for each of the six major immigrant groups: Mexican (18.0 percent of the male immigrant population as of 1980), Cuban (5.3 percent), other Hispanic (9.7 percent), Asian (15.9 percent), white (45.4 percent), and black (5.7 percent), where the "white" and "black" immigrant samples contain the observations which are neither Hispanic nor Asian.[11] Table 2.1 presents the means of basic economic characteristics for the cohorts in each of the immigrant samples, and for their native male counterparts. The table presents the mean (ln) wage rate ($WAGE$), the mean completed years of schooling ($EDUC$), the average age of the group, as well as the number of observations in the sample (N). Throughout the chapter the 1979 wage rate has been deflated to 1969 levels by using the Consumer Price Index. Table 2.1 illustrates the well-known facts that major differences in these socioeconomic characteristics exist both between native and immigrant groups and within each of these populations across national groups.

The empirical analysis reported throughout the chapter is based on the estimates of Equations (2), (3), (9), and (10): the two immigrant cross sections and the two native cross sections. To allow the testing of coefficients across these equations, the four equations were estimated jointly. The Appendix to this chapter presents the complete set of regressions used in the analysis (Table A2.1 provides a description of the variables used in the regression; Table A2.2 presents the estimated regressions; and Table A2.3 presents the means of the socioeconomic characteristics used in the decomposition of cross-section effects into its within- and across-cohort components). The vector of socioeconomic characteristics, X, in the cross-section regressions includes the variables years of completed schooling, years of labor market experience (Age – Schooling – 6), years of labor market experience squared, whether or not health limits work, whether or not married with spouse present, and whether or not the individual resides in an SMSA.[12] The dependent variable is the 1969 or 1979 (ln) wage rate.[13]

Table 2.1
Summary Statistics

Group and Year of Arrival	1970				1980			
	Ln WAGE	EDUC	AGE	N	Ln WAGE	EDUC	AGE	N
White								
1975-79	...	...	...	...	1.32	13.5	38.2	347
1970-74	...	...	...	...	1.28	12.2	38.9	258
1965-69	1.25	11.7	33.1	1,690	1.40	12.2	41.8	370
1960-64	1.41	11.5	35.2	1,288	1.52	12.8	43.5	327
1950-59	1.42	11.6	37.2	3,276	1.53	12.5	45.8	869
<1950	1.53	12.2	43.5	2,595	1.48	12.7	52.6	574
Native	1.31	12.1	35.6	26,045	1.39	12.8	43.0	11,506
Black:								
1975-79	...	...	...	...	.92	11.4	36.7	479
1970-74	...	...	...	...	1.14	12.2	38.0	670
1965-69	1.05	10.7	33.8	145	1.26	12.6	40.7	522
1960-64	1.18	11.9	33.6	67	1.23	13.4	42.2	223
1950-59	1.15	10.6	38.2	81	1.11	11.9	46.3	175
<1950	1.08	10.1	45.5	49	1.08	10.7	49.1	218
Native	.93	10.0	35.3	27,761	1.12	11.2	42.3	7,572
Asian:								
1975-79	...	...	...	...	1.08	13.9	37.8	7,217
1970-74	...	...	...	...	1.34	15.3	37.9	5,176
1965-69	1.13	14.2	32.7	425	1.48	15.6	39.9	3,408
1960-64	1.29	14.0	33.4	195	1.57	15.8	41.5	1,293
1950-59	1.34	13.4	36.8	177	1.49	14.8	44.4	1,334
<1950	1.26	11.2	43.9	152	1.35	11.6	53.1	815
Native	1.31	12.6	35.8	1,441	1.45	13.6	43.0	8,981

Table 2.1 (continued)
Summary Statistics

Group and Year of Arrival	1970				1980			
	Ln WAGE	EDUC	AGE	N	Ln WAGE	EDUC	AGE	N
Mexican:								
1975-79	...	...	...	...	.68	6.3	36.5	1,335
1970-74	...	...	...	...	.90	6.6	35.8	1,719
1965-69	.67	6.4	29.2	415	1.02	6.9	36.8	1,191
1960-64	.92	6.6	32.2	366	1.06	7.2	41.4	926
1950-59	.98	7.1	36.0	559	1.17	8.1	44.7	1,266
<1950	1.05	7.4	42.4	286	1.05	7.4	50.1	603
Native	1.00	9.4	33.5	5,064	1.18	10.3	40.7	11,785
Cuban:								
1975-79	...	...	...	...	.72	11.2	42.0	273
1970-74	...	...	...	...	1.04	9.8	47.5	1,124
1965-69	.95	9.6	39.0	344	1.06	10.2	48.4	1,788
1960-64	1.18	12.2	35.7	428	1.32	13.1	44.4	2,274
1950-59	1.09	10.3	37.9	155	1.22	11.6	47.0	862
<1950	1.25	11.0	44.7	44	1.38	11.2	53.5	172
Native	1.14	11.6	34.1	61	1.29	12.8	41.4	466
Other Hispanic:								
1975-79	...	...	...	...	.89	10.9	36.8	2,467
1970-74	...	...	...	...	1.05	10.8	37.6	3,041
1965-69	1.02	11.1	31.9	459	1.15	11.0	40.3	2,812
1960-64	1.19	11.2	33.9	332	1.27	11.8	42.4	1,774
1950-59	1.31	12.1	36.7	227	1.34	12.3	45.3	1,139
<1950	1.42	13.0	41.8	82	1.35	11.6	51.3	518
Native	1.17	10.8	34.1	3,024	1.29	12.1	41.7	10,301

In this section the discussion will focus on the estimates of the immigrant cross sections (2) and (3). To provide comparability between these results and the literature, Table 2.2 presents the coefficients of the years-since-migration variable obtained from the 1980 cross section for each of the six national groups. The omitted dummy variable in the table is D_{75} (arrivals in 1975–79), so that all coefficients in Table 2.2 measure wage differentials between earlier immigrant cohorts and their most recent counterparts. The results in Table 2.2 tend to mimic those presented in the literature: with relatively minor exceptions, the earnings of immigrants who have been in the United States many years are significantly higher than the earnings of recent arrivals. For example, Asian immigrants who arrived in the early 1970s report about 17 percent higher earnings than the most recent Asian arrivals in the 1980 Census. This differential increases to over 30 percent for the Asian immigrants who arrived in the early 1960s and to over 40 percent for the Asians who immigrated prior to 1950. Similar qualitative conclusions can be drawn for practically all national groups. Thus the 1980 cross-section regressions in the immigrant samples indicate, if anything, the robustness of the years-since-migration variable in cross-section regressions.

Table 2.2

Coefficients of Years-since-Migration Variables in 1980 Cross Section

	Group					
Variable	White Immigrant	Black Immigrant	Asian Immigrant	Mexican Immigrant	Cuban Immigrant	Other Hispanic Immigrant
D70	-.0124	.1801	.1721	.1929	.3722	.1597
	(-.25)	(4.18)	(14.18)	(7.34)	(7.81)	(8.56)
D65	.0665	.2662	.2829	.3044	.3677	.2334
	(1.46)	(5.73)	(20.26)	(10.57)	(7.99)	(12.12)
D60	.1565	.1867	.3474	.3426	.5217	.3177
	(3.32)	(3.12)	(17.15)	(10.91)	(11.53)	(14.39)
D50	.1673	.1434	.3355	.4326	.4902	.3605
	(4.22)	(2.18)	(16.63)	(14.35)	(10.01)	(14.02)
D40	.0883	.1774	.4119	.3749	.6769	.3983
	(1.97)	(2.79)	(15.75)	(9.74)	(9.80)	(11.35)

Note: The *t*-ratios are given in parentheses.
Source: Appendix Table A2.2.

The analysis in the previous section, as summarized by Equation (8), shows how the growth implicit in the cross-section estimates of Table 2.2 can be decomposed into a within-cohort growth and an

Table 2.3

Decomposition of Cross-Section Growth in Immigrant Earnings

Group and Year of Immigration	Cross-Section Growth	Within-Cohort Growth	Across-Cohort Growth
White			
1965-69	.0665	.0029	.0636
	(1.46)	(.20)	(1.61)
1960-64	.1690	-.0111	.1801
	(3.33)	(-.17)	(4.14)
1950-59	.0558	.0089	.0469
	(1.80)	(.59)	(1.54)
Black			
1965-69	.2662	.0041	.2621
	(5.73)	(.10)	(3.35)
1960-64	.0066	-.1540	.1606
	(.10)	(-1.49)	(1.65)
1950-59	-.0831	-.2303	.1472
	(-1.33)	(-2.18)	(1.58)
Asian:			
1965-69	.2829	.1972	.0857
	(20.26)	(4.62)	(2.27)
1960-64	.1754	.1105	.0649
	(8.48)	(1.80)	(1.30)
1950-59	.0204	.0327	-.0123
	(.96)	(.39)	(-.01)
Mexican:			
1965-69	.3044	.1717	.1327
	(10.57)	(3.67)	(2.92)
1960-64	.1497	.0486	.1011
	(5.00)	(.94)	(2.19)
1950-59	.1091	.1024	.0067
	(4.12)	(2.28)	(.20)
Cuban:			
1965-69	.3677	.1031	.2646
	(7.99)	(1.89)	(3.82)
1960-64	.1495	.1037	.0458
	(5.60)	(2.41)	(.94)
1950-59	.0455	.1121	-.0666
	(1.73)	(1.68)	(-1.06)
Other Hispanic:			
1965-69	.2334	.0331	.2003
	(12.12)	(.69)	(4.93)
1960-64	.158	.0058	.1522
	(7.51)	(.01)	(3.39)
1950-59	.0850	.0153	.0697
	(3.67)	(.14)	(1.36)

Note: The t-ratios are given in parentheses.
Source: Appendix Tables A2.2 and A2.3.

across-cohort growth. This decomposition is carried out in Table 2.3 for each of three cohorts which can be matched exactly in the 1970 and 1980 Census files: arrivals in 1965–69, 1960–64, and 1950–59.[14]

Perhaps the best way to understand Table 2.3 is to illustrate its derivation through an example. Consider the group of white immigrants who arrived in the United States during the 1965–69 period. As Table 2.2 shows, these individuals earn roughly 6.7 percent more than the most recent arrivals (i.e., white men who immigrated in 1975–79). Thus the cross-section analysis predicts that over a 10-year period the 1965–69 immigrants will have increased their earnings by 6.7 percent. However, if we compare the earnings of this cohort in 1970 and 1980, as measured by the first term in (8), the cohort actually experienced an insignificant increase in earnings of about 0.3 percent. The difference between the cross-section growth and the within-cohort growth is 6.4 percent. This differential indicates that recently arrived immigrants in 1970 had 6.4 percent higher earnings than recently arrived immigrants in 1980, and it may be indicative of a drop in quality across immigrant cohorts. Thus the decomposition of the cross-section growth predicted for this immi-grant cohort indicates that, in fact, the cohort experienced no earnings growth over the decade and that the entire cross-section growth is ex-plained by earnings differences across immigrant cohorts.

The remaining rows of Table 2.3 replicate this analysis for all other co-horts in the six immigrant groups. The major finding obtained from these results is that there are significant differences in the within-cohort growth experienced by immigrants both within a national group and across na-tional groups. The latter fact is illustrated by the result that within-cohort growth is zero or negative for white and black immigrants, but is over-whelmingly positive for Asian, Mexican, and Cuban immigrants. Thus there are strong racial/ethnic differences in the rate at which the earnings of immigrant cohorts actually increased over the 1970–80 period. Note also that the across-cohort growth is positive in 16 out of 18 cases, and has a t-ratio exceeding 1.5 in 12 out of 18 cases. These results are consistent with the hypothesis that the quality of immigrants has declined over suc-ceeding immigrant cohorts. It is interesting to note that, in fact, the only important negative (but insignificant) across-cohort effect, indicating that the quality of immigrants increased over time, is obtained in the row for Cuban immigrants who arrived in 1950–59. The across-cohort effect in this case measures how these arrivals compare with the Cubans who arrived in 1960–69. The increase in quality suggested by Table 2.3 is con-sistent with the hypothesis that the 1959 political upheaval in Cuba led to the outflow of "better" Cuban immigrants in the first few years of the postrevolution period.

2.4.   The Relative Earnings of Immigrants

As was pointed out earlier, the decomposition of the cross-section growth in Table 2.3 into the within-cohort and across-cohort components is itself not free of bias. If labor market conditions worsened sufficiently between 1969 and 1979, the within-cohort growth of immigrants will be depressed by the fall in the aggregate wage level, and the across-cohort quality change will be exaggerated. It is important to note, however, that the evidence in Table 2.3 suggests that this cannot be the only reason for the difference between cross-section and within-cohort effects. In particular, if the fall in aggregate wage levels was neutral across immigrant cohorts and national groups, the results in Table 2.3 indicate that since some immigrant national groups and/or some cohorts within each group *did* fare quite well during the 1970–80 period, the *relative* differences in the results across the 18 cohorts do measure the variance in the within-cohort growth and the secular quality change among immigrant cohorts.

The analysis in Section 2.2 suggested that a simple way of netting out the influence of the fall in aggregate demand from the estimates was to decompose the cross-section growth in immigrant earnings relative to the native base. One of the most remarkable findings of the cross-section literature on the relative earnings of immigrants is the existence of an overtaking age, at which point immigrants' earnings begin to surpass the earnings of statistically similar native workers. This overtaking point has been dated at between 10 and 15 years after immigration for some immigrant groups.

Before proceeding to the decomposition of the relative change in immigrant earnings over the 1970–80 period, it is useful to provide a set of results comparable to those found in the literature. Table 2.4 presents the difference between the 1980 (ln) earnings of statistically similar immigrants and native workers, evaluated at the mean level of the socioeconomic characteristics of the immigrant cohort.[15] It should be noted that the choice of the reference group is somewhat arbitrary, since the immigrants can be compared either to the white native population or to the immigrants' nationality counterparts in the native population (i.e., Mexican immigrants would be compared to Mexican

American native men, black immigrants to black native men, etc.). Both of these strategies were pursued and since the possibility of overtaking the white native population was quite low for most of the immigrant groups, the analysis is presented using the latter alternative. That is, each immigrant group is compared to its native counterpart.[16]

Table 2.4

Wage Differentials between the Foreign Born and the U.S. Born in 1980 Cross Section

	Group					
Variable	White Immigrant	Black Immigrant	Asian Immigrant	Mexican Immigrant	Cuban Immigrant	Other Hispanic Immigrant
D75	-.0876	-.2521	-.3613	-.2973	-.5287	-.3244
	(-2.64)	(-7.35)	(-31.83)	(-13.32)	(-9.43)	(-19.73)
D70	-.0925	-.0814	-.1736	-.1072	-.1919	-.1754
	(-2.42)	(-2.77)	(-13.65)	(-5.36)	(-3.81)	(-11.54)
D65	-.0126	.0146	-.0805	-.0081	-.2021	-.1258
	(-.39)	(.45)	(-5.69)	(-.49)	(-4.18)	(-8.26)
D60	.0774	-.0731	-.0337	-.0113	-.0251	-.0626
	(2.29)	(-1.49)	(-1.71)	(-.64)	(-.66)	(-3.63)
D50	.0806	-.1087	-.0893	.0383	-.0743	-.0364
	(3.78)	(-1.98)	(-4.59)	(1.50)	(-1.64)	(-1.78)
D40	-.0071	-.0733	-.091	-.0512	.0839	-.0242
	(-.24)	(-1.48)	(-3.72)	(-1.91)	(1.10)	(-.88)

Note: The *t*-ratios are given in parentheses.
Source: Appendix Tables A2.2 and A2.3.

The results in Table 2.4 are consistent with the findings reported in the literature: the earnings of white immigrants overtake the earnings of statistically comparable white native workers within 10–15 years after immigration.[17] All other immigrant groups, however, have slower rates of convergence, even though the other groups are not being compared to the white native base.

Equation (14) presents the methodology by which the cross-section rates of convergence can be decomposed into within-cohort and across-cohort changes in relative earnings.[18] This decomposition is given in Table 2.5. Consider, for example, the results for Mexican immigrants who arrived in 1965–69. According to the cross section, relative to the Mexicans born in the United States, the wage of these immigrants increased about 30 percent within the first ten years after immigration. Note, however, that the cohort actually experienced an increase of only 18.2 percent in their relative earnings during their first decade in the United States. The difference between these two growth rates, about 12.2 per-

Table 2.5

Decomposition of Cross-Section Growth in Immigrant/Native Relative Earnings

Group and Year of Immigration	Cross-Section Growth	Within-Cohort Growth	Across-Cohort Growth
White:			
1965-69	.0665	.0788	-.0123
	(1.46)	(2.22)	(-.37)
1960-64	.1690	.0716	.0974
	(3.33)	(1.89)	(2.21)
1950-59	.0558	.0773	-.0215
	(1.80)	(3.05)	(-.84)
Black:			
1965-69	.2662	-.0308	.2970
	(5.73)	(-.48)	(3.71)
1960-64	.0066	-.1771	.1837
	(.10)	(-1.66)	(1.83)
1950-59	-.0831	-.2668	.1837
	(-1.33)	(-2.45)	(1.87)
Asian:			
1965-69	.2829	.2131	.0698
	(20.26)	(4.07)	(1.55)
1960-64	.1754	.1265	.0489
	(8.48)	(1.81)	(.91)
1950-59	.0204	.0172	.0032
	(.96)	(0.10)	(.22)
Mexican:			
1965-69	.3044	.1823	.1221
	(10.57)	(2.92)	(2.58)
1960-64	.1497	.0563	.0934
	(5.00)	(.93)	(2.00)
1950-59	.1091	.1066	.0025
	(4.12)	(2.01)	(.24)
Cuban:			
1965-69	.3677	-.2424	.6101
	(7.99)	(-1.1 1)	(2.75)
1960-64	.1495	-.0460	.1955
	(5.60)	(-.26)	(1.12)
1950-59	.0455	-.1240	.1695
	(1.73)	(-.62)	(.85)
Other Hispanic:			
1965-69	.2334	.0866	.1468
	(12.12)	(1.77)	(3.31)
1960-64	.1580	.0576	.1004
	(7.51)	(.98)	(2.1)
1950-59	.0850	.0495	.0355
	(3.67)	(0.66)	(.71)

Note: The *t*-ratios are given in parentheses.
Source: Appendix Tables A2.2 and A2.3.

cent, is the across-cohort growth and indicates that recent Mexican immigrants in 1970 did 12.2 percent better (relative to U.S.-born Mexicans) than recent Mexican immigrants in 1980. Thus, relative to the U.S.-born Mexican population, the result in Table 2.5 indicates that the quality of Mexican immigrants may have declined over time.

An additional implication of this result is that the cross-section growth underestimates the number of years that it will take the recent Mexican immigrants to overtake their statistically similar native counterparts. Since the earnings profiles of the Mexican native and foreign men are converging at relatively slow rates, the overtaking point is delayed considerably.

The remaining rows of Table 2.5 indicate that practically all the immigrant cohorts being analyzed experienced strong relative earnings growth over a 10-year period according to the cross-section results. The within-cohort analysis, however, shows that improvements in the relative earnings of immigrants is concentrated within specific race/ethnic groups. For example, earnings profiles of immigrant and native groups of white, Asian, and Mexican workers generally exhibit strong rates of convergence. On the other hand, the results for blacks and Cubans show either little change in the relative earnings of immigrants or a deterioration in their relative earnings over the decade 1970–80.

The results in Table 2.5 also show that the rate of growth in relative immigrant earnings given by the cross-section analysis often exceeds the actual rate of growth experienced by the immigrant cohort. The across-cohort growth is positive and has a t-statistic exceeding 1.5 in 10 of the 18 cohorts under analysis. These positive across-cohort effects state that for the same number of years in the United States, immigrants in earlier cohorts do better (relative to natives) than immigrants in more recent cohorts. Thus the results in Table 2.5 are again consistent with the hypothesis that the quality of immigrant cohorts has been falling over time for many immigrant groups.

It can, of course, be argued that the across-cohort effects are only capturing the fall in demand for immigrant labor that presumably occurred during the 1970s. This argument, however, is not sufficient to explain the results in Table 2.5, since the variation in across-cohort effects across *and* within immigrant groups is quite large. For example, why are the across-cohort changes larger for black and Cuban immigrants than they are for white and Asian immigrants? Further, why are the across-cohort effects so different within specific groups? In the white sample, for instance, two of the across-cohort effects are negative (and insignificant), while one is significantly positive and numerically large. The demand shift hypothesis cannot explain these variations unless it is also argued that demand varied systematically not only across national groups, but also within national groups according to the years since migration. Finally, the demand shift hypothesis must also assume that the demand for immigrant labor declined *relative* to the demand for native labor. The evidence on any of these assumptions is, at present, nonexistent.

The results in Tables 2.3 and 2.5, therefore, raise important doubts about the validity of the inference drawn from cross-section studies that immigrants "assimilate" rapidly in the U.S. labor market. It is important to note that these effects, by focusing solely on the years-since-migration variable, are measuring the impact of assimilation *net* of aging effects. The effect of aging on the relative earnings of immigrants would not be very important if the age coefficients (more precisely, the coefficients of potential labor market experience) were roughly similar in the native and foreign-born earnings functions. The regressions in Appendix Table A2.2, however, suggest that this is not the case. Thus it is worthwhile to conclude the analysis by presenting estimates of the change in the relative wage of immigrants over a 10-year period due solely to the fact that the men are ten years older in 1980 than in 1970.

Using the 1980 cross-section regression in Equation (3), the earnings of immigrants in a particular cohort with T years of potential labor market experience can be defined by

$$(15) \qquad \hat{\gamma}_{i,T} = \bar{Z}\hat{\theta}_i + \hat{\rho}_i T + \hat{\lambda}_i T^2,$$

where $\bar{Z}$ is the mean vector of all the socioeconomic characteristics except for experience and experience squared, and the subscript i indicates that the parameters are drawn from the cross-section regression estimated in the immigrant sample. The predicted earnings for an immigrant who is ten years younger, holding all other factors constant, is given by

$$(16) \qquad \hat{\gamma}_{i,T-10} = \bar{Z}\hat{\theta}_i + \hat{\rho}_i(T - 10) + \hat{\lambda}_i(T - 10)^2.$$

Thus the change in immigrant earnings due solely to the aging of the immigrant over the decade is

$$(17) \qquad \Delta_i = 10\hat{\rho}_i + \hat{\lambda}_i(20T - 100).$$

Using the 1980 cross section estimated in the sample of native men leads, of course, to a similar expression for the aging effect experienced by statistically similar native men:

$$(18) \qquad \Delta_n = 10\hat{\rho}_n + \hat{\lambda}_n(20T - 100).$$

Hence the change in the relative earnings of immigrants due purely to aging is given by

$$(19) \qquad \Delta_i - \Delta_n = 10(\hat{\rho}_i - \hat{\rho}_n) + (\hat{\lambda}_i - \hat{\lambda}_n)(20T - 100).$$

Equation (19) illustrates the obvious fact that the relative earnings of immigrants are affected by aging only if the coefficients of the age variables differ between the immigrant and native earnings functions.

Table 2.6

Estimates of Aging Effect on Immigrant/Native Relative Earnings

Group	Year of Immigration		
	1965-69	1960-64	1950-59
White	.0205	.0163	.0058
	(1.02)	(.87)	(.37)
Black	.0554	.0506	.0115
	(1.81)	(1.73)	(.55)
Asian	-.1485	-.1410	-.1183
	(-8.91)	(-9.21)	(-10.11)
Mexican	-.0789	-.0789	-.0789
	(-3.84)	(-4.95)	(-5.63)
Cuban	-.0687	-.1277	-.0926
	(-1.88)	(-2.85)	(-2.62)
Other Hispanic	-.0944	-.0902	-.0827
	(-6.23)	(-6.53)	(-6.98)

Note: The t-ratios are given in parentheses.
Source: Appendix Tables A2.2 and A2.3.

Table 2.6 presents the estimated aging effects, as defined by Equation (19), for each of the 18 cohorts under analysis. The obvious implication of these results is that for four of the six immigrant groups, pure aging effects lead to a *deterioration* of the relative earnings of immigrants over time. This deterioration is not only statistically significant but is also numerically important. For example, the fact that the immigrant men are ten years older in 1980 than in 1970 lowers the relative earnings of Asians by 12–15 percent, lowers the relative earnings of Mexicans by 7.9 percent, lowers the relative earnings of Cubans by 7–13 percent, and lowers the relative earnings of other Hispanics by 8–9 percent. If these quantities are added to the within-cohort assimilation effects presented in Table 2.5, it quickly becomes apparent that, in fact, the *relative* earnings of immigrants, as a result of relatively low assimilation rates and detrimental aging effects, simply did not increase very much in the decade 1970–80.

The other two immigrant groups – whites and blacks – have aging effects that are positive, but generally insignificant. Only two of the six aging effects estimated for these two groups have a t-ratio exceeding 1.5. Moreover, in the case of whites, the impact of aging on the relative earnings of immigrants is numerically trivial. Thus Table 2.6 reveals that the pure impact of aging seldom works in favor of the immigrants and, in fact, often works to their detriment.

2.5. Summary

This chapter has conducted a reexamination of the empirical basis for two "facts" concerning immigrant wage growth that seem to be found in most cross-section empirical studies of the problem: (1) the earnings of immigrants grow rapidly as they assimilate into the United States; and (2) this rapid growth also leads to immigrants overtaking the earnings of the native workers within 10–15 years after arrival.

The study in this chapter stresses the differences between cross-section and cohort analyses of earnings determination. In particular, cross-section studies of immigrant earnings growth confound the true assimilation impact with across-cohort changes in immigrant quality. The analysis of 18 specific immigrant cohorts in the 1970 and 1980 Public Use Samples of the U.S. census led to three major results:

1. The earnings of a cohort of immigrants grow at a much slower rate than that predicted by cross-section studies. Over the decade 1970–80, the cross-section regression overestimated the true rate of growth experienced by immigrants by as much as 20 percentage points in some immigrant cohorts.

2. The earnings growth of immigrant cohorts relative to the native cohorts is again greatly overestimated by cross-section analysis. The empirical study of specific immigrant cohorts shows that the relative earnings of many of these cohorts experienced little change, or even a slight decline, over the 1970–80 period even though the cross-section regression predicts rapid growth in the relative earnings of immigrants.

3. These results imply that the across-cohort change in immigrant earnings is quite significant, with earlier cohorts earning more at every point of their U.S. labor market career than more recent

cohorts. Although part of this across-cohort result may be due to a hypothesized fall in demand for immigrant labor, the results are also consistent with the hypothesis that the quality of immigrant cohorts has experienced a secular decline.

The analysis in this chapter, therefore, raises serious questions about the economic interpretation of immigrant behavior in the labor market and about the policy question what is the contribution of immigrants to the United States. The main lesson of this chapter, however, is that cross-section studies of immigrant earnings provide useless and misleading insights into the process of immigrant assimilation into the labor market. More generally, the results of the cohort analysis make it clear that an understanding of the immigrant experience in the United States cannot be obtained in a vacuum, free of an institutional framework. The immigration experience cannot be understood without the introduction into the model of the parameters of admission policies, the recurring political and economic upheavals in the sending countries, and the shifts in labor demand for native and foreign-born labor. The study of immigrant earnings, within this institutional framework, will surely lead to a much deeper understanding of the immigration experience.

Appendix

Table A2.1

Definition of Independent Variables in Regression

EDUC	Years of completed schooling
EX PER	Age- EDUC- 6
EXPER2	EXPER squared
MAR	One if married, spouse present; zero otherwise
HLTH	One if health limits work; zero otherwise
SMSA	One if resides in SMSA; zero otherwise
D75	One if immigrated in 1975-79; zero otherwise
D70	One if immigrated in 1970-74; zero otherwise
D65	One if immigrated in 1965-69; zero otherwise
D60	One if immigrated in 1960-64; zero otherwise
DSO	One if immigrated in 1950-59; zero otherwise
D40	One if immigrated prior to 1950;

Table A2.2
Wage Regressions: Dependent Variable = Ln(Wage Rate/10)

Variable	Coefficient t Whites		Coefficient t Blacks		Coefficient t Asians	
1980 native:						
EDUC	.0592	(29.25)	.0497	(16.57)	.0524	(19.68)
EX PER	.0297	(12.86)	.0059	(1.79)	.0348	(12.99)
EXPER2	-.0004	(-9.54)	-.0000	(-.49)	-.0005	(-10.32)
MAR	.2061	(13.57)	.1851	(10.38)	.1897	(11.53)
HLTH	-.1673	(-7.60)	-.1347	(-4.36)	-.1186	(-3.37)
SMSA	.1941	(14.70)	.3043	(13.64)	.1763	(8.11)
CONSTANT	-2.3903	(-56.31)	-2.2262	(-37.72)	-2.2963	(-42.57)
1980 immigrant:						
EDUC	.0556	(16.69)	.0432	(9.02)	.0585	(42.03)
EX PER	.0392	(8.41)	.0234	(3.78)	.0125	(7.35)
EXPER2	-.0006	(-7.23)	-.0004	(-3.32)	-.0003	(-7.60)
MAR	.1378	(4.59)	.0530	(1.56)	.1536	(11.29)
HLTH	-.1504	(-2.71)	.0006	(.01)	-.1168	(-3.61)
SMSA	.1395	(2.95)	.2188	(2.38)	.0125	(.52)
D75	-2.4071	(-25.88)	-2.3996	(-17.85)	-2.2790	(-59.24)
D70	-2.4196	(-25.44)	-2.2194	(-16.24)	-2.1069	(-52.80)
D65	-2.3406	(-24.31)	-2.1334	(-15.03)	-1.9961	(-48.30)
D60	-2.2506	(-22.89)	-2.2129	(-14.80)	-1.9316	(-43.34)
D50	-2.2398	(-23.50)	-2.2562	(-15.29)	-1.9435	(-43.22)
D40	-2.3189	(-23.03)	-2.2222	(-15.82)	-1.8671	(-39.54)
1970 native:						
EDUC	.0690	(49.70)	.0579	(36.77)	.0589	(8.46)
EX PER	.0388	(29.68)	.0262	(18.39)	.0385	(6.39)
EXPER2	-.0006	(-18.76)	-.0004	(-10.79)	-.0007	(-4.55)
MAR	.1822	(18.21)	.1647	(17.15)	.2347	(5.53)
HLTH	-.0925	(-6.25)	-.0161	(-.92)	-.2205	(-2.60)
SMSA	.2175	(27.90)	.3108	(31.69)	.0252	(.33)
CONSTANT	-2.5125	(-121.13)	-2.6055	(-117.50)	-2.2652	(-18.48)
1970 immigrant:						
EDUC	.0466	(24.27)	.0647	(5.15)	.0705	(10.28)
EX PER	.0403	(17.55)	.0150	(1.00)	.0045	(.61)
EXPER2	-.0007	(-13.37)	.0000	(.53)	.0000	(.10)
MAR	.1439	(8.39)	-.0055	(-.06)	.1098	(2.05)
HLTH	-.1162	(-3.92)	.1267	(.64)	-.2165	(-1.98)
SMSA	.1273	(6.67)	.4137	(2.43)	-.0811	(-1.15)
D65	-2.1748	(-57.62)	-2.5982	(-9.74)	-2.2160	(-15.93)
D60	-2.0602	(-51.78)	-2.5375	(-8.95)	-2.0667	(-14.52)
D50	-2.0557	(-53.95)	-2.5593	(-9.15)	-2.0034	(-13.66)
D40	-2.0375	(-49.04)	-2.7399	(-8.93)	-1.9732	(-12.51)
R^2	.174		.129		.171	

63

Table A2.2 (continued)

Wage Regressions: Dependent Variable = Ln(Wage Rate/10)

Variable	Coefficient t		Coefficient t		Coefficient t	
	Mexicans		Cubans		Other Hispanics	
1980 native:						
EDUC	.0531	(25.10)	.0456	(4.12)	.0603	(26.62)
EX PER	.0187	(7.14)	.0285	(2.13)	.0263	(9.58)
EXPER2	-.0002	(-4.59)	-.0005	(-1.79)	-.0003	(-6.23)
MAR	.1733	(10.17)	.1856	(2.56)	.1888	(11.54)
HLTH	-.1092	(-3.81)	.0066	(.05)	-.1234	(-4.73)
SMSA	.1529	(8.41)	.1886	(1.42)	.1502	(8.89)
CONSTANT	-2.2338	(-46.65)	-2.2547	(-8.43)	-2.3984	(-48.89)
1980 immigrant:						
EDUC	.0293	(11.05)	.0329	(13.26)	.0467	(26.99)
EXPER	.0109	(2.73)	-.0017	(-.49)	.0110	(4.10)
EXPER2	-.0002	(-3.44)	-.0000	(-.42)	-.0002	(-3.32)
MAR	.1264	(5.10)	-.1572	(6.89)	.1165	(7.30)
HLTH	-.1132	(-2.56)	-.1003	(-2.03)	-.0642	(-1.67)
SMSA	.1761	(5.78)	-.0324	(-.44)	.0085	(.20)
D75	-2.1736	(-28.77)	-1.9636	(-18.96)	-2.1577	(-35.45)
D70	-1.9807	(-26.09)	-1.5914	(-16.16)	-1.9981	(-32.55)
D65	-1.8692	(-23.92)	-1.5959	(-16.27)	-1.9243	(-30.57)
D60	-1.8310	(-22.41)	-1.4419	(-14.92)	-1.8400	(-28.31)
DSO	-1.7410	(-21.09)	-1.4734	(-14.88)	-1.7972	(-26.97)
D40	-1.7988	(-20.96)	-1.2867	(-11.59)	-1.7594	(-24.81)
1970 native:						
EDUC	.0635	(18.83)	.0488	(1.40)	.0606	(13.16)
EX PER	.0385	(11.58)	.1120	(3.98)	.0378	(8.59)
EXPER2	-.0006	(-7.25)	-.0026	(-3.53)	-.0006	(-5.73)
MAR	.2284	(8.85)	-.0752	(-.33)	.1902	(5.65)
HLTH	-.0750	(-1.82)	-.2708	(-.38)	-.0396	(-.85)
SMSA	.2304	(10.19)	-.0128	(-.03)	.2032	(7.52)
CONSTANT	-2.6573	(-54.04)	-2.4858	(-3.46)	-2.4719	(-36.01)
1970 immigrant:						
EDUC	.0280	(5.00)	.0363	(5.61)	.0448	(7.54)
EX PER	.0292	(4.46)	.0116	(1.42)	.0337	(4.23)
EXPER2	-.0005	(-3.78)	-.0003	(-1.63)	-.0007	(-3.33)
MAR	.1766	(4.11)	.1543	(2.65)	.2399	(5.08)
HLTH	.1234	(1.74)	-.1834	(-2.00)	.1476	(1.60)
SMSA	.3611	(7.71)	.0832	(.69)	.0598	(.70)
D65	-2.4984	(-26.46)	-1.9549	(-11.80)	-2.2848	(-17.64)
D60	-2.3343	(-22.97)	-1.8175	(-11.09)	-2.1701	(-16.02)
DSO	-2.2948	(-22.12)	-1.8504	(-10.99)	-2.1142	(-15.11)
D40	-2.2264	(-19.30)	-1.7065	(-8.76)	-2.0533	(-12.72)
R^2	0.115		0.098		0.122	

Table A2.3

Means of Independent Variables in 1980 Cross Section

Group and Variable	Year of Immigration					
	1975-79	1970-74	1965-69	1960-64	1950-59	<1950
White:						
EDUC	13.52	12.18	12.19	12.79	12.51	12.72
EXPER	18.71	20.75	23.65	24.69	27.33	33.88
EXPER2	475.52	549.67	667.59	729.83	885.92	1253.49
MAR	.78	.80	.85	.79	.83	.82
HLTH	.03	.03	.02	.06	.04	.07
SMSA	.95	.96	.95	.95	.94	.90
Black:						
EDUC	11.39	12.20	12.58	13.35	11.94	10.68
EX PER	19.31	19.83	22.11	22.80	28.39	32.39
EXPER2	474.39	503.72	589.72	614.74	961.35	1186.93
MAR	.72	.75	.72	.78	.64	.72
HLTH	.01	.03	.02	.03	.03	.06
SMSA	.97	.99	.99	.99	.95	.85
Asian:						
EDUC	13.87	15.28	15.58	15.84	14.75	11.61
EX PER	17.92	16.60	18.29	19.62	23.67	35.53
EXPER2	439.17	370.33	431.83	468.53	660.42	1370.26
MAR	.82	.86	.88	.88	.85	.89
HLTH	.03	.02	.01	.01	.03	.05
SMSA	.96	.97	.96	.96	.97	.92
Mexican:						
EDUC	6.35	6.65	6.89	7.17	8.10	7.43
EX PER	24.12	23.18	23.93	28.19	30.59	36.62
EXPER2	683.81	623.22	660.2	911.98	1092.32	1493.32
MAR	.78	.86	.88	.89	.89	.86
HLTH	.02	.03	.04	.04	.05	.08
SMSA	.89	.92	.93	.90	.93	.87
Cuban:						
EDUC	11.18	9.80	10.24	13.10	11.65	11.23
EX PER	24.83	31.73	32.17	25.31	29.39	36.23
EXPER2	745.92	1105.3	1134.69	782.19	984.00	1388.18
MAR	.72	.83	.85	.81	.79	.82
HLTH	.06	.04	.03	.03	.03	.05
SMSA	1.00	.99	.99	.98	.98	.97
Other Hispanic:						
EDUC	10.92	10.83	10.96	11.76	12.30	11.56
EX PER	19.87	20.73	23.30	24.64	26.96	33.77
EXPER2	502.17	527.63	643.44	699.42	841.53	1256.76
MAR	.76	.80	.83	.81	.81	.79
HLTH	.02	.02	.03	.03	.04	.05
SMSA	.98	.98	.98	.98	.96	.96

3

Is the New Immigration Less Skilled Than the Old?

My thinking and writing about immigration actually began early in my career. My PhD dissertation was on the effect of human capital on the distribution of income, both inequality and skewness (Chiswick 1967). Most of the empirical analysis was on the United States. I used my dissertation research as an opportunity (or perhaps an excuse) for my first trip to Israel (summer 1965) to collect articles, books, and data on income distribution over time in Israel. Ruth Klinov of the Hebrew University was most helpful in my obtaining this material.

Intuitively, I felt that the different waves (cohorts) of Jewish immigrants to Israel would impact that country's income distribution in different ways. The migrant cohorts ranged from well-educated European refugees in the 1930s, to the distressed post-World War II European Holocaust survivors, to the primarily low-educated refugees for the poor and less-developed Arab countries (from Morocco to Iraq) in the decade after independence in 1947. Most of these refugee flows arrived without modern Hebrew language skills, which they subsequently acquired. Surely, these sharp skill differences in successive cohorts must have influenced the rate of return on human capital (relative skill differentials) as well as the distribution of skills and

The original version of this chapter was published as: Chiswick, B.R. (1986). Is the New Immigration Less Skilled Than the Old?, in: Journal of Labor Economics, 4(2): 168–92. © 1986 by University of Chicago Press on behalf of the Society of Labor Economists and the NORC at the University of Chicago. The research for this paper has been funded by the Hoover Institution and the Rockefeller Foundation. The author appreciates Robert Wood's research assistance. This paper has benefited from discussions with George Borjas, Carmel U. Chiswick, Evelyn Lehrer, Federico Macaranas, Susan Pozo, and Steven. The title paraphrases the one used by Paul Douglas for his 1919 article on the same subject (Douglas 1919).

hence the distribution of earnings. The Israel case fit my income distribution model very well, and it formed both a section in my dissertation and (somewhat expanded) in my subsequent NBER book Income Inequality (Chiswick 1974).

From 1930 to 1960 the U.S. Census of Population did not ask immigrants when they arrived in the U.S. The 1980 Census microdata file was the first to permit a cohort analysis by comparing it with the 1970 Census date. This resulted in my paper, "Is the New Immigration Less Skilled than the Old?"

Two developments had influenced the change in the earnings profiles of immigrants from 1970 to 1980. One was that over the decade the rate of return on investments in human capital had risen for immigrants as well as for the native-born, thus steepening the immigrants' duration-earnings profile. The second was a shift in the source country of immigrants, away from Canada and Europe towards Latin America and Asia. The growth in Asian immigration was primarily due to the 1965 Amendments to the immigration law and the refugee influx in the 1970s from South-East Asia. The skills of these newer cohorts of immigrants (including language skills) were less readily transferable to the U.S. labor market than the skills of Canadians and Europeans. As a result, they experienced lower initial earnings but a steeper duration-earnings profile.

If immigrant earnings were evaluated at entry, as some have done (e.g., Borjas in Chapter 2 of this volume), it would appear that there had been a decline in immigrant skills relative to the native-born and earlier immigrant cohorts. Yet, if evaluated at tenn years after arrival there was no apparent change over time (Chapter 3 of this volume). Moreover, the number of years in the U.S. at which immigrant earnings caught up with natives' earnings (the "cross-over" point) remained about the same over the decade. Subsequent research has confirmed that, other variables the same, immigrant quality has not declined but the duration-earnings profile has a lower relative starting point and a steeper slope, largely because of the increase in the return to skills and the change in transferability of immigrant skills arising from the change in their countries of origin.

Barry R. Chiswick (2015)

3.1.   Introduction

During the past four decades immigration has shifted from being predominantly European and Canadian in origin to being predominantly Asian and Latin American, and there have been changes in the criteria for rationing immigration visas. These developments may have implications for the skill level of immigrants. Changes in the skills of immigrants may alter the effect of immigration on the level of income of the native population and on the distribution of this income among groups defined by skill and ownership of factors of production. It may also have implications for various aspects of immigration policy, including the maximum number of legal immigrants, the criteria for rationing visas, and the resources and policies for enforcing immigration law.

Table 3.1

Immigrants by Country of Birth and Period of Immigration, 1951–80 (%)

Country	Period of Immigration		
	1971–80	1961–70	1951–60
Europe	17.8	37.3	59.3
United Kingdom	2.7	6.9	8.3
Ireland	.3	1.3	2.6
Italy	2.9	6.2	7.5
Germany	1.5	6.0	13.7
Soviet Union	1.0	.5	1.8
Other	9.4	16.4	25.4
America	42.9	47.6	33.4
Canada	2.6	8.6	10.9
Mexico	14.2	13.3	12.7
Cuba	6.2	7.7	3.1
Other West Indies	10.7	7.9	1.8
Central America	2.9	2.9	1.8
South America	6.3	6.9	2.9
Other	.0	.3	.2
Asia	36.4	13.4	6.2
China[a]	5.6	3.7	1.4
India	3.9	.9	.1
Japan	1.1	1.2	1.8
Vietnam	4.0	.1	.1
Korea	6.1	1.1	.3
Philippines	8.0	3.1	.7
Other	7.7	3.3	1.8
Africa	2.0	1.2	.7
Egypt	.6	.5	.1
Other	1.4	.7	.6
Australia and New Zealand	.4	.4	.2
Other	.4	.2	.2
Total	100.0	100.0	100.0
Number per year	449,330	332,170	251,500

Note: Detail may not add to total because of rounding.
    [a] Includes Taiwan and Hong Kong.
Source: U.S. Bureau of the Census (1983), Table 126: 92.

As recently as the 1950s, 70 percent of legal immigrants arriving in the United States were from Europe and Canada, according to the administrative records of the INS (see Table 3.1). Mexico contributed about 13 percent and other parts of the Western Hemisphere 10 percent, and only 6 percent were from Asia. By the 1970s, however, Europe and Canada contributed only 20 percent. Although Mexico's share showed little change, the proportion of immigrants from other parts of the Western Hemisphere grew to 26 percent of the total, while Asia accounted for an impressive 36 percent.

The change in the source countries of immigration (flows) gradually changes the composition by country of origin of the foreign-born population (stock). It is the stock data that are most relevant for understanding the relation between immigrant quality and the labor market. Table 3.2 shows the stock of foreign-born adult men (age 25–64) in the labor market in 1980 by country of birth and duration of residence as reported in census data.[1] European and Canadian immigrants are clearly a smaller proportion of the recent immigrant cohorts, while the proportion of Asian immigrants has increased. The larger share of Mexican immigrants in the census stock data than in the INS flow data may reflect the enumeration in 1980 of a sizable number of illegal aliens.[2]

There is a literature as to whether migrants tend to be "favorably selected," on the basis of the incentives for migration, the admission criteria of the receiving country, and the institutional constraints within which the migration takes place.[3] This chapter is concerned with the changes over time in the outcome of the selection process, which includes both the "supply" and the "demand" sides for immigrants. Section 3.2 considers various reasons why the quality of immigrants may have changed in the post-World War II period. Section 3.3 examines whether U.S. earnings are systematically different for immigrants from countries whose importance in the immigrant pool has increased in the past four decades. That is, is immigration shifting in favor of countries whose nationals have a poorer performance in the U.S. labor market? The relation between years of schooling and immigrant cohort (i.e., country of origin and period of immigration) is considered in Section 3.4. Section 3.5 considers whether the "unmeasured" dimensions of skill (productivity) have been declining by analyzing changes over time in relative immigrant earnings, other things the same. The purpose is to determine whether recent cohorts of immigrants

Table 3.2

Distribution of Foreign-born Adult Men by Country of Birth and Period of Immigration, 1980ᵃ (%)

Country of Birth	Period of Immigration						
	1975–80	1970–74	1965–69	1960–64	1950–59	Before 1950	All Years
Europe/Canada	21.8	19.2	30.4	37.5	62.5	68.9	38.7
English speakingᵇ	6.8	3.7	7.3	10.2	12.8	21.4	9.7
Other	15.0	15.5	23.1	27.3	49.7	47.5	29.0
Americaᶜ	33.8	46.6	43.8	44.9	23.1	15.3	34.7
Mexico	19.1	24.3	18.0	16.8	13.6	10.0	17.4
Cuba	1.0	4.4	9.0	14.2	3.6	1.2	5.1
British West Indies	2.7	4.3	3.7	1.5	1.2	1.3	2.5
Other	11.0	13.6	13.1	12.4	4.7	2.8	9.7
Asia	32.1	23.6	16.9	10.0	6.8	5.9	16.9
China	5.5	4.9	4.5	3.2	2.1	3.3	4.0
Philippines	5.0	5.9	4.7	2.0	1.6	1.8	3.7
South Asia	7.6	6.8	4.5	2.3	.9	.2	4.0
Southeast Asia	7.1	1.7	1.1	1.4	.7	.1	2.2
Other	6.9	4.3	2.1	1.1	1.5	.5	3.0
Africa	3.8	3.0	2.1	1.5	.8	.6	2.1
Middle East	3.6	3.3	2.4	2.0	1.9	1.1	2.5
Country not reported	5.2	4.3	4.4	4.1	4.8	8.2	5.1
Total	100.0	100.0	100.0	100.0	100.0	100.0	100.0
Number of observations	6,224	6,180	5,250	3,951	6,406	4,062	32,073

Note: Detail may not add to total because of rounding.

ᵃ One-in-a-hundred sample of foreign-born men aged 25–64 in 1980 who worked and had nonzero earnings in 1979.

ᵇ English-speaking developed countries, including Australia, Canada, Ireland, New Zealand, and United Kingdom.

ᶜ Excludes Canada.

Source: U.S. Bureau of the Census (1980) Census of Population, Public Use Sample, C File, 1/100.

have lower earnings profiles than earlier cohorts. Section 3.6 closes the chapter with a synthesis of the findings and a discussion of the implications for immigration policy.

The empirical analyses of earnings and schooling in Sections 3.3 and 3.4 are based on the 1980 Census. This provides sufficiently large samples for analyses by country of origin. The analysis in Section 3.5 requires a comparison of immigrant earnings patterns over time and uses three large cross-sectional samples from the 1970 Census, the 1976 Survey of Income and Education (SIE), and the 1980 Census.[4]

3.2. Changing Circumstances and Immigrant Quality

Immigrant skills can be analyzed within the context of a model of the "supply" of immigrants and the U.S. "demand" for immigrants. In this framework economic factors, such as relative earnings across countries and the cost of migration, and noneconomic push factors, such as revolutions and wars that create refugees, may be viewed as determining immigrant supply. Demand factors for immigrants are reflected in immigration law, which determines the number of and the criteria for rationing visas for legal migrants, and the degree of enforcement (deterrence), which determines the extent of illegal immigration.

3.2.1. Trends in Supply

Trends in immigrant supply can be related to the economic incentives for migration and the noneconomic forces that create refugees.

3.2.1.1. Immigration Incentives and Costs

One hypothesis advanced for a change in immigrant quality over time relates to the greater incentive for immigration for the more able.[5] If the supply of immigrants increases because of an increase in economic rewards from migration, it would be expected that the most able would have a greater incentive for migration and would tend to do so sooner, while the less able would migrate later if at all. This factor may be of some importance in temporarily raising immigrant quality when new sources of immigrants are tapped. However, the potential supply of high-ability immigrants is replenished each year by new cohorts. In addition, the number of immigrants admitted to the United States from most source countries is small relative even to the number of high-ability additions to their labor force.

The difference in the incentive for migration by skill level is related to the ratio of the out-of-pocket costs of migration to the forgone earnings cost. The smaller the out-of-pocket costs relative to the value of the time costs, the smaller is the differential incentive for migration. With the growth in real incomes during the post-World War II period, transportation costs have fallen relative to wages. As a result, it is to be expected that the supply of immigrants would be less intensely favorably self-selected.

3.2.1.2. *Refugees*

People who leave their home country out of fear for the safety of their lives and property are likely to have fewer of the characteristics associated with high labor market performance than are immigrants who come to the United States primarily for jobs (see Chiswick 1978d; 1979). Because economic factors are not the primary determinant of migration for refugees, refugees are less likely to be self-selected on the basis of expected high economic success in the United States, and particularly if the migration was not anticipated, they are less likely to have transferable skills. They have been found to have a more difficult adjustment to the U.S. labor market than economic migrants.

Revolutions, civil wars, and conventional wars between countries typically create refugees. The United States has accepted a large number of refugees in the past four decades, from the Displaced Persons in Europe (in the aftermath of World War II), the Chinese Revolution (since 1949), the Hungarian and Polish uprisings (1956), Cuba (since 1959), and Indochina (since 1975), among other places. Thus while refugee flows are episodic and vary more in magnitude from year to year than the flows of economic migrants, they have been a continuous feature of the U.S. post-World War II immigration experience. However, the magnitude of refugee migration has been growing over the past three decades.

3.2.2. *Trends in Demand*

Trends in the demand for immigrants can be related to the criteria for rationing immigrant visas and the effectiveness with which immigration law is enforced.

3.2.2.1. Occupational and Kinship Visas

By rationing visas the United States has had a measure of control over the size, timing, and sources of migration. During the four decades prior to the 1965 Amendments to the Immigration and Nationality Act, immigration was determined largely by the "national origins" quota system. Under this system immigration from the independent countries in Asia was either barred or severely restricted by extremely low country quotas (about 100 per year), in contrast to the large and often unfilled quotas for Northwestern Europe.[6] During the 1950s most Asian immigrants were refugees or war brides, and they were few in number.

Under the 1965 Amendments, kinship with a U.S. citizen or resident alien is the primary criterion used to ration visas for immigrants from the Eastern Hemisphere. A large immigration from Asia was not expected under the kinship criterion. It had been many decades since the large Chinese and Japanese migrations of the late 19th and early 20th centuries, and few Asian-Americans had immediate relatives in Asia. After 1965, however, the availability of occupational preference visas (for professionals and skilled workers) and for several years "surplus" visas for nonpreference immigrants provided a migration opportunity for Asians with skills or capital to invest in the United States.[7]

As they became established in the United States, the Asian immigrants could sponsor under the kinship preferences the immigration of their relatives who could not qualify for an occupational visa or who would be near the end of the queue for such a visa. With the growth in immigration based on kinship from parts of Europe and Asia, "surplus" visas for nonpreference immigrants disappeared. As a result of both factors, the relative number of Asian immigrants admitted on the basis of their own skill levels declined. Of the Asian immigrants subject to numerical limitation, the proportion who were occupational preference principals (i.e., recipients of labor certifications) declined from 18.2 percent in 1970, to 11.9 percent in 1975, to 8.1 percent in 1981.[8] During this period, there was a decline in the absolute number of Asian immigrants who were occupational preference principals, from nearly 12,000 in 1970 to less than 9,000 in 1981.[9] Thus the increased skill levels that might be expected from the introduction of the rationing of some visas on the basis of skill or investor status may have been mitigated after a fairly short period by the lower skill level of their relatives.[10]

3.2.2.2.   Illegal Immigration
A growing stock of the foreign-born population who are (or who had been) illegal aliens may lower immigrant quality. For a number of reasons there has undoubtedly been an increase in the flow of illegal aliens to the United States, and this too may have increased the proportion of low-skilled workers among the foreign born. An increase in the incentive for migration has arisen in part because of the decline in the costs of transportation and communication relative to wages in the postwar period and in part because of an increasing real wage gap for workers of the same skill level between the United States and some less developed countries. United States immigration law acts as a barrier to the legal entry of many persons interested in migrating. There has, therefore, been an increase in the incentive for illegal migration. The decline in the resources (financial and otherwise) for the enforcement of immigration law relative to the extent of the violations of this law has resulted in an increase in the resident illegal alien population.[11] For low-skilled workers in neighboring low-income countries (e.g., Mexico) the economic incentives for illegal migration are very large.

Illegal aliens tend to be lower-skilled workers, and this does not arise by chance (Chiswick 1984). If there is a nontrivial probability of apprehension and deportation, investments in country-specific skills may be lost involuntarily. Other things the same, workers with internationally transferable skills or with very few skills will suffer the smallest loss if deportation arises. Among the pool of unsuccessful visa applicants, workers with few skills or internationally transferable skills have a greater incentive to become illegal aliens.[12] Since the absolute value of country-specific skills is likely to increase with a worker's overall skill level, illegal aliens would tend to be workers with few or no skills.[13]

In addition, jobs for more highly skilled workers tend to require credentials (e.g., certifications, licenses, union membership, or university degrees), and these may make it more difficult for illegal aliens to mask their status. Finally, since illegal aliens either could not qualify for or were lower in the queue for an occupational preference visa, it would be expected that they are, on average, less skilled than legal immigrants, some of whom were occupational preference principals.

3.2.3.   Summary

Divergent trends may have been affecting the "quality" of immigrants, with some forces increasing immigrant quality and others decreasing quality. The relative strengths of these forces may also vary systematically from source country to source country with the extent of immigration based on skills, kinship, and illegal migration. The opening of skill-based immigration opportunities, particularly for Asians in the late 1960s, undoubtedly tended to raise immigrant quality, other things the same. However, the subsequent increase in the importance of kinship migration from Asia, the increase in refugees and illegal aliens, and the decline relative to wages in the costs of transportation and communication may have had opposite effects.

3.3.   Immigrant Earnings by Country of Origin

The earnings (wage, salary, and self-employment income) of adult foreign-born men are analyzed in this section by country of origin using 1980 Census data for adult foreign-born men.[14] This is done for simple earnings differences and when other variables are the same. Controlling for other demographic and human capital variables narrows the earnings differences. Although the country rankings are generally preserved, there are some notable changes.

In Table 3.3, column 1, simple relative differences in earnings are presented, and no other variables are held constant.[15] Immigrants from the United Kingdom have the highest annual earnings, with Canadian, other European, South Asian, East Asian (except Vietnamese), and other American (except Mexicans) immigrants having successively lower earnings. The Mexicans and the Vietnamese have the lowest earnings. Note that the earnings differences between Europe and Canada, on the one hand, and most of the other countries are very large.

Statistical controls are introduced in Table 3.3, column 2, for period of immigration, level of schooling, total labor market experience, marital status, region of residence (South/non-South), size of place (urban/rural residence), and weeks worked in the year. These statistical controls tend to narrow the earnings differences, particularly for the Vietnamese (i.e., the most recent immigrant group) and the Mexicans (i.e., the group with the lowest level of schooling). Three clusters emerge. Immigrants from the United Kingdom and Canada have very similar earnings (6 percent lower for the Canadians). The next group is immigrants from Europe, the Middle East, South Asia, and other parts of Asia with 11–17 percent lower earnings than U.K. immigrants. This is followed by immigrants from other parts of Asia, the Western Hemisphere, and Africa with 24–32 percent lower earnings than U.K. immigrants.[16]

Table 3.3

Relative Earnings Differences among Foreign-born Adult Men, by Country of Birth, 1980[a]

			Other Variables Held Constant[c]		
			Period of Immigration		
	Overall	All	1965–69	1970–74	1975–79
Country[b]	(1)	(2)	(3)	(4)	(5)
Europe/Canada:					
United Kingdom	d	d	d	d	d
Canada	-.10	-.06	-.10*	.00*	.02*
Ireland	-.20	-.16	-.21	-.16*	.18*
Other Europe	-.20	-.11	-.16	-.24	-.28
Other Americas:					
Mexico	-.56	-.29	-.34	-.41	-.43
Cuba	-.37	-.29	-.37	-.41	-.38
West Indies	-.47	-.30	-.36	-.39	-.41
Other Americas	-.46	-.32	-.39	-.43	-.45
Asia:					
China	-.39	-.29	-.32	-.45	-.45
Philippines	-.36	-.27	-.29	-.36	-.46
South Asia	-.24	-.15	-.05*	-.27	-.39
Vietnam	-.50	-.26	-.22	-.41	-.41
Other Asia	-.30	-.17	-.24	-.30	-.27
Other:					
Middle East	-.32	-.16	-.26	-.34	-.30
Africa	-.39	-.24	-.21	-.43	-.42
Not reported	-.47	-.26	-.36	-.37	-.32

Notes: [a] Men aged 25–64 in 1980 who worked and had nonzero earnings in 1979. Estimated from the regression of the natural logarithm of earnings on the set of country-of-origin dummy variables and additional control variables as noted. The parameter reported is one minus the antilog of the country of origin regression coefficient. When multiplied by 100 it is the percent difference in earnings. The benchmark is immigrants from the United Kingdom.

[b] Canada includes Australia and New Zealand, China includes Taiwan and Hong Kong, and the not reported category indicates the country was not reported.

[c] Control variables are period of immigration, education, experience, experience squared, weeks worked, urban/rural, South/non-South, and marital status. Columns 3–5 are for 5-year periods of immigration.

[d] Benchmark.

* Regression coefficient not statistically significant.

Source: U.S. Bureau of the Census (1980) Census of Population, Public Use Sample, C File, 1/100 Sample.

To what extent have changes in the source countries shifted immigration toward those with relatively lower earnings? A summary measure of the direction and strength of the relation between the proportion of immigrants from a particular country and the relative earnings of immigrants from the country is the correlation coefficient. In Table 3.4 correlation coefficients are presented for immigrants who arrived during the 1950s, 1960s, and 1970s and for three definitions of relative earnings. Clearly, there was a positive relation in the 1950s that became smaller in the 1960s and became negative in the 1970s.[17] That is, over the period U.S. immigration changed from primarily drawing immigrants from countries whose nationals have high relative earnings in the United States to primarily drawing immigrants from countries whose nationals do less well.

Table 3.4

Correlation Coefficient between the Relative Earnings of the Foreign Born (1979) and the Distribution of Immigrants by Country of Origin (1951–80)

| | | Relative Differences in Earnings[a] | |
| | | Other Things the Same[b] | |
Period	Overall (Annual Earnings)	All Periods	Immigrated 1965–69
1951–60	.281	.360	.252
1961–70	.130	.164	.039
1971–80	-.260	-.223	-.256

Notes: [a] Differences in the natural logarithm of earnings by national origin relative to earnings received by immigrants from the United Kingdom (16 categories).
  [b] Controlling for schooling, labor market experience, duration of residence, weeks worked, and residence (urban/rural, South/non-South).
Source: Tables 3.1 and 3.3 above.

3.4. The Level of Schooling of the Foreign Born

There has been a secular rise in the schooling level of adult native-born men in the U.S. labor force. During the decade of the 1970s, the average schooling level of adult men increased by one and a half to two years for nearly all racial and ethnic groups (Table 3.5). Schooling levels have also increased in the immigrant's countries of origin. Yet a similar pattern is not to be found among immigrants to the United States.

Table 3.5

Average Schooling of Adult Native-born Men, by Race and Ethnicity, 1970 and 1980[a] (Years)

Year	White[b]	Mexican	Cuban	Black	Japanese	Chinese	Filipino
1970	11.9	8.9	c	9.9	12.6	12.7	11.1
1980	13.1	10.9	13.3	11.6	14.1	15.0	12.9

Notes: [a] For men aged 25–64 years who worked in the previous year.
[b] Includes Hispanics.
[c] Sample size too small.

Source: U.S. Bureau of the Census (1980) Census of Population, Public Use Sample, C File, 1/1,000 Sample; U.S. Bureau of the Census (1970) Census of Population, Public Use Sample, 5% Questionnaire, 1/1,000 Sample.

The number of years of schooling by period of immigration among foreign-born adult men has varied between 11.5 years and 12.3 years for those who immigrated since 1950 (Table 3.6). The mean of 12.3 years in the 1975–80 cohort is little different from the mean of 12.2 years for the 1950–64 cohorts. For immigrants from Europe and Canada the schooling level was higher in the late 1970s than in the 1950s. Among Mexican immigrants, on the other hand, the schooling level is much lower among more recent cohorts.[18] Among Cubans, the first refugee cohort (1960–64) shows the highest educational attainment. For those from China, the 15 years after the end of the 1949 revolution shows the highest educational attainment.

Among most Asian groups there is a sharp increase in educational attainment associated with the 1965–69 immigration period, with schooling level generally declining thereafter.[19] The pattern for the Asians, including the postrevolution Chinese, is consistent with the hypothesis that the initial effect of opening immigration to Asians under the 1965 Amendments was to favor highly skilled immigrants. However, the subsequent greater reliance on kinship criteria for immigration led to a decline in schooling level.

Looking across countries, there is no clear relation between the growth in the share of immigrants and the level of schooling. While the migration of highly educated Europeans and Canadians declined in relative importance, the immigration of highly educated South and East Asians became relatively more important. In recent years the less well educated group from the Western Hemisphere, particularly Mexico, became relatively more numerous.

The data suggest that recent immigrants are less favorably selected on the basis of their level of schooling. Immigrant schooling levels are lower relative to those born in the United States and relative to

Table 3.6

Years of Schooling of Foreign-born Adult Men by Country of Birth and Period of Immigration, 1980[a] (Means)

Country of Birth	Period of Immigration						All Years
	1975–80	1970–74	1965–69	1960–64	1950–59	Before 1950	
Europe/Canada:							
English speaking[b]	15.3	14.6	14.1	13.4	13.4	12.8	13.7
Other	13.2	10.5	10.8	11.9	12.2	12.7	12.0
America:[c]							
Mexico	6.8	7.0	7.3	7.8	8.6	8.1	7.4
Cuba	11.1	9.9	10.7	13.3	12.1	11.7	11.7
British West Indies	11.8	11.3	12.0	12.3	12.8	11.7	11.8
Other	11.6	11.6	12.1	12.9	13.5	13.6	12.2
Asia:							
China	13.4	13.9	15.1	15.6	15.2	12.3	14.1
Philippines	14.3	15.3	14.7	13.9	14.0	10.8	14.4
South Asia	16.1	17.5	18.5	18.1	16.8	d	17.1
South East Asia	12.6	15.6	16.9	14.8	15.7	d	13.8
Other Asia	14.5	15.1	16.3	15.6	15.6	d	15.0
Middle East	13.0	13.3	13.4	14.7	15.3	13.7	13.7
Africa	15.8	15.8	16.3	15.7	15.4	d	15.7
Not reported	11.9	11.5	11.0	12.1	12.3	11.4	11.7
Total	12.3	11.5	11.7	12.2	12.2	12.1	12.0
Number of observations	6,224	6,180	5,250	3,951	6,406	4,062	32,073

Notes: [a] One-in-a-hundred sample of foreign-born men aged 25–64 in 1980 who worked and had nonzero earnings in 1979.
[b] English-speaking developed countries, including Australia, Canada, Ireland, New Zealand, and United Kingdom.
[c] Excludes Canada.
[d] Fewer than 30 observations in the cell.

Source: U.S. Bureau of the Census (1980) Census of Population, Public Use Sample, C File, 1/100 Sample.

those in the countries of origin than in earlier decades. The growth in western hemispheric immigration, the declining schooling level of western hemispheric (and especially Mexican) immigrants, and the increase in the role of kinship in rationing immigration visas among Asians since the initial phases of the current preference system have had negative effects on the level of schooling of adult foreign-born men in the labor market.

3.5. Immigrant Quality — *Ceteris Paribus*

The third dimension of immigrant quality under investigation is the trend in earnings for immigrants when other readily measured variables, such as labor market experience and schooling, are the same. This analysis provides insights into trends in unmeasured dimensions of immigrant productivity, such as language fluency, the quality of schooling and experience, and ability.

For this analysis to be meaningful, a reference group is required. A comparison with native-born men of the same race and ethnicity would seem appropriate if it is believed there is discrimination or there are important cultural differences that vary on the basis of race or ethnicity.[20] Yet a decline in the economic position of immigrants relative to natives of the same race or ethnicity may be the result of an improvement for the native born, rather than a deterioration in the immigrant's quality. For this reason white non-Hispanic immigrants are also used as the benchmark.

The analysis requires comparable data for at least two points in time. There are only three cross-sectional data files that can be used for the comparison, the 1970 and 1980 Censuses and the 1976 SIE. To as great an extent as possible, the concepts and variables were defined in the same manner for the three data files.[21] However, "nonsampling" errors in comparisons across data collected under somewhat varying methodologies and circumstances may be substantial, and caution is warranted in interpreting findings on changes over time in cohort data.[22]

The data in Table 3.7 compare the earnings of immigrants relative to native-born men of the same race and ethnic origin, other things the same, in the 1970 Census, the 1976 SIE, and the 1980 Census. Relative earning differences are shown at 10 and 20 years after im-

Table 3.7
Differences in Earnings between Foreign-born and Native-born Adult Men, by Race and Ethnicity, 1970–80[a]

Racial/Ethnic Group	1970 Census Relative Earnings Difference		Crossover Year[b]	1976 SIE Relative Earnings Difference		Crossover Year[b]	1980 Census Relative Earnings Difference		Crossover Year[b]
	YSM = 10	YSM = 20		YSM = 10	YSM = 20		YSM = 10	YSM = 10	
White[c]	-.03	.06	13	-.07	.01	17	-.07	.05	15
Mexican[d]	-.05	.04	15	-.01	.05	12	-.11	-.01	21
Cuban[e]	-.16	.03	18	...	...	...	-.21	-.10	N.X.
Asian[f]	-.19	-.04	25	...	...	...	-.13	.04	17
Japanese	-.12	.03	18	...	...	...	.04	.11	7
Chinese	-.26	-.08	N.X.	...	...	...	-.22	-.04	24
Filipino	-.06	.11	13	...	...	...	-.03	.19	11

Notes: [a] The comparison is between foreign-born and native-born men (age 25–64 years who worked and had nonzero earnings in the reference year) of the same race and ethnic origin, except when noted otherwise. Differences in the natural logarithm of earnings evaluated at 10 and 20 years since migration (YSM), controlling for schooling, experience, weeks worked, marital status, and geographic area (nonsouth/south, urban/rural). For the SIE, residence in the 100 largest standard metropolitan statistical areas replaces the urban/rural variable. Experience and YSM are entered as quadratic variables. Data are from a 1/1,000 sample for white men and a 1/100 sample for other groups from the 1970 and 1980 Censuses. The SIE analyses based on weighted regressions. Sample sizes for Cuban and Asian immigrants are too small for statistical analyses in the SIE.

[b] The number of years in the United States at which the earnings of the foreign born equal those of the native born. N.X. means it does not occur.

[c] For comparability, whites includes the "Spanish write-in" in the 1980 Census. Persons who reported a Spanish ancestry in the race question in the 1970 Census and the SIE were recoded as white by the Census Bureau. In the 1980 Census, however, they are separately identified in the "Spanish write-in" category.

[d] Mexican-origin men living in the five southwestern states.

[e] For urban men. The benchmark is native-born white men, as there are too few adult native-born Cuban-origin men.

[f] All Asian race groups.

Source: U.S. Bureau of the Census (1970) Census of Population, Public Use Sample, State File, 5% Questionnaire; U.S. Bureau of the Census (1980) Census of Use Sample, Public Use Sample, C Sample; U.S. Bureau of the Census (1976) Survey of Income and Education (1976), Public Use Sample.

migration. The table also reports the number of years in the United States for which the earnings of the foreign born equal those of the native born if this catch-up occurs.[23] Data are reported in Table 3.8 on earnings differences by race and Hispanic origin in the 1970 and 1980 Censuses in which the benchmark is white non-Hispanic immigrants. Other things the same, the changes over time in the differences in earnings between immigrants and the benchmarks are indices of the changes in relative immigrant quality.

Table 3.8

Differences in Earnings among Foreign-born Men by Race and Ethnicity, 1970–80[a]

	Relative Difference in Earnings	
Race/Ethnic Group	1970 Census	1980 Census
White, non-hispanic	[b]	[b]
Mexican	-.27[c]	-.22[c]
	(-15.0)	(-17.3)
Cuban	-.24	-.22
	(-10.0)	(-11.0)
Japanese	-.07[c]	.13[c]
	(-1.2)	(3.3)
Chinese	-.28	-.23
	(-9.6)	(-11.2)
Filipino	-.22	-.18
	(-7.0)	(-8.2)
Korean	-.13	-.15
	(-1.7)	(-4.6)

Notes: [a] Race/ethnic group regression coefficient (and *t*-ratio) when white non-Hispanic immigrants are the benchmark, controlling for schooling, experience, weeks worked, marital status, geographic distribution (urban/rural, South/non-South), and duration of U.S. residence.
[b] Benchmark.
[c] Significant change in the coefficient from 1970 to 1980.
Source: U.S. Bureau of the Census (1970) Census of Population, Public Use Sample, 5% Questionnaire, 1/100 Sample; U.S. Bureau of the Census (1980) Census of Population, Public Use Sample, C File, 1/100 Sample.

3.5.1. White Immigrants

Among white men (including Hispanics) in 1970, immigrants in the United States for ten years had 3 percent lower earnings than the native born, while immigrants in the United States 20 years had 6 percent higher earnings, *ceteris paribus* (Table 3.7). This 9-percentage-point improvement (between YSM (years since migration) = 10 and YSM = 20) in relative earnings for the 1970 cross-sectional data is also observed over time; the cohort with YSM = 10 in 1970 had earnings in 1980 that were 5 percentage points greater than the native born (compare -3 percent in 1970 for YSM = 10 and 5 percent in 1980 for YSM = 20).[24]

Earnings at ten years of residence are 4 percentage points lower in the 1980 than in the 1970 data. That is, there was a steepening in the cross-sectional effect of duration of U.S. residence on earnings among these white immigrants. The steepening may be reflecting a general increase in investments in and the return from labor market experience.[25] Among native-born white men, evaluated at ten years of experience, the partial effect of experience increased from 2.1 percent in the 1970 Census to 2.8 percent in the 1980 Census. Among foreign-born white men, the partial effect of country-of-origin labor market experience also increased, from 1.2 percent in the 1970 Census to 2.3 percent in the 1980 Census.

The earnings profile of white immigrants relative to white native-born men appears to be 4 percentage points lower in the SIE than in the 1970 Census and 0–4 percentage points lower than in the 1980 Census. About 2 percentage points of this difference may be due to the different statistical control for size of place. The 8 percentage point increase in the relative earnings of white foreign-born men from 10–20 years of residence in the SIE is about the same as in the census.

Thus comparisons among the three large cross-sectional data files suggest no shifting during the 1970s in the height of the earnings profile of white immigrants relative to native-born white men.[26]

3.5.2. Mexican Immigrants

There is a presumption that with the large increase in illegal immigration in the 1970s and the greater efforts to enumerate Mexican-origin people in the 1980 Census, the measured earnings of Mexican immigrants relative to native-born Mexican Americans would have declined over the decade, other things the same. The census data in Table 3.7 for Mexican-origin men in the southwestern states do indicate about a 5 percentage point decline between 1970 and 1980 in the relative earnings of the foreign born, *ceteris paribus*. Even though the 1970 cross section showed the same 9 percentage point increase in relative earnings from YSM = 10 to YSM = 20 observed for all white men, the downward shift in the profile resulted in an actual relative earnings increase of only 4 percentage points.

It is noteworthy that among the native born the unexplained earnings differential between Mexican-origin and white non-Hispanic men declined by 5 percentage points from about 15 percentage points in the 1970 Census to about 10 percentage points in the 1980 Census (Chiswick 1987). This means that there was no change from 1970 to 1980 in the earnings profile of Mexican immigrants relative to native-born non-Hispanic white men. The reasons for the relative improvement for native-born Mexican-origin men and its permanence (or whether it is merely a statistical artifact) are not yet known. Without a better understanding of the reasons for this improvement it may not be possible to determine why Mexican immigrant earnings appear to have declined in the census data, other things the same, relative to native-born Mexican Americans.

As an alternative benchmark Mexican immigrants can be compared with white non-Hispanic foreign-born men, other things the same.

When this is done, Mexican immigrant earnings seem to have *improved* by a statistically significant 5 percentage points from 1970 to 1980 (Table 3.8).

The relative earnings of the more recent Mexican immigrants (YSM = 10) seem to be higher (by 4–10 percentage points) in the SIE than in the two censuses. As a result, the earnings crossover comes earlier in the SIE, at only 12 years. About one-third to one-half of the higher relative earnings of the foreign born in the SIE may be due to the different statistical control for size of place. Among long-term Mexican immigrants (YSM = 20 years), there is still weak evidence for a decline in relative earnings, but these immigrants arrived in the United States prior to the large illegal immigration of the 1970s.

Thus when the three cross-sectional data files are considered and when comparisons are made with alternative benchmarks (e.g., white immigrants and native-born non-Hispanic white men), it is not obvious that the unmeasured dimensions of Mexican immigrant quality have declined over the 1970s.

3.5.3.   *Cuban Immigrants*

When Cuban immigrants are compared to native-born white men, other things the same, it appears that the relative earnings profile has fallen.[27] Relative earnings declined by about 5 percentage points for those in the United States ten years but fell by about 13 percentage

points for those in the United States 20 years. These declines may relate to the refugee experience.

Refugees would be expected to have lower earnings, especially initially, because they are less likely to be self-selected for labor market
success in the United States and because their skills are less readily
transferable. Yet the first group of refugees would contain relatively
more individuals with the greatest transferability of skills and other
assets, while those whose skills have less transferability would be more
likely to emigrate later. As a result, the initial refugees would have low
earnings, other things the same, but later refugee flows would do even
less well. Thus, as suggested in Borjas (1985), cross-sectional data on
earnings may overstate the actual increases in earnings over time for
cohorts of Cuban refugees.

Several words of caution are warranted. Longitudinal data on occupational mobility show steeper increases in occupational attainment
among Cuban refugees than among white immigrants (Chiswick
1978a). This appears inconsistent with the "cohort" data in Table 3.7,
which shows a somewhat smaller rise in relative earnings for Cubans
(6 percentage points) than for white immigrants (8 percentage points).
In addition, the earnings analyses here and in Borjas (1985) bias downward the cohort increase in earnings over the decade by controlling for
schooling level in the same year as the earnings data, rather than schooling level in 1970. While this downward bias occurs for all groups, it is
likely to be more intense for Cuban and other refugees as they invest in
more post-immigration schooling.[28] Thus the downward bias in the estimated growth of earnings would be greater for the Cubans than for other
whites. And there does not appear to have been a change in the relative
earnings of Cuban immigrants (Table 3.8) when compared with non-
Hispanic white immigrants in the 1970 and 1980 Censuses.

3.5.4.   Asian Immigrants

The discussion in Section 3.2 on the effect of the 1965 Amendments
on Asian immigration implies a higher level in the unmeasured dimensions of immigrant quality among the stock of the foreign-born
Asian men residing in the United States in 1980 than in 1970. Among
the Asian foreign born in the United States in 1970 only a very few
(who had entered in the prior three years) immigrated under an occupational preference or investor visa, but this was the case for a much
larger proportion in 1980.

Table 3.7 reports the comparative analysis with the native born for Chinese, Filipino, and Japanese men.[29] For each of these groups there has been an increase in the relative earnings of the foreign born. This rise has been about 4 percentage points among the Chinese and slightly more (with a steepening of the cross-sectional profile) for the Filipinos. Yet the basic pattern for both groups is essentially the same in the two censuses. Among the Japanese, relative earnings profiles have risen more sharply. This may arise from the preponderance of occupational preference principals in the very small male Japanese immigration in the 1970s.

Similar improvements are found when Asian immigrants are compared with white non-Hispanic immigrants (Table 3.8). Other things the same, earnings improved by a statistically significant 20 percentage points for Japanese men and by a statistically insignificant 5 percentage points for Chinese and Filipino men. There were no changes over the decade for Korean immigrants.

3.5.5. Summary

The analysis of the relative earnings of immigrants during the 1970s using three data files suggests that there has been little change for white immigrants, an ambiguous pattern for Mexican immigrants, perhaps a small decline for Cuban immigrants, and a small rise for Asian immigrants. The analysis indicates that cross-sectional earnings profiles are reasonable proxies for cohort or longitudinal changes in earnings when the unmeasured dimensions of skill of immigrant cohorts have not changed materially over time.

3.6.   Summary and Conclusions

This chapter has analyzed whether the newer immigrants, defined in terms of more recent major source countries and more recent cohorts from individual countries, are now less skilled than immigrants who arrived in the decades immediately following World War II.

There has been a shift in the source countries of immigrants. The absolute number and share of immigrants from developed countries (Europe and Canada) have been declining. There have been moderate increases in the number and share from the Western Hemisphere and very rapid increases in the number and share from Asia.

The earnings of immigrants in the United States, whether measured as observed earnings or when other variables are the same, vary by country of origin. Other things the same, U.K. and Canadian immigrants have the highest earnings. Immigrants from Europe, the Middle East, South Asia, and the Other Asia category have earnings 11–17 percent below those of U.K. immigrants. The lowest earnings group includes immigrants from parts of Asia (i.e., China, the Philippines, and Vietnam), Latin America, the Caribbean, and Africa, with earnings 24–32 percent below those from the United Kingdom. Thus, while in the 1950s relatively more immigrants were coming from countries whose migrants tended to have higher earnings in the United States, by the 1970s the relation had reversed.

In general, the Asian immigrants have high levels of schooling compared to European immigrants. The number of Asian immigrants and their schooling level increased sharply with the enactment of the 1965 Amendments, which abolished the very small Asian quotas under the "national origins" quota system. The initial large positive effect of the occupational preference immigration on the level of schooling of Asian immigrants has diminished over time. Recent Mexican immigrants have very low schooling levels, an average of about seven years compared with 11–12 years for immigrants from other parts of Latin America and the Caribbean and from all countries of origin. The growth in illegal Mexican migration undoubtedly contributed to this pattern.

The earnings profiles of immigrants relative to natives of the same racial and ethnic origin or relative to other immigrants, when other measured variables are the same, reflect the unmeasured dimensions of immigrant skill and productivity. For the 1970s, there was little change in the unmeasured dimensions of skill for white immigrants, an ambiguous pattern for Mexican immigrants, perhaps a decline for Cuban immigrants, and a rise for Asian immigrants.

The more recent cohorts of post-Castro refugees may have fewer or less transferable skills, those with greater skills or with the more transferable skills being among the first to have left Cuba. The rise in the profile for Asian immigrants may reflect the increased proportion who were skill tested, that is, who entered under the occupational preferences after the 1965 Amendments. If so, future censuses may show a declining relative earnings pattern for the Asian immigrants.

The analysis indicates a complex answer to the question posed in the title. It suggests that the opening of large-scale nonrefugee immigration from Asia combined with the rationing of visas by skill tended to raise immigrant skill. On the other hand, several factors have tended to lower immigrant skill, whether measured by earnings or by schooling. These factors include the growing proportion of immigrants admitted on the basis of kinship, the growing resident population of illegal aliens, and the growing proportion of immigrants from less developed countries. The lower earnings of immigrants from less developed countries may reflect less readily measured dimensions of skill, such as school quality, and poorer job opportunities in the origin, which lowers the opportunity cost of migration.

These conclusions suggest that, without returning to rationing by country of origin, public policy could raise immigrant skill levels by changing the balance between kinship and the individual's skills in the rationing of visas. This is in the American tradition of being concerned with who a person is rather than to whom a person is related.

4

Self-Selection and the Earnings of Immigrants

After completing my paper on "Assimilation and Changes in Cohort Quality," it was obvious that the next step was to figure out what caused the decline in the earnings potential of successive immigrant cohorts migrating to the United States. It quickly became apparent that the trend was related to the changing national origin mix of the immigrant workforce, a fact that raised a much more important question: why exactly was there such a huge dispersion in the labor market performance of national origin groups in the United States?

Part of the answer was obviously the fact that even if the groups were equally skilled, the extent to which those skills were transferable to the United States likely differed across source countries. What intrigued me, however, was the possibility that the groups were not equally skilled because different types of workers chose to migrate from different countries.

I was fortunate to have been exposed to discussions of self-selection models early on in graduate school. In fact, I was Jim Heckman's research assistant as he was beginning to think about the self-selection issues that eventually led to his Nobel-prize-winning work, and I was exposed to the technical details of

The original version of this chapter was published as: Borjas, G.J. (1987). Self-Selection and the Earnings of Immigrants, in: The American Economic Review, 77(4): 531–53. © 1987 by American Economic Review. The author is grateful to Gary Becker, Stephen Bronars, Richard Freeman, Daniel Hamermesh, James Heckman, Larry Kenny, and Shei Win Rosen for comments on earlier drafts of this paper. The research was funded by a grant from the Ford Foundation to the NBER, and by the National Science Foundation (Grant No. SES-8604973).

self-selection models by Sherwin Rosen when he taught a remarkable class on theoretical labor economics during his visit to Columbia in 1974.

Despite this early exposure, I wasted many months working out various models of immigrant self-selection that focused far too much on the immiration aspect of the problem, and downplayed the insights from the generalized selection models I had learned in graduate school. One morning, while driving from Santa Barbara to Santa Monica, the applicability of the Roy model to the immigration context became completely self-evident and it was obvious that this was just the way to think about immigration. By the end of the day, the entire theoretical section of the paper that eventually appeared in the American Economic Review had been fully fleshed out.

George J. Borjas (2015)

Immigrants in the United States do not make up a random sample of the population from the countries of origin. This is perhaps the most convincing finding in the literature that analyzes how immigrants perform in the U.S. labor market. In the "first-generation" studies of this literature (Chiswick 1978d; Carliner 1980; DeFreitas 1980), cross-section earnings functions were estimated and two conclusions were reached: (1) the age-earnings profile of immigrants is steeper than the age-earnings profile of the native population with the same measured skills; and (2) the age-earnings profile of immigrants crosses the age-earnings profile of natives about ten to 15 years after immigration. Thus, after a relatively short adaptation period, immigrant earnings "overtake" the earnings of comparable native workers. The first of these findings was often explained in terms of the human capital framework: immigrants presumably have stronger investment incentives than native workers, and hence immigrant earnings grow at a faster rate than native earnings. The existence of the overtaking age, however, was explained in terms of the unobserved characteristics of the migrants: Immigrants are a self-selected group and, as a result, immigrants may be "more able and more highly motivated" (Chiswick 1978d: 900) than the native born.

Recently, the focus has shifted from analyses of single cross-section data sets to studies of cohort or longitudinal data (see Chiswick 1985; 1987; and Jasso and Rosenzweig 1986; 1988). The departure point for these studies is the well-known fact that the analysis of a single cross section of data cannot separately identify aging and cohort effects.[1] The cross-section finding that immigrant earnings and years since migration are positively correlated can be explained either in terms of an aging effect (i.e., assimilation) or it may be due to cohort differences in quality (caused by nonrandom return migration propensities and/or secular shifts in the skill mix of immigrants admitted to the United States). These recent studies, in effect, bring to the forefront the question of how cohort quality and immigrant self-selection are related. For example, are immigrants selected from the upper or lower tail of the ability (or income) distribution in the sending countries? Even if immigrants are drawn from the upper tail of the income distribution in the home country, does that ensure that they end up in the upper tail of the U.S. income distribution? Finally, if cohort quality has experienced a secular decline in the postwar period (as my 1985 analysis suggests), what factors are responsible for this change in the selection mechanism determining immigration?

This chapter presents a theoretical and empirical study of these questions. It is assumed that individuals compare the potential incomes in the United States with the incomes in the home countries, and make the migration decision based on these income differentials (net of mobility costs). The use of this standard model allows a systematic analysis of the types of selection biases that are created by this behavior.[2] It will be seen that the common assumption that immigrants are drawn from the upper tail of the "home" income distribution requires a set of conditions that will not be generally satisfied. More importantly, this type of model suggests a few key variables (namely, the characteristics of the relevant income distributions) that "predict" the types of selection biases created by income-maximizing behavior on the part of potential migrants.

The empirical work presented in this chapter analyzes the U.S. earnings of immigrants from 41 countries using the 1970 and 1980 Censuses. Not surprisingly, it is found that the variance in (relative) immigrant earnings across these countries is substantial. Using the theoretical insights, however, the analysis shows that the variance in various measures of the "quality" of immigrants can be explained to a large extent by a few key variables describing economic and political conditions in the countries of origin.

4.1.   Theoretical Framework

Suppose there are two countries: country 0 and country 1. For concreteness, country 0 denotes the home country or the country of origin, while country 1 denotes the United States or the country of destination.[3] Residents of the home country have earnings which are distributed as

(1) $$\ln w_0 = \mu_0 + \varepsilon_0,$$

where $\varepsilon_0 \sim N(0, \sigma_1^2)$. The earnings facing this population if they were to migrate to the United States are given by

(2) $$\ln w_1 = \mu_1 + \varepsilon_1,$$

where $\varepsilon_1 \sim N(0, \sigma_1^2)$, and ε_0 and ε_1 have correlation coefficient ρ.

Equations (1) and (2) describe the earnings distributions facing a given individual that is contemplating emigration to the United States. This framework, due to A. D. Roy, can be interpreted as decomposing individual earnings into a part due to observable socioeconomic variables (μ_0 and μ_1), and a part due to unobserved characteristics (ε_0 and ε_1). The Roy model focuses on the impact of selection biases on the disturbances ε_0 and ε_1. Initially, therefore, variations in socioeconomic variables (which shift μ_0 and μ_1) are ignored, but their role will be discussed later.[4]

The parameter μ_1 is the mean income that residents from the home country would earn in the United States *if all* home country citizens were to migrate to the United States. In general, this level of income need not be the same as that of the U.S. native population since the average skills of the two populations – even in the absence of selection biases – may differ. For simplicity, in the remainder of the discussion it is assumed that these intercountry differences in skill (such as education and age) have been standardized, and hence μ_1 also gives the earnings of the average native worker in the United States.[5]

The migration decision for persons in country 0 is determined by the sign of the index function:

(3) $$I = \ln(w_1/(w_0 + C)) \approx (\mu_1 - \mu_0 - \pi) + (\varepsilon_1 - \varepsilon_0),$$

where C gives the level of mobility costs, and π gives a "time-equivalent" measure of the costs of emigrating to the United States (i.e., $\pi = C/w_0$). Assume that π is constant across all individuals in the country of origin. Since migration to the United States occurs when $I > 0$, the emigration rate from the country of origin is given by

(4) $$P = Pr\left[v > -(\mu_1 - \mu_0 - \pi)\right] = 1 - \phi(z),$$

where $v = \varepsilon_1 - \varepsilon_0$; $z = -(\mu_1 - \mu_0 - \pi)/\sigma_v$; and ϕ is the standard normal distribution function.

Equation (4) neatly summarizes the economic content of the theory of migration proposed by Larry Sjaastad. If follows from (4) that the emigration rate is: (a) a negative function of mean income in the home country; (b) a positive function of mean income in the United States; and (c) a negative function of the costs of emigrating to the United States. There are, however, a number of other implications in the theory that yield important insights into the kinds of selection biases generated by the endogenous migration decision. In particular, consider the conditional means $E(\ln w_0 \mid I > 0)$ and $E(\ln w_1 \mid I > 0)$. The first of these means gives the average earnings of emigrants in the country of origin, while the latter term gives the average earnings of these migrants in the United States. Under the normality assumptions these conditional means are given by

$$(5) \qquad E(\ln w_0 \mid I > 0) = \mu_0 + \frac{\sigma_0 \sigma_1}{\sigma_v} \left(\rho - \frac{\sigma_0}{\sigma_1} \right) \lambda,$$

$$(6) \qquad E(\ln w_1 \mid I > 0) = \mu_1 + \frac{\sigma_0 \sigma_1}{\sigma_v} \left(\frac{\sigma_1}{\sigma_0} - \rho \right) \lambda,$$

where $\lambda = \phi(z)/P$; and ϕ is the density of the standard normal. The variable λ is inversely related to the emigration rate, and takes on a value of zero when $P = 1$ (Heckman 1979). Assume initially that $P < 1$ so that at least part of the home country's population is better off by not emigrating. Then the second terms in (5) and (6) define the kinds of selection biases generated by income-maximizing behavior. Equation (5) shows that the average emigrant may be "better" or "worse" off than the average person in the country of origin depending on $\rho \gtrless \sigma_0/\sigma_1$. Similarly, Equation (6) shows that the average immigrant in the United States may have higher or lower earnings than the average native person depending on $\sigma_1/\sigma_0 \gtrless \rho$. Let Q_0 be the income differential between the average emigrant and the average person in country 0, Q_1 be the income differential between the average immigrant and the average native person in the United States, and $k = \sigma_1/\sigma_0$. There are three cases that are of interest.[6]

Case 1: Positive Selection: $Q_0 > 0$ and $Q_1 > 0$. In this situation the "best" persons leave the country of origin and when they get to the United States, they outperform the native population. A reading of the literature on the earnings of immigrants suggests that this positive selection is most often assumed in the interpretation of those empirical results. Inspection of Equations (5) and (6), however, shows that the necessary (and sufficient) conditions for positive selection to occur are

(7) $$\rho > \min(1/k,\ k) \quad \text{and} \quad k > 1.$$

Thus if ρ is sufficiently high *and* if income is more dispersed in the United States than in the country of origin, the immigrants arriving in the United States are indeed selected from the upper tail of the home country's income distribution and will out-perform the native born.

Case 2: Negative Selection: $Q_0 < 0$ and $Q_1 < 0$. In this type of selection the United States draws persons from the lower tail of the home country's income distribution and these immigrants do not perform well in the U.S. labor market. The necessary (and sufficient) conditions for negative selection to occur are

(8) $$\rho > \min(1/k,\ k) \quad \text{and} \quad k < 1.$$

Negative selection again requires that ρ be "sufficiently" positive but that the income distribution be more unequal in the home country that in the United States.[7]

Case 3: Refugee Sorting: $Q_0 < 0$ and $Q_1 > 0$. The United States draws below-average immigrants (in terms of the country of origin), but they outperform the U.S. native born upon arrival. The necessary (and sufficient) condition for this to occur is

(9) $$\rho < \min(1/k,\ k).$$

These three cases summarize the quality differentials between migrants and the native base in each of the two countries. It seems plausible to argue that for non-Communist countries, ρ is likely to be positive and large. After all, profit-maximizing employers are likely to value the same factors in any market economy. The quality of immigrants in the United States then depends *entirely* on the ratio of variances in the income distributions of the United States and the country of origin. Suppose, for example, that $\sigma_0^2 > \sigma_1^2$. The United States, in a sense, "insures" low-income workers against poor labor market outcomes while "taxing" high-income workers (relative to the country of origin). This opportunity set implies that low-income workers have much greater incentives to migrate than high-income workers, and thus leads to immigrants being negatively selected from the population. Conversely, if $\sigma_1^2 > \sigma_0^2$, the home country now protects low-income workers from poor labor market outcomes and taxes the high-income worker. This opportunity set generates a "brain drain" into the United States. Available data on the distribution of income (World

Bank 1986: 226-7) suggests that income is more unequally distributed in the large number of Third World countries (for example, Mexico, India, etc.) which form the bulk of current immigration to the United States.[8] Income-maximizing behavior is inconsistent with the traditional assumption that the United States draws the "best" workers from a given country and that those workers will (eventually) outperform the U.S. native born.

On the other hand, ρ need not always be positive and strong. It is likely, in fact, that ρ is negative for countries that have recently experienced a Communist takeover. The change from a market economy to a Communist system is often accompanied by structural shifts in the income distribution and, in particular, the confiscation of the financial holdings of entrepreneurs. Immigrants from such systems will be in the lower tail of the "revolutionary" income distribution but will outperform the average U.S. native worker. This result signals the movement of persons who cannot match with the new political structure, but who "seek refuge" and match quite well in a market economy.

These insights are developed under the assumption that selection biases *do* exist (i.e., $P < 1$ and $\lambda > 0$). Since for most countries in Latin America and Asia the mean level of the U.S. income distribution greatly exceeds the mean level of the home country's income distribution, it is unclear why – in the context of an income-maximizing model – the entire population of country 0 does not emigrate to the United States.

There are two reasons why we do not observe wholesale migrations of entire populations to the United States. First, it is not the differences in mean income levels that determine the extent of migration, but the differences in mean income levels *net* of migration costs. These migration costs will be both monetary and psychic, and are likely to be large in countries that have different cultural and social backgrounds than the United States. Second, there are statutory restrictions on the number of legal immigrants the United States will accept from any given country. These quotas play the important role of increasing migration costs of emigrants (if the numerical constraints are binding), since these individuals will presumably have to compete (and invest time and effort) to obtain the relatively scarce visas. Hence mobility costs ensure that only some persons in country 0 find it worthwhile to emigrate and thereby create the selection biases that are apparent in immigration data.

The model outlined above can be used to infer how the quality of immigrants in the United States will differ in the cross section (across different countries of origin) or over time (as economic conditions in the country of origin and in the United States change). The income-maximization hypothesis implies the existence of a reduced-form quality-of-immigrants equation given by

$$(10) \qquad Q_1 = Q_1(\mu_1 - \mu_0 - \pi, \sigma_0, \sigma_1, \rho).$$

To determine the restrictions implied by the behavioral assumption of income maximization it is instructive to recall that $Q_1 = \gamma\lambda$, where $\gamma = (\sigma_0\sigma_1/\sigma_v)(k - \rho)$. The parameter γ does not depend on the size of the flow, while λ does. The impact of any variable α on the quality of immigrants in the United States is given by

$$(11) \qquad \frac{\partial Q_1}{\partial \alpha} = \lambda \frac{\partial \gamma}{\partial \alpha} + \gamma \frac{\partial \lambda}{\partial \alpha}.$$

The first term in (11) holds the size of the flow constant and will be called the "composition" effect. It measures how a change in the ability mix of a constant-sized immigrant pool affects their quality (relative to the U.S. native population). The second term in (11) will be called the "scale" effect and captures what happens to the quality of U.S. immigrants as the size of the flow is changed for any given "mix" (i.e., for constant γ).

Consider what happens to immigrant quality as the mean of the home country's income distribution increases. It can be shown that

$$(12) \qquad \frac{\partial Q_1}{\partial \mu_0} = \frac{\sigma_1\sigma_0}{\sigma_v^2} (k - \rho) \frac{\partial \lambda}{\partial z}.$$

Shifts in γ_0 lead only to a scale effect on Q_1. In addition, it is easy to show that $\partial \lambda/\partial z > 0$.[9] As discussed earlier, the sign of $k - \rho$ determines whether immigrants fall in the upper or lower tail of the U.S. income distribution. Equation (12) shows that $k - \rho$ also determines what happens to the (U.S.) earnings of immigrants as mean income in the home country increases. If $k - \rho$ is negative (immigrants are coming from countries with significantly more unequal income distributions and ρ is "sufficiently" positive), $\partial Q_1/\mu_o < 0$. The intuition for this result follows from the fact that as μ_0 increases the emigration rate falls. The increase in μ_0 improves the position of the "marginal" immigrant so that he no longer migrates. But this marginal immigrant was more productive than the average immigrant. The increase in μ_0, therefore, leads to a reduction in the average quality of the immigrant population. Since the mean of the home country's income distribution and mobility costs play identical roles in the model, Equation (12) also predicts that increases in mobility costs will *decrease* immigrant quality if $k - \rho < 0$.

It is important to note that this result only captures the impact of changes in μ_0 (or migration costs) on the extent of selection bias (Q_1). The increase in μ_0, however, can be induced by either a shift in the skill distribution of the country of origin's population, or by an increase in the country's wealth that is unrelated to skills (for example, the discovery of a large inventory of natural resources). If μ_0 shifts because of the latter factor, Equation (12) correctly predicts the change in observed immigrant earnings (which are given by $\mu_1 + Q_1$). However, if μ_0 shifts due to an increase in the skill level of the population, the change in immigrant earnings will also depend on the term $d\mu_1/d\mu_0$. This derivative will be positive if skills are transferable across countries, and this skill shift may dominate any changes that occur in Q_1 as μ_0 increases. Hence the (relative) earnings of immigrants in the United States may well be a positive function of μ_0 regardless of the sign of Equation (12).[10]

The change in the quality of immigrants due to a mean-preserving increase in the income inequality of the home country is given by

$$(13) \qquad \frac{\partial Q_1}{\partial \sigma_0} = \frac{\sigma_1^2 \sigma_0}{\sigma_v^3}(\rho^2 - 1)\lambda - \frac{\sigma_1 \sigma_0^2}{\sigma_v^3}(k - \rho)(1 - \rho k)\frac{\partial \lambda}{\partial z}z,$$

where the first term gives the composition effect and the second term gives the scale effect. Since $|\rho| \leq 1$, the composition effect will always be nonpositive. An increase in σ_0 reduces the income of the poorest while it improves the position of the richest. Hence the mix of immigrants will include more persons from the lower tail of the distribution.

In addition, a change in σ_0 changes the rate of emigration. Equation (13) shows that the sign of the scale effect depends on the sign of three terms: $(k - \rho)$, $(1 - \rho k)$, and z. The first two of these terms are nothing but the restrictions in Equations (7) and (8). Suppose, for concreteness, that there is negative selection: the least-able persons leave the home country and they perform below the U.S. native average. This implies $k - \rho < 0$ and $1 - \rho k > 0$. Inspection of (13) reveals that the direction of the scale effect depends on the sign of $z = -(\mu_1 - \mu_0 - \pi)/\sigma_v$. If $\mu_1 > \mu_0 + \pi$, so that mean U.S. incomes are higher than foreign incomes even after adjusting for mobility costs, z is negative, the scale effect is negative, and thus immigrants from countries with more income inequality will perform worse in the United States.

The intuition for the workings of the scale effect can be grasped by considering Figure 4.1, which is drawn with $z < 0$ and $\sigma_1 < \sigma_0$. As σ_0 increases, the worst-off persons in country 0 will still want to migrate, while the better-off persons become relatively better off and their migration incentives decline. The emigration rate drops due to the withdrawal of the "best" potential migrants from the market, and thus the quality of the pool that does reach the United States declines.

Figure 4.1

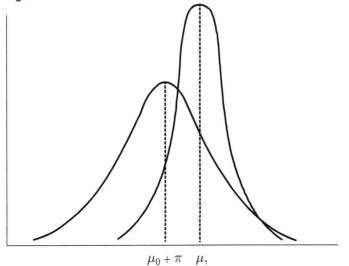

$$\mu_0 + \pi \quad \mu,$$

The last characteristic of the home country's income distribution which determines the quality of immigrants is ρ. It can be shown that

(14) $$\frac{\partial Q_1}{\partial \rho} = \frac{\sigma_1 \sigma_0^3}{\sigma_v^3}(1 - \rho k)\lambda + \frac{\sigma_1^2 \sigma_0^2}{\sigma_v^3}(k - \rho)\,\frac{\partial \lambda}{\partial z}z.$$

Changes in the correlation coefficient also induce two effects. Consider first the composition effect. Its sign depends on $-(1 - \rho k)$, which is negative if there is negative selection. An increase in ρ implies that a better match exists between performance in the United States and in the home country. Since $\sigma_0 > \sigma_1$ this decreases the profitability of migration for the best persons in country 0 and increases it for the worst persons.

In addition, changes in ρ have an impact on the emigration rate, and the scale effect is given by the last term in (14). If the conditions for negative selection hold, $k - \rho < 0$ and the sign of the scale effect will depend on the sign of $-z$. If, as before, we assume $z < 0$, the scale effect of an increase in the correlation coefficient on the quality of immigrants is seen to be positive.

Table 4.1

Summary of Comparative Statics Results

		Positive Selection $Q_0 > 0, Q_1 > 0$	Negative Selection $Q_0 < 0, Q_1 < 0$	Refugee Sorting $Q_0 < 0, Q_1 > 0$
$\partial Q_1 / \partial \mu_0$:	Composition Effect	none	none	none
	Scale Effect	+	-	+
$\partial Q_1 / \partial \sigma_0$:	Composition Effect	-	-	-
	Scale Effect, $z < 0$	-	-	-
	$z > 0$	+	+	+
$\partial Q_1 / \partial \rho$:	Composition Effect	+	+	-
	Scale Effect, $z < 0$	-	-	-
	$z > 0$	+	-	+

A summary of the comparative statics results under the various regimes is provided in Table 4.1. One implication is immediately clear: generalizations about the quality of immigrants in the United States are hard to come by. The model does, however, isolate the key factors that determine the types of selections in the immigrant population and these factors shed some light on my 1985 finding that the quality of immigrants declined in the postwar period. Prior to the 1965 Amendments to the Immigration and Nationality Act, immigration to the United States from Eastern Hemisphere countries was regulated by numerical quotas. These quotas were based on the ethnic population of the United States in 1919 and thus encouraged immigration from (some) Western European countries and discouraged immigration from all other countries. The favored countries have one important characteristic: their income distributions are probably much less dispersed than those of countries in Latin America or Asia. The 1965 Amendments revamped the quota system, established a 20,000 numerical limit for immigration from any single country (subject to both hemispheric and worldwide numerical limits), and led to a substantial increase in the number of immigrants from Asia and Latin America. The new flow of migrants originates in countries that are much more likely to have greater income inequality than the United States. It would not be surprising, therefore, if the quality of immigrants declined as a result of the 1965 Amendments.[11]

4.2.   Empirical Framework

The quality measure Q_1 derived in the previous section is the standardized wage differential between immigrants and natives in the United States. In any given cross section, this wage differential is affected by two factors: (1) differences in the skill composition of the various immigrant cohorts; and (2) the rate of convergence between foreign- and native-born earnings (i.e., the rate of assimilation of immigrants). An empirical framework for measuring these effects thus begins with the specification of the regression model:

$$(15) \qquad \ln w_i(T) = X_i\theta_T + \delta I_i + \alpha_1 I_i y_i + \alpha_2 I_i y_i^2 + \beta_1 I_i C_i + \beta_2 I_i C_i^2 + v_i,$$

where $w_i(T)$ is the wage rate of individual i in cross-section year T; X_i is a vector of socioeconomic characteristics; I_i is a dummy variable set to unity if the individual is foreign born; y_i; represents the number of years the immigrant has resided in the United States; and C_i; is the calendar year of the immigrant's arrival. The parameters α_1 and α_2 capture the impact of assimilation on the (relative) earnings of immigrants, while β_1 and β_2 capture the cohort differentials.[12]

Of course, in a single cross section of data, Equation (15) cannot be estimated since the variables C_i and y_i are related by the identity $T \equiv C_i + y_i$. Substituting this identity in (15) yields

$$(16) \qquad \ln w_i(T) = X_i\theta_T + (\delta + \beta_1 T + \beta_2 T^2)I_i + (\alpha_1 - \beta_2 - 2\beta_2 T)I_i y_i$$
$$+ (\alpha_2 + \beta_2)I_i y_i^2 + v_i.$$

Equation (16) shows that the typical cross-section earnings function estimated in the immigration literature does not identify a single parameter of interest.[13] It is easy to show, however, that if another cross section is available in calendar year T' all the parameters in (15) can be identified.[14] Moreover, the comparison of the two cross-section regressions provides interesting insights about the extent and direction of cohort-quality differentials. Let $\gamma_1 = \delta + \beta_1 T + \beta_2 T^2$, $\gamma_2 = \alpha_1 - \beta_1 - 2\beta_2 T$, and $\gamma_3 = \alpha_2 + \beta_2$ be the coefficients of the immigration variables in the cross section at calendar year T.

This vector will shift over time since

$$(17) \qquad\qquad\qquad \partial\gamma_1/\partial T = \beta_1 + 2\beta_2 T$$

$$(18) \qquad\qquad\qquad \partial\gamma_2/\partial T = -2\beta_2$$

$$(19) \qquad\qquad\qquad \partial\gamma_3/\partial T = 0.$$

The immigration vector in cross-section earnings functions (except for the coefficient of $I \cdot y^2$) is inherently unstable, though the direction of the instability provides insights into the underlying structural changes. For instance, γ_1 (the coefficient of the immigrant dummy) will be shifting down over time if the quality of immigrants is decreasing at the "margin" (i.e., in the cross-section year T). In addition, the age-earnings profile of immigrants (relative to natives) becomes steeper over time (i.e., γ_2 increases) if the decline in the quality of immigrant cohorts has accelerated over the sample period.

The empirical analysis which follows uses the 1970 and 1980 Census cross sections to identify the parameters of interest (δ, α_1, α_2, β_1, and β_2). From these estimates it is possible to calculate measures of three alternative dimensions of cohort quality that underlie the discussion. The first of these dimensions is simply the wage of an immigrant cohort relative to the native base prior to any assimilation taking place; that is, a measure of the "raw" skills a given immigrant cohort brings to the United States. A second dimension is given by the extent to which the quality of successive immigrant cohorts is changing over time, while a third dimension is given by the extent to which the earnings of a specific immigrant cohort grow – above and beyond pure aging effects – in the U.S. labor market. Clearly, there are many ways of defining variables that capture these three facets of the "quality" of immigrants. However, since all possible definitions of a particular dimension of quality are based on the same underlying parameters, there is a high degree of correlation among the alternative measures. Thus, to some extent, the choice of the empirical representation of a given facet of quality is arbitrary. In the following empirical analysis, the three dimensions of quality are defined by:

1. The predicted wage differential in 1979 between the most recently arrived immigrant cohort and the native base. This measure of the quality of a single cohort of immigrants – prior to assimilation taking place – is given by the coefficient of the immigrant dummy variable in the 1980 cross section.

2. The rate of wage growth (relative to natives) for an immigrant cohort that has resided in the United States for ten years. This is the assimilation effect evaluated at $y = 10$, and is given by $\partial \ln w / \partial y|_{y=10} = \alpha_1 + 20\alpha_2$.

3. The predicted wage differential immediately after immigration between the 1979 cohort and the 1955 cohort. This measure of the extent of cohort-quality change is designed to compare the typical immi-

grant that migrated prior to the 1965 Immigration and Nationality Act with the typical immigrant from the most recent wave. Using Equation (15) it is easy to show that this change in cohort quality is given by $24(\beta_1 + 2\beta_2 T - 24\beta_2)$, where T indexes the 1980 cross section.

4.3.   Regression Results from the 1970–1980 Censuses

The data are drawn from the 1970 2/100 U.S. Census (obtained by pooling the 5% SMSA and County Group Sample and the 5% State Sample) and the 1980 5/100 A Sample.[15] The complete samples are used in the creation of the immigrant extracts, but random samples are drawn for the native "baseline" population.[16] The analysis is restricted to men aged 25–64 who satisfied four sample-selection rules: (1) the individual was employed in the calendar year prior to the census; (2) the individual was not self-employed or working without pay; (3) the individual was not in the Armed Forces (as of the survey week); and (4) the individual did not reside in group quarters.[17]

Since labor market conditions changed substantially between 1970 and 1980, the empirical framework derived in the previous section focused on the behavior of immigrant earnings *relative* to the earnings of natives. In this chapter *all* immigrant groups will be compared to a single native base: the group of white, non-Hispanic, non-Asian men.

Forty-one countries were chosen for analysis. The countries were selected on the basis that *both* the 1970 and 1980 Censuses contained a substantial number of immigrants from the country. In particular, it is necessary to have at least 80 observations of persons born in a particular foreign country in the pooled 2/100 1970 Census to enter the sample of the 41 countries.[18] The 41 countries under analysis account for 90.4 percent of all immigration to the United States between 1951 and 1980.

Summary statistics on the immigrant flow in the 1951–80 period are presented in Table 4.2. The first column of Table 4.2 gives the total number of immigrants from each country that arrived in the United States in that period. Although this number is interesting, it is more instructive if it is converted into a percentage of the country of origin's 1980 population. This statistic is presented in the second column and gives the percentage by which the country of origin's population would increase (in 1980) if all the persons who emigrated to the United States in the past three decades returned to their birthplace.

Table 4.2

Immigration Flows to the United States in the 1951–80 Period

Country of Birth	1951-80 Immigration		1951-60 Immigrants as Percent of 1950 Population[a]	1971-80 Immigrants as Percent of 1970 Population[a]
	Total Number (in 1000s)	As Percent of 1980 Population[a]		
Europe:				
Austria	48.1	.6	.4	.1
Czechoslovakia	60.4	.4	.2	.1
Denmark	30.0	.6	.3	.1
France	90.1	.2	.1	.04
Germany	611.5	1.0	.7	.1
Greece	232.3	2.4	.6	1.1
Hungary	93.4	.9	.7	.1
Ireland	120.9	3.5	2.2	.5
Italy	524.8	.9	.4	.2
Netherlands	85.7	.6	.5	.1
Norway	45.1	1.1	.8	.1
Poland	244.9	.7	.5	.1
Portugal	204.2	2.1	.2	1.2
Romania	49.8	.2	.1	.1
Spain	71.2	.2	.04	.1
Sweden	41.9	.5	.3	.1
Switzerland	40.1	.6	.4	.1
United Kingdom	562.9	1.0	.4	.2
USSR	105.4	.04	.02	.02
Yugoslavia	147.0	.7	.4	.2
Asia and Africa:				
China (Taiwan)	331.9	1.9	.4	1.4
Egypt	46.4	.1	.02	.1
India	211.1	.03	.001	.03
Iran	59.1	.2	.01	.2
Israel	48.1	1.3	.7	.9
Japan	131.1	.1	.05	.05
Korea	314.8	.8	.02	.8
Philippines	478.9	.9	.1	1.0
Americas:				
Argentina	81.5	.3	.1	.3
Brazil	43.1	.04	.02	.01
Canada	676.4	2.8	2.0	.5
Colombia	165.5	.6	.4	.6
Cuba	611.9	6.3	1.5	3.2
Dominican Republic	251.9	4.3	.5	3.4
Ecuador	96.7	1.2	.3	.8
Guatemala	45.1	.7	.1	.5
Haiti	100.2	1.8	.1	1.3
Jamaica	221.7	10.3	.6	7.3
Mexico	1399.8	2.0	1.2	1.3
Panama	50.8	2.6	1.2	1.5
Trinidad & Tobago	88.0	8.0	.2	6.0

Note: [a] The population base refers to the country of origin.
Source: U.S. Bureau of the Census (various issues).

This percent ranges from the trivially small (.04 percent of Brazil and the USSR) to the amazingly large (over 10 percent for Jamaica). Of the 41 countries in Table 4.2, 17 of them experienced emigration to the United States which exceeded 1 percent of that country's population.

The national composition of the flows received by the United States over the 1951–80 period did not remain constant over the three decades. The third column gives the flow of immigrants in the 1951–60 decade as a percent of the country's 1950 population; while the fourth column presents the flow of immigrants in 1971–80 as a percent of the country's 1970 population. These statistics document the declining importance of Western European countries as a source of immigrants and the increasing importance of Asia and Latin America. The fact that the characteristics of the sending countries changed drastically during the postwar period implies that the types of selections that distinguish the immigrant population from the native born also changed.

The 1970 and 1980 cross-section regressions were jointly estimated in each of the 41 samples (i.e., the group of immigrants from a specific country of origin pooled with the "white" native base), using the (ln) wage rate in the year preceding the census as the dependent variable. The socioeconomic vector of characteristics X included: years of completed schooling, age, age squared, whether health limits work, whether married, spouse present, and whether resident of an SMSA. The regression framework derived in Section 4.2 implies that the coefficient of the quadratic years-since-migration variable should be constant across censuses. This restriction was satisfied (at the 5 percent level of significance) by 32 of the 41 countries in the data, and hence was imposed on the analysis.

The restricted coefficients of the immigration vector in both the 1970 and 1980 Census cross-sections are presented in the first five columns of Table 4.3. The coefficients of the immigration variables in 1970 differ drastically from the coefficients of the immigration variables in 1980. This difference implies that cross-section regressions do not capture the "true" assimilation impact since cohort effects are confounding the analysis. Consider, for example, Colombia: in 1970, the most recent immigrants earned about 22 percent less than the native base, and their (relative) earnings increased by about 1.7 percent in the first year after immigration. By 1980, the most recent wave of Colombians earned 40 percent less than the *same* native base, and their earnings increased by about 2.2 percent in the first year after immigration.

Table 4.3
Estimates of Model Parameters[a]

Country of Birth	1970 I	1970 $I \cdot y$	1980 I	1980 $I \cdot y$	1980 $I \cdot y^2$	Rate of Assimilation at $y = 10$	1955-79 Change in Cohort Quality
Europe:							
Austria	.0189	.0036	.0321	.0034	-.00003	.0040	.0287
	(.26)	(.75)	(.52)	(.82)	(-.45)	(.66)	(.20)
Czechoslovakia	-.1525	.0147	-.1441	.0127	-.00019	.0088	-.0143
	(-2.48)	(3.34)	(-2.79)	(3.23)	(-2.74)	(1.64)	(-.10)
Denmark	.0838	-.0033	.2018	-.0056	.00009	.0068	.2441
	(.82)	(-.44)	(2.14)	(-.81)	(.72)	(.78)	(1.21)
France	-.0785	.0020	.0999	-.0046	.00005	.0111	.3183
	(-1.28)	(.47)	(2.48)	(-1.33)	(.79)	(2.05)	(2.74)
Germany	.0999	-.0025	.1409	-.0047	.00007	-.0002	.0618
	(3.82)	(-1.37)	(5.40)	(-2.62)	(2.38)	(-.10)	(1.17)
Greece	-.2400	.0115	-.3092	.0141	-.00018	.0049	-.1231
	(-6.70)	(3.73)	(-11.28)	(5.42)	(-3.33)	(1.56)	(-1.75)
Hungary	-.1555	.0173	-.2082	.0145	-.00021	.0036	-.1744
	(-2.98)	(4.12)	(-4.30)	(4.23)	(-3.31)	(.86)	(-1.85)
Ireland	-.0732	.0019	-.0514	.0027	-.00002	.0050	.0666
	(-1.54)	(.53)	(-1.09)	(.78)	(-.28)	(1.26)	(.72)
Italy	.0133	.0060	-.0673	.0065	-.00009	-.0031	-.1855
	(.60)	(3.72)	(-3.45)	(4.58)	(-3.49)	(-1.55)	(-4.07)
Netherlands	.0127	-.0061	.1252	-.0074	.00015	.0062	.2487
	(.23)	(-1.45)	(2.71)	(-2.15)	(2.35)	(1.35)	(2.41)
Norway	.2245	-.0093	.2785	-.0096	.00015	-.0013	.1241
	(2.54)	(-1.55)	(3.77)	(-1.76)	(1.58)	(-.17)	(.71)
Poland	-.1936	.0181	-.2734	.0184	-.00024	.0058	-.1865
	(-5.70)	(7.62)	(-11.08)	(9.61)	(-6.86)	(1.98)	(-3.08)
Portugal	.0797	.0032	-.0913	.0073	-.00012	-.0102	-.3418
	(1.95)	(.86)	(-3.25)	(2.47)	(-1.95)	(-2.77)	(-4.02)
Romania	-.3015	.0263	-.3161	.0229	-.00030	.0136	-.0929
	(-4.23)	(4.97)	(-7.02)	(5.47)	(-3.65)	(2.17)	(-.72)
Spain	-.3547	.0233	-.1920	.0134	-.00022	.0203	.2245
	(-6.15)	(4.32)	(-4.10)	(2.88)	(-2.39)	(3.98)	(1.92)
Sweden	.0128	.0119	.0465	.0099	-.00021	.0080	.0465
	(.13)	(1.90)	(.69)	(1.88)	(-2.14)	(.88)	(.24)
Switzerland	-.0201	.0132	.1467	.0067	-.00015	.0171	.2912
	(-.27)	(2.18)	(2.48)	(1.33)	(-1.56)	(2.56)	(1.97)
United Kingdom	.0607	-.0006	.1271	-.0023	.00002	.0038	.1303
	(2.70)	(-.34)	(7.38)	(-1.61)	(.67)	(1.84)	(2.81)
USSR	-.3509	.0277	-42.99	.0262	-.00035	.0105	-.2144
	(-6.70)	(8.34)	(-18.75)	(11.70)	(-7.67)	(2.22)	(-2.31)
Yugoslavia	-.0659	.0096	-.0920	.0097	-.00009	.0054	-.0608
	(-1.51)	(2.72)	(-2.82)	(3.52)	(-1.61)	(1.49)	(-.79)

Table 4.3 (continued)

Estimates of Model Parameters[a]

Country of Birth	1970 I	1970 $I \cdot y$	1980 I	1980 $I \cdot y$	1980 $I \cdot y^2$	Rate of Assimilation at $y = 10$	1955-79 Change in Cohort Quality
Asia and Africa:							
China (Taiwan)	-.4525	.0227	-.5327	.0254	-.00037	.0114	-.1481
	(-14.34)	(9.43)	(-26.43)	(11.66)	(-8.22)	(4.01)	(-2.44)
Egypt	-.4466	.0421	-.4586	.0396	-.00056	.0260	-.0706
	(-7.00)	(5.67)	(-10.84)	(7.57)	(-4.34)	(4.76)	(-.57)
India	-.2847	.0453	-.4340	.0497	-.00096	.0179	-.2845
	(-7.09)	(9.71)	(-21.41)	(16.75)	(-11.03)	(5.33)	(-3.84)
Iran	-.4078	.0229	-.3101	.0249	-.00031	.0294	.2690
	(-4.71)	(3.03)	(-10.19)	(5.45)	(-2.47)	(4.13)	(1.88)
Israel	-.2998	.0282	-.3397	.0260	-.00041	.0128	-.1314
	(-4.19)	(4.54)	(-8.44)	(5.74)	(-3.84)	(2.11)	(-1.00)
Japan	-.1314	.0010	.1016	-.0049	.00002	.0159	.4616
	(-2.65)	(.19)	(4.31)	(-1.46)	(.18)	(3.60)	(4.78)
Korea	-.5450	.0439	-.4481	.0393	-.00071	.0323	.1544
	(-8.69)	(5.72)	(-19.44)	(9.68)	(-5.40)	(6.31)	(1.37)
Philippines	-.4360	.0265	-.3881	.0266	-.00041	.0233	.1158
	(-13.31)	(11.30)	(-23.14)	(13.33)	9.34)	(7.84)	(1.80)
Americas:							
Argentina	-.2099	.0210	-.2427	.0186	-.00032	.0077	-.1191
	(-3.81)	(3.58)	(-5.80)	(4.13)	(-3.11)	(1.65)	(-1.12)
Brazil	-.1430	.0114	-.0257	.0062	-.00015	.0123	.1941
	(-1.70)	(1.44)	(-.45)	(1.00)	(-1.11)	(1.66)	(1.19)
Canada	.0645	.0003	.1165	-.0013	-.00000	.0030	.0988
	(2.86)	(.17)	(6.06)	(-.91)	(-.21)	(1.50)	(2.17)
Colombia	-.2247	.0169	-.4030	.0219	-.00036	-.0007	-.3444
	(-4.33)	(2.74)	(-12.67)	(5.78)	(-3.71)	(-.17)	(-3.82)
Cuba	-.4612	.0214	-.4517	.0208	-.00025	.0164	.0129
	(-22.20)	(8.89)	(-18.26)	(9.24)	(-5.20)	(9.74)	(.28)
Dominican Republic	-.3293	.0141	-.4556	.0142	-.00018	-.0019	-.3020
	(-5.81)	(2.45)	(-13.91)	(3.62)	(-1.74)	(-.44)	(-3.01)
Ecuador	-.4041	.0242	-.4195	.0210	-.00026	.0127	-.0906
	(-6.06)	(3.28)	(-9.77)	(4.13)	(-1.98)	(2.58)	(-.82)
Guatemala	-.5127	.0408	-.4013	.0298	-.00066	.0222	.0828
	(-5.76)	(5.03)	(-8.97)	(5.09)	(-4.40)	(2.96)	(.51)
Haiti	-.3356	-.0027	-.5234	.0175	-.00011	.0064	-.1130
	(-4.99)	(-.34)	(-13.95)	(3.39)	(-.77)	(1.20)	(-.94)
Jamaica	-.3322	.0165	-.2594	.0097	-.00020	.0095	.0600
	(-6.75)	(4.06)	(-9.33)	(2.92)	(-2.77)	(2.24)	(.64)
Mexico	-.3307	.0191	-.4037	.0206	-.00031	.0078	-.1497
	(-16.57)	(14.80)	(-34.72)	(22.25)	(-15.94)	(4.16)	(-3.61)
Panama	-.3438	.0159	-.2516	.0115	-.00010	.0165	.1476
	(-3.52)	(2.31)	(-4.35)	(2.07)	(-.88)	(2.04)	(.84)
Trinidad & Tobago	-.3091	.0187	-.3257	.0211	-.00024	.0158	.0013
	(-4.02)	(2.59)	(-6.94)	(3.70)	(-1.95)	(2.35)	(.03)

Note: [a] The t-ratios are presented in parentheses. The cross-section regressions hold constant the individual's completed schooling, age, marital status, health, and SMSA residence.

The tilting of the cross-section profile so that later cross sections are steeper and have a more negative constant term implies that the quality of the more recent Colombian immigrant waves is lower than that of the earlier waves. Conversely, consider the immigrants from France: in 1970, the typical French immigrant earned about 8 percent less than a comparable native person, and had earnings growth of about 0.2 percent during that first year after immigration. By 1980, the most recent immigrant earned about 10 percent *more* than the native base, and had earnings growth of minus 0.5 percent during that first year. The flattening of the cross-section profile implies that the quality of French immigrants increased over the sample period.

Three dimensions of cohort quality are implicit in these regression coefficients. The entry wage differential between the 1979 immigrant cohort and the native base is given by the coefficient of the immigrant dummy in the 1980 Census cross-section. Table 4.3 clearly shows that this coefficient has a large variance across countries. The last two columns of Table 4.3 present estimates of the other two dimensions of cohort quality: the assimilation rate defined by the slope of the earnings-assimilation path at $y = 10$; and the rate of change in cohort quality, defined by the earnings differential between the 1979 cohort and the 1955 cohort at the time of arrival in the United States. Since these estimated parameters are functions of the cross-section coefficients of Table 4.3, it is not surprising to find that there is a lot of variance in both of these variables across countries. Immigrants from some countries have high assimilation rates, while immigrants from other countries experience no assimilation at all. Similarly, the rate of cohort-quality change is sometimes positive (thus indicating quality increased between the 1955 and 1979 cohorts) and sometimes negative (thus indicating a quality decrease across cohorts). For example, the most recent immigrant wave from the United Kingdom has an earnings potential that is about 13 percent higher than the wave that arrived in 1955, while the most recent immigrants from India have 28 percent lower earnings than the earlier cohort.

The Roy model suggests that country-specific characteristics of the income distribution (and mobility costs) determine the quality of immigrants in the United States. The important task, therefore, becomes the identification of observable variables which can proxy for these theoretical parameters, and the determination of whether these country-specific variables "explain" the variance in the quality proxies presented in Table 4.3.

4.4. Determinants of Immigrant Quality

Table 4.4 describes the construction and source of country-specific aggregate variables which portray the political and economic conditions (as well as some characteristics of the immigrant populations) of the 41 countries under analysis during the 1950–79 period. Table 4.4 also presents the mean and range of these variables and comparable statistics for the United States.

Three of these variables are designed to capture political conditions in the country of origin. These political measures are obtained from the Cross-National Time-Series Archive (CNTSA), a historical data set containing both political and economic variables for all sovereign countries since 1815 (up to 1973).[19] The CNTSA set contains a variable describing the extent of "party legitimacy," that is, whether or not there is competition among political parties in the electoral system. The measure of party legitimacy is interpreted as an index of political freedom, and is used to construct two variables: (1) a dummy variable set equal to unity if the immigrant's birthplace had a competitive political system during the *entire* 1950–73 period; and (2) a dummy variable set equal to unity if the immigrant's birthplace had a competitive political system at the beginning of the period, but lost its political freedom by the end of the period. The omitted dummy variable indicates whether the birthplace of the immigrant had a noncompetitive political system both at the beginning and at the end of the 1950–73 period.[20] The last index of political stability used is a variable measuring the number of political assassinations (defined as a politically motivated murder or attempted murder of a high government official or politician) that took place in the specific country during the 1950–73 period.

The country-specific vector also includes variables that describe economic conditions in the various countries of origin:

1. The logarithm of per capita Gross National Product in 1980 (in U.S. dollars). In addition, the analysis also uses the average annual percentage change in that variable over the 1963–80 period. These variables, of course, are designed to control for the mean level of the income distribution (as well as changes in that level) in the various countries of origin.
2. The ratio of household income accruing to the top 10 percent of the households to the income accruing to the bottom 20 per-

Table 4.4
Definition of Country-Specific Variables

Variable	Definition and Source	Mean	Minimum	Maximum
Politically Competitive System	= 1 if the country had a competitive party system during the entire 1950-73 period; 0 otherwise. *Source:* Cross-National Time-Series Archive (CNTSA)	.41	-	-
Recent Loss of Freedom	= 1 if the country had a competitive party system at the beginning of the period but had a non-competitive party system at the end of the period; 0 otherwise. *Source:* CNTSA	.20	-	-
Number of Assassinations	Number of politically motivated murders or attempted murders of high government officials or politicians in 1950-73. *Source:* CNTSA.	3.27	0	22
Income Inequality	Ratio of household income of the top 10 percent of the households to the income of the bottom 20 percent of the households. *Source:* World Bank (various issues) and United Nations (1977).	7.50	1.42	30.0
Distance from U.S.	Number of air miles (in thousands) between the country's capital and the nearest U.S. gateway (Los Angeles, Miami, or New York). *Source:* Airline offices contacted by author.	3.37	.18	7.49
English Proficiency	Fraction of 1975-80 cohort of immigrants who speak English well or very well. *Source:* 5/100 A Sample of the 1980 U.S. Census.	.74	.24	1.00
Age at Migration	Mean age at migration. *Source:* 5/100 A Sample of the 1980 U.S. Census.	24.56	12.40	32.40
In (per capita GNP)	(In) 1980 per capita *GNP* in dollars *Source:* U.S. Arms Control and Disarmament Agency (1984).	8.17	5.42	9.62
Rate of Change in Per Capita GNP	Annual rate of change in per capita GNP between 1963 and 1980, defined by: $\ln(GNP_{1980}/GNP_{1963})/17$. *Source:* U.S. Arms Control and Disarmament Agency (1975, 1984).	.03	.004	.07
Rate of Change in Central Government Expenditures	Annual Change in the Percentage of GNP that is accounted for by central government expenditures, defined by $(GOVT_{1980}- GOVT_{1950})/30$, where *GOVT* is the percent of GNP attributable to central government expenditures in year t. *Source:* CNTSA and U.S. Arms Control and Disarmament Agency (1984).	.41	-1.69	2.08
Change in Quota	Change in fraction of population eligible for migration to the U.S., defined by (20000/1979 population) Mathe!! (QUOTA/1950 population), where 20,000 is the maximum number of visas allocated to the country after 1965, and QUOTA is the number of visas allocated prior to 1965. Source: U.S. Immigration and Naturalization Service (1965).	38.90	.28	149.67

cent of the households (circa 1970). Unfortunately, this measure of income inequality does not exist prior to the 1970s for most of the countries under analysis, and hence the change in the extent of income inequality during the last three decades cannot be documented. The empirical analysis which follows will proxy for the change in income inequality by using the change in the fraction of GNP that can be attributed to central government expenditures over that period. Presumably, the greater the role of the government the more taxation and income redistribution that occurs, and hence the less unequal the income distribution will be.

3. The level of mobility costs is proxied by the number of air miles between the country's capital and the nearest U.S. gateway.

Finally, the regressions also include variables that describe relevant characteristics of the immigrant population itself. The two variables in this category are the fraction of the most recently arrived immigrants who speak English well or very well, and the average age at migration. These variables are likely to affect the earnings of immigrants as well as their incentives to invest in human capital, and hence will be important determinants of immigrant quality.

4.4.1. Determinants of the Entry Wage Differential

In the last section a variable measuring the entry wage differential between the foreign born and the native born for the immigrant cohort arriving in 1979 was calculated for each of the 41 countries under analysis. Table 4.5 presents the generalized least squares regressions of this measure of immigrant quality on the country-specific aggregate variables.[21]

The simplest specification in column 1 shows that the variable measuring whether or not the country was politically competitive in the postwar period has a strong positive impact on the immigrant's entry wage. Immigrants from these countries have 27 percent higher relative earnings (at the time of entry into the United States) than immigrants from politically repressive countries. This basic regression also shows that the extent of income inequality has a weak negative impact on the relative quality of immigrants. Immigrants from countries with more income inequality are of lower quality. This result is consistent with the theoretical implications of the Roy model. As income inequality increases, the migration incentives for persons in the upper tail of the distribution decline, thus lowering the average quality of the immigrant population.

Table 4.5

Determinants of the Entry Wage Differential between the 1979 Immigrant Cohort and Native[a]

Country of Origin	Regression			
Characteristics	1	2	3	4
Intercept	-.2214	.1838	-.9934	-.9469
	(-3.88)	(1.06)	(-3.41)	(-3.30)
Politically Competitive System	.2743	.1306	.1101	.1264
	(4.49)	(2.01)	(2.16)	(2.39)
Recent Loss of Freedom	-.0010	-.0511	-.0062	.0136
	(-.01)	(-.75)	(-.12)	(.25)
Number of Assassinations	-.0072	-.0028	.0021	.0044
	(-1.20)	(-.54)	(.51)	(.92)
Income Inequality	-.0084	-.0038	.0039	.0046
	(-1.78)	(-.89)	(1.02)	(1.13)
Distance from U.S.	-	-.0114	-.0031	.0018
		(-.89)	(-.31)	(.09)
English Proficiency	-	.2596	.1980	.2030
		(2.20)	(2.12)	(2.21)
Mean Age at Migration	-	-.0217	-.0149	-.0119
		(-3.55)	(-2.99)	(2.28)
ln (per capita GNP)	-	-	.1164	.1015
			(4.57)	(3.77)
Country in Asia or Africa	-	-	-	-.1145
				(-1.58)
Country in North or South America	-	-	-	-.0640
				(-.73)
R^2	.504	.681	.808	.826

Note: [a] The t-ratios are presented in parentheses.

In column 2 of Table 4.5, the variables measuring mobility costs and the age and English proficiency of immigrants are added to the regression. The results suggest that persons migrating from countries that have 100 percent English proficiency rates have about 26 percent higher relative earnings at the time of entry than immigrants from countries with 0 percent English proficiency rates.[22] Table 4.5 also shows that age at migration has a significant *negative* impact on the initial relative earnings of immigrants in the United States. Hence persons who migrate as youths have an easier time in the U.S. labor market than older immigrants.

The third regression in Table 4.5 adds the level of GNP per capita to the list of exogenous variables. Its impact is strongly positive, and its inclusion increases the explanatory power of the regression to over 80 percent! A 10 percent increase in a country's GNP increases the relative earnings of immigrants by about 1.2 percent. This effect is likely to be caused by the fact that the higher the GNP in the country of origin, the greater the resemblance between that country's economic structure and that of the United States, as well as the greater the skills of the immigrant flow. Hence immigrants from those countries perform quite well in the U.S. labor market. The last regression in Table 4.6 adds continent dummies (the omitted continent is Europe) to control for continent-specific fixed effects. These additional controls do not have a major impact on the coefficient of the other variables.[23]

Table 4.5 shows that controlling for variations in per capita GNP across countries of origin has a major impact on the coefficient of the inequality variable: the latter turns positive (and insignificant). The reason for this shift lies in the very high negative correlation between the two variables ($r = -0.6$). Since high-income countries (mostly in Western Europe) also tend to have the least amount of income inequality, the impact of per capita GNP on initial immigrant quality is likely capturing shifts in both the mean and the variance of the country of origin's income distribution.

The results in Table 4.5, therefore, are not entirely consistent with the theoretical predictions. Note, however, that these regressions do not truly constitute a "test" of the theory. The Roy model shows that selection biases will depend on a number of parameters which are not directly measurable. Table 4.5 attempts to explain intercountry differences in terms of variables which supposedly proxy for these primitive concepts. Clearly the errors introduced in the creation of these variables weaken the link between the theory and the empirical work. Nevertheless, it is important to note that these few country-specific variables "explain" a large fraction of the intercountry differences evident in census data.

4.4.2.   Determinants of the Rate of Assimilation

The assimilation rate is defined by the rate of earnings growth of an immigrant cohort (relative to natives) evaluated at ten years after immigration. Table 4.6 presents the regressions of this variable on the various country-specific proxies.

Table 4.6

Determinants of the Rate of Assimilation[a]

Country of Origin Characteristics	Regression			
	1	2	3	4
Intercept	.0076	-.0240	-.0237	-.0280
	(2.96)	(-3.88)	(-1.50)	(-2.32)
Politically Competitive System	-.0029	-.0068	-.0068	-.0091
	(-1.06)	(-2.66)	(-2.60)	(-4.28)
Recent Loss of Freedom	.0063	.0029	.0030	.0021
	(1.81)	(1.21)	(1.15)	(1.06)
Number of Assassinations	.0008	.0006	.0006	.0008
	(2.68)	(2.36)	(2.14)	(3.07)
Income Inequality	-.0001	-.00002	-.00002	.0002
	(-.50)	(-.11)	(-.10)	(.90)
Distance from U.S.	-	.0003	.0003	-.0027
		(.74)	(.70)	(-2.89)
English Proficiency	-	.0138	.0138	.0122
		(3.27)	(3.20)	(3.70)
Mean Age at Migration	-	.0009	.0009	.0009
		(4.28)	(3.95)	(4.72)
ln (per capita GNP)	-	-	-.00002	.0021
			(-.01)	(1.83)
Country in Asia or Africa	-	-	-	.0151
				(5.11)
Country in North or South America	-	-	-	-.0080
				(-2.08)
R^2	.302	.704	.704	.842

Note: [a] The t-ratios are presented in parentheses.

Assimilation rates are determined by political factors. In particular, immigrants from free countries have lower assimilation rates than immigrants from countries with a long history of political repression, while immigrants from countries that recently lost their political freedom have the highest assimilation rates. These results are consistent with the hypothesis that the costs of return migration for immigrants from politically repressive countries are high, and therefore they have the most incentives to adapt to the U.S. labor market. The same reasoning can also explain the strong positive impact of the number of assassinations on the rate of immigrant assimilation: immigrants from politically unstable countries have greater incentives to assimilate in the U.S. labor market since their return migration may be costly.

The regression in column 2 shows that although distance between the United States and the country of birth has a positive impact on the assimilation rate, the effect is not significant. However, immigrants from countries with higher levels of English proficiency have much higher assimilation rates. In fact, the rate of earnings growth of immigrants from English-speaking countries is 1.4 percentage points higher than that of immigrants from countries with 0 percent English proficiency rates. Similarly, the age at immigration has a strong *positive* impact on assimilation rates. This result is consistent with the hypothesis that immigrants who migrate as youths have little to gain from assimilation per se. On the other hand, the adaptation period is likely to be important for persons who migrate at older ages.

The last two regressions in Table 4.6 include per capita GNP variable and the continent dummies in the list of regressors. These variables have a significant impact on the assimilation rate (in column 4). Immigrants from wealthier countries have higher assimilation rates, and Europeans (the omitted continent) have higher assimilation rates than immigrants from the Americas, but lower assimilation rates than immigrants born in Asia or Africa. Despite the strongly significant impact of the continent dummies, the qualitative effect of most of the other variables in the regression is unaffected.

4.4.3. *Determinants of the Change in Cohort Quality*

Section 4.3 calculated a variable measuring the wage differential between the 1979 immigrant cohort and the 1955 immigrant cohort as of the date of immigration. The regressions analyzing the determinants of cohort quality change are presented in Table 4.7. It should be noted that the specification of these regressions differs slightly from those presented in Tables 4.5 and 4.6 since cohort quality change is likely to be determined by changes in the explanatory variables over the 1954–79 period.

Table 4.7

Determinants of the Rate of Change in Cohort Quality[a]

Country of Origin Characteristics	Regression			
	1	2	3	4
Intercept	-.3194	-.9951	-1.1779	-22202
	(-3.19)	(-3.97)	(-4.08)	(-4.69)
Politically Competitive System	.1760	.1075	.0712	.0630
	(2.54)	(1.60)	(.97)	(.70)
Recent Loss of Freedom	.1256	.1468	.1272	.1310
	(1.67)	(2.16)	(1.81)	(1.33)
Number of Assassinations	.0077	.0156	.0122	.0256
	(1.19)	(2.32)	(1.69)	(2.00)
Rate of Change in Central Government Expenditures	.0698	.0699	.0641	-.0099
	(1.60)	(1.75)	(1.60)	(-.21)
Rate of Change in Per Capita GNP	4.7010	3.0956	1.1567	-1.5321
	(2.27)	(1.60)	(.46)	(-.50)
In (per capita GNP)	-	.0889	.1186	.2443
		(1.93)	(3.22)	(4.15)
Country in Asia or Africa	-	-	.1374	-
			(1.42)	
Country in North or South America	-	-	.0274	-
			(.41)	
Change in Quota	-	-	-	.0034
				(2.26)
R^2	.284	.418	.453	.581

Note [a] The t-ratios are presented in parentheses.

The simple specification in column 1 reveals that cohort quality change is strongly influenced by practically all the variables in the regressions. For example, the quality of cohorts from countries that experienced a shift from political competition to repression increased by about 13 percent (relative to the quality of cohorts from countries that were politically repressive throughout the period). This effect is consistent with the implications of the theory developed in Section 4.1. The change in political structure can be viewed as a change in the correlation coefficient of the earnings of individuals between the home country and the United States. The change toward a repressive government may make the correlation coefficient in earnings across the two countries negative. Thus persons in the "revolutionary" lower tail of the home country's income distribution migrate to the United States and perform quite well in the U.S. labor market.

Table 4.7 also shows that cohort quality change is strongly affected by the average annual change in the percent of GNP that is attributable to expenditures by the central government. Presumably the greater the role of the government, the more income redistribution that takes place and the greater the *decrease* in income inequality over the postwar period. The coefficient of this variable in Table 4.8 is consistent with the theoretical implication.

Table 4.8

Probit Regression on the Emigration Rate[a]

Country of Origin Characteristics	Regression	
	1	2
Intercept	-.6060	-1.1614
	(-1.30)	(-2.46)
Politically Competitive System	.1206	.0801
	(1.13)	(.81)
Recent Loss of Freedom	.1096	-.0365
	(.95)	(-.32)
Number of Assassinations	-.0245	-.0337
	(-2.65)	(-3.65)
Income Inequality	-.0113	-.0145
	(-1.51)	(-2.00)
Distance from U.S.	-.1332	-.1271
	(-6.11)	(-2.68)
English Proficiency	.1661	.0488
	(.94)	(.30)
ln (per capita GNP)	-.1130	-.0441
	(-2.14)	(-.83)
Country in Asia or Africa	-	.3386
		(2.19)
Country in North or South America	-	.2923
		(1.52)
X^2	98.45	108.82

Note: [a] The dependent variable is the probability that an individual migrated to the United States in 1951–80, and is given by the second column of Table 2. The t-ratios are presented in parentheses.

The next two regressions in Table 4.8 add the level of per capita GNP to control for country-specific differences in wealth, and the continent dummies to control for continent-specific fixed effects. The continent dummies are not very significant, but per capita GNP variable does have a strong positive impact on cohort-quality change. Its positive coefficient confirms the finding suggested by the descriptive analysis in Section 4.3: The quality of immigrants admitted to the United States has been increasing over time when the immigrants originate in Western Europe and has been declining over time when the immigrants originate in the less developed countries.

One factor causing systematic quality shifts across immigrant cohorts may have been the change in the quota system mandated by the 1965 Amendments to the Immigration and Nationality Act. Table 4.4 defined a variable that measures the change in the fraction of the home country's population "eligible" for emigration to the United States before and after the 1965 Amendments. Higher levels of this variable imply a reduction in the levels of "mobility costs" faced by potential emigrants. The Roy model suggests that its impact on the rate of cohort-quality change is positive if the correlation coefficient between earning capacities in the two countries is positive and if income is more unequally distributed in the countries of origin than in the United States. The last column of Table 4.7 adds the quota variable to the regression and shows that it indeed has a positive and significant impact on the rate of change in cohort quality. It is important to note that this regression is estimated on only 28 observations since the quota system prior to the 1965 Amendments was applicable only to countries that were in the Eastern Hemisphere.

4.4.4. Determinants of the Emigration Rate

The empirical analysis in this chapter focuses on the determinants of the (relative) earnings of immigrants. It is worth noting, however, that the Roy model also implies that the emigration rate will be a function of the same characteristics of the income distribution, political conditions, and migration costs that determine the relative earnings of immigrants. Therefore, it is important to explore if the emigration rate from the various countries of origin is responsive to shifts in the country-specific variables that have been used throughout this section.

Table 4.8 presents two probit regressions on the emigration rate.[24] The dependent variable is obtained from the second column of the summary statistics presented in Table 4.2, and is the fraction of the country of origin's population that emigrated to the United States in the 1951–80 period. The first of the two regressions includes the political variables, the distance variable (to measure migration costs), and the inequality variable, while the second regression adds the continent dummies.[25]

As expected, the distance between the country of origin and the United States has a negative impact on the emigration rate. The emigration rate is also lower for countries that have high levels of GNP per capita. These results, of course, are consistent with the predictions of the wealth-maximization framework. More interestingly, the second moment of the income distribution (as predicted by the Roy model) plays an important role in the determination of the emigration rate. In particular, countries with more income inequality have lower emigration rates. This negative coefficient is implied by the wealth-maximization framework if there is negative selection in the immigrant pool. Negative selection requires that the correlation between earnings in the United States and in the sending countries be sufficiently positive *and* that the United States has less income inequality than the sending countries. If, in addition, mean income in the United States exceeds mean income in sending countries (adjusted for mobility costs), as income inequality in the home country increases, the migration incentives of the most able decreases while the poorest will still migrate. Hence the emigration rate *declines* due to the withdrawal of high-income persons from the pool of emigrants. The analysis of the emigration rate, therefore, leads to results that are generally consistent with the types of selection biases that have been documented in this chapter.

4.5. Summary

What determines the (labor market) quality of foreign-born persons in the United States? Most of the literature addresses this question simply by assuming that immigrants are a "select" group, and that the selection mechanism somehow sends the most able and the most ambitious persons in any country of origin to the United States. This chapter is an attempt to analyze both the conceptual and empirical foundations for this type of assertion. Among the major findings of the study are:

1. If potential emigrants are income maximizers, foreign-born persons in the United States need not be drawn from the most able and most ambitious in the country of origin. Two conditions must be satisfied in order for positive selection to take place: (a) there is a strong

positive correlation between the earnings a worker may expect in the home country and the earnings the same worker may expect in the United States; and (b) the United States has a more unequal income distribution than the home country. If the income distribution in the sending country is more unequal than that of the United States (and the correlation in earnings is positive and strong), emigrants will be chosen from the *lower* tail of the income distribution in the country of origin.

2. The empirical analysis of the earnings of immigrants from 41 different countries using the 1970 and 1980 Censuses shows that there are strong country-specific fixed effects in the (labor market) quality of foreign-born persons. In particular, persons from Western European countries do quite well in the United States, and their cohorts have exhibited a general *increase* in earnings (relative to their measured skills) over the postwar period. On the other hand, persons from less developed countries do not perform well in the U.S. labor market and their cohorts have exhibited a general *decrease* in earnings (relative to their measured skills) over the postwar period.

3. The empirical analysis of the variance in various dimensions of immigrant incomes shows that a few variables describing political and economic conditions in the various countries of origin explain over two-thirds of the intercountry variance in the mean U.S. incomes of immigrants with the same measured skills. Immigrants with high incomes in the United States relative to their measured skills come from countries that have high levels of GNP, low levels of income inequality, and politically competitive systems.

5

Human Capital and the Labor Market Adjustment of Immigrants: Testing Alternative Hypotheses

In my Labor Department monograph (Chiswick 1980a) I raised the issue of whether the increase in earnings of adult male immigrants with duration in the U.S. observed in a single cross-section, such as the 1970 Census, was a true longitudinal effect or whether it was due to changes in the selectivity of newer immigrants (lower cohort quality) or selective out-migration (the less successful ones were more likely to leave). I extracted the various tests from this monograph, added some additional material, and strengthened the presentation. The result was published as a journal article "Human Capital and the Labor Market Adjustment of Immigrants: Testing Alternative Hypotheses" (reprinted as Chapter 5 of this volume).

The tests demonstrated that country-of-origin differences in the slope of the duration-earnings profiles were consistent with differences in the degree of skill transferability to the U.S. Also, that the increase in earnings in the longitudinal data from the National Longitudinal Survey (NLS) was greater among adult men who were immigrants than among native-born men, which is consistent with the immigrant adjustment model.

There was also a test for selective emigration from the U.S. by schooling level. The distribution of years of schooling among adult immigrant men in the 1970 Census was compared with the distribution for those in the U.S. at least ten years in the 1980 Census. With one exception the distributions

The original version of this chapter was published as: Chiswick, B.R. (1986). Human Capital and the Labor Market Adjustment of Immigrants: Testing Alternative Hypotheses, in: Research in Human Capital and Development: Migration, 4: 1–26. © 1986 by JAI Press Inc.

were similar, suggesting no selective emigration of immigrants by schooling level. The one exception was that men from Mexico with very low levels of schooling had a high propensity for "disappearing" from the data. This was undoubtedly due to the well-known circular migration (high propensity for return migration) among low-skilled – often illegal – migrants from Mexico.

This paper demonstrated that to a first approximation the duration-earnings profiles of immigrants in U.S. cross-sectional data were not a biased estimate of the longitudinal profile.

Barry R. Chiswick (2015)

5.1. Introduction

In the last few years there has been considerable research on the economic adjustment of immigrants in the United States and other countries, as measured by their earnings, occupational status, and employment. The theoretical underpinning of these analyses has been human capital theory and, in particular, the extent of the transferability of skills and the self-selection of migrants.[1] The model has been tested with cross-sectional data, primarily from the censuses of population, but also for other data files for the United States and other countries.[2]

The following hypotheses have been found to be consistent with the data:

1. The economic status of immigrants improves with duration of residence.
2. Refugees experience greater difficulty initially, but because of a steeper improvement in economic position with duration of residence, the differential between refugees and economic migrants narrows with duration of residence.
3. Pre-immigration years of schooling and labor market experience have a smaller effect on economic status in the destination than the schooling and experience of the native born, and the differential is larger for refugees than for economic migrants.
4. The earnings of economic migrants may reach parity with the native born, *ceteris paribus*, after which the foreign born would have higher earnings. This crossover would come later, if at all, for refugees. (Empirically, for white economic migrants in the United States, the crossover occurs at about 15 years of residence.)

Although these patterns are extremely robust, it is not sufficient to show that the data are consistent with a set of hypotheses. Are there other hypotheses that are also consistent with some or all of the observed patterns? The purpose of this chapter is to indicate some plausible alternative hypotheses and to test them with the same data. Two alternative models to the approach outlined here that have been suggested at various seminars and in the literature (for example, Bronfenbrenner 1982; Jasso and Rosenweig 1982) are:

1. *Selective Return Migration* (attrition bias). The rise in economic status with duration of residence is due to the selective return migration (emigration) of the less successful immigrants.
2. *"Luck" as a Determinant of High Earnings.* Immigrants eventually have higher earnings than the native born, not because of greater "ability" but because only those with the good fortune to draw a high earnings profile will move. Either pure luck or some other unobserved component unrelated to ability accounts for the high earnings.

This chapter develops additional tests that can be used to differentiate the original and the alternative hypotheses. The new tests indicate that the data are consistent with the original hypotheses but not the alternative hypotheses. The failure of the alternatives increases confidence in the robustness of the human capital model of immigrant adjustment based on transferability of skills and self-selection for explaining the economic status of immigrants across demographic groups, across geographic areas, and over time.

Section 5.2 is a review of the human capital model of immigrant adjustment and the major hypotheses derived from this approach. The model is based on the self-selection of immigrants and the international transferability of skills. Section 5.3 introduces an alternative hypothesis – that the selective emigration from the United States of less successful immigrants is responsible for the observed rise in earnings, employment, and occupational status with duration of residence of the remaining foreign-born population. This alternative hypothesis is tested with data on the effect of duration of residence for immigrants from countries that differ in the degree of return migration. It is also tested by an examination of the growth in earnings over time among adult men in the National Longitudinal Survey. An additional test uses longitudinal data on the occupational status of immigrants in the 1970 Census. The analyses in Section 5.3 are *"ceteris paribus"*; that is, earnings, employment, and occupational profiles are examined when other variables, including schooling, are the same.

Section 5.4 uses data from the 1960 and 1970 Censuses of population to test for the selective emigration of the foreign born by level of schooling and country of origin. The self-selection model has implications for earnings patterns by immigrant generation, that is, for the earnings of the children and grandchildren of immigrants. These implications do not exist in alternative models. The implications of the self-selection model for earnings by immigrant generation are tested in Section 5.5. The final section is a summary and conclusion.

5.2. The Model and Its Implications

The model of immigrant adjustment is based on the international transferability of skills and the self-selection of immigrants.[3] The model generates implications regarding differences in economic status by nativity, schooling, labor market experience in the countries of origin and destination, and motive for migrating, among other variables.

5.2.1. Transferability of Skills

The extent of the transferability of skills differs by the type of skill and the setting in which it is to be applied. Immigrants whose skills have little transferability will undergo a sharper decline in occupational status at immigration and have lower earnings and higher unemployment (less employment) in the destination. With continued residence in the destination, however, their skills will gradually be modified to increase the transferability of previous investments, and new skills that are more specific to the destination are acquired. Also, the extent of experimental job changes and involuntary layoffs (from low seniority, little firm-specific training, and employer hiring errors) will diminish. As a result, the occupational status, earnings, and employment (weeks worked, or the complement of unemployment) of immigrants will rise with duration of residence.

The labor market disadvantages shortly after immigration are most intense, and the subsequent improvement is strongest, the weaker the transferability of skills. In addition, the effects of pre-immigration schooling and pre-immigration labor market experience on occupational status, earnings, and employment are expected to be weaker for workers with skills that are less readily transferable.

Immigrants may be classified by the similarity of the labor markets in their country of origin to the United States in terms of language, labor market structure, and institutional arrangements. The greater the similarity, the greater the transferability of skills. Thus, English-speaking migrants from developed countries to the United States or Britain would be expected to have more highly transferable skills than otherwise-identical immigrants from other countries.

Motive for migrating is also an important determinant of the transferability of skills of a cohort of immigrants. "Economic migrants" are persons who move primarily because of the attractiveness of the labor market in the destination relative to that in the origin. "Refugees" are those who move largely because of actual or feared persecution for religious, racial, ethnic, political, or social class reasons. Refugees presumably have skills that are less transferable than economic migrants. Economic migrants moved because of the transferability of their skills, and they are more likely to have planned for the move by investments to increase this transferability. For refugees, migration is often an unexpected and unwanted occurrence undertaken to protect their freedom or their lives.

A second category of noneconomic migrant is the "tied-mover." Tied-movers are persons whose migration is determined largely by the migratory behavior of another person, usually a relative (for example, a spouse). Again, since the person's own labor market opportunities are not the primary determinant of the migration decision, tied-movers are likely to have skills that are less readily transferable than those of economic migrants, and they have lower earnings in the destination than economic migrants.[4]

A third category of noneconomic migrants is the "ideological migrant." An ideological consideration (for example, nationalism) rather than conventional economic forces or the persecution associated with refugee migration is the primary migration determinant.[5] Ideological migrants would experience many of the same labor market disadvantages as other noneconomic migrants, although they may have a longer period of preparation.

While the classification of economic migrant, refugee, tied-mover, and ideological migrant is convenient for analytical purposes, empirically it is difficult to identify the motive or motives of particular individuals. Perhaps most Cuban and South Vietnamese "refugees" are truly refugees, but many others may be economic migrants who are using a refugee status as a mechanism to enter the United States. Although many married couples make a joint decision regarding migration, if the husband has more skills and expects greater labor force attachment than the wife, he may be the economic migrant and she may be a tied-mover; yet both elements enter the decision making of each spouse. It seems reasonable to assume, however, that for migration to the United States over the past two to three decades, a greater proportion of the Cubans than the Mexicans and a greater proportion of the Chinese than the Filipinos or Japanese are refugees. Similarly, married female immigrants are more likely to be tied-movers than those who are single at the time of migration.

5.2.2. Self-Selection of Immigrants

As with other forms of investment in human capital, international migration tends to be more profitable for those with higher levels of "ability."[6] Assuming that earnings do not vary with experience, the work life is very long, and migration costs are incurred only in the initial period, then the rate of return on the investment in migration for a low-ability person is approximately

$$r = \frac{W_A - W_B}{C_o + C_d},$$

where W_A and W_B are earnings in the destination and origin of a low-ability worker, C_o is the opportunity (time) cost, and C_d is the direct (out-of-pocket) cost. If the more able have k percent higher earnings in the destination and origin ($k > 0$) but ability does not affect the units of time for making the investment or the direct cost component, the rate of return for the high-ability migrant is:

$$r^* = \frac{(1 + k)W_A - (1 + k)W_B}{(1 + k)C_o + C_d} = \frac{W_A - W_B}{C_o + C_d/(1 + k)},$$

and $r^* > r$ as long as $k > 0$ and $C_d > 0$. Thus, the rate of return from migration is higher for the more able. The intensity of the favorable self-selection is greater the larger the out-of-pocket costs (C_d) of migration.

The incentive for migration by the more able is even greater if high ability makes a person more efficient in the myriad activities involved in migration, thereby reducing the time cost (units of time) and direct costs. For the same percentage reduction in costs, the favorable self-selection is greater the larger the time and direct costs of migration.

If distributions of ability are similar across countries and if immigrants are favorably self-selected on the basis of ability, then immigrants will, on average, have a higher level of ability than does the population in the destination. The favorable self-selection is more intense the larger the costs (particularly out-of-pocket costs) of migration. The ability in question relates to labor market success and may be variously described as entrepreneurial skill, ambition, aggressiveness, allocative decision making, and so forth.

It is the economic migrants who view the migration decision as a conventional human capital investment. For refugees and tied-movers, different incentives are operative. It is therefore expected that economic migrants have greater relevant ability for the labor market than do refugees or tied-movers, other readily measured variables being the same, and that among economic migrants the intensity of the ability differential would be larger the greater the costs of migration.

If economic migrants have greater ability than the native population, they would be expected to have higher earnings once the disadvantages of a foreign origin becomes sufficiently small. Among refugees, however, the combined effects of the lesser transferability of skills (which may not be fully dissipated with a long duration of residence) and the less-intense favorable self-selection implies that they may not reach earnings parity with the native born, but if they do it will be at a longer duration of residence than for economic migrants.

The testing of the model for adult male immigrants in the United States using the 1970 Census of population reveals that the data are consistent with the hypotheses. In particular, controlling for total experience, the occupational status, earnings, and employment of the foreign born rise with the duration of residence; the rise is least intense for English-speaking economic migrants and most intense for refugees. Earnings at arrival and the effects of schooling and pre-immigration labor market experience also vary with the transferability of skills; they are highest for English-speaking economic migrants and lowest for refugees. The regression equations reveal that white economic migrants reach earnings parity with their native-born counterparts at about 15 years of residence, but the crossover is later or nonexistent for refugees. The employment (weeks worked) disadvantage of immigrants disappears at about five to ten years of residence, and it is more intense for refugees than for economic migrants. Analyses of the earnings of immigrants in other countries (Australia, Canada, Britain, and Israel) and the United States at the turn of the century using cross-sectional household survey data are consistent with the model and with the patterns found in the contemporary United States.

5.3.   Selective Emigration of the Foreign Born

A caveat regarding the empirical testing of the model outlined in Section 5.2 is that longitudinal hypotheses are being tested with cross-sectional data. Because of cohort differences, cross-sectional and longitudinal data can generate quite different interpretations.[7] An alternative hypothesis is that, other things the same, the less-successful members of an immigrant cohort reemigrate, either to their country of origin or to a third country. That is, the longer a cohort is in the destination, the smaller its size, but more important for our purposes, the higher its level of ability and economic status (earnings, occupation, and employment). Thus, selective emigration among the foreign born may be responsible for the rise in economic status with duration of residence (Bronfrenbrenner 1982; Jasso and Rosensweig 1982).

The Immigration and Naturalization Service collected data on the emigration of the foreign born from 1908 to 1957, but this activity was suspended because of the poor quality of the data. Indirect techniques have been used to study the issue. The emigration of the foreign born appears to be substantial. It is estimated that during the 1960s, 1.1 million foreign-born persons emigrated, of whom one-quarter (284,000) were men aged 25 to 64 in 1970. This can be compared with the 9.6 million foreign-born persons in the United States in 1970, of whom one-quarter (2.3 million) were men aged 25 to 64. Because the number of foreign-born emigrants was estimated as a residual, it is subject to substantial measurement error (Warren 1979; Warren and Peck 1980).

The rate of foreign-born emigration increases in a recession, is high for new immigrants, and then falls sharply until retirement when there is a second mode, and varies by country of origin. It is greatest for immigrants from Mexico and Canada, lower for Western Europe, and smallest for Cuba and Eastern Europe. Thus, geographic and cultural proximity to the United States and motive for migrating (economic or refugee) influence foreign-born emigration. (See Axelrod 1972; Hansen 1940b; Jasso and Rosensweig 1982; Warren 1979; Warren and Peck 1980; U.S. Bureau of the Census 1960: Series C88–114 and C156–157.)

Information on the self-selection of return migrants is even more scarce and offers ambiguous implications. Vanderkamp's (1972) analysis of short-term interprovincial return migrants in Canada suggests that they were the less-successful migrants. Long and Hansen's (1977) study of black return migrants to the South suggests that both the original migration and the return migration were selective in favor of those with more schooling. DaVanzo (1976) finds that for internal U.S. migration, the return migrants respond to many of the same economic incentives as did the original migrants. Rogers (1984) cites data indicating a variety of motives for return migration, including an original intention that the initial migration is only temporary. She concludes that it is not obvious that return migration reflects negative self-selection.

There are several tests for the selective emigration hypothesis, including comparisons among countries of origin that differ in the extent of reemigration, and analyses of longitudinal data.

5.3.1. Country Differences in Emigration

In spite of the poor quality of the data on foreign-born emigrants, there is reason to believe that emigration varies by country of origin. For example, it is believed that there has been little emigration of the Cuban refugees – few have sought to return to Cuba or to go elsewhere. On the other hand, there is substantial return migration for Canadian, British, and Mexican immigrants.[8] If the return migrants are disproportionately those who have been less successful in the United States, the return migration hypothesis would predict a steeper rise of earnings, occupation, and employment with duration of residence in the United States for Canadian, British, and Mexican immigrants, and a flatter rise for Cuban immigrants. On the other hand, the skill transferability model predicts the smallest rise for the Canadian and British immigrants (English-speaking developed countries), a steeper rise for the Mexican immigrants, and the steepest rise for the Cubans (non-English-speaking refugees).

The empirical evidence supports the skill transferability model. Among adult foreign-born men, other things the same, the partial effect of duration of U.S. residence (entered as a quadratic variable) on annual earnings (expressed in natural logarithms) can serve as the test parameter (Chiswick 1979).[9] The partial effect for adult (age 25–64) white men, when evaluated at ten years, is:

Country of Origin	Percent
All countries	1.12[b]
English-speaking developed countries[a]	0.12[b]
Other countries	1.71[b]
Mexico	1.34[b]
Cuba	2.37[b]

Notes: [a] Includes Canada, the British Isles, Australia, and New Zealand.
[b] Duration of residence and its square are statistically significant at 2.5 percent level, one-tailed test.

That is, the partial effect of duration in the United States is related to skill transferability rather than the degree of return migration.

For an analysis of weeks worked in 1969, immigrants who entered the United States between 1955 and 1959 can serve as the benchmark. The employment "disadvantage" of the 1965 to 1970 immigrant cohort is instructive. The recent Cuban immigrants worked a highly significant 4.6 fewer weeks ($t = -4.76$) than the Cubans who entered during the benchmark period; recent Mexican immigrants worked a significant 1.8 fewer weeks ($t = -2.2$) than their benchmark; for all-white recent immigrants, the disadvantage was 2.7 weeks ($t = -11.5$) (Chiswick 1982b).

A similar test can be performed for nonwhite immigrants. Black immigrants in the United States are primarily from the Caribbean, but they differ in the extent of the transferability of their skills depending on their country of origin. The partial effect of duration of United States residence (evaluated at ten years) on earnings among foreign-born blacks is 1.60 percent overall, but 1.00 percent for those from English-speaking countries and 1.78 percent for those from other (non-English-speaking) countries (Chiswick 1980a, chapter 7). This is consistent with the pattern found among whites.

Among Asian-origin immigrants, the three most numerous groups in the 1970 Census were the Japanese, the Chinese, and the Filipinos. There are no refugees among the Japanese and Filipinos and there are no barriers to their return migration. Among the foreign-born Chinese, however, many are refugees from the mainland – individuals who fled during the Communist Revolution and the periodic persecutions and anarchies since 1949. For many, returning to the mainland is unthinkable, and Hong Kong and Taiwan are "third countries" rather than their origin. When evaluated at ten years, the partial effect of the duration-of-residence variable is 2.7 percent for the Chinese, 2.4 percent for the Japanese, and 1.9 percent for the Filipinos (Chiswick 1979; 1980a, chapter 8). The earnings profile is steeper among Asian-origin immigrants than among white immigrants, presumably because their adjustment is more difficult. As was found among white men, however, the profile is steepest for the Asian-origin group with the largest proportion of refugees. Return migration of the less able is not a compelling interpretation for country-of-origin differences in the slope of the earnings-duration profile. If there were selective emigration of the less-successful immigrants, the slope of cross-sectional profiles relating earnings and employment to duration of residence would be biased upward. The finding that these profiles are flatter where reemigration is most pronounced is inconsistent with the model regarding the transferability of skills and motive for migrating.

5.3.2. Longitudinal Data on Earnings

Longitudinal data can provide a test of the hypothesis that earnings rise with duration of residence among the foreign born when total labor market experience is held constant. By following a cohort of native-born and foreign-born workers over time, earnings ratios would not be confounded by selective emigration.

Longitudinal files with the appropriate data are scarce. Because of the substantial cost of conducting longitudinal surveys, the sample sizes are relatively small. Since the foreign born are about 5 percent of the adult population, the sample size for immigrants is usually very small. Many longitudinal samples do not permit an identification of the foreign born or the year of immigration.

Although it has several deficiencies, the National Longitudinal Survey (NLS) of adult men may be the best longitudinal data file for analyses of the foreign-origin population (Chiswick 1980a, Appendix D). The NLS sample of adult men is a cohort of men aged 45 to 59 in 1966. There are approximately 3,500 white men in the data, but the sample size is reduced when men with missing values for one or more of the relevant variables or who did not work are deleted from the data. In addition, the sample was limited to men aged 64 or less in 1973 (that is, men aged 45 to 57 in 1966). Analyses of earnings (wage, salary, and self-employment income) in 1965 and 1973 were computed for a cohort of 1,338 men, of whom 98 were foreign born. The NLS includes information on nativity, but not year of immigration for the foreign born. However, all of the foreign-born men had immigrated to the United States before 1965.

The average earnings of the foreign born were below that of the native born in 1965 ($8,244 compared with $8,521), but they exceeded those of the native born in 1973 ($11,783 compared with $11,445) (Chiswick 1980a, Appendix D). Controlling for schooling, experience, marital status, weeks worked, and area of residence, the foreign born earned 3.2 percent more than the native born in 1965, although the difference was not statistically significant ($t = 0.52$). In 1973, however, the foreign born had 12.1 percent higher earnings, and the difference was statistically significant ($t = 1.8$). Thus, tracing a cohort of men as it aged suggests that earnings grew more rapidly for the foreign born than for the native born.

The increase in the foreign-born/native-born earnings differential by 8.9 percent over the period of eight years implies a partial effect of duration of residence of 1.1 percent per year. It is quite striking that this same 1.1 percent increase per year of U.S. residence (evaluated at ten years in the United States) was found white men in the 1970 Census. Indeed, since international migration is generally undertaken when men are young adults, since there is a nonlinear effect of duration of residence on earnings, and since the NLS sample is relatively old, a smaller partial effect of duration of residence on earnings would have been expected in the NLS data.

5.3.3.   *Longitudinal Data on Occupation*

The largest sample with longitudinal data[10] on a dimension of economic status is the 1970 Census of population (5 percent questionnaire) which asked occupation in 1965 and in 1970. Although the data on occupation in 1965 are based on a retrospective question and although the time span is short, the data can be used to analyze the occupational change of immigrants. The change in occupational status from 1965 to 1970 can be related to the immigrant's year of immigration and country of origin. The skill-transferability model predicts a decline in occupational status from 1965 to 1970 for immigrants who were in their country of origin in 1965. The decline would vary with the transferability of skill; it would be least intense for economic migrants from English-speaking developed countries and most intense for non-English-speaking refugees. Among immigrants in the United States in 1965, relative to the native born, there would be greater occupational change and a steeper rise in occupational status the more recent the immigration and the less transferable the skills at immigration. Thus, the intensity of this rise would be least for economic migrants from English-speaking developed countries and most intense for refugees. The alternative hypothesis – that the rise in economic status with duration of residence in cross-sectional data arises from the emigration of the less successful – offers no prediction regarding longitudinal changes in occupational status by country of origin.

The empirical analysis focuses on adult white men and the ten broad occupational categories. Other things the same, the foreign born were significantly more likely to experience a change in occupation, particularly those who had been in the United States for fewer than five years and to a lesser extent five to ten years. Among white male immigrants in the United States less than five years, the Cubans experienced the steepest decline in occupational status. This decline is attributable to their refugee-motivated migration rather than to their high level of skill in Cuba. Immigrants from the English-speaking developed countries (mainly Canada and Britain) are also highly skilled, but they experience the least decline in occupational status. Among immigrants in the United States for more than five years, holding period of immigration constant, the Cubans experienced the steepest rise in occupational status, while immigrants from the English-speaking developed countries experienced a relatively small rise.[11] Mexican immigrants are relatively low skilled and they experienced little downward mobility on arrival and little upward mobility in subsequent years.[12] Indeed, small investments in human capital appear to be a characteristic of Mexican-Americans, whether native or foreign born.

Thus, the longitudinal analyses of occupational change in the 1970 Census are consistent with the implications of the skill-transferability model and hypotheses.

5.4. The Schooling of Foreign-born Emigrants

There are no direct data on the characteristics of foreign-born emigrants. There is an indirect test, however, of whether foreign-born emigrants are self-selected in favor of high (or low) levels of schooling. The test suggests that the schooling distribution of the emigrants is not likely to be substantially different from that of foreign-born persons who did not emigrate.

The 1960 and 1970 Censuses of population asked country of birth, but only the 1970 Census asked year of immigration for the foreign born. It is, therefore, possible to compare the schooling distribution in 1960 of an age cohort of immigrants from a country with the "survivors" in the 1970 Census. That is, persons from a particular country in the 1960 Census are compared with those in the 1970 Census who are from the same country, have been in the United States at least ten years, and are ten years older. This is done for men from Europe, Canada, and Mexico. The changes in these schooling distributions over the decade are compared with the change in the distribution for all adult white men in the same age cohorts.

The distributions of schooling for all white men (Table 5.1), 95 percent of whom are native born, shows a small increase in schooling attainment over the decade. This may be due to several factors, such as lower mortality rates for those with higher levels of schooling, the acquisition of more schooling as a cohort ages, or an increase in the over-reporting of schooling level as a cohort ages.[13] If these factors are the same for the native and foreign born, a sharper increase in the level of schooling of the foreign born from 1960 to 1970 would be consistent with a higher rate of emigration for the foreign born with less schooling.[14]

Table 5.1

Frequency Distribution of Schooling in 1960 and 1970 by Age Cohorts for White Men

Years of Schooling Completed	Age in 1960							
	25 to 54		25 to 34		35 to 44		45 to 54	
	1960	1970	1960	1970	1960	1970	1960	1970
0 - 4	3.5	3.3	2.6	2.4	3.3	3.1	4.9	4.8
5 - 7	9.9	8.6	6.9	5.9	8.8	7.7	14.4	13.2
8	14.0	12.9	9.5	8.5	13.0	12.0	20.6	19.7
9 - 11	21.5	20.4	21.4	19.2	21.6	21.0	21.5	21.1
12	28.2	26.7	31.7	33.4	30.8	31.5	21.0	22.6
13 - 15	10.5	10.7	12.3	12.0	10.2	10.8	8.6	8.9
≥ 16	12.4	14.4	15.6	18.6	12.3	13.9	9.0	9.7
Total	100.0	100.0	100.0	100.0	100.0	100.0	100.0	100.0

Note: The published tables do not identify nativity; however, 95 percent are native born.

Source: U.S. Bureau of the Census (1963), Table 1, based on a 5 percent sample of the population; U.S. Bureau of the Census (1973), Table 1, based on a 15 percent sample of the population.

The change in the distribution of schooling for white men and for those born in Europe and Canada are compared in Tables 5.1 through 5.3. There is a tendency for the proportion of men who report the completion of 12 years of schooling to increase over the decade, largely at the expense of the 9–11-year category. This tendency is somewhat larger for the European- and Canadian-born men than it is for all white men. Otherwise, there do not appear to be important differences over the decade in the changes in the schooling distribution by country of origin.

Table 5.2

Frequency Distributions of Schooling in 1960 and 1970 by Age Cohorts for Men Born in Europe

Years of Schooling Completed	Age in 1960							
	25 to 54		25 to 34		35 to 44		45 to 54	
	1960	1970[a]	1960	1970[a]	1960	1970[a]	1960	1970[a]
0 - 4	6.9	6.0	4.7	3.8	5.9	4.8	8.4	7.5
5 - 7	14.5	13.7	11.2	11.5	12.7	12.8	16.6	15.1
8	21.4	19.5	16.4	14.1	16.4	15.5	25.8	24.2
9 - 11	16.5	14.4	16.3	12.2	16.5	14.2	16.5	15.4
12	19.3	23.0	21.2	24.9	23.3	28.1	16.4	19.1
13 - 15	9.6	9.6	13.5	13.5	11.3	10.1	7.3	7.6
≥ 16	11.8	13.9	16.7	19.9	14.2	14.5	8.9	11.0
Total	100.0	100.0	100.0	100.0	100.0	100.0	100.0	100.0
Sample Size	216,018	7,568	40,127	1,560	61,298	2,241	114,594	3,767

Note: [a] Immigrated prior to 1960.
The countries included in the table are United Kingdom, Norway, Sweden, Germany, Austria, Poland, Czechoslovakia, Hungary, Yugoslavia, Lithuania, Finland, the USSR, and Italy.
Source: U.S. Bureau of the Census (1965), Table 2, based on a 25 percent sample of the population; U.S. Bureau of the Census (1970), 1/100 sample, 5 percent questionnaire.

Table 5.3

Frequency Distributions of Schooling in 1960 and 1970 by Age Cohorts for Men Born in Canada

Years of Schooling Completed	Age in 1960							
	25 to 54		25 to 34		35 to 44		45 to 54	
	1960	1970[a]	1960	1970[a]	1960	1970[a]	1960	1970[a]
0 - 4	2.5	2.2	1.7	1.8	1.6	1.1	3.5	3.4
5 - 7	10.9	8.0	8.6	5.8	7.8	6.6	14.9	10.3
8	15.7	15.0	11.3	10.0	12.6	12.3	20.6	19.7
9 - 11	24.5	20.2	24.0	21.9	24.9	20.4	24.3	19.3
12	22.0	25.9	20.3	25.2	26.5	28.2	18.8	24.0
13 - 15	11.1	13.0	14.1	13.7	11.7	14.8	9.2	11.1
≥ 16	13.3	15.7	20.0	21.6	14.9	16.6	8.7	12.3
Total	100.0	100.0	100.0	100.0	100.0	100.0	100.0	100.0
Sample Size	46,656	1.826	8,953	329	17,865	730	19.838	767

Note: [a] Immigrated prior to 1960.
Source: U.S. Bureau of the Census (1965), Table 3, based on a 25 percent sample of the population; U.S. Bureau of the Census (1973), 1/100 sample, 5 percent questionnaire.

Men born in Mexico and living in the United States in 1960 show more dramatic changes in their schooling distribution (Table 5.4).

The proportion of men with less than five years of schooling declined sharply, overall from 50 percent in 1960 to 37 percent in 1970. If this were the result of a disproportionate emigration of men with less than five years of schooling, the proportion in all other schooling groups should increase accordingly. This does, in fact, appear to be the situation. Overall, the proportion with five to seven years of schooling increased from 22 percent to 26 percent (18 percent increase). The proportion with eight or more years of schooling increased from 29 percent to 37 percent (28 percent increase). The 8-percentage-points increase in the proportion of Mexican-born men with eight or more years of schooling can be compared with the 2-percentage-points increase for all white men. Thus, it would appear that either the entire schooling distribution increased substantially during the decade (which is highly unlikely) or the propensity for return migration among men born in Mexico was particularly high for those with less than five years of schooling.

Table 5.4

Frequency Distributions of Schooling in 1960 and 1970 by Age Cohorts for Men Born in Mexico

Years of Schooling Completed	Age in 1960							
	25 to 54		25 to 34		35 to 44		45 to 54	
	1960	1970[a]	1960	1970[a]	1960	1970[a]	1960	1970[a]
0 - 4	49.8	37.2	49.3	32.1	47.5	32.8	52.5	45.8
5 - 7	21.7	26.2	21.7	28.8	21.6	25.3	21.7	24.5
8	8.5	9.8	7.1	9.5	8.9	11.8	9.4	8.3
9 - 11	8.0	10.1	8.4	10.5	8.8	10.6	7.0	9.3
12	6.3	9.1	6.2	10.8	7.3	9.5	5.5	7.1
13 - 15	3.2	3.9	3.9	3.3	3.4	5.2	2.3	3.3
≥ 16	2.5	3.8	3.4	5.0	2.5	4.9	1.6	1.7
Total	100.0	100.0	100.0	100.0	100.0	100.0	100.0	100.0
Sample Size	38,699	1,168	12,585	399	12,967	348	13,148	421

Note: [a] Immigrated prior to 1960.
Source: U.S. Bureau of the Census (1965), Table 4, based on a 25 percent sample of the population; U.S. Bureau of the Census (1973), 1/100 sample, 5 percent questionnaire.

The procedures adopted in this section are rough, primarily because of the absence of data on year of immigration in the 1960 Census. Yet the findings are suggestive. The similar changes in the schooling distributions from 1960 to 1970 for the foreign born from Europe and Canada and all white men suggests that either the number of foreign-born emigrants is relatively small or that their schooling distribution does not differ sharply from that of the foreign born who did not emigrate in the 1960s. For those born in Mexico, however, the data suggest a disproportionate rate of emigration among those with less than five years of schooling, but for those with five or more years of schooling in 1960, the emigration is either very small or does not seem to vary by education. Thus, with the possible exception of Mexican immigrants with less than five years of schooling, there does not appear to be selectivity by schooling level in the emigration of the foreign born.

5.5.   Intergenerational Transmission of Abilities

The model outlined in Section 5.2 implies that the earnings of the foreign-born economic migrants may eventually exceed those of the native born because the former are self-selected on the basis of ability. Once the disadvantages of a foreign origin become sufficiently small with duration in the United States, the greater ability results in equal and then higher earnings. This pattern emerges in the empirical analysis. The relevant ability dimensions are not obvious, and they may vary among individuals. The traits such as entrepreneurship, aggressiveness, persistence, ambition, energy, drive, and so on are dimensions of ability that may not be measured in standardized ability tests.

Suppose that this hypothesis is correct. Also assume that some or all of these unmeasured dimensions of ability can be transmitted from parents to children, either genetically or through the transmission of family values. As with biological traits, a "regression to the mean" may be expected in the transmission of these ability dimensions (Humphrey 1978). That is, the children of high-ability parents would, on average, have an ability level less than that of their parents, but greater than the average. And the children of low-ability parents would, on average, have an ability level greater than that of their parents, but less than the average. Then, the native-born children of immigrants (second generation) would be of higher average ability than those with native-born parents (third and higher generation), and the native-parentage with foreign grandparents (third generation) would be expected to have greater ability than those with native-born grandparents (fourth and higher generation), and so on. Formally, if $A(i)$ is the ability level of the ith immigrant generation, then $A(2) > A(3) > \ldots > A(n-1) > A(n)$, where the differences become smaller between successive generations.

The hypothesis that the foreign born are self-selected on the basis of ability may be contrasted with an alternative hypothesis. Suppose there are no differences in ability between the native and foreign born. There are, however, unmeasured differences in investment in human capital and other unobservables, including pure luck. Potential immigrants who expect to draw a high earnings profile in the United States are more likely to migrate. After overcoming the initial disadvantages of a foreign origin, they have higher earnings, but there are no differences in ability between them and the native born. This hypothesis would not predict ability differences among later immigrant generations. Formally, in terms of ability, $A(2) = A(3) = \ldots = A(n)$.

There are no data files that contain direct measures of ability relevant for the labor market. In this instance, as in others, tests regarding ability differences are indirect. Other things the same, differences in earnings among adult men by immigrant generation may reflect differences in ability. The self-selection model predicts $Y(2) > (Y3) > \ldots > Y(n)$ where $Y(i)$ is the earnings of the ith immigrant generation, and the differences become smaller between successive generations. The alternative model for other unmeasured differences (for example, pure luck) predicts $Y(2) = Y(3) = \ldots = Y(n)$.

Earnings differences, however, are often attributed to discrimination in studies of earnings by race, ethnicity, and national origin. If there is labor market discrimination among the native born by immigrant generation, it is more likely to be against the most recent group, second-generation Americans (one or both parents foreign born). The discrimination hypothesis implies $Y(2) < Y(3) < \ldots < Y(N)$, where the differential decreases between successive generations.[15] Overall, the discrimination hypothesis implies a dampening or even a reversal of the earnings differences by immigration generation predicted from the immigrant self-selection model discussed earlier.

The 1970 Census of population and the National Longitudinal Survey file for adult men permit analyses among the native born by immigrant generation.[16] The 1970 Census (15 percent questionnaire) asked the nativity of the person and the person's parents, thereby permitting a comparative analysis of second-generation Americans and those who are third- and higher-generation Americans. The limited number of generations identified is offset by the large sample size which permits analyses for a range of race and ethnic groups. The NLS file is relatively small, so it is useful only for white men, but it identifies the nativity of the person, his parents, and his four grandparents. Therefore, both sources are used to test the hypotheses.

Among adult white men born in the United States, the 1970 Census data indicate that nearly 20 percent have a foreign-born parent. The men with a foreign-born parent have 15 percent higher earnings, but there are no differences on the basis of parents' nativity in years of schooling or in the partial effect of schooling on earnings in an earnings function. Other things the same, however, second-generation white men earn a statistically significant 4.9 percent ($t =$ 4.67) more than third- and higher-generation Americans. The more favorable geographic location of the foreign parentage – that is, their concentration in the North and urban areas – accounts for most of the other 10 percentage points.

The earnings advantage of the second generation is not an artifact of the all-white sample. When analyses are done within several race-ethnic groups, a consistent pattern emerges for the foreign parentage to earn 5 to 10 percent more than those with native-born parents.[17]

Among adult native-born men, controlling for schooling, experience, marital status, weeks worked, and place of residence, the partial effect on earnings of having foreign-born parents (one or both) is:

Race-Ethnic Group	Coefficient (percent)
White	4.9*
Mexican	5.1*
Mexican (Spanish mother tongue)	8.6*
Black (urban, English mother tongue)	
All states	8.4*
New York State	10.7*
Japanese	5.2
Chinese	4.3
Filipino	9.0

Note: * Statistically significant coefficient at the 2.5 percent level, one-tailed test.

In the National Longitudinal Survey there were 2,822 native-born white men (aged 45 to 59 in 1966) who reported their earnings and other variables relevant for the analysis. The men responded to questions on their parents' and grandparents' nativity.[18] In this sample of older white men, 29 percent reported a foreign-born parent, 24 percent had native-born parents but at least one foreign-born grandparent, and 47 percent had four native-born grandparents. Other things the same, those with foreign-born parents earned 6.4 percent ($t = 2.25$) more than the men with native-born parents. The difference between 6.4 percent in the NLS and 4.9 percent found in the 1970 Census data is not statistically significant.

Among native-born men with native-born parents, the effect of foreign grandparents is positive but small and not statistically significant. Although the t-ratios are below unity, having at least one foreign-born grandparent raises earnings by 1.4 percent, having at least one maternal and one paternal foreign-born grandparent raises earnings by 3.7 percent, and earnings are higher by 0.9 percentage points for each foreign-born grandparent. Thus, between third-generation and fourth- and higher-generation American men there appears to be a small and positive, although statistically insignificant, earnings differential.

The 1970 Census and NLS data for native-born men suggest that, other things the same, there are earnings differences by immigrant generation. The most recent immigrant generation has higher earnings, but the immigrant generation differential narrows and disappears by the third or fourth generation. This pattern is consistent with the hypothesis that the immigrant ancestors were favorably self-selected on the basis of ability and that this characteristic is dissipated with successive generations born in the United States.[19] The pattern is not consistent with the discrimination or adverse self-selection hypotheses.

5.6.   Summary and Conclusions

This chapter has presented alternative models and hypotheses regarding the economic adjustment of immigrants. These models are tested to determine which is more successful for explaining the data.

A model of immigrant adjustment is presented based on human capital theory. It focuses on the international transferability of skills and the self-selection of immigrants in terms of labor market ability. The model generates testable hypotheses, namely, that the economic status of immigrants improves with their duration of residence, that pre-immigration years of schooling and labor market experience have smaller effects than similar investments among the native-born, and that these patterns vary systematically by the transferability of skill and motive for migrating. Another implication is that the greater ability of the favorably self-selected economic migrants would generate a higher economic status for the native-born children of immigrants than those with native-born parents. Several alternative hypotheses are considered. One is that the rise in economic status with duration of residence in cross-sectional data is due to the return migration of the less-successful immigrants. This hypothesis is tested with longitudinal data on earnings and occupation, and by comparing the effect of duration of residence on earnings and employment across countries of origin that differ by the extent of return migration. The rise in earnings with duration of residence, other things the same, is found to be the same in longitudinal and cross-sectional data. These tests support the transferability-of-skill hypothesis rather than selective emigration of the less successful. Although return migration is substantial, it does not appear to be selective with respect to ability or earnings, perhaps because for many the original migration was viewed as temporary and for others noneconomic factors (for example, family obligations) influenced the decision to return.

This conclusion is strengthened by the analysis of the schooling distribution of foreign-born emigrants. There is no compelling evidence of selective out-migration of immigrants with less schooling, with the exception of Mexican nationals with five or fewer years of schooling.

Another alternative hypothesis is that there are no ability differences between the native and foreign born and that the foreign born eventually have higher earnings than the native born because the migrants are those who were lucky enough to draw a high earnings profile or who have high earnings for other reasons unrelated to ability. This hypothesis offers no strong implications for the earnings of the children of immigrants relative to the children of native-born parents, other things the same. A discrimination model or a model of adverse selection of immigrants would imply lower earnings for the children of immigrants. Empirically, among the native born in the United States, those with foreign-born parents earn 5 to 10 percent more than those with native-born parents, and the intergenerational effect appears to diminish with successive immigrant generations. This supports the hypothesis of selective migration on the basis of ability.

The chapter provides further evidence supporting the robustness of the skill-transferability and selective-migration models for explaining the economic adjustment of immigrants.

6

Are Immigrants Favorably Self-Selected? An Economic Analysis

I wrote the paper "Are Immigrants Favorably Self-Selected: An Economic Analysis" for an interdisciplinary collection of articles on immigration (reprinted in Chapter 6 of this volume). I was concerned with what a human capital model would indicate about the selectivity of migrants, whether domestic or international.

A basic human capital model was developed that includes both forgone earnings that vary with ability and out-of-pocket (i.e., direct) costs of migration that do not vary with ability. It demonstrated that those with a higher level of labor market ability in general will have a higher rate of return from investment in migration, whether internal within the same country or international between two countries. This would increase both the probability of migration and the distance migrated. These effects are amplified if, as seems plausible, people with higher levels of labor market ability are also more efficient in using resources – their own time and other inputs (direct costs) – in the migration process. In general, the empirical studies of both internal and international migration support such positive selectivity.

An alternative approach (Borjas, reprinted as Chapter 4 of this volume) uses the "Roy model" to address the same question. In this application the Roy model is based on earnings in the destination relative to the origin, and it assumes that there are no out-of-pocket or direct costs. This assumption

The original version of this chapter was published as: Chiswick, B.R. (2008). Are Immigrants Favorably Self-Selected? An Economic Analysis, in: Brettell, C.B., Hollifield, J.F. (Eds.), Migration Theory. Taking across Disciplines, 2nd edition, New York, NY: Routledge, 63–82. © 2008 by Taylor & Francis Group, LLC.

implies that there are no differences by ability level in the incentives for migration, a hypothesis requiring empirical testing in its own right. My paper (reprinted as Chapter 6 of this volume) provides a test of this hypothesis and finds that it is not supported by the data.

My paper also looks at differences in skill ratios (relative earnings by skill level). Greater inequality (higher skill ratios) in the origin than in the destination would tend to encourage lower-skilled migration. For negative selectivity in migration, however, this effect would have to dominate the positive selectivity effect of direct costs.

This does not mean that there are no circumstances in which selectivity in migration would be less positive or even negative. The human capital model assumed that economic (labor market) factors are the primary determinant of migration. Non-economic migrants, such as tied-movers, refugees, and ideological migrants, would have less intense incentives for favorable selectivity. Sojourners or short-term migrants would also be less favorably selected if destination country human capital is important. Illegal migrants will tend to be less favorably selected, perhaps even negatively selected, if the cost of avoiding detection is positively related to skill (income) levels. Finally, the criteria used by the immigration authorities to ration scarce visas can either enhance positive selectivity (e.g., rationing by skill level) or reduce it (e.g., favoring immigrants in low-skilled household, service, or agricultural occupations).

Barry R. Chiswick (2015)

6.1.   Introduction

The authors of several essays in this volume, including Hasia R. Diner, Susan Hardwick, and Barbara Schmitter Heisler (Chapters 1, 6, 4), express regret regarding the virtual absence of theory in the studies of migration in their respective fields, that is, history, geography, and sociology. The research in their fields is far too often group or time and place specific, with little use of theory to motivate the analysis or to generalize the findings. This criticism is seldom leveled at economics. Indeed, all too often historians, sociologists, and other social scientists complain that economics is much too focused on formalism, with too little interest in specific groups or time and place.[1]

Economics is about the real world in which we live. It is about the study of the choices or opportunities that people have. It is concerned with the allocation of scarce resources (and all resources are scarce), including time, among alternative uses. It is concerned with how individuals, families, business enterprises, and other institutions use these scarce resources for their benefit – whether conceptualized as maximizing utility for individuals, maximizing profits for business firms, or maximizing social welfare for society.

The basic methodology of economics is the scientific method, that is, to develop models based on maximizing behavior, to derive hypotheses from these models, to then test these hypotheses, and if the hypotheses are found to be inconsistent with the data, to revise the model. Hypotheses are maintained only to the extent that they are consistent with the data, that is, the real world. Two guiding principles are Occam's Razor, that simple models are to be preferred to complex ones, and that theory by itself can tell what might be, but that empirical analysis is needed to know what is.

This chapter uses the methodology of economics to address questions raised by Haisia Diner: "Who moves? Why do some human beings get up and shift residence? Why do others stay put?" It focuses on the determinants of selectivity from the *supply side* of migration, that is, the differential incentive among individuals for migration based on their ability, skills, and motive for migration. Another determinant of the characteristics of migrants, particularly for international migrants, is the *demand side* as represented by the mechanism for allocating immigration visas, and the enforcement of immigration law. Recent research demonstrates how the criteria used to ration the limited number of immigration visas among the much larger number of potential visa applicants can substantially influence the quality of the actual immigration flow – their ability, schooling, skills, health, occupational status, and earnings (see, for example, Beach, Green, and Worswick 2007; Chiswick, Lee, and Miller 2006; Chiswick and Miller 2006). A fuller discussion of the determinants and consequences of the demand side, the visa allocation process, is beyond the scope of this chapter.

It is often said that immigrants are different from the people that they leave behind in the origin and the people they join in the destination. They are sometimes described as more aggressive, risk taking, forward looking, and avaricious or entrepreneurial, and sometimes as healthier. Sometimes they are described as fleeing the poverty, repression, and claustrophobia of the place where they were born and raised, and sometimes as being attracted or pulled by the magnet of the wealth ("streets lined with gold"), opportunities, freedom, and anonymity of where they settle.

Economic migrants are those who move from one place of work and residence to another, either within a country or across international boundaries, primarily because of their own economic opportunities. These opportunities may be in the form of earnings, employment, training, or other economic benefits for themselves or their descendants. Their motivations are distinct from those of refugees and those who move because of the migration decisions of others. One of the standard propositions in the migration literature is that economic migrants tend to be favorably *self-selected* on the basis of skills, health, and other characteristics. That is, economic migrants are described as tending, on average, to be more able, ambitious, aggressive, entrepreneurial, healthier, or otherwise have more favorable traits than similar individuals who choose to remain in their place of origin. The favorable selectivity on the basis of labor market and other characteristics would be less intense among those for whom motives other than economic considerations are most important in their migration decision, such as *tied-movers* (those who move because of other family members), refugees (those who move because of real or imagined fears concerning their safety and freedom), and *ideological migrants* (those who move voluntarily for political, religious, or other ideological reasons).

Whether migrants are favorably selected or not is important for understanding the economic, historic, demographic, and sociological consequences of migration for the sending (origin) and receiving (destination) regions, as well as for the migrants themselves. The more highly favorably selected are migrants, the more successful will be their adjustment in the destination and the more favorable their impact on the destination economy and society. Moreover, the more highly favorably selected are the migrants the greater, in general, will be the adverse effect of their departure on their origin. As a consequence, the extent of the favorable selectivity of migrants will affect the impact of migration, and as a result the immigration policies of the destination and emigration policies of the origin, as well as other policies that have indirect effects on the incentives to migrate.[2] Immigration history and, as a result, the histories of the origin and destination regions, are thereby influenced by the degree of selectivity of migrants.

This chapter first develops the human capital model for migration, which serves as the focal point for the discussion of immigrant selectivity ("The Human Capital Migration Model"). It then considers

("Alternative Models") alternative specifications of the migration model, or deviations from the simple human capital model, that are relevant for the issue of migrant selectivity. A review of some of the existing literature forms the basis for the discussion of the empirical testing of the model of migrant selectivity. The chapter closes with a summary and conclusion.

6.2. The Human Capital Migration Model

Consider a simple human capital model of investment as applied to migration (Becker 1964; Sjaastad 1962). Assume that wages in the origin and destination do not vary with the level of labor market experience. That is, for simplicity of exposition, it is assumed there is no on-the-job training and there are no postmigration human capital investments. Also assume that there is a very long (infinite) work life, and that all the costs of migration occur in the first period.[3] These migration costs include forgone earnings (C_f) and direct or out-of-pocket costs (C_d). The indirect or forgone earnings costs are the value of the time devoted to the migration process. The direct or out-of-pocket costs include the expenditure of money for goods and services that are purchased because of the migration. Migration costs are defined broadly to include not merely the airfare or bus ticket and the time in transit, but the full costs of relocating and adjusting, both consumption and labor market activities, from the origin to the destination.[4]

It is easy to show that given these assumptions, the rate of return from migration (r) can then be written (approximately) as:

$$(1) \qquad\qquad r = \frac{W_b - W_a}{C_f + C_d},$$

where w_b represents earnings in the destination and w_a represents earnings in the origin. Migration occurs if the rate of return from the investment in migration (r) is greater than or equal to the *interest cost of funds* for investment in human capital (i). The interest cost of funds for an individual is the person's cost of borrowing or lending money from the capital market. The lower the interest cost of funds is the greater the person's wealth and access to the capital market.[5]

Assume first that there are two types of workers – low-ability and high-ability workers – and that these ability levels are known without cost to the workers and potential employers.[6] The more able may have more innate ability or merely more schooling. Ability may have many dimensions, including ambition, intelligence, learning speed, decision-making proficiency, entrepreneurial skills, aggressiveness, tenacity, health, and so forth.

Let r_l be the rate of return from migration to a low-ability person and let r_h be the rate of return to a high-ability person. If the low- and high-ability individuals have the same interest cost of funds, the person with the higher rate of return from migration will have the greater propensity to migrate. As a first step, assume that in the origin (a) and destination (b) wages are 100k percent higher for the more able than the less able, that is, the ratio of wages in the destination to wages in the origin is independent of level of ability. Then,

$$W_{b,h} = (1 + k)W_{b,l}$$

(2) and

$$W_{a,h} = (1 + k)W_{a,l}.$$

It is assumed that direct costs, which are the out-of-pocket costs associated with migration, do not vary with ability, $C_{d,h} = C_{d,l}$. For example, the airfare is the same regardless of the person's ability. Also assume that greater ability has no effect on efficiency in migration, but because it raises the value of time in the origin, it does raise the value of forgone earnings. Then $C_{f,h} = (1 + k)C_{f,l}$, where C_f is the forgone earnings. The rate of return from migration for the high-ability person can be written as:

$$(3) \qquad r_h = \frac{(1 + k)W_{b,l} - (1 + k)W_{a,l}}{(1 + k)C_{f,l} + C_d} = \frac{W_{b,l} - W_{a,l}}{C_{f,l} + \frac{C_d}{(1 + k)}}.$$

Thus, the rate of return to the high-ability person (r_h) is greater than the rate of return to the low-ability person (r_l) as long as earnings increase with ability ($k > 0$) and there are positive out-of-pocket costs of migration ($C_d > 0$). If the rate of return (r) from the investment is greater for the high-ability person, and if the interest cost of funds (i) is the same, the high-ability person would have a greater economic incentive to migrate. This is what is meant by positive selectivity in migration. The smaller are the direct costs of migration (C_d) relative to the wage premium for higher levels of ability ($1 + k$), the smaller is

$$\frac{C_d}{(1 + k)}$$

and hence the smaller is the differential in the rate of return to those of higher ability relative to those of lesser ability. If there were no out-of-pocket costs associated with migration (C_d equals zero), then $r_h = r_l$, and there would be no selectivity in migration on the basis of ability. Alternatively, suppose there was no labor market premium for a higher level of ability or a particular dimension of ability ($k = 0$). That is, this dimension of ability was not relevant in the labor market. For example, having a higher level of ability playing the board game Monopoly may have no effect on labor market earnings ($k = 0$). Then, $r_h = r_l$, and there is no selectivity in migration on the basis of this dimension of ability.

The preceding model assumed that greater ability enhances efficiency in the labor market in both the origin and destination. Now let us add another assumption: the more able are also more efficient in migration. Just as higher ability enhances productivity in the labor market, these same characteristics may enhance efficiency in investment in human capital. The same investment in migration may require fewer units of time and/or fewer units of out-of-pocket costs for the more able. This may arise if the more able are better decision makers. For example, they know how to find the cheapest airfares.

Since the opportunity cost of migration (C_l) is the product of time units (t) involved in migration multiplied by the value of time in the origin (W_a), opportunity costs can be written as $C_f = tW_a$. Efficiency can be expressed as the more able needing fewer time units to accomplish the same task ($t_h < t_l$). Then, $C_{f,l} = t_l W_{a,l}$ and $C_{f,h} = t_h W_{a,h} = t_h(1 + k)W_{a,l}$, where $t_h < t_l$. This implies relatively lower costs for the more able, and strengthens the argument that r_h, is greater than r_l.

Note that even if there are no out-of-pocket costs ($C_d = 0$), if the more able are more efficient in using time, relative skill differentials that do not vary across regions generate favorable selectivity in migration. That is, if $C_d = 0$, and $t_h < t_l$, using Equation (3), when $C_{f,l} = t_l W_{a,l}$ and $C_{f,h} = t_h(1 + k)W_{a,l}$, then it follows that $r_h > r_l$.

The more able may also be more efficient in utilizing out-of-pocket expenditures ($C_{d,h} < C_{d,l}$) incurred in migration, just as they are more efficient in other activities. If direct costs exist and they are smaller for the more able ($C_{d,h} < C_{d,l}$), the difference in the rate of return from migration is even greater than if there were no ability differences in using the out-of-pocket expenditures required for migration. If

$C_{d,h} = (1 + \lambda)C_{d,l}$ where λ is a direct cost efficiency parameter, and is negative ($\lambda < 0$), then

$$(4) \qquad r_h = \frac{W_{b,l} - W_{a,l}}{C_{f,l} + C_{d,l}\frac{(1 + \lambda)}{(1 + k)}},$$

and r_h is larger relative to r_i the greater the efficiency in handling direct costs (the more negative is λ).

Thus, a human capital model that assumes relative skill differentials are the same in the origin and destination generates favorable selectivity of migration in the supply of migrants if there are out-of-pocket (direct) costs that are not proportional to wages. This favorable selectivity is more intense if those who are more able in the labor market are also more efficient (able) in the migration process, either in using their own time or in using out-of-pocket expenditures.

It is reasonable to assume, however, that migrants will differ in the combination of their own time (forgone earnings) and purchased inputs (direct costs) in the migration and readjustment process. The greater the value of forgone earnings (wages) and the greater a person's efficiency in using purchased inputs relative to their own time, the greater will be the relative use of purchased inputs over their own time. Thus, high-ability migrants may appear to spend more dollars on the migration process (out-of-pocket expenditures) and to use less time than those of lesser ability.[7]

The model can be extended to consider situations in which the relative wage differentials are not the same across countries. Assume that there are no direct costs of migration ($C_d = 0$), and that ability (human capital) does not affect efficiency in time use in migration ($t_h = t_l$). Then,

$$(5) \qquad r_1 = \frac{W_{b,1} - W_{a,1}}{tW_{a,1}} = \frac{1}{t}\left(\frac{W_{b,1}}{W_{a,1}} - 1\right)$$

and

$$(6) \qquad r_h = \frac{W_{b,h} - W_{a,h}}{tW_{a,h}} = \frac{1}{t}\left(\frac{W_{b,h}}{W_{a,h}} - 1\right).$$

Then the ratio of wages in the destination relative to the origin determines migration incentives. If the ratio of wages is the same, the rates of return are the same and there is no selectivity in migration on the basis of skill. If the ratio of wages across regions is greater for those of high ability, that is, W_b/W_a is greater for h than for l, those of high ability have a greater incentive to migrate. If, on the other hand, the ratio of wages across regions is greater for those of low ability, they would have a greater propensity to migrate, other things being the same.

To take an oversimplified example, suppose the wages of low-skilled workers in the United States and Sweden were the same, but highly skilled workers earned relatively more in the United States than in Sweden. Then $\frac{W_{b,l}}{W_{a,l}} = 1$ for the low skilled and $\frac{W_{b,h}}{W_{a,h}} > 1$ for the highly skilled, and highly skilled workers would move from Sweden to the United States. If, on the other hand, the wages of low-skilled workers in the United States were higher than those in Mexico $\left(\frac{W_{b,l}}{W_{a,l}} > 1\right)$, but the wages of highly skilled workers were the same $\left(\frac{W_{b,h}}{W_{a,h}} = 1\right)$, then the low skilled from Mexico would move to the United States. There would be favorable or positive selectivity among migrants to the United States from Sweden and unfavorable or adverse selectivity from Mexico.

Several implications follow from this human capital model regarding the favorable selectivity of economic migrants, that is, those basing their migration decision on the conventionally measured rate of return from migration. The larger the out-of-pocket costs of migration, the lower the propensity to migrate, the lower is the propensity for immigrants to return to their origin, and the greater is the propensity for favorable selectivity in migration. This propensity for favorable selectivity is intensified if those who are more efficient in the labor market are also more efficient in the migration and adjustment process. This effect occurs if migrants are more efficient in using their own time, in using purchased inputs, or in combining their time and purchased inputs. If those with more human capital, for example, those with more schooling and greater proficiency in destination language skills, are more efficient in obtaining and interpreting information and in making decisions (greater allocative efficiency), they would be more efficient in the migration process (Schultz 1975).

The favorable selectivity of migrants is even greater if the relative wage differential between the destination and origin (the ratio of wages in the destination to those in the origin) is greater for the high-ability workers. The favorable selectivity is less intense if the ratio of wages in the destination to those in the origin is smaller for those with high ability. Only if this latter effect is sufficiently large to offset the favorable selectivity effects of out-of-pocket costs and greater efficiency in the migration process will there be no selectivity in migration. In this framework, for there to be negative selectivity in migration even more compressed wage differentials across regions are required for those with high ability relative to those with low ability.

6.3.   Alternative Models

Several alternatives to the simple human capital model presented previously have appeared in the literature to address the issue, either directly or indirectly, of the favorable selectivity of migrants. These include models based on asymmetric information, temporary migration, the Roy model, and noneconomic determinants of migration.

6.3.1.   Asymmetric Information

Katz and Stark (1984; 1987) present a model of asymmetric information. Suppose potential migrants know their true productivity and employers in the origin have, over time, learned the workers' true productivity. Employers in the destination, however, cannot differentiate between high-ability and low-ability migrants. Employers in the origin pay workers wages in accordance with the worker's true productivity since this is known to them, while those in the destination pay workers according to the expected (average) productivity of migrants. High-ability workers will experience a smaller wage differential and higher forgone earnings than low-ability workers, and they will therefore have a smaller incentive to migrate. If employers can never detect true ability differences among migrant workers, there would be adverse selection. The increase in low-ability migration relative to high-ability migration would drive down the expected wage of migrants in the destination, further discouraging high-ability migration.

Employers in the destination would, of course, have an incentive to develop tests or other techniques for distinguishing high-ability from low-ability workers. The lower the cost and the shorter the time interval for identifying ability, the lower the adverse selection effect from asymmetric information. Asymmetric information would appear to be most compelling for low-skilled jobs with a short duration (tenure on the job) that do not involve repeat occurrences. High-wage jobs would warrant investment in information about ability, if only through a trial investment/working period. This might take the form of hiring immigrant workers at low wages until true ability levels are revealed. High-ability workers would be willing to take these jobs as they know that their true ability will be revealed over time, while low-ability workers would avoid these jobs for the same reason. Employers would then be able to discern the ability level of workers for jobs that have a long tenure or that involve repeat occurrences.

6.3.2. Short-Term Migrants

The model developed previously assumed, for simplicity, that workers remained in the destination for a long period of time, and implicitly assumed that there is no location-specific human capital. Suppose, however, there is a short expected duration in the destination because of high expectations of voluntary return migration (guest worker or sojourner migration) or involuntary return migration (deportations of illegal aliens) (Chiswick 1980a; 1986a). Then migrants who made investments in destination-specific human capital would experience a capital loss when they leave the destination, and their origin-specific human capital would have depreciated during their absence from the origin. Therefore, sojourner migrants or illegal aliens, who are concerned about apprehensions and deportations, would tend to avoid country-specific human capital investments and would tend to invest in internationally transferable human capital or very little human capital.

To the extent that there is an incompatibility between country-specific and internationally transferable human capital, which is increased by location-specific occupational licensing and certifications for professional and skilled jobs, temporary migrants would tend to have lower levels of both forms of human capital. This is intensified if country-specific human capital depreciates during absence from the country. This would result in lower skill levels among and illegal aliens than among long-term (permanent) legal migrants. This would give the appearance of less positive self-selectivity among short-term migrants (guest workers, sojourners, and illegal aliens) compared to permanent legal migrants.

This is consistent with analyses of illegal aliens in the United States, which indicate they are disproportionately low-skilled workers, as measured by their level of educational attainment, English language proficiency, occupational status, and earnings. Illegal aliens appear to have lower earnings than workers with legal rights to work who otherwise have similar characteristics, presumably because of their limited job mobility, their shorter expected duration in the destination, and their lower level of unmeasured human capital (see, for example, Rivera-Batiz 1999; Kossoudji and Cobb-Clark 2002).

6.3.3.   *The Roy Model-Relative Skill Differentials*

In a series of studies on selectivity in migration, Borjas (1987b; 1991) presents the Roy model (Roy 1951) as an alternative to the human capital model.[8] It is implicitly assumed that all migration costs are a constant proportion of forgone earnings, that there are no fixed (out-of-pocket) costs, and that ability has no effect on efficiency in migration. As a result, migration incentives are a function of the ratio of wages in the destination to those in the origin (the Roy model), as shown above in Equations (5) and (6). This application of the Roy model is actually a special case of the human capital model.

If the wages of highly skilled workers are similar across countries, a larger relative skill differential (wages of highly skilled to low-skilled workers) in the lower-income origin implies a smaller skill differential for more highly skilled workers, and hence a smaller incentive for them to migrate compared to lower-skilled workers. The reverse follows if there is a smaller relative skill differential in the origin. Borjas (1987b: 552) writes, "If the income distribution in the sending country is more unequal than that of the United States (and the correlation in earnings is positive and strong), emigrants will be chosen from the lower tail of the income distribution in the country of origin." This is not quite correct. As shown earlier, a larger skill differential in the origin than in the destination does not necessarily imply negative selectivity, but rather only less favorable (positive) selectivity.

In an empirical test of the Roy model considering migration to the United States, Borjas (1987b) regresses initial immigrant earnings and the improvement in immigrant earnings, as well as the emigration rate from the origin, on a measure of relative income inequality in the origin. The measure of relative inequality Borjas used is the "[r]atio of household income of the top 10 percent of the households to the income of the bottom 20 percent of the households" (Borjas 1987b: 545). This actually does not test for the effect of household income inequality on positive or negative selectivity in international migration, but only for whether inequality in income in the origin is associated with a greater or lesser degree of selectivity, after controlling for other variables that reflect the effects of positive immigrant selectivity on earnings in the United States. Moreover, this measure of household income inequality may be poorly related to the relevant variable, relative skill differentials. Controlling for other variables, the coefficient on the inequality variable is not statistically significant in analyses of immigrant earnings in the United States, and in half of the specifications has a positive rather than the expected negative sign. Contrary to the conclusion, the test does not offer support for the hypothesis that immigrants from countries with greater skill differentials are drawn from the least able members of the origin labor force.[9]

In his reply to the Jasso and Rosenzweig (1990) critique of his paper, Borjas (1990: 306) repeats: "If earnings between the United States and the source country are positively and strongly correlated, positive selection is observed whenever the United States has more income inequality than the source country and negative selection is observed otherwise." In his new empirical test Borjas (1990: 307) uses as his measure of relative skill differentials a dummy variable for whether the origin country has an income distribution more unequal than the United States. The t-ratio of -1.8 is at the margin of statistical significance, although Borjas asserts confidently that his prediction is "confirmed by the results" (Borjas 1990: 308). It is not clear why he changed the measure of inequality to a dichotomous variable or whether this measure of inequality in this and in the earlier study reflects skill differentials or other dimensions of household income inequality, such as the inequality in human capital and other assets, or differences in household (especially female) labor supply. Moreover, the marginal t-ratio for inequality is in contrast to the very high t-ratios for the effect on immigrant earnings in the United States of country of origin per capita income ($t = 6.4$) and the refugee variable, as measured by whether the origin is a Communist country ($t = -3.6$).

6.3.4. Noneconomic Migrants

Conventionally defined economic variables are not the only determinants of migration. People also move for *noneconomic* reasons, including accompanying or joining family members *(tied-mover)*, for real or perceived threats to their freedom or safety because of their class, religion, race, or other characteristics (refugees), and as voluntary migrants for ideological (including religious) reasons.[10] The favorable selectivity for labor market success would be expected to be less intense among those for whom migration is based primarily on factors other than their own labor market success. Studies of tied-movers and refugees in comparison to economic migrants indicate that the former have higher unemployment rates and lower earnings than statistically comparable economic migrants (Mincer 1978; Chiswick 1978d;

1979; 1980a; 1982b). The earnings disadvantages of tied-movers and refugees are greater initially and diminish with duration of residence, but generally do not disappear.

6.3.5. *Empirical Studies of Selectivity: Migrants and Return Migrants*

A variety of studies have been conducted to test directly for the favorable selectivity of migrants.[11] A series of studies on internal migration in the United States and Canada have found that migrants tend to have higher levels of schooling than nonmigrants who remain in the place of origin, and that the use of selectivity correction techniques indicates that they would have had higher earnings in the origin than nonmovers (see, for example, Islam and Choudhury 1990; Robinson and Tomes 1982; DaVanzo 1976; Vandercamp 1972; Gabriel and Schmitz 1995; Bailey 1993).

An analysis of the earnings of black internal migrants in the United States is instructive (Chiswick 1980a; Long and Hansen 1977; Long and Heitman 1975; Masters 1972). Using data from the 1960 and 1970 U.S. Censuses it has been found that black male migrants from the South to states outside of the South display similar earnings patterns as immigrants. The census provides data on state of birth, state of residence five years before, and current state of residence. Adult black men born in the South, but who have lived outside of the South less than five years, earn significantly less that those born outside of the South, other things being the same. On the other hand, those born in the South who have lived outside the South five or more years earn significantly more than statistically similar black men who were born in and remained in the non-southern states. These findings are consistent with favorable selectivity in migration, with a period of adjustment required in the new (non-South) labor market.

Nearly all of the studies of the selectivity of migrants focus on the level of earnings or schooling of migrants compared to nonmigrants in the origin or destination. Two exceptions are studies by Tidrick (1971) and Finifter (1976). Tidrick conducted a survey among Jamaican university students about their intention to emigrate and whether they would encourage others to emigrate. Using cross-tabulations she shows that both propensities were higher, the higher the social class of the student's family and the higher the student's level of ability. Finifter (1976) reports the findings from a series of Gallup Polls conducted in the United States from 1946 to 1971 that included a question on potential interest in emigrating among Americans. The propensity to express an interest in emigrating from the United States was greater among males, the currently unemployed, those "dissatisfied with the institutions of the American political system" (ideological emigrants), and those with a higher level of education, and declined with age (Finifter 1976: 34–5). Both studies find a positive selectivity in the expressed interest in emigrating.

There is less research on the issue of the selectivity of the emigration of immigrants, of which a special case is return migrants, that is, those who return to their origin. Migrants have a higher propensity for a subsequent move than do nonmigrants, other variables being the same. The former have already demonstrated a propensity to move, and have less human and social capital specific to the initial destination. Return migrants may have human and social capital specific to the origin that has not fully depreciated in their absence. Migrants may depart for a number of reasons, including new information about even better opportunities elsewhere, because ex post there is a realization that the destination did not live up to their expectations, or because economic or political circumstances in the origin or in the destination have changed. Moreover, they may depart because the initial move was intended to be temporary (sojourners), perhaps because they are target earners in the destination, or moving to an initial destination facilitates moving to the ultimate objective (destination) as in stepwise migration. These arguments and the statistical analyses suggest that on average migrants who subsequently emigrate will be somewhat less favorably selected than the original flow of economic migrants, but they appear to be more favorably selected than those who never moved.

DaVanzo (1976) finds that for internal migration in the United States the return migrants respond to many of the same economic incentives as did the original migrants. Long and Hansen's (1977) study of black return migrants to the South suggests that both the original and return migration were selective in favor of those with more schooling. Rogers (1984) cites data indicating a variety of motives for return migration, including an original intention that the initial migration is only temporary. In an analysis of short-term interprovincial return migrants in Canada, Vanderkamp (1972) suggests that they were the less successful migrants. In a study of internal migration in the United States using the National Longitudinal Survey of Youth, Bailey (1993) finds a larger positive effect of a college education on initial migration than on return migration. He interprets this as implying that those with higher levels of education not only have higher rates of migration, but also make fewer errors in their initial migration, suggesting greater efficiency in migration.

Using data from a longitudinal survey of immigrants, Beenstock (1996) studied the return migration of immigrants in Israel. Return migration was greatest among those from the high-income Western democracies who were less successful in adjusting to Israel, among those who migrated as young adults and who did not have children. Return migrants had a lower proficiency in Hebrew (a destination-specific skill) and higher unemployment, other things being the same, before they departed. Immigrants to Israel from high-income Western democracies, primarily ideological migrants, have a high opportunity cost of remaining in Israel.

On the other hand, two recent studies suggest an absence of selectivity in out-migration among immigrants. In another longitudinal study of immigrants in Israel, Beenstock, Chiswick, and Paltiel (2010) analyzed a matched sample of respondents from the 1983 and 1995 Censuses of Israel. Other variables being the same, the earnings in 1983 of those still living in Israel in 1995 were greater than those who died in the intervening 12 years, but did not differ from those known to have emigrated. This suggests no net selectivity in the emigration of immigrants. In a study using the Longitudinal Survey of Immigrants to Australia (LSIA), Chiswick and Miller (2006) find that there was no selectivity in the health status of immigrants who left Australia in the first 3.5 years after immigration.

6.3.6. The Earnings of Migrants and the Children of Immigrants

One of the persistent findings regarding immigrants to the United States is the improvement in their earnings with duration in this country, and that after a period of adjustment of about 15 years, male economic migrants earn about the same and subsequently earn more than adult men born in the United States of the same racial/ethnic origin, level of schooling, and other measure characteristics (see Chiswick 1979; 1980a; 1986b).[12] Among refugees, on the other hand, initial earnings are lower than among economic migrants, but the rate of improvement is greater and the gap diminishes over time, although it does not disappear with duration of residence. Equally striking is that the native-born children of immigrants (second-generation Americans) tend to earn more than the native-born with native-born parents (third- and higher-generation Americans) (Chiswick 1977; 1980a; 1986a). Other things the same, within racial and ethnic groups, this earnings advantage is about 5 to 10 percent, or the earnings equivalent of about one extra year of schooling.

These earnings advantages of immigrants and their native-born children occur in spite of the disadvantages of a foreign origin, including less country-specific knowledge or information and poorer proficiency in English, especially among the immigrant parents.[13] These findings for international and internal migrants are consistent with the hypothesis that economic migrants are favorably self-selected for ability or human capital investment, and that refugees are less intensely favorably selected. When the favorable selectivity of economic migrants just outweighs the disadvantages of a "foreign" origin (less destination-specific human capital, discrimination, etc.), the earnings of immigrants equal those of the native born, and then surpass them. Some of this favorable self-selectivity is transmitted to the immigrant's native-born children, although presumably with a regression to the mean, that is, the effect is dampened across generations.

Thus, the native-born children of immigrants, the second generation, have advantages transmitted from their favorably selected parents (e.g., high ability and motivation), and unlike their parents, the advantages of growing up in the destination culture, language, school system, and economy. Compared to native-born children of native-born parents, the advantages derived from the favorable selectivity of their parents outweigh the disadvantages of their parents' foreign origins. Yet presumably due to a "regression to the mean," across generations there is a diminution of the favorable traits of the immigrant ancestors.

6.4.   Summary and Conclusions

This chapter has explored the theoretical issues and the empirical literature regarding the selectivity of migrants. The analytical framework adopted is equally applicable to internal and international migrants. The analyses indicate a tendency toward the favorable self-selection (supply) of migrants for labor market success on the basis of a higher level of ability broadly defined. The favorable selectivity is more intense: the greater the out-of-pocket (direct) costs of migration, the greater the effect of ability on lowering the costs of migration, and the smaller the wage differences by skill in the lower income origin than in the higher income destination. Favorable selectivity for labor market success can be expected to be less intense for noneconomic migrants, such as refugees, tied-movers, and ideological migrants, and for sojourners (short-term migrants) and illegal aliens.

The theoretical analysis in this chapter applies only to the supply of migrants. The determinants of the demand for migrants are also relevant for international migration as all nation-states have selection criteria for those they will admit. Among countries for whom entry restrictions are binding, the criteria for rationing immigration visas will influence the degree of favorable selectivity of those who actually immigrate. Selection criteria can ration visas on one or more characteristics that enhance labor market earnings, such as schooling level, professional qualifications, age, and destination language proficiency, among other criteria. Alternatively, criteria can be used that are seemingly independent of skill level, such as kinship ties, refugee status, and lotteries.

There will be a tendency for immigrants to be favorably selected under any given selection criteria. Among those who would supply themselves as immigrants, a skill-based system for rationing immigration visas will result in a higher-ability immigrant population than would rationing visas on the basis of other criteria (Chiswick and Miller 2006; Beach, Green, and Worswick, 2007). The overall favorable selectivity of immigrants, therefore, depends on the favorable selectivity of the supply of immigrants and the criteria used to ration admissions.

7

The "Negative" Assimilation of Immigrants: A Special Case

Typically, we think of internal or international migrants as people moving from lower- to higher-income areas. In the research I conducted on immigrants in such high-income countries as the United States, Canada, the United Kingdom, and Australia, I was struck by the extent of migration across or among these countries. Migration is costly, not only in terms of forgone earnings and out-of-pocket costs, but also in terms of leaving family, friends, and a familiar environment. Why would so many workers move from one high-income country to another?

Paul W. Miller and I developed a model of "negative assimilation" to explain this phenomenon (reprinted as Chapter 7 of this volume). If two countries have similar income levels and high skill transferability between them, workers will search in both labor markets for the best job. Under certain circumstances a worker in one country might find a higher wage offer providing economic rent in the other country. This economic rent gives an incentive to migrate but it can be expected to dissipate over time.

In the usual "positive assimilation" model (Chapter 1 of this volume) earnings increase with duration as destination-specific skills increase. In the "negative assimilation" model earnings decline with duration not because skills decrease but because the economic rent that encouraged the move

The original version of this chapter was published as: Chiswick, B.R., Miller, P.W. (2011). The "Negative" Assimilation of Immigrants: A Special Case, in: Industrial and Labor Relations Review, 64(3): 502–25. © 1986 by Cornell University. The authors thank Derby Voon for research assistance. Chiswick acknowledges research support from the Smith Richardson Foundation. Miller acknowledges financial assistance from the Australian Research Council.

diminishes over time. Analyses of census data for the U.S. and for Australia for immigration among the English-speaking developed countries, and for Sweden for immigration among the Nordic countries, support the "negative assimilation" model. These immigrants have higher earnings than the native born on arrival, other measured variables the same, but with time their relative earnings decline to the native-born level.

An important implication of this analysis is that as international skill transferability increases, especially among high-skilled workers in advanced economies, positive assimilation may become less intense and negative assimilation more prevalent.

Barry R. Chiswick (2015)

From the beginning of the research on the economic or labor market assimilation of immigrants, the literature has focused on the degree of improvement in their economic status with duration in their destination country (Chiswick 1978d; 1979). This improvement has been found for all immigrant-receiving countries, time periods, and data sets that have been studied. The theoretical underpinning for this finding is the international transferability of skills. In this chapter, we address whether positive assimilation occurs if skills are highly transferable internationally. Indeed, the question arises, might there be the appearance of negative assimilation, that is, that earnings decline coincident with duration in the destination if the immigrant's skills are highly transferable across countries?

To answer this question, we analyze the earnings of adult, foreign-born men from English Speaking Developed Countries (ESDC) in the 1980, 1990, and 2000 U.S. Censuses.

7.1. The Assimilation Model

The immigrant assimilation model begins with the implicit assumption that immigrants possess a set of skills that they acquired in the lower-income origin that are not perfectly transferable to the higher-income destination. These skills include schooling, on-the-job training, language, labor market information, labor market networks, occupational licensing or credentials, occupation-specific technical training, and the customs or cultural characteristics that influence productivity, and hence earnings, in the origin and destination labor markets. When the immigrant moves from the origin to the destination, at least some of these skills are less than perfectly transferable, giving the immigrant incentives to make explicit (e.g., schooling) or implicit (e.g., learning-by-living) investments in destination-specific skills. Some of these investments may be intended to increase the transferability of skills acquired in the origin, such as when an immigrant physician studies for the Foreign Medical Examination. Other investments may be undertaken to acquire new skills, such as when an immigrant lawyer studies for an MBA.

Immigrants have an incentive to make these investments sooner rather than later for three reasons. First, if these postmigration human capital investments are profitable, in the sense that the net present value of the stream of costs and benefits is positive (or the internal rate of return exceeds the discount rate), the net present value of the investments are greater the sooner they are made. Second, a delay in making these investments reduces the number of future time periods in which immigrants will receive these benefits, thereby lowering the rate of return from the investment. Finally, as duration in the destination increases, explicit investments, and even learning-by-living, will increase immigrants' knowledge and other skills relevant for the destination labor market, thereby raising the opportunity cost of the time devoted to investment in destination skills. This opportunity cost, of course, lowers the net present value and the rate of return on these investments (Ben-Porath 1967).

If skills are not readily transferable internationally, immigrants' earnings will be lower than those for natives with similar skills. Moreover, the greater the extent to which immigrants invest in skills in the destination country, the lower the reported earnings are during the investment period. Earnings then increase as the extent of the investment decreases over time (the most profitable destination investments are made first), and as returns are received on previous investments. As a result, the earnings-duration profile is upward rising, but at a decreasing rate. This accounts for the use of the quadratic duration-of-residence variable in the standard analysis of immigrant postmigration labor market adjustment (Chiswick 1978d). The greater the steepness of the profile, the greater the extent of the investments in destination human capital, and the greater the rate of return from these investments. By implication, the earnings-duration profile would be horizontal if there were no investment, explicit or implicit, in destination human capital.

Let us consider two countries with equal average levels of earnings for individuals with a given level of schooling, labor market information, and other human capital relevant in the origin or destination. Consider, too, the skills to be perfectly internationally transferable between the two countries and that there is no skill employed in one that is not also used in the other country. Moreover, for simplicity, let us assume that in neither the origin nor the destination country are there investments in on-the-job training.

Bear in mind that for each skill level there exists variation in the distribution of wage offers around the mean. Workers in country X search not only in X but also in country Y.[1] A given worker will migrate from X to Y if and only if by random selection he or she receives a sufficiently high wage offer in Y so that this wage offer is greater than the best wage offer in X by an amount sufficient to compensate for the out-of-pocket, time, and psychic costs of migration. Upon receiving this high wage offer, the worker will move from X to Y, and under the assumptions postulated earlier, he will not make any destination human capital investments. Likewise, workers in country Y will search in both countries and some Y workers will move to country X. In this circumstance, migration is a two-way street.

The high randomly drawn wage offer that attracted the migrant from country X to country Y need not persist indefinitely. Since it is a high wage draw from the distribution of wage offers in country Y, with the passage of time the immigrant can expect to experience a "regression to the mean" in his wages, certainly in terms of real wages if not in nominal wages.[2] If this is the case, with the passage of time, there is the appearance of "negative" assimilation in terms of earnings.

Given these possibilities, we want to know whether the immigrant would remain in country Y. The immigrant would return to the origin, X, if the subsequently lowered earnings in the destination, Y, are below his best random draw from country X by an amount sufficient to compensate for the cost of return migration. Some will choose to return to country X; others will remain in the destination, country Y.

The high initial wage offer in the destination country may arise from factors other than random wage draws. For example, it might arise from an unanticipated exogenous increase in demand in the destination labor market for workers with a particular set of skills, perhaps specific to a particular occupation or industry. If so, with the passage of time, as the labor market adjusts, the wages of the immigrants would regress to the mean. Compared to mean wages in the labor market, the relative decline in immigrant wages in these sectors would give the appearance of negative assimilation.[3] Note that if the higher initial wages in the destination of the migrants are due merely to their higher level of ability (or unmeasured dimensions of human capital) their earnings would not decline with duration.

One implication of this model is the propensity for two-way migration and return migration between two countries of equal levels of income and income inequality between which human capital is perfectly transferable.[4] Another implication of the model is that immigrants initially experience higher earnings than the native born in the destination, *ceteris paribus*, with earnings declining toward that of the native born with duration in the destination. The decline in earnings is not the result of deterioration in skills, but rather a decline in earnings for a given set of skills. We refer to the decline in real earnings with duration as negative assimilation.

Suppose the international job search occurs just after leaving school and before marriage and family formation. Shortly thereafter, getting married and having children occur in both the origin and destination. This "family capital" raises the cost of migration, thereby discouraging it, including return migration by immigrants who have experienced negative assimilation. This would strengthen the argument for negative assimilation.

Alternative hypotheses that would give the appearance of negative assimilation in cross-sectional data would, of course, include (a) that there has been an increase over time in the unmeasured dimensions of the quality of immigrants (newer immigrants are more able); or (b) that the most successful in the destination country are more likely to exit (die, return to the origin, or move elsewhere). It is not obvious why there would have been an increase over time in the unmeasured dimensions of skill or ability. This hypothesis is tested, however, by analyzing immigrant-native earnings differentials over time. If immigrant quality increased over time, the ratio of immigrant to native earnings, holding constant duration of residence in the destination, would be higher in recent data than in earlier data, *ceteris paribus*.

It is not obvious why the most successful of the immigrants in the destination country would have a higher propensity to exit from the data. Exit from the data may occur because of death, withdrawal from the labor force, or return migration. There is little analysis on the selectivity, other variables being the same, out of the U.S. labor market of adult male immigrants. Lubotsky (2007) used longitudinal earnings data from U.S. Social Security records to study the effect of selective emigration on the earnings of immigrants. He found selectivity in return migration, with the emigration rate being higher for lower-wage workers. He did not test whether this selectivity also characterized immigrants from English-speaking developed countries. In a matched sample of immigrants in the 1983 and 1995 Censuses of Israel, Beenstock, Chiswick, and Paltiel (2010) found that those who died between 1983 and 1995 had lower earnings in 1983, presumably because they were in poorer health. These researchers also found that there was no difference in 1983 earnings between those who emigrated over the 12-year period and those who were successfully interviewed again in 1995. That is, they found no evidence that among immigrants in Israel the "exits" were positively selected on unmeasured characteristics, other variables being the same. Indeed, within the context of the negative assimilation model, presumably those who experience the steepest regression to the mean, that is, the greatest negative assimilation, would be the most likely to return to their origin. Their exit would reduce the appearance of negative assimilation among those who remain.

7.2. The Application to Immigrants

The model of negative assimilation we have developed has several stringent requirements. Namely, the income levels are the same in both origin and destination countries and the skills acquired and required in one country are perfectly transferable to the other. There are, however, no cases of countries in which these conditions are strictly observed.

Language is a particularly important form of country-specific human capital, and skill transferability is greater among the highly developed economies than between developed and less-developed countries or among less-developed countries. Moreover, among developed countries, those with a high degree of cultural similarity, or that share the same cultural origins, are more likely to have similar labor market institutions. This suggests that an appropriate test of the "negative" assimilation hypothesis for international migrants would be among developed countries that possess a common language and culture, and for which the relevant data exists. The closest approximation in the international arena would be migration among the

English-speaking developed countries (ESDC), namely the United States, Canada, Ireland, Australia, New Zealand, and the United Kingdom. Immigrants to the United States and Australia born in other English-speaking developed countries satisfy these requirements. Moreover, immigrants to Sweden from the other Nordic or Scandinavian countries would also satisfy these criteria.

We performed the main empirical testing of the model of negative assimilation for the United States. Using the 1980, 1990, and 2000 Censuses of Population of the United States (1% PUMS data in 1980; 5% in 1990 and 2000), we analyzed adult male immigrants born in Canada, the United Kingdom (U.K.), Ireland, Australia, and New Zealand.[5] We also performed empirical tests for Australia using the data on the ESDC in the 2001 Census of Australia. We also report findings on immigrant adjustment in Sweden, comparing Nordic and other EU immigrants.

7.2.1.   United States

The estimating equation for the United States regresses the natural logarithm of annual earnings in the year prior to the U.S. Census among adult (aged 25–64) male immigrants from the other English-speaking developed countries on the following characteristics: years of education, years of labor market experience (measured by Age – Years of education – 6), and its square, whether the respondent is currently married (spouse present), the natural logarithm of weeks worked in the reference year, whether a language other than English is spoken by the respondent at home, and, if so, his English language proficiency, and urban/rural and region control variables.[6] The immigration variables include years since migration (YSM) to the United States and country-of-origin dichotomous variables. We provide brief descriptions of all variables in Appendix A. If the negative assimilation hypothesis is to be supported by the data, the coefficient on years since migration would have a negative sign. To test for cohort effects – if the unmeasured dimensions of immigrant quality have increased over time – the ratio of immigrant to native earnings, *ceteris paribus*, would be higher in 2000 than in the earlier census data. We computed separate analyses for the United States by country of origin among the ESDC to ascertain whether the negative assimilation effects are dominated by one origin, or if they are broad-based among the ESDC origins.

The crucial variable for this analysis is the year of immigration. The detail on this in the public use samples for the censuses in the United States has changed over time. As Table 7.1 shows, progressively more detail has been presented over time on the year of immigration, with single years being used in 2000.[7] We followed the literature (e.g., Chiswick 1978d) and formed a continuous variable by using the mid-points of the period of immigration categories for analyses of the 1980 and 1990 Census data. We computed duration in the United States as the census year minus the year of immigration.

Table 7.1

Year of Immigration Data in U.S. Censuses

Census	Number of Categories used for Year of Immigration Data	Year of Immigration Information
1980	6	1975–1980; 1970–1974; 1965–1969; 1960–1964; 1950–1959; Before 1950.
1990	10	1987–1990; 1985–1986; 1982–1984; 1980–1981; 1975–1979; 1970–1974; 1965–1969; 1960–1964; 1950–1959; Before 1950.
2000	In single years	In single years.

Appendix Table A7.1 reports the means and standard deviations for the natural logarithm of earnings and for the explanatory variables. There is a pronounced increase, by nearly one log point, in the natural logarithm of earnings between 1980 and 2000. That is, nominal earnings more than doubled among ESDC immigrants and real earnings increased by about 1.3 percent per year.[8] The mean educational attainment (15.2 years in 2000) increased by 0.7 years over the 20-year period analyzed. Immigrants from ESDC in the 2000 data have resided in the United States for about the same length of time as those in 1980 (19.5 years).

Slightly more than 14 percent of the sample of immigrants from ESDC in the United States reported speaking a language other than or in addition to English at home in the 2000 Census, and about 12 percent did so in each of the earlier data sets (see Table 7.2). The importance of Irish Gaelic among immigrants from Ireland, and French among immigrants from Canada, is shown in Table 7.2. Separate analyses are conducted for "French" Canadians, defined here as immigrants from Canada who speak French at home, and other Canadians. Due to small sample sizes, however, we have not given further consideration to those immigrants speaking Irish Gaelic at home in the United States.

Table 7.2

Percent of Adult Male Immigrants from ESDC in the U.S. by English Proficiency and the Top Five Non-English Languages, by Country of Origin, 2000

| Group | % English Only | Speaks Another Language or Speaks English | | Top 5 Languages Spoken (% speaking them) |
		Very Well/ Well	Not Well/ Not at All	
Total	85.8	13.4	0.7	French (6.60); Spanish (1.18); Irish Gaelic (0.96); German/Austrian/Swiss (0.73); Italian (0.59).
United Kingdom	90.7	8.8	0.6	French (2.23); Spanish (1.07); German/Austrian/Swiss (0.53); Gujarathi (0.41); Polish (0.37).
Ireland	86.2	12.9	0.9	Irish Gaelic (9.39); French (1.35); Spanish (1.27); German/Austrian/Swiss (0.36); Italian (0.25).
Canada	80.6	18.5	0.9	French (12.64); Spanish (1.22); German/Austrian/Swiss (1.02); Italian (0.80); Greek (0.52).
Australia & N.Z.	90.5	9.0	0.5	Greek (1.54); Spanish (1.43); Italian (1.10); French (0.70); German/Austrian/Swiss (0.51).

Source: U.S. Census of Population: 2000 PUMS, 5% sample.

Table 7.3 reports the estimated earnings functions for adult male immigrants from the advanced English-speaking developed countries.[9] These analyses are based on two specifications of the earnings equation: the first contains a quadratic in years since migration (YSM) and the second uses only a linear variable for YSM. The standard model of immigrant labor market adjustment – "positive" assimilation – implies a quadratic specification for years since migration. The negative assimilation model hypothesizes a negative sign but does not indicate whether a linear or a quadratic specification is preferred. Both specifications are applied here.

The estimates reported in Table 7.3 possess all the characteristics of recent research on immigrant earnings, and in particular the steady increase over time for immigrants in the payoff to schooling (from 6.4 percent in 1980 to 10.4 percent in 2000), the decline in the elasticity of earnings with respect to weeks worked (from 1.15 to around unity), and the decline in the North–South earnings differential.[10] Other than marginally significant lower earnings among immigrants from Ireland in 1980, other variables being the same, earnings do not differ significantly from the benchmark, the United Kingdom, across the immigrant groups identified in the analysis.

171

Table 7.3

Analyses of Immigrant Earnings, 25 to 64-Year-Old Male Immigrants from English-Speaking Developed Countries, 1980, 1990 and 2000 U.S. Censuses[a]

Variable	1980		1990		2000	
Constant	3.601	3.630	4.252	4.271	4.526	4.525
	(13.43)	(13.51)	(33.84)	(34.04)	(35.70)	(35.67)
Educational Attainment	0.064	0.064	0.077	0.077	0.104	0.104
	(12.27)	(12.28)	(28.83)	(28.85)	(42.36)	(42.42)
Experience (EXP)	0.058	0.059	0.047	0.047	0.048	0.048
	(10.80)	(11.14)	(19.19)	(19.49)	(19.17)	(19.21)
$EXP^2/100$	-0.094	-0.096	-0.073	-0.074	-0.074	-0.074
	(9.06)	(9.48)	(14.33)	(14.65)	(14.82)	(14.91)
Years Since Migration (YSM)	0.002	-0.003	-0.000	-0.004	-0.007	-0.007
	(0.49)	(2.11)	(0.26)	(6.29)	(4.31)	(13.42)
$YSM^2/100$	-0.011	[b]	-0.007	[b]	0.000	[b]
	(1.15)		(2.06)		(0.09)	
Log Weeks Worked	1.151	1.154	1.129	1.131	0.975	0.975
	(16.84)	(16.93)	(36.02)	(36.13)	(33.56)	(33.62)
Married	0.256	0.255	0.244	0.243	0.256	0.256
	(6.49)	(6.46)	(16.52)	(16.46)	(19.42)	(19.43)
South	-0.173	-0.175	-0.133	-0.134	-0.069	-0.069
	(4.23)	(4.29)	(8.34)	(8.38)	(5.15)	(5.16)
Rural[(c)]	-0.046	-0.048	-0.102	-0.102	-0.295	-0.295
	(0.74)	(0.78)	(5.22)	(5.21)	(6.16)	(6.16)
English Very Well/Well	-0.107	-0.107	-0.073	-0.072	-0.029	-0.029
	(2.29)	(2.29)	(3.29)	(3.26)	(1.66)	(1.66)
English Not Well/Not at All	-0.135	-0.131	-0.041	-0.041	0.074	0.074
	(0.52)	(0.50)	(0.47)	(0.47)	(0.94)	(0.94)
Ireland	-0.092	-0.086	0.003	0.002	-0.003	-0.003
	(1.92)	(1.81)	(0.17)	(0.13)	(0.14)	(0.14)
Canada	0.015	0.016	-0.011	-0.011	-0.007	-0.007
	(0.49)	(0.54)	(0.79)	(0.77)	(0.53)	(0.53)
Australia & New Zealand	-0.074	-0.084	-0.062	-0.065	-0.007	-0.007
	(0.90)	(1.03)	(1.47)	(1.55)	(0.26)	(0.25)
R^2	0.3289	0.3288	0.3061	0.3060	0.2707	0.2707
Sample Size	3,480	3,480	18,046	18,046	21,777	21,777

Notes: [a] Absolute value of heteroskedasticity-consistent t-statistics in parentheses.
[b] Variable not entered.
[c] Definition of variable changes appreciably across data sets.
Source: U.S. Censuses of Population: 1980 1% PUMS; 1990 5% PUMS; 2000 5% PUMS.

Earnings are significantly lower among those who report that in addition to English they speak another language at home, but that they speak English very well or well.[11] This negative effect declines from 11 percent in 1980 to 7 percent in 1990 to a marginally significant 3 percent in 2000. This effect seems to arise primarily from the earnings disadvantage of French-speaking Canadians diminishing over time. The statistically insignificant effect on earnings of speaking English not well or not at all appears to be due to the trivial size of the sample.

The estimates for the variables for duration in the United States (YSM) support the negative assimilation hypothesis. In 1980, neither the linear nor the squared YSM terms were statistically significant when a quadratic YSM specification was used. When only a linear duration variable was employed the statistically significant ($t = -2.11$) coefficient of -0.004 indicated a decline of earnings at 0.4 of one percentage point per year in the United States.

In the 1990 data, when a quadratic YSM specification was used, both coefficients were negative, but only that for the squared variable was statistically significant. When a linear specification was used the statistically significant ($t = 6.29$) estimated coefficient of -0.004 indicated a decline of earnings at 0.4 of one percentage point per year.

For the 2000 data, the quadratic specification showed that the YSM variable had a significant negative coefficient, but the squared YSM term was not significant. The linear specification resulted in a highly significant ($t = -13.42$) negative coefficient on the duration variable, -0.007. That is, there is a decline in ESDC immigrant earnings at the rate of 0.7 of one percentage point per year of duration in the United States.[12] Thus, these results from analyses of the 1980, 1990, and 2000 U.S. Censuses indicate strong support for the negative assimilation hypothesis.[13]

The Table 7.3 results also indicate that the negative assimilation effect has intensified over time. The strengthening of this effect could be an economic phenomenon or the result of the change in the detail on year of immigration used in the analysis (see Table 7.1). To ascertain whether the latter is important, the year of immigration data in the 2000 Census were first recoded into ten categories analogous to those available for the 1990 data, and an alternative YSM variable was created using the mid-points of these categories. The earnings equation using this alternative variable resulted in an estimate of the negative assimilation effect for 2000 of -0.006 (t-ratio $= -13.15$), instead of the -0.007 (t-ratio $= -13.42$) using the full detail.[14] This effect shows that the presentation of the YSM data is of modest importance for the statistical analyses undertaken here. Moreover, this apparent slight diminution of the estimated impact of the duration variable when less detailed categorical information is used strengthens the evidence in support of the negative assimilation hypothesis. It indicates that the effects estimated for 1980 and 1990 are biased somewhat toward zero by the use of the less detailed categorical information on years since migration.

Under the negative assimilation hypothesis, the initial high U.S. labor market entry wage is driven by a favorable draw from the distribution of wage offers. In this situation, the negative relationship between earnings and duration of residence should be less intense, or even non-existent, among immigrants who arrived in the United States as children – they will be tied-movers. The relationship between earnings and years since migration could still be negative for immigrants who arrived as children if the high wage draw for their parents is partly a reflection of initial settlement in a tight labor market, and this results in a favorable initial wage offer for the foreign-born children of immigrants. However, this influence should be weaker the younger the age at migration.

To assess this influence, we estimated separate earnings equations for immigrants who arrived in the United States as children and those who arrived as adults. A difficulty with this approach is that an age at migration has to be inferred from the census self-reports on current age and year of arrival in the United States. The bunching in the data on year of arrival (at years ending in 5 and, particularly, zero) suggests that separating groups that arrived as adults and as children will be imprecise. Consideration is therefore given to a number of ages of arrival as the adult-children threshold, with most emphasis placed on the broad patterns that emerge from this analysis.

Table 7.4 lists selected findings from this analysis by age at migration. This exercise is reported only for the 2000 Census data because of the greater detail on year of arrival and for simplicity using only the linear specification of the duration variable. The coefficients on educational attainment and duration are listed for selected adult-children thresholds, together with the sample sizes.

The results in Table 7.4 for the adult samples are similar for each threshold age and similar to the results in Table 7.3: the payoff to education is a little more than 10 percent, and the coefficient on the YSM variable is between -0.006 and -0.007, with both coefficients highly statistically significant. Among the samples of adults who immigrated as children, the payoff to education is similar to that of adults (11 percent compared to 10 percent) and the coefficient on the YSM variable is smaller in absolute value. The similar coefficient on schooling for the adult immigrants compared to the child immigrants is consistent with the ESDC immigrants entering with a high degree of skill transferability and relatively low costs of immigration (Chiswick and Miller 2008b).[15]

Table 7.4

Selected Estimates of Earnings Functions for Immigrants Arriving as Adults and as Children, 25 to 64-Year-Old Male Immigrants from English-Speaking Developed Countries, 2000 U.S. Census[a]

Arrival Age Threshold for Adults	Arrived as Children			Arrived as Adults		
	Educational Attainment	YSM	Sample Size	Educational Attainment	YSM	Sample Size
12+	0.111	-0.003	5,429	0.102	-0.007	16,348
	(17.15)	(0.88)		(35.84)	(7.78)	
13+	0.109	-0.002	5,696	0.101	-0.006	16,081
	(18.06)	(0.69)		(35.32)	(7.25)	
14+	0.108	-0.004	5,943	0.102	-0.006	15,874
	(18.42)	(1.23)		(35.11)	(7.11)	
15+	0.108	-0.005	6,188	0.102	-0.007	15,589
	(19.17)	(1.99)		(34.88)	(7.05)	
16+	0.107	-0.005	6,475	0.102	-0.007	15,302
	(19.62)	(2.07)		(34.43)	(6.68)	
17+	0.105	-0.004	6,759	0.102	-0.006	15,018
	(20.09)	(2.02)		(33.90)	(6.31)	
18+	0.106	-0.005	7,085	0.102	-0.006	14,692
	(20.97)	(2.59)		(33.30)	(6.00)	

Notes: [a] Absolute value of heteroskedasticity-consistent t-statistics in parentheses. The estimating equation also holds constant labor market experience and its square, log of weeks worked, whether currently married (spouse present), whether the respondent lives in the South or a rural (1980, 1990) or non-metropolitan (2000) area, proficiency in English if a language other than English is spoken at home, and country of origin dichotomous variables (U.K. as benchmark).

Source: U.S. Census of Population: 2000 5% PUMS.

The coefficient on duration is negative in all of the equations in Table 7.4 among adult immigrants; its magnitude is similar to that in Table 7.3 and is highly statistically significant. Among the child immigrants, however, the magnitude is smaller, decreases, and becomes statistically insignificant as older children are excluded. Indeed, the coefficient is not significant in the samples of young children formed using age at arrival of 14 or younger. Nevertheless, the differences in the coefficients on the duration variable between adult and child immigrants are not statistically significant, and the point estimates for the child immigrants support the negative assimilation hypothesis.

Table 7.5 presents estimates of the payoff to schooling and the estimated coefficients for the duration variables from the separate analyses undertaken for immigrants from the United Kingdom, Ireland, Canada and Australia/New Zealand.[16] For the United Kingdom and Canada, where sample sizes are relatively large, the negative assimilation effect is alive and well, and there is evidence for it increasing over time. A similar pattern is evident for the much smaller samples of immigrants from Australia and New Zealand. In the somewhat larger sample for Australia and New Zealand in 2000 (1,250 observations), the coefficient on duration in the quadratic specification is negative and significant, and in the linear specification it is negative, although not statistically significant.

Table 7.5

Selected Estimates of Immigrant Adjustment Earnings Function, 25 to 64-Year-Old Male Immigrants by Country of Origin, 1980, 1990, and 2000 U.S. Censuses[a]

Variable	1980		1990		2000	
United Kingdom: Sample Sizes 1980: 1,268; 1990: 7,439; 2000: 8,917						
Educational Attainment	0.077	0.077	0.085	0.085	0.109	0.109
	(8.68)	(8.67)	(20.15)	(20.19)	(28.08)	(28.09)
Years Since Migration (YSM)	-0.004	-0.002	-0.002	-0.005	-0.009	-0.009
	(0.64)	(1.18)	(0.88)	(5.35)	(3.68)	(11.01)
YSM^2/100	0.005	b	-0.005	b	0.002	b
	(0.35)		(0.93)		(0.38)	
Ireland: Sample Sizes 1980: 367; 1990: 1,857; 2000: 2,029						
Educational Attainment	0.022	0.020	0.051	0.051	0.072	0.072
	(1.50)	(1.37)	(7.51)	(7.48)	(9.26)	(9.24)
Years Since Migration (YSM)	0.027	0.004	0.010	0.002	0.008	-0.001
	(1.58)	(0.70)	(2.01)	(0.89)	(1.40)	(0.67)
YSM^2/100	-0.046	b	-0.018	b	-0.020	b
	(1.33)		(1.95)		(1.77)	
Canada: Sample Sizes 1980: 1,733; 1990: 7,956; 2000: 9,581						
Educational Attainment	0.065	0.064	0.077	0.076	0.108	0.108
	(8.96)	(9.08)	(18.31)	(18.25)	(28.74)	(28.87)
Years Since Migration (YSM)	0.002	-0.004	0.001	-0.004	-0.004	-0.006
	(0.27)	(1.99)	(0.32)	(4.19)	(2.00)	(8.12)
YSM^2/100	-0.014	b	-0.009	b	-0.003	b
	(0.89)		(1.87)		(0.57)	
Australia and New Zealand: Sample Sizes 1980: 112; 1990: 794; 2000: 1,250						
Educational Attainment	0.070	0.069	0.091	0.091	0.104	0.103
	(2.14)	(2.21)	(6.53)	(6.52)	(11.14)	(11.08)
Years Since Migration (YSM)	-0.011	-0.003	-0.000	-0.000	-0.014	-0.004
	(0.35)	(0.55)	(0.03)	(0.11)	(2.21)	(1.42)
YSM^2/100	0.018	b	-0.000	b	0.026	b
	(0.25)		(0.02)		(1.71)	

Notes: [a] Absolute value of heteroskedasticity-consistent *t*-statistics in parentheses.
[b] Variable not entered.
The estimating equation also holds constant labor market experience and its square, log of weeks worked, whether currently married (spouse present), whether the respondent lives in the South or a rural (1980, 1990) or non-metropolitan (2000) area, proficiency in English if a language other than English is spoken at home, and country of origin dichotomous variables (U.K. as benchmark).
Source: U.S. Censuses of Population: 1980 1% PUMS; 1990 5% PUMS; 2000 5% PUMS.

The results for Ireland appear to be different from those of the United Kingdom, Canada, and Australia/New Zealand. In the quadratic specification, the coefficient on the duration term is positive and the squared term is negative, and both are at the margin of being statistically significant in 1990. The coefficients in the quadratic specification indicate a positive effect of duration on earnings, which diminishes with duration and eventually becomes negative (after 28 years in the 1990 data). In the linear specification for Ireland, the coefficients of the duration variable have mixed signs and they are not statistically significant. The lower level of income in Ireland, and the ease (low cost) of migration to the United Kingdom, as distinct from migration to the United States, may be responsible for this effect.

Two further sets of analyses were undertaken to test the robustness of the findings for the United States with respect to the language variable. In the first, the variables for proficiency in the English language were omitted from the specification. It has been shown that English proficiency among immigrants is strongly linked to duration of residence, and the inclusion of the language proficiency variable in the earnings equation could distort measurement of the assimilation effect. Table 7.6 presents the findings for the duration of residence variables from this set of analyses. These estimates mirror those from the earnings function that included the English proficiency variables (compare Table 7.6 with Tables 7.3 and 7.5). The language variable is therefore of little consequence for the quantification of the negative assimilation effect. This is not surprising given that all of the immigrants under study reported that they were born in an English-speaking developed country.

In the second experiment, the data for immigrants born in Canada for 2000 were analyzed separately according to whether the immigrants were French Canadians (defined as speaking French in their home in the United States) or other Canadians. Using the 2000 Census for each sample, the estimate of the assimilation effect was a highly significant -0.006, where the t-ratios were $t = -2.61$ for French Canadians and $t = -7.91$ for other Canadians. This estimate was not sensitive to whether information on the degree of proficiency in English was included in the model. Hence, the negative assimilation effect observed for immigrants from Canada appears to be independent of whether they also speak French at home.

Table 7.6

Selected Estimates of Immigrant Adjustment Earnings Function, 25 to 64-Year-Old Male Immigrants by Country of Origin, Without Language Variables, 1980, 1990, and 2000 U.S. Censuses[a]

Variable	1980		1990		2000	
Total Sample: Sample Sizes 1980: 3,480; 1990: 18,046; 2000: 21,777						
Educational Attainment	0.003	-0.003	-0.000	-0.004	-0.007	-0.007
	(0.54)	(1.90)	(0.28)	(6.17)	(4.36)	(13.41)
YSM^2/100	-0.011	b	-0.007	b	0.001	b
	(1.15)		(1.99)		(0.15)	
United Kingdom: Sample Sizes 1980: 1,268; 1990: 7,439; 2000: 8,917						
Educational Attainment	-0.004	-0.002	-0.002	-0.005	-0.010	-0.009
	(0.59)	(1.05)	(0.85)	(5.35)	(3.70)	(11.00)
YSM^2/100	0.005	b	-0.005	b	0.002	b
	(0.33)		(0.96)		(0.40)	
Ireland: Sample Sizes 1980: 367; 1990: 1,857; 2000: 2,029						
Educational Attainment	0.026	0.004	0.010	0.002	0.008	-0.001
	(1.54)	(0.68)	(2.09)	(1.03)	(1.42)	(0.61)
YSM^2/100	-0.045	b	-0.018	b	-0.020	b
	(1.30)		(1.99)		(1.76)	
Canada: Sample Sizes 1980: 1,733; 1990: 7,956; 2000: 9,581						
Educational Attainment	0.003	-0.004	0.001	-0.004	-0.004	-0.006
	(0.37)	(1.76)	(0.31)	(4.12)	(1.94)	(8.18)
YSM^2/100	-0.015	b	-0.009	b	-0.003	b
	(0.93)		(1.84)		(0.65)	
Australia and New Zealand: Sample Sizes 1980: 112; 1990: 794; 2000: 1,250						
Educational Attainment	-0.010	-0.003	-0.004	-0.002	-0.015	-0.004
	(0.33)	(0.52)	(0.46)	(0.45)	(2.30)	(1.64)
YSM^2/100	0.018	b	-0.006	b	0.025	b
	(0.25)		(0.32)		(1.71)	

Notes: [a] Absolute value of heteroskedasticity-consistent t-statistics in parentheses.
[b] Variable not entered.
The estimating equation also holds constant educational attainment, labor market experience and its square, log of weeks worked, whether currently married (spouse present), whether the respondent lives in the South or a rural (1980, 1990) or non-metropolitan (2000) area, proficiency in English if a language other than English is spoken at home, and country of origin dichotomous variables (U.K. as benchmark).

Source: U.S. Censuses of Population: 1980 1% PUMS; 1990 5% PUMS; 2000 5% PUMS.

7.2.2. Australia

Further evidence regarding the negative assimilation effect among immigrants in the ESDC from other English-speaking countries is provided in a recent study of immigrant earnings in Australia (Chiswick and Miller 2008a, Table 7).[17] Using the Australian 2001 Census data for adult foreign-born men, other variables being the same, earnings increased with duration in Australia among those who were not born in the ESDC. Among those born in the ESDC, however, earnings decreased with duration, other variables being the same (Table 7.7).

Table 7.7

Partial Effect of Duration of Residence on the Earnings of Adult Male Immigrants from the ESDC, 2001 Australian Census

Period of Immigration	ESDC	Other Countries
1991–1995	-0.040	0.011
	(0.92)	(0.32)
1986–1990	-0.055	0.031
	(1.58)	(0.85)
Before 1986	-0.085	0.107
	(3.31)	(3.65)

Notes: The sample size is 3,127, the benchmark immigration category is "Immigrated after 1995," and t-ratios are in parentheses. The estimating equation includes variables for schooling, labor market experience, marital status, and log weeks worked.

Source: Chiswick and Miller (2008a), Table 1: 48.

The coefficients imply 5.5 percent lower earnings for those who migrated to Australia from the ESDC in 1988 compared to those who immigrated in 1998. This compares with a decline of 7 percent over a ten-year period for ESDC immigrants in the U.S. 2000 Census (Table 7.3, last column).

7.2.3. Sweden

Migration among the five Nordic countries might offer another test of the negative assimilation hypothesis. Four Nordic countries – Sweden, Denmark, Norway, and Iceland – are of roughly similar levels of income and the languages are quite similar. Most of the ethnic Swedish and ethnic Finnish migrants from Finland to Sweden know Swedish.[18] Many of the cultural characteristics and institutions are similar across these five countries. Notably, there is unrestricted labor mobility across the Nordic countries.

Pedersen et al. (2008) studied the 2005 wages of immigrants in Sweden from both the ten Eastern European countries that joined the European Union in May 2004 and the four other Nordic countries.[19] According to them, immigrants in Sweden from the EU-10

> have lower wages than the natives and those who have arrived recently have lower wages than those coming earlier, controlling for age, education, and gender. For those coming from the Nordic countries the pattern is quite different. The wage differential is much smaller and

those who have arrived earlier have a wage disadvantage compared to those who arrived in more recent periods. (Pedersen et al. (2008): 105–6, Table 5.8)

Indeed, recent immigrants from each of the four Nordic countries have higher earnings than those born in Sweden, other variables the same, with the earnings advantage declining with duration and eventually becoming negative. This pattern is consistent with the negative assimilation hypothesis.

7.3. Immigrant Versus Native Earnings Over Time

Tables 7.8 and 7.9 list the coefficients of the duration of residence variables from the regression equations estimated on pooled samples of the native and foreign born in the United States for each census year. Table 7.8 contains results for 1990 and 2000 and Table 7.9 contains results for 1980, 1990, and 2000. The analyses differ by the level of detail on the duration of residence variables to the extent permitted by the census with the least amount of information in the set of comparisons conducted (the 1990 Census period of arrival categories when only 2000 and 1990 data are compared, and the 1980 Census categories for period of arrival when 1980, 1990, and 2000 data are compared – see Table 7.1 for details).

For the native born, a 25 percent subset of the 1% PUMS for each census was used in these analyses, a sampling procedure that yielded more than 100,000 observations for this group, which is more than adequate for the comparisons conducted. Column (i) of Table 7.8 reports the mean difference in earnings among adult men between the immigrants from the ESDC and the U.S. native born. The regression equations in Table 7.8 contain the set of standardizing variables used in Table 7.3 and a set of birthplace variables (for immigrants from the United Kingdom, Ireland, Canada, and Australia/New Zealand, respectively). One set of the estimates (Table 7.8, column (ii)) comes from equations that constrain the estimates of each of the human capital and demographic variables from Table 7.3 to be the same for the native and the foreign born. The second set includes a full set of interaction terms between these variables and birthplace (Table 7.8, column (iii)). The inclusion of these interaction terms has minimal impact on the comparisons that can be made across the duration of residence categories. It has, however, a marked impact in some analyses on the magnitude of the native born – immigrant comparisons, *ceteris paribus*, a result consistent with previous findings (e.g., see Funkhouser and Trejo 1995).

Table 7.8

Coefficients on Birthplace and Duration of Residence Variables from Analysis on Pooled Sample of Native-born and Foreign-born Workers, 1990 and 2000 U.S. Censuses[a]

	1990			2000		
	Difference in Mean Earnings[b]	*Without Birthplace Interactions*	*With Birthplace Interactions*	*Difference in Mean Earnings*[b]	*Without Birthplace Interactions*	*With Birthplace Interactions*
Variable	*(i)*	*(ii)*	*(iii)*	*(i)*	*(ii)*	*(iii)*
Birthplace (native-born as benchmark)						
U.K.	0.360	0.149	0.216	0.399	0.315	0.299
	(30.45)	(8.16)	(1.66)	(36.67)	(21.17)	(2.27)
Ireland	0.261	0.182	0.225	0.223	0.319	0.302
	(13.08)	(8.05)	(1.74)	(11.14)	(14.82)	(2.28)
Canada	0.247	0.145	0.206	0.322	0.303	0.289
	(20.66)	(7.50)	(1.58)	(30.33)	(21.02)	(2.20)
Australia & N.Z.	0.248	0.081	0.156	0.392	0.304	0.290
	(5.56)	(1.94)	(1.12)	(13.10)	(11.19)	(2.19)
Duration of Residence (0–4 years as benchmark)						
5–9 yrs	c	0.071	0.051	c	-0.046	-0.056
		(2.88)	(2.09)		(2.31)	(2.82)
10–14 yrs	c	0.060	0.030	c	-0.101	-0.126
		(2.11)	(1.04)		(4.78)	(5.88)
15–19 yrs	c	0.024	-0.010	c	-0.085	-0.118
		(0.84)	(0.36)		(3.81)	(5.27)
20–24 yrs	c	0.035	-0.005	c	-0.117	-0.151
		(1.52)	(0.22)		(4.99)	(6.40)
25–29 yrs	c	0.007	-0.042	c	-0.125	-0.164
		(0.32)	(1.75)		(4.91)	(6.32)
30–39 yrs	c	-0.033	-0.088	c	-0.155	-0.211
		(1.49)	(3.66)		(8.20)	(10.35)
40+ yrs	c	-0.079	-0.145	c	-0.232	-0.303
		(2.57)	(4.34)		(10.73)	(12.62)
R^2	0.0100	0.3749	0.3754	0.0158	0.3316	0.3319
Sample Size	140.344	140,344	140,344	155,254	155,254	155,254

Notes: [a] Absolute value of heteroskedasticity-consistent *t*-statistics in parentheses.
  [b] Difference in mean log earnings from the native born.
  [c] Variable not entered.
  The estimating equation also holds constant educational attainment, labor market experience and its square, log of weeks worked, whether currently married (spouse present), whether the respondent lives in the South or a rural (1980, 1990) or non-metropolitan (2000) area, proficiency in English if a language other than English is spoken at home, and country of origin dichotomous variables, with the native born as the country benchmark.
Source: U.S. Censuses of Population: 1980 1% PUMS; 1990 5% PUMS; 2000 5% PUMS.

Table 7.8 has four main features. First, according to the figures in column (i), the mean earnings of immigrants from the United Kingdom, Canada, and Australia/New Zealand, relative to the native born, increased between 1990 and 2000. The mean earnings of immigrants from Ireland, however, fell by 4 percentage points relative to the mean earnings of the native born over this period. Second, in the 1990 Census data, regardless of the specification of the estimating equation (column (ii) or column (iii)), there is evidence of positive adjustment over the first decade in the United States (earnings were higher for those in the United States five to nine years than those in the United States zero to four years). Beyond this point, however, the estimates are consistent with the negative assimilation hypothesis; earnings decline with a longer duration. Third, the 2000 data exhibit a pattern consistent with the negative assimilation hypothesis across all duration intervals. As Figure 7.1 illustrates, beyond five years of residence, the profiles of the immigrant-native-born earnings differentials by duration of residence for 2000 and 1990, for all intents and purposes, have a negative slope and are parallel.

Figure 7.1

Earnings for Foreign-born Relative to Native-born Adult Men by Duration of Residence Category, Ceteris Paribus, 1990 and 2000 U.S. Censuses

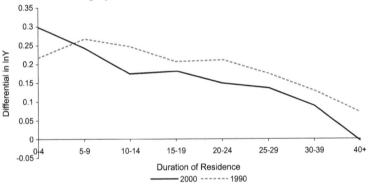

Source: Authors' calculations from Table 7.8, column (iii).

In compiling Figure 7.1, we have used the duration-of-residence co-efficients from the model with birthplace interaction terms. The intercept points are given by the coefficients on the dummy variable for immigrants from the United Kingdom. This brings us to the fourth feature of the results in Table 7.8: the intercept point (or the earnings advantage that immigrants have over the native born, *ceteris paribus*) for 2000 is higher than for 1990. This is generally taken as evidence for an increase over time in the unobservable qualities of immigrants relative to the native born. At each of the other durations of residence, however, the earnings profile for the foreign born for 1990 is above that for 2000. In other words, when looking at the data for 1990 and 2000, the evidence on the unobservable change in the qualities of immigrant cohorts is ambiguous.

Table 7.9

Coefficients on Birthplace and Duration of Residence Variables from Analysis on Pooled Sample of Native-born and Foreign-born Workers, 1980, 1990 and 2000 U.S. Censuses[a]

	1980[b]		1990		2000	
	Without Birthplace	With Birthplace	Without Birthplace	With Birthplace	Without Birthplace	With Birthplace
Variable	Interactions	Interactions	Interactions	Interactions	Interactions	Interactions
Birthplace (native-born as benchmark)						
U.K.	0.048	-0.337	0.149	0.218	0.315	0.307
	(1.13)	(1.24)	(8.19)	(1.68)	(21.19)	(2.33)
Ireland	-0.018	-0.424	0.183	0.228	0.318	0.308
	(0.31)	(1.54)	(8.07)	(1.76)	(14.78)	(2.32)
Canada	0.063	-0.321	0.144	0.206	0.302	0.295
	(1.33)	(1.18)	(7.44)	(1.58)	(20.97)	(2.24)
Australia & N.Z.	-0.038	-0.410	0.082	0.158	0.305	0.298
	(0.47)	(1.46)	(1.95)	(1.13)	(11.20)	(2.24)
Duration of Residence (0–4 years as benchmark)						
5–9 yrs	0.109	0.079	0.071	0.052	-0.046	-0.056
	(1.65)	(1.18)	(2.89)	(2.11)	(2.30)	(2.78)
10–14 yrs	0.127	0.076	0.060	0.031	-0.101	-0.125
	(2.24)	(1.29)	(2.12)	(1.07)	(4.77)	(5.82)
15–19 yrs	0.056	-0.002	0.024	-0.009	-0.085	-0.116
	(1.03)	(0.04)	(0.85)	(0.32)	(3.81)	(5.17)
20–29 yrs	0.050	-0.002	0.020	-0.023	-0.120	-0.154
	(1.03)	(0.04)	(1.00)	(1.09)	(6.19)	(7.78)
301 yrs	-0.007	-0.069	-0.045	-0.100	-0.185	-0.242
	(0.14)	(1.19)	(2.12)	(4.25)	(10.98)	(12.81)
R^2	0.3221	0.3222	0.3748	0.3754	0.3315	0.3318
Sample Size	107,402	107,402	140,344	140,344	155,254	155,254

Notes: [a] Absolute value of heteroskedasticity-consistent t-statistics in parentheses.
[b] The mean earnings advantage in 1980 for the foreign born compared to the native born is 0.258 for immigrants from the U.K., 0.139 for immigrants from Ireland, 0.162 for immigrants from Canada, and 0.126 for immigrants from Australia/New Zealand.
The estimating equation also holds constant educational attainment, labor market experience and its square, log of weeks worked, whether currently married (spouse present), whether the respondent lives in the South or a rural (1980, 1990) or non-metropolitan (2000) area, proficiency in English if a language other than English is spoken at home, and country of origin dichotomous variables, with the native born as the country benchmark.
Source: U.S. Censuses of Population: 1990 5% PUMS; 2000 5% PUMS.

Table 7.9 presents parallel information for the analyses of the 1980, 1990, and 2000 Censuses. The pattern of earnings effects with duration of residence for 1980 is a diluted version of that which characterized the data a decade later, in 1990. The immigrant earnings advantage over the native born in 1990 and 2000 is considerably greater than in 1980, suggesting that the 1980s and 1990s were characterized by different selection among immigrants from English-speaking developed countries than in earlier years. The large negative coefficients on the birthplace variables for 1980 in the specification with birthplace interaction effects are due mainly to different earnings effects of the weeks-worked variable: the coefficient on this for the foreign born was 1.149, and that for the native born 1.062. In comparison, in 2000 the coefficient on the weeks-worked variable was 0.975 for the foreign born and 1.024 for the native born.

The relatively flat earnings duration-of-residence profile in 1980 and the steeper negative profile in 1990 and 2000, together with the increases in the positive immigrant-native-born earnings differential over time, *ceteris paribus*, suggest there may be merit to the estimation of a cohort model. In this application, our approach follows Funkhouser and Trejo (1995).

The cohort model may be written as:

$$\ln Y_i = \alpha + X_i\beta + YSM_i\gamma_1 + YSMSQ_i\gamma_2 + C_i\delta + T_i\phi| + \varepsilon_i,$$

where income (Y) is the annual earnings from wage and salaried employment and self-employment; X_i is the set of human capital and demographic standardizing variables used earlier; YSM_i is the number of years an immigrant has spent in the United States; C_i is a vector of dummy variables indicating the immigrant cohort of arrival; T_i is a vector of dummy variables for the census year; and ε is a stochastic disturbance term. In this earnings equation, γ_1 and γ_2 capture the pattern of immigrant assimilation, and δ captures cohort differences in the intercept of the earnings profile. This specification constrains the coefficients on the X_i variables to be the same across birthplace groups and across time periods, and these restrictions are inconsistent with the evidence in Table 7.3 (for changes over time) and Table 7.8 (statistically significant birthplace interactions). Funkhouser and Trejo (1995: 804) noted that this constraint is not necessary, and they presented estimates from a more general specification that allows the effects of their human capital variables to vary with nativity. Borjas (1995a) also favored a more general model that allows for interactions of the X_i variables with immigrant status and the period effects. We have adopted a general specification that allows the coefficients of the X_i variables to change over time as well as to differ between the native born and foreign born.[20]

Table 7.10

Estimates of Cohort Model for the United States, 1980, 1990, and 2000 U.S. Censuses[a]

Arrival Cohort	Data Sets			
	1990 + 2000		1980 + 1990 + 2000	
1995-2000	0.370	0.379	0.197	0.217
	(4.12)	(4.22)	(2.49)	(2.75)
1990-1994	0.303	0.333	0.142	0.177
	(3.32)	(3.66)	(1.83)	(2.29)
1985-1989	0.223	0.248	0.079	0.102
	(2.47)	(2.76)	(1.03)	(1.34)
1980-1984	0.255	0.298	0.115	0.148
	(2.79)	(3.29)	(1.44)	(1.85)
1975-1979	0.232	0.283	0.085	0.099
	(2.50)	(3.10)	(1.01)	(1.17)
1970-1974	0.218	0.272	0.115	0.130
	(2.31)	(2.93)	(1.24)	(1.40)
1965-1969	0.227	0.278	0.135	0.142
	(2.41)	(2.99)	(1.32)	(1.39)
1960-1964	0.206	0.250	0.111	0.103
	(2.16)	(2.65)	(0.98)	(0.91)
1950-1959	0.191	0.215	0.132	0.096
	(1.97)	(2.23)	(1.01)	(0.74)
Before 1950	0.248	0.211	0.214	0.097
	(2.37)	(2.04)	(1.26)	(0.58)
Years Since Migration	0.003	-0.003	0.001	-0.003
(YSM)	(1.18)	(2.72)	(0.23)	(1.13)
$YSM^2/100$	-0.012	b	-0.014	b
	(2.87)		(4.71)	
R^2	0.3742	0.3742	0.4178	0.4177
Sample Size	295.598	295.598	403.000	403.000

Notes: [a] Absolute value of heteroskedasticity-consistent t-statistics in parentheses.
[b] Variable not entered.
The estimating equation also holds constant educational attainment, labor market experience and its square, log of weeks worked, whether currently married (spouse present), whether the respondent lives in the South or a rural (1980, 1990) or non-metropolitan (2000) area, proficiency in English if a language other than English is spoken at home, and country of origin dichotomous variables, with the native born as the country benchmark.
Source: U.S. Censuses of Population: 1980 1% PUMS; 1990 5% PUMS; 2000 5% PUMS.

We estimated two models: the first is based on a pooling of the data for 1990 and 2000, and the second is based on a pooling of the data for 1980, 1990, and 2000. McDonald and Worswick (1998) have shown that the estimates of (positive) assimilation and cohort differences using a small number of cross-sectional surveys are sensitive to the choice of survey years. In this regard, the weak negative assimilation effect found using the 1980 Census data (see Table 7.3) and the small number of immigrant cohorts (six) distinguished in that data set suggest, a priori, that the findings from analyses that also cover 1980 will be weaker than when the 1980 data are not used. We have estimated both a general specification of immigrant assimilation based on a quadratic in years since migration and a model with years since migration in linear form. Notably, we have not imposed sample inclusions, which are sometimes used to mimic a synthetic cohort (e.g., restrict the analysis to 25 to 44-year-olds in 1980, 35 to 54-year-olds in 1990, and 45 to 64-year-olds in 2000), in this analysis. The sample used is simply a pooled version of the samples used in the separated analyses of the 1980, 1990, and 2000 data earlier in the chapter. Table 7.10 lists the relevant information from this cohort approach.

The results in Table 7.10 present consistent evidence that immigrants in the 1995–2000 cohort have higher earnings relative to the native born than the earlier arrival cohorts, although the advantage is not great. From the analysis based only on the 1990 and 2000 Census data, the variations in earnings by arrival cohort are modest: the smallest earnings effects relative to the native born are associated with the 1950–59 arrival cohort.[21] All other arrival cohorts are associated with positive earnings effects compared to the native born of between 0.21 and 0.37. The analysis based on the 1980, 1990, and 2000 Census data also indicates that the earlier arrival cohorts have a smaller earnings advantage over the native born than the more recent arrival cohorts. In other words, the unmeasured dimensions of immigrant quality have increased over time compared to the native born.

In the models in which years since migration is entered as a quadratic, the squared term is statistically significant whereas the linear term is not. In the simpler specification with only a linear years-since-migration variable, this is negative and statistically significant in the analyses based on the 1990 and 2000 data, and negative but statistically insignificant when the 1980 data are also used. The estimated coefficient is −0.003 in each instance. This compares with values of between −0.003 and −0.007 in the cross-sectional analyses reported earlier in the chapter. In other words, adjustment for differences in the quality of immigrant cohorts, in a situation in which there is an apparent increase in unobserved dimensions of immigrant quality over time, results in a weaker assimilation effect. And yet, the negative assimilation effect remains in the data, particularly when the more recent censuses that appear to be characterized by more pronounced negative assimilation (see Table 7.3) are analyzed.[22]

7.4. Summary and Conclusion

The international migration literature has been dominated to date by empirical testing of the immigrant assimilation hypothesis. The main testable implication of this hypothesis is that immigrant earnings – and other labor market and economic outcomes – will improve with duration of residence in the destination country. Evidence consistent with this hypothesis has been found for all the major immigrant-receiving countries, time periods, and data sets that have been examined.

In this chapter, we have addressed whether such positive assimilation occurs if skills are highly transferable internationally. We hypothesized that in cases in which countries are of approximately equal economic standing and immigrants' skills are highly transferable, international migration among these countries will typically occur when the individual experiences a favorable draw from the distribution of wage offers in the potential destination relative to the wage available in the country of origin and there will be little or no postmigration investment in destination-specific human capital. A relatively high wage offer that attracts the immigrant, particularly if it is a high random wage, need not persist indefinitely. With the passage of time, a "regression to the mean" would be expected, which will be reflected empirically by a negative relationship between earnings and duration of residence in the destination. This "negative" assimilation is not due to a deterioration of skills (quantity of human capital) but due to a relative decline in the wage rate (price).

Our analysis of the earnings of adult, foreign-born men from the English-Speaking Developed Countries (ESDC) in the 1980, 1990, and 2000 U.S. Censuses reveals strong support for the negative assimilation hypothesis. It also indicates that this "negative" assimilation has strengthened over time. An examination of immigrant earnings relative to the earnings of the native born, using both a standard cross-section approach and a cohort model, also showed strong support for the negative assimilation hypothesis. Note that the negative assimilation found among immigrants to the United States born in the other English-Speaking Developed Countries occurs in the same census data in which positive assimilation (earnings increasing with duration) is found for immigrants born in other countries.

Statistical testing rejects the hypothesis that the negative assimilation effect is due to a rise over time in the cohort quality of the ESDC immigrants. For the findings for immigrants from the ESDC (negative assimilation) and for immigrants from other countries (positive assimilation) to be consistent with selective return migration, the return migrants would need to be favorably selected among the former but adversely selected among the latter immigrants. This differential selectivity seems implausible.

The reporting of analyses for immigrants from the other ESDC for Australia (2001 Census) and for Nordic immigrants in Sweden also reveals a relative decline in earnings with duration of residence, whereas the earnings of other immigrants in these countries increase with duration. This is consistent with the negative assimilation hypothesis developed in this chapter.

Whether immigrant earnings assimilation is positive or negative depends on the degree of the international transferability of skills, the extent of postmigration investment in human capital, and the rate of return on this investment.

Negative, rather than positive, assimilation is the pattern that characterizes the earnings-duration of residence relationship among immigrants from the English-speaking developed countries in the United States, Australia, and among Nordic immigrants in Sweden. as with Chiswick's (1978d; 1979) model of three decades ago, we hope future research for other countries, data sets, and time periods will test whether this is a universal finding for immigrants from countries of similar economic standing and very high skill transferability to that of the destination country.

Appendix
Description of Variables for Analysis for the United States

Data Source: 2000 Census of Population of the United States, Public use Microdata Sample (PUMS), 5% sample; 1990 Census PUMS 5% sample; and 1980 Census 1% sample.

Definition of Population: Foreign-born and native-born men aged 25 to 64. The foreign born are limited to those born in Canada, the United Kingdom (and its constituent units), Ireland, Australia, and New Zealand. Only residents of the 50 states and the District of Columbia are considered.

Dependent variable

Earnings (LNEARN): The natural logarithm of earnings in the year prior to the census year for those reporting that they worked in that year. Earnings are the sum of wage and salary and self-employment earnings. Values less than 100, including zero and negative values, are assigned the value 100.

Independent variables

Years of Education (EDUC): This variable records the total years of full-time equivalent education. This has been constructed from the census data on educational attainment by assigning the following values to the census categories: completed less than fifth grade (two years); completed fifth or sixth grade (5.5); completed seventh or eighth grade (7.5); completed ninth grade (9); completed tenth grade (10); completed eleventh grade (11); completed twelfth grade or high school (12); attended college for less than one year (12.5); attended college for more than one year or completed college (14); bachelor's degree (16); master's degree (17.5); professional degree (18.5); doctorate (20).

Potential Experience: This is the individual's age minus years of education minus six.

Years since Migration (YSM): This is computed from the year the foreign-born person came to the United States to stay. For the 1980 and 1990 Censuses, the midpoint of the period of arrival intervals are used.

Log of Weeks Worked: This is the natural logarithm of the number of weeks the person worked in the year prior to the census year (e.g., 1999 for the 2000 Census, and so on).

Marital Status (MARRIED): This is a dichotomous variable that distinguishes individuals who are married, spouse present (equal to 1) from all other marital states.

English Proficiency: Two dichotomous variables are used to summarize the individual's proficiency in spoken English. The first is for those who speak a language other than English at home and speak English very well or well. The second is for those who speak a language other than English at home and speak English not well or not at all. The reference group is those who speak only English at home.

Country of Origin: Separate dichotomous variables for persons born in Canada, the United Kingdom (U.K.) (and its constituent units), Ireland, and Australia/New Zealand. French Canadians are distinguished from other Canadians by whether they report speaking French at home. Because of sample sizes and the similarities of their origins, Australians and New Zealanders are combined.

Location: The size-of-place location variables record residence in a rural area (1980 and 1990 Censuses) and a non-metropolitan area (2000 Census). The southern states (SOUTH) are: Alabama, Arkansas, Delaware, District of Columbia, Florida, Georgia, Kentucky, Louisiana, Maryland, Mississippi, Missouri, North Carolina, Oklahoma, South Carolina, Tennessee, Texas, Virginia, West Virginia.

Table A7.1

Means and Standard Deviations of Variables in Immigrant Earnings Function, 25 to 64-Year-Old Male Immigrants from English-speaking Developed Countries, 1980, 1990, and 2000 U.S. Censuses

Variable	1980	1990	2000
Log Earnings	9.731	10.313	10.725
	(0.97)	(1.03)	(1.02)
Educational Attainment	13.644	14.276	14.866
	(3.60)	(2.94)	(2.70)
Experience (EXP)	25.785	22.327	23.115
	(12.83)	(11.69)	(10.88)
Years Since Migration (YSM)	22.049	21.575	20.480
	(12.63)	(13.87)	(14.71)
Log Weeks Worked	3.827	3.818	3.825
	(0.38)	(0.40)	(0.39)
Married	0.809	0.711	0.677
	(0.39)	(0.45)	(0.47)
South	0.162	0.217	0.258
	(0.37)	(0.41)	(0.44)
Rural[a]	0.074	0.140	0.015
	(0.26)	(0.35)	(0.12)
English Very Well/Well	0.116	0.116	0.134
	(0.32)	(0.32)	(0.34)
English Not Well/Not at All	0.006	0.006	0.007
	(0.08)	(0.08)	(0.09)
United Kingdom	0.364	0.415	0.413
	(0.48)	(0.49)	(0.49)
Ireland	0.105	0.106	0.095
	(0.31)	(0.31)	(0.29)
Canada	0.498	0.434	0.436
	(0.50)	(0.50)	(0.50)
Australia & N.Z.	0.032	0.045	0.057
	(0.18)	(0.21)	(0.23)
Sample Size	3,480	18,046	21,777

Notes: [a] Definition of variable changes appreciably across data sets.
Source: U.S. Censuses of Population: 1980 1% PUMS; 1990 5% PUMS; 2000 5% PUMS.

Table A7.2

Means and Standard Deviations of Variables in Immigrant Adjustment Earnings Function, 25 to 64-Year-Old Male Immigrants from the United Kingdom, 1980, 1990, and 2000 U.S. Censuses

Variable	1980	1990	2000
Log Earnings	9.796	10.377	10.776
	(0.93)	(1.01)	(1.03)
Educational Attainment	14.485	14.747	15.181
	(3.19)	(2.72)	(2.54)
Experience (EXP)	23.973	21.802	23.220
	(12.43)	(11.25)	(10.72)
Years Since Migration (YSM)	19.583	19.322	19.549
	(12.68)	(13.35)	(13.81)
Log Weeks Worked	3.835	3.828	3.828
	(0.38)	(0.39)	(0.39)
Married	0.804	0.714	0.683
	(0.40)	(0.45)	(0.47)
South	0.195	0.248	0.291
	(0.40)	(0.43)	(0.45)
Rural[a]	0.068	0.130	0.011
	(0.25)	(0.34)	(0.10)
English Very Well/Well	0.047	0.064	0.088
	(0.21)	(0.25)	(0.28)
English Not Well/Not at All	0.002	0.003	0.006
	(0.05)	(0.05)	(0.08)
Sample Size	1.268	7.439	8.917

Note: [a] Definition of variable changes appreciably across data sets.
Source: 1980 Census 1% PUMS; 1990 Census 5% PUMS; 2000 Census 5% PUMS.

Table A7.3

Means and Standard Deviations of Variables in Immigrant Adjustment Earnings Function, 25 to 64-Year-Old Male Immigrants from Ireland, 1980, 1990, and 2000 U.S. Censuses

Variable	1980	1990	2000
Log Earnings	9.677	10.278	10.600
	(0.84)	(0.88)	(0.92)
Educational Attainment	12.568	13.233	13.899
	(3.74)	(3.02)	(2.71)
Experience (EXP)	28.311	25.096	23.145
	11.10)	(12.60)	(11.85)
Years Since Migration (YSM)	23.270	22.029	18.982
	10.22)	(14.30)	(13.80)
Log Weeks Worked	3.846	3.816	3.810
	(0.38)	(0.38)	(0.43)
Married	0.809	0.715	0.621
	(0.39)	(0.45)	(0.49)
South	0.076	0.113	0.148
	(0.27)	(0.32)	(0.36)
Rural[a]	0.038	0.080	0.007
	(0.19)	(0.27)	(0.08)
English Very Well/Well	0.093	0.107	0.129
	(0.29)	(0.31)	(0.34)
English Not Well/Not at All	0.000	0.007	0.009
	(0.00)	(0.08)	(0.09)
Sample Size	367	1,857	2,029

Note: [a] U.S. Censuses of Population: 1980 1% PUMS; 1990 5% PUMS; 2000 5% PUMS.
Source: U.S. Censuses of Population: 1980 1% PUMS; 1990 5% PUMS; 2000 5% PUMS.

Table A7.4

Means and Standard Deviations of Variables in Immigrant Adjustment Earnings Function, 25 to 64-Year-Old Male Immigrants from Canada, 1980, 1990, and 2000 U.S. Censuses

Variable	1980	1990	2000
Log Earnings	9.699	10.264	10.699
	(1.01)	(1.05)	(1.03)
Educational Attainment	13.138	13.987	14.729
	(3.68)	(2.99)	(2.77)
Experience (EXP)	27.172	22.606	23.334
	(13.16)	(11.81)	(10.88)
Years Since Migration (YSM)	24.252	24.444	22.447
	(12.44)	(13.71)	(15.64)
Log Weeks Worked	3.815	3.811	3.828
	(0.40)	(0.40)	(0.39)
Married	0.821	0.716	0.685
	(0.38)	(0.45)	(0.46)
South	0.152	0.212	0.254
	(0.36)	(0.41)	(0.44)
Rural[a]	0.086	0.169	0.021
	(0.28)	(0.37)	(0.14)
English Very Well/Well	0.174	0.168	0.185
	(0.38)	(0.37)	(0.39)
English Not Well/Not at All	0.010	0.009	0.009
	(0.10)	(0.09)	(0.09)
Sample Size	1,733	7,956	9,581

Note: [a] Definition of variable changes appreciably across data sets.
Source: 1980 1% PUMS; 1990 Census 5% PUMS; 2000 Census 5% PUMS.

Table A7.5

Means and Standard Deviations of Variables in Immigrant Adjustment Earnings Function, 25 to 64-Year-Old Male Immigrants from Australia or New Zealand, 1980, 1990, and 2000 U.S. Censuses

Variable	1980	1990	2000
Log Earnings	9.663	10.265	10.770
	(0.94)	(1.29)	(1.08)
Educational Attainment	15.496	15.188	15.233
	(3.81)	(3.00)	(2.79)
Experience (EXP)	16.563	17.950	20.613
	(10.73)	(10.37)	(10.09)
Years Since Migration (YSM)	11.895	13.555	14.622
	(12.20)	(12.05)	(12.49)
Log Weeks Worked	3.843	3.799	3.820
	(0.28)	(0.45)	(0.41)
Married	0.688	0.637	0.664
	(0.47)	(0.48)	(0.47)
South	0.214	0.211	0.230
	(0.41)	(0.41)	(0.42)
Rural[a]	0.063	0.103	0.007
	(0.24)	(0.30)	(0.08)
English Very Well/Well	0.080	0.110	0.090
	(0.27)	(0.31)	(0.29)
English Not Well/Not at All	0.000	0.004	0.005
	(0.00)	(0.06)	(0.07)
Sample Size	112	794	1,250

Note: [a] Definition of variable changes appreciably across data sets.

Source: U.S. Censuses of Population: 1980 1% PUMS; 1990 5% PUMS; 2000 5% PUMS.

Part III
Ethnic Networks and Neighborhoods

8

The Self-Employment Experience of Immigrants

One of the features of immigration economics that has kept my interest alive over the years is the fact that there are many applications of the basic economic insights and that these applications address very different and interesting questions. This chapter focuses on one such application – the self-employment of immigrants. In retrospect, this paper was my first attempt at trying to find a mechanism through which the economy benefits from immigration. I sensed that the entrepreneurial activities of immigrants could, in fact, play a substantial role in the economic growth of receiving countries, so that it was important to document the extent and the trends in immigrant self-employment.

An interesting side question is that the incentives for immigrant entrepreneurship are likely to depend crucially on the surrounding characteristics of the neighborhoods where the immigrants settle. Although the implications of this fact are not yet well understood, mainly because the geographic settlement of immigrants is endogenous and it has been difficult to design research strategies that convincingly control for the endogeneity, it is evident that immigrant entrepreneurs have incentives both to employ and to cater to the consumption needs of their ethnic compatriots. These incentives create opportunities and costs for the immigrant population.

George J. Borjas (2015)

The original version of this chapter was published as: Borjas, G.J. (1986). The Self-Employment Experience of Immigrants, in: The Journal of Human Resources, 21(4): 485–506. © 1986 by University of Wisconsin Press. The research for this paper was supported by grants from the Rockefeller Foundation and the Department of Health and Human Services.

8.1. Introduction

The fate of immigrants in the labor market has been studied intensively in the last decade. Generally this literature has demonstrated that earlier waves of immigrants have higher earnings than do more recent waves and that the earnings of immigrants who have been in the U.S. for 10 to 15 years (or longer) exceed the earnings of the native born.[1] Recent work by Borjas (1985) questions the validity of the frequent inference from these cross-section studies that immigrants "assimilate" rapidly into the U.S. labor market. In fact, by following immigrant cohorts over a decade Borjas shows that the cross-section studies confound secular changes in cohort quality with the assimilation process and that most of the earnings growth captured by cross-section regressions is due to a sizable decline in the quality of immigrants admitted to the United States in the post-World War II period.

Despite the important insights these studies provide regarding immigrants in the labor market, a potentially significant aspect of this issue remains unexplored. In particular, it is not uncommon in the sociological literature to assert that a major channel for immigrant assimilation has been the ample availability of self-employment opportunities for immigrants (see, for example, Bonacich and Modell 1980, and Cummings 1980). These studies argue that many immigrants begin their climb up the ladder of economic success by becoming self-employed and catering to customers from the "old country," i.e., consumers who have similar national backgrounds and who demand products that give immigrants a comparative advantage in the production process (due perhaps to common language or to the familiarity with ethnic preferences). Since all studies in the earnings determination literature ignore the self-employment option and/or explicitly focus on the earnings of salaried workers, these studies may give an incomplete picture of how immigrants assimilate into the labor market.

It must be noted, however, that the immigration literature is not alone in its disinterest in self-employment among labor market participants. In fact, the related questions of who the self-employed are and how they do in the labor market have received only the most tangential attention in labor economics.[2] This disinterest could be justified if self-employment was a numerically unimportant component of the labor market. The summary statistics in Table 8.1, however, should quickly dispel this notion. This table presents the self-employment propensities and incomes observed in the 1980 Census for men aged 18–64 in each of 12 major racial/ethnic/nativity groups. Among white male labor force participants, the probability of self-employment is 11.7 percent for the native born and 16.5 percent for the foreign born. These probabilities remain above the 10 percent level for both Asian and Cuban immigrants and fall to about 8 percent for "other Hispanics." The self-employment probabilities are lowest (4 to 5 percent), among both the native and foreign born, in the black and Mexican samples. Table 8.1 also shows differentials by nativity status and ethnic groups in the annual incomes received by self-employed and salaried workers. These statistics indicate that self-employed workers have higher annual incomes than salaried workers (although some of these differences may be due to returns on the physical capital owned by self-employed workers).

Table 8.1

Self-Employment Rates and Incomes

Group	Self-Employment Probability	Mean Annual Income of Salaried Workers	Mean Annual Income of Self-Employed Workers
White			
Immigrant	.165	19594.7	24707.7
Native-born	.117	18014.2	23995.4
Black			
Immigrant	.053	12192.7	16469.9
Native-born	.037	12756.7	15036.8
Asian			
Immigrant	.126	16350.3	25454.5
Native-born	.121	17613.4	24149.6
Mexican			
Immigrant	.042	10158.8	13981.8
Native-born	.056	12932.2	17189.2
Cuban			
Immigrant	.156	14090.2	20670.3
Native-born	.109	13762.7	21249.1
Other Hispanic			
Immigrant	.080	12382.4	22598.6
Native-born	.083	14867.5	21338.9

Source: 1980 U.S. Census.

The fact that more immigrants are self-employed raises the question of what these individuals do in the labor market. Table 8.2 presents the industrial distributions of the native and foreign born by self-employment status. These statistics show that self-employed immigrant workers are significantly more likely to be in a "retail-trade" job than native-born self-employed workers: over 27 percent of self-employed immigrants are in this industry compared to 17 percent of the native-born self-employed population. Since the retail trade industry contains such types of firms as "variety stores," "grocery stores," and "eating and drinking places," Table 8.2 provides some support for the hypothesis that many immigrants assimilate into the U.S. labor market by opening small shops and catering to specialized consumer groups.

Table 8.2
Industrial Distribution by Self-Employment Status

Percent Employed in Industry:	Native Born		Immigrants	
	Salaried	Self-Employed	Salaried	Self-Employed
Agriculture	1.2	9.1	3.9	5.9
Mining	1.2	.5	.6	.1
Construction	9.5	17.6	8.6	13.5
Manufacturing	32	6.8	34.6	9.8
Transportation	11	4.7	7.0	3.6
Wholesale trade	6.0	6.0	5.1	5.2
Retail trade	11.0	17.2	13.1	27.6
Finance	4.6	7.2	4.7	3.9
Business services	4.5	10.6	5.0	9.2
Personal services	1.2	3.5	2.5	5.5
Entertainment	.9	1.2	1.2	1.1
Professional services	10.3	15.9	10.8	14.8
Public administration	6.4	.0	2.9	.0

Source: 1980 U.S. Census.

The statistics in Tables 8.1 and 8.2, therefore, show that self-employment is a significant activity among immigrant (and native-born) men in the labor market and that it deserves careful study. This chapter provides an initial attempt at documenting the differences in self-employment propensities between the native born and the foreign born and at analyzing the impact of assimilation and changes in cohort quality on the self-employment experience of the immigrant population. Section 8.2 of the chapter presents the framework that will guide the empirical analysis. Section 8.3 analyzes the self-employment propensities of immigrants and native-born workers using the 1970 and 1980 U.S. Censuses, while Section 8.4 shows that the "enclave" effect is a major factor in the creation of a gap in self-employment propensities between the foreign born and the native born. Section 8.5 summarizes the results of the study.

8.2. Framework

In deciding whether or not to become self-employed, individual i compares the market wage he would earn as a salaried worker, w_i, with the expected net income from self-employment, y_i. Define the index function:

(1) $$I_i = y_i - w_i = X_i\pi + v_i,$$

where X_i is the vector of observable socioeconomic characteristics which affects y_i and/or w_i. If I_i is positive the immigrant becomes self-employed and is a salaried worker otherwise. The probability of self-employment is then given by:

(2) $$P_i = Pr[I_i > 0] = Pr[v_i > -X_i\pi],$$

and the parameter vector π can be estimated (up to a factor of proportionality) once the stochastic nature of the disturbance v_i is specified.

Little is known about the specification of the variables in the vector X_i in Equation (2). It is reasonable to expect, however, that the standard socioeconomic characteristics of education, age, marital status, etc., which play a major role in the determination of salaries will also play a role in the determination of self-employment incomes, and hence on the self-employment propensity. Individuals who are self-employed differ from salaried workers in two important respects: (1) they have a financial investment in the firm; and (2) they will bear more risk than a salaried worker. Clearly an individual needs time and some skill to acquire the necessary resources to open a business. Thus it would not be surprising if the self-employment propensity was positively correlated with age. In addition, to the extent that education increases the types of skills necessary for an individual to assess the extent of the market and the kinds of goods customers demand, it seems likely that education and self-employment rates would also be positively related. Note, however, that these predictions implicitly assume that marginal increases in both education and age affect self-employment incomes by more than they affect the individual's salaried alternatives.

Self-employed workers risk the possibility that their employees will shirk on the job. Married self-employed persons have a simple way of diminishing this type of risk: hire their spouses. This allocation of labor within the family is optimal since both self-employed workers will have identical incentives – the maximization of family income or self-employment profits – and the shirking problem is thus solved. Hence we would expect that self-employment propensities are greater for married persons than for single persons.

As these examples illustrate, interesting economic hypotheses about the relationship between self-employment incomes (and probabilities) and standard socioeconomic characteristics can easily be derived from basic economic principles. Although the derivation of a complete theory of self-employment is beyond the scope of this chapter, these examples should illustrate that important insights can be obtained from further research along these lines.

Our main interest, of course, is on the determination of self-employment rates for immigrants, and how this process differs from the determination of self-employment rates for native-born men. One key variable which clearly plays a role in determining self-employment rates for immigrants is the number of years that have elapsed since immigration, t_i. Since self-employment requires a relatively large financial investment, it is unlikely that recently arrived immigrants have the financial capability to start a firm soon after immigration. Hence self-employment rates and t_i will be positively correlated. In other words, as immigrants "assimilate" they are also more likely to become self-employed. It is well known, however, that a single cross-section regression of Equation (2) will not provide estimates of this assimilation effect unless it is also assumed that the "quality" of immigrant cohorts has remained stationary over the sample period. The evidence in Borjas (1985), however, has shown that the stationarity assumption is, in fact, invalid in terms of the market wage rate. In particular, the quality of immigrants admitted to the U.S. has declined in the sense that more recent immigrants have lower wage rates than earlier immigrants had at comparable stages of the assimilation experience. Thus cross-section estimates of the effect of t_i on the self-employment probability confound the true assimilation impact with quality differentials among immigrant cohorts.[3]

To derive a general framework that allows the identification of these separate effects, consider the group of immigrants aged 18 to 54 in 1970. Using the 1970 Census, it is convenient to partition this group into four cohorts: arrivals in 1965–69, arrivals in 1960–64, arrivals in 1950–59, and immigrants who arrived prior to 1950. Consider next the group of immigrants aged 28 to 64 in the 1980 Census. The 1980 Census data allows the partitioning of this group of immigrants into six cohorts: arrivals in 1975–79, arrivals in 1970–74, arrivals in 1965–69, arrivals in 1960–64, arrivals in 1950–59, and immigrants who arrived prior to 1950. Note that the last four cohorts defined in the 1980 group exactly match the definitions of the cohorts from the 1970 Census.[4] Given these data, and assuming that the disturbance v_i

follows a logistic distribution, two cross-sectional regressions can be estimated by maximum likelihood:

$$(3) \qquad \ln\!\left(\frac{P_{70}}{1 - P_{70}}\right) = X\gamma_{70} + \alpha_{65}D_{65} + \alpha_{60}D_{60} + \alpha_{50}D_{50} + \alpha_{40}D_{40} + \eta_{70},$$

$$(4) \qquad \ln\!\left(\frac{P_{80}}{1 - P_{80}}\right) = X\gamma_{80} + \beta_{75}D_{75} + \beta_{70}D_{70} + \beta_{65}D_{65} + \beta_{60}D_{60} \\ + \beta_{50}D_{50} + \beta_{40}D_{40} + \eta_{80},$$

where P_t is the probability of self-employment in census year t, X is a vector of socioeconomic characteristics, and the dummy variables indexing years-since-immigration/cohort are defined by: $D_{75} = 1$ if immigrated between 1975 and 1979; $D_{70} = 1$ if immigrated between 1970 and 1974; $D_{65} = 1$ if immigrated between 1965 and 1969; $D_{60} = 1$ if immigrated between 1960 and 1964; $D_{50} = 1$ if immigrated between 1950 and 1959; and $D_{40} = 1$ if immigrated prior to 1950. By definition, the vector X in (3) and (4) does not contain a constant term.

Consider cohort k, where $D_k = 1(k = 40, 50, 60, 65)$. Let $\overline{X}$ give the mean values of the socioeconomic characteristics for the immigrant group as of 1980. Define:

$$(5) \qquad \hat{P}_{70,k} = \left\{1 + \exp\left[-(\overline{X}\hat{\gamma}_{70} + \hat{\alpha}_k)\right]\right\}^{-1},$$

$$(6) \qquad \hat{P}_{80,k} = \left\{1 + \exp\left[-(\overline{X}\hat{\gamma}_{80} + \hat{\beta}_k)\right]\right\}^{-1},$$

$$(7) \qquad \hat{P}_{80,k+10} = \left\{1 + \exp\left[-(\overline{X}\hat{\gamma}_{80} + \hat{\beta}_{k+10})\right]\right\}^{-1},$$

Equations (5) and (6) give the predicted probability of self-employment (evaluated at $\overline{X}$) for the representative member of cohort k in 1970 and 1980, respectively. Equation (7) gives the predicted self-employment probability in 1980 for the cohort who arrived ten years after cohort k. Note that the comparison of cohort k in 1970 and cohort $k + 10$ in 1980 holds constant the number of years since immigration across censuses.

Using the definitions in (5)-(7), the 1980 regression can be used to estimate the cross-section change in the probability of self-employment over a ten year period (net of aging). The cross-section change in the probability is, of course, given by $\hat{P}_{80,k} - \hat{P}_{80,k+10}$. Note, however, that this term can be rewritten as:

(8)
$$\hat{P}_{80,k} - \hat{P}_{80,k+10} = (\hat{P}_{80,k} - \hat{P}_{70,k}) + (\hat{P}_{70,k} - \hat{P}_{80,k+10}).$$

Equation (8) decomposes the cross-section change in the self-employment probability into two parts. The first term in (8) given the change in the probability experienced by cohort k over the 1970–80 decade, and will be called the "within-cohort" change in the self-employment probability. It is worth stressing that this within-cohort change measures the true impact of the assimilation processs on self-employment propensities. The second term in (8) estimates the difference in which occurred over the decade for immigrants with a given number of years since immigration. Thus it compares different cohorts at the same point of their U.S. life cycle and will be called the "across-cohort" change in self-employment propensities. If, for example, the quality decline experienced by immigrant cohorts has affected mainly the level of market earnings, the "across-cohort" effect would be negative since more recent cohorts would find self-employment more profitable than earlier cohorts found it at comparable stages of the assimilation experience. The existence of quality differences among immigrant cohorts, therefore, implies that the cross-section regression provides a biased measure of the impact of assimilation on self-employment propensities.

It should be noted, however, that the within-cohort change defined in Equation (8) can also be a biased measure of the impact of assimilation if aggregate labor market conditions changed sufficiently between 1970 and 1980. For instance, if economic changes over the decade led to a relative decline in the earnings of salaried workers, the probability of self-employment will have experienced a secular increase during the period. This aggregate shift in the probability will bias upwards the within-cohort change and, due to the decomposition in (8), will impart a downward bias on the across-cohort change. One possible solution to this problem is simply to analyze the behavior of the self-employment probability of immigrants *net* of the changes which occurred in the native-born population. Suppose the logit equations determining self-employment propensities for the native born are given by:

(9)
$$\ln\left(\frac{P_{70}}{1 - P_{70}}\right) = X\delta_{70} + \alpha_n + u_{70},$$

(10)
$$\ln\left(\frac{P_{80}}{1 - P_{80}}\right) = X\delta_{80} + \beta_n + u_{80},$$

where the subscript "n" indicates native-born status. Define the self-employment probability of a native-born worker statistically similar to the average immigrant by:

$$\text{(11)} \qquad \hat{P}_{70,n} = \left\{ 1 + \exp\left[-(\overline{X}\hat{\delta}_{70} + \hat{\alpha}_n) \right] \right\}^{-1}.$$

$$\text{(12)} \qquad \hat{P}_{80,n} = \left\{ 1 + \exp\left[-(\overline{X}\hat{\delta}_{80} + \hat{\beta}_n) \right] \right\}^{-1}.$$

The decomposition of the cross-section change in the probability of self-employment net of the secular changes occurring in the native-born population can be written as:

$$\text{(13)} \qquad \hat{P}_{80,k} - \hat{P}_{80,k+10} = \left[(\hat{P}_{80,k} - \hat{P}_{70,k}) - (\hat{P}_{80,n} - \hat{P}_{70,n}) \right]$$
$$+ \left[(\hat{P}_{70,k} - \hat{P}_{80,k+10}) - (\hat{P}_{70,n} - \hat{P}_{80,n}) \right].$$

The first bracketed term in (13) gives the difference between the within-cohort change in the self-employment probability of immigrants and the change in that probability which occurred among native-born workers. Thus it gives the change in self-employment propensities experienced by a specific immigrant cohort net of the change experienced by similar native-born workers. Likewise, the second bracketed term in (13) gives the across-cohort effect net of the economy-wide changes experienced by native-born workers during the 1970–80 period.

8.3. Assimilation and Self-Employment

The data used in the analysis are drawn from the 1970 1/100 Public Use Sample from the U.S. Census (5 percent SMSA and County Group file), and the 1980 A Sample from the U.S. Census (a 5 percent random sample of the population). Due to the very large sample sizes in these data sets, random samples were drawn for some of the larger groups (e.g., white natives in both 1970 and 1980, black natives in 1980, etc.).[5]

The analysis is restricted to male persons aged 18–54 in 1970 and 28–64 in 1980. The five sample selection rules used in both censuses are: (1) the individual is not in the Armed Forces; (2) the individual does not reside in group quarters; (3) the individual is not enrolled in school; (4) the individual worked at some point during 1969 or 1979; and (5) the individual resides in an SMSA. This last restriction prevents the analysis from being biased by the prevalence of self-employment in the farm sector and by the relative absence of immigrants in rural areas. Since previous research has shown that major differences in economic status exist within the male immigrant (and native-born) labor force, the study will be conducted separately for each of six major immigrant groups: Mexican, Cuban, other Hispanic, Asian, white, and black, where the "white" and "black" immigrant samples contain the observations that are neither Hispanic nor Asian.[6] Finally, the definition of self-employment is drawn from the class of worker variables in the 1970 and 1980 Censuses. An individual is classified as self-employed if he is a self-employed worker (business not incorporated) or if he is an employee of his own corporation. Unpaid family workers are excluded from the analysis in this chapter.

Before proceeding to the decomposition suggested by Equations (8) and (13) it is useful to describe the 1980 Census data in terms of a simple cross-sectional regression. In particular, pool the native-born and foreign-born samples in the 1980 Census and estimate the logit regression:

(14) $$\ln\left(\frac{P_{80}}{1 - P_{80}}\right) = Z_i\gamma + \varepsilon_i,$$

where the vector Z_i includes both socioeconomic variables and the years-since-migration vector, and the native-born sample pooled with the immigrant samples is the immigrant's racial/ethnic counterpart in the native-born population. The maximum likelihood estimates of Equation (14) are presented in Table 8.3.

These regressions show that education has a positive (and significant) impact on self-employment rates in all the samples. This result, of course, is consistent with the hypothesis presented earlier that higher education levels increase the individual's ability to provide a service that other persons may desire, or perhaps that higher education levels increase the organizational or managerial skills of workers. Similarly, Table 8.3 shows that self-employment propensities increase with potential labor force experience. The experience coefficient is positive and significant for all racial/ethnic groups except black men. It is of interest to note that black men are also the only group for whom there is zero correlation between marital status and self-employment propensities. In general, married men have higher self-employment rates, due perhaps to the fact that family-owned businesses have an advantage over other firms in solving the shirking problem. As Table 8.3 shows, however, this effect does not exist in the black male sample. This finding probably reflects the high incidence of instability in black marriages. Finally, the regressions in Table 8.3 include a variable measuring the health status of the individual (namely, if health "limits" work). Surprisingly, it is seen that for most of the groups this variable has a *positive* impact on self-employment propensities. It thus seems that the self-employment option expands the opportunities of persons with disabilities and gives them the flexibility of mitigating the negative labor market impacts of bad health.

Table 8.3

Maximum Likelihood Logit Regressions on Probability of Self-Employment[a]

				Group		
Variable[b]	White	Black	Asian	Mexican	Cuban	Other Hispanic
CONSTANT	-3.3575	-4.3717	-4.1438	-4.6183	-3.4602	-4.3481
	(-17.51)	(-11.72)	(-31.48)	(-19.37)	(-21.54)	(-24.55)
EDUC	.0629	.0649	.0692	.0835	.0478	.1112
	(7.53)	(3.72)	(12.69)	(8.76)	(7.23)	(15.93)
EXPER	.0353	.0223	.0520	.0544	.0468	.0347
	(3.25)	(1.04)	(7.68)	(4.07)	(5.05)	(3.31)
EXPER^2	-.0004	.0000	-.0003	-.0006	-.0007	-.0003
	(-1.94)	(.00)	(-2.61)	(-2.45)	(-4.14)	(-1.59)
MAR	.1501	-.0541	.4519	.2829	.4311	.2016
	(2.08)	(-.48)	(7.92)	(3.01)	(6.50)	(3.17)
HLTH	-.0208	.5741	.2902	.2700	.0232	.1834
	(-.17)	(3.05)	(2.91)	(1.97)	(.22)	(1.60)
D40	.4194	.5914	.2117	.2707	.5809	-.0294
	(3.99)	(2.22)	(2.35)	(1.73)	(3.35)	(-.20)
D50	.2706	.8109	.1794	.2132	.4544	.1706
	(2.96)	(3.12)	(2.34)	(1.90)	(5.28)	(1.77)
D60	.3983	.6985	.2512	-.1306	.3867	.1829
	(2.89)	(2.84)	(3.25)	(-.83)	(6.60)	(2.24)
D65	.1980	-.0539	.0765	.0864	.1107	.1471
	(1.38)	(-.22)	(1.31)	(0.20)	(1.54)	(2.05)
D70	.2453	.2785	.2065	-.3678	.2211	-.1419
	(1.44)	(1.44)	(4.01)	(-2.55)	(2.59)	(-1.78)
D75	.1111	.0421	-.4101	-.4693	-.4545	-.4188
	(.70)	(.17)	(-7.34)	(-2.72)	(-2.01)	(-4.24)

Notes: [a] The asymptotic *t*-ratios are given in parentheses.
[b] Key to variables: EDUC = years of completed education; EXPER = age - Educ - 6; MAR = 1 if married, spouse present, 0 otherwise; HLTH = 1 if health limits work, 0 otherwise.

The regressions in Table 8.3 include a vector of years-since-migration dummies that are of more direct concern to the present study. The omitted variable in the vector is the variable for native-born individuals. Two important findings are evident in the table. First, self-employment probabilities are almost always larger for immigrants than for the native born. The exceptions to this result are usually found in the samples of immigrants who have resided in the U.S. fewer than five years. For immigrants who have resided in this country longer than ten years, however, Table 8.3 shows that, without exception, the probability of self-employment is at least as large for immigrants as it is for the native born. A second important finding evident in Table 8.3 is that the probability of self-employment does not increase monotonically with years-since-migration. For example, in the white sample, the logit coefficients of the years-since-migration dummies exhibit little variance (and, in fact, are insignificantly different from each other) during the 1950–75 period. Roughly speaking, therefore, Table 8.3 suggests that, in the absence of quality differences among immigrant cohorts, most of the gap in self-employment propensities between the foreign born and the native born is created within 5 to ten years after immigration. This result differs markedly from the conclusions reached in the cross-section regression on immigrant earnings where it is found that immigrant earnings are a monotonically increasing function of years-since-migration.

As Equations (8) and (13) make clear, however, the cross-section regressions in Table 8.3 say nothing about the assimilation process since they confound the true growth attributable to assimilation with quality differences among immigrant cohorts. These decompositions are presented in Table 8.4 for 18 immigrant cohorts. Two important points should be made about the derivation of the statistics in Table 8.4. First, the vector of socioeconomic characteristics, X, held constant in the logit self-employment regressions includes the variables years of completed schooling, years of labor market experience (defined by Age – Schooling – 6), years of labor market experience squared, whether health problems limit work; and whether married (spouse present). Secondly, to minimize the large number of parameters to be estimated by maximum likelihood, and due to the large number of observations, the coefficients of the socioeconomic variables (γ_{70}, γ_{80}, δ_{70}, δ_{80}) are constrained so that $\gamma_{70} = \gamma_{80} = \gamma$ and $\delta_{70} = \delta_{80} = \delta$. Thus the socioeconomic variables are allowed to have a differential impact between the native- and foreign-born samples, but this impact remained constant over the decade.[7]

The results in Table 8.4 are best understood by illustrating their derivation through an example. Consider the group of white men who arrived in 1965–69. According to the 1980 cross-sectional regression, the probability of self-employment for these men is −.0028 percentage points lower than that of similarly skilled immigrants who arrived ten years later.[8] Thus the cross-sectional regression reveals

Table 8.4

Decomposition of Changes in the Probability of Self-Employment[a]

Group/Year	Cross-Section Growth	Immigrants Only		Relative to Natives	
		Within-Cohort	Across-Cohort	Within-Cohort	Across-Cohort
White					
1965-69	-.0028	.0982	-.1010	.0806	-.0834
	(-.10)	(5.78)	(-5.55)	(6.17)	(-4.70)
1960-64	.0228	.0659	-.0431	.0483	-.0255
	(.72)	(3.05)	(-1.82)	(2.57)	(-1.09)
1950-59	.0002	.0319	-.0317	.0143	-.0141
	(.04)	(2.28)	(-.95)	(.85)	(-.23)
Black					
1965-69	-.0028	.0130	-.0158	.0179	-.0207
	(-.20)	(.64)	(-.75)	(.72)	(-.44)
1960-64	.0281	.0245	.0036	.0294	-.0013
	(1.50)	(.58)	(.11)	(.67)	(-.09)
1950-59	.0369	-.0108	.0477	.0157	.0428
	(1.89)	(-.25)	(1.27)	(.03)	(.79)
Asian					
1965-69	.0525	.1062	-.0537	.1331	-.0806
	(7.95)	(4.62)	(-3.02)	(5.64)	(-5.75)
1960-64	.0088	.1219	-.1131	.1488	-.1400
	(.83)	(3.51)	(-3.39)	(2.21)	(-1.76)
1950-59	.0046	-.0432	.0478	-.0163	.0209
	(.46)	(-1.45)	(1.70)	(-.62)	(1.03)
Mexican					
1965-69	.0247	.0453	-.0206	.0303	-.0056
	(2.66)	(2.71)	(-1.64)	(2.65)	(-1.35)
1960-64	.0094	.0263	-.0169	.0113	-.0019
	(1.09)	(1.80)	(-1.32)	(1.48)	(-.87)
1950-59	.0116	.0184	-.0068	.0034	.0082
	(1.40)	(1.41)	(-.41)	(.43)	(.61)
Cuban					
1965-69	.0551	.1037	-.0486	.0861	-.0310
	(2.34)	(4.95)	(-2.41)	(5.05)	(-2.14)
1960-64	.0336	.1110	-.0774	.0934	-.0598
	(2.48)	(5.18)	(-3.79)	(5.39)	(-3.63)
1950-59	.0308	.0898	-.0590	.0722	-.0414
	(2.43)	(2.70)	(-1.23)	(2.38)	(-.86)
Other Hispanics					
1965-69	.0396	.0614	-.0218	.0552	-.0156
	(5.13)	(3.80)	(-1.75)	(5.34)	(-2.22)
1960-64	.0261	.0261	.0000	.0199	.0062
	(3.19)	(1.45)	(.08)	(1.93)	(0.56)
1950-59	.0017	.0298	-.0281	.0236	-.0219
	(.13)	(1.57)	(-1.27)	(.21)	(-1.51)

Note: [a] The asymptotic t-ratios given in parentheses refer to the respective transformation of the logit coefficients.

little change in self-employment propensities over time. Using Equation (8), however, this quantity can be decomposed into within- and across-cohort changes in self-employment probabilities. This decomposition reveals that as of 1980 this group of immigrants actually had a self-employment probability that was 9.8 percentage points higher than in 1970. Thus the cohort experienced a significant increase in self-employment propensities. Yet, at the same time, this cohort as of 1970 had a self-employment probability 10.1 percentage points lower than the 1980 self-employment probability of men who arrived in 1975–79. Thus the secular changes in the quality mix of these immigrant cohorts have led to an increase in self-employment propensities. In fact, the across-cohort change wipes out the within-cohort change so that in the cross section it appears as if years-since-migration had no impact on the self-employment probability.

Of course, it may well be that these changes between 1970 and 1980 simply reflect economy-wide fluctuations in self-employment incomes. The decomposition in Equation (13) controls for this problem by netting out the change in the self-employment probability achieved by the native-born group. It should be noted, however, that the choice of the native-born reference group is somewhat arbitrary since the immigrant population can be compared to a number of different racial/ethnic native-born men. In this chapter, each immigrant group (except for the Cubans) is compared to its respective ethnic/racial native-born counterpart. In the Cuban case, due to the small sample size (and the even smaller number of self-employed Cuban "natives") the Cuban immigrants are compared to white native-born men.

The last two columns of Table 8.4 conduct the decomposition of the cross-section growth after netting out the change in the self-employment probabilities of the native born. In the case of the 1965–69 white immigrant cohort, the within-cohort change remains positive and significant and is approximately 8.1 percentage points. In other words, the self-employment probability of white immigrants who arrived in 1965–69 increased 8.1 percentage points *above* the increase experienced by white native-born men over the 1970 period. Similarly, the across-cohort change remains negative and significant even after netting out the white native born change so that, indeed, more recent cohorts of immigrants are more likely to opt for self-employment than earlier immigrants.

The remaining rows of Table 8.4 replicate the analysis for all other cohorts in the six immigrant groups. Perhaps the major finding obtained from these results is that there are sizable differences in the within- and across-cohort changes experienced by immigrants both within and across national groups. In general, however, the within-cohort change in the probability of self-employment is positive, while the across-cohort change is negative. For instance, in the decomposition that nets out the change in P_i for the native born, 17 out of 18 within-cohort effects are positive (and 11 of these effects have a t-ratio exceeding unity), while 14 of the across-cohort effects are negative (with 9 of these effects having t-ratios above 1.0 in absolute value). These results, therefore, are consistent with the hypothesis that as immigrants assimilate in the United States the relative gains from self-employment increase. In addition, the results in Table 8.3 also show the existence of a secular shift in the relative gains of self-employment for immigrants. In other words, more recent immigrant cohorts perceive self-employment as a relatively better employment alternative than earlier immigrant cohorts.

Thus two important substantive questions are raised by the results in Table 8.4. First, why does immigrants' assimilation process involve a switch from salaried jobs to self-employment? Second, why do more recent immigrants find self-employment a much more profitable alternative than the earlier waves of immigrants? With respect to the first question, it is clear that self-employment requires a somewhat large financial investment. The most recent immigrants are unlikely to have accumulated the financial resources needed to open a business. Thus it is not too surprising to find that, during their assimilation, immigrants switch from salaried jobs to self-employment opportunities.

The second question posed earlier is somewhat harder to address. A possible factor for the cohort effects is related to the analysis of Borjas (1985). One interpretation of his findings is that salaried opportunities for recent waves of immigrants are substantially worse than the opportunities faced by the earlier waves of foreign-born persons. This implies that the more recent waves of immigrants will find it relatively more profitable to enter self-employment than the earlier waves did (at the same point of their U.S. life cycle). This, however, raises the important question of why salaried opportunities declined more than self-employment opportunities.

A second factor which may be responsible for the cohort effects in Table 8.4 is the change in immigration policy implicit in the 1965 Immigration and Naturalization Act. This law has emphasized family reunification as the primary variable determining visa allocation among potential entrants.[9] Since self-employment opportunities increase greatly when family members can join the firm, the family reunification goal of the current law may well be playing a major role in the self-employment cohort effects. Although the results in Table 8.4 cannot conclusively prove the validity of these hypotheses, it is clear that additional research on the self-employment of immigrants should be conducted to address these important questions.

8.4. Enclaves and the Self-Employment of Immigrants

The finding (discussed in Section 8.3) that the probability of self-employment of immigrants exceeds the probability of self-employment of native-born men for practically all ethnic/racial groups indicates that immigrants have relatively higher self-employment incomes than the native born. This explanation does not really provide an understanding of *why* the nativity differences arise. The sociological literature, however, has presented extensive anecdotal evidence of how immigrants create enclaves by concentrating in specific geographic areas, and of how these enclaves create and expand opportunities for immigrants to become self-employed. These opportunities arise because immigrants from a particular national group are assumed to have a comparative advantage in serving the needs of consumers from that national group. The comparative advantage, of course, is created by informational asymmetries between the immigrants and the rest of the population – asymmetries which may include such factors as better knowledge of consumer preferences and knowledge of the language spoken by the immigrant population.

This hypothesis can easily be tested by analyzing the self-employment propensities of the three Hispanic groups (Mexicans, Cubans, and other Hispanics) studied in the previous section. Since these three groups are much more homogeneous in culture *and* language than the three other groups analyzed earlier (whites, blacks, and Asians), it is likely that enclaves of Hispanics may have opened up self-employment opportunities for Hispanic immigrants. Formally, the enclave hypothesis can be tested by estimating the regression:

$$(15) \qquad \ln\left(\frac{P}{1-P}\right) = Z\gamma + \lambda q_h + v_i,$$

where Z_i is a vector of socioeconomic characteristics, and q_h is the fraction of the SMSA's population that is Hispanic.[10] The enclave hypothesis implies that λ. is positive. In addition, if Equation (15) is estimated separately in the foreign-born and native-born samples, and if immigrants benefit more from the self-employment opportunities opened up by the enclave, one would expect that the impact of q_h on the probability of self-employment is larger in the immigrant than in the native-born sample.

Table 8.5 presents the estimated impact $d_p/dq_h = \beta p(1-p)$ for each of the six Hispanic groups under study, where the derivative is evaluated at the mean self-employment probability of each group. For purposes of comparison the table also presents the impact of q_h on the self-employment probability of non-Hispanic whites. Two important results are apparent. First, the coefficient λ is indeed positive and significant in the Hispanic samples. That is, Hispanics are more likely to be self-employed in areas which have larger Hispanic populations. Moreover, note that the impact of q_h in the non-Hispanic white samples is insignificantly different from zero; hence the results for Hispanics cannot be dismissed as reflecting some unknown area-specific effect. Second, the impact of q_h on the self-employment probability is larger for immigrants than for the native born, and this difference is significant in two of the three Hispanic samples.[11]

Table 8.5

Impact of Enclave on Self-Employment Probabilities[a]

Group	Immigrant	Native-Born	Difference
Mexican	.0869	.0344	.0525
	(6.37)	(3.33)	(2.10)
Cuban	.1975	.1009	.0966
	(5.04)	(.64)	(2.43)
Other Hispanic	.0794	.0114	.068
	(3.64)	(.65)	(2.83)
White	.1751	.1009	.0661
	(.83)	(.64)	(.38)

Note: [a] The asymptotic t-ratios are given in parentheses, and refer to the corresponding logit coefficients.

The regression coefficients reported in Table 8.5 can be used to calculate the increase in the self-employment rates of immigrants (relative to natives) due to the enclave effect. The results from this calculation are reported in Table 8.6. Consider the sample of Mexican men. The average Mexican immigrant lives in a metropolitan area that is 23.7 percent Hispanic, while the average Mexican/American lives in an SMSA that is 25.6 percent Hispanic. The regressions in Table 8.5 report the marginal increase in the self-employment probability due to changes in these proportions. The relevant calculation then shows that the enclave effect increases the self-employment rate of Mexican immigrants by 1.2 percentage points over that of Mexican native-born men. Similar calculations reported in Table 8.6 for the Cuban and other Hispanic samples show that enclave effects increase foreign-born self-employment rates by 1 to 2 percentage points over the native-born base. Hence enclave effects are not only statistically significant, but they are also numerically important.

Table 8.6

Immigrant/Native-Born Differential in Self-Employment Propensities Due to Enclave Effects

| | Fraction Hispanic in SMSA where: | | Predicted Difference in Self-Employment Probability |
	Average Immigrant Resides	Average Nonimmigrant Resides	
Mexican	.237	.256	.012
Cuban	.136	.061	.021
Other Hispanic	.165	.161	.011

These results, however, cannot really answer the fundamental question of *why* enclave effects exist. The fact that the self-employment rates of non-Hispanics whites (reported in the last row of Table 8.5) are not related to the percentage of Hispanic in the SMSA suggests that language (and/or culture) plays an important role in the creation of the enclave effect. A number of additional experiments were conducted to provide a better test of this hypothesis. These experiments included relating the self-employment rates of Asians to the percent of Asians in the SMSA, and conducting a separate analysis of the self-employment rates of immigrants from English-speaking countries. On the whole, however, these preliminary calculations were inconclusive and did not provide any additional insights into the results in Table 8.5, probably because the Asian sample is extremely heterogeneous – both in language and culture. Any future analysis of these individuals will have to segment by country of origin. Similarly, the sample of men from English-speaking countries includes men from the U.K. and Ireland, as well as men from Jamaica and India. The cultural (and racial) differences among these various samples makes it unlikely that a self-employed immigrant from an English-speaking country can be equally efficient in catering to all the groups that make up his "enclave." Future studies of this problem, therefore, will have to consider more closely the roles played by culture, race, and language in differentiating among immigrant and native-born groups.

8.5.   Summary

Self-employment represents an important component of the immigrant experience in the U.S. labor market. Its omission in earlier studies cannot be justified by the presumption that self-employed workers represent a numerically unimportant part of the immigrant labor force. In fact, among large immigrant groups self-employment rates exceed 15 percent of the labor force. This chapter begins the study of the immigrant self-employment experience by analyzing the self-employment rates of 18 immigrant cohorts using the 1970 and 1980 U.S. Census. The major findings are:

1. Assimilation has a sizable impact on self-employment probabilities. The longer the immigrant resides in the United States, the higher the probability of self-employment.

2. Recent immigrant cohorts have higher self-employment rates than earlier cohorts. These across-cohort changes may have been caused by the relative decline of opportunities faced by immigrants in the salaried sector over the last decades.

3. Immigrants are more likely to be self-employed than similarly skilled native-born workers. A major reason for this differential is that geographic enclaves of immigrants increase self-employment opportunities particularly for immigrants who share the same national background (or language) as the residents of the enclave.

The prevalence of self-employment among immigrants (and native-born workers) in the labor market suggests that much additional work is needed in this area. The analysis in this chapter makes clear that continued research of the self-employment option and of self-employment incomes is likely to greatly enhance our understanding of the immigrant assimilation process.

9

Differences in Education and Earnings Across Racial and Ethnic Groups: Tastes, Discrimination, and Investments in Child Quality

I was asked by the National Academy of Education to present a paper at a Conference on the State of Education. I had become interested in the research on tradeoffs between the quantity of children (family size) and their quality (investment per child in their human capital). I also wondered why there were sharp differences across U.S. racial and ethnic groups in education levels and labor market outcomes that seemed to persist over time and across generations. For the State of Education conference I decided to investigate whether the quantity-quality tradeoff model had implications for the persistence of group differences.

I assumed that there were two groups that for exogenous reasons differed in initial conditions in a systematic way. I stacked the deck – for one group additional children would be costly (e.g., urban residence, good job opportunities for women) while for the other group additional children would be inexpensive. Even if both groups are at the same level of utility for the first generation (i.e., on the same indifference curve for the quality-quantity tradeoffs), the different relative prices would induce families in the first group to have fewer children and invest more per child than those in the second group. Their children (generation two) would have fewer siblings and

The original version of this chapter was published as: Chiswick, B.R. (1988). Differences in Education and Earnings Across Racial and Ethnic Groups: Tastes, Discrimination, and Investments in Child Quality, in: The Quarterly Journal of Economics, 103(3): 571–97. © 1988 by the President and Fellows of Harvard College and the Massachusetts Institute of Technology. The research was financed in part by the Center for the Study of the Economy and the State, University of Chicago.

cousins, but a higher level of education and hence higher per-capita income. If the income elasticity of demand for durable "consumer goods" (e.g., cars, houses, and even children) is greater for the quality dimension than for the quantity dimension, the second-generation children as adults would in turn have fewer children and invest more per child, quite aside from the effects of the initial price differences. The result would be persistent differences across racial and ethnic groups in educational attainment and earnings.

This model was shown in the article "Differences in Education and Earnings Across Racial and Ethnic Groups" (reprinted as Chapter 9 of this volume) to be consistent with persistent group differences in education and earnings in the U.S. Moreover, the paper demonstrates that neither discrimination models nor models depending on group differences in "tastes" for investments in children's education are successful for explaining the persistence over time of these group differences in educational attainment and earnings.

Barry R. Chiswick (2015)

9.1. Introduction

Until recently, research in the United States on group differences in socioeconomic success, as measured by schooling, occupation, and earnings, was limited to the comparison of blacks and whites. This focus was understandable for two reasons. First, there was an imperative public policy concern with black–white differences and the implications of historical and contemporary discrimination against blacks. Second, since blacks are the largest and most easily identifiable minority, the available data facilitated research on a black–white dichotomy.[1] As a consequence, much of our thinking regarding group differences in schooling and in the implications of schooling for occupational attainment, earnings, fertility, and other matters is influenced by the black–white pattern (Chiswick and Chiswick 1984). Under this view racial discrimination (past or present) is assumed to be the primary cause of a variety of unfavorable outcomes, including lower levels of schooling and earnings, and a lower rate of return from schooling, for blacks than for whites.

In recent years, however, there has been a return to the turn-of-the-century interest in the multiplicity of racial and ethnic groups in the U.S. population. This interest is in part a consequence of the civil rights activities of the 1960s and 1970s that raised levels of consciousness regarding ethnicity and restored pride in ethnic identity. It is also a consequence of the increase in immigration during the past quarter century, particularly from Latin America and Asia. Data on a variety of racial and ethnic groups are now available and have been studied, with interesting and puzzling patterns emerging.

Within this broader multigroup perspective, Section 9.2 examines data on the mean levels of schooling and earnings, and rates of returns from investments in schooling, for a variety of racial and ethnic groups. Among adult native-born men, those identified as Jews, Chinese, Japanese, and foreign-parentage blacks have high levels of schooling and earnings, while native-born Filipinos, Mexican Americans, American Indians, and native-parentage blacks are far less successful than average. Rates of return are also shown to vary systematically across groups, with the former groups having higher rates than the latter.

Section 9.3 discusses these patterns within the context of a model for the supply and demand for funds for investment in schooling. This permits a test of alternative hypotheses. The evidence suggests that demand conditions vary more across groups than do supply conditions. Since demand curves are higher for those with greater ability, it is inferred that there are group differences in family investments in the "quality" of their children.

Section 9.4 follows this line of reasoning by developing a simple model for the allocation of parental resources. It is shown that if in an initial period two groups are of equal wealth but differ in the price of quantity relative to quality of children, and if these price differences persist, successive generations will differ systematically in fertility, schooling, earnings, and rates of return from schooling.

Evidence is presented in Section 9.5 to test the application of the "quantity-quality" tradeoff model to racial and ethnic groups. Family background, fertility, and female labor force participation are considered. A more favorable family background, in terms of the education and income of parents, fewer siblings with whom to compete for parental time and resources, and more parental time inputs into child care may be responsible for some groups having higher rate of return schedules and hence for their making larger investments in schooling.

Section 9.6 is a summary and conclusion that develops the policy implications of the analysis.

9.2. Multigroup Perspective on Schooling and Earnings

Table 9.1 presents data on earnings and schooling by race and ethnicity from the 1970 Census of Population for adult native-born men.[2] In addition to blacks, the Mexican Americans, Filipinos, and American Indians have lower levels of earnings and schooling than white men. On the other hand, the Chinese and Japanese have higher levels of earnings and schooling than whites, and American Jews have much higher levels of earnings and schooling than other whites.[3] Moreover, among blacks, those with foreign-born parents (primarily of West Indian origin) have a schooling level that exceeds native-parentage blacks and matches that of white men.

Rates of return from investments in schooling are higher for the four minority groups with high levels of schooling than for the less schooled minorities. The statistic in column 4 of Table 9.1 is the partial effect of schooling on earnings in a semi-logarithmic earnings function. Under some simple conditions, this partial regression coefficient is an estimate of the rate of return from schooling (see Becker and Chiswick 1966 or Mincer 1974). Although the correlation is not perfect, groups with higher levels of schooling tend to have higher rates of return. In the 1970 Census data, groups with more than 11.5 years of schooling have schooling coefficients at least equal to 6.5 percent, while groups with less than 11.5 years of schooling have coefficients that are less than 6.0 percent. The positive correlation between schooling level and the measure of the rate of return from schooling is even more striking for subgroups within the three broad racial categories – white, black, and Asian.[4]

This broader perspective on the racial and ethnic composition of the population suggests that the public policy and research questions relevant for the black–white comparison are more complex than has been realized. U.S.-born Jews, Chinese, Japanese, and foreign-parentage blacks in these age cohorts have experienced discrimination in access to higher education and in the labor market. In addition, the Japanese in the Pacific Coast states experienced the disruptions in their schooling and labor market experience arising from the World War II internment. Yet, these groups have achieved a high degree of labor market success, while other groups experiencing discrimination did not.

Much of the race and ethnic studies literature focuses on group-specific models and hypotheses, and it may be that a separate story is

Table 9.1

Earnings, Schooling, and Other Characteristics of Adult Native-born Men by Race and Ethnic Group, 1970[a]

Race and ethnic group	Earnings (1969)	Age (years)	Schooling (years)	Rate of return to schooling[b]	Sample size[c]
	(1)	(2)	(3)	(4)	(5)
White					
All	9,653	42.7	11.9	0.070 (0.0013)	33,878
Native-born parents	9,441	41.7	11.9	0.069 (0.0015)	27,512
Foreign-born parents	10,567	47.1	11.9	0.073 (0.0008)	6,366
Jewish[d]	16,176	49.2	14.0	0.080 (0.0042)	3,719
Non-Jewish[d]	10,431	47.2	11.7	0.068 (0.0010)	57,351
Mexican origin[e]	6,638	39.5	8.9	0.051 (0.0029)	5,197
Black (Urban)					
All	6,126	42.0	9.9	0.044 (0.0013)	26,413
Native-born parents	6,110	42.0	9.9	0.044 (0.0013)	26,137
Foreign-born parents	7,719	39.0	11.8	0.068 (0.0145)	276
Japanese	10,272	43.4	12.7	0.065 (0.0050)	2,063
Chinese	10,406	41.4	13.1	0.067 (0.0078)	627
Filipino	7,173	37.3	11.3	0.045 (0.0118)	335
American-Indian[f]	5,593	40.0	9.9	0.054 (0.0048)	1,894

Notes: [a] The data are for men aged 25 to 64 in 1970 who worked and had nonzero earnings in 1969. Earnings are defined as wage, salary, and self-employment income. The earnings, schooling, and age data are means. The Asian data exclude men in the Armed Forces in 1970, the Jewish/non-Jewish data exclude persons enrolled in school.

[b] Coefficient of schooling from the linear regression of the natural logarithm of earnings in 1969 on schooling, experience, experience squared, marital status dummy variable, geographic distribution, and weeks worked. Geographic distribution is urban/rural and South/non-South, except for the Asian analysis in which it is urban/rural and Hawaii/California/South/Other non-South. The standard error of the regression coefficient is in parentheses.

^c The sampling fractions are 1/1,000 for white men, 1/100 for the Mexican, Jewish/Non-Jewish, and black men, and 2/100 for Asian and American Indian men.

^d The Jewish-Non-Jewish data are for native-born men of foreign parentage (one or both parents foreign born), where Jews are defined as those reporting Yiddish, Hebrew, or Ladino as their mother tongue (language other than or in addition to English spoken in the home when the respondent was a child).

^e White men identified as of Mexican origin in the Hispanic origin question. Over 95 percent of the Mexican origin population was classified as white in the 1970 Census.

^f Excludes men living in Alaska.

Source: The data are from the U.S. Bureau of the Census (1973a), 5 percent and 15 percent questionnaires. For a discussion of the data and the regression equations, see Chiswick (1980a, Chapters 4, 6, and 7; 1982a; 1983a; 1983c).

needed for each group. An alternative approach, however, is adopted in this study. A model is developed in Section 9.4 that can explain the different patterns of success with a minimum of ad hoc reasoning.

9.3.   Testing Alternative Hypotheses

This section presents tests of alternative hypotheses as to why racial and ethnic groups differ in their levels of educational investment. The hypotheses include different "tastes" for schooling, different time preferences, the diaspora effect, discrimination, and differential investment productivity. The tests are done using a model of the investment decision based on the individual's supply and demand for funds for investment in education.

9.3.1.   *Supply and Demand for Funds for Investment*

Regardless of the race or ethnic group, a person can be thought of as making decisions on the optimal level of investment of resources, including time and out-of-pocket expenses, in schooling. The supply of investment funds relates the marginal interest cost to the level of the investment. The demand for investment funds relates the marginal rate of return to the level of the investment. Optimality for the individual occurs when the marginal interest cost of funds equals the marginal rate of return.[5]

The supply curve of investment funds is the marginal interest cost of obtaining funds for investment, including the psychic cost of self-financing investments through lower consumption (see Hirshleifer

1958).[6] It is upward rising if cheaper sources of funds are used before more expensive sources, as would occur, for example, if federally subsidized student loans were used before taking out a second mortgage on the family house. The supply curve is lower, and thus farther to the right (greater funds supplied for the same interest cost of funds), for those who have access to cheaper sources of funds. The supply curve would be lower, for example, for the more wealthy who can self-finance the investment than it would be for those who borrow funds from the capital market (Caplovitz 1963).

The demand curve for investment funds depends on the marginal rate of return on investments in schooling. It is drawn downward sloping under the assumption that beyond some point additional investments command a lower return (see Ben-Porath 1967). This arises in part because eventually schooling raises productivity in the labor market by more than it raises productivity in acquiring more schooling. The demand curve is higher the greater the rate of return on the investment, that is, the greater the benefits from schooling and the lower the cost of acquiring a year of schooling. As a result, the demand curve for funds for investment in schooling is higher for those with greater ability – either innate ability or ability created by greater home-produced human capital.

Optimal investment occurs when the marginal interest cost of funds equals the marginal rate of return on the investment. Group differences in investment in schooling may arise from differences in demand conditions, from differences in supply conditions, or from a combination of the two. If demand conditions vary more than supply conditions (e.g., demand curves $D_0 D_0$ and $D_1 D_1$ and supply curve $S_0 S_0$ in Figure 9.1), groups with higher levels of schooling would tend to have higher rates of return. If supply conditions vary more than demand conditions (e.g., demand curve $D_0 D_0$ and supply curves $S_0 S_0$ and $S_1 S_1$ in Figure 9.1), groups with greater investments would tend to have lower rates of return. Hence, an examination of group differences in schooling levels and rates of return from schooling can provide some insight on whether supply curves or demand curves vary more across race and ethnic groups.

Figure 9.1

Schematic Representation of Supply and Demand for Funds for Investment in Schooling

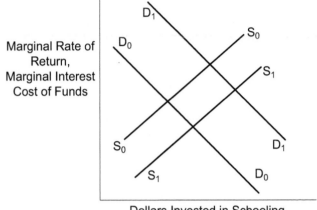

Dollars Invested in Schooling

9.3.2.   Differences in Supply Conditions

It is often said that the high level of schooling of the Chinese, Japanese, Jews, and foreign-parentage blacks arises from a greater preference or "taste" for schooling or from a higher value placed on future consumption compared with current consumption. By implication, the groups with lower levels of schooling do not have such preferences for schooling or do not place as high a current value on future outcomes.

To be other than tautological, a mechanism must be described through which these "taste" factors operate. If there is a "taste" for schooling, perhaps determined by cultural, historical, or other factors, part of the returns are in the form of consumption benefits rather than pecuniary income. Thus, even if the pecuniary benefits and costs of schooling are the same, groups for whom nonmoney consumption benefits are important will be willing to invest more funds at any given interest cost.

Similarly, groups with a lower time preference for current consumption will supply funds at a lower interest cost. Thus, these two hypotheses imply a supply of funds schedule that is farther to the right for the Chinese, Japanese, Jews, and foreign-parentage blacks. Then, if demand conditions do not vary across groups, these four groups would have the observed high levels of schooling. They would, however, also be expected to have lower rates of return from schooling. A variant of the "taste" hypothesis often applied to Jews is the so-called "diaspora" hypothesis. A population that feels insecure in its present residence, either for current or historical reasons, would prefer investments in portable and transferable assets. Portable means that the assets can be easily moved from place to place, and transferable means that the assets are nearly equally productive in all locations. To the extent that human capital is more portable and transferable than other forms of capital, a diaspora population, always fearful of another uprooting, would attach a larger implicit risk premium on nonhuman capital.[7] The result would be a greater supply of funds for human capital investment and a smaller supply of funds for less portable or less transferable investments (e.g., land or plant and equipment). While this implies a higher level of schooling, it also implies a lower rate of return on the investment in schooling.

The empirical relationship between the level of schooling and rates of return suggests that group differences in the supply curve for investment funds vary less than group differences in the demand curve.[8] The simple versions of the taste for schooling, discount rate, and diaspora hypotheses are therefore not consistent with the data.

9.3.3. Discrimination

Group differences in demand conditions may arise from discrimination in access to schooling, in the quality of schooling and in the labor market. Discrimination in the access to and quality of schooling will lower schooling levels, rates of returns from schooling, and earnings. Discrimination in the labor market will generally lower rates of return from schooling and earnings. Even if labor market discrimination is neutral with respect to skill (i.e., it results in the same percentage fall in earnings for all levels of schooling), the rate of return is lowered.[9] Discrimination in access to schooling and in the labor market is the usual explanation for the lower measured rates of return from schooling received by blacks (Smith and Welch 1986).

Although the discrimination hypothesis is consistent with the observation that schooling levels and rates of return from schooling are lower for some minority groups than for whites, it is not consistent with the observation that for other minority groups they are the same or greater than the white magnitudes.

9.3.4.   Productivity of Schooling

An alternative hypothesis considers group differences in the productivity of schooling. Conceptually, this can arise from greater efficiency in acquiring units of skill from a given amount of schooling or from being more efficient in applying these skills in the labor market.[10] It is important to emphasize that group differences in the productivity of schooling are consistent with all racial and ethnic groups having the same distribution of genetically determined ability. Rather, differences in productivity may arise from differences in out-of-school human capital formation (prior to or concurrent with schooling), and tradeoffs that influence the quality of schooling demanded by members of the group.

If group differences in the productivity of schooling vary by more than group differences in the supply of investment funds, a positive relation would appear between levels of schooling and rates of return from schooling. This approach is consistent with not only the observation that some minority groups have low levels of schooling and rates of return, but also that some others have high values for both schooling and its rate of return. Indeed, although the hypotheses discussed in this section are not mutually exclusive, the schooling-productivity hypothesis is the only one that is generally consistent with the observed pattern.

9.4.   Fertility and Child Quality: The Model

Suppose that there are two racial or ethnic groups, A and B, which do not intermarry. In Generation I the two groups are assumed to be alike in all respects, including number of individuals and level of utility. The two groups differ only in the price of quantity relative to the price of quality of children.[11] To take an extreme example, Group A is urbanized (higher cost of space, poorer job opportunities for children, better job opportunities for women), the women are educated (high value of time for child care providers), and there are no psychic or other costs associated with fertility control.[12] For Group B all of these conditions are just the opposite.

Although the two groups are equally wealthy in Generation I, Group A has a higher cost of quantity relative to quality of children than Group B. Group A couples have fewer children and invest more in each child (although perhaps less in total) than Group B.[13] Because of the complementarity of various types of human capital, greater home-produced "child quality" in Group A would be expected to raise the productivity of, and hence the rate of return from, schooling.[14] Thus, higher child quality would appear as a higher marginal rate of return (or demand) schedule in Figure 9.1. As a result, in the second generation, Group B is more numerous. However, the adult members of Group A have higher average skill levels, higher rates of return from schooling, and higher earnings.

Moreover, the same relative price effects that influenced their parents would encourage the second generation of Group A to have lower fertility than Group B and make greater investments in quality per child.[15] Thus, by the third generation each member of Group B has more siblings and cousins than those in Group A, but a smaller level of human capital, a lower return on schooling investments, and lower earnings, and so on for successive generations.

There is, however, an additional consideration. The differences in the skills and earnings between Groups A and B in the second generation imply a positive income effect on fertility. As with most "consumer durables," the income elasticity of demand for quality of children is likely to be much higher than the income elasticity of demand for quantity of children. Perhaps unlike other consumer durables, however, parents generally try to invest equally in all their children.[16] The wealth effect thus implies that the marginal cost of an extra child is greater for higher income parents (Becker and Lewis 1973). This higher price of quantity tends to reduce the number of children, offsetting part or all of the favorable effects of higher income (i.e., the pure income effect) on the number of children. To the extent that there are *fewer* children, increasing child quality is less expensive.

As a consequence of initial exogenous price differences between Group A and Group B, the quantity-quality fertility model generates group differences in fertility, skill formation, rates of return, and earnings; and these differences are transmitted from generation to generation. However, these differences need not increase indefinitely. Some of the variables that are exogenous in one generation may be endogenous over a longer period of time, such as religious practice (see, for example, Newport 1979 and Iannaccone 1988). Other factors may also be operative. For example, in the Easterlin fertility model a group's fertility is positively related to its income relative to expectations based on the income of its parents' generation. This model implies an intergenerational dampening in differences in fertility, and hence in income and schooling.

9.5. Application of the Child Quality Investment Model

The child quality investment model as applied to racial and ethnic groups suggests that fertility rates, female labor supply, and wealth in one generation are relevant variables for analyzing group outcomes in the next generation. Historical data on racial and ethnic minorities in the United States, other than blacks, are very scarce. This section pulls together data on these variables for the racial and ethnic groups considered in Table 9.1. In some instances contemporary data must be used. However, if group differences in relative prices do not vary sharply from generation to generation, contemporary patterns would be reflecting historic patterns.

9.5.1.   Group Differences in Skill Levels Across Generations

Data are not readily available by race and ethnic group on the skills, as measured by income, education, or occupational attainment, of the parents of the current adult population. If it is assumed that there are 30 years from one generation to the next, the cohorts of adults in the United States in 1940 constitute the parent generation of the native-born adult cohorts in 1970.

Educational attainment data for males from the 1940 Census of Population (Table 9.2) can be compared with the educational attainment of U.S.-born members of the same race and ethnic group in the 1970 Census (Table 9.1) to discern intergenerational patterns. As would be expected, most groups with relatively high educational attainments in 1970 had parents with higher than average educational attainment. Relative to whites, the Japanese, and even foreign-origin blacks, had "high" levels of education in 1940 and 1970. On the other hand, American Indians and native-born blacks had low levels in both periods. The relative position of Filipinos declined, while that of the Chinese showed a dramatic increase over the three decades. As will be shown below, in the United States the Chinese are a low-fertility population, while the Filipinos have high fertility rates. These fertility patterns are consistent with the changes in relative educational attainments.

Table 9.2

Median Years of Schooling for Males Age 25 and Over by Race, 1940

Race	Total	Native-born	Foreign-born
White	8.4	8.6	7.3
Black	5.3	5.3	7.6
Urban	6.5	5.5	7.7
Japanese	8.8	12.2	8.3
Chinese	5.6	6.2	5.3
Filipino	7.4	a	a
American Indian	5.7	5.7	a
All races	8.3		

Note: ª The sample size for the foreign born is too small for a comparison by nativity. Persons born in the Philippines were treated as native born in the 1940 Census tabulations.

Source: U.S. Bureau of the Census (1943a) Table 6: 34; and U.S. Bureau of the Census (1943b) Table 31: 271.

Data are not separately reported in the published volumes from the 1940 Census of Population for persons of Mexican origin.

Data from the 1930 Census of Population, however, suggest that Mexican-Americans were much less wealthy than either the Chinese or Japanese.[17]

Since there was little Asian immigration from about 1907 until the 1960s, the ancestors of most adult U.S.-born Asian-Americans lived in this country at the turn of the century. Data from the 1900 Census of Population provide information on the impressive improvements in skills among the Chinese and Japanese. Among men age 18 to 64 in 1900, the Chinese and Japanese, primarily immigrants, had an occupational prestige score (11.8) similar to that of Mexican-Americans (10.9) and blacks (11.9). It was substantially and significantly lower than the score for all native-born white men (23.5) and foreign-born white men (19.7), who were primarily of European origin. Although the Chinese and Japanese had literacy rates (70 percent) that were higher than the Mexicans (56 percent) and blacks (61 percent), they were significantly lower than the literacy rates among native-born white men (96 percent) and foreign-born white men (90 percent). In the course of one or two generations, Americans of Chinese and Japanese ancestry evolved from a low-skilled population to one with higher levels of skill than the majority white population.

There are some data that permit a comparison of the skill level of turn-of-the-century Jewish immigrants with other European immigrants. The 1909 survey conducted by the Dillingham Immigration Commission (1911 report), records of the immigration authorities, and the 1900 and 1920 Censuses of Population are the major sources.

The data suggest that the Jewish immigrants were of a higher level of skill (as defined by occupational status), had a higher literacy rate, and had higher earnings than other immigrants from Eastern and Southern Europe, but not in comparison with immigrants from Northwestern Europe or the native born (Carpenter 1927: 283–92; Kahan 1978; Higgs 1971). American Jews have made considerable gains in their educational and occupational attainment relative to the native-born population (Chiswick 1985). It will be shown later that the fertility rate of American Jews is substantially below that of other whites.

These patterns point to the importance of the intergenerational transmission of wealth in the form of income, schooling, or occupational status.[18] They also suggest that there are changes in relative skill levels from generation to generation. The observed changes in relative skill levels are consistent with the observed patterns of fertility.

9.5.2. *Group Differences in Fertility*

To determine whether group differences in educational attainment are consistent with a quantity-quality tradeoff model, it would be desirable to have data on the mean number of siblings by group for the current cohort of adults. These data are not available directly, but a useful proxy would be the fertility rate for the group at about the time the current cohort was born (Preston 1976). Although black–white fertility comparisons are abundant, historical data for other racial and ethnic groups are scarce. The data that can be used are instructive. They suggest that there was an inverse relationship between number of children and the average educational attainment of these children.

According to Rindfuss and Sweet, "There are two distinctly different age patterns of fertility. American Indians, Mexican Americans, blacks, and whites begin their childbearing early and reach their peak level of fertility by their early twenties. Among these four groups, blacks have an earlier pattern than the other three. The Chinese-Americans and the Japanese-Americans, on the other hand, begin their childbearing substantially later and do not reach their peak level of childbearing until their late twenties" (Rindfuss and Sweet 1977: 145). The later age of childbearing among the Chinese and Japanese women is related to a later age at first marriage (U.S. Bureau of the Census 1973, Tables 1, 5, and 10).

A later age at first marriage for women is associated empirically with higher levels of schooling, including more schooling acquired after marriage (Alexander and Reilly 1981).[19] Hence, a later age at first marriage should be associated with her having fewer children, in part because of a reduced period of exposure to childbearing and in part because of the implications of delayed marriage for the women's own schooling attainment. The lower fertility implies higher average child quality.

Figure 9.2

Total Fertility Rates for Six Racial or Ethnic Groups: 1955–1969

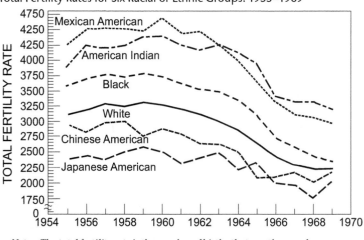

Note: The total fertility rate is the number of births that one thousand women would have in their lifetime if, at each year of age, they experienced the birth rates occurring in the specified year.

Source: Rindfuss and Sweet (1977: 90).

Figure 9.2 shows total fertility rates by year for 1955 to 1969 for six race and ethnic groups.[20] Although earlier fertility data would be more desirable, they apparently do not exist. Note that the fertility rates in Figure 9.2 are virtually the inverse of the level of schooling. In descending order, Mexican-Americans, American Indians, and blacks have higher fertility rates than whites, whereas the Chinese and especially the Japanese have lower fertility rates.[21]

The group differences in fertility rates in the mid-1950s varied by age. Among young women (ages 19–24 years) the Japanese and Chinese had much lower fertility rates than whites and much lower rates than the three high fertility groups. Among older women (age 30–44 years) the ranking is the same but the differences are smaller (Rindfuss and Sweet 1977: 92).[22]

Analysis of Jewish–non-Jewish fertility differences over the past century suggest a consistent pattern of lower fertility among Jews in the United States, Canada, Eastern Europe, and Western Europe, even when the analysis is limited to those living in urban areas (Goldscheider 1967).[23] A study of contraceptive practices in the United States during the 1930s "indicates that a higher proportion of Jews used contraceptives, planned their pregnancies, used more efficient methods of birth control, and began the use of contraception earlier in marriage than Protestants and Catholics" (Goldscheider 1967: 198). A survey conducted in 1957 indicates substantial lower fertility among American Jewish women than all women, even among the older cohort.[24]

Fertility patterns translate into differences in educational attainment in the next generation. Although there has been much research on this issue among whites, recent research shows similar patterns for other racial and ethnic groups. Mare and Winship (1988), for example, analyzed the determinants of school attainment among adult men for seven racial and ethnic groups (white, black, Asian, American Indian, Cuban, Mexican, and Puerto Rican). Controlling for parental schooling and father's occupation, the number of siblings had a consistently significant negative effect on various measures of educational attainment, except among the Asians. One has less confidence in their Asian analysis, however, because of the absence of statistical control for type of Asian origin, nativity, and duration of residence in the United States. These factors would tend to confound the analysis for Asians by more than for other groups.

9.5.3.   Group Differences in Labor Force Participation of Mothers

For the same level of fertility, a higher female labor force participation rate implies greater family money income but less parental time with children. Both greater family money income and more parental time with children would be expected to result in higher quality children. The net impact on child quality of the tradeoff of money for mother's time is not clear a priori.[25] Mother's time in child care would generally be most productive in raising child quality during the preschool and schooling years when children are "time intensive."[26] However, when the children become young adults (i.e., post-high school) they are "goods intensive" and mother's time may be most productive if she engages in market work and uses the earnings to purchase market inputs for the children. These market inputs in the human capital of young adult children include tuition and room and board at college, world travel, food and shelter while obtaining on-the-job training, etc.

Several studies compare racial and ethnic groups as to the effect of the presence of children in the home on female labor supply, both overall and when other variables, including schooling and other family income, are held constant. The detailed regression coefficients are reported in Appendix A. Although these studies use contemporary data, the estimated regression coefficients may be reflecting more fundamental differences in relative prices that do not vary across generations within a group.

Four studies of black–white differences in female labor supply are noteworthy. Bell (1974) used the Survey of Economic Opportunity, Sweet (1973: 82–7 and 96–103) the 1960 Census of Population, Lehrer and Nerlove (1981) the 1973 National Sample of Family Growth, and Reimers (1985) the 1976 Survey of Income and Education. All four studies find a greater labor supply by black women and a smaller depressing effect of the presence of young children on their labor supply.

Reimers (1985) also reports a reduced-form employment equation for Mexican-origin women. She finds a smaller depressing effect of children under age 12 on labor supply for Mexican-origin than for non-Hispanic white women, and the difference is larger the younger the age of the children. There is no differential effect for children age 12 to 17.

A smaller depressing effect of children on female labor supply is not a universal characteristic of minority groups. A study of white women using 1970 Census data examined Jewish–non-Jewish differences in labor supply, overall and when other variables are the same (Chiswick 1986c). Children under age 18 have a greater depressing effect on labor supply for Jewish women. As a consequence, Jewish women with children at home are less likely to work than non-Jewish women, and the difference is greater the younger the children. Among working women with school-age children, the Jewish women are more likely to work part time and part year. But, Jewish women without children at home (no children under 18 years) have a greater labor supply than non-Jewish women when other variables are the same.

In a study of Asian-American women, using 1970 Census and 1980 Census data, Chamnivickorn (1988) shows that other things the same, Filipino women have a greater labor supply than Chinese and Japanese women. The presence of children under age six in the home has a smaller depressing effect on labor supply for the Filipino women. There are no differences among the Asian groups in the effect on female labor supply of children age 6 to 18.

9.5.4.   Group Differences in Intergenerational Transfers

Two studies have examined racial and ethnic group differences in private income transfers (in cash or in kind) received by young adults from other family members, primarily their parents. These transfers can be viewed as a mechanism through which parents can increase the schooling and on-the-job training, and hence the "child quality," of their goods-intensive young adult offspring. Greater transfers from parents to young adult children appear to be made the higher the group's average rate of return on education. That is, greater parental investments in young adult children are made by the same groups that make greater investments in younger children.

Other things the same, blacks and Hispanics receive smaller private transfers than whites, and the differences are greater for young adult than for older children (Chiswick and Cox 1988).

Among white college students, controlling for scholarships, fellowships, and family income, among other variables, Jewish students receive more parental financial support than non-Jewish students (Catsiapis and Robinson 1981).

9.6.   Summary and Conclusion

This chapter has been concerned with racial and ethnic group differences in schooling, earnings, and rates of return from schooling among the native-born population of the United States. The sharp differences in these variables are not easily explained by appealing to discrimination against minorities. Some minorities that have experienced discrimination have high levels of schooling, earnings, and rates of return (e.g., Chinese, Japanese, Jews, and foreign-parentage blacks), while other have low levels (e.g., native-parentage blacks, Mexican-Americans, American Indians, and Filipinos). This does not mean that discrimination in access to schooling and in the labor market has not played a role. What it does imply is that other factors, operating separately or interacting with discrimination, are also relevant and appear to be the dominant explanation.

The ethnic studies literature frequently includes two simple "taste" hypotheses: one is that the more highly educated minorities have a cultural taste or preference for schooling; the other is that they place a higher value on future relative to present consumption (lower discount rate). These hypotheses imply a negative relation between schooling level and rates of return from schooling. Empirically, however, there tends to be a positive relation between the level of schooling and the rate of return from schooling across the race and ethnic groups. These hypotheses are therefore not consistent with the data.

The data suggest that group variations in the rate of return schedules from schooling are greater than variations in the interest cost of funds schedules. Group variations in rates of return arise from differences in the ability to convert the schooling process into earnings. These differences may be a consequence of parental investments (implicit and explicit) in the home-produced components of child quality. Although it is difficult to obtain the most appropriate data for a rigorous testing of the hypotheses, it does appear that members of the more successful groups had parents with higher levels of schooling, had fewer siblings to compete with for parental time and other family resources, and had mothers who were less likely to work when young children were in the household.

A positive relationship between educational attainments across generations reflects the intergenerational transmission of human wealth. There has, however, been some realignment. During the past few decades the relative educational level has been rising for three low-fertility groups, the Chinese, Japanese, and Jews, and declining for a high-fertility group, the Filipinos.

The inverse relation between schooling attainment and family size implies a tradeoff of quality for quantity of children. The tradeoff may arise from differences in relative prices. Children are more expensive the higher the average child quality that is demanded, the higher the value of time of women in the labor market, and the higher the out-of-pocket cost of children. Therefore, groups with more highly educated women and living disproportionately in major metropolitan areas (e.g., Jews, Chinese, Japanese, and foreign-born blacks) may have substituted quality for quantity of children. Price differences may also arise from the fundamental differences that serve to define ethnic groups. For example, groups with religious beliefs that raise the psychic cost of fertility control (e.g., Mexican-Americans and Filipinos) have a larger number of children, and as a consequence make smaller investments of parental time and other resources per child.

Mothers' time may be used in providing child care or in generating money income in the labor market. Both activities may generate higher child quality. Greater time investments in child care during the preschool and schooling years when children are "time intensive" and greater market work during later years when children are "goods intensive" would appear to be optimal. Empirically, the data suggest that among the more successful groups women with children at home tend to have lower labor force participation rates, even after controlling for their higher level of education and husband's income, and fewer children. Perhaps more important, however, the relative difference in participation rates is greater when there are young children present in the home. They appear to have higher participation rates when there are no children at home. In addition, they tend to make larger private transfers to their young adult children.

If race and ethnic group differences in educational attainment and earnings are to a considerable extent a consequence of family decision making, rather than a consequence of direct discrimination in the educational system or in the labor market, group differences in educational attainment and earnings are likely to be more intractable than has been believed. One way that public policy can influence the quantity-quality tradeoff is by reducing the cost of birth control. Other public policies have more ambiguous effects. Income transfer programs (welfare) raise family income, but they do so in proportion to the number of children. Greater public expenditures per pupil in school also subsidize the number of children. The subsidization of the number of children may be an unavoidable consequence of attempts to improve child quality.

This study demonstrates that ad hoc group-specific explanations may not be necessary or even fruitful for understanding the schooling and earnings of the many racial and ethnic groups that comprise the American population. Instead, a relatively simple model in which there are group differences in the relative prices of quantity and quality of children may explain the fertility, human capital investments, and labor market outcomes of these diverse groups. The model may explain differences at a moment in time, as well as changes in relative positions over time.

The hypotheses developed and tested in this chapter must be viewed as preliminary. Much more needs to be learned about the quantity-quality tradeoff and why it appears to vary systematically across race and ethnic groups. In particular, more data and more studies of minority groups, particularly the understudied "successful" minorities, are needed. These studies should identify the determinants of group differences in the price of quantity relative to quality of children and measure the responsiveness of racial and ethnic groups to these price differences. Historical studies are needed to determine some of the roots of group differences in the level of economic welfare and how they have been transmitted from generation to generation over the past century. This information will play a crucial role in the development of more effective public policies to promote higher levels of schooling and home-produced human capital among members of disadvantaged minority groups.

Appendix

This Appendix reports the partial effects of the presence of children in the home on various measures of female labor supply focusing on minority groups.

Black-White Comparison (Bell 1974)

The partial regression coefficients (*t*-ratios in parentheses) are as shown in the following tabulation.

	Dependent variables and groups			
	Full-time participation		Part- or full-time participation	
Children	Black	White	Black	White
Children under age 4	-13.7	-17.5	-14.7	-23.1
(dummy variable)	(-6.3)	(-12.4)	(-6.3)	(-14.2)
Number of children	-1.23	-4.7	-1.9	-3.6
under age 18	(-2.8)	(13.7)	(-4.1)	(-9.5)

Mexican-Black-White Comparison (Reimers 1985)

The dependent variable is labor force participation. The regression coefficients (standard errors in parentheses) are as shown in the following tabulation.

Children	White non-Hispanic	Mexican	Black non-Hispanic
Less than 6 years	-0.431	-0.318	-0.196
	(0.029)	(0.039)	(0.026)
Age 6 to 11	-0.235	-0.064	-0.043
	(0.023)	(0.030)	(0.018)
Age 12 to 17	-0.115	-0.116	-0.109
	(0.018)	(0.025)	(0.015)

The control variables include the women's age, education, nativity, marital status, and spouse's age, education, and nativity, and other family income, among other variables. Most of the Mexican-origin women are native born.

Jewish-Non-Jewish Comparison (Chiswick 1986c)

The partial effects (*t*-ratios in parentheses) are as shown in the following tabulation.

	Dependent variables and groups					
	Labor force participation		Percent of weeks worked		Hours worked per week	
Children	Non-Jewish	Jewish	Non-Jewish	Jewish	Non-Jewish	Jewish
Under Age 6	-0.138	-0.264	-0.117	-0.197	-4.598	-6.913
	(-34.8)	(-11.5)	(-33.7)	(-9.6)	(- 31.4)	(-8.3)
Age 6 to 18	-0.037	-0.062	-0.041	-0.070	-1.60	-2.861
	(-18.1)	(-5.9)	(-22.9)	(-7.5)	(- 21.4)	(-7.5)

The control variables include age, education, marital status, location, and other family income.

Japanese-Chinese-Filipino Comparison (Chamnivickorn 1988)

With Japanese women serving as the benchmark, the partial differential effects (*t*-ratios in parentheses) are as shown in the following tabulation.

Race and children	1970 Census			1980 Census		
	Labor force part.	Weeks worked (percent)	Hours worked	Labor force part.	Weeks worked (percent)	Hours worked
Chinese:						
Under age 6	0.0804	0.0636	1.992	-0.0017	0.0312	-1.157
	(1.88)	(1.60)	(1.11)	(-0.06)	(-1.15)	(-0.94)
Age 6 to 18	0.0026	0.0059	-0.119	-0.0110	-0.0191	0.744
	(0.12)	(0.28)	(-0.13)	(-0.50)	(-0.88)	(0. 75)
Filipino:						
Under age 6	0.1050	0.0689	1.853	0.0553	0.0526	4.877
	(2.36)	(1.66)	(0.99)	(1.91)	(1.83)	(3.72)
Age 6 to 18	0.0066	0.0216	0.244	0.0118	0.0151	0.415
	(0.27)	(0.95)	(0.236)	(0.49)	(0.63)	(0.38)

Pooled regressions for U.S.-born Chinese, Japanese, and Filipino women, also controlling for age, education, marital status, location, other family income, and number and age of children. Samples sizes are 1,493 (1/100 sample) for the 1970 Census and 9,894 (1/20 sample) for the 1980 Census.

10

Ethnic Capital and Intergenerational Mobility

I first began to think about the intergenerational progress of immigrants sometime in the late 1980s. I recall having a vague feeling that the focus of the assimilation literature on what happens during the immigrant's lifetime was somewhat misplaced, since what really mattered is what happens to the progeny of the immigrants one or two generations later. Put differently, does the melting pot really work?

Once I started examining the data, it did not take long for me to realize that the intergenerational correlation between the mean earnings of ethnic groups was far higher than would be expected if we simply looked at the intergenerational correlation between parents and children. In other words, ethnicity itself seemed to play a role in the transmission of skills across generations.

I started to work on my "ethnic capital" hypothesis at a time when the idea of human capital spillovers was revolutionizing how economists thought about the process of economic growth. It quickly became apparent that there was a strong analogy between the economic growth models and the ethnic capital framework: ethnicity played the role of a human capital externality and these externalities could imply that ethnicity mattered, and that it mattered for a very long time.

George J. Borjas (2015)

The original version of this chapter was published as: Borjas, G. J. (1992). Ethnic Capital and Intergenerational Mobility, in: The Quarterly Journal of Economics, 107(1): 123–50. © 1992 by the President and Fellows of Harvard College and the Massachusetts Institute of Technology. I have benefited from discussions. The author is grateful to Julian Betts, John Conlisk, Richard Freeman, Daniel Hamermesh, Lawrence Katz, Alan Krueger, James Rauch, Glenn Sueyoshi, and Stephen Trejo as well as to the Russell Sage Foundation and to the National Science Foundation (Grant No. SES-8809281) for financial support.

10.1. Introduction

The notion that social, cultural, and economic differences between immigrants and natives fade over the course of a few generations is the essence of the assimilation hypothesis.[1] For many years it was generally believed that the melting-pot metaphor correctly described important aspects of the ethnic experience in the United States. Over time the children and grandchildren of immigrants moved out of ethnic enclaves, discarded their social and cultural background, and experienced economic mobility. After a few generations the American-born descendants of the immigrants became indistinguishable from the native population.

Recent sociological and historical research rejects the hypothesis that full assimilation is an unavoidable outcome of the ethnic experience. As Glazer and Moynihan (1963: xcvii) conclude in their classic study Beyond the Melting Pot: "The point about the melting pot ... is that it did not happen... . The American ethos is nowhere better perceived than in the disinclination of the third and fourth generation of newcomers to blend into a standard, uniform national type." Current research in this literature (Perlmann 1988; Steinberg 1989) stresses the fact that the United States remains a multicultural, pluralistic society and cites as evidence the social, cultural, and economic differences that exist and persist among ethnic groups. For instance, Farley (1990) reports that in 1980 U.S.-born workers of Hungarian or Austrian origin earn about 20 percent more than workers of English or Canadian origin, who in turn earn about 20 percent more than workers of Mexican or Puerto Rican origin.[2]

This chapter presents a theoretical and empirical analysis of the extent to which these ethnic differences in skills and earnings are transmitted across generations.[3] The operational hypothesis of the study is that ethnicity acts as an externality in the human capital accumulation process. In particular, the skills of the next generation depend not only on parental inputs, but also on the average quality of the ethnic environment in which parents make their investments, or "ethnic capital." The introduction of ethnic capital into an economic model of intergenerational mobility has one important implication: if the external effect of ethnicity is sufficiently strong, ethnic differences in skills observed in this generation are likely to persist for many generations (and may never disappear).

The empirical analysis uses the General Social Surveys and the National Longitudinal Surveys of Youth. The main insight provided by the evidence is that ethnic capital, as measured by the average skill level of the ethnic group in the father's generation, plays a crucial role in intergenerational mobility, and slows down the convergence in the average skills of ethnic groups across generations. Put differently, the data reveal that the intergenerational progress of workers belonging to ethnic groups that have relatively low levels of human capital is retarded by the low average quality of the group. The empirical evidence also indicates that the role played by ethnic capital in intergenerational mobility partly explains the slow rates of economic progress experienced by blacks.

10.2. Theory

I assume that the link between the skills of parents and children arises because parents invest in the human capital of their children. Obviously, there are many alternative ways of motivating the link in skills across generations. Though it abstracts from many of these considerations, the approach followed here leads to an empirically useful understanding of the role played by ethnicity in intergenerational mobility.

To focus the analysis, I consider a one-person household in generation t. This person has a human capital stock k_t which can be sold to the marketplace at constant price R, or which can be used in the production of the human capital of his children. I assume that workers do not invest in their own human capital, so that the human capital stock of workers in generation $t + 1$ is completely determined by the actions of generation t.

I also assume that the household has only one child. A more general model would allow the household to choose both the quality and quantity of children (Becker and Lewis 1973). Although this assumption can be easily relaxed, the substantive implications of the model are unaffected (and, because of data constraints, the interaction between child quality, child quantity, and intergenerational mobility cannot be fully explored in the empirical analysis presented here).

The parent has a CES utility function defined over the child's quality, which is given by the human capital stock of the child, k_{t+1}, and own consumption C_t,

(1) $$U = U(k_{t+1}, C_t) = \left[\delta_1 k_{t+1}^\rho + \delta_2 C_t^\rho\right]^{1/\rho},$$

where $\rho < 1$, and $\sigma = 1/(1 - \rho)$ is the elasticity of substitution between consumption and child quality.[4]

As already noted, the parent can either sell his human capital to the marketplace or devote a fraction s_t of his time to the production of the child's human capital. Setting the price of C_t as the numéraire implies that

(2) $$R(1 - s_t)k_t = C_t.$$

Up to this point, I have not addressed the role played by ethnicity in the maximization problem. I assume that the average human capital stock of the ethnic group, $\overline{k}_t$, which I call ethnic capital, acts as an externality in the production of the human then given by

(3) $$k_{t+1} = \beta_0(s_t k_t)^{\beta_1}\overline{k}_t^{\beta_2}.$$

Both β_1 and β_2 are assumed to be less than one. It will be seen later that the value of the sum $\beta_1 + \beta_2$ determines whether skill differentials across ethnic groups converge over time.

The production function has three important properties. First, the specification uses the neutrality assumption introduced by Ben-Porath (1967) in his analysis of human capital accumulation over the life-cycle. In Equation (3), $s_t k_t$ is the effective amount of the parent's human capital stock that is devoted to children.

Second, and more important, the production function incorporates the assumption that the average human capital of the ethnic group has an external effect on the production process. As a result, the child's quality depends not only on parental inputs, but also on the average quality of the ethnic environment in which the child is raised (which I assume to be exogenous). Persons who grow up in high-quality ethnic environments will, on average, be exposed to social, cultural, and economic factors that increase their productivity when they grow up, and the larger or more frequent the amount of this exposure, the higher the resulting quality of the worker (for a given level of parental inputs). There are precedents for introducing ethnic capital into the production process in both the economics and sociology literatures.

The literature on the "new" economic growth is motivated by the hypothesis that human capital has external effects on production. The important work of Lucas (1988) uses an aggregate production function similar to (3) and reveals that these externalities provide substantive insights into the process of economic development. A key implication of this approach, which will reappear in a different guise below, is that some countries may remain poor, while others grow richer.[5]

Equation (3) also has strong antecedents in sociology. For instance, Coleman (1988) stresses the concept of "social capital." In Coleman's view, the culture in which the individual is raised, which can be thought of as a form of human capital common to all members of that group, alters his opportunity set, and has significant effects on behavior, human capital formation, and labor market outcomes.[6]

Finally, note that Equation (3) implies that parental time and ethnic capital are complements in the production of child quality. A given level of parental inputs is more productive in environments with higher-quality ethnic capital. This complementarity in production underlies many of the results discussed here.

The maximization of (1), subject to the budget constraint and the technology, generates the household's supply function for time allocated to investing in the human capital of children:

$$(4) \qquad s_t = s(k_t, \bar{k}_t).$$

It is easy to show that the elasticities of s_t with respect to k_t and $\bar{k}_t$ are

$$(5a) \qquad \frac{\partial \log s_t}{\partial \log k_t} = \frac{\rho(\beta_1 - 1)(1 - s_t)}{(1 - s_t)(1 - \rho\beta_1) + s_t(1 - \rho)};$$

$$(5b) \qquad \frac{\partial \log s_t}{\partial \log \bar{k}_t} = \frac{\rho\beta_2(1 - s_t)}{(1 - s_t)(1 - \rho\beta_1) + s_t(1 - \rho)}.$$

In general, utility maximization does not lead to unambiguous predictions about how the fraction of time devoted to investments in children varies with either the parental human capital stock or ethnic capital. The first ambiguity arises because increases in k_t generate both income and substitution effects, and these effects work in opposite directions. In particular, an increase in k_t increases the demand for child quality (because of the income effect), but also makes child quality more expensive. It is evident from (5a) that parental time decreases with k_t when the elasticity of substitution between consumption and child quality is greater than one ($\rho > 0$), and increases otherwise. The easier it is to substitute between child quality and own consumption, the more likely that the substitution effect of an increase in k_t dominates, and parental time declines. In the special case of a Cobb-Douglas utility function ($\rho = 0$), the fraction of time allocated to the production of human capital is independent of the human capital stock of parents.

The variable s_t also varies with respect to the amount of ethnic capital. Changes in $\bar{k}_t$ only alter the shape of the utility function (because ethnic capital does not enter the budget constraint). Equation ($5b$) indicates that s_t and ethnic capital are positively correlated as long as the elasticity of substitution between consumption and child quality is greater than unity. Intuitively, as long as C_t and k_{t+1} are easily substitutable, the household takes advantage of the complementarity in production between the parent's human capital and ethnic capital by devoting more time to their children in advantageous ethnic environments.

Despite the fact that the time devoted by parents to human capital investments in their children depends ambiguously on both parental human capital and on ethnic capital, the relationship between child quality and these variables is unambiguous. In particular, the reduced-form equation determining the human capital stock of children is

$$(6) \qquad k_{t+1} = \beta_0 s(k_t, \bar{k}_t)^{\beta_1} k_t^{\beta_1} k_t^{\beta_2}.$$

In effect, (6) describes the process of intergenerational income mobility (in the absence of stochastic shocks). It is easy to show that

$$(7a) \qquad \frac{\partial \log k_{t+1}}{\partial \log k_t} = \frac{\beta_1(1 - \rho)}{(1 - s_t)(1 - \rho\beta_1) + s_t(1 - \rho)};$$

$$(7b) \qquad \frac{\partial \log k_{t+1}}{\partial \log \bar{k}_t} = \frac{\beta_2(1 - \rho s_t)}{(1 - s_t)(1 - \rho\beta_1) + s_t(1 - \rho)}.$$

There is a positive relationship between child quality and both parental human capital and ethnic capital regardless of the value of the elasticity of substitution between own-consumption and child quality.

To analyze the evolution of the human capital stock across generations for a particular ethnic group, and hence to determine whether the dispersion in human capital across ethnic groups narrows over time, it is useful to consider the special case where all parents in the ethnic group have the same human capital, so that $k_t = \bar{k}_t$. An increase in $\bar{k}_t$, therefore, implies that both parental capital and ethnic capital increase by the same amount. The elasticity of (average) child quality with respect to $\bar{k}_t$ is

$$(8) \qquad \eta = \frac{\partial \log \bar{k}_{t+1}}{\partial \log \bar{k}_t} = \frac{\beta_1(1 - \rho) + \beta_2(1 - \rho s_t)}{(1 - s_t)(1 - \rho\beta_1) + s_t(1 - \rho)}.$$

The average human capital stock of different ethnic groups will converge or diverge across generations depending on whether η is less than or greater than one. Using (8), it follows that

$$(9) \qquad \eta \begin{cases} < 1, & \text{if } \beta_1 + \beta_2 < 1, \\ = 1, & \text{if } \beta_1 + \beta_2 = 1, \\ > 1, & \text{if } \beta_1 + \beta_2 > 1. \end{cases}$$

If the externality introduced by ethnic capital leads to constant returns in the production function, the relative dispersion that exists in human capital among ethnic groups in the parent's generation will persist indefinitely. As in the new literature on economic growth, sufficiently strong externalities can generate human capital growth paths where *relative* differences in skills among ethnic groups do not change over time.[7] If the human capital externality, however, is not sufficiently strong to achieve constant returns to scale, the sum $\beta_1 + \beta_2$ is less than unity, and ethnic differences in human capital will eventually disappear. Nevertheless, a key insight of the model is that the external effects of ethnic capital may greatly retard the process of convergence. In other words, relatively high values of β_2 slow down the regression toward the mean in skills across generations. In the end, the question of how fast the average skills of ethnic groups converge over time can only be resolved by empirical analysis.

10.3. Empirical Framework and Data

The econometric model typically used to assess the extent of intergenerational income mobility is given by[8]

$$(10) \qquad y_{it}(t) = \tau + \delta y_{ij}(t - 1) + \epsilon_{ij}(t),$$

where $y_{ij}(t)$ represents the (log) earnings of person i in ethnic group j in generation t; and $y_{ij}(t - 1)$ represents the (log) earnings of his father. The parameter δ is an inverse measure of the extent of regression toward the mean across generations. Many empirical studies have found that δ lies between 0.2 and 0.3, although recent research (Solon 1992; Zimmerman 1992a) suggests that measurement error leads to a substantial downward bias on the magnitude of the estimated parameter (and hence the estimation of (10) overstates the extent of regression toward the mean).

To the extent that ethnic capital plays an important role in deter-mining the quality of children, Equation (10) misspecifies the inter-generational mobility process. In particular, it ignores the presence of ethnic fixed effects that get partially transmitted across generations. A general specification of the ethnic fixed effects can be written as

$$(11) \qquad y_{ij}(t) = \gamma_1 y_{ij}(t-1) + \sum_j \omega_j(t) C_{ij} + \epsilon_{ij}(t),$$

where C_{ij} is a dummy variable indicating whether individual i is a member of ethnic group j; and the disturbance $\epsilon_{ij}(t)$ is i.i.d. with mean zero and variance σ_ϵ^2. The theoretical model presented above suggests a particular representation for the fixed effects in the vector ω. In par-ticular, they depend on $\bar{y}_j(t-1)$, the average (log) earnings of the ethnic group in the parent's generation. This implies that

$$(12) \qquad \omega_j(t) = \gamma_0 + \gamma_2 \bar{y}_j(t-1) + v_j(t),$$

where $v_j(t)$ is i.i.d. with mean zero and variance σ_v^2. The reduced-form equation summarizing the impact of parental earnings and ethnic capital on child quality is obtained by substituting Equation (12) into (11). Hence

$$(13) \qquad y_{ij}(t) = \gamma_0 + \gamma_1 y_{ij}(t-1) + \gamma_2 \bar{y}_j(t-1) + \xi_{ij}(t),$$

where $\xi_{ij}(t) = \epsilon_{ij}(t) + v_j(t)$. I assume that the random variables ε and v are uncorrelated. Note that because $E(\xi_{ij}(t)\xi_{i'j'}(t))^2 = \sigma_v^2$ for $i \neq i'$, $j = j'$, the disturbance has the stochastic structure of a random ef-fects model, and Equation (13) will be estimated using generalized least squares.[9]

An important implication of Equation (13) is that the transmission parameter describing how the mean skills of the ethnic group evolve across generations is given by the sum of coefficients $\gamma_1 + \gamma_2$. In partic-ular, $(\gamma_1 + \gamma_2) \cdot \bar{y}_j(t-1)$ gives the expected earnings of the offspring of the average father in a particular ethnic group (abstracting from the constant term).

It is of interest to note that as long as ethnic capital plays a key role in the intergenerational transmission of skills, the linkage across generations (as measured by $\gamma_1 + \gamma_2$) may be substantially underes-timated by the coefficient estimated from regressions that ignore the importance of ethnic capital. The expected value of the least-squares estimator of δ in Equation (10) is

$$(14) \qquad E(\hat{\delta}) = \gamma_1 + (1-\pi)\gamma_2 < \gamma_1 + \gamma_2,$$

where $\pi = [\sum_j\sum_i(y_{ij}(t - 1) - y_j(t - 1))^2]/\mathrm{var}\ (y_{ij}(t - 1))$, and is the fraction of the variance of earnings that is explained by variation within ethnic groups (the within-variance). Because most earnings variation in the population is likely to be within groups (rather than across ethnic groups), π is probably large, and the OLS regression of children's earnings on parental earnings may greatly underestimate the intensity of the true linkage in earnings across generations (even in the absence of measurement errors).

The empirical analysis will be conducted on two data sets: the General Social Surveys (GSS) and the National Longitudinal Surveys of Youth (NLSY). The GSS is a series of cross sections that have been collected annually since 1972 (except for 1979 and 1981) by the National Opinion Research Center.[10] Each cross section contains over 1,000 observations, and respondents are asked about their demographic background, political attitudes, and labor market outcomes. Beginning in 1977, each cross section provides information on the respondent's ethnic background, as well as information on whether the respondent, the respondent's parents, and the respondent's grandparents were born in the United States. In addition, these waves of the GSS contain information on the respondent's educational attainment and occupation as well as on the educational attainment and occupation of his parents.

The empirical analysis presented below pools persons aged 18–64 from the 1977–1989 waves, and focuses on the study of intergenerational mobility in educational attainment and in occupation, where the occupation measure is the Hodge-Siegel-Rossi prestige score (Siegel 1971). This prestige score, which resembles the more commonly used Duncan score, is highly correlated with average income in the occupation: the correlation between the prestige score and average earnings was about 0.6. As a way of assessing the cardinal interpretation of the prestige score, I note that a regression of log earnings on the score indicated that a one-point increase in the index increases earnings by 2.4 percent.[11]

The GSS does not contain specific information on the place of birth of the individual's parents or grandparents (other than whether they were born in the United States), so that it is not possible to ascertain the exact national origin of the person. The person's ethnicity, therefore, is obtained from the individual's response to a question that asks "from what countries or part of the world did your ancestors come"? Although most persons in the sample gave only one response to the question, some gave multiple responses. In these cases, I use the main ethnic background (as identified by the respondent).[12] Persons who have missing data on the ethnicity question or on the other variables used in the analysis are omitted from the study.

The more widely used NLSY contains information similar to that available in the GSS. The main difference between the data sets is that respondents in the NLSY are aged 14–21 at the time of the initial survey (in 1979). The data contain information about the father's (and mother's) educational attainment and the father's occupation.

Using the NLSY data, I shall analyze intergenerational mobility in two variables: education and wages. I use the 1987 wave of the NLSY to measure the respondent's education and hourly wage rate (by that time the respondents are 22–29 and only 8 percent of the sample is still enrolled in school). The father's wage is obtained by matching the father's occupation code with average earnings for the occupation obtained from the 1970 Census.[13] I experimented with alternative specifications (such as using an occupational prestige score), with little change in the results.

The NLSY asks respondents "What is your origin or descent"? Hence the self-reported ethnic background variable greatly resembles that available in the GSS, except that the NLSY reports many fewer ethnic groups because more aggregation takes place in the coding.[14] The NLSY, however, permits a separate identification of ethnicity because it reports the specific birthplace of both the father and the mother. For second-generation Americans, there is a high degree of consistency between parental birthplace and self-reported ethnicity. In particular, the NLSY data indicate that if both of the respondent's parents are foreign born, both parents were born in the same country of origin over 90 percent of the time, and the self-reported ethnicity almost always coincides with the parents' birthplace. Among respondents who have only one foreign-born parent, respondents tended to report the national origin of the foreign-born parent as their ethnic background. As with the GSS, persons who did not report an ethnic origin or who have missing data for the other variables used in the study are omitted from the study.

Throughout the analysis, therefore, I categorize individuals into ethnic groups according to their self-reported ethnic identification. To the extent possible (i.e., for the children of immigrants in the NLSY), I conducted a parallel empirical analysis based on the national origin of the parents, and obtained results similar to those presented below.

Table 10.1

Summary Characteristics in GSS, by Ethnic Group

Origin	Education		Occupation		Sample size
	Self	Father	Self	Father	
Arabic	15.200	9.600	54.600	52.600	5
Austria	13.378	9.733	43.000	42.367	45
Belgium	12.333	9.250	37.133	40.067	12
Canada (French)	12.788	10.125	38.496	39.748	104
Canada (Other)	12.911	11.107	40.484	39.813	56
China	14.857	10.429	49.000	34.444	7
Czechoslovakia	12.976	9.368	41.326	38.609	125
Denmark	14.500	10.530	47.912	42.632	66
England and Wales	13.925	11.577	43.920	43.932	1233
Finland	12.708	9.771	38.438	38.229	48
France	13.407	11.429	42.434	42.357	189
Germany	13.175	10.728	41.618	41.224	1653
Greece	13.833	11.458	44.172	44.207	24
Hungary	13.554	10.357	41.702	40.193	56
Ireland	13.151	10.853	41.020	41.328	1043
Italy	13.156	10.294	40.807	38.788	469
Japan	14.579	9.737	49.421	39.474	19
Lithuania	14.130	10.870	44.280	42.040	23
Mexico	11.076	5.890	36.350	31.062	172
Netherlands	12.390	9.968	39.675	40.268	154
Norway	13.288	11.183	41.943	42.383	191
Poland	13.453	10.202	41.725	37.725	258
Portugal	12.800	8.000	34.000	35.583	10
Puerto Rico	12.120	9.760	36.077	36.269	25
Romania	15.125	13.750	46.000	47.000	8
Russia	14.962	11.333	48.009	44.035	105
Scotland	13.969	11.674	43.537	43.549	261
Spain	12.902	9.689	37.683	38.267	61
Sweden	13.843	11.916	44.029	43.372	166
Switzerland	14.053	11.868	45.474	40.053	38
Yugoslavia	12.927	9.146	40.875	37.075	41
Other Hispanic	14.900	11.100	44.818	42.364	10
American	11.452	8.532	40.194	39.224	62
All	13.331	10.726	41.923	41.174	6756

Notes: The sample sizes refer to the education data. There are 7,066 observations for which the occupation data are available.

Further, in both data sets I focus on the link between the respondent's skills (as measured by education, wage rates, or occupation) and those of the father's.[15] The empirical definition of ethnic capital is then given by the mean of the specific skill variable evaluated within the ethnic group in the father's generation.[16] Third, to focus on intergenerational mobility that is not contaminated by comparisons of U.S. residents with parents who resided permanently in the source countries, the empirical study is restricted to persons born in the United States. Finally, to focus on the transmission of ethnicity across generations, I exclude blacks and native Americans (i.e., American Indians) from the study.[17] I shall discuss the empirical relevance of the ethnic capital hypothesis to the study of black intergenerational mobility in what follows.

Table 10.2
Summary Characteristics in NLSY, by Ethnic Group

	Education		Log wage		
Origin	Self	Father	Self	Father	Sample size
China	14.000	14.571	1.831	2.664	7
Cuba	13.444	11.778	2.268	2.452	27
England	12.985	11.977	1.974	2.529	1239
France	12.789	11.813	1.925	2.519	246
Germany	13.288	12.113	2.001	2.503	1168
Greece	14.400	12.550	2.288	2.603	20
Ireland	13.284	12.590	2.041	2.568	714
Italy	13.200	12.297	2.120	2.542	360
Japan	12.667	11.917	2.195	2.144	12
Mexico	12.304	8.079	1.861	2.326	635
Pacific Islander	12.500	8.875	1.662	2.418	8
Philippines	14.071	13.000	2.049	2.628	14
Poland	13.223	11.787	2.018	2.544	188
Portugal	12.043	9.978	2.094	2.532	46
Puerto Rico	11.623	8.084	1.933	2.316	191
Russia	14.698	13.651	2.103	2.650	43
Scotland	14.061	13.520	2.026	2.616	98
Wales	14.571	14.643	2.036	2.692	28
Other Hispanic	12.632	11.059	1.971	2.387	68
American	12.189	10.853	1.914	2.455	502
All	12.941	11.444	1.984	2.496	5619

Notes: The log wages are reported in 1987 dollars. The sample sizes refer to the education data. There are 3,734 observations for which the log wage data are available.

Tables 10.1 and 10.2 report summary characteristics for the variables under analysis for both fathers and children in the GSS and the NLSY data, by ethnic group.[18] A number of findings are immediately apparent. First, the GSS reveals substantial improvement in educational attainment across generations, but little change in the occupational prestige score. The parents of GSS respondents have about 2.5 years fewer schooling than their children, but only about 1 point less in the occupational score (which would translate to about a 2.4 percent increase in earnings). The NLSY also indicates a substantial increase in schooling across generations (of about 1.5 years). Unfortunately, because the father's log wage is obtained by matching the father's occupation to the average earnings in the occupation, and because of the skewed age distribution in the NLSY, it is difficult to ascertain the change in the log wage across generations.

A second finding evident in both the GSS and the NLSY is the huge dispersion in educational attainment, occupational prestige scores, and wages across ethnic groups.[19] In the GSS, for instance, some ethnic groups (such as persons whose ancestors originated in Denmark, Japan, Russia, and Switzerland) have over 14 years of schooling, while others (such as those who originated in Mexico) have 11 years, those from Puerto Rico have 12.1 years, and those who originated in the Netherlands have 12.4 years. The occupational prestige scores show equally wide dispersion, with scores ranging from 36 to about 50 among national origin groups, which imply wage differentials of well over 25 percent across the groups. The NLSY shows equally strong dispersion in both educational attainment and log earnings across national origin groups. The educational attainment of Puerto Ricans or Portuguese workers is about 12 years, while the educational attainment of Germans is 13.3 and that of Russians is 14.7.

In sum, the raw data indicate a substantial improvement in educational attainment across generations, but they also reveal sizable dispersion in skills among ethnic groups for *both* parents and children. It is evident that the ethnic skill differentials found in the parent's generation do not disappear in one generation. The central question that remains, therefore, is to determine the extent to which the intergenerational transmission of skills preserves the ethnic differences or leads to a convergence in the skills of ethnic groups over time.

10.4. Empirical Results

Table 10.3 presents the coefficients estimated from regressions of children's characteristics on the characteristics of the parents.[20] Consider initially the results using educational attainment in the GSS. Column (1) indicates that when the educational attainment of the children is regressed on the educational attainment of the parents, the transmission coefficient is 0.27, which is quite similar to those usually reported in the literature. Note further that controlling for ethnic fixed effects in column (2) has little impact on the estimated coefficient:

the transmission parameter declines from 0.27 to 0.25. Nevertheless, the change in the explanatory power of the regression model associated with including the vector of fixed effects is highly significant at conventional levels (R^2 increases from 0.18 to 0.20 and the associated F-statistic is 6.0; the critical value is only 1.4).

Table 10.3

Intergenerational Transmission Coefficients in GSS And NLSY

a) General Social Surveys

Variable	Education (N = 6, 756)				Occupation (N = 7,066)			
	(1)	(2)	(3)	(4)	(1)	(2)	(3)	(4)
Parental capital	0.2664 (0.0074)	0.2490 (0.0076)	0.2501 (0.0076)	0.2586 (0.0080)	0.1997 (0.0127)	0.1829 (0.0128)	0.1829 (0.0128)	0.1985 (0.0127)
Ethnic capital			0.2265 (0.0466)	0.1455[a] (0.0882)			0.4589 (0.2244)	0.3714[a] (0.2177)
Fixed effects	No	Yes	No	No	No	Yes	No	No
Controls for X	No	No	No	Yes	No	No	No	Yes
R^2	0.177	0.198	0.184	0.210	0.041	0.058	0.046	0.080

b) National Longitudinal Surveys of Youth

Variable	Education (N = 5,619)				Log wage (N = 3, 734)			
	(1)	(2)	(3)	(4)	(1)	(2)	(3)	(4)
Parental capital	0.2665 (0.0072)	0.2566 (0.0077)	0.2570 (0.0075)	0.2556 (0.0073)	0.3465 (0.0283)	0.3257 (0.0205)	0.3257 (0.0291)	0.2983 (0.0284)
Ethnic capital			0.1165 (0.0630)	0.0990 (0.0714)			0.2843 (0.0955)	0.2983 (0.0967)
Fixed effects	No	Yes	No	No	No	Yes	No	No
Controls for X	No	No	No	Yes	No	No	No	Yes
R^2	0.247	0.261	0.248	0.267	0.091	0.104	0.092	0.146

Notes: Standard errors are reported in parentheses. Regressions (3) and (4) use a random effects estimator. Parental capital gives the value of the characteristic observed for the respondent's father, while ethnic capital gives the mean of the characteristic in the ethnic group (evaluated in the father's generation). All GSS regressions control for gender, whether the parents were immigrants, and a vector of dummies indicating the cross section from which the observation was drawn, while all NLSY regressions control for gender, whether the parents were immigrants, and a dummy variable indicating whether the respondent is enrolled in school. In addition, the vector X includes age (and age squared); and a vector of dummies indicating region of residence.

[a] The coefficients of parental and ethnic capital are significantly different from each other at the 10 percent level of significance.

In column (3) I include the ethnic capital variable in the regression. Several findings are worth noting. First, ethnic capital has a positive and significant impact on the educational attainment of respondents in the GSS, holding constant the father's educational attainment. A one-year increase in the average schooling level of an ethnic group increases the average schooling of the next generation by about 0.2 years.

Second, the coefficients of the ethnic capital and the parental education variables have roughly similar magnitudes (and the difference is not statistically significant). In a sense, ethnic capital plays as important a role as the father's human capital in determining the skills of the next generation.

Note also that the intergenerational transmission parameter describing how the mean educational attainment of the ethnic group changes over time is the sum of the coefficients of parental and ethnic capital, which in the education regression for the GSS is 0.48. This number is substantially larger than the 0.27 estimated in column (1) from a regression that ignores ethnic capital. As shown in equation (14), as long as most of the variance in earnings in the population is attributable to within-group differences, studies of intergenerational mobility that ignore ethnic capital greatly overstate the extent of regression toward the mean.

Finally, the fact that the transmission parameter is less than one implies that the external effects of ethnic capital are not sufficiently strong to generate constant or increasing returns in the production of human capital.[21] Nevertheless, the significant role played by ethnic capital in the intergenerational transmission process delays the economic convergence of ethnic groups across generations.

Although the GSS does not contain information on parental income, it does report the occupation of parents and of GSS respondents, as measured by the Hodge-Siegel-Rossi prestige score. The regression coefficients reported in Table 10.3 indicate a strong link in occupational attainment between parents and children. The transmission coefficient in the prestige score is 0.2 when ethnic capital is ignored, and about 0.6 when ethnic capital is introduced. In fact, Table 10.3 suggests that ethnic capital may play an even greater role in the transmission of labor market success (as measured by occupational prestige) than parental capital.[22]

The bottom panel of Table 10.3 reports the regressions estimated in the NLSY. As with the GSS, there is an important link between the educational attainment and wages of parents and children, as well as a link between the skills of NLSY respondents and ethnic capital, though the ethnic capital coefficient is sometimes insignificant. Nevertheless, the comparison of the results obtained using the GSS and the NLSY is remarkable because, despite the difference in the age composition of the samples, the estimated transmission coefficients are similar. Once ethnic capital is taken into account, the NLSY data yield a transmission coefficient of 0.37 for educational attainment and 0.61 for log wages. The respective statistics in the GSS are 0.48 and 0.63. Both data sets, therefore, suggest that ethnic capital is a key determinant of labor market success among ethnic children.[23] As a result, there is substantial linkage in skills across generations.

It is important to note that these findings are not driven by "outlying" ethnic groups. The raw data reported in Tables 10.1 and 10.2 indicate that two Hispanic groups, Mexicans and Puerto Ricans, have much less human capital than other ethnic groups. Because a relatively small number of ethnic groups underlie the empirical analysis, it could be argued that the results are greatly influenced by these outliers. This hypothesis, however, is incorrect. Table 10.4 reports the parental and ethnic capital coefficients estimated in both the GSS and the NLSY after omitting Mexicans and Puerto Ricans from the sample. The ethnic capital coefficient remains positive and (usually) significant when these outlying groups are excluded. In the GSS the intergenerational transmission coefficient (i.e., the sum of the parental and ethnic capital coefficients) is 0.52 for education and 0.62 for occupation. In the NLSY it is 0.50 for education and 0.53 for wages.

Table 10.4

Intergenerational Mobility in Non-hispanic Sample

a) General Social Surveys

Variable	Education (N = 6,559)		Occupation (N = 6,863)	
	(1)	(2)	(1)	(2)
Parental capital	0.2496	0.2602	0.1865	0.2028
	(0.0076)	(0.0081)	(0.0130)	(0.0129)
Ethnic capital	0.2722	0.2429	0.4325	0.3276
	(0.1194)	(0.1018)	(0.2634)	(0.2563)
Controls for X	No	Yes	No	Yes
R^2	0.156	0.195	0.043	0.077

b) National Longitudinal Surveys of Youth

Variable	Education (N = 4,793)		Log wage (N = 3,216)	
	(1)	(2)	(1)	(2)
Parental capital	0.3015	0.2980	0.3372	0.3030
	(0.0087)	(0.0086)	(0.0318)	(0.0310)
Ethnic capital	0.1896[a]	0.2271[a]	0.1980	0.0447[a]
	(0.0581)	(0.0406)	(0.3364)	(0.1930)
Controls for X	No	Yes	No	Yes
R^2	0.265	0.291	0.090	0.144

Notes: Standard errors are reported in parentheses. The regressions use a generalized least-squares random effects estimator. See the notes to Table 10.3 for additional details and for descriptions of variables.

[a] The coefficients of parental and ethnic capital are significantly different from each other at the 10 percent level of significance.

In view of the social and policy implications of the findings, it is important to consider whether the results reported in Tables 10.3 and 10.4 could be attributed to a spurious correlation between ethnic capital and the skills of children. Such a correlation arises if parental skills are measured with error. To illustrate, suppose that the intergenerational mobility process is correctly described by the regression model,

$$(15) \qquad y = \delta x + \epsilon,$$

where y gives the skill level of children, x gives the skill level of parents (and has variance σ_x^2), all variables are measured in deviations from the mean, and subscripts for individuals and ethnic groups are suppressed. The disturbance ϵ is i.i.d. and independent of x. Note that ethnic capital does not enter the "true" model.

Observed parental skills, x_1, are an imperfect measure of x. In particular, $x_1 = x + v_1$, where the random variable v_1 is i.i.d., with mean zero and variance σ_1^2. In addition, v_1 is independent of x and ϵ. It is well-known that the least-squares regression of y on x_1 provides an inconsistent estimate of the parameter δ and that

$$(16) \qquad \text{plim } \hat{\delta} = \left[\sigma_x^2 / (\sigma_x^2 + \sigma_1^2) \right] \delta.$$

Suppose that a different measure of parental skills, x_2, is available, where x_2 gives the average skill level of parents in the ethnic group, or ethnic capital. By construction, $x_2 = x + v_2$, where v_2 is i.i.d., with mean zero, variance σ_2^2, and is independent of ϵ and v_1.[24] Note, however, that v_2 is *not* independent of x because high values of parental skills imply lower values of v_2 within ethnic groups. In fact, corr $(x, v_2) = -\sigma_2/\sigma_x$. Using this notation, the regression model estimated in Table 10.3 is given by

(17) $$y = \theta_1 x_1 + \theta_2 x_2 + \epsilon'.$$

The least-squares estimators of the parameters in (17) have the following properties:

(18a) $$\text{plim } \hat{\theta}_1 = \left[\pi h / (1 - h(1 - \pi)) \right] \delta,$$

(18b) $$\text{plim } \hat{\theta}_2 = \left[(1 - h) / (1 - h(1 - \pi)) \right] \delta,$$

where $h = \sigma_x^2 / (\sigma_x^2 + \sigma_1^2)$; and $\pi = \sigma_2^2 \sigma_x^2$, or the fraction of the true variance that is attributable to within-group variability (i.e., the within-variance). Equations (18a) and (18b) indicate that the coefficients of both parental capital and ethnic capital are inconsistent estimates of the transmission parameter δ. Nevertheless, the estimated coefficients (asymptotically) sum up to the true intergenerational parameter δ. Note that the impact of ethnic capital will be larger the greater the errors in measuring parental skills (and is zero if parental capital is perfectly measured).

Equations (18a) and (18b) can be used to assess the practical importance of the spurious correlation introduced by measurement error in generating the results presented in Tables 10.3 and 10.4. Given plausible values for the primitive parameters of the model, it is possible to predict what the coefficients of parental and ethnic capital would be if the true model did not include ethnic capital and if the observed measure of parental capital was contaminated by measurement error.

Suppose, for instance, that the true $\delta = 0.4$, which is in the high end of the estimates reported in the literature. Suppose also that $\pi = 0.9$, so that most of the variation in parental skills is within-group rather than between-group (in fact, the observed π's are as high as 0.96). Finally, suppose that the noise-to-signal ratio var (v_1)/var (x) is 0.33, so that there is substantial measurement error in the observed measure of parental skills. Equations (18a) and (18b) then predict that the coefficient of parental capital should be 0.29, and that the coefficient of ethnic capital should be 0.11.

The evidence reported in Tables 10.3 and 10.4 indicates that the effect of ethnic capital is generally much larger (and that of parental capital much smaller).[25] In fact, many of the ethnic capital coefficients estimated in Tables 10.3 and 10.4 (particularly in the GSS) are consistent with the measurement error model only if the noise-to-signal ratio is between one and two. It is unlikely, therefore, that the spurious correlation introduced by measurement errors accounts for a large fraction of the estimated impact of the ethnic capital variable.[26]

10.5. Ethnic Capital and Parental Birthplace

It is likely that ethnic capital plays a more important role in the inter-generational transmission process in households whose ancestors are recent arrivals to the United States. As social, cultural, and economic assimilation occurs across generations, the importance of the ethnic enclave diminishes, exposure to ethnic "role models" decreases, and the importance of ethnic capital in intergenerational transmission may decline.

To ascertain the importance of this hypothesis, I reestimated the regressions separately on the sample of second-generation Americans (i.e., children of immigrants), and on the remaining sample of na-tives whose parents were born in the United States. For brevity, this latter sample will be referred to as third-generation Americans, even though it contains workers in the third and higher-order generations. Table 10.5 summarizes the estimated coefficients by generation.

Table 10.5

Intergenerational Mobility for Second- and Third-Generation Americans

Data set/variable	Second generation			Third generation		
	Parental capital	Ethnic capital	Controls for X	Parental capital	Ethnic capital	Controls for X
GSS: Education	0.1741	0.2267	No	0.2620	0.2071	No
	(0.0225)	(0.1079)		(0.0080)	(0.1099)	
GSS: Education	0.1538	0.2568	Yes	0.2744	0.1983	Yes
	(0.0248)	(0.1209)		(0.0085)	(0.0859)	
GSS: Occupation	0.1637	0.7807[a]	No	0.1843	0.3008	No
	(0.0346)	(0.0559)		(0.0137)	(0.4049)	
GSS: Occupation	0.1679	0.6441[a]	Yes	0.2005	0.2244	Yes
	(0.0357)	(0.1492)		(0.0136)	(0.3731)	
NLSY: Education	0.1020	0.0681	No	0.2836	0.1340[a]	No
	(0.0223)	(0.0970)		(0.0080)	(0.0589)	
NLSY: Education	0.1072	0.0317	Yes	0.2816	0.1196[a]	Yes
	(0.0222)	(0.0982)		(0.0078)	(0.0786)	
NLSY: Log wage	0.2162	0.7017	No	0.3385	0.2078	No
	(0.0844)	(0.2255)		(0.0310)	(0.1054)	
NLSY: Log wage	0.2675	0.4188	Yes	0.3048	0.1152	Yes
	(0.0816)	(0.2461)		(0.0303)	(0.2780)	

Notes: Standard errors are reported in parentheses. The regressions use a generalized least-squares random effects estimator. See the notes to Table 10.3 for additional details and for descriptions of variables. The sample sizes are as follows. For the second generation: GSS Education, $N = 796$; GSS Occupation, $N = 947$; NLSY Education, $N = 508$; NLSY log wage, $N = 346$. For the third generation: GSS Education, $N = 5,960$; GSS Occupation, $N = 6,119$; NLSY Education, $N = 5,111$; NLSY log wage, $N = 3,388$.

[a] The coefficients of parental and ethnic capital are significantly different from each other at the 10 percent level of significance.

In general, ethnic capital plays a significant role in intergenerational mobility for both second- and third-generation Americans. The point estimates of the ethnic capital coefficient, however, tend to be greater for the second generation than for the third, particularly in the regressions that link labor market outcomes (i.e., occupation or log wages) across generations.

For instance, the GSS data indicate that the coefficient of ethnic capital on occupational prestige for second-generation workers is over 0.6, while the same coefficient is 0.3 (and has a very large standard error) for third-generation workers. In the NLSY, the coefficient of ethnic capital on log wages is 0.7 for the second generation and 0.2 for the third. In sum, the evidence suggests that the impact of ethnic capital on intergenerational mobility is lower for persons who have resided in the United States for longer periods. Nevertheless, it is important to note that ethnic capital tends to slow down the process of convergence across ethnic groups even in the third generation.

It is also likely that ethnic capital plays a more influential role when both parents are members of the ethnic group than when only one parent is a member. Both the GSS and the NLSY allow a test of this hypothesis. In particular, both data sets provide information on which of the parents (if any) were born outside the United States. In addition, the NLSY reports the specific country of birth for both parents. As noted earlier, the NLSY indicates that the conditional probability that both parents are born in the same source country (given that both are born outside the United States) is over 0.9.

Table 10.6 reports the relevant coefficients from regressions estimated separately for second-generation households where only one parent is foreign born and for households where both parents are foreign born. The evidence is mixed. The GSS education regressions, for example, indicate that ethnic capital has a bigger impact in households where both parents are foreign born. The NLSY results, however, are inconclusive: many of the ethnic capital coefficients are not significantly different from zero. The ambiguous results probably arise because I am using a random effects estimator on relatively small samples.[27]

Despite the mixed picture portrayed by Table 10.6, the preponderance of the evidence summarized in this chapter indicates that ethnic capital plays an essential role in the intergenerational transmission of skills. Although I have stressed the interpretation of the findings in terms of the human capital externality introduced by ethnic environment, this interpretation is not the only one consistent with the data. Such factors as discrimination or lack of access to schools, credit markets, or other institutions can also generate a correlation between the skills of children and the average skills of fathers in the ethnic group (after holding constant the own father's skills).

Table 10.6

Intergenerational Mobility for Second-generation Americans, by Birthplace of Parents

Data set/variable	Both parents born abroad			Only one parent born abroad		
	Parental capital	Ethnic capital	Controls for X	Parental capital	Ethnic capital	Controls for X
GSS: Education	0.1355	0.4995[a]	No	0.2007	0.0446	No
	(0.0360)	(0.1419)		(0.0296)	(0.1787)	
GSS: Education	0.1123	0.6369"	Yes	0.2004	0.1632	Yes
	(0.0399)	(0.1279)		(0.0324)	(0.0390)	
GSS: Occupation	0.1232	0.6290[a]	No	0.2047	0.6373	No
	(0.0529)	(0.2306)		(0.0470)	(0.3183)	
GSS: Occupation	0.1167	0.3142	Yes	0.2122	0.6261	Yes
	(0.0542)	(0.1608)		(0.0483)	(0.3258)	
NLSY: Education	0.1397	-0.0154	No	0.0901	0.0346	No
	(0.0315)	(0.1841)		(0.0307)	(0.2120)	
NLSY: Education	0.1326	-0.0591	Yes	0.1119	0.0995	Yes
	(0.0316)	(0.1811)		(0.0310)	(0.0665)	
NLSY: Log wage	0.5735	0.7482	No	0.1203	0.2995	No
	(0.5480)	(0.4576)		(0.1142)	(0.4570)	
NLSY: Log wage	0.2539	0.2965	Yes	0.2806	0.6988	Yes
	(0.1240)	(0.5073)		(0.1075)	(0.2588)	

Notes: Standard errors are reported in parentheses. The regressions use a generalized least-squares random effects estimator. See the notes to Table 10.3 for additional details and for descriptions of variables. The sample sizes are as follows. For both parents born abroad: GSS Education, $N = 350$; GSS Occupation, $N = 440$; NLSY Education, $N = 199$; NLSY log wage, $N = 147$. For the sample where only one parent is born abroad: GSS Education, $N = 446$; GSS Occupation, $N = 507$; NLSY Education, $N = 309$; NLSY log wage, $N = 199$.
[a] The coefficients of parental and ethnic capital are significantly different from each other at the 10 percent level of significance.

I should note, however, that some of these factors may not necessarily generate a positive correlation between mean skills in the ethnic group in generation t and the skills of children in generation $t + 1$. Suppose, for instance, that statistical discrimination leads to a positive relationship between a worker's wage and the mean skills of his ethnic group (holding constant the individual's skills). Because of the income effect, workers in ethnic groups with high average skills will invest more in their children, while the substitution effect indicates that these workers will invest less in their children. The correlation between what I call ethnic capital and children's skills would then be determined by the parametric specification of the utility function.

In the end, the usefulness of the ethnic capital approach will depend on whether interpreting ethnicity as a human capital externality increases our understanding of the many ethnic differentials observed in the U.S. economy, not just those that have been the focus of this chapter.

10.6. Ethnic Capital and Black Intergenerational Mobility

The empirical analysis presented in the previous sections was based on a sample of ethnic Americans that did not include blacks. The relatively slow economic progress of blacks across generations has been the focus of extensive study (Smith and Welch, 1989). It is fair to conclude that this literature has been unable to explain why the economic progress of blacks lags behind that of many other ethnic or racial groups. It is of substantial interest, therefore, to determine whether the ethnic capital hypothesis can partly explain the relatively slow intergenerational mobility of blacks.

As long as ethnic capital plays an important role in human capital accumulation, the slow progress of blacks arises partly because, as a group, blacks have relatively low levels of human capital. To assess the importance of ethnic capital in retarding black economic growth, I use the regressions estimated among third-generation workers (and reported in Table 10.5) to predict the change in black skills and earnings across generations. The simulation uses the regressions estimated in the sample of third-generation ethnic whites because blacks have been in the United States for several generations.[28] I calculate two alternative predictions: the first uses the regression model that ignores ethnic capital (Equation (10)), while the second uses the model that includes ethnic capital (Equation (13)).

Table 10.7 presents the out-of-sample predictions for black intergenerational mobility using both the GSS and the NLSY.

Consider, for example, educational attainment among black respondents in the GSS. The typical black GSS respondent has 12.3 years of schooling, while his father has 8.7 years. The regression model that ignores the importance of ethnic capital predicts that, given his father's educational attainment, the typical black respondent should have had 12.7 years of schooling, or about half a year more than was actually observed. In contrast, the model that includes ethnic capital predicts that the educational attainment of black respondents should be 12.4, which is closer to the value actually observed.

Table 10.7

Predicted Intergenerational Mobility of Blacks

Data set/variable	Mean of black fathers	Mean of black children	Prediction ignoring ethnic capital	Prediction including ethnic capital	Controls for X
GSS: Education	8.666	12.278	12.726	12.438	No
(N = 1,001)			(0.040)	(0.240)	
GSS: Education	8.666	12.278	12.629	12.353	Yes
			(0.041)	(0.188)	
GSS: Occupation	33.000	35.075	40.310	37.153	No
(N = 1,164)			(0.234)	(1.833)	
GSS: Occupation	33.000	35.075	40.179	37.935	Yes
			(0.246)	(1.782)	
NLSY: Education	10.106	12.641	12.453	12.368	No
(N = 1,926)			(0.030)	(0.073)	
NLSY: Education	10.106	12.641	12.445	12.389	Yes
			(0.033)	(0.040)	
NLSY: Log wage	1.215	1.843	1.936	1.906	No
(N = 1,066)			(0.010)	(0.018)	
NLSY: Log wage	1.215	1.843	1.924	1.905	Yes
			(0.012)	(0.052)	

Notes: Standard errors are reported in parentheses. The sample sizes report the number of blacks over which the relevant characteristics are evaluated. See the notes to Table 10.3 for additional details and for descriptions of variables.

Similarly, the typical black GSS respondent has an occupational prestige score of 35.1, while his father has 33.0. The intergenerational mobility model that ignores ethnic capital predicts that GSS respondents should have a prestige score of about 40.3, about 5 points more than was observed, while the ethnic capital model predicts that respondents should have a score of 37.1, an overprediction of only 2 points. It should be noted, however, that the standard error associated with the predictions that use the ethnic capital model is quite large.

The results using the NLSY data are less suggestive. The prediction of educational attainment is barely affected by the inclusion of ethnic capital. Black respondents in the NLSY have 12.6 years of schooling, while their fathers have 10.1 years. Both regression models predict that NLSY black respondents should have about 12.4 years of schooling. In contrast, the log wage predictions indicate that, given their father's wage, NLSY respondents should have about 3 percent lower wage rates if one uses the model that incorporates ethnic capital.

Overall, the results suggest that the omission of ethnic capital from the analysis of intergenerational mobility tends to overpredict black economic progress. In the GSS data the evidence reveals that the introduction of ethnic capital leads to growth rates in educational attainment and occupation that are somewhat closer to those that were actually observed, although these growth rates are imprecisely estimated. The evidence presented in Table 10.7 does not conclusively prove that the low level of ethnic capital in the black population is the single most important factor retarding black economic progress. Nevertheless, the data suggest that ethnic capital may be playing a role.

10.7. Summary

This chapter presented an analysis of the relationship between ethnicity and intergenerational mobility. The main hypothesis of the chapter is that ethnicity acts as an externality in the production function for human capital. In particular, the quality of the ethnic environment in which a person is raised, which I call ethnic capital, influences the skills and labor market outcomes of the children. This human capital externality, similar to those that motivate much of the new economic growth literature and also similar to the concept of "social capital" in the sociology literature, indicates that differences in skills and labor market outcomes among ethnic groups may persist across generations, and need never converge.

To assess the importance of ethnic capital, I analyzed data from the General Social Surveys and the National Longitudinal Surveys of Youth. The empirical evidence yields two findings. First, ethnic capital plays a major role in intergenerational mobility. The skills and labor market outcomes of today's generation depend not only on the skills and labor market experiences of their parents, but also on the average skills and labor market experiences of the ethnic group in the parent's generation. Second, the introduction of ethnic capital into the analysis provides a very different portrait of intergenerational mobility than that available in the existing literature. In particular, there is much more persistence of skills and earnings capacity across generations than is generally believed. As a result, ethnic differences in skills and labor market outcomes may persist for several generations.

It is apparent that the empirical evidence has an important policy implication. Government interventions designed to increase the average skill level of a racial or ethnic group in one generation significantly improve the economic well-being of all future generations. In addition, these interventions lead to a much faster convergence of average skill levels among the various groups. As a result, models of intergenerational mobility that ignore the significant impact of the policy shocks on the level of ethnic capital may greatly underestimate the economic benefits of these government policies.

Although these results are provocative, this study only represents an initial attempt at analyzing the role played by ethnic capital in the labor market. There are many questions raised by the concept of ethnic capital that I have ignored in both the theoretical and empirical study. Future research, for instance, should consider the link between residential location and ethnic capital. This link leads to a number of interesting issues regarding the migration decisions of ethnic groups, and raises the possibility that parents "choose" particular levels of ethnic capital by migrating to areas that offer the social characteristics they wish to expose to their children.

In addition, the human capital externalities associated with ethnicity in this chapter probably arise in many other contexts. After all, "neighborhood effects" work through a myriad of social, cultural, and economic institutions. In view of the significance of questions relating to social mobility and the economic progress of minorities, it is evident that the further study of these human capital externalities is a promising area for future research.

11

Ethnicity, Neighborhoods, and Human-Capital Externalities

After finishing my initial paper on the ethnic capital hypothesis, the follow-up question asked itself: how was the ethnic externality transmitted? One potential answer lies in the well-known fact that there is a great deal of ethnic residential segregation in most immigrant-receiving countries, so that children belonging to a particular ethnic group are much more likely to be exposed to members of that group than to members of other groups.

I quickly learned that there were two difficult obstacles in examining this general hypothesis. The first is simply the non-random sorting of immigrant ethnic groups across geographic areas. This endogeneity permeates and contaminates almost all attempts to measure the impact of "peer groups." I attempted to solve this problem by focusing on how the nonrandom settlement of parents affects the well-being of the children after the latter grow up. The second obstacle revolves around the data constraints involved in estimating the "neighborhood effects" models in the immigration context. In addition to requiring information on ethnicity, and on parental and children skills, the analysis also requires detailed data on geographic location - preferably at the neighborhood level - at the time the children of immigrants were growing up. I am certain that the severe data constraints have hampered continued progress in this very important set of questions.

George J. Borjas (2015)

The original version of this chapter was published as: Borjas, G. J. (1995). Ethnicity, Neighborhoods, and Human-Capital Externalities, in: The American Economic Review, 85(3): 365–90. © 1995 by American Economic Association. The author is grateful to Julian Betts, Thomas MaCurdy, James Rauch, Glenn Sueyoshi, Stephen Trejo, and Finis Welch for helpful comments, and to the National Science Foundation and the Russell Sage Foundation for financial support.

Ethnic neighborhoods have long been a dominant feature of American cities (and of cities in many other countries). In fact, segregation by race and ethnicity often defines the invisible line that creates a neighborhood. These neighborhoods insulate people of similar backgrounds and foster a set of cultural attitudes, social contacts, and economic opportunities that affect workers throughout their lives.

In earlier work (Borjas 1992; 1994a), I have argued that ethnicity has an external effect on the human-capital accumulation process.[1] Persons raised in advantageous ethnic environments will be exposed to social and economic factors that increase their productivity, and the larger or more frequent the amount of this exposure, the higher the resulting "quality" of the worker. As with the models that dominate the new growth literature, sufficiently strong ethnic externalities may delay the convergence of ethnic differentials indefinitely. My earlier empirical work indicated that the earnings of children are affected strongly not only by parental earnings as in the usual models of intergenerational income mobility, but also by the mean earnings of the ethnic group in the parents' generation (which I called "ethnic capital"). As a result, the ethnic spillover effect retards intergenerational improvement for relatively disadvantaged ethnic groups and slows down the deterioration of skills (i.e., the regression toward the mean) among the more advantaged groups.

The process through which the ethnic externalities are transmitted, however, is not well understood. This paper investigates one possible mechanism, ethnic neighborhoods. The insight that human-capital externalities and geography are linked is not new. In his pathbreaking work, Robert E. Lucas (1988) cites the crowding of similarly skilled workers into a small number of city blocks as a key determinant of the economic development of cities. Similarly, William Julius Wilson's (1987) influential work on the creation and growth of the underclass argues that blacks who live in poor neighborhoods are not exposed to "mainstream" role models, thus hampering the economic mobility of blacks.

This paper presents an empirical study of the link between geography and ethnic externalities. The analysis uses the 1/100 Neighborhood File of the 1970 Public Use Sample of the U.S. Census and a specially designed version of the National Longitudinal Surveys of Youth (NLSY). The census data group workers into one of over 40,000 neighborhoods, while the NLSY File groups workers into one of 1,978 zip codes. Hence it is possible to determine the extent to which ethnic groups segregate in particular neighborhoods and the impact of this segregation on the process of human-capital accumulation and inter-generational mobility.[2]

The main finding of the analysis is that residential segregation and the influence of ethnic capital on the process of intergenerational mobility are intimately linked. In particular, the impact of ethnic capital on the skills of the next generation arises partly because the ethnic-capital variable is an excellent proxy for the socioeconomic background of the neighborhood where the children were raised, and these neighborhood characteristics influence intergenerational mobility. In other words, the ethnic-capital model provides an alternative way of capturing neighbor-hood effects. Ethnic capital, however, plays an additional role in inter-generational mobility. Even among persons who grow up in the same neighborhood, ethnic capital matters when children are exposed fre-quently to other persons who share the same ethnic background.

11.1. Ethnicity and Neighborhoods

Because little is known about the residential clustering of many of the ethnic groups used in the empirical analysis which follows, it is useful first to document the link between ethnicity and residential segregation.[3] The descriptive analysis is based initially on data drawn from the 1/100 Neighborhood File of the 1970 U.S. Census (15 percent questionnaire). These data not only contain the individual-level de-mographic variables typically available in census files, but also group individuals into one of 42,950 "neighborhoods." Neighborhoods are contiguous and relatively compact (roughly the size of a census tract), and they have an average population of 4,000 persons (U.S. Bureau of the Census 1973d). Although the specific geographic location of a neighborhood cannot be determined (other than its location in one of the nine census regions), the data file reports a number of demo-graphic characteristics describing the neighborhood (such as the frac-tion of persons who are either first- or second-generation Americans, and the fraction of persons who are college graduates).

I restrict the analysis to persons aged 18–64. I begin by document-ing the residential segregation of immigrants and second-generation Americans, and the extent to which residential segregation changes across generations. A person is an immigrant if he or she was born outside the United States (or its possessions); a person is a second-gen-eration American if either parent was born outside the United States.

All other persons are grouped and labeled "third-generation" Americans, although this sample obviously includes higher-order generations. The 1970 Census does not provide any information on the ethnic ancestry of persons in the "third" generation.

As already noted, the neighborhood file reports the proportion of the population in each neighborhood that is either first or second generation. This statistic was calculated by the Bureau of the Census using all available observations in the neighborhood (i.e., the 15 percent sample of respondents who filled out the relevant questionnaire). I use these data to estimate the fraction of persons in the neighborhood who are either first or second generation for the average person in a number of demographic groups.

Table 11.1 summarizes the extent of residential segregation. The first row reports that the average immigrant resided in a neighborhood where 32.7 percent of the population was either first- or second-generation. This pattern of residential location differs significantly from what one would expect if immigrants were randomly allocated across neighborhoods. The 1970 Census indicates that only 16.6 percent of the population was first or second generation.

Table 11.1

Residential Segregation in the 1970 Census

Neighborhood characteristics of average person in:	Percentage of population in neighborhood that is:				
	First generation	First or second generation	Black	Hispanic	Sample size
First generation	15.3	32.7	6.9	10.2	63,099
Second generation	6.7	28.2	4.3	5.2	156,134
Third generation	3.8	13.8	11.7	3.9	905,213
Hispanics:					
First generation	22.2	36.7	6.5	35.0	10,713
Second generation	9.4	27.3	5.1	33.0	10,801
Third generation	8.9	21.9	11.4	28.8	25,202
Third generation:					
Blacks	3.1	8.0	54.7	3.7	109,533
Whites	3.7	14.4	5.6	3.1	771,359

Notes: The "white" sample includes all nonblack, non-Hispanic third-generation workers. The population proportions are as follows: immigrants, 4.8 percent; first or second generation, 16.6 percent; blacks, 11.1 percent; and Hispanics, 4.4 percent.

Source: U.S. Bureau of the Census (1973d).

Because the aggregate characteristics reported in the neighborhood file do not include the proportion of the neighborhood's population that is foreign born, I calculate this statistic by combining the birthplace data reported in each individual's record with the aggregate neighborhood characteristics provided by the Census Bureau.[4] The typical immigrant lives in a neighborhood that is 15.3 percent immigrant, even though only 4.8 percent of the population was foreign born.

Residential segregation persists into the second generation. As the second row of Table 11.1 shows, the average second-generation American resides in a neighborhood that is 28.2 percent first or second generation. The 1970 Census does not provide any information on ancestry past the second generation. As a result, I cannot determine how the pattern of residential segregation changes beyond the second generation for most groups. Intergenerational changes in residential segregation, however, can be documented for the subpopulation of Hispanics, the vast majority of whom are foreign born or have parents or grandparents who are foreign born.[5] Table 11.1 indicates that there is very little movement of Hispanics out of Hispanic neighborhoods even in the third generation. The average Hispanic immigrant lives in a neighborhood that is 35 percent Hispanic; the average second-generation Hispanic lives in one that is 33 percent Hispanic; and the typical third-generation Hispanic lives in one that is 29 percent Hispanic. The fraction of Hispanics in the population is only 4.4 percent. The clustering of Hispanics into Hispanic neighborhoods, therefore, is prevalent and persistent.[6]

In addition to the clustering of first- and second-generation persons into certain neighborhoods, there is substantial segregation by ethnic group. To document the differences across national origin groups, I focus on the 39 largest groups in the data. These 39 groups include 83.7 percent of all first-generation Americans, and over 95 percent of all second-generation Americans. The national origin of immigrants is, of course, determined by their country of birth. The national origin of a second-generation person is determined by the father's birthplace (unless only the mother was foreign born, in which case it is determined by the mother's birthplace). Table 11.2 lists the 39 national-origin groups used in the analysis.

I first calculated the proportion of the population who are either first or second generation and who have a particular ethnic ancestry. This number is reported in the first column of the table and represents the probability that a first- or second-generation person from that group will be found in a particular neighborhood *if* the ethnic group is distributed randomly across neighborhoods. Most of the groups make up relatively small fractions of the population: only 0.8 percent of the population, for instance, is first- or second-generation Irish.

Table 11.2 reveals that immigrants and their children, regardless of national origin, cluster in neighborhoods that have large numbers of first- or second-generation Americans. The typical second-generation person of English ancestry resides in a neighborhood that is 23.5 percent first or second generation; the respective statistic for Irish persons is 31.3 percent, for Italians 32.0 percent, and for Mexicans 27.8 percent. There is little evidence, therefore, that only economically disadvantaged groups are crowded into ethnic neighborhoods.

Table 11.2

Residential Segregation in the 1970 Census, by National Origin Group

		First generation			Second generation		
		Percentage of population in neighborhood that is:			Percentage of population in neighborhood that is:		
National origin	Percentage of population in group	First or second generation	Same ethnicity	Sample size	First or second generation	Same ethnicity	Sample size
Austria	0.6	34.5	2.0	883	30.1	2.1	6,007
Azores	0.04	37.1	8.0	184	30.5	3.5	320
Belgium	0.07	28.9	0.4	250	21.8	0.7	573
British West Indies	0.03	24.8	0.8	175	24.0	0.8	188
Canada	1.8	25.7	6.2	6,843	24.8	7.4	13,085
Cuba	0.3	48.7	21.3	3,119	27.6	4.7	270
China	0.2	38.5	9.2	1,617	33.5	6.2	635
Czechoslovakia	0.5	34.6	2.3	797	25.6	2.9	4,571
Denmark	0.2	24.9	0.5	289	20.2	0.9	1,608
England	0.8	24.3	1.5	3,113	23.5	1.5	6,367
Finland	0.1	29.1	1.5	194	25.5	3.9	1,200
France	0.2	28.7	0.4	811	23.8	0.3	1,184
Germany	1.7	27.2	2.9	5,930	21.9	3.2	13,089
Greece	0.3	38.3	2.6	1,147	28.3	1.1	1,913
Hungary	0.4	34.3	2.6	1,020	28.0	1.9	3,472
Ireland	0.8	36.2	4.6	1,434	31.3	3.3	7,137
Italy	2.8	37.7	15.3	5,193	32.0	12.1	26,476
Jamaica	0.06	28.4	2.2	507	22.3	1.5	163
Japan	0.2	26.1	3.2	1,020	33.7	12.6	1,716
Latvia	0.04	27.0	0.2	245	33.1	0.1	260
Lebanon	0.05	27.0	0.3	118	23.7	0.4	476
Lithuania	0.2	36.2	3.7	325	30.6	1.5	2,128
Mexico	1.3	35.4	22.6	5,746	27.8	18.1	8,412
Netherlands	0.2	23.9	1.8	689	21.5	3.9	1,725
Northern Ireland	0.1	29.4	0.3	233	28.1	0.2	573
Norway	0.3	28.5	1.8	422	22.1	3.0	3,203
Other West Indies	0.04	28.8	2.5	254	25.5	1.3	250
Philippines	0.2	31.0	5.9	1,477	30.1	6.5	606
Poland	1.7	40.2	9.1	2,846	32.0	7.8	15,182
Portugal	0.1	40.9	11.2	654	32.7	6.8	1,030
Romania	0.1	38.6	0.8	373	34.5	0.7	1,150
Scotland	0.3	27.5	0.7	1,013	24.4	0.7	2,517
Sweden	0.4	29.1	1.4	445	22.3	1.7	4,284
Switzerland	0.1	26.7	0.6	315	20.3	0.8	947
Syria	0.04	30.9	1.7	103	27.9	0.8	387
Turkey	0.06	36.6	0.2	251	33.0	0.3	459
USSR	1.2	38.8	7.0	1,738	34.9	7.8	12,067
Wales	0.1	23.7	0.1	99	21.3	0.3	529
Yugoslavia	0.3	31.9	2.7	930	25.1	2.4	2,309
Sample of 39 countries	-	32.9	8.3	52,802	28.3	6.6	148,468

Note: The residential-segregation measures give the percentage of the population in the neighborhood that belongs to the specified ethnic group for the average person in the sample.

Source: U.S. Bureau of the Census (1973d).

To document how type-j ethnics cluster in specific neighborhoods, I calculate the fraction of the neighborhood's population that has the same ethnicity as the average type-j person. The Census Bureau does not report the fraction of the population in each neighborhood that belongs to each of the groups. Hence I calculated this statistic from within the 1/100 sample. Because the family members of a type-j ethnic are likely to be type-j ethnics, and because the 1/100 Census File is a random sample of households, the stratified sampling scheme introduces an upward bias in the calculation of the fraction of the neighborhood's population that is type j. I choose a conservative index of within-group residential segregation and calculate (for each person in the data) the proportion of persons in the neighborhood who reside outside the household unit and who are type-j ethnics.[7] Table 11.2 reports the average of this statistic for each of the groups. In view of the relatively small sample size available for each neighborhood (the mean and median number of observations in a neighborhood is 26, and the interquartile range is 9, from 21 to 30), some caution is required in the interpretation of the data.

The probability that type-j ethnics live near other type-j ethnics is much higher than one would expect if type-j ethnics were randomly distributed across neighborhoods. Among second-generation workers, the typical person of Irish ancestry lives in a neighborhood that is 3.3 percent Irish, although first- and second-generation Irish make up only 0.8 percent of the population; the typical Italian lives in a neighborhood that is 12.1 percent Italian, although Italians make up only 2.8 percent of the population; and the typical Mexican lives in a neighborhood that is 18.1 percent Mexican, although Mexicans make up only 1.3 percent of the population. Among the 39 national-origin groups, the typical immigrant lives in a neighborhood in which 8.3 percent of the population shares the same ethnic background, and the typical second-generation person lives in a neighborhood in which 6.6 percent of the population shares the same background.

Table 11.3

Residential Segregation in the 1970 Census, by Demographic Characteristics

Neighborhood characteristics of average person in:	Percentage of population in neighborhood that is				Sample size
	First or second generation	Black	Hispanic	Same ethnicity	
First generation:					
Age:					
18-34	31.7	7.9	11.9	8.7	21,532
35-64	33.2	6.3	9.3	8.2	41,567
Education:					
Less than 12 years	35.5	7.3	13.3	11.7	30,590
12 years	30.8	6.6	7.8	5.8	17,000
13-15 years	29.5	6.1	7.4	4.6	7,959
16 or more years	29.1	6.4	5.7	3.4	7,550
Year moved to house:					
Before 1960	32.5	6.3	7.4	7.7	13,623
1960-1966	33.9	6.3	10.0	8.8	18,690
1967-1970	32.1	7.4	11.6	8.3	30,786
Second generation:					
Age:					
18-34	27.4	4.9	7.6	6.6	31,824
35-64	28.5	4.1	4.6	6.5	124,310
Education:					
Less than 12 years	28.7	4.8	6.7	8.4	61,896
12 years	28.1	3.9	4.4	6.0	56,725
13-15 years	27.4	3.9	4.6	4.7	19,311
16 or more years	27.8	3.8	3.3	4.2	18,212
Year moved to house:					
Before 1960	29.4	4.4	4.3	7.4	65,585
1960-1966	28.5	3.9	5.4	6.5	45,926
1967-1970	26.3	4.3	6.2	5.4	44,623
Third generation:					
Age:					
18-34	14.5	11.4	4.1	-	425,477
35-64	13.2	11.9	3.7	-	479,477
Education:					
Less than 12 years	11.5	16.5	4.3	-	346,392
12 years	14.5	9.4	3.6	-	334,888
13-15 years	15.9	8.1	3.9	-	129,884
16 or more years	17.0	6.7	3.3	-	94,049
Year moved to house:					
Before 1960	13.9	11.4	3.3	-	242,945
1960-1966	13.6	12.3	3.8	-	255,798
1967-1970	13.9	11.4	4.3	-	406,470

Source: U.S. Bureau of the Census (1973d).

I conclude the descriptive analysis of the census data by document-ing that ethnic residential segregation exists across a number of de-mographic and skill groups. Table 11.3 shows that there is little differ-ence in ethnic residential segregation across age groups. The typical second-generation person aged 18–34 resides in a neighborhood that is 27.4 percent first or second generation, while the respective statistic for an older person is 28.5 percent. In addition, the differences in residential segregation across education groups are often small. The typical high-school dropout in the second generation lives in a neighborhood that is 28.7 percent first or second generation, while the respective statistic for the typical college graduate is 27.8 percent. Finally, the data indicate that internal migration decisions among first- and second-generation Americans do not seem to alter the ethnic composition of their residential environments. Second-generation persons who have lived in the same house for over ten years live in a neighborhood that is 29.4 percent first or second generation, while the respective statistic for persons who have lived in the house fewer than three years is 26.3 percent.

The NLSY reveals even stronger patterns of residential segregation. The analysis uses a version of the NLSY that identifies the subset of persons who resided in the same zip code in 1979, at the time the survey of young persons (aged 14–22) began. Hence it is possible to determine whether NLSY respondents live near other NLSY respondents who share the same ethnic background.[8]

Ethnicity is determined from the response to the question: "What is your origin or descent?" Although most persons in the NLSY gave only one response to the question, about one-third of the respondents gave multiple answers. In these cases, I used the main ethnic background (as identified by the respondent) to classify people into ethnic categories.

For each person in the data, I calculated the probability that other NLSY respondents in the zip code had the same ethnic background. The NLSY, however, surveyed other persons in the family unit who were in the "correct" age range (i.e., 14–22 in 1979). As a result, there are large numbers of siblings in the data: 27 percent of the respondents have one sibling, and an additional 19 percent have at least two siblings in the data. To avoid the bias introduced by this sampling scheme, I calculated the residential-segregation measures on the sample of nonrelated persons who reside outside the household unit.[9] Moreover, because the NLSY oversampled blacks and other minorities, I used the sampling weights in the calculations.

The segregation indexes are reported in Table 11.4 for the 25 ethnic groups identifiable in the NLSY.[10] There is strong evidence of residential segregation. The average black lived in a neighborhood that was 63.4 percent black, while the average Mexican lived in a neighborhood that was 50.3 percent Mexican. Overall, the typical NLSY respondent lived in a neighborhood where 30.4 percent of other nonrelated respondents shared a common ethnic background.[11]

Table 11.4
Residential Segregation in the NLSY, by National Origin Group

Ethnicity	Percentage of population in group	Percentage of population in neighborhood with same ethnic background	Sample size
American	7.6	18.2	743
American Indian	5.9	12.9	624
Asian Indian	0.2	2.0	22
Black	14.9	63.4	3,055
Chinese	0.2	3.5	26
Cuban	0.4	33.3	117
English	18.9	23.9	1,587
Filipino	0.4	5.0	44
French	3.5	5.6	316
German	17.4	25.7	1,420
Greek	0.4	7.2	31
Hawaiian	0.1	0.2	20
Irish	11.0	14.3	956
Italian	6.2	16.3	498
Japanese	0.2	0.0	20
Korean	0.1	0.0	6
Mexican	4.1	50.3	1,174
Other Hispanic	0.9	9.3	214
Polish	3.1	12.8	242
Portuguese	0.6	19.7	97
Puerto Rican	1.2	29.8	328
Russian	0.6	0.3	47
Scottish	1.5	4.6	122
Vietnamese	0.0	0.0	1
Welsh	0.5	1.0	35
All	-	30.4	11,745

Source: National Longitudinal Surveys of Youth (NLSY).

Note that this statistic is much larger than the respective statistic in the census data, where only 7–8 percent of a neighborhood's population belonged to the same group. The census results, however, underestimate the extent of residential segregation because all third-generation workers are classified as nonethnics (because no information is provided on the ethnic background of third-generation persons). As a result, even though the typical immigrant in the census lives in a neighborhood where 8.3 percent of the population is composed of first- or second-generation persons who belong to the same ethnic group, a much larger fraction of the neighborhood's population might be composed of third-generation workers who also belong to the same ethnic group. The NLSY avoids this problem because all persons in the data (regardless of generation) report their ancestry.

11.2. Econometric Framework

My objective is to determine the relationship between ethnic externalities and neighborhood effects in the intergenerational transmission process. The econometric model underlying the analysis is given by

$$(1) \qquad y_{ij} = \beta_1 x_{ij} + \beta_2 \bar{x}_j + \varepsilon_{ij},$$

where y_{ij} measures the skills (such as educational attainment or the log wage) of person i in ethnic group j; x_{ij} gives the skills of his father; and x_j gives the average skills of the ethnic group in the father's generation (which I call ethnic capital). Note that $\bar{x}_j$ takes on the same value for all persons in group j. All variables are measured in deviations from the mean.

Equation (1) can be derived from a model in which utility-maximizing parents invest in their children, and in which ethnicity has an external effect on the production of children's skills (Borjas 1992). As a result of the ethnic spillover, the human capital of children depends not only on parental inputs (as measured by the exogenous human capital of the parents), but also on the external effect of ethnicity, as summarized by the average skills of the ethnic group.

The spillover effects underlying the ethnic-capital model have much in common with the human-capital externalities that are at the heart of the recent literature on economic growth (Romer 1986; Lucas 1988), as well as with the notions of social capital and neighborhood effects that are stressed routinely in the sociology literature (Coleman 1988; 1990; Wilson 1987). If the ethnic externality is sufficiently strong, skill differentials observed among ethnic groups can persist for many generations and may never disappear. Note that the expected skills of the son of the average father in ethnic group j are given by

$$(2) \qquad E(y_{ij}) = (\beta_1 + \beta_2)\bar{x}_j.$$

The sum $\beta_1 + \beta_2$, therefore, determines whether the mean skills of ethnic groups converge across generations; hence $\beta_1 + \beta_2$ is an inverse measure of the rate of "mean convergence."[12] If the sum of coefficients is less than 1, ethnic differences converge over time; if it is greater than 1, ethnic differences diverge across generations.

As I have already shown, ethnic groups cluster in particular neighborhoods. This clustering suggests that part of the ethnic-capital effect in Equation (1) may be capturing the influence (if there is one) of the neighborhood's socioeconomic background on intergenerational mobility. Suppose, for example, that ethnic groups are completely segregated so that there is one ethnic group per neighborhood. The ethnic-capital variable $\bar{x}_j$ would then also represent the mean skills of the neighborhood, and the coefficient β_2 in (1) would capture the total impact of the ethnic spillover and of the neighborhood's socioeconomic background. The coefficient of ethnic capital would be significant even if ethnicity did not have a direct impact on intergenerational mobility, but neighborhood characteristics mattered.

The data do not exhibit this extreme type of segregation. Ethnic groups, however, are likely to cluster by skill level, so that unskilled ethnic groups live together in low-income neighborhoods and skilled ethnic groups live in high-income neighborhoods. The ethnic-capital variable would again be correlated with the skill level of the neighborhood, and the ethnic-capital coefficient could be capturing neighborhood effects (i.e., the impact of the neighborhood's overall socioeconomic background), rather than the direct effect of ethnicity. In effect, the ethnic-capital model "works" because ethnic capital proxies for the relevant neighborhood characteristics that influence the intergenerational transmission process. If ethnicity did not have a direct impact on intergenerational mobility, controlling for the relevant neighborhood characteristics (such as mean income and education) would drive the ethnic-capital coefficient down to zero.

Ethnic capital might still matter, *above and beyond neighborhood effects*, if intragroup contacts within a neighborhood are more frequent or are more influential than intergroup contacts.[13] Children who belong to ethnic group j are then exposed to a different set of values, social contacts, and economic opportunities than children who belong to other ethnic groups but who grow up in the same neighborhood. In effect, the aggregate socioeconomic characteristics of the neighborhood are not a sufficient statistic summarizing the environment facing type-j persons. As a result, ethnic capital influences the intergenerational-mobility process even after controlling for neighborhood effects. Ethnicity per se has an impact on intergenerational mobility.

The empirical work presented in this paper decomposes the impact of the ethnic-capital coefficient into neighborhood effects (the extent to which the ethnic-capital variable proxies for neighborhood characteristics that influence all persons who reside in the same neighborhood, regardless of ethnic background) and into an ethnic effect. A simple way of determining the extent to which the impact of ethnic capital (i.e., the coefficient β_2) operates through neighborhood effects is to expand the model in (1) to include a vector of neighborhood fixed effects:

$$(3) \qquad y_{ij} = \delta_1 x_{ij} + \delta_2 \bar{x}_j + \sum_k \theta_k D_{ij}^k + \varepsilon'_{ij},$$

where D_{ij}^k is a dummy variable set to unity if person i in ethnic group j resides in neighborhood k. The parameter vector $(\theta_1, ..., \theta_k)$ gives the neighborhood fixed effects, which are assumed to be exogenous.[14] The coefficients δ_1 and δ_2 measure the within-neighborhood impact of parental skills and of ethnic capital. As long as neighborhoods matter in the transmission of skills, the "net" rate of mean-convergence (i.e., net of neighborhood effects) implied by the fixed-effects model, $\delta_1 + \delta_2$, is conceptually different from the "gross" rate implied by Equation (1), $\beta_1 + \beta_2$.

Equations (1) and (3) can be estimated directly in the NLSY data discussed earlier. It is unusual, however, to come across data that contain all the requisite information: ethnicity, the skills of two generations of workers, and neighborhood of residence. Nevertheless, a relatively complete analysis of the relationship between ethnic capital and neighborhood effects can be conducted even if the data do not provide any information on parental background (as is the case with the 1970 Census neighborhood file). In particular, suppose *mean* parental skills in the group, $\bar{x}_j$, are observed even if parental skills are not (the source of the data on $\bar{x}_j$ will be discussed later). The individual-level data available for second-generation workers in the 1970 Census can then be used to estimate the following regression models:

$$(4) \qquad y_{ij} = \beta x_j + \omega_{ij}$$

$$(5) \qquad y_{ij} = \delta \bar{x}_j + \sum_k D_{ij}^k + \omega'_{ij}.$$

Because Equations (4) and (5) regress individual-level data on an aggregate measure of ethnic skills, I call this type of model a "semi-aggregate" regression. It is easy to show that the following proposition holds:

PROPOSITION 1: $$E(\hat{\beta}) = \beta_1 + \beta_2$$

Data on parental skills, therefore, are not required to estimate the gross rate of mean convergence. Because the mean skills of the ethnic group instrument for parental skills, the omitted-variable bias introduced by leaving out parental skills is simply the "recovery" of the coefficient β_1. It would now be useful to determine whether $E(\hat{\delta}) = \delta_1 + \delta_2$, so that the net rate of mean convergence can also be estimated without information on parental skills. I proceed to show that this is indeed the case in an important special case and that the difference between the gross and net rates of mean convergence is attributable solely to the change in the ethnic-capital coefficient.

Consider first how the coefficients of parental and ethnic capital in Equation (1) change when neighborhood fixed effects are introduced into the model. The probability limits of the estimated coefficients in (1) when the true model is given by (3) are given by Equations (6) and (7), at the top of the following page, where $\Delta = \mathrm{Var}(x_{ij})\mathrm{Var}(\overline{x}_j) - \mathrm{Var}(\overline{x}_j)^2$; p_k is the fraction of the population that lives in neighborhood k; $E(x_{ij}|k)$ is the mean value of skills among parents who live in neighborhood k, where the expectation is evaluated over all i and j; and $E(\overline{x}_j|k)$ is the mean value of the ethnic-capital variable among all persons who live in neighborhood k,

(6)
$$\text{plim } \hat{\beta}_2 = \delta_2 + \frac{\mathrm{Var}(x_{ij})}{\Delta} \left\{ \sum_{e >} \sum_k p_e p_k \left(\theta_e - \theta_k \right) \right.$$
$$\left(\left[E(x_{ij}|e) - E(x_j|e) \right] - \left[E(x_{ij}|k) - E(\overline{x}_j|k) \right] \right) \right\}$$

(7)
$$\text{plim } \hat{\beta}_2 = \delta_2 + \frac{\mathrm{Var}(\overline{x}_j)}{\Delta} \left\{ \sum_{e >} \sum_k p_e p_k \left(\theta_e - \theta_k \right) \left[E(\overline{x}_j|e) - E(\overline{x}_j|k) \right] \right\}$$
$$- \frac{\mathrm{Var}(\overline{x}_j)}{\Delta} \left\{ \sum_{e >} \sum_k p_e p_k (\theta_e - \theta_k) \left[E(x_{ij}|e) - E(x_{ij}|k) \right] \right\}$$

where the expectation is again evaluated over all i and j.

In general, the introduction of neighborhood effects affects the coefficients of both parental skills and ethnic capital. Suppose, however, that type-τ ethnics residing in region k are a random sample of the population of type-τ ethnics, so that the skill distribution of type-τ ethnics in region k is the same as their skill distribution in the population. This assumption implies

(8)
$$E(x_{i\tau}|k) = \overline{x}_\tau$$

where the expectation in the left-hand side is taken over all i in group τ in neighborhood k, while the right-hand side simply gives the level of ethnic capital for group τ. I refer to (8) as the "skill-invariance" assumption. Equation (8) implies $E(\overline{x}_j|k) = E(xjlk)$, $\forall k$, so that the bracketed term in (6) vanishes. It is useful to summarize this result as the following proposition.

PROPOSITION 2:

If the distribution of type-j ethnics across neighborhoods is skill-invariant, plim $\hat{\beta}_1 = \delta_1$, so that the coefficient of parental skills is unaffected by the introduction of neighborhood fixed effects.

Note that the skill-invariant geographic assignment of type-j workers is distinct from and weaker than assuming that type-j ethnics are distributed randomly across neighborhoods.

The skill-invariance assumption is also useful in determining the relationship between the estimator $\hat{\delta}$ [from Equation (5)] and the net rate of mean convergence. This relationship is summarized by the next proposition.

PROPOSITION 3:

If the distribution of type-j ethnics across neighborhoods is skill-invariant, then plim $\hat{\delta} = \delta_1 + \delta_2$.

As before, it is unnecessary to have information on parental skills in order to estimate the rate of mean convergence (net of neighborhood effects).

The results can now be used to determine why the two rates of mean convergence estimable in census data might differ. Because the coefficient of parental skills is unaffected by the introduction of neighborhood fixed effects, the difference between the "gross" and "net" rates of mean convergence is attributable *entirely* to the change in the coefficient of the ethnic-capital variable (assuming the skill-invariance assumption holds). Therefore, the inclusion of neighborhood fixed effects into semi-aggregate regressions can be used to assess the relationship between ethnic capital and geography. I summarize this result in the following proposition.

PROPOSITION 4:

Suppose the distribution of type-j ethnics is skill-invariant. The difference in the estimated rates of mean convergence $\hat{\beta}$ and $\hat{\delta}$ gives the impact of neighborhood effects on the ethnic-capital coefficient.

Because of the practical importance of these results, it is worth stressing that the skill-invariance assumption is unlikely to hold strictly in the data. The analysis of the census data presented below uses two alternative measures of skills (educational attainment and log wages) to estimate the rate of mean convergence. Even if there were no skill differentials among type-j workers residing in different neighborhoods, the restriction in (8) would be violated if there exist neighborhood wage differentials that are independent of skills. These differentials imply that the mean wage of type-j parents in a particular neighborhood differs from the measure of ethnic capital for group j. Therefore, the analysis must control for regional wage differentials prior to applying the results presented here. The construction of an index of regional wage differentials at the neighborhood level is discussed later.

A more difficult problem with the skill-invariance assumption is simply that the skill distribution of type-j ethnics probably does differ across neighborhoods.[15] I will show shortly, however, that the restriction implied by skill invariance is not grossly inconsistent with the geographic sorting of type-j ethnics.

Finally, the discussion has assumed that the ethnic-capital effect is constant across neighborhoods and persons. This need not be the case. In fact, the ethnic-capital model implies that the spillover effects of ethnicity should be larger for persons who are more frequently exposed to an ethnic environment. Put differently, the ethnic-capital effect should be larger for those children who grow up in neighborhoods where many of the residents share the same ethnic background. The empirical analysis presented below investigates the extent to which the ethnic-capital effect depends on the ethnic composition of the neighborhood.

11.3. Results

I initially use the sample of second-generation workers in the 1970 Census file (U.S. Bureau of the Census 1973d) to analyze the relationship between ethnic externalities and neighborhood effects. I restrict the analysis to second-generation men aged 18–64, who worked in the civilian sector in the year prior to the census, who were not enrolled in school, and who were not self-employed. As before, the ethnic group of the second-generation worker is defined in terms of the father's birthplace (unless only the mother was foreign born, in which case it is defined in terms of the mother's birthplace). I use two alternative measures of the worker's skills: educational attainment and log wage rates. Because census data do not directly link the skills of second-generation Americans with the skills of their immigrant parents, I use the 1/100 Public Use Sample of the 1940 Census to estimate the mean skills of the national origin group in the parent's generation. It is likely that (adult) second-generation persons enumerated in the 1970 Census are the children of the immigrants who arrived in the period prior to 1940.[16]

Table 11.5

Skills of Immigrant and Second-Generation Workers

Country of origin	Immigrants in 1940 Census			Second generation in 1970 Census		
	Educational attainment	Low wage	Sample size	Educational attainment	Low wage	Sample size
Austria	6.7	-0.349	1,210	11.9	1.550	2,134
Azores	5.0	-0.672	63	9.6	1.232	104
Belgium	7.8	-0.483	138	11.4	1.475	197
British West Indies	8.1	-0.810	58	12.2	1.368	68
Canada	9.2	-0.427	2,741	12.0	1.431	4,720
China	6.3	-1.176	139	13.6	1.447	206
Cuba	8.6	-0.655	42	12.0	1.372	82
Czechoslovakia	6.8	-0.345	817	11.3	1.453	1,749
Denmark	9.2	-0.392	327	12.0	1.405	553
England	9.5	-0.313	1,656	12.5	1.508	2,255
Finland	6.5	-0.539	244	11.3	1.457	390
France	9.0	-0.430	248	12.3	1.450	281
Germany	8.8	-0.467	2,943	11.7	1.463	4,558
Greece	6.9	-0.737	518	12.7	1.484	694
Hungary	7.1	-0.378	809	11.7	1.509	1,298
Ireland	8.3	-0.445	1,326	12.3	1.508	2,645
Italy	5.4	-0.475	4,784	11.2	1.454	10,148
Japan	9.5	-0.849	141	12.5	1.476	662
Lithuania	4.5	-0.479	451	12.0	1.511	766
Mexico	4.4	-1.120	1,192	9.2	1.133	2,959
Netherlands	8.8	-0.557	292	11.7	1.487	623
Northern Ireland	8.3	-0.401	280	12.8	1.533	200
Norway	8.6	-0.441	606	12.0	1.457	987
Other West Indies	8.3	-0.821	119	11.9	1.353	87
Philippines	7.8	-1.009	233	11.9	1.268	188
Poland	5.4	-0.407	2,610	11.3	1.492	5,769
Portugal	4.7	-0.577	212	10.2	1.357	383
Romania	7.4	-0.339	300	13.2	1.647	428
Scotland	9.6	-0.326	862	12.4	1.511	901
Sweden	8.6	-0.378	1,038	12.3	1.503	1,534
Switzerland	9.5	-0.461	242	12.0	1.488	329
Syria	6.7	-0.547	105	12.5	1.576	131
Turkey	7.2	-0.523	211	13.7	1.644	144
USSR	7.0	-0.363	2,418	13.1	1.654	4,313
Wales	9.4	-0.426	100	12.4	1.441	189
Yugoslavia	5.4	-0.340	512	11.7	1.449	928

Table 11.5 reports the average educational attainment and log wages for the 36 ethnic groups that can be identified in both the 1940 and 1970 Censuses with sufficiently large numbers of observations. These 36 ethnic groups make up 97.4 percent of working immigrant men in 1940, and 95.5 percent of the second-generation working men in

1970. There is substantial dispersion in skills and wages across national-origin groups, and there is a strong positive correlation between the skills of the immigrant group in 1940 and the skills of the corresponding second-generation group in 1970.

To calculate the variable measuring mean skills in the parent's generation (i.e., the empirical measure of ethnic capital), I pool the sample of immigrant and native men in the 1940 Census (for a total of 231,606 observations) and estimate the following regression model:

$$(9) \qquad x_{ij} = Z_{ij}\alpha + \sum_j \gamma_j G_{ij} + \varepsilon_{ij},$$

where x_{ij} gives the skills of person i in national-origin group j; Z_{ij} is a vector of socioeconomic characteristics including age, age squared, and region of residence; and G_{ij} is a dummy variable set to unity if person i belongs to group j (natives are the omitted group). The regression is estimated separately using educational attainment and the log wage rate as dependent variables. The parameter vector $(\gamma_1, \ldots, \gamma_2)$ gives the empirical measure of ethnic capital for the j groups.

Table 11.6 reports the estimated rates of mean convergence. Equations (4) and (5) give the basic specification of the model, except that the regressions also control for the second-generation worker's age and age squared. The regressions use a random-effects estimator which allows for an ethnic-group-specific component in the error term.[17] Consider initially the middle panel reporting the transmission coefficients obtained in the log-wage regression model. Column (i) indicates that the rate of mean convergence (or $\beta_1 + \beta_2$ in terms of the model in the previous section) is 0.45, in line with the results of earlier work (Borjas 1992; 1993).

The next column controls for the bias introduced by regional wage differentials. As noted earlier, the skill-invariance assumption is violated if some ethnic groups have relatively high wage levels simply because they live in high-wage areas. To control for regional wage variation, I estimated the following regression in the sample of *third-generation* workers in the 1970 neighborhood file:

$$(10) \qquad w_i = X_i\alpha + \sum_k \psi_k D_i^k + \varepsilon_i,$$

where w_i gives the log wage of person i; X is a vector of standardizing variables (including educational attainment, age, age squared, marital status, and dummy variables indicating whether the person is black or Hispanic); and D_i^k is a dummy variable indicating whether person i resides in neighborhood k. The vector $(\psi_1, \ldots, \psi_K)$ gives the skill-

Table 11.6

Estimates of Intergenerational Correlation in 1970 Census

Variable	Regressions using neighborhood file				Regressions using county group file		
	(i)	(ii)	(iii)	(iv)	(v)	(vi)	(vii)
Education:							
Mean of group in 1940	0.3649 (0.0828)	-	0.1707 (0.0457)	0.2670 (0.0557)	0.3628 (0.0833)	-	0.3316 (0.0709)
Includes neighborhood fixed effects	no	-	yes	no	-	-	-
Includes county fixed effects	-	-	-	-	no	-	yes
Includes neighborhood characteristics	no	-	no	yes	no	-	no
Log wage:							
Mean of group in 1940	0.4549 (0.0781)	0.3974 (0.0662)	0.2191 (0.0578)	0.2474 (0.0362)	0.4607 (0.0874)	0.3710 (0.0694)	0.3938 (0.0772)
Includes skill-adjusted wage level	no	yes	no	yes	no	yes	no
Includes neighborhood fixed effects	no	no	yes	no	-	-	-
Includes county fixed effects	-	-	-	-	no	no	yes
Includes neighborhood characteristics	no	no	no	yes	no	no	no
Log wage, adjusted for education:							
Mean of group in 1940	0.2038 (0.0400)	0.1767 (0.0321)	0.1101 (0.0413)	0.1020 (0.0193)	0.2132 (0.0511)	0.1589 (0.0352)	0.1701 (0.0440)
Includes skill-adjusted wage level	no	yes	no	yes	no	yes	no
Includes neighborhood fixed effects	no	no	yes	no	-	-	-
Includes county fixed effects	-	-	-	-	no	no	yes
Includes neighborhood characteristics	no	no	no	yes	no	no	no

Notes: Standard errors are reported in parentheses; the sample size is 53,703. All regressions include a second-order polynomial in the worker's age. The neighborhood characteristics included in column (iv) are the fraction of persons in the neighborhood with at least 12 years of schooling, the fraction with at least 16 years of schooling, the labor-force participation rates of men and women, the unemployment rate, the fraction of persons working in professional occupations, the fraction of families below the poverty line, and the fraction of families that earn at least $15,000 annually. The regressions use a random-effects estimator.

adjusted neighborhood wage level. This wage level is included as an additional regressor in the intergenerational earnings equations, and the resulting transmission coefficient is reported in column (ii) of Table 11.6.[18] The transmission coefficient falls to 0.40 (a drop of about 0.05 units).

Column (iii) of the table adds the vector of neighborhood fixed effects into the regression.[19] Controlling for the neighborhood fixed effects reduces the estimated transmission parameter substantially, to about 0.2. Assuming that the skill-invariance assumption holds, the transmission coefficient changes because the estimate in column (iii) "nets out" the relationship between the ethnic externality and neighborhood effects (but leaves unchanged the impact of parental skills). It is interesting to note that the resulting coefficient of 0.2 is roughly the same as the coefficient of parental capital in my earlier work (Borjas 1992). It seems as if neighborhood effects account for most (if not all) of the ethnic influence in the intergenerational-transmission process. Ethnic capital seems to be a very good proxy for the relevant characteristics of the neighborhood's economic and social environment which influence the intergenerational-transmission process *and* which are common to all persons living in the same neighborhood, regardless of ethnicity.[20]

The last three columns of Table 11.6 use the 1/100 County Group File of the 1970 Public Use Sample (15 percent questionnaire) to estimate an identical model in a sample of second-generation workers defined exactly as in columns (i)-(iii). This census file reports the metropolitan area (instead of the neighborhood) of current residence. Persons who live outside metropolitan areas are grouped into economically similar "county groups." A total of 408 metropolitan areas and country groups are identified in the data.

Not surprisingly, the transmission coefficient reported in column (v) is almost identical to the respective statistic in column (i). To control for regional wage variation, I estimated a regression in the sample of third-generation workers similar to (10) with county-group dummies instead of neighborhood dummies. The skill-adjusted county wage level was then introduced as an additional regressor in the model. This reduced the coefficient to about 0.37, which is roughly the same as the analogous coefficient in column (ii).

The coefficient in the last column of Table 11.6, however, differs drastically from the respective coefficient in column (iii). Controlling for county fixed effects barely affects the estimated transmission coefficient; it remains at about 0.4. Put differently, the ethnic-capital variable and the vector of county fixed effects are uncorrelated. There is no evidence, therefore, that ethnic capital has anything to do with geography at the county level. At the neighborhood level, however, geography is intimately linked to the ethnic-capital effect.[21]

The top panel of Table 11.6 reports the transmission coefficients obtained from regressions which use the worker's educational attainment as the dependent variable. The results are virtually identical to those obtained in the log-wage regressions. Including the neighborhood fixed effects reduces the transmission coefficient from 0.36 to 0.17, while adding in the county dummies barely changes the estimated parameter (it declines to 0.33).[22]

Finally, the bottom panel of Table 11.6 reports the transmission coefficients obtained in a log-wage regression that also includes the educational attainment of the second-generation worker as a regressor. Although the transmission rates are much smaller (because the transmission that occurs through educational attainment is netted out), adding neighborhood fixed effects changes the estimated coefficients in exactly the same way as in the top two panels of the table.

In sum, the analysis reveals a link between ethnic capital and neighborhood effects, but it provides no information about which set of neighborhood characteristics are being proxied by the ethnic-capital variable. Column (iv) of Table 11.6 shows that the neighborhood fixed effects can be summarized in terms of a small number of neighborhood characteristics. The neighborhood characteristics included in the regression are: the percentage of the neighborhood's population that has at least a high-school diploma; the percentage with at least a college diploma; the labor-force participation rates of men and women; the unemployment rate; the percentage of workers employed in professional occupations; the percentage of families below the poverty level; and the percentage of families with at least $15,000 in household income. All of these neighborhood characteristics were calculated by the Census Bureau (and are included in the Public Use Sample).

The inclusion of these aggregate neighborhood characteristics reduces the transmission coefficient from 0.36 to 0.27 in the education regressions, and from 0.4 to 0.25 in the log-wage regressions. In other words, a small vector of variables that are common to all persons living in the neighborhood, regardless of ethnic background, can explain over half of the drop in the ethnic-capital coefficient.[23]

It seems, therefore, that a large part of the impact of ethnic capital is simply disguising for neighborhood effects which have nothing to do with ethnicity. This interpretation of the results, of course, depends on the validity of the skill-invariance assumption. As shown in Section 11.2, when the distribution of persons across neighborhoods is skill-invariant, including neighborhood effects in semi-aggregate regressions reduces the estimated rate of mean convergence solely because the ethnic-capital coefficient is "standing in" for neighborhood effects.

Parental skills are not observed in the census data, so that it is not possible to assess directly the validity of the skill-invariance assumption. I can test, however, whether the geographic distribution of second-generation workers rejects the skill-invariance assumption. Consider the following regression model:

$$(11) \qquad y_{ijk} = \gamma_0 G + \gamma_1 (G \times D) + \varepsilon_{ijk},$$

where y_{ijk} gives the skills of second-generation worker i in group j in neighborhood k; G gives a vector of dummy variables indicating the worker's ethnic group; and D gives a vector of dummy variables indicating the worker's neighborhood. The skill-invariance assumption states that the mean skills of a worker in ethnic group j are independent of the neighborhood of residence, so that the coefficient vector γ_1 is zero.

I calculated the analysis-of-variance decomposition implied by (11) using both the educational attainment and log wage of workers in the second generation.[24] To net out the impact of regional wage differentials on the analysis, the worker's log wage is deflated by the skill-adjusted neighborhood wage level defined earlier. Despite the very large samples used in the analysis, testing the hypothesis that the coefficient vector γ_1 differs from zero yields F statistics that are barely above the critical value of 1; the F statistic in the educational-attainment regression was 1.21, and the F statistic in the log-wage regression was 1.18. In contrast, the F statistic testing the significance of the group effect (i.e., whether the coefficient vector γ_0 was zero) was 17.2 in the educational-attainment regressions and 95.9 in the log-wage regressions, substantially above the critical value of 1.4.[25]

I now use the NLSY (where parental skills are observed *and* where it is unnecessary to maintain the skill-invariance assumption) to confirm that there is a very strong link between neighborhood effects and the ethnic-capital coefficient. The analysis uses the 1990 wave of the NLSY, by which time the respondents were aged 25–33 and only about 5 percent were still enrolled in school. Equations (1) and (3) give the basic specifications of the models. The regressions also control for age, gender, whether the person is a first- or second-generation American, and whether the person was enrolled in school in 1990.

As with the analysis of census data, I use two measures of skills: educational attainment and the log wage rate. Each NLSY respondent in 1979 reported the father's education and occupation (which was coded using the 1970 Census codes). I constructed a wage for each father by matching the father's occupation code with the average log wage in the occupation, as reported by the 1970 Census.

To obtain a measure of ethnic capital, I used the 1/100 1980 U.S. Census to calculate the mean educational attainment and mean log wage for each of the ethnic groups in the parents' generation.[26] The census data report the ancestral background of U.S.-born residents (obtained from questions resembling the self-reported ethnic background in the NLSY). To increase the probability that the average skills of the ethnic milieu corresponded to that in which the NLSY respondents were raised, I restrict the 1980 Census sample to men aged 35–64.

Table 11.7 reports the summary statistics of the variables used in the analysis. There are sizable ethnic differentials in educational attainment and log wages among NLSY respondents and their parents. Table 11.8 reports the estimates of the ethnic-capital model. The coefficients in the first column of the top panel reveal that the educational attainment of NLSY respondents depends on both the father's education and on the mean education of the ethnic group in the parents' generation. The estimated rate of mean convergence is 0.44. The introduction of a vector of 510 county dummies in the second column reduces both of the coefficients somewhat; the parental coefficient falls from 0.24 to 0.2, and the ethnic-capital coefficient falls from 0.20 to 0.14. Column (iii) investigates the relationship between ethnic capital and neighborhoods by introducing a vector of 1,937 dummies indicating the zip code of residence.[27] The parental coefficient declines further to 0.17, and the ethnic-capital effect evaporates (the coefficient falls to 0.04). Net of neighborhood effects, therefore, the rate of mean convergence is only 0.21, about half the size of the gross rate, and the decline is mostly due to the weakening of the ethnic-capital effect. The NLSY results, therefore, strongly confirm the implications of the analysis of the census neighborhood data.[28]

Table 11.7

Skills of Ethnic Groups in the NLSY

National origin	Educational attainment			Log wage			Sample size
	NLSY respondents	NLSY fathers	Census men	NLSY respondents	NLSY fathers	Census men	
American	12.4	10.9	11.2	2.099	1.292	1.945	480
American Indian	12.1	10.2	11.2	1.977	1.285	1.904	429
Asian Indian	14.0	11.9	16.7	1.684	1.464	2.180	7
Black	12.8	10.1	11.0	1.948	1.177	1.852	1,795
Chinese	15.2	10.0	13.8	2.403	1.146	1.955	16
Cuban	13.4	11.0	11.3	2.403	1.293	1.876	69
English	13.0	11.9	12.9	2.085	1.353	2.093	1,125
Filipino	13.9	13.0	13.8	2.471	1.388	2.009	21
French	12.8	11.7	11.7	2.074	1.329	2.123	203
German	13.4	12.2	12.9	2.167	1.317	2.115	1,009
Greek	14.3	12.4	12.8	2.330	1.404	2.081	21
Hawaiian	12.7	9.5	12.1	2.470	1.282	2.006	6
Irish	13.4	12.6	12.8	2.219	1.401	2.098	651
Italian	13.4	12.3	12.6	2.345	1.375	2.141	347
Japanese	13.4	11.9	14.1	2.093	0.907	2.194	13
Korean	15.5	13.5	14.9	1.982	1.058	2.007	4
Mexican	12.3	7.4	9.0	2.015	1.114	1.808	723
Other Hispanic	13.1	10.5	11.4	2.217	1.254	1.893	102
Polish	13.4	11.8	13.0	2.242	1.389	2.164	171
Portuguese	12.0	8.8	10.5	2.159	1.267	1.984	59
Puerto Rican	11.9	7.9	9.6	2.249	1.156	1.798	170
Russian	15.0	13.6	15.3	2.666	1.486	2.324	39
Scottish	14.4	13.5	13.8	2.224	1.458	2.158	86
Welsh	14.8	14.5	13.8	1.987	1.542	2.150	23

Source: NLSY, U.S. Bureau of the Census (1973d), own calculations.

The remaining two panels of Table 11.8 reestimate the model using the (log) wage and the adjusted wage. The estimate of the rate of mean convergence using the log wage is 0.70, which is higher than the one found in the census. The introduction of county dummies reduces the rate of mean convergence to 0.57, with the ethnic-capital coefficient remaining unchanged. Finally, the introduction of neighborhood fixed effects reduces the coefficient of ethnic capital to 0.05, which is statistically insignificant. Note, however, that the coefficient of parental capital has declined by about 0.13 units, which indicates that the geographic distribution of NLSY respondents is not consistent with the skill-invariance assumption.[29]

Table 11.8

Estimates of the Ethnic-capital Model in the NLSY

Variable	Regression			
	(i)	(ii)	(iii)	(iv)
Education:				
Parental skills	0.2404	0.2005	0.1745	0.1784
	(0.0666)	(0.0669)	(0.0718)	(0.0849)
Ethnic capital	0.2004	0.1356	0.0376	0.1480
	(0.0465)	(0.0301)	(0.0288)	(0.0504)
Includes county fixed effects	no	yes	no	no
Includes neighborhood fixed effects	no	no	yes	no
Includes neighborhood characteristics	no	no	no	yes
Log wage:				
Parental skills	0.3774	0.2645	0.2500	0.2460
	(0.0371)	(0.0398)	(0.0418)	(0.0480)
Ethnic capital	0.3190	0.3107	0.0458	0.0229
	(0.1559)	(0.1116)	(0.1331)	(0.1636)
Includes county fixed effects	no	yes	no	no
Includes neighborhood fixed effects	no	no	yes	no
Includes neighborhood characteristics	no	no	no	yes
Log wage, adjusted for education:				
Parental skills	0.1765	0.1158	0.1214	0.1221
	(0.0369)	(0.0394)	(0.0410)	(0.0476)
Ethnic capital	0.0759	0.1581	-0.0231	-0.0584
	(0.1571)	(0.1141)	(0.1289)	(0.1621)
Includes county fixed effects	no	yes	no	no
Includes neighborhood fixed effects	no	no	yes	no
Includes neighborhood characteristics	no	no	no	yes

Notes: Standard errors are reported in parentheses. The sample size is 7,569 for the educational-attainment regressions and 4,261 for the log-wage regressions. All regressions include variables indicating the worker's age, gender, whether the person is first generation or second generation, and whether the person is enrolled in school in 1990. The neighborhood characteristics included in column (iv) are the average educational attainment and the average log wage of parents in the neighborhood. The regressions use a random-effects estimator.

Source: Own calculations.

The last column of Table 11.8 shows what happens to the parental and ethnic-capital coefficients when I introduce a small vector of neighborhood characteristics (rather than zip-code dummies) to control for neighborhood effects. Because the NLSY file does not contain any population estimates of economic or social characteristics in the zip code, all neighborhood-specific variables must be calculated from within the data and contain substantial sampling error. I estimated the mean education and log wage of the parents of NLSY respondents in each zip code. Controlling for these two characteristics reduces the ethnic-capital coefficient by about 0.05 units in the education regression and by almost 0.3 units in the log-wage regression. As with the census, a small vector of neighborhood characteristics that are common to all persons living in the neighborhood helps explain why the ethnic-capital variable matters (particularly in the log-wage regressions).[30]

11.4. Ethnic Capital and the Ethnic Composition of the Neighborhood

The evidence suggests that, to a large extent, the ethnic-capital effect summarizes the impact of neighborhood characteristics (common to all the residents of the neighborhood) on the intergenerational-transmission process. In view of this result, it is worth asking whether ethnicity per se plays any role in intergenerational mobility, above and beyond the influence of parents and neighborhoods.

Ethnicity is likely to play a more important role among persons who grow up in a segregated ethnic environment. After all, these persons will probably experience (and be influenced by) more frequent social, cultural, and economic intragroup contacts. The analysis in the preceding section ignored this implication of the model because It assumed that the ethnic-capital coefficient was constant across workers. To determine whether ethnicity plays an independent role among workers raised in segregated neighborhoods, I now allow the ethnic-capital coefficient to vary according to the extent of residential segregation in the neighborhood.

In particular, I interact both the ethnic-capital variable and the parental-skills variable (when available) with dummies indicating the proportion of persons in the neighborhood who share the same ethnic background. The regression model also includes the dummy variables indicating the proportion of the neighborhood's population who belong to the respondent's ethnic group (so as to allow for different constant terms). Finally, I estimate the models both with and without neighborhood fixed effects.[31]

The evidence is summarized in Table 11.9. Consider initially the results obtained from the 1970 Census file. Even after controlling for neighborhood effects, both the education and log-wage regressions show that the rate of mean convergence is larger among persons who live in highly segregated neighborhoods. The education regressions, for example, indicate that the net rate of mean convergence is 0.15

Table 11.9

Estimates of Intergenerational Correlation, by Ethnic Composition of Neighborhood

Ethnic composition of neighborhood	Education				Log wage			
	(i)		(ii)		(i)		(ii)	
	Parental skills	Ethnic capital	Parental skills	Ethnic capital	Parental skills	Ethnic capital	Parental skills	Ethnic capital
A. 1970 Census								
Percentage with same ethnicity:								
0 percent	-	0.2458 (0.1195)	-	0.1467 (0.0781)	-	0.2567 (0.1020)	-	0.1322 (0.0447)
Between 0 percent and 15 percent	-	0.3206 (0.1410)	-	0.2261 (0.0930)	-	0.4702 (0.1320)	-	0.2920 (0.0653)
More than 15 percent	-	0.5325 (0.2338)	-	0.2711 (0.2166)	-	0.6769 (0.1496)	-	0.3782 (0.1091)
B. NLSY								
Percentage with same ethnicity:								
Less than 5 percent	0.2748 (0.0126)	0.1482 (0.0791)	0.2071 (0.0131)	0.0491 (0.0257)	0.4636 (0.0719)	0.1850 (0.2085)	0.3178 (0.0758)	0.0290 (0.1422)
Between 5 percent and 33 percent	0.2933 (0.0116)	0.2699 (0.0863)	0.2014 (0.0125)	0.0439 (0.0267)	0.4198 (0.0654)	0.2189 (0.2092)	0.3292 (0.0737)	0.0152 (0.1440)
More than 33 percent	0.1965 (0.0105)	0.2998 (0.0848)	0.1311 (0.0105)	0.1188 (0.0268)	0.3828 (0.0575)	0.2958 (0.2094)	0.2586 (0.0618)	0.1429 (0.1253)
Includes neighborhood fixed effects?	no		yes		no		yes	

Notes: Standard errors are reported in parentheses. The census regressions include a second-order polynomial in the worker's age. The NLSY regressions control for the worker's age, gender, whether the person is first or second generation, and whether the person is enrolled in school in 1990. The census regressions have 53,703 observations; the NLSY education regressions have 7,569 observations, and the NLSY log-wage regressions have 4,261 observations. The regressions use a random-effects estimator.

Source: Own calculations.

for those who live in neighborhoods where none of the neighbors share the same ethnic background; 0.23 for those who live in neighborhoods where at most 15 percent of the population share the same ethnic background; and 0.27 for those who live in neighborhoods where over 15 percent of the population has the same ethnic background.[32] In the log-wage regressions, the respective statistics are 0.13, 0.29, and 0.38.

It is worth stressing that these estimates of the rate of mean convergence net out neighborhood effects. If the impact of parental skills is constant across neighborhoods, the evidence suggests that ethnicity might be playing an important role for persons who live in segregated neighborhoods, above and beyond the influence of parents and neighborhoods.

This implication is partially confirmed by the analysis of the NLSY data, where the rate of mean convergence can be decomposed into the parental and ethnic effects. The educational-attainment regressions, for instance, show that (even after controlling for neighborhood fixed effects) the ethnic-capital coefficient increases from 0.05 for children who grew up in areas where fewer than 5 percent of the nonrelated neighbors have the same ethnic background to 0.12 for children who grew up in areas where at least 33 percent of the neighbors share the same ethnicity. Similarly, the ethnic-capital coefficient in the log-wage regressions rises from 0.03 for those who grew up in "integrated" neighborhoods to 0.14 for the children raised in the most "segregated" neighborhoods (although many of these coefficients have large standard errors).

The NLSY results suggest that not only does the ethnic-capital coefficient increase as the neighborhood becomes more segregated, but also the coefficient of parental skills decreases. The log-wage regressions, for instance, indicate that the parental coefficient (net of neighborhood effects) declines from 0.32 for persons raised in the most integrated neighborhoods to 0.26 for persons raised in the most segregated neighborhoods. The relative unimportance of parental skills for persons raised in segregated neighborhoods might indicate that group influences "take over" as the neighborhood becomes more segregated.

Because the coefficients of parental skills and ethnic capital move in different directions as persons are raised in more segregated neighborhoods, the rate of mean convergence (net of neighborhood effects) only increases slightly in the NLSY log-wage regressions, from 0.35 for persons living in integrated neighborhoods to 0.40 for persons raised in segregated neighborhoods. In the educational-attainment regressions, however, the net rate of mean convergence is roughly the same (around 0.25) across the various types of neighborhoods.

11.5. Ethnic Capital and Measurement Error

Many of the results presented in this paper are consistent with a different interpretation of the ethnic-capital effect. Suppose that parental skills are measured with error. The ethnic mean then provides a very good instrument for parental skills. As a result, part of the parental influence on intergenerational mobility would be captured by the coefficient of the ethnic-capital variable, even if ethnic capital did not enter the model (see Borjas (1992) for a formal derivation of the biases introduced by measurement error). The greater the noise-to-signal ratio in parental skills, the greater the ethnic-capital coefficient.

This interpretation of the results is particularly important in light of recent evidence that measurement error in parental skills imparts a sizable downward bias on the correlation between the earnings of fathers and sons (Altonji and Dunn 1991; Solon 1992; Zimmerman 1992b). Prior to these studies, it was generally believed that the coefficient of parental skills in an intergenerational-transmission equation was on the order of 0.2 (see, for example, the survey by Becker and Tomes 1986). The recent studies, which typically use panel data to average parental earnings over a number of years (and thus "wash out" the measurement error introduced by transitory changes in earnings), report much higher coefficients, on the order of 0.3–0.4.

The empirical results presented in this paper suggest transmission coefficients (as defined by the rate of mean convergence) that are typically above 0.4. In fact, the rate of mean convergence was roughly 0.5–0.7 for children raised in segregated neighborhoods. Taken at face value, therefore, the evidence suggests that ethnic capital might play an important role even if the intergenerational correlation between parents and children was as high as 0.3–0.4.

The NLSY data permit a more detailed analysis of some of the biases introduced by measurement error. As noted earlier, there are large numbers of siblings in the data, with each sibling independently reporting ethnic background, as well as the parent's education and occupation. The correlation among the siblings' responses is high, but it is far from unity. For example, the correlation between a sibling's report of the father's education and the father's average educational attainment as reported by all other siblings is 0.9; the respective statistic for the father's occupational earnings is 0.8; and nearly 30 percent of the respondents identify most with an ethnic background that differs from the "main" ancestry reported by at least one other sibling (although typically the other siblings report the alternative ancestry as a second or third ethnic background). The availability of other sources of information on parental skills and ethnic background suggests that these alternative measures of the variables can be used as instruments in the intergenerational-transmission equation. The instrumental-variables (IV) estimates of the transmission parameter can then be used to assess the practical importance of the bias introduced by measurement error in parental skills and ethnic background.[33]

I restrict the analysis to NLSY respondents who have at least one sibling in the data. For those who have only one sibling (58 percent of the sample), the instruments are given by the sibling's response. For those who have more than one sibling, the instruments are defined as the average response of all other siblings. The instruments are the average skills of the father (either educational attainment or log occupational wage) as reported by the other siblings in the data and a set of dummy variables indicating the ethnic background of the other siblings.[34] The regressions use the IV random-effects estimator proposed by Jerry A. Hausman and William E. Taylor (1981).[35]

A comparison of the IV estimates in the first row of Table 11.10 with the corresponding ordinary least-squares (OLS) estimates in Table 11.8 indicates that the coefficient of parental skills increases both in the education regression (from 0.24 to 0.28) and in the log-wage regression (from 0.38 to 0.48). The results also indicate that the IV estimates of the ethnic-capital coefficient remain sizable and significant. In particular, the coefficients are 0.18 and 0.30 in the education and log-wage regressions, respectively, only slightly below the OLS estimates reported in Table 11.8. It is evident, therefore, that measurement error in parental skills or in ethnic background cannot account for the results.

The remaining rows of the table interact the measures of parental skills and ethnic capital with dummy variables indicating the proportion of persons in the zip code who share the same ethnic background as the worker. The coefficients in Table 11.10 resemble those reported

Table 11.10

Instrumental-Variable Estimates of Intergenerational Correlation in the NLSY

	Education				Log wage			
	(i)		(ii)		(i)		(ii)	
Model	Parental skills	Ethnic capital	Parental skills	Ethnic capital	Parental skills	Ethnic capital	Parental skills	Ethnic capital
All workers	0.2781	0.1772	0.1984	0.0885	0.4776	0.3000	0.1366	0.4433
	(0.0111)	(0.0658)	(0.0129)	(0.0510)	(0.0764)	(0.2879)	(0.0978)	(0.2723)
Interactions with percentage of population that has same ethnicity:								
Less than 5 percent	0.3360	0.1230	0.2912	0.0090	0.5384	0.2516	0.1460	0.3955
	(0.0210)	(0.0675)	(0.0242)	(0.0546)	(0.1435)	(0.3010)	(0.1623)	(0.2852)
Between 5 percent and 33 percent	0.3378	0.1076	0.2387	0.0765	0.4209	0.2794	0.1439	0.5579
	(0.0202)	(0.0670)	(0.0224)	(0.0533)	(0.1379)	(0.2977)	(0.1785)	(0.2465)
Greater than 33 percent	0.1963	0.2357	0.1350	0.1677	0.4744	0.3248	0.2848	0.3436
	(0.0168)	(0.0660)	(0.0176)	(0.0532)	(0.1154)	(0.2929)	(0.1354)	(0.2805)
Includes neighborhood fixed effects?	no		yes		no		yes	

Notes: Standard errors are reported in parentheses. The census regressions include a second-order polynomial in the worker's age. The NLSY regressions control for the worker's age, gender, whether the person is first or second generation, and whether the person is enrolled in school in 1990. The instruments used in the regression include the average skills of the father (either educational attainment or the log occupational wage) as reported by the other siblings in the data; and the average of a set of dummy variables indicating the ethnic background reported by the other siblings. The NLSY education regressions have 3,157 observations; the NLSY log-wage regressions have 1,978 observations. The regressions use a random-effects estimator.

Source: Own calculations.

earlier, particularly in the education regressions. The coefficient of parental skills is smaller and the ethnic-capital coefficient is larger among workers who grew up in segregated neighborhoods (even after controlling for neighborhood effects). The impact of parental education, for instance, declines from 0.29 to 0.14 (in an IV model which includes neighborhood effects) for workers who live in more segregated neighborhoods, while the ethnic-capital coefficient rises from 0.01 to 0.17. In view of the small sample sizes and large standard errors, however, many of these differences are not statistically significant.[36]

11.6. Summary

It is increasingly evident that ethnic skill differentials tend to persist from generation to generation. Part of the correlation arises because of the linkage between parental skills and the skills of children. Even if ethnicity did not matter, the children of skilled parents are likely to have above-average skills. This correlation, however, is not sufficiently high to account for the sluggish rate at which the mean skills of ethnic groups converge over time. To explain the slow rate of convergence, recent work borrows from the new growth literature and stresses the importance of ethnic externalities in the human-capital accumulation process. This ethnic spillover implies that the skills of ethnic children depend not only on parental skills, but also on the mean skills of the ethnic group in the parents' generation. The intergenerational transmission of this ethnic fixed effect explains why it takes a relatively long time for ethnic skill differentials to converge.

This paper investigates the nature of the ethnic externality. The study focuses on one possible channel through which the ethnic externality might operate, the ethnic neighborhood. Using the Neighborhood File of the 1970 U.S. Census and the National Longitudinal Surveys of Youth, I documented substantial residential segregation by ethnicity. Even though only 16.6 percent of the population in 1970 was first or second generation, the typical immigrant resided in a neighborhood that was 32.7 percent first or second generation, and the respective statistic for second-generation workers was 28.2 percent. In addition, there was a strong likelihood that persons belonging to a particular ethnic group reside in a neighborhood where a relatively high number of persons share the same ethnic background.

The empirical analysis indicated that the rate of mean convergence in the skills of ethnic groups was significantly reduced after controlling for neighborhood fixed effects. This finding indicates that much of the ethnic-capital effect works through the fact that low-income ethnic groups cluster in low-income neighborhoods, and these neighborhood effects influence intergenerational mobility. The analysis, however, also revealed that neighborhood effects cannot account for the entire impact of ethnicity on intergenerational mobility, particularly for persons residing in ethnically segregated neighborhoods. Ethnicity has an impact above and beyond both parental and neighborhood effects for persons who are frequently exposed to a particular ethnic environment.

There are many related issues and questions that are not addressed in this paper. For instance, what happens to the nature and impact of ethnic externalities as the groups intermarry? How do the different ethnic influences clash when disparate ethnic and racial groups cluster in the same neighborhoods? What are the policy implications of the interactions among ethnic externalities, residential segregation, and intergenerational mobility? Because of the underlying significance of these questions, the study of the links between race or ethnicity and human-capital externalities is sure to remain a fertile ground for future research.

12

Ethnic Networks and Language Proficiency Among Immigrants

This paper, with Paul W. Miller, uses data for Australia to investigate the relationship between destination language proficiency, ethnic enclaves, and ethnic networks among immigrants. Several previous studies of immigrants' destination language proficiency have used a minority language concentration measure as an index of the size of the immigrant enclave. Our study also finds highly significant negative effects on English speaking, reading, and writing proficiency among immigrants who live in an area with a high concentration of people speaking their own language. We then control for variables that describe the ethnic network in which a person lives, including the spouse's language, whether the respondent has other relatives in Australia, and the extent of ethnic language media (press, radio, and TV) in Australia. When these are included in the regression equation the coefficient of the linguistic concentration measure becomes very small and is insignificant.

For analyses of immigrant dominant language proficiency direct measures of the immigrant networks and enclaves are to be preferred, but if they are not available the linguistic concentration index serves as a useful proxy.

Barry R. Chiswick (2015)

The original version of this chapter was published as: Chiswick, B. R., Miller, P. W. (1996). Ethnic Networks and Language Proficiency among Immigrants, in: Journal of Population Economics, 9: 19–35. © 1996 by Springer-Verlag. The survey Issues in Multicultural Australia 1988 analyzed in this paper was made available by the Social Science Data Archives at the Australian National University.

12.1. Introduction

Immigrants in the main immigrant receiving countries (such as Australia, Canada, Germany, Israel, and the United States) acquire fluency in the dominant language of the destination with the passage of time, and the possession of these skills enhances prospects for economic success (Chiswick and Miller 1992; 1995). Consequently, knowledge of the process through which the language skills are acquired is important for understanding immigrant well-being. Much of the research into language proficiency has focused on individual characteristics that affect language choice and proficiency, for example, educational attainment, duration of residence, and exposure to the dominant language prior to migration. It has been shown, for example, that destination language fluency rates are higher among the better educated, among those in the country for a longer period of time, and among those exposed to the language prior to migration. There are also systematic effects by marital status, family composition, country of origin, and motive for migrating. Estimation of language choice and proficiency models using different data sets for the same country, and using similar specifications for different countries, reveals that these individual effects are remarkably robust (Chiswick and Miller 1992; 1994b; 1995).

At the same time, researchers have been aware that group effects may alter the costs of, and benefits to, language acquisition, and thus affect fluency rates. Evans (1986: 243), for example, outlines but does not test three hypotheses concerning group differences. She suggests that members of a large immigrant community, or of an immigrant group that has large enclave markets, or a more inward-looking perspective will have less economic incentive to acquire dominant language fluency. Similarly, Chiswick (1991: 156) suggests that for inhabitants of the Los Angeles area, the presence of a sizable, Spanish-speaking community could reduce the incentive for Hispanic immigrants to acquire English-language skills. Clyne (1991: 88) notes that in Australia "...the rate of language maintenance/shift varies in accordance with the relative size of the community in a particular state (or capital city)." Veltman (1983: 215), on the basis of an examination of regional differences in the rates of acquiring English fluency in the United States, claims that "The existence of this basic pool of people usually speaking the minority language may have a braking effect on the anglicization of immigrants." Dustmann (1994) attributes the lower fluency of Turkish immigrants in Germany to their being the most numerous non-Germanic immigrant group and their reduced exposure to German because of linguistic enclaves. In these studies, however, the differences in dominant language fluency rates reported by linguistic origin were not systematically related to any single group identifier, suggesting that they may reflect regional economic differences or other unmeasured variables rather than group linguistic effects per se.

A more promising line of inquiry into the identification of group linguistic effects is contained in Chiswick and Miller (1992; 1995). In this research into variations in dominant language fluency rates among immigrants, a variable for the fraction of the regional population that, whether native or foreign born, speaks the same origin-language as the respondent is included in the micro-level equation. Comparable statistical analyses undertaken for Australia, Canada, Israel, and the United States reveal that the minority-language concentration measure is an important determinant of dominant language fluency. Immigrants living in regions that have a relatively high representation of their language group are less likely to be fluent in the dominant language, other things being the same. The statistically significant effect is strongest in Australia and about the same in Canada, Israel, and the United States. The effect of the minority language concentration measure persists even when analyses are done within countries of origin for each of these four major destinations.

The minority language concentration measure may well be a proxy for an array of variables not available in the census data studied to date that are associated with greater group density. For example, to what extent is the concentration effect reflecting the intensity of interaction with friends or social/ethnic networks? Group differences in the effect on language fluency of simple measures of linguistic concentration may well reflect differences in these more fundamental variables.

The primary focus of this chapter is to explore this issue with a unique data set that can be used to study various dimensions of the linguistic environment in which immigrants live. A second purpose is to exploit more fully information on three dimensions of language proficiency, that is, reading, writing, and speaking, that are available in these data. Most census and survey data mechanically limit themselves to one dimension, speaking fluency, yet this may not be the most salient characteristic. Indeed, some recent research on special samples of immigrants in the United States, Israel, and Germany suggest the greater importance of literacy rather than fluency in the destination language in an analysis of earnings (see Beenstock 1993; Chiswick 1991; Dustmann 1994).

Section 12.2 introduces the data from the survey Issues in Multicultural Australia 1988, while Section 12.3 briefly describes the estimating equation. Section 12.4 presents estimates of models of language skill that consider proficiency in speaking, reading and writing. The relationship between a group minority-language concentration variable and various ethnic variables as determinants of language skills is decomposed using a method outlined in Johnson and Solon (1986). A summary and conclusion are contained in Section 12.5.

12.2. The Data

The analyses presented here are based on the survey *Issues in Multicultural Australia 1988* undertaken on behalf of the Office of Multicultural Affairs in the Department of the Prime Minister and Cabinet in the Federal Government of Australia. This survey contains detailed information on language use and the interaction of the individual with the environment that appear to be unique among contemporary data sets. In particular, in addition to the demographic and skill-level data collected in most surveys (e.g., age, years since migration, and educational attainment), information was collected on English-language reading, writing, and speaking skills, on the number of the respondent's relatives in Australia, on ethnic identification, and on affiliation with ethnic/social clubs.

In the statistical analyses reported here respondents are coded as being proficient in spoken English (SPEAK) if English is the first language spoken at home or, if a language other than English is the first language spoken at home but the respondents' spoken English is "very good." The respondent is not fluent if English is not the first language spoken at home and if the person's speaking skills are only "good," "fair," or "poor." Proficiency in reading (READ) and writing (WRITE) are defined in a similar manner.

The *Issues in Multicultural Australia 1988* data set comprises four separate independent random samples: the Australian population aged 15 years and over (1,552 cases); second-generation Australians (823 cases); immigrants from non-English speaking countries (986 cases);

and immigrants who had arrived in Australia from July 1, 1981 until the date of the survey (1,141 cases). These four samples provide 4,502 observations, of whom 2,532 were born overseas. Given the focus on English-language fluency, this study is restricted to immigrants from non-English speaking countries. The study covers the language proficiencies of adults age 15 to 64. This is a slightly wider age group than usual in studies using the large samples in census data (Evans (1986): ages 20 to 64, Chiswick and Miller (1995): ages 25 to 64). The country of origin and age restrictions and the deletion of the few observations with missing data result in a sample with 2,032 observations.

The sampling frames of the four samples collected in the *Issues in Multicultural Australia 1988* survey differ, and the ideal approach is to conduct separate analyses for each sample (see, for example, Kee 1990). The small sample sizes for immigrants, however, suggest that a more practical alternative is to pool the data from the three relevant surveys (see, for example, Chapman and Iredale 1993). Models estimated from the pooled data were checked against similar models estimated using a random sample from the 1986 Australian Census of Population and Housing (see Appendix Table A12.2). The qualitative conclusions that can be drawn from the parallel analyses are the same and the magnitudes of many of the coefficients are very similar, particularly with respect to the minority language concentration variable (-0.060 in the census analysis and -0.058 in the 1988 survey analysis). For all practical purposes, therefore, the pooled survey data can be viewed as having been drawn from the same statistical population as the census sample.

Following Chiswick and Miller (1994a), both males and females are included in the analysis. The means and standard deviations of the variables used in the analysis are reported in Appendix Table A12.1.

12.3. A Model of Dominant Language Fluency

Language use and proficiency may be analyzed within a human capital framework (see, for example, Breton 1978a; b; Chiswick and Miller 1992; 1995). Within this framework, attention is focused on the factors that affect the costs of, and returns from, the investment in human capital. Chiswick and Miller (1995) discuss these in terms of three fundamental variables: exposure to the language, efficiency in second language acquisition, and economic benefits from language fluency. Exposure to the language has three components: exposure prior to immigration, time units of exposure in the destination, and the intensity of exposure per unit of time in the destination. Both the characteristics of the individual and of the environment in which an individual lives may affect these variables.

The variables included in the estimating equation are discussed in depth in Chiswick and Miller (1995), and their empirical counterparts employed in the current analysis are defined in Appendix B. In particular, it has been found for Australia, as well as for the United States, Canada, Israel, and Germany, that destination language fluency increases with duration of residence and level of education and decreases with age at immigration. There are systematic differences by country of origin, with refugees and sojourner migrants having the lowest fluency and those with greater pre-immigration exposure to the destination language having the highest level of fluency among the immigrants.

The minority group language concentration variable provides a measure of the intensity of exposure in the destination country to the language of the origin through the medium of linguistic enclaves (Chiswick and Miller 1992; 1995). Where there is a large concentration of minority language speakers, linguistic enclaves may form in which the language of the country of origin is used, at least in part, as a language of the home, at work and in the community. This would lower the benefits and increase the costs of learning the language of the destination. For example, respondents dwelling in areas with high minority-language concentration ratios may have a relatively large number of family members near by, or may limit their interactions to ethnic clubs or organizations or ethnic media which require a critical mass to function.

Reflecting this situation, the language equation estimated in previous studies and outlined above is augmented in this study with variables for ethnic affiliation, social/ethnic club membership, ethnic media, and relatives in the destination. The construction of these variables is described in Appendix B. Including variables for these linguistic-ethnic influences in the analysis will facilitate an assessment of the determinants of the minority-language enclave effect.

Three foreign media variables were constructed from independent sources for use in the analysis and add to the data file. The first is the number of Australian newspapers published in the language other than English reported by the respondent. There are no newspapers published in many community languages with small representation in Australia, whereas there are 15 published in Greek, 14 in Turkish, and 10 in Italian. The second variable recorded the weekly hours of broadcast time in each community language on the 11 radio stations with the most hours of non-English broadcasts. This variable ranges in value from 0 h for small language groups to 68 h for Greek, 52 h, for Italian and 33 h for Spanish. The third variable is the annual number of hours of transmission in origin languages on the government-run Special Broadcasting Service multicultural TV channel. This variable ranged in value from zero for many languages to high values for Italian (256 h), German (197 h), and French (137 h).

In addition, a variable that records whether English was used in the home when the respondent was 14 years of age is included in the model. The primary role of this variable is to control for initial language skills. It is not possible to do this in most data sets, although a notable exception is Chiswick (1991) where statistical controls for English language skills at the time of migration to the United States are entered in the language fluency model.

12.4. Estimation and Decomposition

Models of English speaking (SPEAK), reading (READ), and writing (WRITE) skills are presented in this section (Table 12.1). All estimates reported in Table 12.1 are obtained using OLS. There are two well-known problems with this method of estimation when the dependent variable is dichotomous: the residuals are heteroskedastic and the predicted values may lie outside the range of the unit interval. Reestimation of the models using a logit estimation procedure does not lead to any changes in the substantive findings of the analysis (see Appendix Table A12.3). Accordingly, because the OLS estimates are easier to interpret (and consistent standard errors may be computed following White 1980) and are amenable to analysis using the methodology of Johnson and Solon (1986), priority is given to the OLS results.

It should be noted that the survey design means that the analyses of the three dependent variables are not independent: all individuals who report English as the first language spoken at home are classified as fluent in each of these skills. As these account for between 80 and 85 percent of the fluent group, the analyses should reveal similar patterns.

The analyses are presented for a pooled sample of males and females. F-tests of structural differences between the determinants of language

Table 12.1

Regression Estimates of English-language Fluency Among Adult Immigrants from Non-English-speaking Countries, Australia, 1988 (Dependent Variables: SPEAK, READ, WRITE)

Variable	SPEAK		READ		WRITE	
	(1)	(2)	(3)	(4)	(5)	(6)
Constant	0.168	0.325	0.117	0.280	0.097	0.266
	(2.90)	(5.24)	(2.00)	(4.49)	(1.66)	(4.25)
Age	-0.004	0.004	-0.004	0.004	-0.004	-0.003
	(4.55)	(4.08)	(4.40)	(4.00)	(3.88)	(3.49)
Education	0.017	0.016	0.027	0.026	0.024	0.023
	(7 .05)	(6.84)	(10.88)	10. 74)	(9.87)	(9.82)
Years since migration (YSM)	0.025	O.D25	0.022	0.022	0.021	0.021
	(9.72)	(9.85)	(8.42)	(8.62)	(8.30)	(8.52)
YSM squared/100	-0.024	0.028	-0.018	0.022	-0.017	-0.021
	(4.05)	(4.97)	(3.04)	(3.95)	(2.85)	(3.79)
Female	-0.026	0.024	-0.041	0.040	-0.017	-0.015
	(1.51)	(1.47)	(2.40)	(2.39)	(0.99)	(0.93)
Married	-0.075	0.060	-0.078	0.058	-0.073	0.065
	(3.69)	(2.57)	(3.86)	(2.57)	(3.53)	(2.77)
English at age 14	0.225	0.191	0.205	0.172	0.228	0.194
	(9.58)	(8.26)	(9.14)	(7 .81)	(9.83)	(8.44)
Northern Europe	0.248	0.150	0.229	0.132	0.217	0.119
	(7.97)	(4.83)	(7.45)	(4.25)	(6.79)	(3. 75)
Eastern Europe	-0.014	0.023	-0.023	0.034	-O.D78	-0.084
	(0.33)	(0.55)	(0.51)	(0.80)	(1.79)	(2.01)
Arabian countries	-0.008	0.035	0.006	0.049	-0.014	0.034
	(0.20)	(0.88)	(0.15)	(1.21)	(0.34)	(0.84)
South Asia	0.213	0.070	0.207	0.067	0.206	0.062
	(5.73)	(1.84)	(5.52)	(1.74)	(5.49)	(1.61)
Philippines	0.360	0.241	0.406	0.291	0.371	0.248
	(6.54)	(4.61)	(8.69)	(6.36)	(7.25)	(5.07)
Vietnam	-0.190	0.117	-0.204	0.134	-0.197	-0.117
	(6.08)	(3.37)	(6.24)	(3.72)	(6.13)	(3.31)
Other Asia	-0.042	0.141	-0.082	0.179	-0.075	-0.176
	(1.18)	(3.90)	(2.25)	(4.88)	(2.11)	(4.90)
South and Central America	-0.040	0.026	-0.077	0.066	-0.070	-0.049
	(0.70)	(0.47)	(1.30)	(1.17)	(1.21)	(0.90)
Africa	0.243	0.047	0.240	0.044	0.239	0.039
	(4.02)	(0.76)	(3.91)	(0.73)	(3.95)	(0.64)
Other countries	0.323	0.143	0.317	0.141	0.316	0.134
	(6. 71)	(2.94)	(6.79)	(3.01)	(6.68)	(2.82)
Minority-language concentration	-0.050	0.003	-0.046	0.005	-0.052	0.002
	(5.17)	(0.23)	(4.90)	(0.42)	(5.41)	(0.19)
Foreign marriage	a	0.222	a	0.223	a	-0.224
		(9.00)		(9.20)		(9.16)
Family	a	0.046	a	0.057	a	-0.058
		(2.32)		(2.86)		(2.94)
Ethnic press	a	0.041	a	0.039	a	-0.045
		(4.72)		(4.42)		(5.19)
Ethnic press squared	a	0.002	a	0.002	a	0.002
		(3.22)		(2.99)		(3: 75)
R^2	0.4268	0.4658	0.4297	0.4690	0.4327	0.4746
Sample Size	2032	2032	2032	2032	2032	2032

Notes: ª Variable not entered.
The benchmark country category is Southern Europe
t-statistics in parentheses computed using White's (1980) heteroskedasticity-consistent covariance matrix estimator.

Source: *Issues in Multicultural Australia Survey 1988*.

fluency for males and females were conducted for each of the six models listed in Table 12.1. There was evidence that the models for males and females were not the same in only two cases (Equations (1) and (4)), and even then the test statistics were at the margin of significance. Separate analyses for males and females are therefore not reported. This contrasts with the statistically significant difference in the structure by gender reported in Chiswick and Miller (1994a) for Australia using the census. The difference is most likely associated with the much larger sample sizes available in the census.

Language speaking, reading, and writing skills are markedly lower in regions where there is a relatively high concentration of minority language speakers. The coefficient on the minority language concentration variable in a simple (one variable) linear regression is -0.088 (t = 7.96) for SPEAK, -0.093 (t = 8.47) for READ, and -0.095 (t = 8.61) for WRITE. That is, in a region where an additional 1 percent of the population speaks the same minority language as the respondent, the fluency rate is expected to be around 9 percentage points lower than otherwise.

For the reasons noted previously, this group effect in a simple regression will undoubtedly capture some unmeasured individual effects (omitted variables bias). The nature of the relationship can be determined in a straightforward manner. Let β_s be the estimated coefficient on the minority language concentration variable obtained from a simple regression with SPEAK, READ, or WRITE as the dependent variable, and β_m be the estimated coefficient on this variable from a multiple regression (with the same dependent variable) that includes I control variables for individual characteristics. Then:

$$\beta_m - \beta_s = -\sum_{i=1}^{I}\beta_i b_{ic},$$

where β_i is the estimated coefficient on the ith control variable, and b_{ic} is the coefficient from a simple regression of the ith control variable on the minority language concentration measure (see Johnson and Solon 1986).

As a first step in implementing this approach, multiple regression equations are estimated that include both the group and individual effects. Two specifications of the estimating equation are presented in Table 12.1 for each of the fluency measures. The first equation includes variables that are thought less likely to be closely related to the minority language concentration variable. The second specification includes "foreign marriage," "family," and "ethnic media" variables that are alternative dimensions of linguistic enclaves.

The three media variables for access to foreign language newspapers and radio and TV broadcasts are highly positively inter-correlated. When all three are entered in the estimating equation at the same time, the ethnic press variable is statistically significant, whereas the ethnic radio and ethnic TV variables are not. Only the ethnic press variable is therefore included in the specifications reported in what follows. To allow the impact of the ethnic press variable to vary with the number of newspapers available, a quadratic form is used.

Replacing the ethnic press variable by the ethnic radio variable results in no material change to the results. However, the ethnic TV variable is not statistically significant in an equation that includes the minority-language concentration variable. Broadcast time on the Special Broadcasting Service TV channel is allocated on the basis of the number of speakers of various languages *and* the availability of suitable films (Clyne 1991: 149). Presumably it is the second of these conditions that accounts for the different performance of the ethnic TV variable.

A variable recording membership in a social/sports club that was identified with a particular ethnic group was insignificant in each equation, as was a variable that recorded whether the respondent identified with a non-Australian ethnic or cultural group. The latter variable was marginally significant when the ethnic media variable was omitted. These variables were not included in the specifications reported in this chapter.

Focusing first on the equation for speaking skills, the variable age (or age at migration given that years since migration are held constant) is negatively related to speaking fluency (Table 12.1, column 1). Each additional year of age leads to 0.4 of one percentage point lower fluency. This effect is about one-half of that reported from analyses of 1981 and 1986 Australian Census data (Chiswick and Miller 1995), but the discrepancy appears to be associated with the inclusion in the current analysis of a variable for language used at age 14 (see, for example, the results in Appendix Table A12.2).

Language fluency rises with educational attainment, the estimated effects indicating 1.7 percentage points higher fluency per additional year of education. When education is divided into pre- and post-migration schooling the coefficients are the same. Hence, the strong finding of complementarity of the various types of human capital skills among immigrants reported in Chiswick and Miller (1995) carries over to the current analysis.

There is a curvilinear relationship between English language proficiency and years since migration, with language skills increasing at a decreasing rate with years of residence in Australia. Evaluated at a duration of ten years, the partial effect of English language proficiency with respect to duration of residence is 2.0 percentage points. This declines to 1.6 percentage points after 20 years of residence in Australia, but remains positive throughout the range of the data.

Current language skills depend on the use of the English language (either as a first or second language) in the home when the respondent was a youth (age 14). The partial effect of this variable (23 percentage points) is quite large. The most important role this variable plays in the analysis is standardizing for English language fluency as a youth.

Language proficiency rates vary across birthplace groups, even after excluding from the data immigrants from English-speaking countries and controlling statistically for speaking English in the home at age 14. English language fluency is greater among immigrants from countries in which English is a common second language and is lower among refugees. Compared to the Southern European control group, English-language proficiency rates are 25 percentage points higher for immigrants from Northern Europe, 36 percentage points higher for those from the Philippines, and 21 percentage points higher for immigrants from South Asia. Rates of English language proficiency are 19 percentage points lower for immigrants from Vietnam, of whom nearly all are refugees. Language fluency rates do not differ between the Southern European benchmark group and immigrants from Arab countries, Other Asia, Eastern Europe, and South and Central America.

Finally, the estimated coefficient on the minority language concentration variable is negative and highly significant. The magnitude of -0.050 indicates that a 1-percentage-point increase in the representation of persons in the region of residence speaking the same minority language as the respondent is associated with a decline in the English proficiency rate of 5 percentage points. This partial effect is much lower than the 9-percentage-point reduction determined from a simple (one variable) regression in which the concentration measure is the only variable. This suggests that some of the individual variables incorporated into the Table 12.1 column (1) specification must be correlated with the propensity to form language enclaves. Yet, there are no substantive changes in the coefficients of the other variables when the concentration measure is deleted from the equation in column (1).

In the Table 12.1, column (2) equation, three variables that are most obviously related to minority language enclaves – foreign marriage, family in Australia, and ethnic press – are included in the equation. The impacts of these variables are negative, and highly significant. Where the respondent is married and the spouse speaks the same minority language, English-language speaking skills are 22 percentage points lower than if the spouse was not of the same language group. Language skills are lower (by 5 percentage points) when the respondent has at least one family member (other than a spouse and children) present in Australia. Tests reveal that it is the presence of at least one family member, rather than the number of such members, that is important. Language skills are reduced, at a decreasing rate, the greater the number of foreign language newspapers, that is, by 2.5 percentage points per additional newspaper when evaluated at the mean number (four) of foreign language newspapers.

The ethnic network variables are also associated with a reduction to statistical and practical insignificance of the estimated effect of the minority-language concentration variable (from -0.050, $t = -5.2$ to 0.003, $t = -0.2$). When the foreign marriage variable is added to the Table 12.1 column (1) specification by itself, the coefficient on the minority-language concentration variable is -0.036 ($t = -3.89$), and when the foreign marriage and family variables are added to the Table 12.1 column (1) specification (but not the ethnic press variables), the coefficient on the minority-language concentration variable is -0.035 ($t = -3.75$).

These findings indicate that in the restricted specification in Table 12.1, column (1), the minority-language concentration variable was a proxy for ethnic interaction factors captured in column (2) by the foreign marriage, family in Australia, and ethnic press variables. This is consistent with the intention behind the inclusion of the minority-language concentration variable in previous studies where alternative measures were not available.

Columns (3) to (6) in Table 12.1 present estimates for models of English reading and writing skills. The pattern of effects for the models of speaking, reading, and writing skills are generally the same. There are, however, some important differences. Education has a stronger effect on English reading and writing skills than it does on speaking skills. In other words, the degree of complementarity between education and English reading and writing skills is greater than that between education and English-speaking skills. As it seems reasonable to view reading and writing as more advanced skills, this finding is intuitively appealing. Moreover, while there is no gender difference in speaking and writing skills, female immigrants have poorer English reading skills than males, other things being the same.

The impact of the inclusion of the ethnic control variables in the equations for English reading and writing skills on the coefficients of the minority-language concentration variable is similar to what was found in the English-speaking equation. The estimated coefficient declines to statistical and practical insignificance.

The t-ratios below unity imply that the adjusted coefficient of determination would increase if the minority-language concentration variable were deleted from the equation.

The inclusion of the three ethnic variables in the even numbered equations in Table 12.1 also raises the adjusted coefficient of determination of the equations. The increase of 3 to 4 percentage points in the (unadjusted) coefficient of determination is statistically significant. The inclusion of the three ethnic variables has no material influence on the coefficients of the other variables in the analysis, with the exception of the variable for being married. Those who are married to a spouse not of the same language origin have significantly higher levels of English language skills than those who are single, but those who are married to a spouse from the same linguistic-country group have even lower fluency than those who are single.

Table 12.2 presents a decomposition of the influence of the individual characteristics on the coefficient of the minority-language concentration variable. Birthplace, age, education, English usage at age 14, foreign marriage, and the ethnic press variables make positive contributions to the difference between the estimated impacts of the minority-language concentration variable in multiple and simple regressions. Years since migration, marital status, and the gender variables make negative contributions.

Table 12.2

Decomposition of the Influence of Regressors on the Estimation of the Minority-language Concentration Effect

	SPEAK	READ	WRITE
Difference between impacts estimated in multiple and simple regressions	0.0903	0.0978	0.0971
Derives from:			
Education	0.0139	0.0217	0.0198
Age	0.0079	0.0078	0.0068
Birthplace	0.0160	0.0155	0.0127
Years since migration[a]	-0.0348	-0.0322	-0.0319
Language at age 14	0.0133	0.0120	0.0136
Marital status	-0.0018	-0.0018	-0.0020
Female	-0.0001	-0.0001	0.0000
Foreign marriage	0.0249	0.0250	0.0251
Family	0.0021	0.0025	0.0026
Ethnic press[a]	0.0488	0.0472	0.0504

Note: [a] Includes effect of squared term.

Source: Table 12.1 and auxiliary regressions computed from the *Issues in Multicultural Australia Survey 1988*.

Consider the positive contribution for education of 0.0139 in the equation for speaking skills (Table 12.2). Education is associated with greater dominant language fluency (Table 12.1), but there is a negative correlation between education and the minority-language concentration variable, that is, better educated immigrants are less likely to live in language enclaves. Consequently,

$$-\beta_{EDUC}b_{EDUC,CONC}$$

is positive. As a result, controlling for education will reduce the impact of minority language concentration on language fluency.

Years since migration has a positive effect on dominant language fluency. There is a positive correlation in these data between years since migration and the minority-language concentration variable, perhaps reflecting the different waves of migration to Australia, with earlier groups coming mainly from Europe while the more recent groups have a much wider representation across Europe and Asia, and hence a lower concentration measure.

Consequently,

$$-\beta_{YSM}b_{YSM,CONC}$$

is negative.

It is apparent from Table 12.2 that the reduction in the impact on dominant language fluency of the language enclave variable when the analysis is switched from a simple regression to a multiple regression framework is mainly due to the ethnic press (4.88 percentage points) and foreign marriage variables (2.49 percentage points). In other words, much of the substantial 8 to 9-percentage-point effect of the minority-language concentration variable in a simple regression is due to effects associated with the more limited interactions an immigrant will have with the English language when the immigrant has access to ethnic-language media or when their spouse was born in the same linguistic-country group as the immigrant.

12.5. Conclusion

Dominant language fluency among immigrants has been shown in previous research to be adversely affected by residence in a region with a relatively large number of individuals that speak the same origin-language as the immigrant. Comparable statistical analyses conducted for Australia, Canada, Israel, and the United States reveal that this relationship is remarkably robust.

The origins of the effect of the minority-language concentration measure are explored in this chapter using a unique sample for Australia. It is demonstrated that the minority-language concentration measure reflects interactions in the marriage market, with family (other than a spouse and children) in Australia, and with ethnic media, and hence with formal ethnic networks. The addition of variables reflecting these concepts reduces to statistical and practical insignificance the estimated impact of the minority-language concentration variable, but results in only minor changes in other estimated effects. Thus, previous research which used the simple minority-language concentration index because other measures of language interaction were not available could not reveal the mechanism through which this process operated. When these variables are available they should be included in the analysis. Yet, the analysis also reveals that the simple minority-language concentration index can serve as a reasonable proxy for these other dimensions when the data are not available.

The analysis also shows that the model that was successful for analyzing the determinants of English speaking skills among immigrants in Australia is also successful for analyzing English reading and writing skills. The most noteworthy difference is that education is more important for explaining reading and writing than it is for explaining English speaking proficiency.

Appendix A

Table A12.1

Means and Standard Deviations of Variables

Variable	Mean	Standard Deviation
Age	37.40	11.45
Education	12.74	3.69
Years since migration	12.74	12.29
Years since migration squared	313.25	480.98
Female	0.424	0.494
Married	0.729	0.444
English at age 14	0.283	0.451
Northern Europe	0.106	0.308
Eastern Europe	0.064	0.244
Southern Europe	0.214	0.410
Arabian countries	0.079	0.269
Southern Asia	0.130	0.337
Philippines	0.044	0.205
Vietnam	0.134	0.341
Other Asia	0.126	0.332
South and Central America	0.030	0.169
Africa	0.030	0.171
Other countries	0.043	0.204
Minority-language concentration	0.751	1.096
Foreign marriage	0.429	0.495
Family	0.700	0.458
Ethnic press	3.910	4.480
Ethnic press squared	35.347	57.215
SPEAK	0.496	0.500
READ	0.527	0.499
WRITE	0.501	0.500
Sample size	2032	

Source: Issues in Multicultural Australia Survey 1988 and for the ethnic press variable, Clyne (1991) Tables 20, 21 and 22.

Appendix Table A12.1 presents the means and standard deviations of the variables used in the statistical analysis. Appendix Table A12.2 presents estimates of a model of English-speaking skills among adult immigrants based on the 1988 *Issues in Multicultural Australia* (IMA) survey together with results from a comparable model based on the 1986 Australian Census of Population and Housing, 1 percent random sample of immigrants. The estimations are self-weighting; hence new arrivals are given relatively greater weight in the analyses based on the IMA. The pattern of the coefficients in the equation using the IMA survey is very similar to that obtained from the analysis of the large, random sample from the 1986 Census.

Appendix Table A12.3 presents logit equations parallel to the OLS equations in Table 12.1. The substantive interpretations are the same.

Table A12.2

Regression Estimates of English-language Fluency Among Adult Immigrants from Non-English-speaking Countries

Variable	1986 Census	1988 Survey
Constant	0.267	0.288
	(9.11)	(5.07)
Age	-0.009	-0.007
	(22.23)	(7.30)
Education	0.034	0.019
	(25.14)	(7.53)
Years since migration	0.016	0.020
	(34.30)	(20.94)
Female	-0.044	-0.022
	(5.40)	(1.24)
Married	-0.038	-0.075
	(3.63)	(3.61)
Small urban location	-0.008	-0.039
	(0.52)	(0.88)
Rural location	0.032	0.005
	(2.07)	(0.13)
Northern Europe	0.267	0.258
	(19.83)	(8.32)
Eastern Europe	0.064	-0.065
	(3.94)	(1.52)
Arabian countries	-0.025	-0.030
	(1.27)	(0.73)
South Asia[b]	0.201	0.303
	(13.16)	(8.16)
Philippines	a	0.441
		(8.33)
Vietnam	-0.228	-0.212
	(11.21)	(6.76)
Other Asia[b]	a	-0.063
		(1.75)
South and Central America	-0.082	-0.044
	(2.68)	(0.76)
Africa	0.316	0.293
	(15.90)	(4.79)
Other countries	0.422	0.426
	(25.03)	(9.00)
Minority language concentration	-0.060	-0.058
	(16.74)	(5.81)
Sample size	10157	2032
R^2	0.3422	0.3964

Notes: [a] Variable not entered.

[b] Due to limited country-of-origin categories in the 1986 Census, the South Asia group includes a small number of cases from unidentified other parts of Asia.

The benchmark country category is Southern Europe.

t-statistics in parentheses computed using White's (1980) heteroskedasticity-consistent covariance matrix estimator.

Source: Column (1): Australian Census of Population and Housing, 1986. Column (2): *Issues in Multicultural Australia Survey 1988*.

Table A12.3

Legit Estimates of Models of English-language Fluency Among Adult Immigrants from Non-English-speaking Countries, Australia, 1988 (Dependent Variables: SPEAK, READ, WRITE)

Variable	SPEAK		READ		WRITE	
Constant	-1.881	-0.891	-2.463	-1.526	-2.529	-1.562
	(4.42)	(1.91)	(5.67)	(3.23)	(5.85)	(3.30)
Age	-0.040	-0.039	-0.037	-0.308	-0.034	-0.033
	(5.46)	(5.09)	(5.08)	(4.87)	(4.66)	(4.34)
Education	0.117	0.119	0.190	0.199	0.173	0.183
	(5.96)	(5. 73)	(9.15)	(8.98)	(8.44)	(8.33)
Years since migration	0.172	0.178	0.154	0.161	0.149	0.156
(YSM)	(7 .80)	(7 .60)	(6.85)	(6. 73)	(6.78)	(6.66)
YSM2/100	-0.145	-0.179	-0.109	-0.140	-0.104	-0.139
	(2.66)	(3.08)	(1.92)	(2.33)	(1.90)	(2.37)
Female	-0.209	-0.219	-0.323	-0.331	-0.138	-0.131
	(1.67)	(1.67)	(2.54)	(2.51)	(1.09)	(0.99)
Married	-0.475	0.508	-0.511	0.530	-0.467	0.525
	(3.19)	(2.71)	(3.40)	(2.73)	(3.13)	(2.77)
English at age 14	1.558	1.515	1.565	1.491	1.588	1.531
	(9.30)	(8.51)	(8.80)	(7 .93)	(9.29)	(8.43)
Northern Europe	2.366	1.697	2.167	1.484	1.880	1.198
	(7.25)	(4.96)	(6.60)	(4.31)	(6.25)	(3. 75)
Eastern Europe	0.074	-0.090	-0.036	-0.205	-0.376	-0.578
	(0.27)	(0.30)	(0.13)	(0.70)	(1.38)	(1.94)
Arabian countries	0.205	0.402	0.248	0.461	0.114	0.335
	(0.83)	(1.49)	(1.01)	(1.74)	(0.46)	(1.25)
South Asia	1.299	0.162	1.204	0.110	1.188	0.063
	(5.17)	(0.55)	(4.76)	(0.37)	(4. 76)	(0.21)
Philippines	2.161	1.163	2.785	1.780	2.316	1.277
	(6.10)	(3.03)	(6.55)	(3.94)	(6.08)	(3.12)
Vietnam	-1.127	-0.710	-1.097	-0.700	-1.161	-0.706
	(4.08)	(2.38)	(4.24)	(2.49)	(4.35)	(2.44)
Other Asia	0.064	-0.783	-0.217	-1.074	-0.215	-1.108
	(0.27)	(2.81)	(0.91)	(3.89)	(0.90)	(3.98)
South and Central America	0.088	0.158	-0.167	-0.144	-0.162	-0.085
	(0.24)	(0.39)	(0.45)	(0.37)	(0.44)	(0.21)
Africa	1.550	0.020	1.502	-0.060	1.458	-0.102
	(4.16)	(0.05)	(3.91)	(0.15)	(3.88)	(0.25)
Other countries	2.116	0.545	2.200	0.645	2.104	0.524
	(5.48)	(1.30)	(5.30)	(1.44)	(5.25)	(1.21)
Minority-language concentration	-0.304	0.033	-0.291	0.034	-0.318	0.029
	(5.22)	(0.43)	(4.92)	(0.45)	(5.40)	(0.38)
Foreign marriage	[a]	-1.481	[a]	-1.491	[a]	-1.480
		(8.47)		(8.33)		(8.44)
Family	[a]	-0.249	[a]	-0.311	[a]	-0.339
		(1.74)		(2.16)		(2.35)
Ethnic press	[a]	-0.326	[a]	-0.312	[a]	-0.356
		(5.31)		(5.13)		(5.82)
Ethnic press squared	[a]	0.016	[a]	0.015	[a]	0.018
		(4.02)		(3.85)		(4.61)
Chi-squared	1110.1	12367.0	1130.2	1253.3	1119.7	1254.2
Sample size	2032	2032	2032	2032	2032	2032

Note: [a] Variable not entered

Asymptotic t-statistics in parentheses. The benchmark country category is Southern Europe.

Source: Issues in Multicultural Australia Survey 1988.

Appendix B
List of Variables

English language proficiency (SPEAK, READ, WRITE): The survey asks "Is English the first language spoken at home?" Respondents answering "Yes" were not asked additional questions on their English language skills. Respondents answering "No" were then asked how well they speak, read, and write English, with five response categories: Very Good, Good, Fair, Poor, and Very Poor. SPEAK is set to one for individuals who report that English is the first language spoken at home, or if a language other than English is the first spoken in the home, speak English "very good." The SPEAK variable is set to zero where a language other than English is reported as the first spoken in the home and the respondent speaks English either "good," "fair," "poor," or "very poor." READ (English reading skills) and WRITE (English-writing skills) are defined in a similar manner.

Age: Age in years for those age 15 to 64.

Years of education: This variable records the total years of full-time education. It has been created from the "Age Left School" and "Qualifications" variables. Years of education is calculated as age left school minus 5. Individuals who possess a trade certificate or diploma have been assigned an additional two years of education, individuals who possess a bachelor's degree an additional 3.5 years of education, and individuals who have a higher degree have been assigned an additional six years of education.

Years since migration: The years since migration variable is computed as current age minus age on arrival.

Female: A binary variable, equal to one for females and zero for males.

Marital status: Married is a binary variable, defined to equal one for individuals who are married.

English at age 14: English was spoken in the home when the respondent was age 14.

Birthplace: The following birthplace regions were formed from the country codes available in the original data: Britain, Northern Europe, Southern Europe, Eastern Europe, Arabian countries, Philippines, Vietnam, South Asia (which primarily comprises the regions of British influence), Other Asia, Canada, United States, British West Indies, South and Central America, Africa, New Zealand, Other countries (including country not specified). Immigrants from Britain, Canada,

United States, British West Indies, and New Zealand are viewed as being from English-speaking countries and are deleted from the analysis. Immigrants from Southern Europe are used as the control group.

Ethnic affiliation: This is a binary variable coded to one where the respondent identified with a non-Australian ethnic or cultural group which was regarded as either very important or fairly important to him.

Family present: The FAMILY variable is a binary variable set equal to one if the respondent had either a mother, father, sibling, or other relative (grandparents, grandchildren, aunts, uncles, parents-in-law, and brothers- and sisters-in-law) in Australia.

Social membership: The SOCIAL variable is a binary variable that is set equal to one where the respondent belonged to a social/sports club that was identified with a particular ethnic or cultural group.

Foreign marriage: Binary variable is set equal to one where the respondent's spouse was born in the same linguistic-country group as the respondent.

Location: Three binary variables were formed, the first for the benchmark group of individuals living in the major urban areas, the second for individuals living in "other urban areas," and the third for individuals living in "rural" areas. The "rural" and "urban" variables were insignificant in the analyses, see, for example, Appendix Table A12.2, and therefore are not included in the analyses reported in the text.

Minority-language concentration: This variable is defined as the percentage of the population aged 15–64 in the region (defined broadly using information on location) in which the respondent lives that reports the same minority language as the respondent. The 12 minority languages coded in the Household Sample File of the 1986 Census from which the language data are derived are used in the construction of the variable. These are: Arabic/Lebanese, Chinese, Dutch, French, German, Greek, Italian, Maltese, Polish, Serbian and Croatian, Spanish, and Vietnamese. It is set equal to zero for all other languages.

Ethnic press: This variable is defined as the number of Australian newspapers in 1986 in the language other than English reported by the respondent. Thirty languages are identified.

Ethnic radio: This variable is defined as the weekly hours of broadcasts in 1986 in the non-English language of the respondent on the 11 radio stations in Australia with the most non-English broadcasts. Transmission times for over 60 languages are available.

Ethnic TV: This variable is defined as the annual hours of community language broadcasts on the multicultural, Special Broadcasting Service, TV station in 1986/87. This station is government run and can be received in all of Australia. Broadcast times for over 30 languages are available. According to Clyne (1991: 149), "Time allocation is made on an annual basis, taking into consideration number of speakers and the availability of suitable films."

Note: All variables are dichotomous except education, age, duration in the destination, the minority concentration measure, and the ethnic media variables. All of the variables are from the *Issues in Multicultural Australia Survey 1988*, except for the three ethnic media variables from Clyne (1991), Tables 20, 21, and 22.

13

Do Enclaves Matter in Immigrant Adjustment?

I grew up in Brooklyn, New York at a time of intense residential differentiation of neighborhoods by ethnic groups. There were African-American, Irish, Italian, Jewish, and Puerto Rican areas. Small mom-and-pop grocery stores, butcher shops, and bakeries (there were no supermarkets) carried goods catering to the preferences of their respective ethnic customers. So, too, the ethnicity of the neighborhoods could be identified by houses of worship that were also specific to each ethnic group. We did not have the terminology of "ethnic enclaves" or "ethnic goods," but we understood the concepts very well.

Fast forward a few decades and I am doing research on immigrant adjustment. I became interested in why immigrants and ethnic groups tend to concentrate geographically. I hypothesized that their choice of location might be affected by their linguistic skills, or limited proficiency in English, and by their desire to consume "ethnic goods," including ethnic foods and entertainment, houses of worship, and the intangible preference to live among others of a similar background.

This resulted in several papers on enclaves, networks, ethnic goods, and, among other things, their impact on earnings. One of these studies, co-authored with Paul W. Miller, was published as "Do Enclaves Matter in Immigrant Adjustment?" (Chapter 13 in this volume). In this paper immigrant enclaves are measured by a linguistic concentration index and the "ethnic goods" concept is developed and explored using data from the U.S. Census. Ethnic goods are cheaper the larger the size of the enclave, if only because of easier access, more competition, and economies of scale.

The original version of this chapter was published as: Chiswick, B.R., Miller, P.W. (2005). Do Enclaves Matter in Immigrant Adjustment?, in: City and Community, 4(1): 5–35. © 2005 by American Sociological Association.

We demonstrated theoretically and showed empirically that immigrants from non-English-speaking origin countries living in larger ethnic enclaves take longer to become proficient in English. Immigrant earnings are related to their human capital; earnings being lower for those less proficient in English. Other factors the same, including their own English language proficiency, immigrant earnings are lower if they live in a larger ethnic (linguistic) enclave. The latter phenomenon may be a compensating differential if desirable ethnic consumer goods are less expensive in enclave communities. If so, the cost of living is lower within the enclave and an immigrant would require a higher wage offer as an incentive to relocate elsewhere.

Barry R. Chiswick (2015)

13.1. Introduction

This chapter is concerned with the issue of immigrant/ethnic concentrations, that is, the tendency of immigrants to concentrate geographically by ethnicity or country of origin within the host country.[1] In particular, it is concerned with the consequences of enclaves or concentrations for two characteristics of immigrant adjustment – destination language proficiency and labor market earnings. Other aspects of immigrant life influenced by concentrations, including political participation and influence, are beyond the scope of this chapter.

There are two basic research questions of interest. One is the effect of immigrant concentrations on proficiency in destination language skills. The other is the direct effect of the immigrant's proficiency in the destination language and the effects of these immigrant concentrations on their labor market earnings. In particular, this study separates the direct effects and indirect effects via language proficiency of immigrant concentrations on earnings. The application is to the United States. The methodology developed, however, could be applied to any immigrant-receiving country for which there is appropriate census or survey data.

The section "Immigrant Concentrations: Hypotheses" provides a brief introduction to the broader setting within which the issue of immigrant concentrations arises. Testable hypotheses are developed, with a particular emphasis on ethnic goods. "The Data" section discusses the data used in the empirical analysis. In the "Analysis of Language" section a model of dominant language acquisition is presented and estimated, with a particular focus on the effects of immigrant/linguistic concentrations on dominant language proficiency. "Analysis of the Earnings" section is the analysis of the earnings of immigrants with a particular focus on the effects of the immigrant's destination language skills and living in a linguistic concentration area on the respondent's labor market earnings. The chapter closes with a summary and conclusion, with implications for public policy.

13.2. Immigrant Concentrations: Hypotheses

13.2.1. Immigrant Flows

A characteristic of the late 20th century that is surely to continue into at least the early 21st century is an increase in the movement of people across international borders (Chiswick and Hatton 2003). International migration has increased into the traditional immigrant-receiving countries, such as the United States, Canada, and Australia. Yet, international migration into traditional countries of emigration has also become commonplace. Italy, Ireland, Germany, and Japan, among others, are now experiencing large net in-migration, or where restricted by law, as in Japan, pressures for in-migration as evidenced by illegal flows.

These migration flows have, in part, been "East" to "West," that is, from the former Soviet Union and the Eastern block countries to the United States, Canada, Germany, and Israel. More pronounced, however, are the migration flows from the "South" to the "North," more precisely, from less developed countries to highly developed economies. Unprecedented immigration flows have been experienced from Latin America to North America, from Africa to Western Europe, and from Asia to North America, Western Europe, Australia, and Japan (Chiswick and Hatton 2003).

An important characteristic of these international migration flows is that the immigrants are "different" from the natives. As was true of the immigration flows from Southern and Eastern Europe to North America at the turn of the 20th century, the immigrants to the developed countries at the turn of the 21st century "sound" and "look" different.

In spite of the world becoming a smaller place with the ease (falling cost) of the transmission of information and ideas, and the falling cost of transportation for people and goods, and hence the "Westernization" of much of the world, new immigrants are frequently distinctive. Although distinctive clothing, especially for men, is less common than in the past, immigrants as a group frequently differ from natives as a group in appearance, religion, customs, belief-systems, language, and other characteristics associated with ethnicity.

13.2.2. Immigrant Concentrations

The immigrant groups typically have a spatial distribution in their host countries that differs sharply from that of the native born. For obvious reasons, new immigrants typically settle in areas based on three characteristics (Bartel 1989).[2] The first is "ports" of entry, near seaports in the past, near airports in the current era. The second is where family and friends (co-ethnics) from earlier migrations have settled. Even if the location choice of the first settler from the ethnic group is purely random among a set of equally attractive locations in a destination country, once that first settler is established, future settlers are no longer indifferent among destination sites. The third is where the jobs are, that is, where the immigrants are most able to gain employment that makes best use of their skills, or lack thereof. With the passage of time "ports of entry" and "family and friends" become less central and economic factors relatively more central in deciding where to live in the host country, and immigrants tend to disperse to some extent.

Some interpret the "family and friends" or chain migration effect on immigrant formations of concentrations as "clannishness." Yet to say it is clannishness is to beg the question as "clannishness" per se has no content. An alternative interpretation, however, is that settling in areas with others from the same origin provides for economies in communication, information, consumption, and in the labor market.

Where new immigrants differ from the host population in terms of language skills, communication in all spheres of life are that much more difficult. These communication costs can be reduced if the host population were to learn the immigrant's language. Yet, it is not cost effective for a majority host population speaking the dominant language to learn the myriad of new languages that minority immigrants bring with them from various linguistic backgrounds.

These communication costs are reduced when immigrants learn the dominant language of the destination country. Yet, this learning can be costly and cannot be done instantaneously in the destination. Thus, to varying degrees, new immigrants from a different linguistic origin tend to lack complete proficiency in the dominant language of the host economy, unless dominant language proficiency is a requirement for entry. Moreover, as with the production of other forms of human capital and of market goods and services, beyond some point, costs per unit of improved proficiency increase with a faster speed of language acquisition. Thus, the optimal acquisition of dominant language proficiency among immigrants takes time and, for some, full proficiency may never be obtained in their lifetime.

Finally, these communication costs for the immigrants can be reduced by living and/or working in a linguistic concentration area (Bauer, Epstein, and Gang 2005). Not all members of the group need dominant language proficiency, and the earlier arrivals and those more efficient in language acquisition are more likely to become proficient. They can serve as either direct or indirect translators for communication between the enclave and the host society. The demand for this specialized function increases with the size of the linguistic minority group and decreases as the members of the group learn the dominant language or as the native population learns the immigrant language.

Even aside from issues of language skills, immigrant/ethnic concentrations provide information networks that can be very valuable in social interaction, consumption, and employment activities. Natives of an area have acquired location-specific human capital, which includes information obtained directly and indirectly through established networks. Not being connected to host country information networks when they arrive, immigrants have an incentive to create or "import" information networks through living in geographic concentrations with other new and longer-term immigrants from the same origin.

13.2.3. Ethnic Goods

Immigrants tend to differ from the native or host population in many dimensions related to ethnicity. They may differ in the foods they eat, the clothing they wear, the holidays they celebrate, the religion they practice, the media they read or hear (e.g., newspapers and radio), their social organizations, and the languages they speak, among other characteristics.[3] There is frequently a tension among immigrants between preserving the culture of the "old country" in the new setting and adopting the culture of the host country.

Let us call "ethnic goods" the consumption characteristics of an immigrant/ethnic group not shared with the host population, or with other immigrant groups, broadly defined to include market and non-market goods and services, including social interactions for themselves and their children with people of the same origin.[4] To the extent that "ethnic goods" are distinctive and are important in the market basket, immigrants from a particular origin have a different market basket than the native born and immigrants from other origins. The full cost of consumption of these ethnic goods varies with the price of purchased market goods and services and the value of time, but also with the importance and distinctiveness of the ethnic goods and the size of the group.[5]

There are certain fixed costs and economies of scale in the production and distribution of ethnic goods. Social interaction with others of the same origin (including finding an appropriate marriage partner) may involve little in the way of conventional market goods and services, but importantly involves the number of other individuals in the group. The cost would decrease (presumably at a decreasing rate) the larger the size of the group.[6] Up to a point, an ethnic religious institution (e.g., church, mosque, temple, or synagogue) or an ethnic school for the children of immigrants has a lower per capita cost for members for the same type of facility providing the same level of services to the congregants or students if it is in a larger rather than in a smaller ethnic community.[7] There are fixed costs for buildings and hiring religious officials, among other items, including the probability that enough individuals will show up on a given occasion for the religious service.

The cost of "importing" into the community ethnic-specific goods (e.g., saris, Chinese vegetables, kosher meats) also varies with the size of the market because of economies of scale. Indeed as the size of the community increases, the manner of "importation" may change from a family making a trip to a larger nearby community, to collective/cooperative efforts to place periodic bulk orders, to the establishment of a single (monopoly) outlet, to many competitive outlets selling the product. The full price declines, the larger the size of the community.

The cost of living in an area then depends on the relative cost of ethnic goods, broadly defined, and the importance and distinctiveness of ethnic goods in the person's market basket. The cost of ethnic goods is lower, the larger is the size of the particular ethnic/immigrant community. The share of ethnic goods in the market basket is likely to be lower, the closer culturally the group is in the origin to the host society, the greater the extent of assimilation into the host society, the longer the immigrant's duration of residence in the destination, and among the native-born descendants of immigrants.

Ethnic goods have implications for living in an ethnic concentration area as well as for geographic differences in earnings. If ethnic goods, defined broadly, are an important part of the market basket, the person faces a higher real cost of living where ethnic goods are more expensive (an area where fewer co-ethnics live) than where they are less expensive (a high ethnic concentration area). Then the ethnic immigrant would be indifferent between a similar job in a high-concentration area and a low-concentration area only if the latter provided a higher nominal wage that was just sufficient to compensate for the higher cost of living.[8]

Thus, ethnic goods can result in different geographic concentrations of various immigrant groups and differences in the pattern of regional wage differentials across immigrant groups and between immigrants and natives. The general observation would be lower nominal wages, the larger the size of the concentration, other variables being the same. Note that the "ethnic goods" hypothesis regarding the negative relation between the concentration measure and earnings is an equilibrium situation based on differences in the real (ethnic-specific) cost of living. It reflects compensating wage differentials.[9]

When a new immigrant group initially arrives in a destination it may be indifferent among alternative regions in the destination that are equally attractive in terms of job opportunities and ports of entry. The initial settlers would tend to be immigrants with a lower demand for ethnic goods. Subsequent immigrants from this ethnic group will not be indifferent among the alternative destinations as ethnic goods will be cheaper where their co-ethnics have already settled. With the ethnic community established, those with a higher demand for ethnic goods would find immigration much more attractive.

New ethnic concentrations away from the original center in the destination can be formed under any one of several scenarios. An individual with a very low demand for ethnic goods may settle elsewhere and gradually (and perhaps inadvertently) serve as a nucleus for others to follow. An individual with a high demand for ethnic goods may randomly receive a very high wage offer from the distribution of wage offers and settle in a new area. This person may serve as a nucleus and may even have an economic incentive to subsidize ethnic goods to encourage others to join him or her in the new location. Moreover, if a very "large" number of immigrants settle in the initial location and they are less than perfect substitutes in production for native workers, under the crowding hypothesis their wages decline relative to what they could earn in alternate locations with fewer (perhaps none) of their group. If the wage gap compensates for the higher cost of living because of ethnic goods, a second enclave can be established. Thus, the number of enclaves or areas of concentration will vary systematically with the size of the immigrant/ethnic group and the distinctiveness and intensity of the demand for ethnic goods.

13.2.4. Immigrant "Crowding"

An alternative to the "ethnic goods" hypothesis is a labor supply or "crowding" hypothesis. If there are a large number of immigrants with a given skill level, and if they are not good substitutes in production for others with the same skill level, their earnings would be depressed as indicated in the previous paragraph. This is, however, a disequilibrium situation as immigrant workers with a given level of skill could receive higher real wages outside the enclave. The internal mobility of immigrant and native-born labor, and other factors of production, as well as goods and services, would bring about factor price equalization, eliminating the negative relation between concentration and earnings.

The "crowding hypothesis" is not likely to be compelling for the United States. The United States has highly fluid labor, capital, and product markets where inter-regional mobility is the norm rather than the exception. The largest single group of immigrants is from Mexico, and they tend to have low levels of skill, without a high degree of specialized skills.[10] As such, they are good substitutes in production for other low-skilled labor, whether native born or foreign born. Among the non-Mexican immigrants, the countries and languages of origin are numerous and skill levels are more highly varied. It is difficult to think of any groups in the U.S. that are sufficiently large and specialized with a low substitutability with native-born and other foreign-born workers. To the extent that a sudden exogenous infusion of immigrant labor with specialized skills impacts a local labor market, disequilibrium earnings differentials would emerge, but would be dissipated over time with internal mobility of factors of production (including immigrant labor) and tradable goods. The persistence over time of immigrant concentrations is not consistent with the implications of the crowding hypothesis effect on wages.

13.2.5. Consequences of Concentrations

Limited destination language proficiency is likely to reduce the earnings potential of immigrants (Chiswick and Miller 1992; 1995). It raises the cost or lowers the efficiency of job search and in many jobs may restrict access (e.g., if there is a need to pass a test that requires proficiency) or merely lower productivity. There may also be discrimination in the labor market by the native population (either as employers, co-workers, or consumers) against those who are less proficient in the dominant language or who speak it with an accent. Working within a linguistic enclave is a mechanism for sheltering oneself from, or mitigating the adverse labor market consequences of, limited destination language proficiency.

Living and working within a linguistic concentration area has feedback effects on destination language proficiency. The greater the extent to which an individual can avoid communicating in the destination language, the slower is likely to be the rate of acquisition of dominant language skills. Consider two individuals: one lives in a large linguistic concentration area where one can work, consume, socialize, and engage in other activities using the origin language and the other lives in a linguistically isolated area; communication can be done only in the dominant language. The latter may have a more difficult initial adjustment, but has a stronger incentive to acquire destination language skills and has greater exposure that facilitates learning the destination language.

Thus, what has emerged in many developed countries is the existence of distinct immigrant communities that differ in language, culture, and other characteristics from the host society. These immigrant/linguistic concentrations are expected to have an adverse effect on the immigrant's acquisition of dominant language skills. The immigrant's dominant language skills, as well as the size of the linguistic concentration area, will also affect the person's earnings, other things being the same. Greater proficiency would have a positive effect, and a larger concentration a negative effect on nominal earnings. These hypotheses are tested in the empirical analysis.

13.3.   The Data

13.3.1.   Defining the Population Under Study

The empirical analysis is performed using data from the 1990 Census of Population of the United States for adult male immigrants.[11] The U.S. Census provides a very large sample, a rich array of variables, and immigrants from diverse origins arriving at various periods of time. The analysis at this stage is limited to adult (nonaged) males as the analysis for females or aged males becomes more complex because of the need to model labor supply decisions, in addition to the language and earnings equations. Moreover, the formation of enclaves or concentrations is taken as exogenous for the individual in the empirical analysis, although there was a discussion in Section 13.3 as to why such concentrations are formed.

The data for the statistical analysis are from the 5 percent Public Use Microdata Sample from the 1990 Census. The sample is limited to males aged 25 to 64 years who were foreign born, but not from an English-speaking developed country. Thus, the native born, those born in a U.S. territory (e.g., Puerto Rico), born at sea, or born abroad of American parents are excluded, as are those born in the United Kingdom, Ireland, Canada, Australia, and New Zealand.

13.3.2.   Defining the Variables

The English language proficiency variable comes from question number 15 in the census long form. Respondents were asked if there was a language other than English spoken at home (other than just a few words), and if so the identity of that language and how well they spoke English, where the response categories were Very Well, Well, Not Well, and Not at All. For the purpose of this analysis, the foreign born who spoke only English or who spoke another language but reported that they spoke English "very well" or "well" were considered fluent; those who spoke English "not well" and "not at all" were considered not fluent.

The other dependent variable is earnings, which is the sum of wage, salary, and self-employment income in 1989. Those with earnings of less than $100, including those with negative earnings, were assigned a value of $100. Those who worked 0 weeks in 1989 were deleted from the sample for the analysis of earnings.

The enclave variable is a minority language concentration measure (CON).[12] The 24 languages other than English most frequently spoken in the United States were identified. The speakers of these top 24 languages constitute around 94 percent of those reporting a foreign language spoken at home. For each of these 24 languages, for the 50 states and the District of Columbia, the percent age of the states' population aged 18 to 54 years (whether native or foreign born) speaking that language, was computed. The concentration measure for each respondent is the percentage speaking the person's origin language in the state of current residence. For other languages, since the number of speakers is too low, the percentage was assumed to be zero. Those who reported speaking only English were assigned the mean value of the concentration ratio for foreign-language speakers in their birthplace group.

Within states, the density of population is less in rural areas than in urban areas. A variable for residence in a rural area (RURAL) is included because of a smaller concentration of origin language speakers in rural than in urban centers. The other explanatory variables are straightforward and are discussed in Appendix B and as the variables are introduced in the text.

13.3.3. *The Statistical Techniques*

The main statistical methodology that is employed is ordinary least squares (OLS) with standard errors corrected for heteroskedasticity, and where indicated below instrumental variables (IV) analysis.

13.4. Analysis of Language
13.4.1. *The Language Model*

This section presents the development of the model for dominant language proficiency. While largely based on previous work, in particular Chiswick and Miller (1995; 1998a), the model is expanded to include new variables (refugees, persons from former colonies of English-speaking countries, and persons who lived abroad five years earlier). Particular attention is given to the variable measuring the degree of minority language concentration (CON).

The language proficiency model adopts a human capital approach in which destination language proficiency (LANG) is a function of three fundamental determinants, namely, "exposure," "efficiency," and "economic incentives." Since the application is to the English language for immigrants in the United States in the 1990 Census, the discussion of these variables will be in this context. The principles apply to any destination language, country, and data set.

13.4.1.1. Exposure Variables

"Exposure" refers to exposure to the destination language either pre- or post-immigration. The census identifies country of birth, but provides no other information on pre-immigration experiences relevant for acquiring English language proficiency. A set of country-of-origin dichotomous variables is included in the analysis to control for country of origin fixed effects. Western Europe (other than the U.K. and Ireland) is the benchmark. Moreover, a dichotomous variable is created for whether the origin was a colony (COLONY) of an English-speaking country, that is, of either the United States or the United Kingdom. Recall that respondents born in current U.S. territories are excluded from the analysis.

Postimmigration exposure to English can be measured in time units and in intensity per unit of time. Time in the destination is measured as the number of years since migration and its square (YSM, YSMSQ). It is expressed as a quadratic variable to allow for the effect of an extra year in the United States to be larger in the early years than in subsequent years.

The duration variable refers to when the immigrant first came to the United States to stay. Exposure to English in the United States may have been interrupted by sojourns outside the country after the initial migration. For immigrants in the United States for more than five years the variable "lived abroad five years ago" (ABROAD5) is unity if this was the situation, otherwise it is zero. It is expected that, other variables being the same, having lived outside the United States would be associated with lesser proficiency in English compared to otherwise similar immigrants who did not live elsewhere in 1985.

Intensity of exposure per unit of time in the United States can be measured by several variables. Of particular interest is the minority language concentration measure (CON), which is computed on a state level, as discussed earlier. Within states the density of population is less in rural areas than in urban areas. A variable for residence in a rural area (RURAL) is included because of a smaller concentration of origin language speakers in rural than in urban areas within states.

For immigrants from Mexico the analysis also includes an index for Spanish language media, namely, a variable for the number of radio stations in Spanish normalized for the size of the state in square miles and population (RADIO) (Chiswick and Miller 1998a). Because of possible endogeneity in this variable, a predicted value (IV technique) rather than an observed value for radio is used.

A marital status variable (MARR is unity if married, spouse present) is also included here. It is not possible in the 1990 Census to distinguish between pre- and postmigration marriages, but it was possible to do so in the 1980 Census (Chiswick and Miller 1992).

13.4.1.2. Efficiency Variables

"Efficiency" refers to the ability to convert exposure into language skills. Greater efficiency means more language skills are acquired for the same level of exposure. The efficiency variables include age at migration (age with years since migration held constant), years of schooling, whether the respondent may have been a refugee, and a measure of the "distance" between the origin language and English.

Older immigrants (AGE) at arrival have greater difficulty learning a new language. Age is entered as a quadratic variable (age and its square) as it is expected that an extra year of age at migration would have a larger adverse effect among younger than among older immigrants.

Those with more schooling (EDUC) are assumed to be more able and to have more knowledge of the structure of languages, and hence are likely to be more efficient in learning new languages, including the destination language. It may also be that those with more schooling in the origin were exposed to English at higher grades prior to immigration, or that schooling in the United States enhanced proficiency.[13]

The refugee variable (REFUGEE) is included because refugees tend to be less favorably selected for a successful adjustment in the destination than are economic migrants. The migration decision of refugees is influenced to an important extent by factors other than the expectation of a successful economic adjustment. The refugee variable is based on country of birth and period of immigration.

Another efficiency variable is "linguistic distance" (DISTANCE), that is, a measure of how difficult it is for non-English speakers to learn English (see Chiswick and Miller 1998a). For example, Korean would be more "distant" from English than would be French. The more "distant" is the origin language from English, the lower the efficiency in learning English and hence the lower the expected proficiency in English.

13.4.1.3. Economic Variables

"Economic incentives" is the most difficult conceptual variable to model. In principle, one would like to add an explanatory variable that measures the expected increment in earnings for a unit increase in proficiency for each respondent. Given currently available data it is not possible to do this. It has been found that immigrants with higher levels of schooling have a greater economic return from becoming proficient (Chiswick and Miller 2003). That is, that there is a complementarity between language skills and education in generating labor market earnings. This effect on incentives to invest in destination language skills would be captured by the education variable (EDUC).

The economic benefits in the labor market and in other activities from increased proficiency in English would be greater the longer the expected duration in the United States. Immigrants from countries with a high propensity for return migration would expect a shorter period in the U.S. data on emigration (EMIG) by country of origin are used for this purpose, but not for Mexico (Ahmed and Robinson, 1994). The methodology for developing the country-specific emigration rates in Ahmed and Robinson (1994) is not applicable to Mexico because of the 1986 amnesty and the very large proportion of illegal aliens among the foreign born from Mexico.

Immigrants from countries farther from the United States are more likely to be favorably self-selected as they have higher costs of migration (Chiswick 1999). This implies a higher level of efficiency in learning English. They also have a lower return migration rate, again because of the higher migration costs. Those from origins at a greater distance from the United States are, therefore, expected to be more fluent (Chiswick and Miller 1998a). This is measured as the number of miles (XMILES) from the major city in the origin to New York, Miami, or Los Angeles, whichever is the shortest. It is entered as a quadratic variable. While state-specific (fixed) effects are not held constant because the concentration ratio is based on state data, a control variable is entered for southern states (SOUTH).

13.4.2. Statistical Analysis

The means and standard deviations of the language variable (LANG) and the explanatory variables, overall and separately for Mexican and non-Mexican immigrants, are reported in Table A13.1. The regression

Table 13.1

Regression Estimates of Language Equation, Adult Foreign-born Men by Origin, 1990

Variable	Total Sample[a]	Excludes Immigrants from Mexico[a]	Immigrants from Mexico Only[b]
Constant	0.409	0.478	0.440
	(26.28)	(26.76)	(10.64)
Age	-0.01	-0.011	-0.006
	(15.69)	(16.59)	(3.96)
Age squared/100	0.003	0.006	-0.003
	(4.96)	(7.55)	(1.33)
Years of education	0.029	0.030	0.028
	(141.10)	(119.57)	(64.67)
Years since migration (YSM)	0.021	0.018	0.027
	(100.30)	(83.11)	(48.35)
YSM squared/100	-0.025	-0.023	-0.027
	(56.69)	(50.82)	(22.23)
Married	0.033	0.020	0.053
	(19.29)	(11.02)	(12.06)
Rural	0.010	0.021	0.002
	(3.00)	(6.93)	(0.26)
South	0.013	0.010	0.028
	(7.16)	(5.41)	(5.75)
S. Europe	-0.028	-0.033	c
	(9.47)	(10.88)	
E. Europe	-0.047	-0.063	c
	(12.19)	(15.41)	
USSR	-0.03	-0.039	c
	(4.75)	(6.19)	
IndoChina	-0.09	-0.093	c
	(9.19)	(9.22)	
Philippines	0.024	0.014	c
	(3.43)	(1.78)	
China	-0.123	-0.128	c
	(17.17)	(16.15)	
S. Asia	-0.011	-0.02	c
	(1.38)	(2.26)	
Other Asia	-0.036	-0.044	c
	(3.27)	(3.91)	
Korea	-0.202	-0.207	c
	(21.62)	(18.04)	
Japan	-0.108	-0.116	c
	(10.74)	(9.84)	
Middle East	0.010	0.009	c
	(2.52)	(1.10)	
Sub-Saharan Africa	0.032	0.028	c
	(6.28)	(2.79)	
Mexico	-0.067	c	c
	(12.10)		
Cuba	0.044	0.040	c
	(5.17)	(3.97)	

Table 13.1 (continued)

Regression Estimates of Language Equation, Adult Foreign-born Men by Origin, 1990

Variable	Total Sample[a]	Excludes Immigrants from Mexico[a]	Immigrants from Mexico Only[b]
C. and S. America (Spanish)	-0.019	-0.042	c
	(4.10)	(8.25)	
C. & S. America (non-Spanish)	0.219	0.208	c
	(32.97)	(30.76)	
Minority language concentration	-0.004	-0.003	-0.010
	(17.81)	(9.73)	(7.84)
Linguistic distance	-0.005	-0.006	c
	(0.36)	(0.44)	
Miles from origin/1,000	0.050	0.054	c
	(14.57)	(15.19)	
Square of miles from origin/1,000	-0.034	-0.038	c
	(9.16)	(10.19)	
Refugee	-0.123	-0.138	c
	(32.12)	(35.19)	
Colony	0.012	0.013	c
	(3.53)	(3.90)	
Resident overseas 5 years ago	-0.069	-0.046	-0.073
	(11.34)	(6.76)	(3.13)
Emigration rate	c	-0.01	c
		(2.37)	
Spanish radio	c	c	-21.98
			(4.11)
R^2	0.3244	-0.006	d
Sample size	237,766	(0.44)	68,512

Notes: [a] Equation estimated using ordinary least squares.
[b] Equation estimated using instrumental variables (IV) estimator.
[c] Variable not applicable.
[d] R^2 not defined for the IV Model. IV estimator used for Spanish Radio variable.
t-statistics have been computed using White's (1980) heteroskedasticity-consistent covariance matrix estimator.

Source: 1990 Census of Population of the United States, Public Use Microdata Sample, 5 percent sample.

equations for English language proficiency are reported in Table 13.1 for all immigrants, non-Mexican immigrants, and Mexican immigrants.

The data are found to be consistent with the hypotheses developed earlier. In particular, English language proficiency is greater the higher the level of schooling, the longer the duration of residence (quadratic effect), the younger the age at immigration (negative effect of age), among those from a former British or American colony, and from countries more distant from the United States. It is less among refugees, among transients (i.e., immigrants who first came to the United States more than five years earlier – prior to 1985 – but who were outside the United States in 1985), and where the expected duration in the United States (emigration rate variable) is shorter. The linguistic distance variable is not statistically significant when country of origin fixed effects are included in the analysis, as is the case in Table 13.1, but it is significant with the expected negative effect when the country dichotomous variables are excluded from the equation. This arises from the close relation between country of origin and language of origin.

The minority language concentration variable (CON) is highly statistically significant as is the rural variable (RURAL), which is a proxy for the concentration of foreign-language speakers within areas in states. According to the regression for all immigrants, going from a minority language concentration of zero to the mean value of 7.8 percent lowers the probability of being fluent in English by 3.1 percentage points, which is 4.2 percent of the mean proficiency of 0.73 or 73 percent. Rural residence (5.5 percent of the foreign born) raises proficiency by 1.0 percentage point overall and by 2 percentage points among non-Mexican immigrants.

Among Mexican immigrants three variables reflect the effect of the linguistic concentration of Spanish speakers. One is the direct minority language concentration measure, the second is the rural variable, while the third is the (predicted) Spanish-language radio station variable. The minority concentration measure and the radio station variable, but not the rural variable, are highly statistically significant with the expected negative signs. Thus, the analysis of English language proficiency among immigrants from non-English origins in the United States indicates that the data are consistent with the model based on exposure, efficiency, and economic variables. Moreover, it is found that linguistic concentrations or enclaves are associated with a lesser proficiency in English among all, Mexican, and non-Mexican immigrants.

13.5. Analysis of Earnings

13.5.1. The Earnings Model

The econometric analysis of earnings is based on the human capital earnings function, modified for immigrant adjustment (Chiswick 1978d). In this specification, the natural logarithm of annual earnings (LNEARN) is regressed on years of schooling (EDUC), years of potential labor market experience and its square (EXP, EXPSQ), duration in the United States and its square (YSM, YSMSQ), the natural logarithm of weeks worked (LNWW), marital status (MARR), and place of residence (RURAL, SOUTH). Three dichotomous variables are added to the equation which take the value of unity for immigrants whose race is black, are Veterans of the U.S. Armed Forces, and who are citizens of the United States. Two other variables are also added to this equation, the respondent's proficiency in English (LANG), which is unity for those fluent in English, as previously defined, and zero otherwise, and the minority language concentration measure (CON).

13.5.2. Statistical Analysis

The earnings equation is estimated separately for all immigrants, Mexican immigrants, and non-Mexican immigrants. The means and standard deviations of the variables are reported in Table A13.2, while Tables A13.3–A13.5 report the regression equations for each group. A basic earnings function in these tables is reported in column (i) without the language and concentration variables, column (ii) adds the English language proficiency variable (LANG), column (iii) adds the concentration variable (CON) to the basic equation, column (iv) adds both variables, while column (v) substitutes a predicted English language proficiency variable obtained through the IV technique. (The auxiliary equation is reported in Table A13.6.) A summary of the language and concentration variable results are presented in Table 13.2.

Table 13.2

Partial Effects on Earnings of the Language and Concentration Variables, Adult Foreign-born Men from Non-English-Speaking Countries, 1990

Variables	Total Sample		Excludes Immigrants from Mexico		Immigrants from Mexico Only	
	OLS	IV	OLS	IV	OLS	IV
Proficient in English	0.148	0.592	0.151	0.678	0.146	[a]
	(31.60)	(16.53)	(22.40)	(16.40)	(23.52)	
Minority language concentration	-0.0056	-0.0039	-0.007	-0.005	-0.0033	[a]
	(15.25)	(9.62)	(11.77)	(7.85)	(7.13)	

Note: [a] IV equation is not computed for Mexico; *t*-ratios are in parentheses.
Full regression equations are reported in column (iv) and column (v) of Tables A13.3–A13.5. OLS refers to ordinary least squares. IV refers to instrumental variables technique using predicted value of respondent's proficiency in English.

Source: Tables A13.3–A13.5.

13.5.2.1. Ordinary Least Squares Analysis

As has been found elsewhere, the basic determinants of earnings among immigrants are also found to be important here (see Tables A13.3-A13.5). For immigrants from non-English speaking countries, earnings increase with years of schooling (by about 5 percent per year of schooling), duration in the United States (at a decreasing rate), pre-immigration labor market experience (total experience when duration is held constant), and weeks worked (with an elasticity of annual earnings with respect to weeks worked close to unity), and are higher for married men (by about 20 percent) and citizens (9 percent). Earnings are lower for immigrants who are veterans of the U.S. Armed Forces (8 percent), and among those living in rural areas (4 percent) and in the South (11 percent).

Similar patterns are found when the analysis is done separately for non-Mexican and for Mexican origin immigrants (Tables A13.4 and A13.5).[14] Note that the effects of several variables reflecting human capital are smaller for Mexican immigrants than for other immigrants. These include schooling, experience, and weeks worked, but not duration in the United States.

The OLS analysis in Tables A13.3-A13.5 indicates that earnings are about 15 percent higher for all immigrants, Mexican immigrants, and non-Mexican immigrants who are proficient in English, compared to those lacking proficiency. The difference is statistically significant and the magnitude of the effect and level of significance do not vary with whether the concentration measure is included in the analysis.

Assuming a long working life, the real rate of return on the investment in language proficiency can be estimated (approximately) as $r = b/k$, where r is the real rate of return, b is the regression coefficient of the language proficiency variable, and k is the number of full-year equivalents of lost earnings (including out-of-pocket expenditures and forgone earnings), to go from not proficient ("not well," "not at all") to proficient (English only, "very well" or "well"). Then, if the coefficient of the language variable is $b = 0.15$ and if the full cost is the equivalent of a full year's potential earnings ($k = 1$), the rate of return is about 15 percent. If the cost were the equivalent of two years of full-time equivalent earnings ($k = 2.0$), the rate of return on the investment would be about 7.5 percent. If proficiency required the equivalent of only five months' forgone earnings ($k = 0.5$), the estimated rate of return would be about 30 percent. The rate of return would be even higher if the positive effects of proficiency on weeks worked in the year were included in the calculation and if the consumption benefits from English language proficiency could be estimated. Thus, investments in English language skills appear to be profitable for immigrants from non-English-speaking countries.

The concentration measure is also statistically significant in all three analyses. Earnings are lower where the concentration index is higher.[15] The coefficient and level of significance are also largely invariant with respect to the inclusion in the analysis of the respondent's fluency in English. Among all immigrants, going from a zero concentration area to the mean level (7.8 percent) lowers earnings by about 4.4 percent (i.e., 7.8 times 0.0056 from Table A13.3, column (iv)). For non-Mexican immigrants (mean concentration 3.9 percent) it lowers earnings by about 2.7 percent. Among Mexican immigrants, the mean of the concentration ratio is much higher (18.1 percent), but the coefficient of the concentration ratio is lower (-0.0033 compared to -0.0070 for other countries). For Mexican immigrants, the effect of going from a zero concentration to the mean concentration ratio is to lower earnings by about 6.0 percent. Thus, other variables the same, including the respondent's own proficiency in English, living in a linguistic/ethnic concentration area lowers the earnings of immigrants.[16] Moreover, the estimated magnitude of the effect is in a reasonable range.

The effect of the concentration ratio on earnings varies systematically with the level of education. If an education-concentration ratio interaction term is added to the regression in Table A13.3, column (iv), it has a negative and highly significant effect.[17] That is, the adverse effect on earnings from living in a high-concentration area is greater the higher the level of schooling.[18] There is no effect for those with only five years of schooling, but the negative effect of living in a high-concentration area grows larger at higher levels of schooling. Alternatively, this can be expressed as the effect of education on earnings is smaller in the high-concentration (enclave) area than in an area where fewer other individuals speak the same origin language.

13.5.2.2. Instrumental Variables Analysis
There are several potential econometric problems with the OLS analysis using the respondent's reported level of English language proficiency. One problem is that language skills may be endogenous to, that is, determined by, earnings. Those who anticipate higher earn-

ings if they were to become proficient will make greater investments to acquire proficiency (Chiswick and Miller 1995).

A second problem is that there may be substantial measurement error in reported language skill. Purely random measurement error would bias the coefficient toward zero, but the measurement error need not be purely random (Kruger and Dunning 1999). For example, those who are more successful in the labor market for unmeasured reasons may be more likely to overestimate their English language skills. A positive correlation in the measurement error terms could bias the coefficient upward.

A third problem is that there may be dimensions of ability that are not in the equation, but which enhance both English language proficiency and earnings. Those with greater innate ability among the foreign born may have superior English language skills and earn more, even though the higher earnings may be unrelated to their English proficiency. Yet there are no independent measures of ability in these data. This form of omitted variables bias would tend to overstate the true effect of language skills on earnings in an OLS equation.

Instrumental variables is a statistical technique that can, in principle, correct for these potential problems by using a predicted rather than the observed value of language proficiency. An auxiliary regression is computed (Table A13.6), which includes at least some variables that are not in the earnings function and which has a more complex functional form (various quadratic and interaction terms) to permit statistical identification. This auxiliary regression is used to obtain predicted values of the language variable, and it is these values, rather than the reported or observed values, that are used in the earnings equation. Because the statistical identification is so dependent on variables that vary across countries of origin, a reliable IV model cannot be estimated using these data for immigrants from only one country, Mexico.

The results for the IV earnings function are reported in column (v) in Tables A13.3 and A13.4 and are summarized in Table 13.2 for all and non-Mexican immigrants. The IV technique results in a very large coefficient for the language proficiency variable. It implies about 80 percent higher earnings for those proficient in English in the all immigrant analysis.[19] Yet, similar very large coefficients on destination language skills have been found elsewhere and for other countries using this technique.[20] Perhaps the unbiased effect of English language fluency on earnings among immigrants is somewhere between the OLS and the IV estimates. Yet, even the OLS estimate of about 15 percent implies a large payoff from obtaining English language skills.

13.6. Summary and Conclusion

13.6.1. Summary

This chapter has been concerned with whether immigrant linguistic concentrations or enclaves affect immigrant adjustment in terms of destination language proficiency and earnings.

The reasons for the development of these concentrations are discussed. New immigrants tend to settle near ports of entry, where previous immigrants from their origin (friends and family) have settled and where their employment opportunities are best. The "friends and family" or chain migration effect is a consequence of economies in communication, information, consumption, and the labor market.

"Ethnic goods" are market and nonmarket goods and services consumed by members of an immigrant/ethnic group that are not consumed by others. Ethnic-specific goods are an important factor in location choice. Because of economies of scale in the production of ethnic goods, the full cost of ethnic goods is lower the larger the size of the immigrant/ethnic group. Then an immigrant would be indifferent between working in two alternative areas (equal real wages) only if the area with the high cost ethnic goods (lower concentration ratio) provided a higher nominal wage.

Several hypotheses emerge from the analysis. Linguistic concentrations are expected to have an adverse effect on the destination language proficiency of immigrants. Greater proficiency is expected to result in higher earnings and a larger ethnic/immigrant concentration is expected to have a negative effect on nominal earnings.

The modeling of the language equation is based on three fundamental variables: exposure (pre- and post-immigration) to the destination language, efficiency in destination language acquisition, and economic incentives for destination language acquisition. Variables are developed to measure the effects of these concepts. The concentration ratio and the rural variable measure, in part, post-immigration exposure to the destination language. The earnings equation is based on the standard human capital earnings function augmented for immigrant adjustment. Two additional variables are the immigrant's proficiency in the destination language and the minority language concentration ratio.

The empirical testing is done using adult (nonaged) male immigrants in the United States from non-English speaking countries as reported in the 1990 Census 5 percent microdata sample. Immigrant language skills are found to vary positively with exposure to the destination language, efficiency in language acquisition, and economic incentives. In particular, English language proficiency is greater the higher the level of schooling, the longer the duration of residence, the younger the age at immigration, the further the origin from the United States, if the origin was a colony of the United States or the United Kingdom, if the immigrant was not a refugee, has a lower probability of return migration, and among immigrants who do not go back and forth between their origin countries and the United States. A smaller minority language concentration ratio and living in a rural area, and hence living among a lower density of origin language speakers, are both associated with greater proficiency in English. Among immigrants from Mexico, greater access to Spanish language radio stations is associated with poorer English language skills.

Annual earnings are found to increase with skill level (schooling, experience, duration in the United States), and weeks worked, and are higher among married men, those living in urban areas outside the South, those who are citizens, and those who are not black. Veteran status is associated with higher earnings among Mexican immigrants, but lower earnings among other immigrants. In the OLS analysis earnings are higher by about 15 percent for those proficient in English, compared to those lacking fluency, and are lower for those living in an area with a higher minority language concentration ratio. The earnings advantage from proficiency is even greater when the respondent's English language proficiency is estimated using the IV technique.

13.6.2. *Policy Implications*

The answer to the question in the title is "yes." Enclaves matter for immigrant adjustment. Immigrant linguistic concentrations are associated with a lower level of proficiency in the destination language (English). Poorer English language skills result in lower nominal and real earnings. Even after controlling for one's own language skills, living within an immigrant/ethnic concentration area also results in lower nominal earnings, presumably because of the ethnic goods effect. Thus, linguistic concentrations have both an indirect effect (via destination language skills) and a direct effect on lowering the observed earnings of immigrants. The direct effect of concentration on earnings may be an equilibrium situation, where earnings differences are compensating differentials reflecting geographic differences in the cost of ethnic goods.

Immigrant/linguistic concentrations serve a useful role. They provide information networks and channels of communication in consumption and in the labor market for those without, or with only limited, destination-specific information and language proficiency, and they lower the cost of ethnic goods. On the other hand, they tend to retard the acquisition of, or investment in, destination-specific skills (e.g., language proficiency) and to lower nominal earnings. The assimilation or adjustment of immigrants is enhanced the smaller the extent of the immigrant/ethnic concentration.

It would be difficult to implement incentives for immigrants to settle outside of concentrated areas for their group. Focusing immigration on countries of origin "culturally similar" to the United States would be an unwarranted return to the pernicious national origins quota system in place from 1921 to 1965. A reduced emphasis on family ties in issuing immigration visas, and placing a greater emphasis on the applicant's own skills is likely to increase the diversity of origins and reduce the extent of immigrant-linguistic concentrations.

Yet, in the highly mobile United States these concentrations tend to be first generation, and at most also second generation, phenomena. Reliance on self-correcting mechanisms is likely to be the most effective public policy, such as the acquisition of English language skills and the decline in the importance in the market basket of ethnic goods with a longer duration of residence.

Appendix A

Table A13.1

Means and Standard Deviations of Variables, Sample Used for Language Model

Variable	Total Sample	Excludes Immigrants from Mexico	Immigrants from Mexico Only
English proficiency	0.730	0.808	0.524
	(0.44)	(0.39)	(0.50)
Age	37.79	40.92	36.83
	(10.63)	(10.75)	(9.69)
Years of education	11.63	13.09	7.80
	(4.99)	(4.27)	(4.69)
Years since migration	15.21	15.43	14.64
	(11.08)	(11.51)	(9.84)
Married	0.655	0.673	0.610
	(0.48)	(0.47)	(0.49)
Rural	0.055	0.042	0.089
	(0.23)	(0.20)	(0.28)
South	0.237	0.234	0.244
	(0.43)	(0.42)	(0.43)
S. Europe	0.078	0.107	[a]
	(0.27)	(0.31)	
E. Europe	0.036	0.049	[a]
	(0.19)	(0.22)	
USSR	0.016	0.022	[a]
	(0.12)	(0.15)	
IndoChina	0.048	0.066	[a]
	(0.21)	(0.25)	
Philippines	0.051	0.070	[a]
	(0.22)	(0.26)	
China	0.062	0.085	[a]
	(0.24)	(0.28)	
S. Asia	0.049	0.067	[a]
	(0.21)	(0.25)	
Other Asia	0.012	0.016	[a]
	(0.11)	(0.13)	
Korea	0.031	0.044	[a]
	(0.17)	(0.20)	
Japan	0.015	0.020	[a]
	(0.12)	(0.14)	

Table A13.1 (continued)

Variable	Total Sample	Excludes Immigrants from Mexico	Immigrants from Mexico Only
Middle East	0.060	0.083	a
	(0.24)	(0.28)	
Sub-Saharan Africa	0.024	0.034	a
	(0.15)	(0.18)	
Mexico	(0.276)	0.00	1.00
	(0.45)	(0.00)	(0.00)
Cuba	0.051	0.070	a
	(0.22)	(0.26)	
C. and S. America (Spanish)	0.125	0.173	a
	(0.33)	(0.38)	
C. and S. America (non-Spanish)	0.009	0.012	a
	(0.09)	(0.11)	
Minority language concentration	7.784	3.816	18.178
	(8.87)	(6.19)	(5.95)
Linguistic distance	0.515	0.542	a
	(0.15)	(0.17)	
Miles from origin	3841.1	4756.6	a
	(2574.9)	(2475.4)	
Refugee	0.096	0.133	a
	(0.29)	(0.34)	
Colony	0.147	0.203	a
	(0.35)	(0.40)	
Resident overseas 5 years ago	0.019	0.017	0.025
	(0.14)	(0.13)	(0.16)
Emigration rate	a	2.049	a
		(0.76)	
Spanish radio	a	a	0.002
			(0.01)
Sample size	237,766	169,253	68,512

Note: Standard errors are in parentheses.
 [a] Variable not applicable.
Source: 1990 Census of Population of the United States, Public Use Microdata Sample, 5 percent sample.

Table A13.2

Means and Standard Deviations of Variables, Sample Used for Earnings
Model

Variable	Total Sample	Excludes Immigrants from Mexico	Immigrants from Mexico Only
Natural log of earnings	9.787	9.942	9.387
	(1.03)	(1.04)	(0.90)
English proficiency	0.747	0.830	0.535
	(0.43)	(0.38)	(0.50)
Labor market experience	22.76	22.41	23.63
	(11.46)	(11.53)	(11.25)
Years of education	11.79	13.30	7.90
	(4.92)	(4.11)	(4.68)
Years since migration	15.43	15.75	14.60
	(10.85)	(11.30)	(9.52)
Married	0.673	0.691	0.627
	(0.47)	(0.46)	(0.48)
Rural	0.057	0.044	0.091
	(0.23)	(0.20)	(0.29)
South	0.240	0.238	0.244
	(0.43)	(0.43)	(0.43)
Race (Black)	0.033	0.044	0.004
	(0.18)	(0.21)	(0.06)
Citizen	0.417	0.484	0.247
	(0.49)	(0.50)	(0.43)
Veteran	0.068	0.083	0.030
	(0.25)	(0.28)	(0.17)
Log weeks worked	3.752	3.774	3.693
	(0.47)	(0.46)	(0.51)
S. Europe	0.078	0.108	[a]
	(0.27)	(0.31)	
E. Europe	0.036	0.050	[a]
	(0.19)	(0.22)	
USSR	0.013	0.019	[a]
	(0.12)	(0.14)	
IndoChina	0.041	0.057	[a]
	(0.20)	(0.23)	

Table A13.2 (continued)

Variable	Total Sample	Excludes Immigrants from Mexico	Immigrants from Mexico Only
Philippines	0.053	0.073	[a]
	(0.22)	(0.26)	
China	0.061	0.085	[a]
	(0.24)	(0.28)	
S. Asia	0.051	0.071	[a]
	(0.22)	(0.26)	
Other Asia	0.011	0.016	[a]
	(0.11)	(0.12)	
Korea	0.031	0.043	[a]
	(0.17)	(0.20)	
Japan	0.015	0.021	[a]
	(0.12)	(0.14)	
Middle East	0.059	0.082	[a]
	(0.24)	(0.27)	
Sub-Saharan Africa	0.024	0.034	[a]
	(0.15)	(0.18)	
Mexico	0.279	0.00	1.00
	(0.45)	(0.00)	(0.00)
Cuba	0.051	0.069	[a]
	(0.22)	(0.25)	
C. and S. America (Spanish)	0.127	0.176	[a]
	(0.33)	(0.38)	
C. and S. America (non-Spanish)	0.009	0.012	[a]
	(0.09)	(0.11)	
Minority language concentration	7.834	3.850	18.129
	(8.88)	(6.21)	(6.00)
Sample size	212,381	150,680	61,700

Note: Standard errors are in parentheses.

    [a] Variable not applicable.

Source: 1990 Census of Population of the United States, Public Use Microdata Sample, 5 percent sample.

Table A13.3

Regression Estimates of Earnings Equation, Adult Foreign-born Men from Non-English Speaking Countries, 1990

Variable	OLS				IV
	(i)	(ii)	(iii)	(iv)	(v)
Constant	5.063	5.006	5.074	5.017	4.845
	(173.18)	(171.67)	(173.47)	(171.96)	(150.58)
Years of education	0.049	0.045	0.048	0.045	0.035
	(91.10)	(83.48)	(90.24)	(82.85)	(35.19)
Experience	0.023	0.025	0.023	0.025	0.029
	(35.72)	(38.04)	(35.77)	(38.04)	(38.55)
Experience squared/100	-0.037	-0.038	-0.038	-0.038	-0.041
	(31.33)	(32.20)	(31.47)	(32.30)	(33.27)
Years since migration (YSM)	0.028	0.025	0.028	0.025	0.017
	(49.29)	(43.73)	(49.76)	(44.24)	(18.36)
YSM squared/100	-0.039	-0.035	-0.039	-0.036	-0.026
	(30.24)	(27.56)	(30.54)	(27.88)	(16.85)
Log of weeks worked	0.970	0.964	0.967	0.963	0.952
	(135.52)	(134.94)	(135.43)	(134.88)	(131.21)
Married	0.213	0.208	0.214	0.209	0.195
	(55.22)	(54.02)	(55.43)	(54.23)	(47.54)
Rural	-0.037	-0.038	-0.043	-0.044	-0.047
	(4.67)	(4.89)	(5.43)	(5.58)	(5.89)
South	-0.112	-0.113	-0.109	-0.11	-0.113
	(26.11)	(26.36)	(25.40)	(25.71)	(25.90)
Race (Black)	-0.182	-0.19	-0.187	-0.195	-0.218
	(12.36)	(12.95)	(12.68)	(13.22)	(14.48)
Veteran	-0.078	-0.08	-0.079	-0.081	-0.085
	(10.25)	(10.48)	(10.39)	(10.61)	(11.12)
Citizen	0.090	0.082	0.088	0.080	0.056
	(21.36)	(19.35)	(20.87)	(18.94)	(11.83)
S. Europe	-0.063	-0.06	-0.058	-0.056	-0.049
	(6.23)	(5.98)	(5.70)	(5.51)	(4.85)
E. Europe	-0.077	-0.073	-0.077	-0.074	-0.062
	(6.40)	(6.09)	(6.44)	(6.13)	(5.14)
USSR	-0.133	-0.125	-0.134	-0.127	-0.103
	(7.37)	(6.95)	(7.43)	(7.02)	(5.65)
IndoChina	-0.282	-0.27	-0.283	-0.271	-0.236
	(23.21)	(22.31)	(23.31)	(22.42)	(19.02)
Philippines	-0.224	-0.234	-0.217	-0.227	-0.259
	(21.11)	(22.07)	(20.39)	(21.39)	(23.42)
China	-0.274	-0.254	-0.27	-0.251	-0.193
	(24.10)	(22.41)	(23.73)	(22.11)	(15.84)
S. Asia	-0.021	-0.028	-0.023	-0.029	-0.049
	(1.83)	(2.41)	(2.00)	(2.55)	(4.13)
Other Asia	-0.201	-0.203	-0.202	-0.203	-0.208
	(10.45)	(10.54)	(10.49)	(10.57)	(10.70)
Korea	-0.233	-0.209	-0.233	-0.209	-0.137
	(14.95)	(13.41)	(14.94)	(13.43)	(8.25)
Japan	0.347	0.357	0.347	0.357	0.389
	(18.75)	(19.45)	(18.76)	(19.44)	(20.97)

Table A13.3 (continued)

Variable	OLS				IV
	(i)	(ii)	(iii)	(iv)	(v)
Middle East	-0.098	-0.104	-0.099	-0.105	-0.122
	(8.26)	(8.77)	(8.36)	(8.85)	(10.18)
Sub-Saharan Africa	-0.064	-0.07	-0.062	-0.068	-0.087
	(3.38)	(3.71)	(3.29)	(3.62)	(4.54)
Mexico	-0.341	-0.313	-0.235	-0.218	-0.167
	(37.39)	(34.39)	(21.28)	(19.80)	(14.23)
Cuba	-0.242	-0.216	-0.172	-0.153	-0.095
	(21.54)	(19.22)	(14.35)	(12.77)	(7.44)
C. and S. America (Spanish)	-0.244	-0.227	-0.168	-0.158	-0.129
	(25.62)	(23.89)	(15.93)	(15.05)	(11.96)
C. and S. America (non-Spanish)	-0.081	-0.1	-0.073	-0.092	-0.15
	(3.61)	(4.45)	(3.27)	(4.12)	(6.47)
Proficient in English	a	0.151	a	0.148	0.592
		(32.26)		(31.60)	(16.53)
Minority language concentration	a	a	-0.0062	-0.0056	-0.0039
			(16.75)	(15.25)	(9.62)
R^2	0.4157	0.4185	0.4164	0.4190	b
Sample size	212,381	212,381	212,381	212,381	212,381

Notes: [a] Variable not entered;
 [b] R^2 not defined for the IV Model.
 IV estimator used for proficient in English variable. t-statistics have been computed using White's (1980) heteroskedasticity-consistent covariance matrix estimator.

Source: 1990 Census of Population of the United States, Public Use Microdata Sample, 5 percent sample.

Table A13.4

Regression Estimates of Earnings Equation, Adult Foreign-born Men from Non-English Speaking Countries Other than Mexico, 1990

Variable	OLS				IV
	(i)	(ii)	(iii)	(iv)	(v)
Constant	4.824	4.757	4.839	4.773	4.542
	132.90)	(131.27)	(133.15)	(131.52)	(111.69)
Years of education	0.058	0.055	0.058	0.054	0.041
	(85.04)	(77.84)	(83.96)	(76.98)	(33.96)
Experience	0.023	0.025	0.024	0.025	0.030
	(29.48)	(31.39)	(29.80)	(31.64)	(33.21)
Experience squared/100	-0.037	-0.038	-0.038	-0.039	-0.042
	(24.66)	(25.42)	(25.05)	(25.77)	(26.90)
Years since migration (YSM)	0.026	0.024	0.027	0.024	0.016
	(37.82)	(33.87)	(38.05)	(34.15)	(15.63)
YSM squared/100	-0.037	-0.034	-0.038	-0.035	-0.024
	(24.46)	(22.43)	(24.66)	(22.64)	(13.87)
Log of weeks worked	0.994	0.991	0.994	0.990	0.978
	108.94)	(108.53)	(108.89)	(108.50)	(105.98)
Married	0.218	0.215	0.217	0.215	0.205
	(44.77)	(44.23)	(44.70)	(44.18)	(40.86)
Rural	-0.002	-0.005	-0.006	-0.009	-0.018
	(0.18)	(0.43)	(0.50)	(0.72)	(1.48)

Table A13.4 (continued)

Variable	OLS				IV
	(i)	(ii)	(iii)	(iv)	(v)
South	-0.087	-0.088	-0.091	-0.091	-0.093
	(16.22)	(16.38)	(16.85)	(16.95)	(16.90)
Race (Black)	-0.189	-0.197	-0.196	-0.203	-0.228
	(12.25)	(12.77)	(12.65)	(13.13)	(14.40)
Veteran	-0.093	-0.095	-0.094	-0.095	-0.101
	(11.12)	(11.33)	(11.18)	(11.38)	(11.90)
Citizen	0.107	0.098	0.105	0.097	0.069
	(19.99)	(18.41)	(19.63)	(18.12)	(11.85)
S. Europe	-0.028	-0.025	-0.023	-0.02	-0.012
	(2.72)	(2.46)	(2.18)	(1.96)	(1.17)
E. Europe	-0.069	-0.063	-0.071	-0.065	-0.045
	(5.66)	(5.21)	(5.81)	(5.36)	(3.67)
USSR	-0.133	-0.123	-0.136	-0.125	-0.09
	(7.28)	(6.74)	(7.44)	(6.90)	(4.84)
IndoChina	-0.266	-0.251	-0.269	-0.253	-0.199
	(21.30)	(20.11)	(21.50)	(20.32)	(15.19)
Philippines	-0.225	-0.232	-0.217	-0.225	-0.253
	(20.62)	(21.33)	(19.91)	(20.66)	(22.53)
China	-0.274	-0.251	-0.27	-0.248	-0.169
	(23.67)	(21.67)	(23.33)	(21.39)	(12.94)
S. Asia	-0.041	-0.044	-0.043	-0.047	-0.058
	(3.45)	(3.75)	(3.69)	(3.96)	(4.85)
Other Asia	-0.207	-0.206	-0.209	-0.207	-0.203
	(10.68)	(10.63)	(10.77)	(10.71)	(10.36)
Korea	-0.237	-0.208	-0.238	-0.21	-0.112
	(14.94)	(13.17)	(15.01)	(13.26)	(6.40)
Japan	0.339	0.353	0.338	0.352	-0.402
	(18.12)	(18.99)	(18.07)	(18.93)	(21.06)
Middle East	-0.105	-0.108	-0.107	-0.11	-0.121
	(8.72)	(9.01)	(8.89)	(9.16)	(9.99)
Sub-Saharan Africa	-0.071	-0.074	-0.068	-0.071	-0.082
	(3.63)	(3.78)	(3.48)	(3.65)	(4.17)
Cuba	-0.23	-0.203	-0.141	-0.12	-0.051
	(19.99)	(17.56)	(10.42)	(8.93)	(3.48)
C. and S. America (Spanish)	-0.217	-0.197	-0.124	-0.112	-0.067
	(22.14)	(20.07)	(10.21)	(9.17)	(5.25)
C. and S. America (non-Spanish)	-0.06	-0.077	-0.052	-0.069	-0.129
	(2.62)	(3.36)	(2.25)	(3.00)	(5.44)
Proficient in English	a	0.154	a	0.151	0.678
		(22.82)		(22.40)	(16.40)
Minority language concentration	a	a	-0.0076	-0.007	-0.005
			(12.71)	(11.77)	(7.85)
R^2	0.3770	0.3792	0.3776	0.3797	b
Sample size	150,680	150,680	150,680	150,680	150,680

Notes: [a] Variable not entered;
[b] R2 not defined for the IV Model.
IV estimator for proficient in English variable. t-statistics have been computed using White's (1980) heteroskedasticity-consistent covariance matrix estimator.

Source: 1990 Census of Population of the United States, Public Use Microdata Sample, 5 percent sample.

Table A13.5

Regression Estimates of Earnings Equation, Adult Foreign-born Men from Mexico, 1990

Variable	OLS			
	(i)	(ii)	(iii)	(iv)
Constant	5.208	5.194	5.279	5.254
	(115.30)	(115.28)	(114.92)	(114.70)
Years of education	0.027	0.024	0.027	0.024
	(29.94)	(26.67)	(29.77)	(26.58)
Experience	0.015	0.016	0.015	0.016
	(12.23)	(13.35)	(12.11)	(13.23)
Experience squared/100	-0.026	-0.026	-0.025	-0.026
	(12.74)	(12.90)	(12.64)	(12.81)
Years since migration (YSM)	0.029	0.025	0.029	0.025
	(29.47)	(25.36)	(29.82)	(25.70)
YSM squared/100	-0.037	-0.033	-0.037	-0.033
	(15.40)	(13.69)	(15.57)	(13.85)
Log of weeks worked	0.918	0.913	0.918	0.913
	(82.30)	(81.83)	(82.25)	(81.79)
Married	0.207	0.199	0.208	0.200
	(33.54)	(32.43)	(33.78)	(32.65)
Rural	-0.098	-0.099	-0.105	-0.105
	(10.58)	(10.73)	(11.27)	(11.29)
South	-0.184	-0.184	-0.174	-0.175
	(26.73)	(26.81)	(24.85)	(25.16)
Race (Black)	-0.039	-0.055	-0.038	-0.054
	(0.82)	(1.16)	(0.80)	(1.14)
Veteran	0.087	0.078	0.085	0.076
	(4.73)	(4.24)	(4.63)	(4.17)
Citizen	0.042	0.028	0.040	0.026
	(6.17)	(4.04)	(5.86)	(3.82)
Proficient in English	a	0.149	a	0.146
		(23.98)		(23.52)
Minority language concentration	a	a	-0.0039	-0.0033
			(8.53)	(7.13)
R^2	0.4080	0.4135	0.4086	0.4139
Sample size	61,700	61,700	61,700	61,700

Note: ᵃ Variable not entered;
t-statistics have been computed using White's (1980) heteroskedasticity-consistent covariance matrix estimator.

Source: 1990 Census of Population of the United States, Public Use Microdata Sample, 5 percent sample.

Table A13.6

Regression Estimates of Language Equation Used in IV Estimation, Adult Foreign-born Men by Origin, 1990

Variable	Total Sample	Excludes Immigrants from Mexico
Constant	0.350	0.398
	(25.24)	(24.06)
Experience	-0.007	-0.007
	(23.10)	(21.09)
Experience squared/100	0.004	0.004
	(6.62)	(6.87)
Years of education	0.022	0.022
	(67.15)	(65.15)
Years since migration (YSM)	0.013	0.012
	(54.17)	(44.62)
YSM squared/100	-0.019	-0.016
	(41.42)	(33.24)
Married	0.028	0.016
	(15.33)	(8.35)
Rural	0.010	0.020
	(3.07)	(6.62)
South	0.005	0.004
	(2.53)	(2.15)
Citizen	0.064	0.055
	(33.65)	(27.59)
Race (Black)	0.068	0.065
	(12.22)	(11.61)
Veteran	0.019	0.012
	(8.46)	(5.17)
Natural logarithm of weeks worked	0.026	0.022
	(14.14)	(10.77)
S. Europe	-0.055	-0.056
	(18.47)	(18.16)
E. Europe	-0.072	-0.087
	(18.72)	(20.88)
USSR	-0.039	-0.053
	(6.22)	(8.22)
IndoChina	-0.156	-0.134
	(15.12)	(12.78)
Philippines	-0.065	-0.038
	(9.10)	(4.72)
China	-0.163	-0.144
	(21.67)	(17.56)
S. Asia	-0.102	-0.072
	(12.31)	(7.79)
Other Asia	-0.12	-0.1
	(10.44)	(8.15)
Korea	-0.242	-0.196
	(25.25)	(16.82)
Japan	-0.137	-0.101
	(13.30)	(8.42)
Middle East	-0.038	0.008
	(9.17)	(0.99)
Sub-Saharan Africa	-0.081	-0.024
	(10.71)	(2.04)
Mexico	-0.11	[a]
	(18.91)	

Table A13.6 (continued)

Variable	Total Sample	Excludes Immigrants from Mexico
Cuba	-0.024	-0.008
	(2.66)	(0.73)
C. and S. America (Spanish)	-0.057	-0.053
	(11.40)	(9.84)
C. and S. America (non-Spanish)	0.106	0.133
	(13.69)	(15.99)
Minority language concentration (CON)	0.028	0.022
	(7.61)	(5.76)
Linguistic distance	-0.002	0.009
	(0.16)	(0.59)
Miles from origin/1,000	0.035	0.047
	(8.43)	(10.12)
Square of miles from origin/10 m.	-0.012	-0.023
	(2.85)	(5.08)
Refugee	-0.116	-0.113
	(28.94)	(27.36)
Colony	0.019	0.022
	(5.70)	(6.57)
Resident overseas 5 years ago	-0.066	-0.045
	(10.37)	(6.37)
Emigration rate	a	-0.033
		(7.61)
CON × years of education/1,000	-0.024	0.103
	(0.84)	(2.12)
CON × experience/1,000	-0.206	-0.27
	(17.89)	(15.59)
CON × YSM/1,000	0.527	0.666
	(50.63)	(37.23)
CON × linguistic distance	-0.078	-0.078
	(9.26)	(9.11)
CON × miles from origin/1 m	0.181	-0.349
	(1.40)	(2.41)
CON × emigration rate	a	0.003
		(8.00)
R^2	0.3345	0.3164
Sample Size	212,381	150,680

Notes: ᵃ Variable note entered;
t-statistics have been computed using White's (1980) heteroskedasticity-consistent covariance matrix estimator.
Source: 1990 Census of Population of the United States, Public Use Microdata Sample, 5 percent sample.

Appendix B

Definitions of Variables

The variables used in the statistical analyses are defined here. Mnemonic names are also listed where relevant. The means and standard deviations are reported in Appendix A1 and A2 for the samples used in the analysis of language attainment and earnings, respectively.

Data Source: 1990 Census of Population, Public Use Microdata Sample, 5 percent sample of the foreign born, except where noted otherwise.

Immigrant Adjustment

Definition of Population: The sample used in this study comprises foreign-born men aged 25 to 64, born in countries other than the English-speaking developed countries (UK, Ireland, Canada, Australia, New Zealand), territories of the United States, at sea, or born abroad of American parents. Those who worked 0 weeks in 1989 were deleted from the analysis of earnings, as they were not labor force participants.

Dependent Variables

English Language Fluency (LANG): LANG is set equal to 1 for individuals who speak only English at home, or if a language other than English is spoken in the home, who speak English either "very well" or "well." The variable is set to 0 where a language other than English is spoken in the home and the respondent speaks English either "not well" or "not at all."

   Earnings (LNEARN): The natural logarithm of the sum of wage or salary income and self-employment income (either nonfarm or farm) received in 1989. Individuals with earnings less than $100, including those with negative earnings, were assigned a value of $100.

Explanatory Variables

Minority Language Concentration (CON): Each respondent is assigned a measure equal to the percentage of the population aged 18 to 64 in the state in which he lives, who reports the same non-English language as the respondent. In the construction of this variable, only the 24 largest language groups nationwide are considered. In descending order they are: Spanish; French; German; Italian; Chinese; Tagalog; Polish; Korean; Vietnamese; Japanese; Portuguese; Greek; Arabic; Hindi; Russian; Yiddish; Thai; Persian; French Creole; Armenian; Hebrew; Dutch; Hungarian; Mon-Khmer (Cambodian). These constitute 94 percent of all responses that a language other than English is used at home. Representation in the other language groups is so small numerically that the proportions are approximately zero, and this value is assigned. Those who reported speaking only English are assigned the mean value of the CON measure for other language speakers of their birthplace group.

Location: The two location variables record residence in a rural area (RURAL) or in the southern states (SOUTH). The states included in the latter are: Alabama, Arkansas, Delaware, District of Columbia, Florida, Georgia, Kentucky, Louisiana, Maryland, Mississippi, Missouri, North Carolina, Oklahoma, South Carolina, Tennessee, Texas, Virginia, West Virginia.

Birthplace (BIRTH): A number of non-English speaking birthplace regions are considered in the analyses: Western Europe; Southern Europe; Eastern Europe; former Soviet Union; Indochina; South Asia (which comprises the regions of British influence, for example, India, Nepal, Pakistan); Other South-East Asia; Korea; Japan; Middle East and North Africa; Sub-Saharan Africa; Mexico; Cuba; Central and South America (Spanish influence); Central and South America (non-Spanish influence). The benchmark group (omitted category) in the regression analysis is Western Europe.

Colony (COLONY): Countries that are current or former colonies of English-speaking countries are coded 1. All other countries are coded 0. Dependencies of the United Kingdom, United States, Australia, New Zealand, and South Africa are coded as colonies under this definition.

Years Since Migration (YSM): The categorical census information on year of immigration is converted to a continuous measure using the following values: 1987 to 1990 (1.75 years); 1985 to 1986 (4.25 years); 1982 to 1984 (6.75 years); 1980 to 1981 (9.25 years); 1975 to 1979 (12.75 years); 1970 to 1974 (17.75 years); 1965 to 1969 (22.75 years); 1960 to 1965 (27.75 years); 1950 to 1959 (35.25 years); before 1950 (49.75 years).

Lived Abroad 5 Years Ago (ABROAD5): This dichotomous variable is defined only for immigrants who have resided in the United States for more than five years. It is set equal to 1 if the individual lived abroad in 1985, otherwise it is set equal to 0 for immigrants in the United States five or fewer years and for longer duration immigrants living in the United States in 1985.

Radio (RADIO): The number of radio stations broadcasting entirely or nearly entirely in Spanish in the state were obtained from Willard (1994: B566-B567). In 1994, there were 315 Spanish language radio stations broadcasting in 25 states. Chiswick and Miller (1998a) present details. The number of Spanish-language radio stations in the state was normalized by the area of the state to give the number of radio stations per 1,000 square miles. Then this variable was normalized by the number of Spanish speakers in the state of residence to give the number of Spanish language radio stations per unit of area per 10,000 Spanish speakers. This variable provides an index of the intensity of the infrastructure supporting the Spanish language in the state of residence. There were too few radio stations broadcasting in languages other than Spanish to compute a meaningful index for other languages. Because of the possible endogeneity of this variable, an IV approach was used.

Marital Status (MARR): This is a binary variable that distinguishes individuals who are married, spouse present (equal to 1) from all other marital states.

Years of Education (EDUC): This variable records the total years of full-time education. It has been constructed from the census data on educational attainment by assigning the following values to the census categories: completed less than fifth grade (2.5 years); completed fifth through eighth grade (7 years); completed ninth grade (9); completed tenth grade (10); completed 11th grade (11); completed 12th grade or high school (12); attended or completed college (14); Bachelor's degree (16); Master's degree (17.5); Professional degree (18); Doctorate (20).

Refugee (REFUGEE): This variable is constructed to identify the major sources of post-World War II refugees to the United States. It is defined only for immigrants who migrated at age 25 and older. Individuals who migrated from Cambodia, Laos, or Vietnam in 1975 or later, Iran in 1980 or later, Cuba in 1960 or later, or the USSR and Baltic States are assigned a value of one for this variable. All other immigrants are assigned a value of 0.

Linguistic Distance (DISTANCE): This is a measure of the difficulty of learning a foreign language for English-speaking Americans. It is based on a set of language scores (LS) measuring achievements in speaking proficiency in foreign languages by English-speaking Americans at the U.S. Department of State, School of Language Studies, reported by Hart-Gonzalez and Lindermann (1993). It is described in detail in Chiswick and Miller (1998a, Appendix B). For the same number of weeks of instruction, a lower score (LS) represents less language facility, and, it is assumed, greater linguistic distance between English and the specific foreign language. For example, French is scored at 2.5 (in a range from 1 to 3), while Japanese is scored at 1.0. The language groups reported in the Hart-Gonzalez and Lindermann (1993) study are then matched to language codes in the 1990 Census using the Ethnologue Language Family Index published by Grimes and Grimes (1993). Adam Makkai, Professor of Linguistics, University of Illinois at Chicago, assisted in the matching of language codes, and in expanding the list of languages for which scores were assigned.

In the construction of this variable, foreign-born persons who speak only English at home and hence do not report speaking a non-English language are assigned the mean value of the linguistic score measure for individuals reporting a foreign language from their birthplace group.

The variable in the regression equations is linguistic distance, which is 1 divided by the linguistic score, DISTANCE = 1/LS.

Emigration Rate (EMIG): Yearly emigration rates of the foreign born by country of birth and sex are computed by dividing the yearly emigration levels between 1980 and 1990 from Ahmed and Robinson (1994) by the number of immigrants of the specific birthplace-gender group in 1980 from the 1980 U.S. Census. Thirty-three countries are separately identified in the data, together with seven residual regions.

Direct-Line Distances (MILES): The miles between the major city in the immigrant's country of origin and the nearest large port of entry in the United States (New York, Miami, Los Angeles) are constructed from data in Fitzpatrick and Modlin's (1986) Direct Line Distances, United States Edition.

Years of Experience (EXP): This is computed as Age – Years of education – 5 (that is, EXP =AGE- EDUC- 5). A quadratic specification is used.

Log of Weeks Worked (LNWW): The number of weeks worked in 1989 is used in natural logarithmic form.

Race: This is a dichotomous variable, set to 1 if the individual is black, and set to 0 for all other racial groups (white, Asian, and Pacific Islander groups, American Indian, Other groups).

Veteran Status (VETSTAT): This is a dichotomous variable, set to 1 where the respondent is a veteran of the U.S. armed forces. In all other cases it is set to 0.

Citizen (CITIZEN): This is a dichotomous variable, set to 1 for individuals who are naturalized citizens.

Part IV
Language and Human Capital

14

Speaking, Reading, and Earnings among Low-skilled Immigrants

Although my research on immigration began because of a concern in the U.S. about growing illegal immigration in the 1970s, most of my work focuses on the foreign born living in several countries (U.S., Australia, Canada, Israel, and U.K.), as reported in census and survey data. There were, and still are, little data explicitly on the undocumented or illegal alien population or labor force. To generate some data, I was Principal Investigator for two surveys, conducted by the Survey Research Laboratory of the University of Illinois. One of these was a survey of employees, identified by the I-213 form (deportable aliens located) on file in the INS Chicago District Office, matched to a random sample of employers not identified in these files. This survey resulted in my book Illegal Aliens: Their Employment and Employers (Chiswick 1988b).

The other survey was of illegal aliens apprehended during a single year (October 1986–September 1987) by the Los Angeles District Office of the INS who had been in the United States for at least four days at the time of apprehension. The paper "Speaking, Reading, and Earnings among Low-Skilled Immigrants" (reprinted as Chapter 14 of this volume) uses this sur-

The original version of this chapter was published as: Chiswick, B.R. (1991). Speaking, Reading, and Earnings among Low-Skilled Immigrants, in: Journal of Labor Economics, 9(2): 149–70. © 1991 by University of Chicago Press. The survey analyzed in this article was financed by a grant from the Immigration and Naturalization Service, U.S. Department of Justice, and was conducted by the Survey Research Laboratory, University of Illinois. The research for this article was financed by grants from the Sloan Foundation and the Institute of Government and Public Affairs, University of Illinois. The author appreciates the research assistance of Xiao-Bo Li and the comments received from Evelyn Lehrer, Luis Locay, Evelina Tainer, and François Vaillancourt.

vey to analyze the determinants of English speaking and reading proficiency and their effects on the earnings of these primarily low-skilled immigrants. These data were analyzed before the U.S. Census (later the American Community Survey) asked questions on English speaking proficiency; data on reading skills are still not collected by the Census Bureau. One of the important findings in this study is that in this population English reading skills have a larger impact on earnings than do English speaking skills.

Barry R. Chiswick (2015)

The growing literature on the economic adjustment or economic assimilation of immigrants has focused on the human capital that is embodied in them, the relevance of this human capital to the destination labor market, and postmigration human capital investments. One important aspect of human capital is "language capital," that is, the speaking, reading, and writing skills in one or more languages.

Language capital, particularly spoken language, is partially developed during the course of a child's maturation, for example, the development of speaking fluency in one's "mother tongue." Important investments are made in school and elsewhere in developing further one's language capital in the mother tongue. For most immigrants, however, their mother tongue is not the majority or dominant language spoken in the destination. An immigrant who does not know the dominant language might find a language-minority enclave within which mother-tongue skills can be fruitfully used. A language-minority enclave may, however, limit training opportunities and job mobility, whether it is geographic, occupational, or employer mobility, and thereby limit earnings opportunities. Furthermore, greater dominant language skills would enhance productivity in the enclave and the nonenclave labor market by increasing efficiency in job search and through greater productivity on the job. There is, therefore, a labor market incentive to acquire dominant-language skills. Whether, and under what circumstances, this incentive is worth the cost is of keen interest.

This article is concerned with both the determinants of fluency in dominant-language skills and how these skills are translated into labor market earnings. A unique data set, a sample of illegal aliens apprehended in the Los Angeles area, is used to study the issue.[1]

Section 14.1 briefly reviews the literature on the nexus between language and earnings in the labor market for immigrants. It indicates the strengths and limitations of this literature. The data used for this study are described in Section 14.2. Section 14.3 is a multiple regression analysis of the determinants of fluency in speaking and reading English. This includes longitudinal changes in speaking skills. Section 14.4 is a regression analysis of the determinants of earnings focusing on the roles of fluency in speaking and reading English. The article closes (Section 14.5) with a summary and conclusion, including suggestions for the collection of data on immigrant populations.

14.1.   Language and Earnings

Ever since its recent development, the literature on the economic status of immigrants has been concerned with the "Americanization" or adjustment of immigrants (Chiswick 1978d). One of the important interpretations of the variable for duration in the destination has been the acquisition of destination-specific skills, including labor market information and language skills. The earliest research, using the 1970 Census of Population, was limited by the absence of data on language skills, except for what could be inferred from country of birth.[2]

Substantial progress on the role of language in immigrant adjustment could not be made until the 1976 Survey of Income and Education (SIE) became available. The SIE asked a battery of questions about languages spoken and the use of these languages.[3] The 1980 Census furthered research on language and earnings by including a self-reported question on fluency in spoken English at the time of the census, as well as a question on languages currently spoken in the home other than English, a pattern repeated in the 1990 Census questions.

Two data deficiencies in the SIE and the 1980 Census are corrected in the survey data studied in this article. First, the survey asked for self-reported fluency in English at the time of *first* arrival in the United States, as well as the SIE/Census question on fluency at the time of interview.[4] Second, the survey included a question on self-reported fluency in reading English at the time of interview. Furthermore, the survey methodology included a bilingual interviewer and both English and Spanish versions of the survey instrument. This methodology should reduce reporting errors and nonresponse on the part of those least fluent in English.

Most of the American studies of English language fluency have focused on Hispanics. The earliest study was by McManus and his colleagues and concluded that once language skills are taken into account "the differentials in wages which are associated with Hispanic ethnicity, U.S. nativity, schooling abroad and time in the United States are no longer statistically significant" (see McManus, Gould, and Welch 1983: 121). They then indicate that the interpretation is not that these factors are unimportant but rather that "their effects are mediated through" measured English language skills. These findings, however, are the result of a specification error.[5]

Other studies have used the SIE and the 1980 Census for the United States and 1971 and 1981 Canadian Census data to analyze the effect of dominant and minority language proficiency at time of interview on the earnings or occupational status of immigrants.[6] In general, the studies find that dominant language fluency, entered directly or using an instrumental variables approach, explains some (perhaps one-third) of the observed immigrant-native earnings differential, other variables the same, and accounts for some of the effect of duration in the destination on earnings.

Veltman (1988: 545–6) notes that "no comprehensive account of the language shift process has as yet been produced for immigrants, although several relevant variables have been suggested." He cites only age at migration and length of time in the destination. Using the 1976 SIE data on Hispanics and univariate analysis, he confirms findings reported elsewhere that the propensity to speak English decreases with age at migration and increases with duration in the United States. He did not use the SIE data on schooling or other variables and, of course, did not have data on English fluency at migration. Chiswick and Miller (1992) used the 1980 U.S. and the 1981 Canadian Censuses to analyze dominant language fluency as a function of demographic, human capital, household characteristic, and minority-language concentration variables. They also analyzed the effect of dominant language fluency on earnings and the endogeneity of language skills. Their analyses were, of course, limited by the variables available in the censuses.

Research on the role of language in the labor market has been limited by the absence of data on English speaking ability at immigration. Furthermore, the research has not been able to resolve the issue as to whether speaking ability is sufficient or whether the speaking variable is reflecting some of the effects of an important unmeasured variable with which it is correlated, fluency in reading English. The analysis in this chapter addresses both issues.

14.2.   The Survey Data

The data for this study are from a survey of illegal aliens apprehended by the Los Angeles District Office of the Immigration and Naturalization Service (INS) during the 12-month period starting October 1986.[7] The survey instrument was administered to all illegal aliens detained and processed during this period who satisfied the following criteria: age 15 and over, in the United States for at least 4 days during the current stay, non-violent, and not held for felony prosecution. The interviewer was fully bilingual in English and Spanish, and the survey instrument was available in both languages. The interviewer was clearly identified as not being an employee or agent of INS, and the interviews were conducted in private. The questionnaire was designed to elicit information on the income, employment, and household structure of the illegal alien population of the United States who would not be eligible for legalization under the Immigration Reform and Control Act of 1986.[8] In addition to standard demographic, skill, and labor market questions the survey included the following language questions:

1. What languages did you usually speak at home as a child? (Circle all that apply.) Spanish, English, Other (specify).
2. How well did you speak English when you first came to the United States? Would you say: Very well, Well, Not well (a little bit), or Not at all?
3. Currently how well do you *speak* English? Would you say: Very well, Well, Not well (a little bit), or Not at all?
4. Currently how well do you *read* English? For example, an English language newspaper. Would you say: Very well, Well, Not well (a little bit), or Not at all?

Self-assessment of language skills is always problematical. A test of English language competency that may be more reliable would be very costly to implement for a large sample. The procedure adopted here also has the advantage of comparability to questions asked by the U.S. Bureau of the Census on English speaking fluency. Reliability should be enhanced by the survey procedure of having a bilingual interviewer and English and Spanish versions of the questionnaire. Furthermore, there is no reason to believe the procedure generates systematic biases in the interpretation of the findings.

The survey resulted in 836 completed interviews for males. There were only 14 refusals, for an interview refusal rate of only 1.6 percent. The item nonresponse rates were also very low. The average length of the interview was 36 minutes and did not differ between Mexican and non-Mexican men. Among the 836 men, 94 percent of the interviews were conducted in Spanish, 4 percent in English (primarily for men from Canada and the Eastern Hemisphere), and 2 percent in English and Spanish. In only two instances was it not possible to conduct the interview because a translator fluent in a third language was not available.

The sample demonstrates characteristics typical of illegal aliens in the Los Angeles labor market (Chiswick 1984; 1988b; 1989; Kossoudji and Ranney 1986; and Massey 1987). In the sample, 84 percent of the men were from Mexico, 11 percent from Central America, 2 percent from South America, and 3 percent from Canada and the Eastern Hemisphere. Half of the Mexican men were born in the northern part of the Central Plateau, the home of 22 percent of the population of Mexico.

The mean age of the sample was young, only 23 years. The average for the Mexican men was 22 years and about 28 years for the others. They had a relatively short mean duration in the United States during their current stay, 1.5 years overall, 1.4 years for the Mexicans, and 2.2 years for the others. However, the Mexican men were more likely to have had previous stays or episodes; 28 percent for the Mexicans, only 15 percent for the others. The schooling levels in this population are very low. The mean level of schooling outside the United States was 7.1 years overall and 7.0 years for both the Mexican and other Latin American aliens. It was 8.3 years for the Canadian/European men and 13.2 years for the other Eastern Hemisphere men. This generally low educational attainment was not substantially augmented by schooling in the United States. Among the Mexican men 77 percent had no schooling in the United States, and another 14 percent had less than one year. Among the non-Mexican men, 61 percent had no U.S. schooling, and another 20 percent had less than one year. Among the small number currently enrolled in school, about half reported enrollment in an "English-as-a-second-language" program for both the Mexican and other aliens.

Reflecting the languages spoken in their countries of origin, nearly all of the Mexican and other Latin American aliens reported that only Spanish was spoken in the home when they were a child. Among the 18 Asian, African, and Middle Eastern aliens, all reported a language other than English, but nearly 40 percent also reported English was spoken in the home when they were a child.

14.3. Speaking and Reading English

This section analyzes the English language speaking and reading skills of the sample of aliens. Although several studies have included analyses of current English language proficiency, this study is unique in being able to analyze speaking fluency at immigration and fluency in both speaking and reading English at the time of interview. This section first analyzes the speaking skills of the aliens. It closes with the analysis of English reading skills.

14.3.1. Speaking English

The aliens came to the United States with very poor English language skills. Among the Mexican men, nearly 80 percent reported that they could not speak English at all, another 20 percent reported that they spoke "not well," only 1 percent reported speaking "well," and none said "very well." For the men from other countries, English language skills at migration were only slightly higher: 70 percent spoke "not at all," nearly 20 percent reported "not well," 8 percent spoke "well," and only 5 percent (primarily from Canada and the United Kingdom) spoke "very well."

Language skills increased by the time of the interview, in spite of the short duration in the United States. Among the Mexican migrants, the proportion reporting that they spoke English "not at all" fell by half from four-fifths to two-fifths (see Table 14.1). Those reporting "not well" increased from one-fifth to over one-half. And 6 percent reported speaking "well" or "very well," in contrast with the 1 percent prior to coming to the United States.

Table 14.1

English Speaking Fluency of Mexican Men

When First Came to United States	At Time of Interview				Total	%
	Very Well	Well	Not Well	Not at All		
Very Well	0	0	0	0	0	.0
Well	2	3	1	0	6	.8
Not Well	1	15	119	1	136	19.3
Not at All	2	19	252	291	564	79.9
Total	5	37	372	292	706[a]	...
%	.7	5.2	52.7	41.4	...	100.0

Note: [a] One nonrespondent to both questions.

The male aliens from other countries experienced greater improvements in their speaking skills (see Table 14.2). Less than 30 percent reported that they spoke English "not at all," a decline from nearly 70 percent at arrival. And nearly 30 percent reported speaking "well" or "very well," more than doubling the 13 percent at arrival.

Table 14.2

English Speaking Fluency of Non-Mexican Men

When First Came to United States	At Time of Interview				Total	%
	Very Well	Well	Not Well	Not at All		
Very Well	6	0	0	0	6	4.7
Well	2	8	0	0	10	7.8
Not Well	1	10	13	0	24	18.6
Not at All	2	8	44	35	89	69.0
Total	11	26	57	35	129	...
%	8.5	20.2	44.2	27.1	...	100.0

The data on English language proficiency prior to first coming to the United States and at the time of interview permit a multivariate analysis of the determinants of increased fluency in English. It is hypothesized that, controlling for language skills at arrival, the longer aliens are in the United States, the greater their fluency in English. It is also hypothesized that, due to the complementarity of schooling and language fluency, in a low-fluency population those with higher levels of schooling would have a greater increase in English language fluency. Furthermore, the effect of a higher level of schooling would be greater the longer the duration of residence. That is, controlling for initial speaking ability, education would have no separate effect at arrival but would have an increasing effect with duration of residence. Finally, it is hypothesized that the greater extent of temporary migration of Mexican aliens, because of the low cost of to-and-from migration, and the existing Spanish-speaking Mexican-origin enclave in the Los Angeles area would retard their investments in developing English fluency.[9]

The variables used in the econometric analysis of speaking English (and the analyses which follow for reading English and for earnings) are defined in the Appendix.[10] The multiple regression analysis of speaking English is reported in Table 14.3. The dichotomous dependent variable SPEKWELL takes the value of one if the respondent reports speaking English "well" or "very well" at the time of interview; otherwise it is zero.[11] The equations are computed overall and separately for Mexican and other Latin American men, using ordinary least squares (OLS) and logit analysis.[12]

The first two columns in Table 14.3 report the simple linear regression for speaking well or very well (SPEKWELL) both with and without the statistical control variables for initial English speaking ability. The explanatory power of the equation is increased significantly (from 34 percent to 39 percent) when speaking skills at arrival are held constant. Perhaps most important, the partial effects of education and Canadian/Eastern Hemisphere origin are biased upward when speaking skills at arrival are not held constant. That is, part of the greater fluency of those with more schooling and from Canada/Eastern Hemisphere is due to their greater English fluency at arrival. There is little substantive difference between the results of the OLS specification and the logit specification (cf. Table 14.3, columns 2 and 6).

Controlling for speaking skills at arrival, there is a highly significant positive relationship between the ability to speak English well or very well and variables for duration in the United States, schooling, and a non-Mexican origin (Table 14.3). Overall, an extra year in the United States during the current stay is associated with a 3-percentage-point higher probability of speaking well or very well, but the effect differs by country of origin. It is only 2 percentage points for Mexican aliens and 7 percentage points from other Latin American aliens, and the difference is statistically significant (Table 14.3, columns 4 and 5).

An additional year of schooling is also associated with a higher probability of speaking well or very well. Overall the effect is 1.3 percentage points per year of schooling. However, it is 1.0 percentage point for Mexican aliens and 2.4 percentage points for other Latin American aliens. Again the difference is statistically significant.

Table 14.3, column 3, analyzes SPEKWELL by including interaction variables. As hypothesized, differences in schooling at immigration have no effect on language skills when initial speaking skills are held constant. However, the effect of a higher level of schooling increases with duration in the United States. At three years in the United States, an extra year of schooling raises the proportion speaking well or very well by 2.0 percentage points overall. Separate regressions by origin indicate the effect is 1.7 percentage points for Mexicans and 3.2 percentage points for other Latin American men.

The analysis indicates that older migrants have more difficulty adapting to English. As hypothesized, at arrival there is no effect of age on English skills, but the age-duration interaction variable indicates that the improvement in English-language skills with duration is significantly slower for older migrants, other variables the same. It is slower by 1.3 percentage points for each year difference in age.

Table 14.3

Analysis of Fluency in Speaking English (SPEKWELL) by Country of Origin, OLS, and Logit

Variable	OLS					Logit All[a]
	All	All	All	Mexico	Other Latin American Countries	
AGE	-.0003	-.0007	.0018	.0003	.0004	-.0374
	(-.216)	(-.592)	(1.376)	(.199)	(.128)	(-1.21)
EDUC	.0178	.0135	.0049	.0105	.0243	.2984
	(6.405)	(4.891)	(1.548)	(3.595)	(3.151)	(4.86)
DURNOW*	.0317	.0292	.0243	.0212	.0706	.3372
	(8.401)	(8.004)	(1.776)	(5.602)	(5.862)	(6.09)
SPOKE1	b	.4199	.3896	b	.6282	21.675
		(3.458)	(3.290)		(2.419)	(.0006)
SPOKE2	b	.4195	.4141	.6446	.3430	3.7311
		(6.239)	(6.316)	(7.278)	(1.328)	(2.97)
SPOKE4	b	-.0745	-.0694	-.0602	-.0700	-1.0672
		(-3.639)	(-3.473)	(-2.870)	(-.979)	(-3.01)
OTHLATIN	.0423	.0452	-.0552	b	b	.6307
	(1.651)	(1.835)	(1.649)			(1.42)
OTHER	.7576	.5905	.6671	b	b	3.3483
	(13.492)	(7.621)	(6.927)			(2.99)
(EDUC)(DURNOW*)	b	b	.0051	b	b	b
			(4.587)			
(AGE)(DURNOW*)	b	b	-.0013	b	b	b
			(-2.920)			
(OTHLAT)(DURNOW*)	b	b	.0366	b	b	b
			(3.328)			
(OTHER)(DURNOW*)	b	b	-.0878	b	b	b
			(-2.497)			
CONSTANT	-.1101	.0101	.0095	-.0115	-.1506	-4.5847
	(-3.028)	(-.248)	(-.212)			(-5.36)
R^2	.3438	.3947	.4439	.1732	.4940	...
Adjusted R^2	.3397	.3886	.4263	.1671	.4621	...
N	802	802	802	680	102	802

Note: Men who spoke only some English (SPOKE3) before coming to the United States are the benchmark in cols. (2)-(5). In the pooled equation Mexican men are also the benchmark. t-ratios are in parentheses.
[a] Logit analysis final value of log-likelihood ratio = -134.7. There are very few observations in the SPOKE 1 category.
[b] Variable not included.

The level and improvement in language skills also varies by country of origin. Although in Table 14.3, column 3, other Latin American aliens have a poorer fluency at arrival than Mexican aliens (coefficient = -0.055, t = -1.65), their skills increase more sharply with duration (coefficient = 0.037, t = 3.3), and they surpass the Mexican aliens after 18 months.[13]

The small sample of other aliens (Canadian and Eastern Hemisphere = OTHER) initially have much greater proficiency in English (Table 14.3, column 3, coefficient = 0.667, $t = 6.927$). However, the interaction term indicates the difference narrows with duration (coefficient = -0.087, $t = -2.497$).

The primary purpose of the SPOKE variables in Table 14.3 is to control for initial conditions.[14] The coefficients indicate the not surprising result that those who had greater English speaking fluency at arrival were more likely to have greater fluency at the time of interview.

In summary, controlling for English speaking ability at immigration, spoken English fluency improves with duration in the United States after immigration. This improvement is steeper for those with higher levels of schooling, who are younger at immigration, and who came from Latin American countries other than Mexico. Those with greater speaking fluency at arrival also have greater fluency at the time of interview.

14.3.2. Reading English

It is unfortunate that questions on English literacy no longer appear in most surveys and censuses that have been used to study immigrant labor. Believing that this is still an important issue, especially for low-skilled immigrants, I included a question in the survey instrument on the self-reported ability to read English at the time of interview. The responses could fall into one of four categories: "very well," "well," "not well," or "not at all."

The Mexicans reported very low skills in reading English. Nearly two-thirds of the Mexican men reported "not at all," and one-third reported "not well." For other nationals, the situation was somewhat better. Nearly half reported "not at all," over a third reported "not well," and nearly one-quarter reported "well" or "very well." Aliens who had been in the United States for three or more years during their current stay had a higher level of reading ability than more recent arrivals (see Table 14.4). Yet, only 11 percent of the Mexicans and 37 percent of other nationals in the United States for 3 or more years read English "well" or "very well."

Table 14.4

Ability to Read English at the Time of Interview by Country of Origin and Duration in the United States

Reading Ability	Mexico[a]		Other Countries		Total
	Less Than 3 Years	3 or More Years	Less Than 3 Years	3 or More Years	
Very Well	2	1	5	6	14
Well	15	13	5	13	46
Not Well	162	67	21	22	272
Not at All	392	51	46	11	500
Total	571	132	77	52	832

Note: [a] Duration not reported for three Mexican males, and reading ability not reported for a fourth.

It is to be expected that English speaking fluency would be an important determinant of English reading skills. Those more fluent in speaking English would be more adept at learning how to read and at increasing their fluency. Therefore, the determinants of speaking skills discussed earlier are also determinants of reading skills. Yet the inquiry here is whether reading fluency is related to demographic and human capital variables after controlling for speaking fluency.

The acquisition of reading skills is a form of investment in human capital. The accumulated stock of reading capital would increase with greater exposure to the United States, even when speaking skills are held constant. This implies that reading skills would increase with the duration of the current residence in the United States. It also implies that, for aliens from countries where multiple stays in the United States are not uncommon (such as Mexico), reading skills would increase with age when duration of the current stay is held constant.

Because of the complementarity among types of human capital, the costs involved in acquiring English reading skills would be smaller for those with more schooling, while the benefits from doing so would be larger. The effect of schooling, however, is expected to increase with the length of time in the United States.

The regression equations are reported in Table 14.5 for the dichotomous dependent variable, READWELL, which is unity for those who read "well" or "very well," using both OLS and logit analysis.[15] The simplest functional forms are presented in Table 14.5, columns 1–3, which examine the effects of adding speaking fluency to a reading skills equation. As indicated in column 1, English reading skills are significantly greater among those with more schooling, who have been in the United States a longer period of time, and who are of Canadian/Eastern Hemispheric origin. The addition of English speaking skills at immigration (STSPWELL) significantly increases the explanatory power of the equation (adjusted R^2 increases from 0.32 to 0.45). The inclusion of STSPWELL reduced by about one-quarter the partial effects on reading skills of schooling and duration and reduces by almost two-thirds the coefficient on Canada/Eastern Hemisphere, but these explanatory variables remain highly significant. Controlling for speaking skills at immigration, each extra year of schooling increases the probability of reading English well or very well by 1.3 percentage points, while each extra year in the United States raises it by 2.3 percentage points. Furthermore, as would be expected, those who spoke English well or very well at immigration had greater reading ability in English at the time of interview.

In column 3 of Table 14.5, the variable for English speaking skills at migration is replaced by the same variable at the time of the interview (SPEKWELL). Presumably because similar processes enhance speaking and reading skills, this substitution increases the explanatory power of the equation (adjusted R^2 increases from 0.45 to 0.57). Since current speaking skills have already been shown to increase with schooling level and duration in the United States, substituting current for initial speaking fluency lowers the partial effects of these variables. However, even after controlling for current English speaking skills, current reading ability is significantly greater for those with more schooling, in the United States a longer period of time, from Canada/Eastern Hemisphere, and for those who immigrated at an older age.

The logit equation in Table 14.5, column 5, demonstrates the statistical importance of the same variables as in the OLS analysis: schooling, duration, English speaking skills, and country of origin (cf. Table 14.5, columns 3 and 5).

Table 14.5

Regression Analysis of Fluency in Reading English Well or Very Well (READWELL), OLS, and Logit

Variable	OLS				Logit[a]
	(1)	(2)	(3)	(4)	(5)
AGE	.0018	.0010	.0019	.0009	.0654
	(1.66)	(1.08)	(2.25)	(.79)	(1.94)
EDUC	.0168	.0131	.0072	.0060	.2433
	(6.78)	(5.82)	(3.56)	(2.27)	(3.01)
DURNOW*	.0266	.0229	.0095	-.0155	.1852
	(7.92)	(7.52)	(3.41)	(-1.33)	(2.49)
STSPWELL	[b]	.7051	[b]	.7319	[b]
		(13.43)		(11.01)	
SPEKWELL	[b]	[b]	.5390	[b]	4.4105
			(21.42)		(8.36)
OTHLATIN	.0096	.0105	-.0132	-.0495	-.6697
	(.42)	(.51)	(-.72)	(-1.77)	(-1.01)
OTHER	.6177	.2326	.2093	.3742	.3472
	(12.35)	(4.34)	(4.74)	(4.47)	(.44)
(AGE)(DURNOW*)	[b]	[b]	[b]	.0003	[b]
				(.76)	
(EDUC)(DURNOW*)	[b]	[b]	[b]	.0043	[b]
				(4.54)	
(OTHLAT)(DURNOW*)	[b]	[b]	[b]	.0228	[b]
				(2.46)	
(OTHER)(DURNOW*)	[b]	[b]	[b]	-.0743	[b]
				(-2.47)	
(STPSWELL)(DURNOW*)	[b]	[b]	[b]	-.0149	[b]
				(-1.18)	
CONSTANT	-.1551	-.1139	-.0958	-.0577	-8.4380
	(-4.79)	(-3.87)	(-3.69)	(-1.72)	(-6.88)
R^2	.3277	.4519	.5738	.4804	...
Adjusted R^2	.3234	.4478	.5705	.4732	...
N	802	802	802	802	802

Notes: Mexican men are the benchmark. t-ratios are in parentheses.
[a] Logit analysis, final value of log-likelihood function = -72.1.
[b] Variable not included.

Interaction variables are added to the equation in Table 14.5, column 4, and regressions were also computed separately by country of origin. If speaking skills at migration are controlled for, an extra year of schooling increases English reading skills, with the partial effect increasing with the duration of residence. At three years of residence an extra year of schooling increases the probability of reading well or very well by 1.9 percentage points. The partial effect is 1.3 percentage points per year of schooling overall, but it is smaller for Mexican immigrants, 1.0 percentage point, compared to 2.1 percentage points for other Latin Americans. Age, however, shows no statistically significant effect on reading skills when initial speaking skills are held constant.

The partial effect of duration of residence is a highly statistically significant 2.3 percentage points per year in this sample controlling for initial speaking fluency. This effect varies with schooling level: it is larger for those with more schooling (Table 14.5, column 4). It also varies by country of origin, being larger for the other Latin American migrants than for the Mexicans.

In summary, the analysis indicates that English reading ability among low-skilled immigrants is related to their overall skill level. Reading fluency is significantly greater for those with more schooling, in the United States a longer period of time, more fluent in speaking English at immigration, and from Canada/Eastern Hemisphere countries. Duration in the United States has a larger positive impact for those more schooling and for Latin American men other than Mexicans.

14.4. Earnings

This section reports the results of the multiple regression analysis of earnings for the sample of illegal aliens. Two dependent variables are considered: the usual weekly earnings during the current stay and the most recent hourly wage in the current stay. Because of missing values for one or more of the variables in the analysis, particularly the earnings variables, the analysis of usual weekly earnings is for about 380 observations, and the analysis for hourly wages is for 605 observations.[16]

Following standard practice, the natural logarithm of earnings is regressed on demographic and human capital variables.[17] It is hypothesized that earnings increase with the level of schooling attainment (EDUC), labor market experience in the current stay (DURNOW*), and total labor market experience (T) and that earnings are lower for those who are not currently married (SPOUSEAB). It is also hypothesized that earnings are greater for those more fluent in English (SPEKWELL and READWELL). The regression analysis of usual weekly earnings is presented in Table 14.6 with a statistical control for the natural logarithm of usual hours of work per week (LNHOURS/WK) in columns 1 and 2 but not in columns 3 and 4. When hours per week are held constant, the coefficients of the other variables in the equation measure their effects on usual earnings per hour worked. Columns 2 and 4 include the speaking and reading variables (SPEKWELL and READWELL). The regression analysis for the most recent hourly wage is reported in Table 14.7 for the full sample and separately by country of origin, where the regressions in this table differ by the inclusion of the language variables.

Table 14.6

Regression Analysis of the Natural Logarithm of the Usual Weekly Earnings during the Current Stay (Dependent Variable: LNWKEARN)

Variable	(1)	(2)	(3)	(4)
EDUC	.01906	.01447	.02370	.01967
	(2.500)	(1.858)	(2.599)	(2.102)
T	.01122	.01055	.01339	.01263
	(1.655)	(1.566)	(1.641)	(1.548)
TSQ	-.00024	-.00024	-.00038	-.00038
	(-1.429)	(-1.439)	(-1.920)	(-1.894)
DURNOW*	.01961	.01441	.03779	.03276
	(2.405)	(1.678)	(3.895)	(3.254)
SPOUSAB	-.08312	-.08742	-.13167	-.13818
	(-1.644)	(-1.736)	(-2.177)	(-2.283)
LNHOURS/WK	.72461	.73138	a	a
	12.804	(12.972)		
SPEKWELL	a	-.02862	a	.05836
		(-.320)		(.538)
READWELL	a	.26992	a	.16031
		(2.467)		(1.209)
OTHWHEM	-.03722	-.04660	-0.05654	-.06784
	(-.730)	(-.914)	(-0.923)	(-1.102)
OTHER	-.07369	-.25913	-0.23439	-.40360
	(-.671)	(-1.955)	(-1.779)	(-2.516)
CONSTANT	2.26849	2.29021	4.87120	4.91345
R^2	.3686	.3811	.0912	.0993
Adjusted R^2	.3550	.3644	.0743	.0777
N	380	380	385	385

Note: Mexican men are the benchmark. t-ratios are in parentheses.
a Variable not included.

As has been shown elsewhere, schooling has a highly significant effect on the earnings of the illegal alien (see, e.g., Chiswick 1984; 1988b; Kossoudji and Ranney 1986; and Massey 1987). In these data, weekly or hourly earnings rise by about 2 percent and 3 percent, respectively, for each additional year of schooling. The effect is somewhat larger, 3.5–4 percent, for the aliens from other Latin American countries. These partial effects are comparable to coefficients found in other analyses for illegal aliens, although they are lower than what is found in studies of legal immigrants (Chiswick 1984; 1988b).

Table 14.7

Regression Analysis of the Natural Logarithm of the Most Recent Hourly Wage during the Current Stay (Dependent Variable: LNWAGENW)

Variable	All Countries			Mexico (4)	Other Latin American Countries (5)
	(1)	(2)	(3)		
EDUC	.02962	.02814	.02587	.02266	0.03434
	(4.065)	(3.778)	(3.456)	(2.630)	(2.304)
T	.02226	.02183	.02153	.01846	.03405
	(3.389)	(3.315)	(3.281)	(2.443)	(2.401)
TSQ	-.00036	-.00035	-.00035	-.00029	-.00060
	(-2.223)	(-2.169)	(-2.179)	(-1.590)	(-1.674)
DURNOW*	.01370	.01153	.00927	.01445	-.03593
	(1.726)	(1.398)	(1.120)	(1.560)	(-1.770)
SPOUSAB	-.04835	-.05039	-.04908	-.02105	-.10868
	(-.941)	(-.980)	(-1.958)	(-.338)	(-1.135)
SPEKWELL	a	.07669	-.04529	-.07627	.06082
		(.969)	(-.478)	(-.684)	(.318)
READWELL	a	a	.25881	.31667	.35649
			(2.326)	(2.320)	(1.623)
OTHLATIN	-.04827	-.05247	-.05277	a	a
	(-.951)	(-1.030)	(-1.039)		
OTHER	-.00520	-.06365	-.15758	a	a
	(-.046)	(-.493)	(-1.169)		
CONSTANT	1.09180	1.10725	1.12692	1.13753	1.03475
R^2	.0672	.0687	.0771	.0580	.2692
Adjusted R^2	.0563	.0562	.0631	.0447	.2044
Sample size	87	605	605	605	502

Note: Mexican men who are the benchmark in the pooled equations. t-ratios are in parentheses.
[a] Variable not included.

Labor market experience in the United States during the most recent stay (DURNOW*) has a significant effect on usual weekly earnings (Table 14.6). When hours of work are not held constant and there are no controls for language fluency (Table 14.6, column 3), the partial effect of duration in the United States during the current stay is 3.8 percent per year, with a t-ratio of 3.9. The statistical control for usual hours of work lowers the partial effect of current U.S. experience to 2.0 percent ($t = 2.4$) because usual hours worked per week increases with duration. The partial effect of duration on usual weekly earnings is reduced from 3.8 percent to 3.3 percent (or when hours are held constant, from 2.0 percent to 1.4 percent) when the language variables are held constant. When the most recent hourly wage is the dependent variable, the coefficient of the duration variable is smaller and is less significant (Table 14.7). Indeed, when the language variables are included in the hourly wage equation, duration in the United States is not statistically significant. Controlling for language skills reduces the effect of duration in the United States on the hourly wage because, as was shown earlier, English language fluency itself increases with duration.

The coefficients of the variables for total labor market experience (T) and its square (TSQ) and marital status (SPOUSAB) are not sensitive to the inclusion of language variables. In Table 14.6, those who are not married have lower usual weekly earnings (by about 13 percent). About one-third of this differential arises because they work fewer hours and two-thirds because they earn less even when hours worked are held constant (about 8 percent lower earnings). In the analysis of hourly wages, however, there is generally no significant marital status effect.

Other variables the same, there is no difference in usual weekly earnings or hourly wages between Mexican and other Latin American aliens and no effect of adding statistical controls for language fluency. By way of contrast, although the coefficient is always negative, Canadian and Eastern Hemisphere aliens (OTHER) show no significant weekly earnings or hourly wage difference from the Mexican men when language variables are not included in the equation.[18] When English language fluency is held constant, however, the usual weekly earnings of the Canadian/Eastern Hemisphere illegal aliens (OTHER) are significantly lower than the earnings of Mexican aliens.[19]

Last, consider the coefficients of the English language fluency variables, SPEKWELL and READWELL. Alternative specifications, the most informative of which are presented in Tables 14.6 and 14.7, indicate that the variable for reading English consistently has a larger coefficient and a higher t-ratio than the variable for speaking. In the analysis for weekly earnings with a control for hours worked per week (Table 14.6, column 2), reading well or very well increases earnings by a highly statistically significant 31 percent (converting the coefficient of 0.27 to a percent increase), while the speaking coefficient is very small and not significant (coefficient of -3 percent, $t = -0.3$). In the analysis of hourly wages (Table 14.7, column 3), reading well or very well increases wages by a highly statistically significant 30 percent (converting the coefficient of 0.26 to a percent increase). Comparable findings appear when separate analyses are performed for Mexican and other Latin American aliens speaking fluency has no separate effect, and reading well or very well increases wages by a statistically significant 37 percent and 42 percent, respectively, for the Mexican and other Latin American men.

Thus, reading skills dominate speaking skills in the analysis of the effect of English language fluency on earnings. Furthermore, the inclusion of language fluency variables reduces, but do not eliminate, the measured effect on earnings of experience in the U.S. labor market. Finally, the inclusion of language variables alters the relative differences in earnings by country of origin. The relative earnings of Hispanic aliens is enhanced when there is an adjustment for their lower level of fluency in English.

14.5. Summary and Conclusion

This article is concerned with the determinants of English language fluency and the effects of English language fluency on the earnings of a sample of low-skilled aliens. Using special survey data on over 800 illegal aliens, the analysis shows the importance of certain variables that are not available in the Census Bureau data that have been used previously to study immigrant labor market activities. These variables are English speaking fluency at migration and English reading fluency.

Using longitudinal data from self-reported responses to questions on English speaking fluency at arrival in the United States and at the time of interview, I show that English speaking fluency improves with duration in the United States. The improvement is greater for those with higher levels of schooling, presumably because of the complementarity of schooling and language acquisition and utilization. The improvement with duration is also greater for those who came to the United States at a younger age, reflecting the greater ease of language acquisition for younger people. The improvement with duration is slower for Mexican aliens. This may reflect the greater temporary nature of their stays and the adverse effects on English language acquisition of living in a language-minority enclave. Furthermore, tests indicate that analyses of English speaking fluency result in upward-biased estimated effects of schooling and non-Mexican origin if fluency at arrival is not held constant.

The men in the sample reported very poor English reading skills, particularly the Mexican nationals. The regression analysis of English reading ability demonstrates the large and highly significant effect of English speaking skills at migration and at the time of interview. Yet, even after speaking skills are controlled for, there are important effects on reading of demographic and human capital variables. Reading skills increase with schooling level and duration in the United States, and the increase with duration is greater for those with more schooling. This presumably reflects the complementarity of various types of human capital. Age at immigration apparently has no independent effect on reading fluency when speaking fluency at immigration is held constant, but it has a positive effect when speaking fluency at the time of the interview is held constant. Hispanic aliens reported poorer English reading skills than those from Canada/Eastern Hemisphere, even when other variables are the same. This may be reflecting adverse impacts on the acquisition of English reading skills of living in a language-minority enclave.

The analyses of the usual weekly earnings and most recent hourly wages of the illegal aliens show patterns consistent with other studies. Earnings increase with level of schooling, total labor market experience, and experience in the U.S. labor market. Adding variables for English language fluency (speaking and reading) reduces, but does not eliminate, the partial effect of duration in the United States on earnings. The coefficients of the schooling, marital status, and total experience variables are not affected.

In the analyses of weekly earnings and hourly wages, the variable measuring English reading proficiency dominates the variable measuring English speaking skills. That is, measures of reading skills are more important statistically for understanding labor market outcomes than merely measures of speaking English.

These findings indicate the importance of English language proficiency, especially reading and writing skills, for the labor market success of immigrants. They also suggest that future surveys of immigrants should include questions on English proficiency at arrival as well as at the time of interview and that questions on reading skills may be more useful than merely asking the respondent's fluency in spoken English. Furthermore, tests designed by the immigration authorities to evaluate the applicant's likely adjustment to the U.S. labor market for purposes of legalization, immigration, or naturalization would be more effective if they also measure English reading skills.

Appendix

Table A14.1

List of Variables Used in the Statistical Analysis

Variable	Code	Description
	SPEKWELL, READWELL	Dichotomous variable, equal to unity if speak English or read English well or very well; zero otherwise.
Language skills	SPOKE1, SPOKE2, SPOKE3, SPOKE4	English speaking ability when came to the United States for the first time: 1 = very well, 2 = well, 3 = not well, 4 = not at all.
	STSPWELL	Dichotomous variable equal to unity if SPOKE1 or SPOKE2 are unity; otherwise zero.
Earnings	LNWKEARN, LNWAGENW	The natural logarithm of the usual weekly earnings, current stay or of the most recent hourly wage, current stay.
Schooling	EDUC	Total years of schooling.
	AGE	Age in years.
Age and experience	T	Years of labor market experience. (Age - schooling - 5, or years since age 15, for those with 10 or fewer years of schooling.)
Marital status	SPOUSAB	Dichotomous variable, equal to unity if divorced, widowed, or never married; zero otherwise.
Duration in United States	DURNOW*	Years in the United States, current stay. DURNOW* = (year and month of interview) minus (year and month last entered).
Hours of work	LNHOUR/WK	The natural logarithm of hours worked per week, current stay.
Country of birth[a]	MEXICO, OTHLATIN, OTHER	Dichotomous variable, equal to unity if born in Mexico, another Latin American country, or another country.

Note: [a] OTHLATIN includes Belize, Colombia, Chile, Costa Rica, El Salvador, Equador, Guatemala, Honduras, Nicaragua, Peru, and Venezuela. OTHER includes Canada, India, Iraq, Israel, Italy, Korea, Lebanon, Morocco, Nigeria, Pakistan, Philippines, Syria, Taiwan, and United Kingdom.

15

Educational Mismatch: Are High-skilled Immigrants Really Working in High-Skilled Jobs, and What Price Do They Pay If They Are Not?

Although there is a continuing concern with low-skilled, often illegal immigrants, in recent years there has been an increase in research and public policy interest at the other end of the skill distribution – high-skilled immigrants. The United States and most of the other advanced economies have altered their policies toward temporary workers and permanent immigrants to attract high-skilled immigrants. In 2009 I organized a conference for the American Enterprise Institute on High-Skilled Immigration in a Global Labor Market. Paul W. Miller and I co-authored a paper for this conference, "Educational Mismatch: Are High-Skilled Immigrants Really Working in High-Skilled Jobs, and What Price Do They Pay if They Are Not?" This paper was published in the conference volume (Chiswick 2011, reprinted as Chapter 15 of this volume).

Educational mismatch refers to workers in jobs for which they are "overeducated" or "undereducated" (i.e., their formal schooling level is greater or less than is typical for workers in that occupation). Overeducation is more

The original version of this chapter was published as: Chiswick, B.R., Miller, P.W. (2010). Educational Mismatch: Are High-Skilled Immigrants Really Working at High-Skilled Jobs and What Price Do They Pay If They Are Not?, in: Chiswick, B.R. (Ed.), High Skilled Immigration in a Global Labor Market, Washington DC: American Enterprise Institute Press, 111–54. © 2010 by American Enterprise Institute Press. The authors thank Derby Voon for research assistance and Charles Beach and other participants at the American Enterprise Institute (AEI) 2009 conference, "High-Skilled Immigration in a Globalized Labor Market" as well as seminar participants at the University of Illinois at Chicago and the Australian National University, for helpful comments. Chiswick and Miller acknowledge research support from AEI, and Miller acknowledges financial assistance from the Australian Research Council.

typical among workers who are highly educated (think of someone with a PhD driving a taxi) while undereducation is more typical for workers with little schooling (think of a very low-educated immigrant taxi driver).

There are several problems associated with overeducated workers. One is the sheer waste of human capital – skills that they possess are not being put to their full and most productive use. Programs and policies designed to attract high-skilled workers are undermined to the extent that these workers cannot secure employment commensurate with the very skills that qualified them for a visa. Moreover, high-skilled workers who cannot work at their skill level have a greater incentive to return to their country of origin or to move on to a third country. It is not sufficient to have an immigration policy that encourages high-skilled immigration if there are few incentives to encourage them to remain permanently.

In "Educational Mismatch..." Paul W. Miller and I show the extent of over- and undereducation and analyze the determinants of educational mismatch among high-skilled adult male immigrants in the United States in comparison with their native-born counterparts. High-skilled immigrants are shown to have a higher propensity for being overeducated within their occupations, but this propensity is greatest for recent arrivals. As these immigrants improve their language skills, acquire credentials, and develop new networks relevant for the U.S. labor market they move up the occupational ladder and the degree of their overeducation declines (job matching improves).

Among high-skilled immigrants, the returns to required or typical years of schooling in their occupation is high and comparable to that of the native born, while the returns to years of overeducation (or undereducation) is very low, sometimes even zero or negative, for both immigrants and the native born. Higher educational attainment opens the door to higher-paying occupations, but within these occupations variations in years of schooling have little effect on earnings. The implications of these findings for immigration/temporary worker policies and for postmigration adjustment policies are explored in this paper.

Barry R. Chiswick (2015)

The United States is home to millions of immigrants. Its "golden door" has been open to many flows of immigrants, including "the wretched refuse of your teeming shore," as termed in Emma Lazarus's 1883 poem engraved on the base of the Statue of Liberty. In addition to these "huddled masses," however, from colonial times to the present, the United States has attracted many skilled immigrants.[1] High-skilled immigrants currently in the United States are the subject of this chapter.

Figure 15.1

Total Legal Permanent-Resident Visas and Employment-Preference Visas Issued in the United States, Fiscal Years 1987–2007

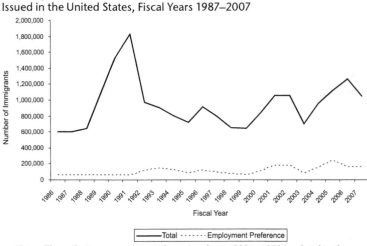

Note: The spike in permanent-resident visas from 1989 to 1992 is related to the granting of ammesty to nearly 3 million illegal migrants under the 1986 Immigration Reform and Control Act.

Source: U.S. Department of Homeland Security (2006) and (2008).

Figure 15.1 displays the flow of legal permanent residents (LPRs) into the United States for fiscal years 1987–2007. These numbers reflect both new arrivals and adjustments of status among those already living in the United States. Permanent-residence status is primarily gained on the basis of a family relationship with a U.S. citizen or LPR, with permanent residency based on skills (employment preferences) serving as a much smaller, but the second-largest, category of admissions (see Table 15.1 for a breakdown of 2007 admissions). Figure 15.1 also provides information on the number of LPRs in the employment-preference categories.[2] The number of immigrants entering the United States in the employment-preference categories has increased considerably over the past two decades. In 1986, they numbered 56,617, or 9.4 percent of to-tal immigration, while in response to 1990 legislation to increase the number of immigrants admitted based on employer preferences, they numbered 162,176 in 2007, or 15.4 percent of total immigration. How-ever, in both years nearly half of immigrants in this category consisted of spouses and minor children of principal applicants.

Understanding how employment-preference immigrants perform in the U.S. labor market is important from the perspective of guid-ing the mix of immigrants, that is, whether relatively more low- or high-skilled immigrants should be granted entry to the United States. Unfortunately, visa category information is not available in the data sets – such as from the decennial censuses – that are otherwise most useful for labor-market analyses of immigrants in the United States. Therefore, this chapter looks at all skilled foreign-born workers, as reported in the U.S. census, regardless of their visa status, including those on temporary work visas (such as H1-B visa recipients).

Table 15.1

Immigration to the United States by Type of Visa, Fiscal Year 2007

Type of Visa	Immigrants (Thousands)	
Immediate Relatives of U.S. Citizens	494	⎱ 688
Family-Sponsored Preferences	194	⎰
Employment-Based (and their families)	162	
Diversity	42	
Refugees, Asylum Recipients, Parolees	138	
Other	20	
Total	**1,052**	

Note: Detail may not add to total due to rounding.
Source: U.S. Department of Homeland Security (2008).

This chapter adopts perspectives from the overeducation and undereducation literature. This literature proposes that there is a "usual" education level for each occupation. Some workers will have this level of education, and will therefore be regarded as being matched to the typical educational requirements of their jobs. Other workers will have a higher level of education than that which is usu-al in their job. These workers with "surplus" years of schooling are viewed as being overeducated.[3] Still other workers will have a lower level of education than that which is usual in their job. Such work-ers are viewed as being undereducated. Chiswick and Miller (2008b; 2009) show that, for analyses of the United States and Australia, this framework yields important insights into the international transfer-ability of human capital for immigrant workers across all skill levels, but this chapter will focus on high-skilled immigrant workers.

This chapter will include a discussion of how a "mismatch" of education and occupation in the labor market is determined. While the factors that bring about this mismatch for the native born also apply for immigrants, two additional factors (skill transferability and selectivity in migration) also apply for immigrants. Following this, the chapter provides an overview of data on the education levels of the native- and foreign-born population. Next is a brief review of a selection of previous studies in the overeducation and undereducation literature.[4] The broad aim of this review is to highlight methodological issues pertinent to a study of high-skilled immigrants. The chapter then outlines the empirical framework adopted in this study and provides information on the data sources. The statistical analyses of the extent of the educational mismatch and the earnings consequences of these mismatches are then presented. The final section concludes with a summary and the policy implications of the findings.

15.1.   Why Do Education Mismatches Occur?

Consider the typical or usual level of education in an occupation. Why would there be education mismatches, that is, individuals whose educational attainment differs from the norm for their occupation?

The usual level or norm is merely a measure of central tendency. Depending on the particular technology that they employ, or the educational attainment of the labor market from which they draw their labor supply, firms may have a different optimal level of education for their workers in a particular occupation compared to the occupation as a whole nationwide. Workers also differ by age, so there are cohort differences in when they received their formal schooling, when they joined the labor force, and the extent of their labor market experience. Mismatches related to cohorts may arise if there has been an upgrading of educational requirements for new hires, but longer-term employees are retained because of their seniority or because their greater on-the-job training (labor market experience) compensates for their falling behind the educational norms for new hires. The mismatches here would be overeducated new hires and undereducated established workers compared to the average worker currently in place.

Workers clearly differ in characteristics that may be difficult, if not impossible, to measure in survey or census data, but which may be revealed in the labor market. These unmeasured characteristics include dimensions of worker and allocative (decision-making) ability, efficiency, ambition, aggressiveness, energy, job dedication, favorable and unfavorable personality traits, and so on. On the one hand, those with higher levels of desirable unmeasured abilities can attain a higher occupation level for the same amount of schooling, and thereby may appear to be undereducated. On the other hand, those who the market evaluates as being deficient in beneficial unmeasured traits are more likely to be relegated to occupations that are at a lower level compared to their schooling, and hence appear to be overeducated given their occupation.

The reasons just discussed for educational mismatches would apply equally to native-born and foreign-born workers. There are, however, immigrant-specific factors that may contribute to a greater mismatch of education and occupation among the foreign-born population in the labor market: the limited international transferability of skills and selectivity in migration.

For most immigrants to a destination, skills acquired in the country of origin are not perfectly transferable. These skills include information about how labor markets operate, as well as destination language skills. There may be occupation-specific skills that are not readily transferable because of differences related to types of technology (such as English measures versus the metric system or legal systems based on English common law versus those based on the Napoleonic code). There may be differences in levels of technology because of differences in capital-to-labor ratios or relative-factor prices (for example, high-technology medicine in the United States versus low-technology medicine in the former Soviet Union and the developed countries). Moreover, there may be barriers to entry in occupations in immigrants' destination countries that they trained for and practiced in their origin countries (examples include occupational licensing, union regulations, and governmental requirements, such as citizenship). In addition, cultural differences may make it difficult for immigrants in certain occupations to transfer their skills to the labor market in their destination country.[5]

Immigrants and those who assist their integration into the destination country's labor market frequently express concern about the nonrecognition of premigration skills, whether acquired in school or on the job. In some instances nonrecognition results from requirements for occupational licensing, but it may also arise when risk-averse employers and consumers do not know how to evaluate foreign credentials compared to credentials earned in the destination country.[6] Further, discrimination against immigrants can also reduce their ability to transfer their skills in whole or in part to their destination country.

A lower degree of transferability of skills from an immigrant's origin country to the destination leads to a greater occupational downgrade for the immigrant. This increases the likelihood that immigrants will appear to be overeducated for the occupations they ultimately hold in the destination country. Over time, immigrants who stay in the destination country generally invest in destination human capital, either by modifying (or increasing the transferability of) premigration skills, or by acquiring new skills altogether. Thus, immigrants' occupational levels improve, thereby diminishing the extent to which they are seen as overeducated.

Selectivity in immigration is the other immigrant-specific factor that can contribute to a mismatch in immigrant education and occupation. For several reasons, economic migrants tend to be favorably selected for labor market success in their destination country (Chiswick 1999; 2008). Indeed, economic migrants have success in the destination country as their primary goal by definition (this relates to the supply of immigrants). Moreover, some immigrants are specifically granted visas because of their high levels of skill (relating to the demand for immigrants), although the relative importance of employment-based visas varies across destinations. The considerations that lead to self-selection for economic immigration and the considerations that lead employers to sponsor immigrants suggest that such immigrants are likely predisposed to be successful.

Other measured variables being equal, including educational attainment, these circumstances indicate that immigrants are more likely to have higher unmeasured dimensions of ability than others in their origin country who do not emigrate. If these unmeasured dimensions of ability are similarly distributed among the native-born population in the origin and destination countries, by implication the immigrants will also have, on average, a higher level of unmeasured dimensions of ability than the native-born population in the destination country. If the usual educational attainment in an occupation is based on the native-born population, a higher level of unmeasured ability would enable immigrants to attain a higher occupational level in the destination country than native-born workers with the same level of schooling might attain. Alternatively, such immigrants might gain employment in the same occupation as more highly educated natives. Immigrants in this situation would appear to be undereducated for their occupation level.

In summary, one would expect to observe workers in the labor market who appear to be over- or undereducated relative to the usual educational attainment for their occupation. Along with the factors relevant for the native-born population, immigrants face two additional factors that may lead to an education-occupation mismatch. Less-than-perfect international transferability of skill tends to result in overeducated immigrants, that is, immigrants who are more likely to be employed in occupations for which the usual schooling level is lower than the level they have attained. In contrast, the favorable selectivity of immigrants tends to lead to undereducated immigrants for their occupation, that is, immigrants who are more likely to be working in occupations in which the usual education level is higher than that which they have attained. The issue of skill transferability becomes more intense as skill levels increase, while the issue of selectivity becomes more intense as the ratio of out-of-pocket or direct costs of immigration relative to the opportunity cost of time increases, that is, the effects will be stronger for lower-skilled workers (Chiswick 1999; 2008; Chiswick and Miller 2008b). As a result, in a study of high-skilled immigrants, it is to be expected that immigrants with an educational mismatch will tend to be overeducated.

15.2. Education Levels of the Native- and Foreign-born Populations

Figure 15.2 presents information on the distribution of education levels of native- and foreign-born males 25 years old and older in 1999.[7] This figure shows that only around 14 percent of native-born males left school before completing high school, while 33 percent are classified as high school graduates, 18 percent attended college but did not receive a degree, 7 percent attained an associate's degree, 18 percent a bachelor's degree, 6 percent a master's degree, and 4 percent attained either a professional degree or doctorate.

The data for foreign-born males show a much lower mean and greater inequality in the distribution of schooling. A major difference occurs among those who left school very early. Only 14 percent of native-born males did not complete high school, but 34 percent of foreign-born males are in this category. This relatively high representation of those leaving school early is responsible for the mean level of education for the foreign born being nearly 1.5 years lower than the mean level of education for the native born (11.76 years of education for foreign-born males compared with 13.13 years for native-born males in 1999).

Figure 15.2

Distribution of Educational Attainment Levels of Adult Males by Nativity, 1999

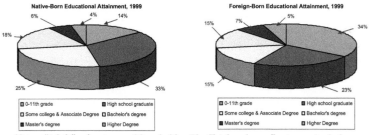

Notes: "Adult" refers to ages 25 and older. The "higher degree" category includes those with degrees above the master's level, including professional degrees (such as M.D. or LLB) and doctorates (Ph.D.).

Source: U.S. Department of Labor. Bureau of Labor Statistics (1999).

The foreign- and native-born populations are more similar in categories denoting higher levels of education. Among the foreign born, 15 percent have bachelor's degrees, compared with 18 percent of native-born males. Foreign-born males are slightly more likely to have attained degrees above a bachelor's than native-born males; 7 percent of the foreign-born population holds a master's degree, compared to 6 percent among the native-born population, and 5 percent of foreign-born males have attained either a professional degree or doctorate, compared to 4 percent of native-born males. Foreign-born males are more heavily represented at the lowest and – albeit to a smaller extent – the highest educational levels.

There are various ways to define the skilled-immigrant group that is the focus of this study: the group could include the approximately 28 percent of the population in each birthplace group (native or foreign) who have attained bachelor's degrees or higher, or the group could be more restrictive and consist only of those who have attained master's degrees or higher. The second option would include 12 percent of the immigrant population and 10 percent of the native-born population. The following analyses consider both definitions.[8]

15.3. Literature Review of the ORU Technique

The overeducation and undereducation literature has been used to examine the allocation of workers across the overeducated, undereducated, and correctly matched educational categories in the United States. This literature has also examined how educational mismatches affect earnings. The latter research has been based on a variant of the human capital earnings function that has been termed the ORU specification (representing overeducation, required education, and undereducation). In this model the dependent variable is the natural logarithm of earnings ($\ln Y_i$) and the variable for actual years of education is decomposed into three terms. This produces the following specification:

(1) $$\ln Y_i = \alpha_0 + \alpha_1 \text{Over\_Educ}_i + \alpha_2 \text{Req\_Educ}_i + \alpha_3 \text{Under\_Educ}_i + \ldots + u_j,$$

where
   Over_Educ = years of surplus or over education,
   Req_Educ = the usual or reference years of education,
   Under_Educ = years of deficit or under education,
and the actual years of education equals Over_Educ + Req_Educ - Under_Educ. Note that for each individual, "Over_Educ" and "Under_Educ" cannot both be positive.[9] Either one or both must be zero. Equation (1) also contains other variables generally included in earnings functions, such as years of labor market experience, marital status, location, veteran of the U.S. Armed Forces, and race/ethnicity; as well as variables specific to the foreign born, such as duration of residence in the United States and citizenship status.

All studies report a high incidence of educational mismatches in the U.S. labor market. In most studies, Equation (1) is estimated on samples of all workers, though separate analyses are often undertaken for particular groups of interest. For example, Rumberger (1987) reported findings from estimations undertaken on separate samples of men and women. Duncan and Hoffman (1981) present results for four gender-race groups (white men, black men, white women, black women). Chiswick and Miller (2008b) conduct separate analyses for foreign-born and native-born male workers and, among the foreign born, for country of origin.

Some analyses extend the disaggregation of the sample beyond that based on nativity, gender, or race to consider occupations (Rumberger 1987; Verdugo and Verdugo 1989). Rumberger (1987: 31), for example, argued that "we would expect the estimated return to required and surplus schooling to vary across occupations just as the estimated return to actual schooling varies across occupations." Rubb (2003: 54) explains that "the theory behind the occupational analysis is that some occupational groups may be better suited than others in using the surplus human capital of the overeducated workers." Rumberger's 1987 study was based on only five broad categories of occupations: (i) professional/managerial, (ii) support, (iii) craft, (iv) operative, and (v) service. Verdugo and Verdugo (1989) expanded the occupation-specific analyses to nine occupations. Other studies have focused only on particular skill segments of the labor force. Rubb (2003) and Duncan and Hoffman (1981), for example, studied the links between overeducation and earnings among workers with postcollege schooling.

In analyses of earnings, the return to the usual number of years of education for a particular occupation (α_2) is typically much higher than the return to actual years of education (β_1) (Hartog 2000). Years of education above those that are usual in a particular job are associated with a payoff that is much lower than the payoff for each year of education up to the point that is usual within an occupation $(\alpha_2 > \alpha_1)$, whereas years of undereducation are associated with an earnings penalty compared to those correctly matched $(\alpha_2 > |\alpha_3|)$. These earnings effects, however, have been shown to vary by nativity, occupation, and skill level.

Chiswick and Miller (2008b) report that the payoff to a year of education (generally) in the 2000 U.S. population census was 10.6 percent for native-born males and only 5.2 percent for foreign-born males. That is, each additional year of schooling is expected to be associated with 10.6 percent higher earnings among the native born, but with only 5.2 percent higher earnings among the foreign born. The payoff to a year of education that is usual in a person's job did not differ by nativity: it was 15.4 percent for the native born and 15.3 percent for the foreign born. A year of surplus schooling was associated with a payoff of 5.6 percent for the native born and of 4.4 percent for the foreign born. In comparison, the earnings penalty associated with a year of undereducation was -6.7 percent for the native born and only -2.1 percent for the foreign born.

Vahey (2000) examined the incidence and returns to educational mismatch in Canada with a modification to the ORU model. Thus, the estimating equation was:

$$(2) \quad \ln Y_i = \gamma_0 + \gamma_1 \text{Over\_Educ}_i^A + \gamma_2 \text{Req\_Educ}_i^A + \gamma_3 \text{Under\_Educ}_i^A + \ldots + u_i$$

where the superscript "A" on the ORU variables simply indicates an alternative definition. In particular, Vahey (2000) defined $\text{Req\_Educ}_i{}^A$ as a vector of dichotomous variables for each usual level of education. Because the usual level of education was rarely more than one level from the attained level of education, in Vahey's empirical analysis a restricted specification was employed, where $\text{Over\_Educ}_i{}^A$ and $\text{Under\_Educ}_i{}^A$ comprised, for each usual level of schooling, single dichotomous variables for overeducation and undereducation regardless of the number of years.

The analyses of overeducation and undereducation have shown that knowledge of educational mismatch can enhance understanding of labor market outcomes. The efforts to extend the analyses to consider variation across education levels and across occupations revealed that this extension can be useful, although the limitations of these earlier studies prevent strong conclusions from being drawn. The analyses presented in what follows, based on the large Public Use Microdata Sample from the 2000 U.S. population census, overcome these limitations and demonstrate the considerable potential of a study disaggregated by occupation that uses more detailed information regarding the required level of school and schooling mismatches.

15.4. Measurement of Mismatches and Data

This section reviews the way the "required" or "usual" level of education is measured. It also presents a brief overview of the data used.

The method used to identify the "required" or "usual" level of education in this study is the realized-matches (RM) technique.[10] This is based on the actual educational attainments of workers in each occupation and, therefore, reflects the outcome of the labor market matching process. Either the mean of educational attainments within each occupation (as in Verdugo and Verdugo 1989) or the modal educational attainment (as in Cohn and Khan 1995) may be used.

The analyses reported below are based on the 2000 U.S. population census 5 percent Public Use Microdata Sample and use the approximately five hundred occupations that are separately identified. This data set contains information on labor market outcomes (earnings, occupation) and demographic characteristics (educational attainment, age, marital status, veteran of U.S. Armed Forces, English proficiency, location, and, among the foreign born, citizenship and duration of residence in the United States). While this data source covers the entire population, the analyses are based on 25 – 64-year-old men who worked in paid employment in 1999.[11] The analyses are restricted to those in nonmilitary occupations, as these are the most likely to respond to market forces. Separate analyses are conducted for native-born workers and for foreign-born workers. Both wage and salary earners and the self-employed are covered by the study. All foreign-born men and a 15 percent random sample of native-born men from the 5 percent sample meeting the sample restrictions are included in the analysis.

The modal level of education of native-born workers in the 2000 U.S. population census data is used to determine the usual level of education in each of the approximately five hundred occupations. The focus on native-born male workers is appropriate because the economic majority group sets the norm for all workers in the occupation.[12] This RM measure ranges from 12 years of schooling to the professional degree and doctorate categories (there are seven educational categories in total).

15.5. Statistical Analyses

The statistical analyses that follow have several main sections. The first contains a brief overview of the incidence of educational mismatch in the U.S. labor market. This is followed by a section that presents the analyses of the determinants of earnings for high-skilled workers: workers with a bachelor's degree or higher, and workers with a master's degree or higher. Next, the analyses of earnings for the skilled workers are conducted separately by major occupation. This permits assessment of whether some occupations are able to utilize any surplus educational attainments more effectively than others. That section is followed with the analysis of earnings, which is undertaken using the more flexible specification of the ORU model Vahey introduced (2000). This approach offers advantages for understanding whether the apparent inability of the labor market to effectively utilize surplus schooling depends on the usual level of schooling for a given occupation. The final section reports findings from an analysis of the effects of education – actual years, usual years, and surplus years – on earnings by duration of residence in the United States.

15.5.1. The Incidence of Skill Mismatch

Table 15.2 lists the percentage of correctly matched education and mismatched education in the U.S. labor market based on the modal education level for each individual's occupation by nativity, skill level, and occupation, using data on adult males from the 2000 U.S. population census. The data for the native born are in standard font (first row) and the data for the foreign born are in italics (second row) for each occupation. The first three columns of the table cover all educational attainments, while the final two columns are for the two definitions of high-skilled workers used in this study. When all workers are considered, information is presented on undereducation, correctly matched education, and overeducation. When only high-skilled workers (defined as those having attained a bachelor's degree and higher or a master's degree and higher) are considered, however, undereducation is not a material issue, as very few workers are in this category; so only the incidence of overeducation is presented, with the balance of the workforce being considered correctly matched.

Across all occupations (see the first row of data in Table 15.2) the rate of correctly matched education among the native born is around 40 percent, and the rates of undereducation and overeducation are 26 percent and 33 percent, respectively. The rate of being overeducated among the foreign born is similar to that of the native born (29 percent). The foreign born, however, are far more likely than the native born to be undereducated (45 percent compared to 26 percent) and are far less likely than the native born to be in the correctly matched group (26 percent compared to 40 percent).

The patterns in the incidence of educational match and mismatch across occupations are affected by two sets of factors. First, the usual level of education varies by occupation, from 12 years in some occupations (such as in sales and related) to a doctorate in other occupations

Table 15.2

Percentage of Overeducation, Correctly Matched Education, and Undereducation by Nativity, Skill Level, and Occupation, Males Ages Twenty-five to Sixty-four Years

Occupation	All Education Levels			Bachelor's Degree +	Master's Degree +
	Undereducated (i)	Correctly Matched (ii)	Overeducated (iii)	Overeducated (iv)	Overeducated (v)
All Occupations	26.3	40.2	33.4	50.3	69.7
	45.0	26.0	29.1	62.5	79.0
Management,	32.3	36.1	31.5	45.2	86.7
	36.9	28.1	35.0	57.8	96.5
Business and	23.9	45.2	30.9	35.3	100.0
Financial Operations	33.5	40.4	26.1	46.0	100.0
Computer and	22.3	40.2	37.5	37.8	97.5
Mathematical Science	46.0	38.4	15.4	55.5	99.2
Architecture and	18.2	42.9	38.9	33.8	100.0
Engineering	41.1	38.4	20.6	55.3	100.0
Life, Physical, and	39.3	43.8	16.9	42.4	69.4
Social Sciences	41.4	40.6	18.0	43.4	50.7
Community and	17.6	38.7	43.7	24.0	42.8
Social Service	20.9	33.2	45.9	29.6	51.0
Legal	11.6	79.0	9.4	12.2	7.3
	23.7	57.2	19.1	26.6	18.1
Education, Training, and	46.0	41.1	12.9	48.8	80.4
Library	52.0	32.9	15.1	55.2	71.6
Arts, Design, Entertainment,	16.0	38.3	45.8	30.1	100.0
Sports, and Media	22.2	30.2	47.5	43.3	100.0
Health Care Practitioner and	14.5	62.5	23.0	19.6	20.4
Technical	19.0	65.5	15.4	22.8	23.5
Health Care Support	51.1	31.2	17.7	100.0	100.0
	51.7	22.7	25.6	100.0	100.0
Protective Service	34.3	26.0	39.7	84.4	100.0
	41.3	25.2	33.5	91.6	100.0
Food Preparation	39.5	34.3	26.2	100.0	100.0
	20.5	20.8	58.7	100.0	100.0
Building and Grounds	31.4	44.2	24.5	100.0	100.0
Cleaning and Maintenance	15.7	19.6	64.7	100.0	100.0
Personal Care and Service	44.2	32.3	23.5	78.4	100.0
	35.3	25.4	39.3	91.4	100.0
Sales and Related	43.5	29.5	27.1	78.4	100.0
	44.3	21.7	34.0	91.4	100.0
Office and	47.0	24.8	28.2	99.8	100.0
Administrative Support	45.3	18.4	36.3	99.8	100.0
Farming, Fishing,	26.3	40.7	33.0	100.0	100.0
and Forestry	5.1	9.2	85.7	100.0	100.0
Construction and Extraction	33.2	44.1	22.6	100.0	100.0
	17.1	21.9	61.0	100.0	100.0
Installation, Maintenance,	33.6	40.6	25.8	100.0	100.0
and Repair	30.2	24.6	45.3	100.0	100.0
Production	37.6	46.0	16.4	100.0	100.0
	25.9	22.8	51.3	100.0	100.0
Transportation and	30.1	47.7	22.2	78.4	100.0
Material Moving	24.8	25.3	49.9	95.3	100.0

Note: For each occupation the data in the first row are for the native born and the data in the second row (italics) are for the foreign born. Based on realized matches (RM) procedure (mode).

Source: U.S. Census Bureau (2005).

(such as in the life, physical, and social sciences). Second, the proportion of highly educated workers varies across occupations. Hence, the mean actual years of education by occupational group in Table 15.2 ranges from 12.19 years to 18.05 years among the native born, and from 9.24 years to 17.77 years among the foreign born.[13]

In the fourth column of Table 15.2, the analysis is restricted to workers with at least a bachelor's degree. Thus, by definition, these workers have a higher mean level of actual years of education than the sample of all workers. This tends to increase the percentage of overeducated workers.

The results in column iv of Table 15.2 show that in approximately one-third of the occupational groups, all of the workers with at least a bachelor's degree are overeducated, regardless of nativity. The foreign born have a greater rate of overeducation than the native born in the remaining occupations. Furthermore, when the analysis focuses on the group with a master's degree or higher (see Table 15.2, column (v), all the workers are overeducated in over half of the occupational groups regardless of nativity. The incidences of overeducation are similar for both the native born and the foreign born in the remaining occupations, with the exception of the legal occupation group, where the rate of overeducation for the foreign born is only 18 percent and the rate for the native born is only 7 percent.

The incidence of educational mismatches can also be considered by duration in the United States, as is shown in Table 15.3. Among high-skilled workers in the United States for ten or more years in 2000, the extent of overeducation declines with duration of residency. This suggests that with longer residencies in the U.S. labor market, immigrants are more likely to acquire the U.S.-specific skills, credentials, and reputation that permit more workers to get jobs in occupations commensurate with their educational attainment. Note, however, that the degree of overeducation is lower for those in the U.S. fewer than ten years in 2000 compared with those who have resided in the United States for between ten and 19 years. The better occupational matching of the foreign born who came to the United States in the 1990s may reflect cohort differences arising from the 1990 Immigration Act. That legislation had two major effects on this issue. First, it increased the number of labor certification/employer-sponsored visas, and workers entering under these visas are more likely to be better matched than those entering under other visas, such as the family-based, diversity, or refugee visas. Secondly, the act created the H1-B (temporary worker) visas for employer-sponsored high-skilled workers, for which, again, workers are better matched (there are fewer overeducated workers).

Thus, educational mismatch, especially for highly educated workers, is a major feature of the U.S. labor market. Its importance increases when the focus is on the most highly skilled workers. Indeed, in many occupations, all of the most highly educated workers are categorized as overeducated. This would be expected to have major implications for these workers' earnings. These implications are explored in the subsections that follow.

Table 15.3

Percentage of Overeducation, Correctly Matched Education, and Undereducation for Foreign-born Males Ages 25 to 64, by Duration of U.S. Residency and Skill Level

Duration of U.S. Residency	All Skill Levels			Bachelor's Degree	Master's Degree
	Under-educated	Correctly Matched	Over-educated	Over-educated	Over-educated
(years)	(i)	(ii)	(iii)	(iv)	(v)
All Durations	45.0	26.0	29.1	62.5	79.0
0-9	42.6	28.2	30.2	62.7	80.0
10-19	48.5	24.0	27.5	67.1	83.7
20-29	46.5	25.3	28.1	59.4	75.5
30+	38.3	29.5	32.2	57.8	73.4

Notes: Numbers are based on the realized-matches procedure (mode).
Source: U.S. Census Bureau (2005).

15.5.2. Analyses for High-Skilled Workers

Table 15.4 presents results from the estimation of the standard and ORU models of earnings determination on a sample restricted to workers with at least a bachelor's degree.

The payoff to actual years of education for skilled workers is 11.1 percent for the native born and 10.6 percent for the foreign born. These estimates are greater than those for the full sample of all male workers (of 10.3 and 5.3 percent, respectively), indicating a nonlinearity in the returns to education, particularly among the foreign born. At first glance this might suggest that the limited international transferability of formal schooling is less of an issue for high-skilled immigrants than for less-skilled immigrants. Chiswick and Miller (2008b), however, present a decomposition of the lower payoff to schooling for the foreign born than for the native born

Table 15.4

Estimates of Standard and ORU Models of Earnings for Skilled (Bachelor's or Higher Degree) Males Ages 25 to 64 Years by Nativity

Variable	Native Born		Foreign Born	
	Standard	ORU	Standard	ORU
Constant	4.073	4.131	4.669*	4.297
	(52.08)	(54.16)	(71.98)	(67.29)
Educational Attainment	**0.111**	(a)	**0.106**	(a)
	(42.49)		**(49.52)**	
Usual Level of Education	(a)	**0.122**	(a)	**0.140***
		(47.85)		**(64.45)**
Years of Overeducation	(a)	**0.020**	(a)	**0.019**
		(7.15)		**(8.34)**
Experience	0.057	0.059	0.031*	0.039*
	(48.12)	(50.65)	(25.67)	(32.55)
Experience Squared/100	-0.122	-0.124	-0.074*	-0.085*
	(39.64)	(41.38)	(24.61)	(29.17)
Log Weeks Worked	0.999	0.979	0.972	0.945
	(59.77)	(59.75)	(73.07)	(72.22)
Married	0.302	0.271	0.972*	0.215*
	(48.67)	(44.59)	(73.07)	(34.64)
South	-0.031	-0.034	-0.061*	-0.054*
	(5.43)	(6.01)	(9.86)	(9.12)
Metropolitan	0.333	0.308	0.147*	0.154*
	(36.82)	(34.82)	(8.28)	(8.96)
Veteran of U.S. Armed Forces	-0.056	-0.043	-0.128*	-0.106*
	(7.22)	(5.68)	(8.97)	(7.70)
Black	-0.188	-0.162	-0.296*	-0.262*
	(17.17)	(14.98)	(30.40)	(27.70)
English Very Well	-0.072	-0.064	-0.141*	-0.110*
	(5.37)	(4.79)	(18.76)	(27.70)
English Well	-0.068	-0.055	-0.403*	-0.304*
	(1.97)	(1.64)	(42.61)	(32.84)
English Not Well/Not at All	-0.109	-0.099	-0.690*	-0.492*
	(1.97)	(2.35)	(49.40)	(35.70)
Years Since Migration (YSM)	(a)	(a)	0.009	0.011
			(9.81)	(12.23)
YSM Squared/100	(a)	(a)	-0.005	-0.011
			(2.41)	(6.07)
Citizen	(a)	(a)	0.035	0.024
			(4.95)	(6.07)
Adjusted R^2	0.230	0.259	0.278	0.322
Sample Size	100,885	100,885	100,968	100,968

Notes: Heteroskedasticity-consistent *t*-statistics in parentheses; * indicates that the estimated coefficient for the foreign born is significantly different from that for the native born; (a) indicates the variable is not relevant or not entered into the estimating equation; coefficients of the education variables are in bold.

Source: U.S. Census Bureau (2005)

into the components due to the international transferability of human capital skills and due to selection in migration. They sugge st that the latter factor, which is likely to be more prevalent among the less educated, is of far greater importance than the former factor. The finding in Table 15.4, which excludes those with less than a bachelor's degree, appears to reinforce the findings from the Chiswick and Miller (2008b) analyses.

The payoff to labor-market experience is higher in the analyses for the high-skilled group of workers than for all workers. It is 3.26 percent for native-born, skilled workers for each year of experience (evaluated at ten years) compared to 2.20 percent for all native-born workers. The payoff to pre-immigration labor market experience is 1.62 percent for foreign-born, skilled workers, compared to 0.86 percent for all foreign-born workers. Thus, there appear to be complementarities between formal education and labor market experience, particularly among the foreign born. This suggests that with additional years of formal schooling, immigrants receive greater earnings for skills acquired on the job prior to immigration.

The earnings payoff to an additional year of living in the United States among high-skilled immigrants, holding total labor market experience constant, is 0.80 percent, which is about the same as the payoff for all immigrants (0.82 percent).

Finally, the earnings penalties associated with limited English skills are greater when the focus is on skilled immigrants than when all immigrants are considered. For example, among immigrants, skilled workers who self-report that they speak English well have earnings 40 percent lower than the earnings of skilled immigrants who speak only English at home. When all immigrants are included in the analysis, this earnings penalty is only 25 percent. To put this another way, among immigrants there is evidence of a complementarity between English-language skills and formal education, with a greater earnings return to English proficiency among skilled immigrants. Among the native born, almost all of whom speak only English at home regardless of schooling level, the change in sample from all workers to skilled workers (bachelor's degree and above) is associated with only minor changes in the estimated coefficients of the English-language variables.

The coefficients on the ORU variables in Table 15.4 differ by up to 4 percentage points compared with those in a regression for all male workers (compared with Chiswick and Miller 2008b). Thus, the payoff to years of usual education, as measured by the RM procedure, falls

Table 15.5

Estimates of Standard and ORU Models of Earnings for Highly Skilled (Master's or Higher Degree) Males Ages 25 to 64 Years, by Nativity

Variable	Native Born		Foreign Born	
	Standard	ORU	Standard	ORU
Constant	3.775	3.695	5.663*	5.231*
	(26.57)	(26.72)	(49.87)	(46.52)
Educational Attainment	**0.110**	**(a)**	**0.055***	**(a)**
	(19.37)		**(13.43)**	
Usual Level of Education	**(a)**	**0.132**	**(a)**	**0.091***
		(23.67)		**(22.00)**
Years of Overeducation	**(a)**	**0.027**	**(a)**	**-0.018***
		(4.50)		**(4.20)**
Experience	0.069	0.069	0.034*	0.041*
	(31.39)	(32.16)	(18.51)	(22.75)
Experience Squared/100	-0.154	-0.153	-0.076*	-0.087*
	(27.66)	(28.14)	(16.62)	(19.51)
Log Weeks Worked	1.056	1.024	0.936*	0.909*
	(39.25)	(38.85)	(45.18)	(44.64)
Married	0.326	0.295	0.268*	0.245*
	(27.87)	(25.78)	(26.89)	(25.11)
South	-0.030	-0.033	-0.054	-0.049
	(2.97)	(3.27)	(5.93)	(5.53)
Metropolitan	0.336	0.331	0.097*	0.133*
	(20.66)	(21.06)	(3.71)	(5.28)
Veteran of U.S. Armed Forces	-0.020	0.000	-0.153*	-0.132*
	(1.49)	(0.03)	(5.91)	(5.28)
Black	-0.179	-0.143	-0.368*	-0.132*
	(7.81)	(6.39)	(24.02)	(22.59)
English Very Well	-0.072	-0.060	-0.09	-0.078
	(2.96)	(2.51)	(8.30)	(6.97)
English Well	-0.026	-0.011	-0.424*	-0.336*
	(0.44)	(0.19)	(29.36)	(23.54)
English Not Well/Not at All	-0.191	-0.021	-0.816*	-0.590*
	(2.00)	(2.17)	(35.27)	(25.38)
Years Since Migration (YSM)	(a)	(a)	0.016	0.016
			(11.51)	(12.21)
YSM Squared/100	(a)	(a)	-0.017	-0.021
			(6.22)	(7.92)
Citizen	(a)	(a)	0.068	0.053
			(6.08)	(4.86)
Adjusted R^2	0.221	0.251	0.269	0.307
Sample Size	36,572	36,572	47,539	47,539

Notes: Heteroskedasticity-consistent *t*-statistics in parentheses; * indicates that the estimated coefficient for the foreign born is significantly different from that for the native born; (a) indicates the variable is not relevant or not entered into the estimating equation; coefficients of the education variables are in bold.
Source: U.S. Census Bureau (2005).

by 2–3 percentage points when the focus is shifted from all workers to workers with at least a bachelor's degree, whereas the payoff to years of surplus schooling falls by up to 4 percentage points. [14]

Table 15.5 lists results for the more stringent definition of skilled workers, that is, of workers with a master's, professional, or doctorate degree. These findings show that the payoff to education is 11 percent for the native born and only 5.5 percent for the foreign born. This difference in the payoff to education is comparable to that reported from the analyses based on all workers, but contrasts with the findings for workers with a bachelor's degree or higher (Table 15.4), where the payoffs for the native born and foreign born are about the same, at 11 percent. This difference may be due to the relatively high earnings among the native born with a professional degree – which involves fewer years of schooling than a doctorate – compared to the earnings of those with a doctorate, and the increased numerical importance of workers with professional degrees when the more stringent definition of skilled workers is used. [15]

The payoff to a year of labor market experience (evaluated at ten years) for native-born workers with a master's degree or higher is 3.82 percent, about 17 percent higher than the 3.26 percentage-point effect for native-born workers with at least a bachelor's degree. Among the foreign born, however, the payoffs to experience acquired in the country of origin and in the United States for the high-skilled group in Table 15.5 are slightly higher than the payoffs established using the broader definition of skilled immigrants in Table 15.4. [16] However, the earnings effects associated with very limited English-language skills are greater among immigrants with a master's degree or higher than were reported in Table 15.4. This further emphasizes the complementarity between formal schooling and English language proficiency in the immigrant workforce.

15.5.3. *Analyses by Occupation*

Do some occupations use surplus skills more effectively than elsewhere in the economy? This question can be addressed through the ORU model via a smaller gap between the payoffs to the years of education that are usual for a worker's occupation and to years of education that are considered surplus in the occupation. [17]

The coefficients on the education variables (actual years of education, usual years of education, and surplus years of education) for each skill-birthplace group are presented in Appendix B. Sets of simple correlations between the estimated coefficients on the various education variables are presented in Table 15.6 (bachelor's degree and above) and Table 15.7 (master's degree and above). Shaded figures in the lower cells in each of these tables are for the foreign born, while the figures in the top, unshaded cells are for the native born. Correlations with the mean level of schooling in the occupation (computed by nativity) are also provided to illustrate how these payoffs vary with the educational level for the occupation.

Table 15.6

Correlation Coefficients among Payoffs of Education and Mean Level of Education From Analyses Disaggregated by Occupation and Nativity, Skilled (Bachelor's Degree or Higher) Males Ages 25 to 64 Years

Foreign Born / Native Born		Level of Education				
		Actual	Usual	Surplus	Gap	Mean
Level of Education	Actual	—	0.49*	0.18	0.24	0.84*
	Usual	0.52*	—	0.41	0.46*	0.19
	Surplus	0.52*	0.15	—	-0.63*	0.08
	Gap	0.19	0.85*	-0.40	—	0.08
	Mean	0.72*	0.11	0.31	-0.07	—

Notes: Table based on realized-matches procedure; shaded cells represent correlations for the foreign born. "Actual" represents the payoff to actual years of schooling; "usual" the payoff to usual years of schooling; "surplus" the payoff to years of surplus schooling; "gap" the difference between payoff to usual and surplus years of schooling; and "mean" the mean educational attainment of the occupation; * denotes coefficients significant at the 5 percent level.
Source: Appendix B.

Table 15.7

Correlation Coefficients among Payoffs of Education and Mean Level of Education From Analyses Disaggregated by Occupation and Nativity, Highly Skilled (Master's Degree or Higher) Males Ages 25 to 64 Years

Foreign Born / Native Born		Level of Education				
		Actual	Usual	Surplus	Gap	Mean
Level of Education	Actual	—	0.49*	0.77*	-0.12	0.73*
	Usual	0.54*	—	0.18	0.73*	0.47
	Surplus	0.92*	0.46*	—	-0.54*	0.29
	Gap	-0.19	0.68*	-0.34	—	0.20
	Mean	0.59*	0.07	0.33	-0.20	—

Notes: Table based on realized-matches procedure; shaded cells represent correlations for the foreign born. "Actual" represents the payoff to actual years of schooling; "usual" the payoff to usual years of schooling; "surplus" the payoff to years of surplus schooling; "gap" the difference between payoff to usual and surplus years of schooling; and "mean" the mean educational attainment of the occupation; * denotes coefficients significant at the 5 percent level.
Source: Appendix B.

Consider the findings for the foreign born with a bachelor's degree or higher (Table 15.6). The payoff to actual years of education within the broad occupational categories ranges from less than zero and very small positive amounts in a number of occupations to 17.4 percent in the group for health care practitioners and technical occupations (see Appendix Table B15.1).

Education is rewarded more highly in the more skilled occupations. Thus, there is a simple correlation coefficient of 0.72 between the payoff to actual years of education and the mean level of education (as a measure of overall skill) in an occupation. The mean payoff to actual years of education for the 20 occupations included in this analysis is 7.3 percent, which is 3.3 percentage points lower than the 10.6 percent reported in the pooled (across all occupation groups) analyses in Table 15.4.[18] This shows that about one-third of the payoff to schooling among skilled immigrants is due to interoccupational mobility across the major occupation groups included in the census data.

The payoffs to years of usual education within the broad occupational category are listed in the second column of Appendix Table B15.1. There is one negative payoff to usual education – for the community and social services occupation group. This is due to the combination of relatively low earnings and a high usual level of education for the clergy. Apart from this anomaly, the payoff to usual education ranges from zero (arts, design, entertainment, sports, and media; personal care and services; and construction and extraction) to 25.6 percent (architecture and engineering) among those with a bachelor's degree or higher level of schooling. The payoff to usual education is positively correlated across occupations with the payoff to actual years of education ($r = 0.52$). However, there is no association between the payoff to usual education and the mean level of education in the occupation ($r = 0.11$). The mean payoff to usual years of education across the 20 occupations is 14.9 percent, which is of the same order of magnitude as the 14.0 percent reported in Table 15.4. Within the sample analyzed, the usual education variable takes into account movements to occupations where the worker's schooling is at the usual level. The fact that there is little change in the payoffs to usual schooling when the major occupation groups in the census data are held constant suggests that the payoff to matching occurs mainly within the major occupation groups, rather than across occupations. Schooling may be used to qualify for a higher-status occupation, but there is a sorting/matching process within these occupations that is very important to the earnings-determination process.

The payoffs to years of overeducation range from zero (in eight occupations) to over 15 percent (in education, training and library, and health care support). The mean payoff to years of overeducation is 5.2 percent, which compares favorably with the 4.6 percent for the analyses across occupations in Table 15.4.

The absence of a pattern to the ways the payoffs to years of surplus education and usual education change across occupations shows up clearly when the gap between these payoffs is linked to the mean level of schooling: the simple correlation coefficient is -0.07. That is, surplus schooling is not used effectively in high-skilled occupations, nor is it used effectively in less-skilled occupations.

Similar patterns are evident for the native born and for the high-skilled groups, and when the WSA procedure is used to construct the usual level of schooling for each occupation (Chiswick and Miller 2010a). This reinforces the conclusion that there is minimal evidence that some sections of the economy are immune to the ineffective use of surplus schooling. Whether this conclusion carries across to all levels of schooling is considered in the next section.

15.5.4. *Analyses by Level of Education*

Vahey's theoretical estimating equation includes dichotomous variables for each level of overeducation and undereducation for a given level of usual education (2000). In other words, for a usual level of education of a bachelor's degree, for example, workers who hold a master's degree would be represented by one dichotomous overeducation variable, those who hold professional degrees by a separate dichotomous overeducation variable, and workers who hold a doctorate by a further separate dichotomous overeducation variable. In the same way, workers who only completed tenth grade or who only hold a high school diploma would be represented by particular dichotomous undereducation variables if they were working in occupations with a usual level of education of a bachelor's degree. In some instances, however, this flexible approach would result in very small samples in specific overeducation and undereducation groups. Indeed, for this reason Vahey considered only one variable for overeducation and one for undereducation at each usual level of education (2000).

In the current analysis, however, the maximum detail on the extent of overeducation is incorporated into the estimating equation.

This follows from the aim of the section, which is to assess whether the difficulties in using surplus education are equally prevalent across all levels of education. These analyses are undertaken only for the sample of skilled workers with at least a bachelor's degree.

Given the array of findings from this approach, a graphical presentation of the main results is provided. Figure 15.3 presents the relevant findings for the foreign born, and Figure 15.4 provides comparable results for the native born using the realized-matches (RM) approach.

Figure 15.3

Results from Flexible Specification of ORU Model in Equation 2 for Foreign Born, based on Realized-Matches Procedure

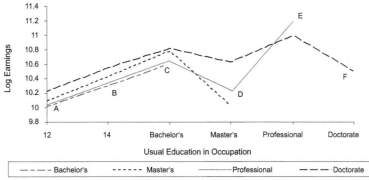

Source: U.S. Census Bureau (2005).

Figure 15.4

Results from Flexible Specification of ORU Model in Equation 2 for Native Born, based on Realized-Matches Procedure

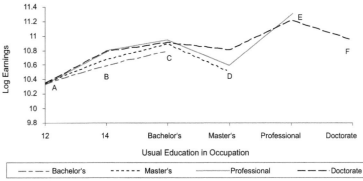

Source: U.S. Census Bureau (2005).

Figures 15.3 and 15.4 have the natural logarithm of earnings on the vertical axis and the usual level of education in the occupation on the horizontal axis.[19] Earnings by usual level of education profiles are presented for each of four actual levels of education: bachelor's degree, master's degree, professional qualifications, and doctorates. The first line to consider is the short line for workers with a bachelor's degree that is truncated where the usual level of education for an occupation is a bachelor's degree; it has the letters A, B, and C positioned on it.

If workers with a bachelor's degree are employed in an occupation where the usual level of education is a bachelor's degree, they will be correctly matched in terms of educational attainment. These workers are represented in Figure 15.3 by the point C. If workers with a bachelor's degree are employed in an occupation where the usual level of education is 12 or 14 years, they are overeducated for their occupation. Workers in these situations are represented in Figure 15.3 by the points A and B, respectively. The highest earnings among workers with a bachelor's degree occur when these workers are correctly matched, that is, they are working in occupations in which the usual level of education is a bachelor's degree (point C). The overeducated workers earn considerably less than the correctly matched workers (21 percentage points lower earnings if working in an occupation where the usual level of schooling is 14 years, at point B, and 45 percentage points less if working in an occupation where the usual level of schooling is 12 years, at point A). The fact that points A and B are lower than point C shows that among holders of bachelor's degrees, years of surplus education are not used as effectively in the labor market as are years of correctly matched education.

Now consider the earnings by usual level of education profile for individuals who possess a master's degree. This is the dotted line that is truncated at point D. Across the usual education levels of 12 years to a bachelor's degree, where workers with a master's degree would be overeducated, this profile is a little above the profile for workers who possess a bachelor's degree and is essentially parallel. There is thus some advantage to having a master's degree rather than a bachelor's degree if overeducated. Note, however, that the higher qualification does not greatly assist in overcoming the difficulties degree-qualified workers have in getting adequate reward for their schooling if they are working in an occupation for which they are classified as overeducated.

The foreign-born men with a master's degree who are correctly matched to the usual educational requirements of their job earn less than workers who have master's degrees and who work in jobs that require only a bachelor's degree. The master's degree appears to offer access to a particular set of occupations that are relatively poorly paid (schoolteachers and social workers, for example). This may explain why only 9 percent of the foreign-born workers with a master's degree are correctly matched in terms of levels of education.

Foreign-born workers with either professional qualifications or doctorates (the lines truncated at E and F, respectively) earn amounts similar to workers with either a bachelor's degree or a master's degree when working in occupations where the usual level of education is from 12 years of education to a bachelor's degree. Compared to when working in occupations where a bachelor's degree is usual, workers with either professional qualifications or doctorates tend to earn even less if they work in an occupation where a master's degree is usual. They earn more, however, than workers with a master's degree who work in an occupation where the usual level of education is a master's degree. These slightly higher earnings are the modest rewards to the surplus years of education.

Workers with a professional degree who are correctly matched to the usual educational requirements of their jobs have very high earnings (point E), whereas workers with a doctorate who are correctly matched tend to have much more modest salaries (point F). Figures 15.3 and 15.4 also demonstrate that those with doctorates working in occupations where the usual level of education is a professional qualification actually earn more than their counterparts who work in occupations where a doctorate is the usual level of education.[20] Again, this evidence shows that earnings follow the usual level of education in the occupation rather than the actual years of education for the individual. Workers' occupations govern their relative success in the labor market, not simply their years of education, although years of education, in part, influence the occupations that they can attain.

These analyses show that if a skilled worker works in an occupation that requires between 12 years of education and a bachelor's degree, surplus years of schooling are used ineffectively, and the extent of ineffectiveness is largely invariant to the actual level of schooling. In the small group of occupations with usual levels of schooling greater than a bachelor's degree, the pattern of earnings effects is irregular, but this pattern supports the view that earnings are more strongly related to the usual level of education for the job than to an individual's actual years of education.

Figure 15.4 shows information on the earnings rewards to overeducation and correctly matched education by the level of schooling for native-born, high-skilled workers. The earnings by usual level of education profiles for each of the levels of schooling (bachelor's, master's, professional, and doctorates) for the native born are largely the same as those discussed for the foreign born. Thus, the ineffective use of surplus years of education that occurs at each level is not a foreign-born phenomenon: it is a labor market phenomenon.

15.5.5.   *Analysis of the Effect of Education by Duration of U.S. Residency*

The analysis can be extended by asking whether the effect of education on earnings varies systematically with duration of residency in the United States. To answer this question, the education variables in the standard and ORU equations are interacted with the variables for duration of residency and duration-squared. These interaction terms are highly statistically significant. Based on the regression results with these variable interactions, Figures 15.5 and 15.6, respectively, plot the partial effects of education on earnings with respect to years since migration for immigrants with at least a bachelor's degree and at least a master's degree. The effects of education on earnings with respect to years since migration for educational attainment (standard analysis) and for usual level and years of overeducation (ORU analysis) show that the partial effects increase, albeit at a decreasing rate, with duration of residency in the United States. That is, educational attainment has a greater positive effect on earnings the longer an individual's U.S. residency.

However, the partial effects are systematically higher for the usual level education than for the respondent's actual level of schooling. Most dramatic is the consistently very low effect on earnings of years of overeducation across the range of years since migration. Indeed, the effect of overeducation on earnings is negative until about nine years of U.S. residency for those with at least a bachelor's degree and until about 20 years of U.S. residency for those with at least a master's degree.

Figure 15.5

Partial Effects of Education on Earnings by Duration of U.S. Residency, Skilled Foreign-born Adult Males

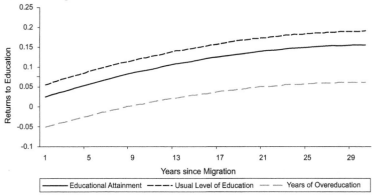

Notes: "Skilled" refers to bachelor's degree or higher. "Adult" refers to ages 25 to 64 years.
Source: U.S. Census Bureau (2005).

Figure 15.6

Partial Effects of Education on Earnings by Duration of U.S. Residency, Highly Skilled Foreign-born Adult Males

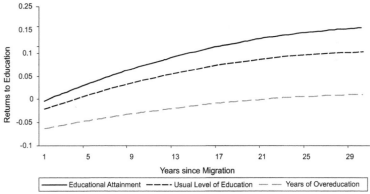

Notes: "Highly skilled" refers to master's degree or higher. "Adult" refers to ages 25 to 64 years.
Source: U.S. Census Bureau (2005).

15.6. Conclusion

This chapter is concerned with the consequences of a mismatch between educational attainment (measured by formal schooling) and employment among high-skilled, adult male immigrants in the United States and the extent to which such a mismatch affects earnings. The ORU education decomposition methodology is employed with mismatches identified based on a realized-matches approach (modal educational level in the occupation). The empirical analyses focus on the foreign born, but, for comparative purposes, parallel analyses are conducted for the native born. The empirical analyses are conducted using the Public Use Microdata Sample of 5 percent of the U.S. population from the 2000 U.S. population census. Skilled immigrants are defined as those with at least a bachelor's degree, and parallel analyses are conducted at a higher level for those with at least a master's degree.

While there has been a long history of high-skilled migration to the United States, the provisions of the 1990 Immigration Act increased the number of permanent and temporary visas to the United for these workers. In 2007, of the nearly 1.1 million who became immigrants, 162,000 received a permanent-resident visa under an employment-based category; half of these were the spouses and minor children of the principal applicants.

Educational mismatches refer to the difference in the educational attainment of a worker and the usual or typical (modal) level of education of those working in a given occupation. These mismatches can result from several causes, including occupational-skill upgrading for younger cohorts of workers and unmeasured worker-productivity characteristics that may be positive or negative. Among immigrants, mismatches may also arise from the limited international transferability of skills and selectivity in migration, or they may be the result of labor-market discrimination against immigrants. Educational mismatches due to overeducation and undereducation are expected to occur among both native- and foreign-born workers.

Conducting an empirical analysis necessitates the identification of a required or usual level of education in each occupation. An RM approach was used, which refers to what actually occurs in the labor market as reflected by the modal level of education in each of the approximately five hundred occupations identified in the 2000 U.S. census.

Over all educational levels among adult men, there are greater mismatches among immigrants than among the native born. Among all immigrants, only 26 percent were correctly matched (compared to 40 percent for the native born), with 45 percent undereducated and 29 percent overeducated (in contrast to 26 percent and 33 percent, respectively; for the native born). Among high-skilled workers, however, 63 percent of immigrants with a bachelor's degree or higher were overeducated for their occupations (compared to 50 percent of the native born), while among those with a master's degree or higher, fully 79 percent of immigrants are considered overeducated (70 percent of the native born). Nearly all of the rest were correctly matched; that is, their own education was equal to that of the modal education in their occupation. Except for the immigrants who arrived in the 1990s, the extent of correct matching of education and occupation increases as duration of U.S. residency increases. Thus, among the highly educated, particularly among immigrants, there is a high degree of "surplus" education. But is this surplus education wasted?

When the analysis is limited to those with a bachelor's degree or higher, earnings among both the foreign and native born increase by about 11 percent per year of schooling. When years of education is divided into years of usual (modal) education in the worker's occupation and years of overeducation, the effect on earnings of usual education is about 13 percent for both nativity groups, whereas the effect of years of overeducation is about 2 percent per surplus year for both groups. Thus, whereas the return to years of required or usual schooling is high, the returns to education in excess of what is needed for one's occupation are extremely low.

When the analysis is limited to those who have attained a master's degree or higher, the educational coefficients are less stable but tell a similar story: workers receive high returns to years of usual education and extremely low returns (even negative returns among immigrants) for years of overeducation.

When separate analyses are conducted by broad occupational categories, similar patterns emerge. Such analyses generally show a high return to years of usual education and very little or no returns to years of surplus education. When analyses are performed by educational level, the most striking feature is that perhaps the group with the greatest number of years in school (those who receive a doctorate) tends to have relatively low earnings compared to the group of individuals who attained a professional degree. Among high-skilled immigrants, the return to surplus education is actually negative in the first ten to 20 years of U.S. residency, after which the returns become positive but remain very small.

The very low return to years of overeducation indicates that, among the highly educated, educational attainments beyond what is required for the occupation in which one works are not productive. This is true for native- as well as foreign-born workers. This means earnings are influenced more by the educational norms in a particular occupation than by an individual's educational level.

The private and social losses in economic welfare are substantial for all workers (whether native or foreign born) who are not employed in the higher-level occupations that might make better use of their educational credentials. This has implications for immigration and absorption policy. It suggests that, in general, employment-based immigrant visas are more likely to attract high-skilled immigrants who will be working in jobs better matched to their educational attainment than is the case for family refugee visa recipients. An employer-sponsored, targeted-employment approach might result in better educational matches than one that does not require an employment sponsor. Even a points system for rationing visas, as used in Canada and Australia, might be improved by adding a set of points for prearranged employment or for having a particular set of skills in high demand.[21] Proactive efforts to facilitate the adjustment of high-skilled, new immigrants in the labor market might be most productive. These could include specific programs for English-language training, obtaining a U.S. certification or occupational license, or even learning how to navigate the job-search process in the United States for particular occupations.

The analyses reported in this chapter focus on high-skilled male immigrants and are based on a single cross section of data. They demonstrate that including demand-side considerations (such as the usual level of education in the occupation) in addition to the usual supply-side factors (such as the actual educational attainment of workers) has considerable merit. This research could be extended in a number of ways, including by undertaking separate analyses for high-skilled females, conducting analyses of low- and medium-skilled workers, and using data from earlier censuses in synthetic cohort models. Disaggregating the analysis by age at migration could permit a study of differences in the effects on income of schooling acquired in the United States and schooling acquired abroad. Conducting separate analyses for each of the major foreign-born groups in the United States and relating the estimates of the RM specification to characteristics of the immigrants' countries of origin, such as the internationally standardized scores from the Programme for International Student Assessment (PISA), may provide a means of determining how the quality of schooling acquired abroad influences the estimated effects of surplus schooling.[22] A study of the sensitivity of the estimates to the specification of the empirical model (such as more extensive controls for U.S. region of residence, race, as well as interaction effects between the more important regressors) might also be considered.

Appendix A: Definitions of Variables

Table A15.1
Dependent and Explanatory Variables Used in the Statistical Analyses

Dependent Variables	
Income in 1999	Natural logarithm of earnings in 1999 (where earnings are defined as gross earnings from all sources).
Explanatory Variables	
Years of Education	This variable records the total years of full-time equivalent education. It has been constructed from the U.S. census data on educational attainment by assigning the following values to the census categories: completed less than fifth grade (2 years); completed fifth or sixth grade (5.5); completed seventh or eighth grade (7.5); completed ninth grade (9); completed tenth grade (10); completed eleventh grade (11); completed twelfth grade, no diploma (11.5); completed high school (12); attended college for less than one year (12.5); attended college for more than one year or completed college (14); completed bachelor's degree.(16); completed master's degree (17.5); completed professional degree (18.5); completed doctorate (20). Further discussion of these years-of-schooling equivalents is presented in the text.
	Note: (a) As with other census data, the values for educational attainment are self-reported responses. While academic degrees may have required different years of schooling for immigrants educated in some countries of origin, U.S. values are used in the analysis.
	(b) Sensitivity tests were performed using eighteen, twenty, and twenty-one years of schooling for the master's, professional, and doctorate degrees, respectively. The findings are essentially invariant with respect to this alternative set of years of schooling. Vocational and technical training for a specific trade that does not require an advanced degree beyond the bachelor's is excluded from the category of professional degrees.
Usual Level of Education	This variable records the typical years of education. It is constructed using the modal level of education of the native-born workers in the respondent's occupation of employment based on the realized-matches procedure.
Years of Overeducation	The overeducation variable equals the difference between a worker's actual years of education and the years of education required for the worker's job where the number is positive. Otherwise, it is set equal to zero.
Logarithm of Weeks Worked in 1999	This is the natural logarithm of the number of weeks an individual worked in 1999.

Table A15.1 (continued)

Experience	Potential labor-market experience is computed as age minus years of education minus 6.
Location	The two location variables record residence in a metropolitan area or in one of the southern states. The latter includes Alabama, Arkansas, Delaware, District of Columbia, Florida, Georgia, Kentucky, Louisiana, Maryland, Mississippi, Missouri, North Carolina, Oklahoma, South Carolina, Tennessee, Texas, Virginia, and West Virginia.
Marital status	This is a dichotomous variable set equal to one for individuals who are married (and whose spouse is present in the household) and set equal to zero for all other marital states.
Veteran	This is a dichotomous variable set equal to one for someone who has served in the U.S. Armed Forces and set equal to zero otherwise.
Race	This is a dichotomous variable that distinguishes between individuals who are black and all other races.
English Language Proficiency	Three dichotomous variables (speaks English very well, well, and not well or not at all) are used to record respondents' English language proficiency.
Years Since Migration	This is computed from the year a foreign-born person came to the United States to stay.
Citizenship	This is a dichotomous variable set equal to one for foreign-born workers who are U.S. citizens.

Note: Population is defined as native- and foreign-born employed men, ages 25 to 64 years.

Source: U.S. Census Bureau (2005). The statistical analyses relied on the 5 percent sample of the population from the U.S. census microdata file for the foreign born and a 15 percent random sample of the 5 percent sample for the native born.

Table A15.2

Means and Standard Deviations of Variables in Earnings Equation for Skilled (Bachelor's Degree or Higher) Males Ages 25 to 64 Years, by Nativity

Variable	Native Born	Foreign Born
Log Income	10.800	10.650
	(0.98)	(1.03)
Educational Attainment	16.744	17.046
	(1.10)	(1.29)
Usual Level of Education	15.335	15.121
	(1.93)	(2.10)
Years of Overeducation	1.447	1.960
	(1.72)	(1.93)
Experience	20.008	18.322
	(10.07)	(9.94)
Experience Squared	501.808	434.95
	(426.05)	(410.70)
Log Weeks Worked	3.855	3.812
	(0.34)	(0.40)
Married	0.704	0.695
	(0.46)	(0.46)
South	0.330	0.272
	(0.47)	(0.45)
Metropolitan	0.890	0.971
	(0.31)	(0.17)
Veteran of U.S. Armed Forces	0.192	0.045
	(0.39)	(0.21)
Black	0.053	0.076
	(0.22)	(0.27)
English Very Well	0.046	0.537
	(0.21)	(0.50)
English Well	0.005	0.196
	(0.07)	(0.40)
English Not Well/Not at All	0.004	0.060
	(0.06)	(0.24)
Years Since Migration (YSM)	N/A	16.683
		(11.82)
YSM Squared	N/A	418.13
		(526.92)
Citizen	N/A	0.514
		(0.50)
Sample Size	100,885	100,968

Source: Authors' calculations based on U.S. Census Bureau (2005).

Appendix B: Regression Analyses of Effects of Education on Earnings

Table B15.1

Selected Estimates from Standard and ORU Models of Earnings by Occupation, Skilled (Bachelor's Degree or Higher), Foreign-born Males Ages 25 to 64 Years

Occupation	Educational Attainment	Usual Education	Over-education	Mean of Education	Sample Size
Management	0.078	0.175	0.050	16.914	15,175
	(11.93)	(21.56)	(7.64)		
Business and Financial Operations	0.099	0.149	0.098	16.762	7,171
	(8.81)	(7.15)	(8.69)		
Computer and Mathematical Science	0.038	0.146	0.028	16.925	11,360
	(6.47)	(13.27)	(4.76)		
Architecture and Engineering	0.074	0.256	0.064	16.992	9,231
	(14.32)	(21.21)	(12.27)		
Life, Physical, and Social Sciences	0.054	0.039	0.047	18.464	3,133
	(7.07))	(4.92)	(5.17)		
Community and Social Services	0.004	-0.129	0.020	17.200	2,097
	(0.40)	(6.66)	(1.45)		
Legal	0.132	0.173	0.079	18.095	1,360
	(5.78)	(6.82)	(2.08)		
Education, Training, and Library	0.157	0.140	0.169	18.095	6,769
	(28.57)	(13.07)	(22.53)		
Arts, Design, Entertainment, Sports, and Media	0.031	0.047	0.031	16.724	3,071
	(1.62)	(1.51)	(1.63)		
Health Care Practitioner and Technical	0.174	0.224	0.016	18.023	9,384
	(22.92)	(30.99)	(1.52)		
Health Care Support	0.156	0.209	0.152	16.978	495
	(5.14)	(3.63)	(4.99)		
Protective Service	0.016	0.159	0.002	16.515	1,088
	(0.56)	(5.28)	(0.06)		
Food Preparation	-0.011	0.109	-0.014	16.549	1,901
	(0.61)	(3.45)	(0.75)		
Personal Care and Service	0.004	0.064	0.001	16.541	730
	(0.12)	(1.78)	(0.05)		
Sales and Related	0.051	0.155	0.045	16.545	9,578
	(4.42)	(12.19)	(3.96)		
Office and Administrative Support	0.053	0.172	0.053	16.546	5,506
	(5.06)	(11.81)	(4.99)		
Construction and Extraction	-0.010	-0.005	-0.010	16.622	2,413
	(0.57)	(0.14)	(0.57)		
Installation, Maintenance, and Repair	0.034	0.062	0.036	16.524	2,230
	(1.82)	(2.34)	(1.93)		
Production	0.069	0.092	0.069	16.583	3,824
	(5.57)	(2.07)	(5.55)		
Transportation and Material Moving	-0.005	0.130	-0.005	16.583	3,123
	(0.32)	(5.95)	(0.34)		

Note: Heteroskedasticity-consistent t-statistics in parentheses.
Source: U.S. Census Bureau (2005).

Table B15.2

Selected Estimates from Standard and ORU Models of Earnings by Occupation, Skilled (Bachelor's Degree or Higher), Foreign-born Males Ages 25 to 64 Years

Occupation	Educational Attainment	Usual Education	Over-education	Mean of Education	Sample Size
Management	0.065	0.133	0.017	16.627	19,193
	(9.27)	(16.51)	(2.34)		
Business and Financial Operations	0.080	0.157	0.077	16.486	9,722
	(6.69)	(9.40)	(6.42)		
Computer and Mathematical Science	0.058	0.132	0.045	16.461	5,182
	(5.67)	(9.23)	(4.41)		
Architecture and Engineering	0.044	0.233	0.378	16.497	6,060
	(4.94)	(15.06)	(4.22)		
Life, Physical, and Social Sciences	0.087	0.080	0.093	17.469	2,398
	(9.57)	(8.50)	(8.64)		
Community and Social Services	0.061	-0.043	0.068	17.061	3,439
	(6.43)	(3.10)	(4.96)		
Legal	0.155	0.148	0.020	18.312	4,498
	(7.92)	(6.40)	(0.57)		
Education, Training, and Library	0.100	0.071	0.098	17.295	9,878
	(21.71)	(7.50)	(16.03)		
Arts, Design, Entertainment, Sports, and Media	-0.029	0.008	-0.030	16.438	3,635
	(1.12)	(0.19)	(1.16)		
Health Care Practitioner and Technical	0.230	0.263	0.081	17.898	6,299
	(25.71)	(30.56)	(5.95)		
Health Care Support	0.233	0.073	0.228	16.776	226
	(3.90)	(0.76)	(3.87)		
Protective Service	0.007	0.115	0.012	16.269	2,499
	(0.34)	(4.64)	(0.58)		
Food Preparation	-0.018	0.121	-0.013	16.279	731
	(0.46)	(2.35)	(0.34)		
Personal Care and Service	0.074	0.083	0.074	16.423	742
	(1.63)	(1.71)	(1.63)		
Sales and Related	0.024	0.127	0.022	16.287	11,704
	(1.49)	(7.80)	(1.36)		
Office and Administrative Support	0.048	0.160	0.041	16.349	5,299
	(3.19)	(9.08)	(2.74)		
Construction and Extraction	0.013	-0.021	0.012	16.316	2,183
	(0.57)	(0.34)	(0.53)		
Installation, Maintenance, and Repair	-0.050	-0.073	-0.049	16.268	1,439
	(1.43)	(1.90)	(1.42)		
Production	0.023	-0.079	0.024	16.341	2,307
	(0.97)	(0.63)	(1.01)		
Transportation and Material Moving	-0.008	0.178	-0.012	16.299	2,406
	(0.28)	(6.64)	(0.47)		

Note: Heteroskedasticity-consistent t-statistics in parentheses.
Source: U.S. Census Bureau (2005).

Table B15.3

Selected Estimates from Standard and ORU Models of Earnings by Occupation, Highly Skilled (Master's Degree or Higher), Foreign-born Males Ages 25 to 64 Years

Occupation	Educational Attainment	Usual Education	Over-education	Mean of Education	Sample Size
Management	0.033	0.149	0.026	18.010	6,883
	(2.63)	(8.90)	(2.09)		
Business and Financial Operations	0.022	0.142	0.020	17.881	2,912
	(0.81)	(3.16)	(0.75)		
Computer and Mathematical Science	-0.012	0.079	-0.020	17.866	5,677
	(1.16)	(4.37)	(1.80)		
Architecture and Engineering	0.056	0.276	0.055	18.037	4,478
	(6.14)	(9.79)	(6.07)		
Life, Physical, and Social Sciences	0.044	0.005	0.019	19.122	2,461
	(3.61)	(0.34)	(1.26)		
Community and Social Services	-0.008	-0.156	0.002	18.064	1,242
	(0.44)	(4.81)	(0.13)		
Legal	0.093	0.153	0.068	18.547	1,115
	(2.04)	(2.85)	(1.20)		
Education, Training, and Library	0.209	0.207	0.209	18.777	5,065
	(25.22)	(14.20)	(22.02)		
Arts, Design, Entertainment, Sports, and Media	-0.010	0.064	-0.011	17.942	1,150
	(0.26)	(0.99)	(0.28)		
Health Care Practitioner and Technical	0.029	0.156	-0.051	18.605	7,310
	(1.42)	(7.63)	(2.44)		
Health Care Support	0.089	0.127	0.091	18.419	201
	(1.24)	(1.44)	(1.28)		
Protective Service	-0.104	0.116	-0.110	17.968	284
	(1.42)	(1.57)	(1.64)		
Food Preparation	0.011	0.196	0.004	18.067	487
	(0.21)	(2.88)	(0.08)		
Personal Care and Service	0.034	0.085	0.038	18.150	184
	(0.50)	(1.16)	(0.57)		
Sales and Related	-0.028	0.106	-0.016	17.867	2,807
	(1.01)	(3.61)	(0.60)		
Office and Administrative Support	0.032	0.182	0.052	17.971	1,517
	(1.20)	(5.17)	(1.95)		
Construction and Extraction	-0.125	-0.223	-0.129	18.016	751
	(2.33)	(2.66)	(2.38)		
Installation, Maintenance, and Repair	-0.073	-0.040	-0.070	17.938	611
	(1.42)	(0.62)	(1.36)		
Production	0.059	0.008	0.061	18.026	1,089
	(1.98)	(0.10)	(2.06)		
Transportation and Material Moving	0.076	0.281	0.073	17.980	911
	(1.85)	(6.70)	(2.13)		

Note: Heteroskedasticity-consistent *t*-statistics in parentheses.
Source: U.S. Census Bureau (2005).

Table B15.4

Selected Estimates from Standard and ORU Models of Earnings by Occupation, Highly Skilled (Master's Degree or Higher), Native-born Males Ages Twenty-five to Sixty-four Years

Occupation	Educational Attainment	Usual Education	Over-education	Mean of Education	Sample Size
Management	0.003	0.059	-0.001	17.810	6,680
	(0.19)	(3.24)	(0.04)		
Business and Financial Operations	-0.020	0.072	-0.021	17.737	2,735
	(0.60)	(1.41)	(0.61)		
Computer and Mathematical Science	0.018	0.054	0.012	17.806	1,337
	(0.75)	(1.79)	(0.52)		
Architecture and Engineering	-0.008	0.155	-0.006	17.761	1,691
	(0.34)	(3.76)	(0.25)		
Life, Physical, and Social Sciences	0.096	0.093	0.107	18.588	1,328
	(6.16)	(6.04)	(5.98)		
Community and Social Services	0.013	-0.068	0.022	17.890	1,976
	(0.74)	(2.81)	(1.22)		
Legal	0.058	0.093	-0.018	18.546	4,100
	(1.47)	(2.20)	(0.43)		
Education, Training, and Library	0.110	0.087	0.125	18.165	5,770
	(15.16)	(7.84)	(13.62)		
Arts, Design, Entertainment, Sports, and Media	-0.109	-0.188	-0.111	17.808	902
	(1.54)	(1.92)	(1.57)		
Health Care Practitioner and Technical	0.123	0.205	0.011	18.541	4,714
	(4.26)	(7.27)	(0.37)		
Health Care Support	0.451	-0.130	0.365	18.241	78
	(2.61)	(0.59)	(2.32)		
Protective Service	-0.001	0.074	-0.007	17.696	397
	(0.02)	(0.98)	(0.11)		
Food Preparation	-0.278	-0.200	-0.272	17.926	102
	(2.62)	(1.35)	(2.56)		
Personal Care and Service	0.010	0.046	0.023	17.846	174
	(0.08)	(0.34)	(0.18)		
Sales and Related	-0.071	0.094	-0.043	17.714	1,964
	(1.39)	(1.80)	(0.87)		
Office and Adminastrative Support	-0.009	0.106	-0.002	17.791	1,034
	(0.23)	(2.23)	(0.05)		
Construction and Extraction	0.127	-0.021	0.125	17.884	371
	(2.27)	(0.07)	(2.18)		
Installation, Meintenance, and Repair	-0.134	-0.085	-0.136	17.826	208
	(1.42)	(0.79)	(1.43)		
Production	0.028	0.127	0.023	17.834	414
	(0.42)	(1.50)	(0.35)		
Transportation and Material Moving	-0.130	0.112	-0.062	17.744	414
	(1.50)	(1.28)	(0.75)		

Note: Heteroskedasticity-consistent *t*-statistics in parentheses.
Source: U.S. Census Bureau (2005).

Part V

Impact on the Economy

16

The Economic Benefits from Immigration

I have always been puzzled by the fact that, depending on the context, economists often end up stressing either the costs or the benefits of a particular policy. In the case of international trade, for example, trade economists have traditionally emphasized the benefits from free trade, and downplayed the concurrent distributional impacts. In the case of the impact of remittances, development economists usually emphasize the benefits from income inflows to developing countries, but ignore the costs that the income outflows impose on the sending immigrant communities. Similarly, in the context of immigration, the literature through the mid-1990s seemed to always focus on the costs of immigration on receiving countries, as measured by the distributional impact on the native wage structure or by the implications of the trends in declining skills of successive immigrant cohorts.

It has always been intuitively obvious to me that immigration is great for some people and not so great for others, and it is this duality that first drew me into working out the implications of factor demand theory for calculating the benefits from immigration. I had taught the basic model that isolated the immigration surplus in labor economics classes for some years, and probably even tried plugging in a number or two into the formulas. But I honestly

The original version of this chapter was published as: Borjas, G.J. (1995). The Economic Benefits from Immigration, in: The Journal of Economic Perspectives, 9(2): 3–22. © 1995 by American Economic Association. The author is grateful to John Conlisk, Vincent Crawford, Richard Freeman, Claudia Goldin, Daniel Hamermesh, Valerie Ramey, James Rauch, Michael Rothschild, Carl Shapiro, Joel Sobel, Timothy Taylor, and Stephen Trejo for helpful comments, and to the Sloan Foundation and the National Science Foundation for research support.

thought that if I wrote a paper simulating this very simple textbook model, it could not possibly be taken very seriously. The opportunity to actually write down the model, carry out the simulation, and extend the framework to the heterogeneous labor context finally presented itself when I was invited to organize a symposium on immigration for the Journal of Economic Perspectives.

The analysis, I believe, teaches three very valuable lessons: (1) the net economic benefits from immigration arise from complementarities between immigrants and other factors of production; (2) there must be a distributional impact if there is to be a net gain for the receiving country; and (3) it is impossible to manipulate the competitive labor market model to generate huge net gains from immigration in an economy as large as that of the United States. Despite these lessons, I have always been struck by the seriousness attached to the resulting "estimates" by participants in the policy debate. These numbers are not estimates in the sense that they are implied by a careful examination of real-world data; rather, they are the outcome of a calculation that follows mechanically from the algebraic structure of the assumed model. It would be very interesting to see some pathbreaking work that actually tried to estimate the gains that accrue to those agents who presumably benefit from the presence of immigrants.

George J. Borjas (2015)

The rapid increase in the size of the immigrant flow reaching the United States, the major changes in the national origin composition of the immigrant population, and the decline in the skills of immigrants relative to the skills of native workers have rekindled the debate over immigration policy. The current debate revives the old concerns over immigrants "taking jobs away" from native workers and finding it difficult to adapt in the American economy, as well as questions whether immigrants pay their way in the welfare state.

A large literature investigates each of these issues in detail; Borjas (1994b) offers a survey. The empirical evidence indicates that more recent immigrant waves will remain economically disadvantaged throughout their working lives; that this disadvantage may be partly transmitted to their offspring; that recent immigrants are more likely to participate in welfare programs than natives; and that immigration may have contributed to the increase in wage inequality observed during the 1980s.

Table 16.1 summarizes some of the key trends in immigrant skills and welfare participation. The relative educational attainment of successive immigrant waves fell dramatically in recent decades. In 1970, the typical immigrant who had just arrived in the United States had 11.1 years of schooling, as compared to 11.5 years for the typical native worker. By 1990, the typical immigrant who had just arrived in the United States had 11.9 years of schooling, as compared to 13.2 years for natives. The data also reveal a corresponding decline in the relative wage of immigrants. The most recent arrivals enumerated in the 1970 Census earned 16.6 percent less than natives. By 1990, the wage disadvantage between the most recent immigrant wave and natives had grown to 31.7 percent.

Table 16.1

Socioeconomic Characteristics of Immigrants and Natives in the United States, 1970–1990

Group/Variable	1970	1980	1990
Natives:			
Mean Educational Attainment (in years)	11.5	12.7	13.2
Percent of Households Receiving Public Assistance	6.0	7.9	7.4
All Immigrants:			
Mean Educational Attainment (in years)	10.7	11.7	11.6
Percent Wage Differential Between Immigrants and Natives	+.9	- 9.2	15.2
Percent of Households Receiving Public Assistance	5.9	8.7	9.1
Recent Immigants (< 5 years in U.S.):			
Mean Educational Attainment (in years)	11.1	11.8	11.9
Percent Wage Differential Between Immigrants and Natives	-16.6	27.6	-31.7
Percent of Households Receiving Public Assistance	5.5	8.3	8.3

Note: Educational attainment and relative wages are calculated in the sample of working men aged 25–64. The fraction of households receiving public assistance is calculated in the sample of households where the household head is at least 18 years old.

Source: Author's tabulations from 1970, 1980, and 1990 Public Use Samples of U.S. Census.

Because less-skilled workers tend to qualify for and participate in public assistance programs, the deteriorating skill composition of the immigrant flow may have increased the fiscal costs of immigration substantially. Table 16.1 shows that immigrants were less likely than natives to receive public assistance in 1970. By 1990, the welfare participation rate of immigrant households had risen to 9.1 percent, or 1.7 percentage points higher than the participation rate of native households.

Overall, the available evidence extensively documents the various costs that immigration imposes on native workers and taxpayers. Surprisingly, the literature does not address an equally important set of issues: Do natives benefit from immigration? Where do these benefits come from? How are these benefits dispensed to the native population? And how large are the benefits? The absence of any serious discussion regarding the gains from immigration is puzzling because costs must be contrasted with benefits before we conclude that immigrants are a "boon or bane" for the United States.[1] If the economic benefits from immigration are sufficiently large, for example, the costs resulting from increased expenditures in social programs can be reinterpreted as the outlay on an investment that has a very high rate of return.

This chapter uses a simple economic framework to describe how natives benefit from immigration, provides a back-of-the-envelope calculation of these benefits, and suggests the parameters of an immigration policy that would maximize the economic benefits. The discussion indicates that natives do benefit from immigration mainly because of production complementarities between immigrant workers and other factors of production, and that these benefits are larger when immigrants are sufficiently "different" from the stock of native productive inputs. The available evidence suggests that the economic benefits from immigration are relatively small, on the order of $7 billion, and almost certainly less than $25 billion, annually. The discussion also indicates, however, that these gains could be increased considerably if the United States pursued an immigration policy that attracted a more skilled immigrant flow.

The analysis presented below discusses the impact of immigration on a host country within a competitive, market-clearing framework. In this context, as long as there are no externalities, an application of the fundamental theorems of welfare economics and the principles of free trade suggests that allowing factors of production to move from one country to another increases total welfare and efficiency. Because of the potential implications of the results, however, it is important to point out at the outset that the discussion ignores some very important issues. For example, by focusing on the economic benefits accruing to natives residing in the host country, the study ignores the impact of immigration both on the immigrants themselves and on the persons who remain in the source countries. Similarly, by focusing on a competitive economy with market-clearing and full employment, the analysis ignores the potentially harmful effects of immigration when there is structural unemployment in the host economy, and jobs might be a "prize" captured partly by immigrants.

16.1. The Immigration Surplus

We begin by specifying the production technology in the host country (which, for concreteness, will be the United States throughout the discussion). Suppose that the technology can be summarized in terms of an aggregate production function with two inputs, capital (K) and labor (L), so that output $Q = f(K, L)$. The workforce is composed of N native workers and M immigrant workers. Initially, let's assume that all capital is owned by natives, so that we ignore the possibility that immigrants might augment the host country's capital stock. We will also ignore skill differentials among immigrant and native workers and assume that all workers are perfect substitutes in production (hence $L = N + M$). Finally, we will assume that the supplies of capital and of both native- and foreign-born labor are perfectly inelastic.[2]

The aggregate production function exhibits constant returns to scale. As a result, the entire output is distributed to the owners of capital and to workers. The equilibrium in this economy prior to the admission of M immigrants requires that each factor price equals the respective value of marginal product. Suppose that the price of capital is initially r_0 and the price of labor is w_0. The price of the output is the numéraire (so that the input prices are measured in units of output). Before the admission of immigrants, therefore, the national income accruing to natives, Q_N, is the price of capital times the quantity used, plus the price of labor times the number of workers hired, or $Q_N = r_0 K + w_0 N$.

Figure 16.1 illustrates this initial equilibrium in the labor market. Because the supply of capital is inelastic, the area under the marginal product of labor curve (MP_L) gives the economy's total output. Prior to the entry of immigrants, therefore, the national income accruing to natives Q_N is given by the trapezoid $ABN0$.

What happens to national income when immigrants enter the country? The supply curve shifts, and the market wage falls to w_1. National income is now given by the area in the trapezoid $ACL0$. Part of the increase in national income, however, is distributed directly to immigrants (who get $w_1 M$ in labor earnings). Inspection of Figure 16.1 thus reveals that the increase in national income accruing to natives, or the *immigration surplus*, is given by the triangle BCD. Because the market wage equals the productivity of the last immigrant hired, immigrants increase national income by more than what it costs to employ them.

Figure 16.1
The Immigration Surplus

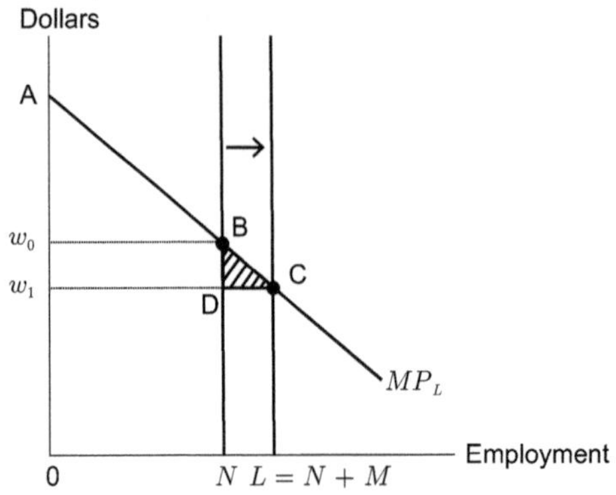

Note that if the demand curve for labor were perfectly elastic, so that immigrants had no impact on the wage rate, immigrants would receive the entire additional product, and natives would gain nothing from immigration. An immigration surplus arises only when the native wage falls as a result of immigration. Although native workers get a lower wage rate, these losses are more than offset by the increase in income accruing to capitalists, through a higher rental price of capital r.

The immigration surplus is given approximately by the area of the triangle BCD, which can be calculated as $\frac{1}{2} \times (w_0 - w_1) \times M$. By manipulating this formula, it is easy to show that the immigration surplus, as a fraction of national income, equals:[3]

$$\frac{\Delta Q_N}{Q} = -\frac{1}{2}sem^2,$$

where s is labor's share of national income; e is the elasticity of factor price for labor (that is, the percentage change in the wage resulting from a 1 percent change in the size of the labor force); and m is the fraction of the workforce that is foreign born ($m = M/L$).

What does this formulation imply about the size of the immigration surplus in the United States? The share of labor income is on the order of 70 percent, and the fraction of immigrants in the workforce is slightly less than 10 percent. The vast empirical evidence on labor demand, surveyed recently by Hamermesh (1993), suggests that the elasticity of factor price for labor is on the order of -0.3, so that a 10 percent increase in the number of workers reduces the wage by 3 percent.[4] The immigration surplus, therefore, is only on the order of 0.1 percent of GDP (that is, one-tenth of 1 percent!). The economic gains from immigration in a $7 trillion economy, therefore, are relatively small, about $7 billion per year or less than $30 per native-born person in the United States. Even if we assume that the elasticity of factor price is -1 (so that a 10 percent increase in labor supply decreases the native wage rate by 10 percent), the gains from immigration would still be on the order of $25 billion per year.

It is important to note that the immigration surplus is proportional to the elasticity of factor price for labor e. If the increase in labor supply greatly reduces the wage, natives *as a whole* gain substantially from immigration. If the native wage is not very sensitive to the admission of immigrants, the immigration surplus is nearly zero. The elasticity of factor price is small (in absolute value) when the labor demand curve is elastic. In other words, the immigration surplus is small when labor and capital are easily substitutable. The elasticity of factor price is large (in absolute value) when the labor demand curve is inelastic, implying that natives have much to gain from immigration when labor and capital are more complementary. The immigration surplus, therefore, arises because of the complementarities that exist between immigrants and native-owned capital.[5]

Even though the immigration surplus is small, immigration has a substantial economic impact. In particular, immigration causes a large redistribution of wealth from labor to capital. In terms of Figure 16.1, native workers lose the area in the rectangle $w_0 BDw_1$, and this quantity plus the immigration surplus accrues to capitalists. Expressed as a fraction of GDP, the net change in the incomes of native workers and capitalists are approximately given by:[6]

$$\frac{\text{Change in Native Labor Earnings}}{Q} = sem(1 - m),$$

$$\frac{\text{Change in Income of Capitalists}}{Q} = -sem(1 - m).$$

If the elasticity of factor price is -0.3, native workers lose about 1.9 percent of GDP, or $133 billion in a $7 trillion economy; native capital gains about 2.0 percent of GDP, or $140 billion. The small immigration surplus of $7 billion thus disguises a sizable redistribution of wealth from workers to the users of immigrant labor.

The relatively small size of the immigration surplus – particularly when compared to the very large wealth transfers caused by immigration – probably explains why the debate over immigration policy has usually focused on the potentially harmful labor market impacts rather than on the overall increase in native income. In other words, the debate stresses the distributional issues (the transfer of wealth away from workers) rather than the efficiency gains (the positive immigration surplus). If the social welfare function depends on *both* efficiency gains and the distributional impact of immigration, the slight benefits arising from the immigration surplus may well be outweighed by the substantial wealth redistribution that takes place, particularly since the redistribution goes from workers to owners of capital (or other users of immigrant services).

Putting aside the distributional impact of immigration, it is of great interest to compare the immigration surplus with estimates of the fiscal cost of immigration. Recent estimates of the *net* fiscal benefits (that is, of the difference between the taxes paid by immigrants and the cost of services provided to immigrants) range from a positive net fiscal benefit of about $27 billion calculated by Passel and Clark (1994), to a $16 billion net loss reported by Borjas (1994b), to a net loss of over $40 billion estimated by Huddle (1993).

It is doubtful, however, that *any* of these numbers estimates accurately the gap between the taxes paid by immigrants and the cost of services provided to immigrants. For example, Passel and Clark conclude that immigrants pay their way in the welfare state and contribute a net $27 billion to native taxpayers by assuming that immigrants do not increase the cost of most government programs other than education and social welfare programs. In contrast, Borjas assumes that the marginal cost of providing immigrants with a vast array of public services equals the average cost of providing these same services to natives. We do not know by how much immigrants increase the cost of freeways, national parks, and even national defense. As a result, accounting exercises that claim to estimate the net fiscal impact of immigration should be viewed with a great deal of suspicion. Because the immigration surplus is only on the order of $7 billion, however, it is evident that the net economic benefits from immigration are very small and could even be negative.

16.2. Some Problems with the Calculation of the Immigration Surplus

A number of restrictive assumptions are built into the calculation of the immigration surplus.

For example, the analysis assumes that immigration augments only the economy's labor endowment. What if immigration also augments the host country's capital stock? Interestingly, the immigration surplus might be even smaller if immigrants bring in capital. To see why, suppose that immigrants increase both the size of the labor force and the capital stock by 100 percent (perhaps through the use of "investor visas" requiring that immigrants invest in the host country). Because the production function has constant returns to scale, this type of immigration would not change the factor prices r and w. As a result, immigration would have *no* impact on the national income accruing to natives. As long as immigrants replicate the existing economy, therefore, immigrants get the total returns from their product, and the immigration surplus is zero.

The calculation of the immigration surplus also assumes that immigrants *do* have an impact on the earnings of native workers. This assumption seems to contradict much of the available empirical evidence (Borjas 1994b; Friedberg and Hunt 1995). Many studies have found a negative, but weak, correlation between the native wage in a particular labor market and the immigrant share of the workforce in the locality. This weak correlation is then interpreted as evidence that immigrants do not reduce the earnings of native workers.

It is important to note, however, that the weak correlation between the native wage and the immigrant share need not indicate that immigrants have little impact on native earnings opportunities. In particular, the interpretation of this correlation as a causal relationship between immigration and native wages presumes that the local labor markets are closed (once immigration takes place). Metropolitan areas in the United States, however, are not closed economies; labor, capital, and goods flow freely across localities and tend to equalize factor prices in the process. As long as native workers and firms respond to the entry of immigrants by moving to areas offering better opportunities, there is no reason to expect a correlation between the wage of natives in a particular locality and the presence of immigrants. As a result, the cross-section or time-series comparison of local labor markets may be masking the "macro" effect of immigration.

A number of recent studies suggest that natives respond to immigration by "voting with their feet" (Filer 1992; Frey 1994). In particular, natives tend to move out of areas where immigrants choose to live, and this migration flow may have accelerated during the 1980s, resulting in what has been called "the new white flight." To the extent that these migration flows (as well as flows of capital and goods) disperse the adverse impact of immigration on the wage over the entire economy, the weak correlations reported in the literature bear no relationship to the structural parameter required to estimate the immigration surplus. Moreover, some recent empirical studies that look more closely at the impact of immigration on the aggregate economy (rather than on a particular locality) find that immigration may have had a significant impact on the relative wage of unskilled workers during the 1980s (Borjas, Freeman, and Katz 1992; Topel 1994).

The conclusion that the immigration surplus is .1 percent of GDP assumes that the elasticity of factor price for labor is -.3, so that a 10 percent increase in the size of the labor force reduces the wage level by about 3 percent. If the native wage is *less* responsive to immigration, the immigration surplus would be correspondingly *smaller*. If we wish to believe that native workers are unaffected by immigration, therefore, we would also be forced to conclude that immigrants get the entire fruits of their labor and that there is no immigration surplus. Ironically, even though the debate over immigration policy views the possibility that immigrants lower the wage of native workers as a harmful consequence of immigration, the economic benefits from immigration arise only when immigrants *do* lower the wage of native workers.[7]

16.3.   External Effects and the Immigration Surplus

A number of recent studies have argued that an increase in trade generates external returns in the aggregate economy (see, for example, Helpman and Krugman 1985). Immigration expands the size of the market. It can introduce many new interactions among workers and firms, so that both workers and firms might "pick up" knowledge without paying for it. As a result, even though the production technology at the firm level has constant returns to scale, the external effects resulting from immigration might lead to increasing returns on the aggregate.

To represent these external effects, suppose that the firm's production function is given by $Q_F = f(K, L)Q_E^{\gamma}$, where Q_F is the representative firm's output and Q_E is the aggregate output in the economy (which the firm takes as given). As immigrants expand the scale of the economy, the marginal product of both labor and capital increases (assuming $\gamma > 0$). The parameter γ gives the percentage increase in the marginal product of labor or capital resulting from a 1 percent increase in aggregate output.

As illustrated in Figure 16.2, the external effects of immigration can increase the size of the immigration surplus substantially. As the economy expands, the marginal product of labor curve shifts from MP_L to MP'_L. The change in national income accruing to natives is then given by the sum of the triangle BCD and the area of the trapezoid $ABEF$, which measures the impact of immigration on natives' total product. The Appendix shows that the immigration surplus, as a fraction of GDP, in the presence of external effects is approximately given by:

$$\frac{\Delta Q_N}{Q} = -\frac{1}{2}sem^2 + \frac{\gamma sm}{1 - \gamma}(1 - sm),$$

where the first term gives the area of the triangle, and the second term gives the change in the value of natives' total product attributable to external effects.

Figure 16.2

The Immigration Surplus in the Presence of External Effects

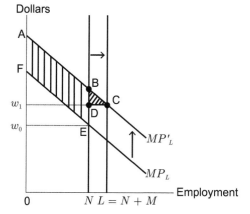

As before, suppose that the share of labor income is approximately 0.7, and that immigrants make up 10 percent of the workforce. If we assume that the elasticity of marginal product with respect to aggregate output (or y) is 0.05, the external effects increase the national income accruing to natives by about 0.3 percent of GDP, or $21 billion. If y is 0.1, external effects increase the immigration surplus by 0.7 percent of GDP, or about $49 billion. Adding the $7 billion surplus resulting from the triangle implies that the total contribution of immigrants to native income would be between $30 billion and $55 billion.

Although models that incorporate external effects in the aggregate economy are used frequently in modern discussions of the gains from trade, there is little empirical evidence supporting the existence, let alone measuring the magnitude, of the external effects (for an exception, see Dekle and Eaton 1999). As a result, the numerical exercise presented here should not be interpreted as indicating that immigrants contribute substantially to the incomes of natives, but rather as giving a ballpark estimate of what the gains would be *if* immigration indeed generated increasing returns in the aggregate economy. Despite the current popularity of external effect models in the theoretical international trade literature, it is difficult to imagine that immigrants entering an economy as large as that of the United States could generate these types of externalities. Most likely, immigration would lead to increased congestion and decreasing returns to scale because other factors of production remain fixed.

16.4. Immigrant Skills and the Immigration Surplus

The previous section illustrates how and why the gains from immigration arise in competitive economies. Perhaps the most restrictive aspect of the model is that it ignores the skill differentials that exist both within and across the and immigrant populations. Because immigration policy can encourage or prevent the admission of certain classes of workers, it is of interest to investigate the relationship between the immigration surplus and the skill composition of the immigrant flow. In other words, which type of immigrant flow, a skilled flow or an unskilled flow, generates the largest increase in national income for native workers?

16.4.1. A Simple Case: Ignoring Capital

To illustrate how the skill composition of the immigrant flow affects the economic gains from immigration, consider the case where there are only two skill classes in the workforce, skilled workers (L_S) and unskilled workers (L_U), and initially ignore the role of capital in the production process. The fraction of skilled workers in the native population is b, and the respective fraction among immigrants is β. We assume that the supply of workers to the labor market is perfectly inelastic. Finally, suppose that the aggregate production function is linear homogeneous and that there are no external effects, so that $Q = f(L_S, L_U)$.

Under these conditions, the immigration surplus is positive as long as the skill composition of the immigrant flow differs from that of native workers (that is, as long as β is not equal to b). If the skill composition of immigrants were the same as that of natives, the constant returns to scale production function implies that the wages of skilled and unskilled workers are unaffected by immigration, and hence natives have nothing to gain from immigration. (This result, of course, parallels our earlier discussion where the production function depends on labor and capital, and immigrants increase both labor and capital by the same proportion.) As stressed earlier, a key lesson of economic analysis is that natives benefit from immigration only if immigrants are different from natives.

If the skill composition of immigrants differs from that of natives, the magnitude of the immigration surplus depends on exactly how different immigrants are. Figure 16.3 illustrates the relationship between the immigration surplus and the skill composition of the immigrant flow (as measured by β, the fraction of immigrants who are skilled).[8] The left panel shows the situation when 50 percent of the native workforce is skilled (or $b = 1/2$). As noted earlier, there is no immigration surplus if half of the immigrant flow is also composed of skilled workers. Natives do gain, however, whenever the skill composition of immigrants differs from that of natives. In fact, the immigration surplus is maximized when the immigrant flow is composed of exclusively unskilled or exclusively skilled workers. Either policy choice generates an immigrant flow that is very different from the native workforce, and hence maximizes the immigration surplus. Because 50 percent of natives are skilled, there is no particular advantage (from the point of view of maximizing the immigration surplus) to admitting either an all-skilled or an all-unskilled immigrant flow.[9]

Figure 16.3

The Immigration Surplus and Immigrant Skills, in a Model Without Capital

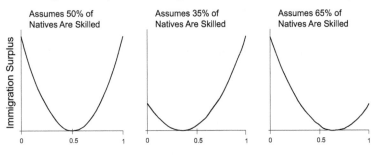

Economic incentives for pursuing an immigration policy that selects either an all-skilled or an all-unskilled immigrant flow arise when the native workforce is predominantly skilled or predominantly unskilled. Suppose, for example, that the native workforce is relatively unskilled (or $b < 1/2$). As illustrated in the middle panel of Figure 16.3, the immigration surplus is maximized by admitting immigrants who complement the native workforce, and this is accomplished by admitting only skilled workers. If, in contrast, the native workforce is relatively skilled (as illustrated in the right panel of the figure), the immigration surplus is maximized when immigrants are unskilled.

The United States presumably has a relatively skilled workforce. Economic analysis thus implies that, *in the absence of capital*, the immigration surplus would be maximized by pursuing an immigration policy that only admitted unskilled workers. This type of immigration policy maximizes the economic gains to natives by fully exploiting the production complementarities between immigrants and natives.

16.4.2. *Capital and the Skills of Immigrants*

The conclusion that an unskilled immigrant flow maximizes the immigration surplus in the United States hinges crucially on the assumption that capital plays no role in the production process. To see how the existence of a native-owned capital stock affects the relative gains to skilled and unskilled migration flows, suppose that the technology in the host country is given by the linear homogeneous production function $Q = f(K, L_S, L_U)$. As before, we assume that all factors of production are supplied inelastically to the economy.

It is instructive to compare the immigration surplus resulting from two alternative policy choices. Suppose initially that the United States decides to admit only skilled immigrants. As shown in the Appendix, the immigration surplus (as a fraction of GDP) would then be given by:

$$\frac{\Delta Q_N \text{ if U.S. admits only skilled immigrants}}{Q} = -\frac{1}{2}\frac{s_s e_{ss}}{p_s^2} m^2,$$

where s_s is the share of income that goes to skilled workers, e_{ss} is the elasticity of factor price for skilled workers (that is, the percentage change in the wage of skilled labor resulting from a 1 percent change in the number of skilled workers); and p_s is the fraction of the workforce that is skilled.[10]

If the United States instead pursues an immigration policy that admits only unskilled workers, the immigration surplus is given by a parallel formulation:

$$\frac{\Delta Q_N \text{ if U.S. admits only unskilled immigrants}}{Q} = -\frac{1}{2}\frac{s_U e_{UU}}{p_U^2} m^2,$$

where s_U is the share of income that goes to unskilled workers; e_{UU} is the elasticity of factor price for unskilled workers (that is, the percentage change in the wage of unskilled labor resulting from a 1 percent change in the number of unskilled workers); and p_U is the fraction of the workforce that is unskilled.

Note that each immigration surplus is proportional to the relevant elasticity of factor price. As long as the immigration of skilled workers reduces the wage of skilled workers or the immigration of unskilled workers reduces the wage of unskilled workers, there is a positive immigration surplus regardless of whether the United States admits exclusively skilled or exclusively unskilled workers.

Which immigration policy leads to a larger immigration surplus? Although there is a great deal of dispersion in the estimated elasticities, many studies surveyed in Hamermesh (1993, chapter 3), suggest that the elasticity of factor price is greater (in absolute value) for skilled workers than for unskilled workers. The fact that the wages of skilled workers are more responsive to a shift in supply than the wages of unskilled workers (that is, $e_{SS} < e_{ss}$) introduces a new set of incentives that suggest the immigration surplus may be larger when the immigrant flow is composed of skilled workers.

To see this point, suppose that the fraction of skilled workers in the native workforce is one-half. Suppose also that immigration is relatively small, so that the fraction of skilled workers in the population (p_S) is approximately one-half. Our earlier discussion indicated that as long as we ignored capital, the immigration surplus was maximized whenever the immigrant flow was either exclusively skilled or unskilled. The introduction of capital, however, implies that as long as $e_{SS} < e_{UU}$, the United States is better off admitting an exclusively skilled immigrant flow.[11]

A skilled immigrant flow generates a larger immigration surplus partly because of the production complementarities that exist between skilled labor and capital. A very negative elasticity of factor price for skilled workers implies that skilled workers are highly complementary with other factors of production. In contrast, a numerically small elasticity of factor price for unskilled workers implies that unskilled workers are not highly complementary with other factors of production. Because the complementarities across factors play a central role in generating the gains from immigration, the immigration surplus is maximized when the immigrant flow is skilled. In other words, the complementarity between capital and skills provides an economic rationale for admitting skilled workers.[12]

Of course, this conclusion is reinforced if we allow for the possibility that the human capital imported by immigrants has external effects in production. It is also reinforced by the fact that unskilled immigrants are more likely to increase expenditures on such government programs as unemployment compensation and means-tested entitlement programs, and are less likely to pay sufficient taxes to offset those costs.

Figure 16.4 illustrates the relationship between the immigration surplus and the fraction of the immigrant flow that is skilled in an economy with capital (assuming that 50 percent of the native workforce is skilled). As drawn, the immigration surplus is at a minimum when the immigrant flow is "mixed" in terms of skilled and unskilled workers.[13] Because skilled workers are more complementary with other inputs than unskilled workers, however, the host country benefits more from the admission of an exclusively skilled immigrant flow. This conclusion, of course, may change if the native workforce is predominantly skilled. In particular, when the native workforce is predominantly skilled, the gains from admitting a skilled immigrant flow resulting from capital-skill complementarity might be outweighed by the gains from admitting immigrants who differ from native workers.

Figure 16.4

The Immigration Surplus and Immigrant Skills, in a Model With Capital (assuming 50 percent of natives are skilled)

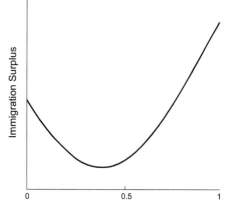

Fraction of Immigrants Who Are Skilled

As noted earlier, there is a great deal of uncertainty regarding the values of the elasticities that determine the immigration surplus in this model. Nevertheless, the simulations reported in Table 16.2 show that altering the skill composition of the immigrant flow can generate sizable gains for natives. If half of the natives are skilled, and if the elasticities of actor price are -.4 and -.75 for unskilled and skilled workers, respectively, the immigration surplus would be $14 billion if only unskilled immigrants are admitted, but would jump to $47.3 billion if only skilled immigrants are admitted. Even if the native workforce were predominantly skilled (so that 75 percent of the natives are skilled), these elasticity values suggest that the immigration surplus would increase from $22.4 to $28.0 billion if the United States pursued a more selective immigration policy. The complementarities in production between skilled workers and capital, therefore, may be sufficiently strong to suggest that natives gain if the immigrant flow is composed of exclusively skilled workers, even if the native workforce is predominantly skilled.

Table 16.2

Estimates of Immigration Surplus (in billions of dollars)

	25% of Natives are Skilled; 30% of National Income Goes to Skilled Workers	50% of Natives are Skilled; 45% of National Income Goes to Skilled Workers	75% of Natives are Skilled; 60% of National Income Goes to Skilled Workers
Admit Only Unskilled Immigrants: Elasticity of Factor Price for Unskilled Workers is:			
-.2	5.0	7.0	11.2
-.4	10.0	14.0	22.4
-.6	14.9	21.0	33.6
Admit Only Skilled Immigrants: Elasticity of Factor Price for Skilled Workers is:			
-.5	84.0	31.5	18.7
-.75	126.0	47.3	28.0
-1.0	168.0	63.0	37.3

Notes: The calculations assume that the GDP in the United States equals $7 trillion; that the share of national income accruing to capital is 30 percent; and that immigrants make up 10 percent of the workforce.

Source: Own calculations.

It is important to stress that the simulation results reported in Table 16.2 only suggest how a shift in the skill composition of the immigrant flow influences the immigration surplus. To calculate or predict the immigration surplus resulting from particular immigration policies, we would have to provide a much more complete description of what is meant by "skilled" and "unskilled" workers, as well as obtain robust estimates of the elasticities of factor price, which ultimately determine the size of the immigration surplus.

16.5. Conclusion

The family of economic models summarized in this chapter provides the foundation for a positive theory of immigration policy. If we are willing to maintain the hypothesis that immigration policy should increase the national income of natives, the government's objective function in setting immigration policy is well defined: maximize the immigration surplus net of the fiscal burden imposed by immigrants on native taxpayers. The optimal size and skill composition of the immigrant flow would equate the increase in the immigration surplus resulting from admitting one more immigrant to the marginal cost of the immigrant.

It is reasonable to suppose that the net fiscal costs of immigration are larger for unskilled immigrant flows. After all, unskilled immigrants are more likely to use many government services *and* pay lower taxes. In addition, there are economic reasons, arising mainly from the complementarity between capital and skills, that suggest that the immigration surplus might be larger when the immigration flow is composed exclusively of skilled workers. It seems, therefore, that on purely efficiency grounds there is a strong economic case for an immigration policy that uses skill filters in awarding entry visas.

The analysis, however, also revealed that these efficiency considerations may not be the most important consequences of choosing among alternative immigration policies. Immigration also generates a sizable redistribution of wealth in the economy, reducing the incomes of natives who are now competing with immigrant workers in the labor market and increasing the incomes of capitalists and other users of immigrant services.

It is worth stressing that the discussion in this chapter considers only the "demand side" of the immigration market. The United States can attract only those immigrants who wish to enter the country.[14] If economic conditions in the United States are particularly attractive to unskilled workers from other countries, the demand side of the immigration market might only grant visas to skilled workers, but the supply side suggests that only unskilled workers are willing to make the move. It is possible, therefore, that ruling out the immigration of unskilled workers may greatly reduce the size of (and perhaps even cut off) the immigrant flow.

Finally, the positive theory of immigration policy suggested by the discussion is based on the idea that, distributional issues aside, the main objective of immigration policy should be to increase the national income accruing to natives. It is far from clear that immigration policy *should* pursue this objective. The immigration statutes reflect a political consensus that incorporates the conflicting social and economic interests of various demographic, socioeconomic, and ethnic groups, as well as political and humanitarian concerns. Nevertheless, the economic approach is useful because it tells us what we are giving up by pursuing immigration policies that minimize or ignore economic considerations.

Appendix:
The Mathematics of Calculating Surplus

The Immigration Surplus

To show how the immigration surplus can be calculated in more complicated models, it is instructive to provide an algebraic derivation of the surplus given by the triangle BCD in Figure 16.1. The linear homogenous production function is given by $Q = J(K, L)$, where $L = N + M$. The national income accruing to natives is $Q_N = wN + rK$. Assuming that native workers and capital are inelastically supplied to the economy, immigration increases Q_N by the amount:

$$(A1) \qquad \Delta Q_N = \left(K\frac{\partial r}{\partial L} + N\frac{\partial w}{\partial L} \right)\Delta L,$$

where $\Delta L = M$.

It is well known that when the derivatives in $(A1)$ are evaluated at the initial equilibrium (where $L = N$), the infinitesimal increase in national income accruing to natives is zero (Bhagwati and Srinivasan, 1983: 294). To calculate finite changes, therefore, we evaluate the immigration surplus using an "average" rate for $\partial r/\partial L$ and $\partial w/\partial L$, where the average is defined by:

$$\frac{1}{2}\left(\frac{\partial r}{\partial L} \Big|_{L=N} + \frac{\partial r}{\partial L} \Big|_{L=N+M} \right),$$

with a similar definition for the average rate of change in the wage. Because evaluating the immigration surplus at $L = N$ leads to a zero value for ΔQ_N, this approximation implies that the finite change in the immigration surplus is half the gain obtained when Equation $(A1)$ is evaluated at $L = N + M$. Using this property and converting Equation $(A1)$ into percentage terms yields:

$$(A2) \qquad \frac{\Delta Q_N}{Q} = \frac{1}{2}\left[(1 - s)e_{KL} + s(1 - m)e_{LL} \right]m,$$

where $s = wL/Q$; $m = M/L$; $e_{LL} = d \log w/d \log L$; and $e_{KL} = d \log r/d \log L$. A weighted average of factor price elasticities adds up to zero (Hamermesh 1993), so that $(1 - s)e_{KL} + se_{LL} = 0$. Substituting this fact into $(A2)$ yields the area of the triangle reported in the text.

If there are external effects, the production function for the representative firm is given by $Q_F = f(K, L)Q_E^\gamma$. Because the firm ignores the external effects, input prices are given by the marginal productivity conditions $r = f_K Q_E^\gamma$ and $w = f_L Q_E^\gamma$. Equation $(A1)$ still gives the change in national income accruing to natives. Immigration changes input prices, and these changes depend on the external effects. To calculate the derivatives $\partial r/\partial L$ and $\partial w/\partial L$, therefore, we use the equilibrium condition $Q = f(K, L)^{1/1(1-\gamma)}$. The equation in the text reporting the magnitude of the immigration surplus in the presence of external effects is obtained by evaluating the contributions of external effects to the immigration surplus at the point where $L = N + M$.

The Surplus and Immigrant Skills

To conserve space, the immigration surplus is derived only for the model that includes capital; a similar approach can be used to derive the equation reported in note 8 in the text. The concave linear homogeneous production function is given by:

$$(A3) \qquad Q = f(K, L_S, L_U) = f(K, bN + \beta M, (1 - b)N + (1-\beta)M),$$

where b and β denote the fraction of skilled workers among natives and immigrants, respectively. The wage of each factor of production (capital, skilled workers, and unskilled workers) is determined by the respective marginal productivity condition. The increase in national income accruing to natives is:

$$(A4) \qquad \Delta Q_N = \left(\frac{K\partial r}{\partial M} + bN\frac{\partial w}{\partial M} + (1 - b)N\frac{\partial w_U}{\partial M}\right)M.$$

Define $e_{ij} = \partial \log w_i/\partial \log X_j$ (where $X_j = K, L_S, L_U$), or the elasticity of factor price. If we convert Equation $(A4)$ into percentage terms, evaluate the various derivatives at the "average" point, and use the condition that a weighted average of elasticities of factor price equals zero, we obtain:

$$(A5) \qquad \frac{\Delta Q_N}{Q} = \frac{s_S e_{SS}\beta^2 m^2}{2p_S^2} - \frac{s_U e_{UU}(1 - \beta)^2 m^2}{2p_U^2} - \frac{s_S e_{SU}\beta(1 - \beta)m^2}{2p_S p_U}$$

$$- \frac{s_U e_{US}\beta(1 - \beta)m^2}{2p_S p_U},$$

where s_S and s_U are the shares of national income accruing to skilled and unskilled workers, respectively, and p_S and p_U are the shares of the workforce that are skilled and unskilled. The equations reported in the text giving the immigration surplus when the immigrant flow is exclusively skilled or unskilled are obtained by evaluating the immigration surplus in $(A5)$ at the values of $\beta = 1$ or $\beta = 0$.

To show that the immigration surplus is positive, note that the elasticity of factor price $e_{ij} = s_j c_{ij}$, where c_{ij} is the elasticity of complementarity (defined as $c_{ij} = f_{ij}f/f_if_j$). We can then rewrite $(A5)$ as:

$$(A6) \quad \frac{\Delta Q_N}{Q} = \frac{s_S^2 c_{SS}\beta^2 m^2}{2p_S^2} - \frac{s_U^2 c_{UU}(1-\beta)^2 m^2}{2p_U^2} - \frac{s_S s_U c_{SU}\beta(1-\beta)m^2}{p_S p_U}.$$

The concavity of $f(K, L_S, L_U)$ implies that:

$$f_{SS} \le 0, \quad \begin{vmatrix} f_{SS} & f_{SU} \\ f_{US} & f_{UU} \end{vmatrix} \ge 0, \quad \text{and} \quad \begin{vmatrix} f_{SS} & f_{SU} & f_{SK} \\ f_{US} & f_{UU} & f_{UK} \\ f_{SK} & f_{KU} & f_{KK} \end{vmatrix} \le 0.$$

The linear homogeneity of the production function implies that the determinant of the three-by-three matrix is zero. We can write the production function in its intensive form as $Q = K \, q(L_S/K, L_U/K)$. Assuming that q is strictly concave implies that $f_{SS}f_{UU} - f_{SU}^2 > 0$, so that $c_{SS}c_{UU} - c_{SU}^2 > 0$. This assumption guarantees that the isoquants between skilled labor and unskilled labor, for a given capital, have the usual convex shape. Using this restriction, it can be shown that the immigration surplus in $(A6)$ is positive. The relationship between the immigration surplus and β illustrated in Figure 16.4 is obtained by differentiating $(A6)$ twice with respect to β (and evaluating these derivatives at $p_S = p_U = 1/2$). Using various restrictions implied by $c_{SS}c_{UU} - c_{SU}^2 > 0$ and assuming that $c_{SS} < c_{UU}$, it can be shown that the first derivative is positive at $\beta = 1$ and that the second derivative is positive everywhere, so that $(A6)$ is convex. The relationship between the immigration surplus and β therefore is either upward-sloping (and convex) throughout or has the U-shape illustrated in Figure 16.4.

17

The Labor Demand Curve is Downward Sloping: Reexamining the Impact of Immigration on the Labor Market

Although I had done some work that attempted to measure the labor market impact of immigration in the 1980s, I had always been dissatisfied with how those papers turned out. I had initially used a structural approach in the spatial correlation genre – assuming a specific functional form for the production function and comparing outcomes across cities. Nevertheless, I felt that I had not quite cracked the technical puzzle presented by this very important economic and policy issue.

I returned to the question in joint work with Richard Freeman and Larry Katz in the mid-1990s (the main paper appearing in the Brookings Papers on Economic Activity series in 1996), but again the work left me dissatisfied. Even though we had shifted the emphasis away from the local labor market to the national labor market, the analysis relied on simulating a standard textbook model of labor supply and labor demand, using off-the-shelf elasticity estimates.

I intuitively felt that there had to be a better way of measuring the labor market impact of immigration that avoided the pitfalls of the spatial correlation approach and that did not rely entirely on simulations. Over a period of several years, I experimented with many alternative approaches,

The original version of this chapter was published as: Borjas, G. J. (2003). The Labor Demand Curve Is Downward Sloping: Reexamining the Impact of Immigration on the Labor Market, in: The Quarterly Journal of Economics, 118(4): 1335–74. © 2003 by Oxford University Press. The author is grateful to Daron Acemoglu, Joshua Angrist, David Autor, Richard Freeman, Daniel Hamermesh, Lawrence Katz, Michael Kremer, Casey Mulligan, and Stephen Trejo for helpful comments and suggestions, and to the Smith-Richardson Foundation for financial support.

including the examination of labor market outcomes along industries and occupations, but I was still not satisfied.

One day in the summer of 2002, while sitting at a conference, some of the data experimentation finally led me to recognize that supply shocks differed over time, across education groups, and even across age groups within the same education category. I sensed that this variation could be exploited to measure the labor market impact of immigration. It was immediately clear to me what the paper would look like, and, in fact, an early draft of the descriptive section of the study was ready within a month. After adding the structural estimation using the nested CES framework a few months later, I finally felt that the difficult conceptual issues involved in measuring the labor market impact of immigration could be resolved.

George J. Borjas (2015)

"After World War I, laws were passed severely limiting immigration. Only a trickle of immigrants has been admitted since then ... By keeping labor supply down, immigration policy tends to keep wages high." Paul Samuelson, *Economics* (1964)

17.1.   Introduction

Do immigrants harm or improve the employment opportunities of native workers? As Paul Samuelson's assertion suggests, the textbook model of a competitive labor market predicts that an immigrant influx should lower the wage of competing factors.[1]

Despite the intuitive appeal of this theoretical implication and despite the large number of careful studies in the literature, the existing evidence provides a mixed and confusing set of results. The measured impact of immigration on the wage of native workers fluctuates widely from study to study (and sometimes even within the same study), but seems to cluster around zero. A widely cited survey by Friedberg and Hunt (1995: 42) concludes that "the effect of immigration on the labor market outcomes of natives is small." Similarly, the 1997 National Academy of Sciences report on the economic impact of immigration argues that "the weight of the empirical evidence suggests that the impact of immigration on the wages of competing native workers is small" (Smith and Edmonston 1997: 220). These conclusions are potentially inconsistent with the textbook model because the immigrant supply shock in recent decades has been very large, and most studies of labor demand (outside the immigration context) conclude that the labor demand curve is not perfectly elastic (Hamermesh 1993).

This chapter presents a new approach for thinking about and estimating the labor market impact of immigration. Most existing studies exploit the geographic clustering of immigrants and use differences across local labor markets to identify the impact of immigration. This framework has been troublesome because it ignores the strong currents that tend to equalize economic conditions across cities and regions. In this chapter I argue that by paying closer attention to the characteristics that define a skill group – and, in particular, by using the insight that both schooling *and* work experience play a role in defining a skill group – one can make substantial progress in determining whether immigration influences the employment opportunities of native workers.

My analysis uses data drawn from the 1960–1990 U.S. Decennial Censuses, as well as the 1998–2001 Current Population Surveys, and assumes that workers with the same education but different levels of work experience participate in a national labor market and are not perfect substitutes. It turns out that immigration – even within a particular schooling group – is not balanced evenly across all experience cells in that group, and the nature of the supply imbalance changes over time. This fact generates a great deal of variation – across schooling groups, experience cells, and over time – that helps to identify the impact of immigration on the labor market. Most importantly, the size of the native workforce in each of the skill groups is relatively fixed, so that there is less potential for native flows to contaminate the comparison of outcomes across skill groups. In contrast to the confusing array of results that now permeate the literature, the evidence consistently suggests that immigration has indeed harmed the employment opportunities of competing native workers.

17.2. Measuring the Labor Market Impact of Immigration

The laws of supply and demand have unambiguous implications for how immigration should affect labor market conditions in the short run. The shift in supply lowers the real wage of competing native workers. Further, as long as the native supply curve is upward sloping, immigration should also reduce the amount of labor supplied by the native workforce.

If one could observe a number of closed labor markets that immigrants penetrate randomly, one could then relate the change in the wage of workers in a particular skill group to the immigrant share in the relevant population. A negative correlation (i.e., native wages are lower in those markets penetrated by immigrants) would indicate that immigrants worsen the employment opportunities of competing native workers.

In the United States, immigrants cluster in a small number of geographic areas. In 1990, for example, 32.5 percent of the immigrant population lived in only three metropolitan areas (Los Angeles, New York, and Miami). In contrast, only 11.6 percent of the native population clustered in the three largest metropolitan areas housing natives (New York, Los Angeles, and Chicago). Practically all empirical studies in the literature, beginning with Grossman (1982), exploit this demographic feature to identify the labor market impact of immigration. The typical study defines a metropolitan area as the labor market that is being penetrated by immigrants. The study then goes on to calculate a "spatial correlation" measuring the relation between the native wage in a locality and the relative number of immigrants in that locality. These correlations are usually negative, but very weak.[2] The best known spatial correlations are reported in Card's (1990) influential study of the Mariel flow. Card compared labor market conditions in Miami and in other cities before and after the *Marielitos* increased Miami's workforce by 7 percent. Card's difference-in-differences estimate of the spatial correlation indicated that this sudden and unexpected immigrant influx did not have a discernible effect on employment and wages in Miami's labor market.[3]

Recent studies have raised two questions about the validity of interpreting weak spatial correlations as evidence that immigration has no labor market impact. First, immigrants may not be randomly distributed across labor markets. If immigrants endogenously cluster in cities with thriving economies, there would be a spurious positive correlation between immigration and wages.[4] Second, natives may respond to the wage impact of immigration on a local labor market by moving their labor or capital to other cities. These factor flows would reequilibrate the market. As a result, a comparison of the economic opportunities facing native workers in different cities would show little or no difference because, in the end, immigration affected every city, not just the ones that actually received immigrants.[5]

Because the local labor market may adjust to immigration, Borjas, Freeman, and Katz (1997) suggested changing the unit of analysis to the national level. If the aggregate technology can be described by a CES production function with two skill groups, the relative wage of the two groups depends linearly on their relative quantities. By restricting the analysis to two skill groups, the "factor proportions approach" precludes the estimation of the impact of immigration – there is only one observation at any point in time (usually a census year), giving relative wages and relative employment. As a result, the typical application of this approach compares the actual supplies of workers in particular skill groups with those that would have been observed in the absence of immigration, and then uses outside information on labor demand elasticities to simulate the consequences of immigration. The immigrant flow to the United States in the 1980s and 1990s was relatively low-skill. Not surprisingly, the Borjas-Freeman-Katz (1997) simulation finds that immigration worsened the relative economic status of low-skill workers.

Despite all of the confusion in the literature, the available evidence teaches two important lessons. First, the study of the geographic dispersion in native employment opportunities is not an effective way for measuring the economic impact of immigration; the local labor market can adjust in far too many ways to provide a reasonable analogue to the "closed market" economy that underlies the textbook supply-and-demand framework. Second, the factor proportions approach is ultimately unsatisfactory. It departs from the valuable tradition of empirical research in labor economics that attempts to estimate the impact of labor market shocks by directly observing how those shocks affect some workers and not others. For a given elasticity of substitution, the approach mechanically predicts the relative wage consequences of supply shifts.

Ideally, one would want to estimate directly how immigration alters the employment opportunities of a particular skill group. As noted earlier, by aggregating workers into groups based on educational attainment, there is just too little variation to examine how supply shocks affect relative wages. However, the human capital literature emphasizes that schooling is not the only – and perhaps not even the most important determinant of a worker's skills. The seminal work of Becker (1975) and Mincer (1974) stressed that skills are acquired both before and after a person enters the labor market. I will assume that workers who have the same schooling, but who have different levels of experience, are imperfect substitutes in production. As a result, a skill group should be defined in terms of both schooling and labor market experience.

To see how this insight can provide a fruitful approach to the empirical analysis of the labor market impact of immigration, consider the following example. Recent immigration has increased the relative supply of high school dropouts substantially. The labor market implications of this supply shock dearly depend on how the distribution of work experience in the immigrant population contrasts with that of natives. After all, one particular set of native high school dropouts would likely be affected if all of the new low-skill immigrants were very young, and a very different set would be affected if the immigrants were near retirement age.

It is unlikely that similarly educated workers with very different levels of work experience are perfect substitutes (Welch 1979; Card and Lemieux 2001). The definition of a skill group in terms of both education and experience provides a great deal more independent variation in the immigrant supply shock that can be used to identify how immigration alters the economic opportunities facing particular groups of native workers.

17.3. Data

The empirical analysis uses data drawn from the 1960, 1970, 1980, and 1990 Public Use Microdata Samples (PUMS) of the Decennial Census, and the 1999, 2000, and 2001 Annual Demographic Supplement of the Current Population Surveys (CPS). I pool all three of the CPS surveys and refer to these pooled data as the "2000" cross-section. The analysis is restricted to men aged 18–64 who participate in the civilian labor force. A person is defined to be an immigrant if he was born abroad and is either a noncitizen or a naturalized citizen; all other persons are classified as natives. Appendix A provides a detailed description of the construction of the data extracts and of the variables used in the analysis.

As noted previously, I use both educational attainment and work experience to sort workers into particular skill groups. In particular, I classify the men into four distinct education groups: persons who are high school dropouts (i.e., they have less than 12 years of completed schooling), high school graduates (they have exactly twelve years of schooling), persons who have some college (they have between 13 and 15 years of schooling), and college graduates (they have at least 16 years of schooling).

The classification of workers into experience groups is bound to be imprecise because the census does not provide any measure of labor market experience or of the age at which a worker first enters the labor market. I initially define work experience as the number of years that have elapsed since the person completed school. This approximation is reasonably accurate for most native men, but would surely contain serious measurement errors if the calculations were also conducted for women, particularly in the earlier cross sections when the female labor force participation rate was much lower.

Equally important, this measure of experience is also likely to mismeasure "effective" experience in the sample of immigrants, i.e., the number of years of work experience that are valued by an American employer. After all, a variable that roughly approximates "Age – Education – 6" does not differentiate between experience acquired in the source country and experience acquired in the United States. I address this problem in Section 17.6.

I assume that the age of entry into the labor market is 17 for the typical high school dropout, 19 for the typical high school graduate, 21 for the typical person with some college, and 23 for the typical college graduate. Let A_T be the assumed entry age for workers in a particular schooling group. The measure of work experience is then given by (Age $- A_T$). I restrict the analysis to persons who have between 1 and 40 years of experience.

As noted in Welch's (1979) study of the impact of cohort size on the earnings of baby boomers, workers in adjacent experience cells are more likely to influence each other's labor market opportunities than workers in cells that are further apart. Throughout much of the analysis, I will capture the similarity across workers with roughly similar years of experience by aggregating the data into five-year experience intervals, indicating if the worker has one to five years of experience, six to ten years, and so on.

Consider a group of workers who have educational attainment i, experience level j, and are observed in calendar year t. The (i, j, t) cell defines a skill group at a point in time. The measure of the immigrant supply shock for this skill group is defined by

$$(1) \qquad p_{ijt} = \frac{M_{ijt}}{(M_{ijt} + N_{ijt})},$$

455

where M_{ijt} gives the number of immigrants in cell $(i,\ j,\ t)$, and N_{ijt} gives the corresponding number of natives. The variable p_{ijt} measures the foreign-born share of the labor force in a particular skill group.

Figure 17.1

The Immigrant Supply Shock, 1960–2000

a) High School Dropouts

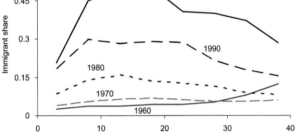

b) High School Graduates

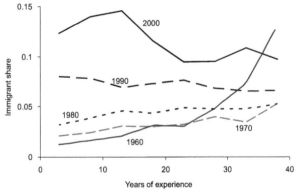

c) Some College

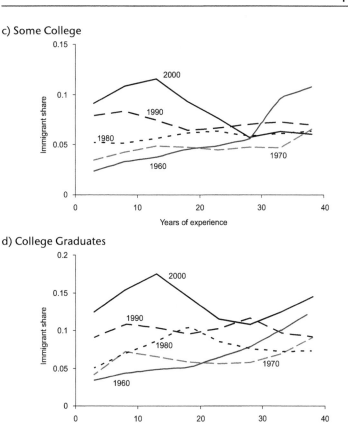

d) College Graduates

Note: Within each education group, workers are aggregated into experience groups defined in five-year intervals. The figures use the midpoint of each experience interval to illustrate the trends.

Source: 1960, 1970, 1980, and 1990 Public Use Microdata Samples (PUMS) of the Decennial Census and the 1999, and 2000 Annual Demographic Supplement of the Current Population Surveys (CPS).

The various panels of Figure 17.1 illustrate the supply shocks experienced by the different skill groups between 1960 and 2000 (Appendix B reports the underlying data). There is a great deal of dispersion in these shocks even within schooling categories. It is well known, for instance, that immigration greatly increased the supply of high school dropouts in recent decades. What is less well known, however, is that this supply shift did not affect equally all experience groups within the population of high school dropouts. Moreover, the imbalance in the supply shock changes over time. As

Panel A of the figure shows, immigrants made up half of all high school dropouts with ten to 20 years of experience in 2000, but only 20 percent of those with less than five years. In 1960, however, the immigration of high school dropouts increased the supply of the most experienced workers the most. Similarly, Panel D shows that the immigrant supply shock for college graduates in 1990 was reasonably balanced across all experience groups, generally increasing supply by around 10 percent. But the supply shock for college graduates in 1960 was larger for the most experienced groups, while in 2000 it was largest for the groups with five to 20 years of experience.

The earnings data used in the chapter are drawn from the sample of persons who worked in the year prior to the survey and reported positive annual earnings, are not enrolled in school, and are employed in the wage and salary sector. Earnings are deflated to 1999 dollars by using the CPI-U series. Table 17.1 summarizes the trends in log weekly wages for the various native groups. Not surprisingly, there is a great deal of dispersion in the rate of decadal wage growth by education and experience. Consider, for instance, the sample of college graduates. In the 1970s, wage growth was steepest for college graduates with 31–35 years of experience. In the 1990s, however, the wage of college graduates grew fastest for workers with 11–20 years of experience. In sum, the data reveal substantial variation in both the immigrant supply shock and native labor market outcomes across skill groups.

Before proceeding to a formal analysis, it is instructive to document the strong link that exists between log weekly wages and the immigrant share within schooling-experience cells. In particular, I use the data reported in Table 17.1 to calculate the decadal change in log weekly wages for each skill group, and the data summarized in the various panels of Figure 17.1 (and reported in Appendix B) to calculate the decadal change in the group's immigrant share. Figure 17.2 presents the scatter diagram relating these decadal changes after removing decade effects from the differenced data. The plot clearly illustrates a negative relation between wage growth and immigrant penetration into particular skill groups, and suggests that the regression line is not being driven by any particular outliers. Put simply, the raw data show that weekly wages grew fastest for workers in those education-experience groups that were least affected by immigration.

Table 17.1

Log Weekly Wage of Male Native Workers, 1960–2000

Education	Years of experience	1960	1970	1980	1990	2000
High school dropouts	1-5	5.535	5.758	5.722	5.494	5.418
	6-10	5.920	6.157	6.021	5.839	5.751
	11-15	6.111	6.305	6.166	6.006	5.932
	16-20	6.188	6.360	6.286	6.087	5.989
	21-25	6.201	6.413	6.364	6.180	6.034
	26-30	6.212	6.439	6.368	6.268	6.036
	31-35	6.187	6.407	6.419	6.295	6.086
	36-40	6.175	6.377	6.418	6.295	6.168
High school graduates	1-5	5.940	6.132	6.090	5.837	5.773
	6-10	6.257	6.476	6.343	6.159	6.140
	11-15	6.392	6.587	6.497	6.309	6.273
	16-20	6.459	6.639	6.609	6.415	6.323
	21-25	6.487	6.664	6.638	6.495	6.406
	26-30	6.478	6.677	6.662	6.576	6.414
	31-35	6.450	6.674	6.667	6.572	6.493
	36-40	6.435	6.622	6.657	6.548	6.460
Some college	1-5	6.133	6.322	6.237	6.085	6.013
	6-10	6.412	6.633	6.472	6.387	6.366
	11-15	6.535	6.752	6.641	6.534	6.489
	16-20	6.604	6.805	6.762	6.613	6.591
	21-25	6.634	6.832	6.764	6.711	6.626
	26-30	6.620	6.841	6.789	6.771	6.648
	31-35	6.615	6.825	6.781	6.740	6.662
	36-40	6.575	6.728	6.718	6.658	6.623
College graduates	1-5	6.354	6.612	6.432	6.459	6.458
	6-10	6.625	6.891	6.702	6.766	6.747
	11-15	6.760	7.032	6.923	6.908	6.943
	16-20	6.852	7.109	7.043	7.005	7.046
	21-25	6.876	7.158	7.087	7.112	7.051
	26-30	6.881	7.146	7.085	7.122	7.084
	31-35	6.867	7.095	7.079	7.095	7.074
	36-40	6.821	7.070	6.985	6.950	6.944

Note: The table reports the mean of the log weekly wage of workers in each education-experience group. All wages are deflated to 1999 dollars using the CPI-U series.

Source: 1960, 1970, 1980, and 1990 Public Use Microdata Samples (PUMS) of the Decennial Census and the 1999, and 2000 Annual Demographic Supplement of the Current Population Surveys (CPS).

Finally, the validity of the empirical exercise reported below hinges on the assumption that similarly educated workers who have different levels of experience are not perfect substitutes. Studies that examine this question, including Welch (1979) and Card and Lemieux (2001), find less than perfect substitutability across experience groups. Nevertheless, it is of interest to document that (for given education) immigrants and natives with similar levels of experience are closer substitutes than immigrants and natives who differ in their experience.

Figure 17.2

Scatter Diagram Relating Wages and Immigration, 1960–2000

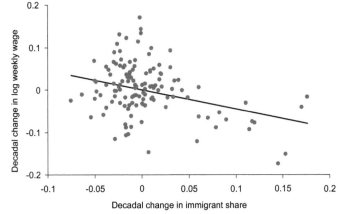

Note: Each point in the scatter represents the decadal change in the log weekly
wage and the immigrant share for a native education-experience group. The
data have been adjusted to remove decade effects. The regression line in the
figure weighs the data by $(n_0 n_1)/(n_0 + n_1)$, where n_0 is the sample size of the
cell at the beginning of the decade, and n_1 the sample size at the end. The
coefficient of the regression line is -.450, with a standard error of .172.

Source: 1960, 1970, 1980, and 1990 Public Use Microdata Samples (PUMS) of the
Decennial Census and the 1999, and 2000 Annual Demographic Supplement
of the Current Population Surveys (CPS).

I use Welch's (1999) index of congruence to measure the degree of
similarity in the occupation distributions of immigrants and natives.
The index for any two skill groups k and l is defined by

(2)
$$ G_{kl} = \frac{\sum_c (q_{kc} - \bar{q}_c)(q_{lc} - q_c)/\bar{q}_c}{\sqrt{\left(\sum_c (q_{kc} - \bar{q}_c)^2/\bar{q}_c\right)\left(\sum_c (q_{lc} - \bar{q}_c)^2/\bar{q}_c\right)}}, $$

where q_{hc} gives the fraction of group h ($h = k$, l) employed in occupation c, and $\bar{q}_c$ gives the fraction of the entire workforce employed
in that occupation. The index G_{kl}, which is similar to a correlation
coefficient, equals one when the two groups have identical occupation distributions and minus one when the two groups are clustered
in completely different occupations.

I calculate the index of congruence in the 1990 Census. I use the
three-digit census occupation codes to classify male workers into the
various occupations, and restrict the analysis to workers in nonmilitary occupations. To minimize the problem of having many occupa-

tion-experience cells with few observations, I aggregate workers into ten-year experience bands. Table 17.2 reports the calculated indices for each of the education groups. The occupation distributions of immigrants and natives with the same experience are generally more similar than the distributions of immigrants and natives with different levels of experience. Moreover, the congruence index falls, the larger the disparity in work experience between the two groups.

Table 17.2

Index of Congruence in Occupation Distributions within Education Groups, 1990

| Education-experience of | Experience of corresponding immigrant group | | | |
native groups:	1-10 years	11-20 years	21-30 years	31-40 years
High school dropouts				
1-10 years	0.709	0.714	0.671	0.619
11-20 years	0.525	0.631	0.628	0.585
21-30 years	0.410	0.527	0.567	0.566
31-40 years	0.311	0.435	0.496	0.518
High school graduates				
1-10 years	0.682	0.611	0.498	0.405
11-20 years	0.279	0.379	0.387	0.338
21-30 years	0.030	0.184	0.297	0.272
31-40 years	-0.035	0.126	0.276	0.311
Some college				
1-10 years	0.649	0.571	0.474	0.291
11-20 years	0.147	0.401	0.492	0.336
21-30 years	-0.052	0.230	0.432	0.407
31-40 years	-0.066	0.217	0.458	0.489
College graduates				
1-10 years	0.756	0.710	0.639	0.531
11-20 years	0.561	0.673	0.674	0.593
21-30 years	0.430	0.597	0.661	0.619
31-40 years	0.422	0.599	0.688	0.691

Note: Equation (2) defines the index of congruence. The index is calculated separately for each pair of native and immigrant groups.
Source: 1990 Public Use Microdata Samples (PUMS).

Consider the group of native workers who are high school dropouts and have 11 to 20 years of experience. The index of congruence with immigrants who have the same experience is 0.63. This index falls to 0.53 for immigrants who have one to ten years of experience, and to 0.59 for immigrants with 31 to 40 years. Similarly, consider the native workers who are college graduates and have fewer than ten years of experience. The index of congruence with immigrants who have the same experience is 0.76, but this index falls to 0.71 for immigrants who have 11 to 20 years of experience, to 0.64 for immigrants who have 21 to 30 years, and to 0.53 for immigrants who have more than 30 years. In sum, the occupation distributions of immigrants and natives (for a given level of education) are most similar when one compares workers who have roughly the same level of work expenence.

17.4. Basic Results

Let y_{ijt} denote the mean value of a particular labor market outcome for native men who have education i ($i = 1, \ldots, 4$), experience j ($j = 1, \ldots, 8$), and are observed at time t ($t = 1960, 1970, 1980, 1990, 2000$). Much of the empirical analysis reported in this chapter stacks these data across skill groups and calendar years and estimates the model:[6]

$$
\begin{aligned}
(3) \qquad y_{ijt} = {} & \theta p_{ijt} + s_i + x_j + \pi_t + (s_i \times x_j) + (s_i \times \pi_t) \\
& + (x_j \times \pi_t) + \varphi_{ijt},
\end{aligned}
$$

where s_i is a vector of fixed effects indicating the group's educational attainment, x_j is a vector of fixed effects indicating the group's work experience, and π_t is a vector of fixed effects indicating the time period. The linear fixed effects in Equation (3) control for differences in labor market outcomes across schooling groups, experience groups, and over time. The interactions $(s_i \times \pi_t)$ and $(x_j \times \pi_t)$ control for the possibility that the impact of education and experience changed over time, and the interaction $(s_i \times x_j)$ controls for the fact that the experience profile for a particular labor market outcome differs across schooling groups.

The dependent variables are the mean of log annual earnings, the mean of log weekly earnings, and the mean of fraction of time worked (defined as weeks worked divided by 52 in the sample of all persons, including nonworkers). Unless otherwise specified, the regressions are weighted by the sample size used to calculate y_{ijt}. The presence of the education-experience interactions in (3) implies that the impact of immigration on labor market outcomes is identified from changes that occur within education-experience cells over time. The standard errors are clustered by education-experience cells to adjust for possible serial correlation.

The first row of Table 17.3 presents the basic estimates of the adjustment coefficient 8. Consider initially the results when the dependent variable is the log of weekly earnings of native workers. The coefficient is -0.572, with a standard error of 0.162. It is easier to interpret this coefficient by converting it to an elasticity that gives the percent change in wages associated with a percent change in labor supply. Let $m_{ijt} = M_{ijt}/N_{ijt}$, or the percentage increase in the labor supply of group (i, j, t) attributable to immigration. Define the "wage elasticity" as[7]

$$(4) \qquad \frac{\partial \log w_{ijt}}{\partial m_{ijt}} = \frac{\theta}{(1 + m_{ijt})^2}.$$

Table 17.3

Impact of Immigrant Share on Labor Market Outcomes of Native Education-Experience Groups

	Dependent variable		
Specification:	Log annual earnings	Log weekly earnings	Fraction of time worked
1. Basic estimates	-0.919	-0.572	-0.529
	(0.582)	(0.162)	(0.132)
2. Unweighted regression	-0.725	-0.546	-0.382
	(0.463)	(0.141)	(0.103)
3. Includes women in labor force counts	-0.919	-0.637	-0.511
	(0.661)	(0.159)	(0.148)
4. Includes log native labor force as regressor	-1.231	-0.552	-0.567
	(0.384)	(0.204)	(0.116)

Note: The table reports the coefficient of the immigrant share variable from regressions where the dependent variable is the mean labor market outcome for a native education-experience group at a particular point in time. Standard errors are reported in parentheses and are adjusted for clustering within education-experience cells. All regressions have 160 observations and, except for those reported in row 2, are weighted by the sample size of the education-experience-period cell. All regression models include education, experience, and period fixed effects, as well as interactions between education and experience fixed effects, education and period fixed effects, and experience and period fixed effects.
Source: Own calculations.

By 2000, immigration had increased the number of men in the labor force by 16.8 percent. Equation (4) implies that the wage elasticity-evaluated at the mean value of the immigrant supply increase – can be obtained by multiplying θ by approximately 0.7. The wage elasticity for weekly earnings is then -0.40 (or -0.572 × 0.7). Put differently, a 10 percent supply shock (i.e., an immigrant flow that increases the number of workers in the skill group by 10 percent) reduces weekly earnings by about 4 percent.

Table 17.3 indicates that immigration has an even stronger effect on annual earnings, suggesting that immigration reduces the labor supply of native male workers. A 10 percent supply shock reduces annual earnings by 6.4 percent and the fraction of time worked by 3.7 percentage points. Note that the difference in the coefficients from the log annual earnings and the log weekly earnings regressions gives the coefficient from a log weeks worked specification. A simple supply-demand framework implies that the labor supply elasticity for workers can be estimated from the ratio of the immigration effect on log weeks worked and log weekly earnings. The point estimate for this ratio is 0.6. This estimate lies above the range reported by Juhn, Murphy, and Topel (1991), who report labor supply elasticities between 0.1 and 0.4.[8]

The remaining rows of Table 17.3 conduct a variety of specification tests to determine the sensitivity of the results. The coefficients reported in the second row, for example, indicate that the results are similar when the regressions are not weighted by the sample size of the skill group. In the third row the regression redefines the measure of the immigrant share p_{ijt} to include both male and female labor force participants. Despite the misclassification of many women into the various experience groups, the adjustment coefficients remain negative and significant, and have similar values to those reported in the first row. The last row of the table addresses the interpretation problem that arises because a rise in p_{ijt} can represent either an increase in the number of immigrants or a decline in the number of native workers in that skill group (e.g., the secular decline in the number of natives who are high school dropouts). Row 4 of the table reports the adjustment coefficient when the regression adds the log of the size of the native workforce in cell (i, j, t) as a regressor. The wage elasticity for log weekly earnings is -0.39 and significant. In short, the parameter a in Equation (3) is indeed capturing the impact of an increase in the size of the immigrant population on native labor market outcomes.[9]

I also estimated the regression model within schooling groups to determine whether the results are being driven by particular groups, such as the large influx of foreign-born high school dropouts. With only one exception, Table 17.4 shows that the impact of immigration on the weekly earnings of particular schooling groups is negative and significant. The exception is the group of college graduates, where the adjustment coefficient is positive and has a large standard error. Note, however, that the regression estimated within a schooling group cannot include experience-period interactions to control for secular changes in the shape of the experience-earnings profile. As a result, the coefficient of the immigrant share variable may be measuring a spurious correlation between immigration and factors that changed the wage structure differentially within schooling groups. It is probably not coincidental that the adjustment coefficient is positive for college graduates, the group that experienced perhaps the most striking change in the wage structure in recent decades.[10]

Table 17.4

Impact of Immigrant Share on Native Labor Market Outcomes, by Education Group

Dependent variable:	High school dropouts	High school graduates	Some college	College graduates	At least high school graduates
1. Log annual earnings	-1.416	-2.225	-0.567	1.134	-1.184
	(0.313)	(0.622)	(0.421)	(0.436)	(0.668)
2. Log weekly earnings	-0.947	-2.074	-1.096	0.610	-0.335
	(0.164)	(0.510)	(0.461)	(0.440)	(0.612)
3. Fraction of time worked	-0.086	0.393	0.567	0.300	-1.040
	(0.073)	(0.251)	(0.385)	(0.499)	(0.211)

Note: The table reports the coefficient of the immigrant share variable from regressions where the dependent variable is the mean labor market outcome for a native education-experience group at a particular point in time. Standard errors are reported in parentheses and are adjusted for clustering within experience cell (in the first four columns) and within education-experience cells (in the last column). All regression are weighted by the sample size of the education-experience-period cell. The regressions reported in the first four columns have 40 observations and include experience and period fixed effects. The regressions reported in the last column have 120 observations and include education, experience, and period fixed effects, as well as interactions between education and experience fixed effects, education and period fixed effects, and experience and period fixed effects.
Source: Own calculations.

Finally, the last column of Table 17.4 estimates the regressions using only the groups of natives with at least a high school education. The coefficients generally suggest that the sample of high school dropouts is not the group that is driving much of the analysis. Although the adjustment coefficients remain negative for all the dependent variables, it is insignificant for log weekly earnings. In the case of log annual earnings, however, the wage elasticity is around -0.8, suggesting that immigration had an adverse impact on native workers even when the regression ignores the information provided by the workers who experienced the largest supply shock in the past few decades.[11]

17.5. A Comparison with the Spatial Correlation Approach

In contrast to the studies that calculate spatial correlations between wages in local labor markets and measures of immigrant penetration, the evidence presented in the previous section indicates that immigrants have a sizable adverse effect on the wage of competing workers. This discrepancy suggests that it might be instructive to examine how the results of the generic spatial correlation regression would change if that analysis defined skill groups in terms of both education and experience.

Suppose that the relevant labor market for a typical worker is determined by his state of residence (r), education, and experience.[12] I use the 1960–2000 Census and CPS files to calculate both the immigrant share and the mean labor market outcomes for cell (r, i, j, t). I then use these aggregate data to estimate regressions similar to those presented earlier, but the unit of analysis is now a state-education-experience group at a particular point in time.

Table 17.5 reports the estimated coefficient of the immigrant share variable from this regression framework. The first column of the table presents the coefficient from the simplest specification, which includes the state, education, experience, and period fixed effects, as well as interactions between the state, education, and experience fixed effects with the vector of period fixed effects, and interactions between the state and education fixed effects. This regression, in effect, estimates the impact of immigration on the *change* in labor market outcomes experienced by a particular education group in a particular state. The adjustment coefficients for the various dependent variables are negative and mostly significant. The adjustment coefficient in the log weekly earnings regression is -0.124, with a standard error of 0.042. Note that the implied adverse impact of immigration resulting from this specification is far smaller than the effects reported in the previous section.

The second column of Table 17.5 adds a three-way interaction between the state, education, and experience fixed effects. This specification, therefore, examines the impact of immigration on the wage growth experienced by a particular education-experience group living in a particular state. The adjustment coefficients are more negative (-0.217 in the log weekly wage specification) and statistically significant. In short, defining a skill group in terms of both education and experience implies that immigration has a more adverse impact than a specification that ignores the experience component.

Table 17.5

Impact of Immigrant Share on Labor Market Outcomes of Native State-Education-Experience Groups

Dependent Variable:	(1)	(2)	(3)	(4)
1. Log annual earnings	-0.115	-0.276	-0.253	-0.217
	(0.079)	(0.053)	(0.046)	(0.068)
2. Log weekly earnings	-0.124	-0.217	-0.203	-0.183
	(0.042)	(0.039)	(0.038)	(0.050)
3. Fraction of time worked	-0.038	-0.100	-0.078	-0.119
	(0.030)	(0.015)	(0.015)	(0.021)
Controls for:				
(State × period), (education × period), (experience × period), (state × education) fixed effects	Yes	Yes	Yes	Yes
(State × education × experience) fixed effects	No	Yes	Yes	Yes
(Education × experience × period) fixed effects	No	No	Yes	Yes
(State × education × period), (state × experience × period) fixed effects	No	No	No	Yes

Note: The table reports the coefficient of the immigrant share variable from regressions where the dependent variable is the mean labor market outcome for a native state-education-experience group at a particular point in time. Standard errors are reported in parentheses and are adjusted for clustering within state-education-experience cells. All regressions are weighted by the sample size of the state-education-experience-period cell and include state, education, experience, and period fixed effects. The regressions on log annual earnings or log weekly earnings have 8,153 observations; the regressions on the fraction of time worked have 8,159 observations.

Source: Own calculations.

The third column of the table further expands the model by allowing for period effects to vary across education-experience cells, while the fourth column presents the full specification of the regression that allows for all possible three-way interactions between the state, education, experience, and period fixed effects. This regression specification effectively identifies the wage impact by using only variation in immigration at the (state × education × experience × period) level. The coefficient is negative and significant (-0.183 in the log weekly wage specification), and it is numerically much smaller than the coefficients reported in the previous section.

In fact, it is instructive to contrast the difference in the results reported in the last column of Table 17.5 with the evidence reported in Table 17.5. The key difference between the two sets of estimates is the assumption made about the geographic boundary of the labor market. The estimated wage elasticity for log weekly earnings is 0.13 when a state's geographic boundary limits the size of the market, and -0.40 when the worker participates in a national market. One interesting interpretation of this discrepancy is that there is sufficient spatial arbitrage – perhaps due to interstate flows of labor and capital – that tends to equalize opportunities for workers of given skills across regions. The spatial arbitrage effectively cuts the national estimate of the impact of immigration by two-thirds.[13] Put differently, even though immigration has a sizable adverse effect on the wage of competing workers at the national level, the analysis of wage differentials across regional labor markets conceals much of the impact.

17.6. Refining the Definition of Skills

17.6.1. Measuring Effective Experience

Up to this point, labor market experience has been defined as the time elapsed since entry into the labor market for both immigrants and natives. The evidence indicates that U.S. firms attach different values to experience acquired abroad and experience acquired in the United States (Chiswick 1978d). These findings suggest that one should use the "effective experience" of an immigrant worker before assigning that worker to a particular schooling-experience group, where effective experience measures the years of work exposure that are valued in the U.S. labor market. Let A denote age, A_m the age of entry into the United States, and A_r the age of entry into the labor market. The years of effective experience for an immigrant worker are given by

$$(5) \qquad X = \begin{cases} \alpha(A_M - A_T) + \beta(A - A_m), & \text{if } A_m > A_T \\ \gamma(A - A_T), & \text{if } A_m \leq A_T, \end{cases}$$

where α translates a year of source country experience acquired by immigrants who migrated as adults (i.e., $A_m > A_T$) into the equivalent value of experience acquired by a native worker, β rescales the value of a year of U.S. experience acquired by these adult immigrants, and γ rescales the experience acquired by immigrants who migrated as children (i.e., $A_m \leq A_T$).

The parameters α, β, and γ can be estimated by using the standard model of immigrant assimilation, a model that also accounts for differences in immigrant "quality" across cohorts (Borjas 1985). Suppose that we pool data for native and immigrant workers in two separate cross sections (such as the 1980 and 1990 Censuses). A generic regression model that can identify all of the relevant parameters is

$$(6) \qquad \log w = s_i + \phi_D I^D + \lambda_N N(A - A_T) + \lambda_c I^c (A - A_T),$$

$$+ \lambda_{D0} I^D (A_m - A_T) + \lambda_{D1} I^D (A - A_m) + \kappa Y + \rho \pi + \varphi,$$

where w gives the weekly wage of a worker observed in a particular cross section, s_i gives a vector of education fixed effects, I^c indicates whether the immigrant entered the country as a child, I^D indicates whether the immigrant entered as an adult, N indicates whether the worker is native born ($N = 1 - I^c - I^D$), Y gives the calendar year of entry into the United States (set to zero for natives), and π indicates whether the observation is drawn from the 1990 Census.

The coefficient λ_N gives the market value of a year of experience acquired by a native worker; λ_c gives the value of a year of experience acquired in the United States by a "child immigrant"; and λ_{D0} and λ_{D1} give the value of a year of source country experience and of U. S. experience acquired by an adult immigrant, respectively. The weights that define an immigrant's effective experience are

(7) $$\alpha = \frac{\lambda_{D0}}{\lambda_N}, \quad \beta = \frac{\lambda_{D1}}{\lambda_N}, \quad \gamma = \frac{\lambda_c}{\lambda_N}.$$

Although the generic regression model in (6) is pedagogically useful, it ignores the curvature of the experience-earnings profile, and also ignores the possibility that the returns to education differ among the various groups. Further, it is preferable to define the calendar year of an immigrant's arrival as a vector of dummy variables indicating the year of arrival, rather than as a linear time trend. I estimated this more general model using the pooled 1980 and 1990 data. Table 17.6 reports the relevant coefficients from this regression.

The experience coefficients for natives and for immigrants who migrated as children have almost identical numerical values, so that a marginal year of experience is valued at the same rate by employers (although the tiny numerical difference is statistically significant). This implies that the weight γ is estimated to be 1.0. In contrast, the value of an additional year of source country experience for adult immigrants (evaluated at the mean years of source country experience) is 0.006, while the value of an additional year of U. S. experience for these immigrants is 0.024. The value of a year of experience for a comparable native worker is 0.015. The implied weights are $\alpha = 0.4$ and $\beta = 1.6$.

Table 17.6

Impact of Different Types of Labor Market Experience on the Log Weekly Earnings of Natives and Immigrants

Coefficient of:	Group		
	Natives	Child immigrants	Adult immigrants
Source country experience	—	—	0.012
			(0.001)
Source country experience squared ÷ 10	—	—	-0.003
			(0.000)
U.S. experience	0.056	0.058	0.032
	(0.000)	(0.001)	(0.002)
U.S. experience squared ÷ 10	-0.010	-0.010	-0.004
	(0.001)	(0.000)	(0.001)
Mean value of:			
Source country experience	—	—	10.6
U.S. experience	16.7	13.0	10.8
Marginal value of an additional year of experience for immigrants:			
Source country experience	—	—	0.006
			(0.001)
U.S. experience	—	0.033	0.024
		(0.001)	(0.001)
Marginal value of an additional year of experience for natives, evaluated at mean value of relevant sample of immigrants	—	0.031 (0.000)	0.015 (0.000)

Note: Standard errors are reported in parentheses. The regression pools data from the 1980 and 1990 Censuses and has 1,141,609 observations. The dependent variable is the log of weekly earnings. The regressors include: dummy variables indicating if the worker is an adult immigrant or a child immigrant; a vector of variables indicating the worker's educational attainment, interacted with variables indicating if the worker is an adult or a child immigrant; experience (and its square) for native workers; experience (and its square) for immigrants who arrived as children; source country experience (and its square) for immigrants who arrived as adults; experience in the U.S. (and its square) for immigrants who arrived as adults; dummy variables indicating the calendar year in which the immigrant arrived (1985–1989, 1980–1984, 1975–1979, 1970–1974, 1965–1969, 1960–1964, 1950–1959, and before 1950), and the interaction of this vector with a dummy variable indicating if the immigrant arrived as an adult; and a dummy variable indicating if the observation was drawn from the 1990 Census.

Source: Own calculations.

I used these weights to calculate the effective experience of each immigrant, and then reclassified them into the schooling-experience cells using the predicted measure of effective experience.[14] The top row of Table 17.7 reports the estimated adjustment coefficients. The effects are roughly similar to those reported in the previous section. For example, the weekly earnings regression implies that the wage elasticity is -.30, and the effect is statistically significant.

Table 17.7

Impact of Immigrant Share on Labor Market Outcomes of Native Skill Groups, Using Effective Experience and Effective Skills

Specification:	Dependent variable		
	Log annual earnings	Log weekly earnings	Fraction of time worked
1. Effective experience	-1.025	-0.422	-0.611
	(0.506)	(0.210)	(0.118)
2. Using quantiles of wage distribution	-0.562	-0.606	-0.048
	(0.329)	(0.158)	(0.167)

Note: The table reports the coefficient of the immigrant share variable from regressions where the dependent variable is the mean labor market outcome for a native skill group (defined in terms of education-experience in row 1 or education-quantile in row 2) at a particular point in time. The quantile definition of skill groups is based on the worker's placement in each of 20 quantiles of the (within-education) native weekly wage distribution. Standard errors are reported in parentheses and are adjusted for clustering within education-experience cells (row 1) or within education-quantile cells (row 2). All regressions are weighted by the sample size of the education-experience-period cell (row 1) or the education-quantile-period cell (row 2). The regressions reported in row 1 have 128 observations; those reported in row 2 have 400 observations. The models in row 1 include education, experience, and period fixed effects, as well as interactions between education and experience fixed effects, education and period fixed effects, and experience and period fixed effects. The models in row 2 include education, quantile, and period fixed effects, as well as interactions between education and quantile fixed effects, education and period fixed effects, and quantile and period fixed effects.

Source: Own calculations.

17.7. Measuring Effective Skills

The notion of effective experience raises a more general question about the overall comparability of the skills of immigrants and natives. The U. S. labor market differentiates the value of human capital embodied in immigrants and natives along many dimensions. For example, the value that firms attach to schooling will probably differ between the two groups, as well as among immigrants originating in different countries. It is of interest, therefore, to devise a simple way of summarizing the differences in "effective skills" that exist between immigrants and natives within a schooling category. It seems sensible to assume that similarly educated workers who fall in the same general location of the wage distribution have roughly the same number of efficiency units because employers attach the same value to the *entire* package of skills embodied in these workers.

To conduct this classification of workers into skill groups, I restrict the analysis to workers who have valid wage data. In each cross section and for each of the four schooling groups, I sliced the weekly wage distribution of *native* workers into 20 quantiles. By construction, 5 percent of natives in each schooling group fall into each of the quantiles. I then calculated how many of the immigrant workers in each schooling group fall into each of the 20 quantiles. The immigrant supply shock is defined by

$$(8) \qquad \hat{p}_{ikt} = \frac{M_{ikt}}{(M_{ikt} + N_{ikt})},$$

where M_{ikt} and N_{ikt} give the number of foreign-born and native-born workers in schooling group i, quantile k ($k = 1, \ldots, 20$), at time t.

Consider the regression model:

$$(9) \qquad y_{ikt} = \theta \hat{p}_{ikt} + s_i + q_k + \pi_t + (q_k \times s_i) + (s_i \times \pi_t)$$
$$+ (q_k \times \pi_t) + \varphi_{ikt},$$

where q_k is a vector of fixed effects indicating the quantile of the cell. The second row of Table 17.7 reports the adjustment coefficients estimated from this specification of the model. Despite the very different methodological approach employed to define the skill groups, the estimated coefficient in the log weekly earnings regression is similar to those reported above. The estimate of θ is -0.606 (with a standard error of 0.158), implying a wage elasticity of -0.42. In sum, the evidence suggests that the clustering of immigrants into particular segments of the wage distribution worsened the wage outcomes of native workers who happened to reside in those regions of the wage distribution.[15]

17.8. A Structural Approach to Immigration and Factor Demand

17.8.1. Theory and Evidence

Up to this point, I have not imposed any economic structure in the estimation of the wage effects of immigration. As in most of the studies in the spatial correlation literature, I have instead attempted to calculate the correlation that indicates whether an increase in the number of immigrants lowers the wage of competing native workers.

An alternative approach would impose more structure by specifying the technology of the aggregate production function.[16] This structural approach would make it possible to estimate not only the effect of a particular immigrant influx on the wage of competing native workers, but also the cross effects on the wage of other natives. An empirically useful approach assumes that the aggregate production function can be represented in terms of a three-level CES technology: similarly educated workers with different levels of work experience are aggregated to form the effective supply of an education group; and workers across education groups are then aggregated to form the national workforce.[17]

Suppose that the aggregate production function for the national economy at time t is

$$(10) \qquad Q_t = \left[\lambda_{Kt} K_t^\nu + \lambda_{Lt} L_t^\nu \right]^{1/\nu},$$

where Q is output, K is capital, L denotes the aggregate labor input; and $\nu = 1 - 1\sigma_{KL}$, with σ_{Kl} being the elasticity of substitution between capital and labor $(-\infty < \nu \le 1)$. The vector λ gives time-variant technology parameters that shift the production frontier, with $\lambda_{Kt} + \lambda_{Lt} = 1$. The aggregate L_t incorporates the contributions of workers who differ in both education and experience. Let

$$(11) \qquad L_t = \left[\sum_i \theta_{it} L_{it}^\rho \right]^{1/\rho},$$

where L_{it} gives the number of workers with education i at time t, and $\rho = 1 - 1/\sigma_E$, with σ_E being the elasticity of substitution across these education aggregates $(-\infty < \rho \le 1)$. The θ_{it} give time-variant technology parameters that shift the relative productivity of education groups, with $\sum_i \theta_{it} = 1$. Finally, the supply of workers in each education group is itself given by an aggregation of the contribution of similarly educated workers with different experience. In particular,

$$(12) \qquad L_{it} = \left[\sum_j \alpha_{ij} L_{ijt}^\eta \right]^{1/\eta},$$

where L_{ijt} gives the number of workers in education group i and experience group j at time t, and $\eta = 1 - 1/\sigma_x$, with σ_x being the elasticity of substitution across experience classes within an education group $(-\infty < \eta \le 1)$. Equation (12) incorporates an important identifying assumption: the technology coefficients α_{ijt} are constant over time, with $\sum_j \alpha_{ij} = 1$.

The marginal productivity condition implies that the wage for skill group (i, j, t) is

$$(13) \qquad \log w_{ijt} = \log \lambda_{Lt} + (1 - \nu) \log Q_t + (\nu - \rho) \log L_t + \log \theta_{it}$$
$$+ (\rho - \eta) \log L_{it} + \log \alpha_{ij} + (\eta - 1) \log L_{ijt}.$$

As Card and Lemieux (2001) show in their recent study of the link between the wage structure and cohort size, it is straightforward to implement this approach empirically. In particular, note that the marginal productivity condition in (13) can be rewritten as

$$(14) \qquad \log w_{ijt} = \delta_t + \delta_{it} + \delta_{ij} - \tfrac{1}{\sigma_x} \log L_{ijt},$$

where $\delta_t = \log \lambda_{Lt} + (1 - \nu) \log Q_t + (\nu - \rho) \log L_t$, and is absorbed by period fixed effects; $\delta_{it} = \log \theta_{it} + (\rho - \eta) \log L_{it}$, and is absorbed by interactions between the education fixed effects and the period fixed effects; and $\delta_{ij} = \log \alpha_{ij}$ and is absorbed by interactions between education fixed effects and experience fixed effects. The regression model in (14), therefore, identifies the elasticity of substitution across experience groups.

Moreover, the coefficients of the education-experience interactions in (14) identify the parameters $\log \alpha_{ij}$. I impose the restriction that $\sum_j \alpha_{ij} = 1$ when I estimate the α_{ij} from the fixed effect coefficients.[18] As indicated by Equation (12), the estimates of α_{ij}, and σ_x permit the calculation of L_{it}, the CES-weighted labor aggregate for education group i. I can then move up one level in the CES technology, and recover an additional unknown parameter. Let $\log w_{it}$ be the mean log wage paid to the average worker in education group i at time t. The marginal productivity condition determining the wage for this group is

$$(15) \qquad \log w_{it} = \delta_t + \log \theta_{it} - \tfrac{1}{\sigma_E} \log L_{it}.$$

This equation is closely related to the model estimated by Katz and Murphy (1992: 69) that examines how the wage differential between college and high school graduates varies with relative supplies. Note that σ_E cannot be identified if the regression included interactions of education-period fixed effects to capture the term $\log \theta_{it}$. There would be 20 such interaction terms, but there are only 20 observations in the regression (four education groups observed at five different points in time). To identify σ_E, I adopt the Katz-Murphy assumption that the technology shifters can be approximated by a linear trend that varies across education groups.

It is important to note that ordinary least squares regressions of Equations (14) and (15) may lead to biased estimates of σ_x and σ_E because the supply of workers to the various education groups is likely to be endogenous over the 40-year period spanned by the data. The economic question at the core of this chapter, however, suggests an instrument for the size of the workforce in each skill group: the number of immigrants in that group. In other words, the immigrant influx into particular skill groups provides the supply shifter required to identify the labor demand function. This instrument would be valid if the immigrant influx into particular skill groups were independent of the relative wages offered to the various skill categories. It is likely, however, that the number of immigrants in a skill group responds to shifts in the wage structure. Income-maximizing behavior on the part of potential immigrants would generate larger flows into those skill cells that had relatively high wages. This behavioral response would tend to build in a positive correlation between the size of the labor force and wages in a skill group. The regression coefficients, therefore, understate the negative wage impact of a relative supply increase.[19]

The three-level CES technology offers a crucial advantage for estimating the impact of immigration within a structural system of factor demand. My analysis defines 33 factors of production: 32 education-experience skill groups plus capital. A general specification of the technology, such as the translog, would require the estimation of 561 different parameters (or $n(n + 1)/2$). The three-level CES approach drastically reduces the size of the parameter space; the technology can be summarized in terms of three elasticities of substitution. Obviously, this simplification comes at a cost: the CES specification restricts the types of substitution that can exist among the various factors. The elasticity of substitution across experience groups takes on the same value for workers in adjacent experience categories as for workers who differ greatly in their experience; the elasticity of substitution between high school dropouts and high school graduates is the same as that between high school dropouts and college graduates; and the elasticity of substitution between capital and labor is the same for all the different types of workers.

Finally, note that the empirical implementation of the three-level CES technology described above does not use any data on the aggregate capital stock, making it difficult to separately identify the value of σ_{KL}.[20] I will discuss later a plausible assumption that can be made about this parameter to simulate the impact of immigration on the labor market.

The first step in the empirical application of the model is to estimate Equation (14) using the sample of 160 (i, j, t) cells. The IV estimate of this regression equation is[21]

(16) $$\log w_{ijt} = \delta_t + \delta_{it} + \delta_{ij} - \underset{(0.115)}{0.288} \log L_{ijt}.$$

The implied elasticity of substitution across experience groups is 3.5. This estimate of σ_x is similar to the Card-Lemieux (2001) estimate of the elasticity of substitution across age groups. The Card-Lemieux estimates for U.S. data range from 3.8 to 4.9.

I use the implied estimate of the elasticity of substitution and the (transformed) coefficients of the education-experience fixed effects to calculate the size of the CES-weighted labor aggregate for each education group. I then estimate the marginal productivity condition for the education group given by (15). The IV regression estimate is[22]

(17) $$\log w_{it} = \delta_t$$

+ linear trend interacted with education fixed effects $- \underset{(0.646)}{0.741} \log L_{it}.$

Alternatively, I can bypass the calculation of the CES-weighted labor aggregate for each education group, and simply use the actual number of workers in the group (L_{it}^*). The IV regression estimate is

(17′) $$\log w_{it} = \delta_t$$

+ linear trend interacted with education fixed effects $- \underset{(0.582)}{0.759} \log L_{it}^*.$

Both specifications imply that σ_E is around 1.3. The regressions reported in (17) and (17′) have only 20 observations (four education groups observed at five different points in time), so that the elasticity of substitution is not measured precisely. Nevertheless, the implied elasticity is similar to the Katz-Murphy (1992) estimate of 1.4, despite the different data and methodology.[23] In sum, the evidence indicates that workers within an experience group are not perfect substitutes, but there is clearly more substitution among similarly educated workers who differ in their experience than among workers with different levels of education.

17.8.2.   Simulating the Wage Effects of Immigration

Hamermesh (1993: 37) shows that the factor price elasticity giving the impact on the wage of factor y of an increase in the supply of factor z is[24]

(18)
$$\varepsilon_{yz} = \frac{d\log w_y}{d\log L_z} = s_z \frac{Q_{yz}Q}{Q_y Q_z},$$

where s_z is the share of income accruing to factor z; and $Q_y = \partial Q/\partial L_y$, $Q_z = \partial Q/\partial L_z$, and $Q_{yz} = \partial^2 Q/\partial L_y \partial L_z$.

The three-level CES technology implies that the own factor price elasticity giving the wage impact of an increase in the supply of workers with education i and experience j is

(19)
$$\varepsilon_{ij,ij} = \frac{1}{\sigma_x} + \left(\frac{1}{\sigma_x} - \frac{1}{\sigma_E}\right)\frac{s_{ij}}{s_i} + \left(\frac{1}{\sigma_E} - \frac{1}{\sigma_{KL}}\right)\frac{s_{ij}}{s_L} + \frac{1}{\sigma_{KL}} s_{ij},$$

where s_{ij} gives the share of income accruing to group (i, j); s_i gives the share of income accruing to education group i, and s_L gives labor's share of income. Similarly, the (within-branch) cross-factor price elasticity giving the impact on the wage of group (i, j) of an increase in the supply of group (i, j'), with $j \neq j'$, is

(20)
$$\varepsilon_{ij,ij'} = \left(\frac{1}{\sigma_x} - \frac{1}{\sigma_E}\right)\frac{s_{ij'}}{s_i} + \left(\frac{1}{\sigma_E} - \frac{1}{\sigma_{KL}}\right)\frac{s_{ij'}}{s_L} + \frac{1}{\sigma_{KL}} s_{ij'}.$$

Finally, the (across-branch) cross-factor price elasticity giving the impact on the wage of group (i, j) of an increase in the supply of group (i', j'), with $i \neq i'$ and $j' = (1, \ldots, j, \ldots 8)$, is

(21)
$$\varepsilon_{ij,i'j'} = \left(\frac{1}{\sigma_E} - \frac{1}{\sigma_{KL}}\right)\frac{s_{i'j'}}{s_L} + \frac{1}{\sigma_{KL}} s_{i'j'}.$$

The calculations of the factor price elasticities in (19)-(21) require information on the factor shares. I assume that labor's share of income is 0.7, and use the 1990 Census to calculate the share of total annual earnings accruing to each education-experience cell. I use these total annual earnings to apportion the labor shares accruing to the various groups.[25] Based on the coefficients estimated above, I set $\sigma_x = 3.5$ and $\sigma_E = 1.3$. Finally, the calculations require an assumption about σ_{KL}. Hamermesh (1993: 92) concludes that the aggregate U.S. economy can be reasonably described by a Cobb-Douglas production function, suggesting that σ_{KL} equals one. I impose this restriction in the analysis.

Table 17.8 reports the estimated elasticities. The own elasticity varies from -0.30 to -0.36, with a weighted mean of -0.33 (where the weight is the size of the native labor force as of 2000).[26] The table also reports the cross elasticities within an education branch. Without exception, these cross elasticities are negative, and their weighted mean is -0.05.

Table 17.8

Estimated Factor Price Elasticities, By Skill Group

Education	Years of experience	Own elasticity	Cross elasticity (within education branch)	Cross elasticity (across education branches)
High school dropouts	1-5	-0.313	-0.028	0.002
	6-10	-0.330	-0.044	0.003
	11-15	-0.344	-0.059	0.004
	16-20	-0.341	-0.056	0.004
	21-25	-0.339	-0.053	0.004
	26-30	-0.352	-0.066	0.004
	31-35	-0.358	-0.072	0.005
	36-40	-0.361	-0.076	0.005
High school graduates	1-5	-0.316	-0.030	0.012
	6-10	-0.335	-0.050	0.020
	11-15	-0.343	-0.057	0.023
	16-20	-0.337	-0.051	0.020
	21-25	-0.333	-0.047	0.019
	26-30	-0.330	-0.044	0.017
	31-35	-0.323	-0.037	0.015
	36-40	-0.315	-0.029	0.012
Some college	1-5	-0.318	-0.032	0.012
	6-10	-0.339	-0.054	0.020
	11-15	-0.349	-0.063	0.024
	16-20	-0.348	-0.063	0.024
	21-25	-0.339	-0.054	0.020
	26-30	-0.324	-0.038	0.015
	31-35	-0.313	-0.028	0.010
	36-40	-0.305	-0.019	0.007
College graduates	1-5	-0.317	-0.031	0.017
	6-10	-0.335	-0.049	0.026
	11-15	-0.341	-0.056	0.030
	16-20	-0.348	-0.062	0.033
	21-25	-0.332	-0.046	0.025
	26-30	-0.318	-0.032	0.017
	31-35	-0.309	-0.023	0.013
	36-40	-0.302	-0.016	0.009

Note: Equations (19)-(21) define the factor price elasticities in the three-level CES framework. For a given percent change in the numbers of workers of any specific group: the own factor price elasticity gives the percent change in that group's wage; the cross elasticity within an education branch gives the percent change in the wage of a group with the same education but with different experience; the cross elasticity across education branches gives the percent change in the wage of groups that have different educational attainment.

Source: Own calculations.

Finally, the table reports the cross elasticities across education branches. These cross elasticities are positive and small, with a weighted mean of 0.02. It is worth noting that the cross-branch elasticities reported for high school dropouts are very close to zero. This result follows from the definition of the elasticity in Equation (21). Because the share of income accruing to high school dropouts is small, an influx of low-skill immigrants is bound to have only a tiny impact on the wage of workers in other education groups.[27] As an example, consider the wage effects of a 10 percent increase in the number of college graduates who have 16–20 years of experience. The elasticities calculated for this group indicate that their own wage would drop by 3.5 percent, that the wage of other college graduates (with different levels of experience) would fall by -0.6 percent, and that the wage of all workers without a college degree would rise by 0.3 percent.

I use the elasticity estimates reported in Table 17.8 to calculate the wage impact of the immigrant influx that entered the United States between 1980 and 2000. The marginal productivity condition for the typical worker in education group s and experience group x can be written as $w_{sx} = D(K, L_{11}, \ldots, L_{18}, \ldots, L_{41}, \ldots, L_{48})$. Assuming that the capital stock is constant, the net impact of immigration on the log wage of group (s, x) is[28]

$$(22) \qquad \Delta \log w_{sx} = \varepsilon_{sx,sx} m_{sx} + \sum_{j \neq x} \varepsilon_{sx,sj} m_{sj} + \sum_{i \neq s} \sum_{j} \varepsilon_{sx,ij} m_{ij},$$

where m_{ij} gives the percentage change in labor supply due to immigration in cell (i, j). Because the size of the native labor force in each skill group is shifting over time, I define m_{ij} as

$$(23) \qquad m_{ij} = \frac{M_{ij,2000} - M_{ij,1980}}{0.5(N_{ij,1980} + N_{ij,2000}) + M_{ij,1980}},$$

so that the baseline population used to calculate the percent increase in labor supply averages out the size of the native workforce in the skill cell and treats the preexisting immigrant population as part of the "native" stock.

Table 17.9 summarizes the results of the simulation. The large immigrant influx of the 1980s and 1990s adversely affected the wage of most native workers, particularly those workers at the bottom and top of the education distribution. The wage fell by 8.9 percent for high school dropouts and by 4.9 percent for college graduates. In contrast, the wage of high school graduates fell by only 2.6 percent, while the wage of workers with some college was barely affected. Overall, the immigrant influx reduced the wage of the average native worker by 3.2 percent.

Table 17.9

Wage Consequences of Immigrant Influx of the 1980s and 1990s (Predicted change in log weekly wage)

Years of experience	High school dropouts	High school graduates	Some college	College graduates	All workers
1-5	-0.065	-0.021	0.004	-0.035	-0.024
6-10	-0.101	-0.027	0.001	-0.042	-0.029
11-15	-0.128	-0.036	-0.009	-0.059	-0.041
16-20	-0.136	-0.033	-0.011	-0.055	-0.039
21-25	-0.108	-0.025	-0.008	-0.049	-0.033
26-30	-0.087	-0.023	0.000	-0.049	-0.029
31-35	-0.066	-0.022	0.001	-0.050	-0.027
36-40	-0.044	-0.013	0.008	-0.056	-0.022
All workers	-0.089	-0.026	-0.003	-0.049	-0.032

Note: The simulation uses the factor price elasticities reported in Table 17.8 to predict the wage effects of the immigrant influx that arrived between 1980 and 2000. The calculations assume that the capital stock is constant. The variable measuring the group-specific immigrant supply shock is defined as the number of immigrants arriving between 1980 and 2000 divided by a baseline population equal to the average size of the native workforce (over 1980–2000) plus the number of immigrants in 1980.

Source: Own calculations.

These predictions assume that the elasticity of substitution between capital and labor equals one. Equations (19)-(21) imply that the adverse wage effects of immigration are larger if there is less substitution between capital and labor than implied by the aggregate Cobb-Douglas specification. For example, the predicted wage effect for each skill group is about one percentage point lower (i.e., more negative) when $\sigma_{KL} = 0.75$, so that the wage of the average native worker would then fall by 4.2 percent.

17.9. Conclusion

The concern over the adverse labor market impact of immigration has always played a central role in the immigration debate. The resurgence of large-scale immigration in recent decades stimulated a great deal of research that attempts to measure these labor market effects. This research effort, based mainly on comparing native employment opportunities across regions, has not been entirely successful. The weak spatial correlations typically estimated in these studies, although often construed as showing that immigrants do not lower native wages, are difficult to interpret. In fact, economic theory implies that the more that firms and workers adjust to the immigrant supply shock, the smaller these cross-region correlations will be – regardless of the true impact of immigration on the national economy.

This chapter introduces a new approach for estimating the labor market impact of immigration. The analysis builds on the assumption that similarly educated workers who have different levels of experience are not perfect substitutes. Defining skill groups in terms of educational attainment and work experience introduces a great deal of variation in the data. In some years, the influx of immigrants with a particular level of schooling mainly affects younger workers; in other years it mainly affects older workers. In contrast to the existing literature, the evidence reported in this chapter consistently indicates that immigration reduces the wage and labor supply of competing native workers, as suggested by the simplest textbook model of a competitive labor market. Moreover, the evidence indicates that spatial correlations conceal around two-thirds of the national impact of immigration on wages.

My estimates of the own factor price elasticity cluster between -0.3 and -0.4. These estimates, combined with the very large immigrant influx in recent decades, imply that immigration has substantially worsened the labor market opportunities faced by many native workers. Between 1980 and 2000, immigration increased the labor supply of working men by 11.0 percent. Even after accounting for the beneficial cross effects of low-skill (high-skill) immigration on the earnings of high-skill (low-skill) workers, my analysis implies that this immigrant influx reduced the wage of the average native worker by 3.2 percent. The wage impact differed dramatically across education groups, with the wage falling by 8.9 percent for high school dropouts, 4.9 percent for college graduates, 2.6 percent for high school graduates, and barely changing for workers with some college.

Although the comparison of workers across narrowly defined skill classifications reveals a sizable adverse effect of immigration on native employment opportunities, it is worth noting that we still do not fully understand *why* the spatial correlation approach fails to find these effects. I suspect that we can learn a great deal more about the labor market impact of immigration by documenting the many adjustments that take place, by workers and firms, both inside and outside the labor market, as immigration alters economic opportunities in many sectors of the economy. For instance, my analysis ignored the long-run capital adjustments induced by immigration, the role played by capital-skill complementarities, and the possibility that high-skill immigration (e.g., scientists and high-tech workers) is an important engine for endogenous technological change.

The adverse wage effects documented in this chapter tell only part of the story of how the U.S. economy responded to the resurgence of large-scale immigration. The interpretation and policy implications of these findings require a more complete documentation and assessment of the many other consequences, including the potential benefits that immigrants impart on a host country.

Appendix A: Variable Definitions

The data are drawn from the 1960, 1970, 1980, 1990 Public Use Microdata Samples of the U.S. Census, and the pooled 1999, 2000, 2001 Annual Demographic Supplement of the Current Population Surveys. In the 1960 and 1970 Censuses, the data extracts form a 1 percent random sample of the population. In 1980 and 1990 the immigrant extracts form a 5 percent random sample, and the native extracts form a 1 percent random sample. The analysis is restricted to men aged 18–64. A person is classified as an immigrant if he was born abroad and is either a noncitizen or a naturalized citizen; all other persons are classified as natives. Sampling weights are used in all calculations involving the 1990 Census and the CPS.

Definition of education and experience. I categorize workers in four education groups: high school dropouts, high school graduates, persons with some college, and college graduates, and use Jaeger's (1997: 304) algorithm for reconciling differences in the coding of the completed education variable across surveys. I assume that high school dropouts enter the labor market at age 17, high school graduates at age 19, persons with some college at age 21, and college graduates at age 23, and define work experience as the worker's age at the time of the survey minus the assumed age of entry into the labor market. I restrict the analysis to persons who have between 1 and 40 years of experience. Throughout much of the chapter, workers are classified into one of eight experience groups. The experience groups are defined in terms of five-year intervals (1–5 years of experience, 6–10, 11–15, 16–20, 21–25, 26–30, 31–35, and 36–40).

Counts of persons in education-experience groups. The counts are calculated in the sample of men who do not reside in group quarters and participate in the civilian labor force (according to the information provided by the labor force status variable for the reference week).

Annual and weekly earnings. These variables are calculated in the sample of men who do not reside in group quarters, are employed in the civilian labor force, are not enrolled in school, report positive annual earnings, weeks worked, and weekly hours, and are not self-employed (as determined by the class of worker variable). In the 1960, 1970, and 1980 Censuses, the top coded annual salary is multiplied by 1.5. In the 1960 and 1970 Censuses, weeks worked in the calendar year prior to the survey are reported as a categorical variable. I impute weeks worked for each worker as follows: 6.5 weeks for 13 weeks or less, 20 for 14–26 weeks, 33 for 27–39 weeks, 43.5 for 40–47 weeks, 48.5 for 48–49 weeks, and 51 for 50–52 weeks. The average log annual earnings or average log weekly earnings for a particular education-experience cell is defined as the mean of log annual eantings or log weekly earnings over all workers in the relevant population.

Fraction of time worked. This variable is calculated in the sample of men who do not reside in group quarters, are not enrolled in school, and are not in the military (as indicated by the labor force status variable for the reference week). The fraction of time worked for each person is defined as the ratio of weeks worked (including zeros) to 52. The group mean used in the analysis is the mean of this variable over the relevant population, which includes persons with zero hours worked.

Appendix B

Percent of Male Labor Force That Is Foreign Born, by Education and Experience, 1960–2000

Education	Years of experience	1960	1970	1980	1990	2000
High school dropouts	1-5	2.6	3.9	8.5	18.4	20.8
	6-10	3.6	5.4	13.9	29.7	44.9
	11-15	3.6	6.2	15.8	28.1	49.8
	16-20	4.3	6.7	13.5	28.9	50.0
	21-25	4.4	6.0	12.5	28.5	40.5
	26-30	5.2	5.5	11.2	21.4	40.0
	31-35	8.0	5.4	8.8	17.7	37.1
	36-40	12.3	5.8	7.9	15.3	28.4
High school graduates	1-5	1.2	2.1	3.2	8.0	12.3
	6-10	1.6	2.4	3.8	7.8	14.0
	11-15	2.0	3.1	4.6	6.9	14.5
	16-20	3.1	3.0	4.3	7.3	11.5
	21-25	3.0	3.2	4.8	7.6	9.4
	26-30	4.8	4.0	4.8	6.8	9.5
	31-35	7.3	3.4	4.7	6.5	10.8
	36-40	13.0	5.3	5.2	6.6	9.7
Some college	1-5	2.3	3.5	5.2	7.9	9.1
	6-10	3.3	4.2	5.1	8.3	10.8
	11-15	3.7	4.9	5.6	7.4	11.6
	16-20	4.6	4.8	6.1	6.4	9.3
	21-25	4.9	4.5	6.3	6.6	7.6
	26-30	5.5	4.7	5.8	7.0	5.7
	31-35	9.6	4.7	6.1	7.2	6.3
	36-40	10.7	6.5	6.3	6.9	6.0
College graduates	1-5	3.4	4.1	5.0	9.0	12.4
	6-10	4.3	7.2	6.9	10.8	15.4
	11-15	4.8	6.5	8.5	10.3	17.5
	16-20	5.0	5.8	10.5	9.5	14.6
	21-25	6.4	5.6	8.5	10.2	11.5
	26-30	7.8	5.7	7.6	11.6	10.8
	31-35	10.0	6.9	7.2	9.6	12.4
	36-40	12.5	9.0	7.2	9.1	14.5

Source: 1960, 1970, 1980, and 1990 Public Use Microdata Samples (PUMS) of the Decennial Census and the 1999, 2000, and 2001 Annual Demographic Supplement of the Current Population Surveys (CPS).

18

Does Immigration Grease the Wheels of the Labor Market?

As mentioned in the preface to Chapter 16, I have been keenly interested in isolating and documenting mechanisms through which receiving countries benefit from immigration. One lesson from my 1995 paper in the Journal of Economic Perspectives was that the competitive labor market model implied very modest net gains for a country like the United States. Since then I have been searching for alternative sources of gains that the standard textbook model of the labor market might miss. This paper represents one of my efforts in this search.

It is obvious that if migration costs were mostly fixed costs, income-maximizing behavior would lead the self-selected sample of immigrants to settle in those localities where they face the best economic opportunities. The native workforce faces similar costs of migration, but those costs would discourage many natives from moving, and hence native labor mobility would not fully arbitrage wage differences across localities. Since income-maximizing immigrants will settle in those regions that offer the highest wages, they can play a central role in arbitraging geographic wage differences, generating further gains for the receiving country in the process.

My simulation of simple models of this process suggested that these gains were not likely to be numerically large. Nevertheless, the approach may

The original version of this chapter was published as: Borjas, G.J. (2001). Does Immigration Grease the Wheels of the Labor Market?, in: Brookings Papers on Economic Activity, 32(1): 69–134. © 2001 by The Brookings Institution. The author is grateful to Donald Davis, Richard Freeman, Edward Glaeser, Daniel Hamermesh, Lawrence Katz, Dani Rodrik, Mark Rosenzweig, Robert Shimer, Robert Topel, Steven Trejo, and Andrew Weiss for helpful comments, and to the Smith Richardson Foundation and the National Science Foundation for research support.

*have more important implications in labor markets or time periods when
the native population is relatively non-mobile.*

George J. Borjas (2015)

Most studies of the economic impact of immigration are motivated
by the desire to understand how immigrants affect various dimensions of economic status in the population of the host country. This
motivation explains the persistent interest in determining whether
immigrants "take jobs away" from native workers, as well as the attention paid to measuring the fiscal impact that immigration inevitably
has on host countries that offer generous welfare benefits.[1]

For the most part, the existing literature overlooks the factor that
places immigration issues and the study of labor mobility in general at the core of modern labor economics. The analysis of labor
flows, whether within or across countries, is a central ingredient in
any discussion of labor market equilibrium. Presumably, workers
respond to regional differences in economic opportunities by voting with their feet, and these labor flows improve labor market efficiency.

In this chapter I emphasize this different perspective to analyzing
the economic impact of immigration: immigration as grease on the
wheels of the labor market. Labor market efficiency requires that the
value of the marginal product of workers be equalized across labor
markets, such as U.S. metropolitan areas, states, or regions. Although
workers in the United States are quite mobile, particularly when compared with workers in other countries, this mobility is insufficient to
eliminate geographic wage differentials quickly. The available evidence suggests that it takes around 30 years for the equilibrating flows
to cut interstate income differentials by half.[2]

I argue that immigration greases the wheels of the labor market
by injecting into the economy a group of persons who are very responsive to regional differences in economic opportunities.[3] My
empirical analysis uses data drawn from the 1950–90 U.S. Censuses
to analyze the link between interstate wage differences for a particular skill group and the geographic sorting of immigrant and native
workers in the United States. The evidence shows that interstate dispersion of economic opportunities generates substantial behavioral
differences in the location decisions of immigrant and native workers. New immigrant arrivals are much more likely to be clustered
in those states that offer the highest wages for the types of skills

486

that they have to offer. In other words, new immigrants make up a disproportionately large fraction of the "marginal" workers who chase better economic opportunities and help equalize opportunities across areas. The data also suggest that wage convergence across geographic regions is faster during high-immigration periods. As a result, immigrant flows into the United States may play an important role in improving labor market efficiency.

The chapter presents a simple theoretical framework for calculating this efficiency gain from immigration. Simulation of this model suggests that the efficiency gain accruing to natives in the United States – between $5 billion and $10 billion annually – is small relative to the overall economy, but not relative to earlier estimates of the gains from immigration (which are typically below $10 billion). It seems, therefore, that the measurable benefits from immigration are significantly magnified when estimated in the context of an economy with regional differences in marginal product, rather than in the context of a one-region aggregate labor market.

18.1. Framework

The intuition underlying the hypothesis developed in this chapter is easy to explain.[4] There exist sizable wage differences across regions or states in the United States, even for workers with particular skills looking for similar jobs.[5] Persons born and living in the United States often find it difficult (that is, expensive) to move from one state to another. Suppose that migration costs are, for the most part, fixed costs, and that these are relatively high. The existing wage differentials across states may then fail to motivate large numbers of native workers to move, because the migration costs swamp the interstate differences in income opportunities. As a result, native internal migration will not arbitrage interstate wage differentials away.

In contrast, newly arrived immigrants in the United States are a self-selected sample of persons who have chosen to bear the fixed cost of the geographic move. Suppose that once this fixed cost is incurred, it costs little more to choose one state as the destination over another. Income-maximizing immigrants will obviously choose the destination that offers the best income opportunities. Newly arrived immigrants will then tend to live in the "right" states, in the sense that they are clustered in the states that offer them the highest wages.

In short, the location decisions of immigrant workers should be much more responsive to interstate wage differentials than those of natives. As a result, immigrants may play a crucial – and neglected – role in a host country's labor market: they are "marginal" workers whose location decisions arbitrage wage differences across regions. The immigrant population may therefore play a disproportionate role in helping the national labor market attain an efficient allocation of resources.

18.1.1. The Location Decisions of Native Workers and Immigrants

This hypothesis can be formalized as follows. Consider initially the interstate migration decision faced by workers born in the United States. Let w_{jk} be the wage paid in state j to a native worker with skills k (for example, a worker with a high school diploma). The worker currently lives in state b. The sign of the index function determines the worker's internal migration decision:

$$(1) \qquad I = \max_j \left\{ w_{jk} \right\} - w_{bk} - C,$$

where C gives the migration costs. Although these include both variable and fixed costs, I assume that they are mostly fixed. Perhaps the most important fixed cost is the disutility suffered by the migrant who leaves family and friends behind and begins life in a new and uncertain environment. The native worker migrates if $I > 0$.[6]

What does the index function in Equation (1) imply about the equilibrium sorting of native workers across states? Suppose that the fixed costs of moving are very high, so that the wage gap between the current state of residence and the state offering the highest wage cannot cover the migration costs. In this extreme case, the geographic distribution of native workers is determined solely by the random allocation that occurs at birth and has little to do with interstate differences in economic opportunities. Because native workers do not respond to interstate wage differentials, these differences will persist (in the absence of other equilibrating flows).

Of course, native workers do in fact move from state to state. Some natives will find that the wage differential between the highest-paying state and the current state of residence is sufficient to cover the fixed migration costs. But many others will find that these migration costs act as a wedge, preventing them from taking full advantage of interstate differences in economic opportunities. As a result, the native working population will not be sorted efficiently, and many native workers end up living in states where their marginal product is not maximized.

Capital flows across localities could help to equilibrate the national economy. In the short run, however, moving physical capital – whether plant or equipment – across localities is expensive. As a result, the adjustment of capital stocks will depend largely on new investment, a process that is gradual and can take many years. In what follows I simplify the exposition by assuming that the capital stock is fixed.

Immigrants are born in country 0 and are income maximizers. Their index function is

$$(2) \qquad I = \max_j \left\{ w_{jk} \right\} - w_{0k} - C.$$

Since the wage differential between the United States and many other countries far exceeds the differences that exist between regions in the United States, it is likely that many residents of other countries will find it optimal to move to the United States.[7] More important, the self-selected sample of foreign-born workers observed in survey data collected in the United States is composed of persons for whom the index I defined in Equation (2) is positive. Suppose then that a particular immigrant worker chooses to live in state ℓ. For immigrants in the United States, this residential choice *must* satisfy the condition

$$(3) \qquad w_{\ell k} = \max_j \left\{ w_{jk} \right\}.$$

Put differently, immigrants in the United States will reside in the state that pays the highest wage for the skills they possess. Note that the condition in Equation (3) holds regardless of the level of fixed costs, the magnitude of interstate dispersion in wages, or the size of the wage differential between the United States and the source country. Relatively high fixed costs (or a relatively high wage in the source country) simply imply that there will be fewer immigrants. But the sample of foreign-born workers who choose to move will still end up in the right state.

This hypothesis has a number of interesting implications. First, because many native workers are "stuck" in the state where they were born, and immigrant workers are clustered in the states that offer the best economic opportunities, immigrants and natives will be observed living in different states. Moreover, different types of immigrants – depending on their skills – will also be living in different states. In short, the labor supply of immigrant workers to a particular regional labor market should exhibit greater sensitivity to interstate wage differentials than the labor supply of natives.

Second, the group of immigrants whose location decisions are most responsive to regional differences in economic opportunities should be the sample of newly arrived immigrants. Over time, economic opportunities will probably change differently in different states, and the sample of new immigrants will become like the sample of natives in one very specific way: they all get trapped in the state where they reside. As a result, earlier immigrant waves should be found living in different states than the newest immigrants.

Third, the insight that the location decisions of a particular group of workers – recent movers – are most sensitive to interstate wage differences is not specific to immigrants. It applies to *any* group of movers, whether foreign born or native born. As a result, the location decisions of the self-selected sample of native workers who have chosen to move across states should also be quite sensitive to interstate wage differentials.

Finally, the clustering effect implicit in Equation (3) has important implications for studies of labor market equilibrium and for estimates of the benefits from immigration. Native migration flows, perhaps because of relatively high fixed migration costs, cannot fully arbitrage away the regional wage differences. The immigrant flow, in contrast, is self-targeted to those regions of the country where their productivity is highest. As I will show shortly, this clustering effect greases the wheels of the labor market, by speeding up the process of wage convergence, and improves economic efficiency. It is important to emphasize that these gains from immigration differ conceptually from the productivity gains typically stressed in the literature.[8] The productivity gains arise because immigrants and natives complement each other in the production process, and estimates of these gains explicitly assume that the national labor market is in a "single-wage" equilibrium.

Obviously, these strong theoretical implications follow from a framework that uses very restrictive assumptions. In particular, I ignore the many factors other than wage differentials that determine the location decisions of both immigrants and natives. For example, the resurgence of immigrant flows into the United States since 1965 has led to the creation of large ethnic enclaves in many American cities, but in the context of this model it is unclear that these ethnic enclaves arise exogenously. For instance, the first immigrant arriving in the United States from country n may have chosen to live in region j because that region maximized his or her income opportunities.[9] If most workers in a particular national origin group have roughly similar skills, it would not be too surprising if most new immigrants from that source country also settle in region j. But the ethnic networks that link immigrants in the United States with their source countries also help transmit valuable information about income opportunities to potential migrants. These information flows reduce the costs of migration to specific regions for particular ethnic groups and could lead to a different geographic sorting than that predicted by the income maximization model with fixed migration costs. Any empirical analysis of the magnetic effects generated by interstate differences in labor market opportunities, therefore, must incorporate relevant information about these ethnic networks.

18.1.2. *Welfare Implications*

Why does the greater sensitivity of immigrants than natives to regional wage differentials generate economic gains? How large are those gains? And do they accrue to immigrants or to the native population?

Before addressing these questions, it is instructive to review how the benefits from immigration arise in the traditional, one-sector model. Suppose the production technology in the host country can be described by a linear homogeneous aggregate production function with two inputs, capital and labor (L), the price of the output being the numéraire. Suppose further that all workers, whether native or foreign born, are perfect substitutes in production. Finally, assume that natives own the entire capital stock in the host country and that the supply of all factors of production is perfectly inelastic.

In a competitive equilibrium, the price of each factor equals its marginal product. Figure 18.1 illustrates the initial pre-immigration equilibrium, with N native workers employed at a wage of w. Because the supply of capital is fixed, the area under the curve representing the marginal product of labor (f_L) gives the economy's total output. National income, all of it accruing to natives, is then given by the trapezoid $ABN0$.

Figure 18.1

Immigration Surplus in a Single-Region Economy with Homogeneous Labor and Fixed Capital

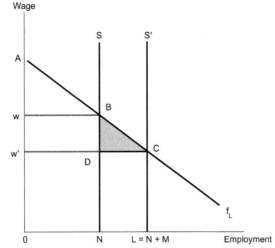

Source: Author's model as described in the text.

The entry of M immigrants shifts the supply curve to S' and lowers the market wage to w'. The area in the trapezoid ACL0 now gives national income. Part of the increase in national income is distributed directly to immigrants (who get $w'M$ in labor earnings). The area in the triangle BCD is the increase in national income that accrues to natives, or the "immigration surplus." Note that the immigration surplus arises because natives own all of the capital, and the additional labor raises the return to this fixed capital stock. The immigration surplus, as a fraction of GDP, is[10]

(4)
$$\text{surplus} = \tfrac{1}{2}\, s\delta m^2,$$

where s is labor's share of national income, δ is the absolute value of the factor price elasticity (or $-d \ln w / d \ln L$), and m is the fraction of the workforce that is foreign born. To illustrate, suppose that labor's share of income is 0.7, that the factor price elasticity is 0.3 (so that a 10 percent increase in labor supply lowers wages by 3 percent), and that immigrants make up 10 percent of the workforce (as in the United States today). Equation (4) then implies that the immigration surplus is on the order of 0.1 percent of GDP, or roughly $10 billion annually.

Now consider the nature of the gains from immigration in a multi-region economy where there are wage differences across regions in the initial equilibrium.[11] Suppose the United States has two regions and that the *same* linear marginal product schedule, f_L, gives the labor demand curve in each. The total (and fixed) number of natives in the economy is N, with a fraction λ of the natives living in region 1. For concreteness, assume that $\lambda < 0.5$. Further suppose that labor is supplied inelastically in each region, with supply curves S_1 and S_2, respectively. As before, natives own the entire capital stock, which is fixed within each region. Figure 18.2 illustrates the initial equilibrium. The supply imbalance between the two regions implies that w_1, the wage in region 1, exceeds w_2, the wage in region 2.

Since capital is fixed in each region, one can write the quadratic production function in region j ($j = 1, 2$) as

$$(5) \qquad Q_j = \alpha L_j - \beta L_j^2,$$

Figure 18.2

Total Gain from Complete Immigration in a Two-Region Economy[a]

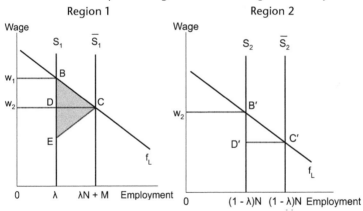

Note: [a] Assumes homogeneous labor and fixed capital. Under complete
          immigration, exactly enough immigrants enter region 1 to equalize wages
          between the two regions.
Source: Author's model as described in text.

where L_j gives the number of workers in region j, and $\beta > 0$. This quadratic production function generates the linear marginal product curves in Figure 18.2. The initial wage of workers in region 1 equals w_1

$= \alpha - 2\beta\lambda N$, and the wage in region 2 is $w_2 = \alpha - 2\beta(1 - \lambda)N$. These wages are assumed to be positive over the relevant range of employment. I assume initially that natives are immobile, so that the regional wage differential is not arbitraged away by internal migration.

Suppose the United States decides to admit M immigrants. It is useful to write M in terms of the number and geographic distribution of natives in the labor markets. In particular, the difference in the number of natives residing in the two regions is $N_2 - N_1 = (1 - 2\lambda)N$. The number of immigrants can then be written as

(6) $$M = k(1 - 2\lambda)N.$$

The parameter $k = 1$ when the number of immigrants exactly equals the supply imbalance between the two regions. If all of these immigrants were to enter region 1 (as income-maximizing behavior on the part of immigrants would imply), immigration would completely equalize wages between the two regions. In terms of Figure 18.2, this case of "complete immigration" would shift the supply curve in region 1 to $\overline{S}_1$, and the single wage in the national economy would be w_2. For simplicity, I will assume that $0 \le k \le 1$ throughout the analysis.

Let θ be the fraction of immigrants who choose to live in region 1. The total number of workers in each region can then be written as

(7) $$L_1 = \lambda N + k\theta(1 - 2\lambda)N$$

(8) $$L_2 = (1 - \lambda)N + k(1 - \theta)(1 - 2\lambda)N,$$

and GDP in this two-region economy with immobile native workers is given by

(9) $$Q = \alpha\big[N + k(1 - 2\lambda)N\big] - \beta\big[\lambda N + k\theta(1 - 2\lambda)N\big]^2 - \beta\big[(1 - \lambda)N + k(1 - \theta)(1 - 2\lambda)N\big]^2.$$

The parameter θ equals 1 when the geographic sorting of immigrants in the United States is the sorting that maximizes immigrant income. Not surprisingly, this type of immigrant behavior also maximizes GDP for the *entire* U.S. population (which now includes both natives and immigrants). Put differently, Q is maximized at $\theta = 1$ for a given volume of immigration. Figure 18.2 illustrates the nature of this result for the special case where $k = 1$. The increase in GDP to the entire country if all immigrants were to migrate to region 1 equals the area under the demand curve between points B and C. In contrast, the increase in GDP if all immigrants were to migrate to region 2 equals only the area under the demand curve between the points B' and C'. Comparing these two polar cases makes it clear that the net increase in GDP attributable to optimizing behavior on the part of immigrants is given by the shaded triangle BCE.

In an important sense, this result summarizes the economic content of the statement that immigration greases the wheels of the labor market: income-maximizing behavior leads to a more efficient allocation of resources and maximizes GDP per capita in the host country. This type of immigrant behavior speeds up the process of adjustment to long-run equilibrium, and the larger national output may impart benefits to some sectors of the economy. In the absence of any redistribution mechanism, however, it turns out that the immigrants get to keep much of the increase in GDP that can be attributed to their locating in the high-wage region. As a result, it is important to examine to what extent natives benefit from the fact that income-maximizing immigrants cluster in high-wage regions and thereby improve market efficiency. Consider again the case where natives are immobile. The income accruing to natives is then given by

(10) $$Q_N = Q - w_1 M_1 - w_2 M_2.$$

The maximization of Equation (10) with respect to θ indicates that the relation between Q_N and θ is U-shaped. In fact, the value of Q_N is the same at the two polar extremes of $\theta = 0$ and $\theta = 1$, and the income accruing to natives is minimized when $\theta = 0.5$, regardless of the value of k. Put differently, natives gain the most when immigrants cluster in one region, regardless of where they cluster, and natives gain the least when immigrants allocate themselves randomly across regions.

Figure 18.2 also illustrates the intuition behind this result for the special case where $k = 1$. Suppose that all immigrants cluster in the high-wage region ($\theta = 1$). The net gain to natives is then given by the triangle BCD. In contrast, suppose that all of the immigrants end up in the low-wage region ($\theta = 0$). The net gain to natives then equals the triangle $B'C'D'$, which is obviously equal in area to triangle BCD. The assumption of identical and linear demand curves in the two regions effectively builds in the result that the net gain to natives is the same whenever there is complete clustering, regardless of where immigrants cluster.[12]

This conclusion also depends crucially on the assumption that the native workforce is immobile. It is easy to show that natives benefit more when immigrants cluster in high-wage regions as long as natives can move across regions and it is costly to make that internal move. After all, the initial regional wage gap would have eventually motivated some native workers to move across regions. The clustering of income-maximizing immigrants in the high-wage region reduces the number of natives who need to engage in internal migration and hence reduces the migration costs that natives have to incur.

To illustrate this point in a simple framework, suppose that immigrants enter the country first, and that natives then base their internal migration decisions on the post-immigration regional wage gap. Suppose further that, although costly, the internal migration of natives is instantaneous and complete, in the sense that all natives who need to move to equalize wages across regions do so immediately. The number of natives who need to move across regions is then given by

$$(11) \qquad R = \frac{L_2 - L_1}{2} = \frac{\left[(1 - 2\lambda)\,1 + k\,(1 - 2\theta)\right]N}{2}.$$

Define the "net" income accruing to natives as

$$(12) \qquad Q_N = Q - wM_1 - wM_2 - C(R),$$

where $w = w_1 = w_2$, and $C(R)$ gives the migration costs associated with R native workers moving across regions, with $C'(R) > 0$. Because natives "fill in" to arbitrage the regional wage gap regardless of where immigrants choose to cluster, it should be evident that the quantity $Q - wM_1 - wM_2$ in Equation (12) is independent of θ. In the end, half of the labor force end up in region 1 and half in region 2, and wages are equalized. The relationship between Q_N and θ, therefore, depends entirely on how the geographic sorting of immigrants affects migration costs. Inspection of Equations (11) and (12) shows that the larger the fraction of immigrants who cluster in the high-wage region (that is, the greater is θ), the fewer natives need to move across regions, the lower is the level of migration costs, and the larger is the net income that accrues to the native population.[13]

In fact, the increase in migration costs that natives must incur if immigrants are to cluster in the low-wage region can be substantial and may well swamp any benefits resulting from the clustering effect. Let R_0 be the number of natives who would have to move to equate wages if all immigrants clustered in the low-wage region ($\theta = 0$), and let R_1 be the number of natives who would have to move if all immigrants clustered in the high-wage region ($\theta = 1$). Equation (11) then implies that

$$(13) \qquad \frac{R_0}{R_1} = \frac{1 + k}{1 - k}.$$

The implications of Equation (13) are easily grasped with a numerical example. Suppose $k = 0.5$, so that half as many immigrants enter the country as complete immigration would require. The ratio in Equation (13) then equals 3. In other words, native migration is three times as large when immigrants cluster in the low-wage region as when they cluster in the high-wage region. The additional migration costs, therefore, could easily outweigh the benefits that immigrants impart to natives when they cluster in the low-wage region.[14]

In sum, the endogenous clustering of immigrants in the high-wage region is optimal in two different ways: it increases total national income, *and* it maximizes the income that accrues to natives net of migration costs. By moving the economy from an initial equilibrium with a regional wage gap to a new equilibrium with either a single national wage (in the case of complete immigration) or a smaller regional wage gap, immigrants generate two distinct types of benefits for natives.[15] First, they raise national income through the traditional immigration surplus: because the capital stock is fixed, immigrants increase the profits of native capitalists by more than they lower the earnings of native workers. Second, they help narrow the gap between marginal products in the two regions, maximize the increase in GDP that accrues to natives, *and* reduce the volume of migration costs that natives would have had to incur. It is this second type of gain that results from the fact that immigration greases the wheels of the labor market.

In a multiregion framework *and* for a given volume of immigration, it seems sensible to define the gains that accrue to natives from the geographic sorting of immigrants in another way. How much do natives benefit from the income-maximizing behavior of immigrants relative to how much they would have benefited if the immigrants had chosen locations in some other way? Obviously, this operational definition of the gain is inherently ambiguous, because one must first define the nonoptimal behavior that might determine the geographic distribution of immigrants. Throughout the analysis, I define the baseline as the income that would have accrued to natives if immigrants had simply replicated the geographic sorting of the native population. In other words, suppose that a fraction λ of the immigrants choose to live in region 1. The gain that accrues to natives is then given by

$$(14) \qquad\qquad \Delta_N = Q_N|_{\theta=1} - Q_N|_{\theta=\lambda}.$$

The variable Δ_N includes two distinct types of benefits. First, an immobile native population gains as immigrants cluster rather than replicate the regional distribution of the native population. In the simple framework presented in this section, the benefits that arise from immigrant clustering are the same regardless of whether immigrants cluster in the high-wage or the low-wage region.[16] However, the fact that natives eventually move in response to interregional wage differences – together with the fact that these moves are costly – implies that Δ_N captures an additional benefit: the reduced costs of internal migration. In the remainder of the chapter I will refer to the sum of the two types of benefits captured by the variable Δ_N as the *efficiency gain* from immigration. The efficiency gain thus measures how much natives gain from a fixed volume of immigration simply because immigrants choose to settle in high-wage regions.

It is worth stressing that the choice of a baseline in Equation (14) plays a crucial role in any calculation of the efficiency gain. The arbitrary nature of this choice, however, does not alter an important implication of the analysis: without *any* intervention on the part of the native population, immigration by income-maximizing persons not only maximizes national income but also maximizes the efficiency gain, the additional net income that accrues to the native population.

Figure 18.3 illustrates the nature of the efficiency gain defined in Equation (14). For simplicity, I show the labor market conditions in region 1 only, and I ignore the savings in migration costs. Initially, the labor market is in equilibrium with wages w_1 and w_2. As drawn, $\lambda = 0.25$, so that one-quarter of the natives live in region 1 and the rest in region 2 (with supply curves S_1 and S_2, respectively). Suppose there is complete immigration and that all immigrants locate in the high-wage region ($k = 1$ and $\theta = 1$). The economy is now in a single-wage equilibrium, and natives gain by the size of the triangle formed by the union of areas a, b, and c.

Figure 18.3

Gains Accruing to Natives under Optimal and Nonoptimal Sorting[a]

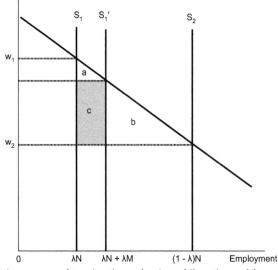

Note: [a] Assumes complete migration and an immobile native workforce.
Source: Author's model as described in text.

Suppose instead that immigrants did not behave optimally in making their location decisions, and suppose further that $\theta = 0.25$, so that immigrants replicate the geographic sorting of the native population. This sorting of immigrants shifts the supply curve in region 1 to S'_1. The immigrants who locate in the high-wage region generate a gain of triangular area a for natives, whereas those who locate in the low-wage region generate a gain of area b for natives. It is evident that the optimal sorting increases native income over that with the nonoptimal sorting by the rectangular area c. This rectangle is the gain accruing to natives, for a given volume of immigration, over and above that from a sorting that simply replicates the geographic sorting of the native population.[17]

Note that the theoretical framework presented in this section makes extensive use of the assumption that the two regions of the economy have the same labor demand curve. The theoretical implications are less straightforward when the two regions have different demand curves, as could result from underlying differences in the (fixed) endowment of physical capital. It is still the case, of course, that total GDP increases most when immigrants cluster in the high-wage region. Abstracting from the savings in migration costs, however, natives now have the most to gain when immigrants cluster in the region with the more inelastic demand curve.[18] After all, for a fixed number of immigrants, the size of the triangle that accrues to natives is larger when the demand curve is steeper. The region with the more inelastic demand is not necessarily the region with higher wages. However, it should be clear that the bunching of immigrants in the "wrong" region – from the perspective of total economic efficiency – would lead, in the long run, to more native migration and increase migration costs for the native population. It might also greatly reduce any gains arising from immigrants pursuing a location strategy that does not maximize their income.

Finally, the one-period framework summarized in this section shows that the interaction among immigrants clustering in high-wage regions, the regional wage structure, and native internal migration can increase the income accruing to the native population. A more complete description of this interaction requires embedding the income-maximizing behavior of immigrants in a multiperiod model of native internal migration, one that allows for natives to adjust slowly to the presence of regional wage differences. This dynamic model is presented in what follows and used to provide a back-of-the-envelope calculation of the efficiency gain.

18.2. Data

I examine the link between interstate wage differentials and the location decisions of immigrants and natives using data from the 1960–90 Public Use Microdata Samples of the decennial census. The sample extracts used in the analysis include all civilian workers aged 18 to 59 who do not live in group quarters. The immigrant extracts form a 5 percent random sample of the population in 1980 and 1990, and a 1 percent random sample in 1960 and 1970. The native extracts form a 1 percent random sample in all years. I define a worker to be an immigrant if he or she was born abroad and is either a noncitizen or a naturalized citizen; all other persons are classified as natives.

I begin the empirical analysis by constructing a log wage index to measure the relative wage of a skill group in a particular state at a particular time. Five skill groups are defined in terms of educational attainment: less than nine years of schooling, nine to 11 years of schooling, 12 years of schooling (high school graduates), 13–15 years of schooling, and at least 16 years of schooling (college graduates).[19] The wage index is calculated as follows. Let $w_{ijk}(t)$ be the wage of worker i, residing in state j, belonging to skill group k, in census year t. I then used the sample of *native* workers to estimate the following regression model separately in each census for the years 1960, 1970, and 1980:[20]

$$(15) \qquad \ln w_{ijk}(t) = X_{ijk}(t)\beta(t) + v_{jk}(t) + u_{ijk}(t),$$

where $X_{ijk}(t)$ gives a vector of socioeconomic characteristics indicating the worker's sex and age (defined as a vector of dummy variables indicating whether the worker is aged 18–24, 25–34, 35–44, 45–54, or 55–64); $v_{jk}(t)$ gives a vector of fixed effects for state-education groups (j, k) at time t; and $u_{ijk(t)}$ is the error term, assumed uncorrelated with all the independent variables in the model. The dependent variable and all the variables in vector X are normalized to have a mean of zero in each census. The log wage index $v_{jk}(t)$ can then be interpreted as the (adjusted) wage differential, in percent, between the wage in state-education group (j, k) and the mean wage in the United States at time t. Note that the log wage index does not adjust for cost-of-living differences across states. The empirical analysis reported here will control for these differences by including a vector of state fixed effects in second-stage regression models.

Figure 18.4 illustrates the interstate variation in the log wage index revealed by the 1960 and 1980 Census data for selected education groups. Not surprisingly, there is a great deal of dispersion in adjusted wages across states, so that different states offer different opportunities to similarly skilled workers.[21] Consider, for instance, the wage opportunities available to a college graduate in 1980. If he or she chose to live in Wyoming, the state at the 20th percentile (so that ten states offered lower wages), the log wage index took on a value of 0.18. If that college graduate chose instead to live in Nevada, the state at the 80th percentile, the log wage index took on a value of 0.35. In other words, interstate wage differentials are sizable even when we ignore the ten states at each end of the wage distribution.

Figure 18.4

Interstate Dispersion in Adjusted Wages, by Educational Attainment, 1960 and 1980[a]

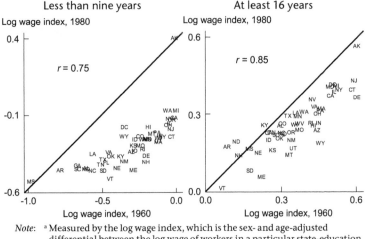

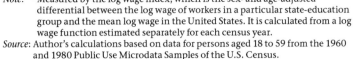

Note: [a] Measured by the log wage index, which is the sex- and age-adjusted differential between the log wage of workers in a particular state-education group and the mean log wage in the United States. It is calculated from a log wage function estimated separately for each census year.

Source: Author's calculations based on data for persons aged 18 to 59 from the 1960 and 1980 Public Use Microdata Samples of the U.S. Census.

Although high-wage states tend to offer high wages to all workers regardless of educational attainment, this correlation is far from perfect. In 1980 the correlation between the log wage index of workers with less than nine years of schooling and that of college graduates was only 0.72.[22] To illustrate how the same state may offer relatively different opportunities to different types of workers, consider the log wage indices for New York and California. Both are high-wage states, but New York's wage advantage is particularly pronounced for highly educated workers. In 1980 16 states paid higher wages than New York to workers with less than nine years of schooling, but only five states paid higher wages to college graduates. In contrast, California's wage offer to workers with less than nine years of schooling was the fourth highest in the nation, but its wage offer to college graduates was only the ninth highest.

Finally, Figure 18.4 shows that the relative wages that states offer to workers with particular skills change over time. The correlations between the 1960 and the 1980 log wage indices range from 0.75 to 0.92, depending on the education group. As a result, workers in a given education group might wish to live in different states at different times.

For instance, Washington, D.C., offered the eighth-highest wage to college graduates in 1960. By 1980, however, the District's offer to college graduates had risen to become the third highest in the nation. There are, therefore, substantial wage differences across states for particular skill groups. This chapter argues that immigrants should be particularly responsive to these differences. This hypothesis, however, would seem to contradict a well-known stylized fact: immigrants have clustered and continue to cluster in a relatively few states. In 1990, 74 percent of newly arrived immigrants (those who had been in the country for less than five years) lived in one of the six main immigrant-receiving states: in descending order these are California, New York, Florida, Texas, New Jersey, and Illinois. In contrast, only 36 percent of natives lived in those states.

Table 18.1

Newly Arrived Immigrant Population in the Six Largest Immigrant-Receiving States, by Educational Attainment, 1970 and 1990

State	Less than nine years		Nine to eleven years		Twelve years		Thirteen to fifteen years		At least sixteen years	
	1970	1990	1970	1990	1970	1990	1970	1990	1970	1990
	Percent of new immigrants[a]									
California	22.0	50.1	22.3	41.9	21.4	32.7	25.7	33.2	17.8	26.5
New York	23.4	9.2	24.6	14.8	24.4	18.6	19.8	14.1	19.1	14.9
Florida	9.1	5.6	6.7	8.1	6.7	8.1	5.8	7.8	3.2	5.0
Texas	5.2	10.1	2.6	7.2	3.2	5.1	2.6	5.4	3.9	5.2
New Jersey	8.9	2.9	7.3	4.1	6.8	5.8	3.7	4.7	4.7	6.3
Illinois	7.0	4.4	5.3	3.9	5.6	5.0	6.3	4.3	7.7	4.7
	Percent of new immigrants relative to percent of natives (ratio)									
California	4.1	9.4	2.7	4.9	2.2	4.4	1.7	2.6	1.5	2.2
New York	3.3	1.7	2.8	2.3	2.9	2.9	2.4	2.3	1.9	1.8
Florida	2.9	1.3	2.1	1.6	2.3	1.8	1.9	1.6	1.1	1.2
Texas	0.8	1.2	0.4	1.0	0.7	0.9	0.4	0.8	0.7	0.8
New Jersey	2.9	1.3	2.1	1.5	1.9	1.9	1.2	1.7	1.2	1.6
Illinois	1.4	1.2	1.0	1.0	1.0	1.1	1.1	0.9	1.4	1.0

Note: [a] New immigrants have been in the United States less than five years.
Source: Author's calculations based on data for persons aged 18 to 59 from the 1970 and 1990 Public Use Microdata Samples of the U.S. Census.

Although this clustering might raise serious doubts about the validity of my argument, it is simply not true that all immigrants cluster in the same states. It turns out that different types of immigrants tend to live in different states, and that the nature of the clustering has changed over time. Table 18.1 describes the geographic distribution of newly arrived immigrants. In 1990 half of all new immigrants with less than nine years of schooling lived in California, compared with only a quarter of those with a college education. In contrast, 9.2 percent of immigrants with less than nine years of schooling, and 14.9 percent of immigrants who were college graduates, lived in New York. Overall, the data reveal that although fewer than 20 percent of immigrants who were high school dropouts lived outside the six main immigrant-receiving states, almost 40 percent of immigrants with a college degree did so.

Moreover, the differences in the geographic sorting of immigrants cannot be fully accounted for by the job structures offered by the various states. As the bottom panel of Table 18.1 shows, the ratio of the percentage of immigrants with less than nine years of schooling who live in California to the percentage of similarly skilled natives who live there rose from 4.1 percent to 9.4 percent between 1970 and 1990. In contrast, the same ratio for college graduates rose only from 1.5 to 2.2 during that period. In sum, the stylized fact that most immigrants move to the same states misses an important part of the story: there is a great deal of dispersion in the residential choices made by different types of immigrants.

The theory advanced by this chapter suggests that the relative supplies of immigrants and natives to various states will depend on interstate wage differentials. As noted earlier, I calculated the log wage indices in census year t (where $t = 1960, 1970, 1980$). I now calculate the measures of relative supplies by analyzing the location decisions of immigrants who arrived *soon after* the year in which the log wage index is calculated. Let $M_{jk}(t^*)$ be the number of immigrants who arrived "soon after" time t, reside in state j, and belong to skill group k, and let $M_k(t^*)$ be the total number of new immigrants who belong to that skill group. The group of newly arrived immigrants is composed of persons who entered the United States in the five-year period after the log wage index is measured, so that $t^* = t + 5$. The variables $N_{jk}(t^*)$ and $N_{k(t^*)}$ give the corresponding numbers of native workers in the state-education groups at that particular time. I then define the index of relative supply for the state-education group (j, k) at time t^* as[23]

$$(16) \qquad Z_{jk}(t^*) = \frac{M_{jk}(t^*) \,/\, M_k(t^*)}{N_{jk}(t^*) \,/\, N_k(t^*)}.$$

The variable $Z_{jk}(t^*)$ measures the relative supply of newly arrived immigrants in education group k to state j. The denominator effectively "deflates" the supply of immigrant workers in a particular skill group to a particular state by the relative importance of that state in the employment of similarly skilled native workers. The relative supply index equals 1 when immigrant and native workers belonging to the same education group have the same geographic distribution. The index would be greater than 1 if immigrants in education group k were overrepresented in state j.

I estimated the index of relative supply for each state-education group using the 1970, 1980, and 1990 Censuses. Each census provides information on the person's state of residence five years before the census. To minimize the amount of time that elapses between the measurement of the log wage index (time t) and the observation of a state of residence for a worker (time t^*), I used the mid-decade measure of location to calculate the relative supply indices. In other words, the 1960 log wage index (calculated from the 1960 Census) will be related to the 1965 relative supply measure (calculated from the 1970 Census), and similarly for the 1970s and the 1980s.

Table 18.2

Relative Labor Supply of New Immigrants in High- and Low-Wage States, by Educational Attainment[a]

Census year and educational attainment	New immigrants relative to natives		New immigrants relative to earlier immigrants	
	five highest-wage states	five highest-wage states	five highest-wage states	five highest-wage states
1960				
Less than nine years	2.681	0.017	1.237	0.333
Nine to eleven years	1.937	0.262	1.095	2.258
Twelve years	1.688	0.368	1.045	1.792
Thirteen to fifteen years	1.480	0.397	1.046	1.306
At least sixteen years	1.238	0.289	0.890	0.956
1970				
Less than nine years	1.250	0.022	0.770	0.328
Nine to eleven years	1.003	0.065	0.739	0.307
Twelve years	1.029	0.207	0.737	0.670
Thirteen to fifteen years	0.921	0.264	0.790	0.958
At least sixteen years	1.083	0.384	0.885	1.214
1980				
Less than nine years	4.964	0.045	1.210	0.691
Nine to eleven years	2.709	0.082	1.196	0.513
Twelve years	2.360	0.143	1.217	0.523
Thirteen to fifteen years	1.880	0.192	1.134	0.721
At least sixteen years	1.920	0.312	1.143	0.850

Notes: [a] High- and low-wage states are those with high and low values, respectively, of a log wage index calculated for the indicated census year and skill group. The index measures the sex- and age-adjusted differential between the log wage of workers in the indicated education group in a given state and the mean log wage in the United States. Relative supply indexes are calculated from pooled data for the five highest-wage and the five lowest-wage states. New immigrants are those entering the United States within five years after the log wage index is measured; earlier immigrants have been in the country for at least five years.

[b] Calculated as newly arrived immigrants from a particular state-education group as a percentage of all newly arrived immigrants in that education group, divided by the same ratio for natives (or earlier immigrants).

Source: Author's calculations based on data for persons aged 18 to 59 from the 1960–90 Public Use Microdata Samples of the U.S. Census.

The cross-sectional relationship between the log wage index and the index of relative supply is summarized in Table 18.2. For each of the five education groups, the table differentiates between the states paying the highest and those paying the lowest wages. The highest-paying states for an education group are those where the log wage index for that group ranks in the top five, and the lowest-paying states are those where the log wage index ranks in the bottom five. For each set of states I then calculated the average index of relative supply. Table 18.2 strongly suggests a behavioral clustering effect for new immigrants, at least in the cross section. Consider, for example, the geographic distribution of workers who are high school graduates. In 1980 the relative supply index in the five "best" states for high school graduates is 2.4. In contrast, new immigrants are relatively absent from the five states that offer the lowest wages for high school graduates: the relative supply index in the "worst" states is 0.14. Generally, new immigrants tend to be overrepresented in the states that offer the highest wages, and underrepresented in the states that offer the lowest wages.[24]

It turns out that the newest immigrant arrivals are overrepresented in high-wage states not only relative to natives, but also relative to immigrants who arrived in earlier waves. To show this, the last two columns of the table use a slightly different definition of the relative supply index. Let $E_{jk}(t^*)$ be the number of immigrants in earlier waves who reside in state j and belong to skill group k at time t^*, and let $E_k(t^*)$ be the total number of these earlier immigrants belonging to that skill group. The earlier immigrants have been in the United States for at least five years before the measurement of the log wage index.[25] One can then define an alternative relative supply index:

(17)
$$Z'_{jk}(t^*) = \frac{M_{jk}(t^*) \,/\, M_k(t^*)}{E_{jk}(t^*) \,/\, E_k(t^*)}.$$

Equation (17) provides a simple way of netting out the impact of ethnic networks on residential choice. Suppose that these networks lower the costs of migrating to the areas where the ethnic enclaves are located by transmitting information about economic opportunities in those areas and by providing a welcoming environment (in terms of language and culture) to new immigrants. If these networks are very effective and new immigrants simply move to the areas where their compatriots already reside, the new immigrants should be living in exactly the same places as the older immigrants. In contrast, if new immigrants are more responsive to the changing economic environment, they will be overrepresented relative to the older immigrants in those states that offer the highest wages for their particular skills.

The calculations reported in Table 18.2 suggest that the two cohorts of immigrants locate themselves in somewhat different states, with the new immigrants tending to be overrepresented in those states that offer the best economic opportunities for their skills (this was particularly true in 1980).[26] Consider, for example, workers who have between nine and 11 years of schooling. In 1980 the relative supply index defined in Equation (17) was 1.2 in the five states offering the highest wages, but only 0.5 in the five states offering the lowest.

The descriptive analysis in this section thus finds sizable interstate wage differentials among workers who have similar skills and a tendency for different types of immigrants to live in different states. Most important, the interstate wage differentials seem to be correlated with the residential choices made by new immigrants – relative to the choices made by natives and by earlier immigrant waves.

18.3.   Empirical Results

Admittedly, this cross-sectional correlation between regional wage differentials and the subsequent location decisions of new immigrants could be spurious, because immigrants, for reasons unrelated to economic opportunities, may simply be moving to those states (such as California and New York) that happen to pay high wages. It turns out, however, that the relative supply of immigrants to a particular state varies over time in response to relative wage changes in that state. Consider the following first-difference regression model:

$$(18) \qquad Z_{jk}(t_1{}^*) - Z_{jk}(t_0{}^*) = \theta\left[v_{jk}(t_1) - v_{jk}(t_0)\right] + \eta_j + \gamma_k + \varphi_t + \varepsilon,$$

where η_j is a state fixed effect, γ_k is an education fixed effect, and φ_t is a period fixed effect. The unit of observation in this regression is a state-education group during a particular decade. (For example, it may be the change in the relative supply index observed for high school graduates between the early 1960s and the early 1970s, or that for college graduates between the early 1970s and the early 1980s.) The data are pooled across the two decades, so that the regression has

510 observations (two periods × five education groups × 51 states, the 51st being the District of Columbia).

To illustrate the nature of the regression in Equation (18), consider the observation that measures the change in the relative supply of new immigrants between the 1970s and the 1980s. The variable $Z_{jk}(t_1^*)$ gives the relative supply index (as of 1985) for the new immigrants with skills k who arrived between 1980 and 1984, whereas $v_{jk}(t_1)$ gives the log wage index as of 1980. Similarly, the variable $Z_{jk}(t_0^*)$ gives the relative supply index (as of 1975) for the new immigrants with skills k who arrived between 1970 and 1974, whereas $v_{jk}(t_0)$ gives the log wage index as of 1970. The parameter θ then estimates the sensitivity of the relative supply index to the wage changes that occurred within a particular state-education group over the decade.[27]

18.3.1. Basic Regressions

Table 18.3 reports estimates of θ from alternative specifications of the model in Equation (18). Each coefficient in the table comes from a different specification. All regressions are weighted by $(n_0^{-1} + n_1^{-1})$, where n_t gives the number of observations in the state-education group (j, k) at time t.

The coefficients reported in the first row of Table 18.3 are from regressions that do not include the state and education fixed effects in Equation (18); those in the second row are estimated from models that do. The state fixed effects play a particularly important role because they control for state-specific changes in the cost of living over the decade (as well as for any other state-specific factors that might change the relative supply of immigrants).[28] The regression results are not affected qualitatively by the inclusion of the state and education fixed effects. Therefore I will limit the discussion to the results obtained from the more general (and preferred) specification.

In the first data column of the table, the relative supply index compares, for each state, the *total* number of immigrants – regardless of the year of migration – with the number of natives. In the second data column the index compares the number of earlier immigrants with that of natives, and in the third data column the index compares the number of new immigrants with that of natives (the relative supply index defined in Equation (16)). The last column uses the relative supply index defined in Equation (17), which contrasts the residential locations of new immigrants and earlier immigrants, bypassing the location choices made by native workers altogether.

Table 18.3

Estimating the Sensitivity of Relative Labor Supply of Immigrants to Inter-state Wage Differences[a]

| | | Estimated coefficient on log wage index | | | |
Sample and specification	Fixed effects in model?[b]	Immigrants relative to natives	Earlier immigrants relative to natives	New immigrants relative to natives	New immigrants relative to earlier immigrants
1960–80	No	0.580	-0.245	1.150	1.149
		(0.295)	(0.277)	(0.355)	(0.360)
1960–80	Yes	0.643	-0.56	1.754	2.145
		(0.253)	(0.250)	(0.373)	(0.438)
1960–70	Yes	-0.525	-0.551	0.258	1.554
		(0.585)	(0.496)	(0.936)	(1.092)
1970–80	Yes	-0.476	-0.613	0.507	3.019
		(0.831)	(0.886)	(0.556)	(0.751)
1960–80, men only	Yes	0.817	-0.409	1.993	3.557
		(0.307)	(0.305)	(0.438)	(0.971)
1960–80, women only	Yes	0.499	-0.674	1.526	1.830
		(0.219)	(0.230)	(0.360)	(0.495)
1960–80, IV[c]	Yes	-2.752	0.327	2.254	44.356
		(6.588)	(5.521)	(7.936)	(44.479)

Notes: [a] The dependent variable for each specification is the change in the relative supply index over a given period. The independent variable is the change in the log wage index. Standard errors are reported in parentheses. The multiple-decade specifications pool the data for 1960–70 and 1970–80 and have 510 observations (five education groups in 51 states over two periods). These regressions include a dummy variable for the decade from which the observation was drawn. Regressions estimated for single decades have 255 observations. All regressions are weighted by $(n_0^{-1} + n_1^{-1})$, where n_t gives the number of observations for the state-education group in year t.
[b] Specifications with fixed effects include vectors indicating the state of residence and educational attainment.
[c] Instrumental variables regression using as an instrument the previous decade's wage growth in that state-education group.
Source: Author's calculations using data for persons aged 18 to 59 from the 1950–90 Public Use Microdata Samples of the U.S. Census.

The positive regression coefficient reported in the first cell of each of the first two rows indicates that the relative supply of immigrants in a particular skill group rose in those states where the wage offered to that skill group was also rising. The sensitivity of immigrant supply to interstate wage differentials, however, differs across immigrant groups. In particular, the location choices of earlier immigrants relative to those of natives are not positively related to within-state changes in the log wage index. In contrast, new immigrants are very responsive to wage changes. To get a sense of how responsive they are, it is useful to convert the coefficient θ into a relative supply elasticity, $d \ln Z / d \ln v$. Abstracting from scale effects, this elasticity gives the percentage change in the relative number of immigrants who choose to reside in a particular state for a given percentage change in the wage. This elasticity is given by the ratio θ / Z. The mean value of the relative supply index for new immigrants (in the 1980s) is 1.4. The estimated supply elasticity for new immigrants relative to natives is then 1.3 (1.754 ÷ 1.4).

The regression results reported in the first three data columns of Table 18.3 ignore the possibility that nonwage factors, such as the pull of ethnic enclaves on potential migrants, may partly determine the residential choices of immigrants relative to those of natives. As I argued earlier, one can partly net out the impact of ethnic enclaves by comparing the residential locations of new immigrants with those of earlier immigrants. The last column of the table reports the regression coefficients from the model that uses this alternative index of relative supply.

The evidence indicates that the location decisions of new immigrants exhibit greater sensitivity to interstate wage differentials than do those of earlier immigrants. The relative supply elasticity is also 1.3.[29] The analysis thus suggests that, even when one controls for idiosyncratic factors that help determine the location decisions of immigrants in the United States, it is still the case that the supply of new immigrants to particular labor markets is very responsive to the regional wage structure.

In their studies of the impact of immigration on native wages, Borjas, Richard Freeman, and Lawrence Katz, as well as Robert Schoeni, report that the sign of the geographic correlation between past immigration and current wages seems to depend on the period under analysis.[30] In some decades the correlation between wage growth in a particular labor market and immigration into that labor market is positive, whereas in other decades it is negative. It is important, therefore, to investigate whether the evidence supporting the excess sensitivity hypothesis holds up in different periods. The third and fourth rows of Table 18.3 reestimate the regressions using the 1960–70 and the 1970–80 periods, respectively. The excess sensitivity hypothesis is roughly consistent with the evidence in each of the decades under analysis, although the results are stronger for the 1970–80 period.

The fifth and sixth rows of Table 18.3 replicate the (pooled) analysis in the samples of men and women, respectively. The relative supply elasticities tend to be more positive for men than for women.[31] The weaker supply elasticity found among women is consistent with the hypothesis that the location decision of female immigrants is strongly influenced by family considerations. For instance, the sample of female immigrants may contain many tied-movers and tied-"stayers," contaminating the correlation between a worker's wage and the migration decision.[32] The sample of female immigrants likely contains many women whose location decisions are tied to those of their foreign-born husbands, or who are tied-stayers because they are married to native men and hence face relatively high fixed costs of moving across states.

Finally, there may be some contemporaneous correlation between wage growth in a particular state-education group in any given decade and the residual ε in Equation (18).[33] One common solution to this problem is to use as an instrument for the decade's wage change the wage change experienced by the same state-education group in the *previous* decade. This procedure requires estimating the log wage index in the 1950 Census, to get the change in the log wage index for each group during 1950–60. I reestimated the regression model in Equation (14) on data from the 1950 Census, using the same sample restrictions and variable definitions as in the analysis of the subsequent censuses.[34]

The last row of Table 18.3 reports the instrumental variables regression estimates. Although the evidence is qualitatively consistent with the results implied by the ordinary least-squares coefficients, the instrumental variables procedure leads to unstable results, with coefficients that fluctuate dramatically across specifications and have very large standard errors. Part of the problem is that the wage growth experienced by a particular state-education group in decade $\tau - 1$ may not be a valid instrument for the wage growth in decade τ. In fact, there is only a very weak correlation in wage growth across decades. The correlation between wage growth in a given (j, k) cell across subsequent decades is –0.04.[35] Because the log wage index predicted from the first-stage regression is effectively constant within state-education groups, the instrument has relatively little variance relative to the error in the equation.[36]

18.3.2. Sensitivity of Regression Results

Because the analysis emphasizes the residential location decisions made by immigrants, it is useful to account for some of the characteristics that help differentiate the immigrant population in the United States. As we have seen, immigrants tend to cluster in relatively few states, and this clustering has been particularly pronounced in California. In 1990, 33.8 percent of immigrants resided in California, up from 14.6 percent in 1960. As shown in the last section, California tends to be a high-paying state for all workers, regardless of their educational attainment. Suppose that immigrants cluster in California simply because it is geographically close to some important source countries (such as Mexico), or because it offers amenities (such as a pleasant climate) that provide a more welcoming environment for new immigrants. The positive correlation between the relative supplies of immigrants and interstate wage differences within a skill group could then arise spuriously. The first row of Table 18.4, however, shows that the empirical results are not affected when the relative supply regressions exclude all state-education groups that refer to workers in California. Even outside California, new immigrants are more sensitive to interstate wage differentials than either earlier immigrants or natives.

Table 18.4

Robustness of Estimated Relative Supply Effect to Changes in Sample Specification[a]

	Estimated coefficient on log wage index			
Sample	Immigrants relative to natives	Earlier immigrants relative to natives	New immigrants relative to natives	New immigrants relative to earlier immigrants
Workers outside California	0.484	-0.689	1.642	2.272
	(0.166)	(0.172)	(0.401)	(0.488)
Natives and non-Mexican immigrants	0.811	-0.813	3.042	3.182
	(0.210)	(0.181)	(0.503)	(0.542)
Natives and non-Mexican immigrants outside California	0.274	-0.889	1.949	3.400
	(0.158)	(0.197)	(0.430)	(0.605)
Natives and European immigrants	-0.260	-0.882	1.847	2.253
	(0.184)	(0.204)	(0.429)	(0.675)
Natives and Asian immigrants	0.920	-0.711	1.372	1.568
	(0.449)	(0.532)	(0.750)	(0.980)
Natives and Hispanic immigrants	1.276	-0.275	1.616	2.446
	(0.241)	(0.430)	(0.592)	(0.965)
Natives and nonrefugee immigrants	0.522	-0.684	1.753	2.003
	(0.246)	(0.249)	(0.344)	(0.369)

Note: [a] Using the 1960–80 specification with fixed effects (see Table 18.3). Standard errors are reported in parentheses.

Source: Author's calculations using data for persons aged 18 to 59 from the 1950–90 Public Use Microdata Samples of the U.S. Census.

One could also argue that the key results may be driven by the predominance of the Mexican population in the immigrant flow. In 1990 about 22 percent of immigrants living in the United States had been born in Mexico, and 58 percent of these Mexican immigrants were living in California, a state that offered relatively high wages. As the second and third rows of Table 18.4 show, the results are similar when the regressions are reestimated in samples that either exclude Mexican immigrants or exclude both Mexican immigrants and workers living in California.

It is also worth investigating whether the relative supply of immigrants to particular states exhibits excess sensitivity even when we estimate the models within particular national origin groups. To calculate the relative supply indices in sufficiently large samples, the analysis must use broadly defined groups, such as European immigrants, Asian immigrants, and Latin American immigrants. The evidence obtained from these regressions, however, is consistent with the basic thrust of the evidence. The relative supply of new immigrants within these aggregated groups – even when compared with the relative supply of their previously arrived compatriots – shows excess sensitivity to interstate wage differentials.

Finally, I have assumed throughout the analysis that newly arrived immigrants can freely choose their residential location when they enter the United States. One group of immigrants, however, has relatively little choice over where to reside when they first enter the country, namely, refugees. The U.S. Department of State assigns individual refugees to sponsoring private voluntary agencies that provide them with a variety of social services, including initial resettlement in the United States.[37] These sponsoring agencies determine the location of resettlement, which depends partly on the match between a refugee's socioeconomic background and the availability of jobs and services in particular localities – as perceived by the sponsoring agency. As a result, the initial location of refugees could well be consistent with the key implications of the model proposed in this chapter, but it may not be. Unfortunately, the census does not contain any information on the type of visa used by an individual to enter the United States. To approximate the refugee population, therefore, I classify all immigrants who originate in the main refugee-sending countries as refugees and all other immigrants as nonrefugees.[38]

The last row of Table 18.4 reports the coefficients estimated from the sample of nonrefugees. The evidence clearly indicates that the location decision of nonrefugees is consistent with the hypothesis proposed in this chapter: they are disproportionately more likely to choose to live in the high-wage states. It would be of interest to estimate the regression model in the sample of refugees. The refugee population, however, is relatively small, hovering around 10 percent of the immigrant population during the period under study. The data lack sufficient variation, therefore, to allow a full-scale study of the relationship between the location of refugees (as chosen by the sponsoring agency) and interstate wage differentials.

18.3.3.   Native Internal Migration

Up to this point, the empirical analysis has emphasized that the self-selected sample of new immigrants is very responsive to interstate wage differentials. In fact, the basic idea developed in this chapter applies equally well to the self-selected sample of native workers who choose to move across states. Just as new immigrants should be clustered in the states that offer the highest wages for their types of skills, so the self-selected sample of native movers should also be clustered in those states that offer the highest wages for *their* skills.[39]

The census reports a worker's state of residence five years before the census date.[40] One can then use these data to create two alternative samples of natives: native movers, who moved across state lines during the relevant five-year period, and native stayers, who remained in the same state over the five-year period. It would seem ideal to replicate the regression analysis in Equation (18) by defining a new relative supply index that compares the location decisions of the native movers with those of the native stayers. Unfortunately, this comparison is not quite right. Consider the data available for the 1980s. The 1980 log wage index was calculated using the 1980 Census. The 1990 Census provides the eventual geographic location of native movers – as of 1990 – for those natives who moved between 1985 and 1990. The sample of native stayers that can be defined in these data, therefore, contains both natives who did not move after 1985 and natives who moved between 1980 and 1985 but did not move thereafter. In short, the so-called sample of native stayers is contaminated by the presence of some native movers.

In fact, the regression coefficients reported in the first data column of Table 18.5 suggest that native movers are *less* responsive to interstate wage differences than native stayers. One can try to circumvent the measurement problem by using alternative control groups. The second data column of the table refines the definition of native stayers by estimating the relative supply index only in the subsample of stayers who are 40–50 years old – that is, among workers who are past their prime years for internal migration but before the retirement age. This subsample of stayers, therefore, is likely to contain relatively few movers. In fact, there is now a very weak positive correlation between the relative supply index and relative wages in the fixed-effects specification, suggesting that native movers are somewhat more likely to reside in those states that pay the highest wages for the skills they have to offer.

Table 18.5

Estimating the Sensitivity of Relative Labor Supply of Native Internal Migrants to Interstate Wage Differences[a]

Specification	Estimated coefficient on log wage index			
	Native movers relative to native "stayers"	Native movers relative to older native "stayers"	Native movers relative to earlier immigrants	Native movers relative to new immigrants
Without fixed effects	-1.064	-1.28	3.421	-9.919
	(0.184)	(0.236)	(1.895)	(7.406)
With fixed effects	-1.372	0.517	3.716	-22.005
	(0.221)	(0.441)	(2.406)	(9.478)

Note: [a] Using the 1960–80 specification with fixed effects (see Table 18.3). Standard errors are reported in parentheses. Older native "stayers" are those aged 40–50. New immigrants are those entering the United States within five years after the log wage index is measured; earlier immigrants have been in the country for at least five years.

Source: Author's calculations using data for persons aged 18–59 from the 1960–90 Public Use Microdata Samples of the U.S. Census.

One way of avoiding the measurement problem altogether is simply to ignore the group of native stayers and compare the native movers with immigrants. The third data column of Table 18.5 defines the relative supply index by contrasting the location decisions of native movers with those of earlier immigrants. As long as there are substantial migration costs, the sample of earlier immigrants is "stuck" in the states where they first entered the United States, so that this sample approximates an immobile native sample. Table 18.5 reports that the relative supply of native movers is more sensitive to interstate wage differentials than that of the earlier immigrants.

Finally, one can also define the relative supply index by contrasting the location of native movers with that of newly arrived immigrants.

If the two groups were equally responsive to interstate wage differentials, the estimated impact of the log wage index would be zero. The regression coefficient, however, is negative and significant when the fixed effects are included, indicating that newly arrived immigrants are more responsive to interstate wage differentials than the self-selected sample of native movers.

Overall, the evidence reported in Table 18.5 does not support the hypothesis that native movers behave "just like" new immigrants. Part of the problem arises from the data: the construction of the census data prevents the correct calculation of the relevant group of native stayers. It may also be the case, however, that the data simply are not consistent with the theory that native movers are income maximizers. The available evidence in the internal migration literature suggests that natives respond to interstate wage differentials and move to high-wage states. However, much of this evidence is somewhat dated and does not directly address the possibility that, in recent years, net native migration to Sunbelt states may have been motivated by reasons other than income maximization.[41] This possibility increases the importance of immigrant flows in arbitraging regional wage differentials.

Between 1985 and 1990, 10.9 million native workers (11.0 percent of the native workforce) moved across state lines. During the same period, 880,000 "preexisting" immigrants (11.3 percent of the immigrants who arrived before 1985) also moved across state lines.[42] Finally, 2.1 million new immigrant workers entered the U.S. labor market during the same period. The new immigrants, therefore, accounted for 15.1 percent of all workers who moved across state lines between 1985 and 1990, even though these workers accounted for only 1.9 percent of the workforce in 1990. The flow of new immigrants into the United States, therefore, has a disproportionate impact on the evolution of the regional wage structure – even if all native movers are income maximizing when making their migration decisions. The new immigrants make up many of the marginal workers whose location decisions help equilibrate the national labor market and improve labor market efficiency.

18.4. Immigration and Wage Convergence

The labor supply responses documented in the previous section suggest that the geographic distribution of new immigrants in the United States should help reduce regional wage differentials. This finding has significant macroeconomic implications, for it suggests that regional wage convergence will be faster among those skill groups and in those periods that experience high levels of immigration.

A large literature examines the rate of wage convergence across states in the United States.[43] These studies typically estimate the generic regression model

$$(19) \qquad \ln w_{j,t+1} - \ln w_{jt} = \alpha + \beta \ln w_{jt} + \varepsilon_{jt},$$

where w_{jt} is the wage in state j at time t, and β is the convergence coefficient, which will be negative if there is wage convergence across states. The values of β (measured at an annual rate) estimated in the literature range around -0.02, suggesting that the half-life of interstate wage differentials is roughly 35 years.[44] The hypothesis examined in this chapter suggests that there exists a structural relationship linking the coefficient β in any particular labor market and the size of the immigrant flow into that market between periods t and $t + 1$.

I use data drawn from the 1950–90 Censuses to estimate a particular specification of the regression model in Equation (19). Recall that my empirical framework has differentiated across skill groups throughout the analysis. Consider the following convergence regression model:

$$(20) \qquad v_{jk,t+1} - v_{jkt} = \alpha_{kt} + \beta_{kt} v_{jkt} + \varepsilon_{jkt},$$

where $v_{jk}(t)$ is the log wage index estimated for workers in state j and skill group k in census year t, and the parameter β_{kt} is the convergence coefficient describing the evolution of the regional wage structure for that skill group in the $(t, t + 1)$ time period. I annualized the dependent variable by dividing by ten, so that β gives the annual rate of regional wage convergence. I estimated the regression model in Equation (20) separately for each skill group in each time period 1950–60, 1960–70, 1970–80, and 1980–90. The empirical analysis, therefore, yields a total of 20 estimated convergence coefficients (five education groups over four periods).

Table 18.6 summarizes the convergence coefficients estimated for each of the cells. Sixteen of the coefficients are negative, and only one of the four positive coefficients is significantly different from zero. The mean convergence coefficient (weighted by the inverse of the square of the standard error) is -0.02, which is quite similar to the "consensus" convergence coefficient reported in the literature.

Table 18.6

Estimated Wage Convergence and Immigrant Penetration, by Educational Attainment

Decade and educational attainment	Convergence coefficient[a]	Standard error	Immigrant penetration[b]
1950-60			
Less than nine years	0.004	0.004	-4.231
Nine to eleven years	0.009	0.006	-4.32
Twelve years	-0.004	0.004	-4.316
Thirteen to fifteen years	-0.014	0.007	-3.836
At least sixteen years	-0.03	0.006	-3.633
1960-70			
Less than nine years	-0.025	0.003	-3.574
Nine to eleven years	-0.022	0.003	-4.233
Twelve years	-0.016	0.004	-3.987
Thirteen to fifteen years	-0.005	0.005	-3.547
At least sixteen years	-0.004	0.006	-3.123
1970-80			
Less than nine years	-0.04	0.003	-2.625
Nine to eleven years	-0.046	0.004	-3.723
Twelve years	-0.037	0.005	-3.764
Thirteen to fifteen years	-0.045	0.005	-3.069
At least sixteen years	-0.037	0.004	-2.72
1980-90			
Less than nine years	-0.018	0.008	-1.821
Nine to eleven years	-0.008	0.014	-2.784
Twelve years	-0.002	0.015	-3.658
Thirteen to fifteen years	0.014	0.015	-2.898
At least sixteen years	0.023	0.011	-2.693
Sample mean, 1950-90	-0.022	n.a.	-3.571

Notes: [a] Estimated by Equation (20) and weighted by $(n_0^{-1} + n_1^{-1})^{-1}$, where n_t gives the number of observations for the state-education group in year t.
[b] Measured as the log ratio of the total number of immigrants in a particular skill group who entered the United States over the sample period to the size of the native-born population in that skill group at the beginning of the period.
Source: Author's calculations using data for persons aged 18 to 59 from the 1950–90 Public Use Microdata Samples of the U.S. Census.

The hypothesis developed in this chapter suggests that there should be greater wage convergence in those labor markets (defined for a particular skill group over a particular time period) that experience larger immigrant flows. Let the index of immigrant penetration in a particular labor market be given by

$$(21) \qquad g_{kt} = \frac{\ln M_k(t, t+1)}{N_{kt}},$$

where $M_k(t, t+1)$ is the total number of immigrants in skill group k who entered the United States between periods t and $t+1$, and N_{kt} is the native-born population in skill group k at the beginning of the period. I then test the theoretical implication that high immigration leads to faster wage convergence by estimating the following second-stage regression model:

$$(22) \qquad \beta_{kt} = a + bg_{kt} + \xi_t.$$

Because the dependent variable in Equation (22) is subject to sampling error, I weight the regression by the inverse of the square of the standard error. This procedure helps adjust for any potential heteroskedasticity in the disturbance.

Figure 18.5 presents a scatter diagram illustrating the basic data available for the second-stage regression. (The area of the circles corresponds to the weights of the convergence coefficients as described above.) There is a clear downward-sloping relationship between the convergence coefficient in any particular market (defined by time period and skill group) and the relative number of immigrants entering that labor market.

Figure 18.5

Relationship between Wage Convergence and Immigrant Penetration, 1950–90

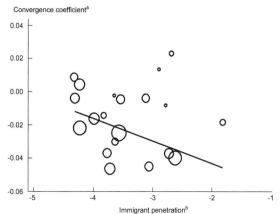

Notes: [a] Each circle represents a convergence coefficient estimated in a particular decade for a particular skill group. Estimates are weighted by the inverse of the square of the standard error of the convergence coefficient; the larger the area of the circle, the larger the weight of that estimate in the regression.
[b] Immigrant penetration is measured as the log ratio of the number of immigrants in a particular skill group who arrived during a particular decade to the number of natives in that skill group at the beginning of the decade.
Source: Author's calculations based on data for persons aged 18 to 59 from the 1950–90 Public Use Microdata Samples of the U.S. Census.

Table 18.7 reports the results of estimating the basic regression models on these data. The simplest specification, reported in the first row, takes each of the 20 labor markets as independent observations; a numerically strong and statistically significant correlation is found between convergence and immigration.

Table 18.7

Explaining Wage Convergence with Immigrant Penetration[a]

Specification	Coefficient on immigrant penetration[b]	R^2	No. of observations
Without fixed effects	-0.013	0.229	20
	(0.006)		
With education fixed effects	-0.021	0.366	20
	(0.008)		
With education and period fixed effects	-0.001	0.753	20
	(0.005)		

Notes: [a] The dependent variable for each specification is the convergence coefficient estimated in a particular decade for a particular skill group (see Table 18.6). The independent variable is the measure of immigrant penetration for that decade and skill group. Standard errors are reported in parentheses. Regressions are weighted by the inverse of the square of the standard error of the estimated convergence coefficient.
[b] See Table 18.6.
Source: Author's calculations using data for persons aged 18 to 59 from the 1950–90 Public Use Microdata Samples of the U.S. Census.

To illustrate the magnitude of the correlation, consider the following thought experiment. Suppose the convergence coefficient is on the order of –0.02, implying a half-life of regional wage differences of 35 years. In the 1950s the average value of m_k (across skill groups) was equal to –4.1. Put differently, immigration during this decade increased labor supply by around 1.6 percent. By the 1980s the average value of m_k was –2.5, and total immigration increased labor supply by around 9.8 percent. The magnitude of the coefficient b in Equation (22) ($b = -0.013$) implies that this increase in immigration would lower the convergence coefficient by 0.021 unit, or from –0.02 to –0.04. The half-life of interstate wage differentials would then be cut in half, to 17.3 years. Immigration, therefore, seems to significantly speed up the process of wage convergence. And this speeding up occurs precisely because immigration introduces into the U.S. labor market a sizable group of persons who are particularly responsive to interstate wage differentials.

The remaining rows of Table 18.7 show estimates of the basic second-stage model using increasingly general specifications. The second row, for example, adds education fixed effects to the basic model.

The addition of these education fixed effects implies that the relationship between wage convergence and immigration is now being estimated *within* education groups – identifying the impact of immigration from the time variation in the size of the immigrant flow for a particular skill group. The coefficient b remains negative and is actually larger, again suggesting that immigration plays an important role in determining the speed of wage convergence in the U.S. labor market.

The last row of Table 18.7 adds variables indicating period fixed effects (that is, the decade in which the convergence coefficient was estimated). The coefficient b remains negative, but it is no longer statistically (or numerically) significant. This is not too surprising, since there is little variation left in the sample of 20 convergence rates to identify the relationship between immigration and the speed of wage convergence.

Overall, the empirical analysis of interstate wage convergence yields results consistent with the key hypothesis of this chapter. Immigration greases the wheels of the labor market by introducing workers who are very responsive to regional wage differentials into the host country's labor market. As a result, immigrants speed up the process of wage convergence and improve labor market efficiency.

18.5. Estimating the Efficiency Gain

Equation (14) defined the efficiency gain from immigration as the net increase in GDP accruing to natives that results from the clustering of immigrants in high-wage regions relative to what would have been observed if immigrants had simply replicated the geographic sorting of the native population. The calculation of the efficiency gain requires that I first specify how natives respond to regional wage differentials. In particular, how would the regional wage structure have evolved in the absence of immigration? And how do natives respond to the entry of immigrants in different markets?

The speed of adjustment by natives plays an important role in calculations of the efficiency gain. Suppose, for example, that natives are very responsive to regional wage differentials and that migration costs are relatively low. Then the entry of M immigrants into the high-wage region generates only a short-run efficiency gain, because natives would have eliminated the wage gap between the two regions quickly and at very low cost. In this scenario the fact that immigration greases the wheels of the labor market is unlikely to play an important role in a cost-benefit analysis of immigration. If, however, migration costs are relatively high, and relatively few natives move across regions, the efficiency gain generated by immigration could be sizable and long lasting.

A simple model helps to formalize these ideas.[45] Suppose the United States has two regions ($j = 1, 2$) and that the production function is the same in each:

$$(23) \qquad\qquad Q_{jt} = A \, L_{jt}^{\beta},$$

where Q_{jt} is the value of output in region j at time t, L_{jt} is employment, and $\beta < 1$. The regional labor demand function implied by this technology is

$$(24) \qquad\qquad \ln w_{jt} = \alpha - \delta \ln L_{jt},$$

where w_{jt} is the wage in region j at time t, and $\delta = 1 - \beta > 0$. A fraction $\lambda < 0.5$ of the native population lives in region 1 at time 0. The total number of native workers in the labor market, $N = L_{10} + L_{20}$, is assumed fixed. The wage gap between the two regions before any immigrants enter the economy is

$$(25) \qquad\qquad \ln w_{10} - \ln w_{20} = -\delta \ln \frac{\lambda}{1 - \lambda}.$$

Suppose that the United States admits M immigrants at the end of time 0 and that a fraction θ of these immigrants settle in region 1. The numbers of immigrants who settle in regions 1 and 2, respectively, are given by

$$(26) \qquad\qquad M_1 = \theta \, k(1 - 2\lambda)N,$$

$$(27) \qquad\qquad M_2 = (1 - \theta) \, k(1 - 2\lambda)N.$$

As before, the parameters k and θ help to measure the extent to which immigrants arbitrage wage opportunities across the two labor markets. In the special case of $k = 1$, the immigrant flow is sufficiently large to potentially bring the two labor markets into a single-wage equilibrium without any native internal migration. If all of these immigrants settled in the high-wage region, so that θ is also equal to 1, immigration would be "complete" and would bring about an immediate equalization of wages across regions.

Regional wage differentials induce a supply response in the native-born population, but this response occurs with a lag. For simplicity, assume that only natives move across regions and that their supply response is described by the following lagged adjustment function:

$$(28) \qquad \ln\frac{L_{1,t+1}}{L_{2,t+1}} - \ln\frac{L_{1t}}{L_{2t}} = \sigma\,(\ln w_{1t} - \ln w_{2t}),$$

where $\sigma \geq 0$ is the labor supply elasticity. In other words, the rate of change in the regional allocation of labor between times t and $t + 1$ depends on the regional wage gap at time t.

Some tedious algebra reveals that the adjustment mechanism in Equation (28) implies that the regional employment and wage differentials at time t are given by

$$(29) \qquad \ln L_{1t} - \ln L_{2t} = (1 - \delta\sigma)^t \ln\frac{\lambda + \theta k(1 - 2\lambda)}{(1 - \lambda) + (1 - \theta)k(1 - 2\lambda)},$$

$$(30) \qquad \ln w_{1t} - \ln w_{2t} = -\delta(1 - \delta\sigma)^t \ln\frac{\lambda + \theta k(1 - 2\lambda)}{(1 - \lambda) + (1 - \theta)k(1 - 2\lambda)}.$$

I assume that $0 < (1 - \delta\sigma) < 1$ so that the national labor market converges to a single-wage equilibrium over time.

Finally, it is costly for natives to engage in internal migration. Suppose that these migration costs at time t are given by the following quadratic cost function:[46]

$$(31) \qquad C_t = \phi R_t^2,$$

where R_t gives the number of natives who move at time t. It is easy to show that the number of internal migrants is approximated by[47]

$$(32) \qquad R_t = \tfrac{1}{4}\sigma(N + M)\ln\frac{w_{1t-1}}{w_{2t-1}}.$$

The present value of GDP accruing to natives, net of migration costs, is given by

$$(33) \qquad Q_N = \sum_{t=0}^{\infty}\left[\frac{1}{(1 + r)^t}\left(AL_{1t}^\beta + AL_{2t}^\beta - w_{1t}k\theta(1 - 2\lambda)N\right.\right.$$

$$\left.\left. - w_{2tk}(1 - \theta)(1 - 2\lambda)N - \phi R_t^2\right)\right]_.,$$

where r is the rate of discount. Let $Q_{N}|_{\theta=1}$ be the net income accruing to natives if immigrants are income maximizers and cluster in the high-wage region, and let $Q_{N}|_{\theta=\lambda}$ be their net income if immigrants replicate the geographic sorting of the native population. The measure of the efficiency gain from immigration defined earlier is simply the difference between these two quantities.

The magnitude of the efficiency gain will obviously depend on the value of the supply elasticity σ. Rather than assume a particular numerical value, I build into the simulation a behavioral assumption about native migration. Suppose that native migration decisions are efficient, in the sense that native migration maximizes the value of national income accruing to natives, net of migration costs. It is well known that if natives have perfect foresight and the migration response by native workers is efficient, the quadratic cost function leads to the lagged adjustment function in Equation (28).[48] The supply elasticity σ is then a sufficient statistic to summarize how native migration responds optimally to changes in the regional wage gap. The assumption of efficient migration greatly simplifies the estimation of the efficiency gain that accrues to natives. The annualized efficiency gain is given by[49]

$$(34) \qquad \Delta_N = \left(\max_{\sigma 1} rQ_N|_{\theta=1} - \max_{\sigma\lambda} rQ_N|_{\theta=\lambda} \right),$$

where σ_1 is the supply elasticity measuring optimal native migration behavior when all of the immigrants choose to live in the high-wage region, and σ_λ is that elasticity when a fraction λ of the immigrants choose to live in the high-wage region. The separate maximization of each stream of national income ensures that the "right" number of natives move in each period under either regime.

Table 18.8 reports estimates of Δ_N for alternative values of the parameters.[50] The table also reports the supply elasticities that maximize the efficiency gain in Equation (34). All of the simulations assume that the real rate of interest is 3 percent, that the parameter β is 0.7 (so that the elasticity δ in the labor demand function is 0.3), that there are 100 million native workers in the economy, and that GDP in the pre-immigration regime is $10 trillion.[51] Finally, the relation between the immigrant share of the workforce ($m = M/N$) and the fraction of natives who reside in region 1 is

$$(35) \qquad m = k(1 - 2\lambda).$$

Table 18.8

Estimates of Efficiency Gains from Immigration Accruing to Natives under Selected Parameter Values

Item	Initial regional wage gap[a]		
	Low (0.06)	Moderate (0.12)	Sizable (0.25)
Parameter			
λ^{b}	0.45	0.40	0.30
k^{c}	1.00	0.50	0.25
Low migration cost[d]			
Net efficiency gain[e]	2.7	4.7	6.9
σ_1^{f}	0.0	0.6	0.4
σ_λ^{g}	0.3	0.3	0.3
High migration cost			
Net efficiency gain	3.5	6.1	9.0
σ_1	0.0	0.4	0.3
σ_λ	0.2	0.2	0.2
Prohibitive migration cost			
Net efficiency gain	4.6	7.9	12.4
σ_1	0.0	0.3	0.2
σ_λ	0.1	0.1	0.1
Net efficiency gain	10.3	13.2	22.0

Notes: [a] Difference in the log wage index before immigration.
[b] The fraction of natives that live in the high-wage region.
[c] The size of the immigrant flow relative to the supply imbalance between the two regions.
[d] Average cost of migration equals half of annual income. For medium cost, average cost of migration equals annual income, and for high cost it equals twice annual income.
[e] Efficiency gain (in billions of dollars) accruing to natives is the difference between the income that accrues to natives if all immigrants settle in the high-wage region and that if immigrants replicate the geographical distribution of the native population.
[f] The supply elasticity that maximizes native income (net of migration costs) when immigrants cluster in the high-wage region.
[g] The optimal supply elasticity when immigrants replicate the initial native geographical distribution.
Source: Author's calculations based on the theoretical model.

All of the simulations impose the restriction that $m = 0.1$, so that immigration increases labor supply by 10 percent. This assumption greatly restricts the range of valid values for k and λ.

Suppose that $\lambda = 0.4$ (or, equivalently, that $k = 0.5$), so that 40 percent of natives live in the high-wage region, and that the observed volume of immigration is half as large as required to bring about an immediate equalization of wages across regions. In this scenario the initial wage gap between the two regions is 12.2 percent. The simulations in Table 18.8 then indicate that the efficiency gain accruing to natives is modest. Consider first the case where natives are immobile, so that the supply elasticity of natives is set to zero, regardless of how many immigrants enter the country and where they settle. The last panel of the table shows that the annual efficiency gain from immigration is $13.2 billion.

Suppose now that immigration costs are "low," in the sense that the average cost of a native moving from region 2 to region 1 is half the income per worker in the country ($35,000).[52] The efficiency gain accruing to natives falls to $4.7 billion. The efficiency gain is now relatively small because the low migration costs imply that natives would have quickly moved across regions anyway, so that there is little to be gained from immigration. The efficiency gain accruing to natives increases to $7.9 billion when migration costs are "high," in the sense that the migration cost per worker, on average, is twice as large as income per worker.

The efficiency gains are substantially larger when there is a larger regional wage gap in the pre-immigration period, that is, when income-maximizing immigrants have the most to contribute to the narrowing of regional wage differences. Consider, for instance, the situation when $\lambda = 0.3$, so that the initial wage gap between the two regions is 25.4 percent. The efficiency gain accruing to natives is now approximately twice that calculated when the pre-immigration regional wage gap was only 12.2 percent, and ranges from $6.9 billion to $12.4 billion annually.

Although these efficiency gains are trivial in the context of a $10 trillion economy, they are not trivial when compared with the traditional immigration surplus stressed in earlier calculations. After all, the efficiency gain measured here accrues to natives *in addition* to the immigration surplus that arises from having more workers in an economy with a fixed (and native-owned) capital stock. The efficiency gain from immigration measures how much a *fixed* volume of immigration increases native income simply because the immigrants tend to cluster in the high-wage region. As I showed earlier, the immigration surplus is approximately $10 billion when the factor price elasticity is 0.3. It turns out that the estimates of the efficiency gain roughly double the measured benefits from immigration.

The simulations reported in Table 18.8 may be unsatisfactory in one important way. As noted earlier, many studies in the wage convergence literature report that the half-life of differences in income per capita across U.S. states is around 30 years. It turns out, however, that the assumption of efficient migration built into the simulations implies a faster rate of convergence. The simulations yield an estimate of σ_1 (the supply elasticity when all immigrants cluster in the high-wage region) of 0.3 to 0.4 in the medium-cost scenario. This supply elasticity, in turn, implies that the half-life of the initial wage gap is around five to seven years.[53]

Suppose that the empirical finding of a 30-year half-life for regional wage differences is correct. The simplest explanation of the inconsistency between the simulations and this empirical finding is that migration costs are far higher than assumed in the calculations.[54] In fact, the exercise would generate a half-life of 30 years if I assumed that the average migration cost was around three times income per worker, or $210,000. Although this estimate of migration costs may seem implausible, it is less so when viewed in the context of *actual* migration flows across regions or countries. Consider, for example, the migration flow between Puerto Rico and the United States. Although there are no legal restrictions on the movement of Puerto Ricans to the U.S. mainland, a large income gap has persisted between these two regions for many decades.[55] The Penn World Tables report that in 1955 (chain-indexed) GDP per capita in the United States was four times as large as in Puerto Rico. Even by 1999, GDP per capita, adjusted for purchasing power parity, was still 3.5 times as large in the United States.

Not surprisingly, many Puerto Ricans have taken advantage of the huge income gap over the decades. Nearly 25 percent of Puerto Ricans migrated to the United States between the 1940s and the 1980s.[56] However, the interesting question is not why 25 percent of Puerto Ricans chose to migrate, but why 75 percent of Puerto Ricans chose *not* to. The Puerto Rican case, I conjecture, strongly suggests that migration costs could easily swamp income differentials that are perhaps on the order of three- to fourfold.

Of course, smaller income gaps across countries would induce even less migration. The recent experience of the European Union, as it extended membership to such low-wage countries as Spain and Portugal, is instructive. In 1990, for instance, GDP per capita in France was 80 percent greater than that in Greece, 70 percent greater than in Portugal, and 44 percent greater than in Spain.[57] Yet despite much concern that the accession of Greece, Portugal, and Spain into the European Union might generate substantial migration flows, these flows never materialized.

Consider, for example, what happened to migration to Germany – one of the EU countries with the highest GDP per capita – after the initial expansion. The number of Greek nationals living in Germany grew from 356,000 to 363,000 between 1994 and 1996, the number of Spanish nationals remained at about 132,000, and the number of Portuguese nationals grew from 118,000 to 131,000.[58] And the number of foreign-born nationals from the acceding countries was roughly stable in the other EU countries. It seems, therefore, that the income differences between the original EU ountries and the initial wave of acceding countries, large as they were, were not sufficiently large to generate substantial migration flows. In short, there is strong circumstantial evidence suggesting that migration costs play a crucial role in inhibiting labor flows across regions or countries. This fact, of course, increases the importance of immigration as grease on the wheels of the labor market of the host country's economy.

In the end, the hypothesis of efficient migration, and its link to migration costs and the actual size of population flows across regions, raises a number of important questions about the process of native internal migration, questions that remain unexplored in a literature that seems ripe for rediscovery.

18.6. Conclusion

Migration costs prevent many native-born workers from moving to those states that offer the best economic opportunities. Immigrant workers, in contrast, form a self-selected sample of persons who have chosen to incur those migration costs. As long as migration costs are mainly fixed costs, newly arrived immigrants in the United States will choose to live in those states that offer them the best economic opportunities. As a result, new immigrants should be clustered in those states that offer them the highest wages, and the location decisions of immigrant workers should be much more responsive to interstate wage differentials than those of natives.

This chapter has tested this hypothesis using data drawn from the decennial censuses. The evidence indicates that new immigrants do indeed make different location decisions than native workers and than earlier immigrants. Moreover, these differences are strongly related to interstate wage differences within a particular skill group. In other words, new immigrants who have particular skills to offer are more likely to reside in those states that happen to offer the highest wages for those skills. The endogenous sorting of newly arrived immigrants to high-wage areas, in fact, speeds up the process of regional wage convergence.

The empirical evidence, therefore, suggests that immigrants may play an important – and neglected – role in the U.S. economy: They make up a disproportionately large fraction of the marginal workers whose location decisions arbitrage differences across labor markets. Put differently, immigration improves labor market efficiency. Moreover, it turns out that part of this efficiency gain accrues to natives, suggesting that existing estimates of the benefits from immigration may be ignoring a potentially important source of these benefits. However, a back-of-the-envelope calculation suggests that the efficiency gain is probably below $10 billion a year.

The analysis also has provocative implications for the interpretation of studies that analyze how immigration affects the labor market opportunities of native workers. Most studies in this literature attempt to estimate the impact of immigration by comparing the wages of native workers in different geographic areas and relating these geographic differences to measures of immigrant penetration in the local labor markets.

Because immigrants deliberately choose to enter those labor markets that offer the highest wages, it will be very difficult to document that increased immigration lowers the native wage in the penetrated geographic areas. The literature has typically attempted to control for this endogeneity problem by using instrumental variables, where the instrument for the measure of immigrant penetration in the local labor market is typically a variable indicating the number of immigrants who resided in that labor market at some point in the past. The evidence presented in this chapter suggests that this is not a valid instrument. Immigrants cluster in those labor markets that offer them the best opportunities for the skills that they bring to the country, and hence the size of the preexisting stock of immigrants will not, in general, be uncorrelated with the wages offered by a particular locality.

The evidence presented in this chapter suggests that there is much left to learn about the macroeconomic consequences of immigration. For the most part, the immigration literature in labor economics evaluates various aspects of the microeconomic impact of immigration or measures how immigrants perform in the host country's labor market. The fact that immigration speeds up the process of wage convergence raises a number of new questions, such as the link between immigration and economic growth, that deserve careful empirical investigation.

Finally, most of the studies in the immigration literature emphasize some measure of the cost that immigrants impose on various sectors of the host country's economy – whether they be the wage losses suffered by native workers or the increase in taxes borne by native taxpayers. Remarkably little attention has been paid to the possibility that immigrants impart a variety of benefits to the host country's economy. A great deal of research remains to be done to better understand the source and magnitude of these benefits.

19

Native Internal Migration and the Labor Market Impact of Immigration

After introducing the national labor market approach in my 2003 Quarterly Journal of Economics paper, it was obvious that the next step should be to try to disentangle why the spatial correlation approach led to different results than the national labor market approach. One obvious factor that would account for the discrepancy was the possibility that flows of inputs or goods across local labor markets would diffuse the impact of immigration to the national economy.

This chapter presents a simple theoretical framework that helps us understand the implications of these regional adjustments, when the adjustment mechanism is driven by native internal migration. It turns out that a simple parameterization of the supply and demand functions in a local labor market has important implications about the relationship between the spatial correlation and the wage impact estimated in national-level studies. Specifically, the impact of immigration estimated at the local level is a "deflated" measure of the national labor market impact, where the deflator is a parameter that measures the extent to which natives respond to migration by moving to other localities.

George J. Borjas (2015)

The original version of this chapter was published as: Borjas, G.J. (2006). Native Internal Migration and the Labor Market Impact of Immigration, in: The Journal of Human Resources, 41(2): 221–58. © 2006 by University of Wisconsin Press. The author thanks Alberto Abadie, Richard Freeman, Edward Glaeser, Daniel Hamermesh, Lawrence Katz, Robert Rowthorn, and Stephen Trejo for very helpful comments on an earlier draft, and the Smith-Richardson Foundation for research support.

19.1.   Introduction

Immigrants in the United States cluster in a small number of geographic areas. In 2000, for example, 69.2 percent of working-age immigrants resided in six states (California, New York, Texas, Florida, Illinois, and New Jersey), but only 33.7 percent of natives lived in those states. Similarly, 38.4 percent of immigrants lived in four metropolitan areas (New York, Los Angeles, Chicago, and San Francisco), but only 12.2 percent of natives lived in the four metropolitan areas with the largest native-born populations (New York, Chicago, Los Angeles, and Philadelphia).

Economic theory suggests that immigration into a *closed* labor market affects the wage structure in that market by lowering the wage of competing workers and raising the wage of complements. Most of the empirical studies in the literature exploit the geographic clustering of immigrants to measure the labor market impact of immigration by defining the labor market along a geographic dimension – such as a state or a metropolitan area. Beginning with Grossman (1982), the typical study relates a measure of native economic outcomes in the locality (or the change in that outcome) to the relative quantity of immigrants in that locality (or the change in the relative number).[1] The regression coefficient, or "spatial correlation," is then interpreted as the impact of immigration on the native wage structure.

There are two well-known problems with this approach. First, immigrants may not be randomly distributed across labor markets. If immigrants tend to cluster in areas with thriving economies, there would be a spurious positive correlation between immigration and wages either in the cross section or in the time-series. This spurious correlation could attenuate or reverse whatever measurable negative effects immigrants might have had on the wage of competing native workers.[2]

Second, natives may respond to the entry of immigrants into a local labor market by moving their labor or capital to other localities until native wages and returns to capital are again equalized across areas. An interregion comparison of the wage of native workers might show little or no difference because the effects of immigration are diffused throughout the national economy, and not because immigration had no economic effects.

In view of these potential problems, it is not too surprising that the empirical literature has produced a confusing array of results. The measured impact of immigration on the wage of native workers in local labor markets fluctuates widely from study to study, but seems to cluster around zero. In recent work (Borjas 2003), I show that by defining the labor market at the national level – which more closely approximates the theoretical counterpart of a closed labor market – the measured wage impact of immigration becomes much larger. By examining the evolution of wages in the 1960–2000 period within narrow skill groups (defined in terms of schooling and labor market experience), I concluded that a 10 percent immigrant-induced increase in the number of workers in a particular skill group reduces the wage of that group by 3 to 4 percent.

In this chapter, I explore the disparate findings implied by the two approaches by focusing on a particular adjustment mechanism that native workers may use to avoid the adverse impacts of immigration on local labor markets: internal migration. A number of studies already examine if native migration decisions respond to immigration. As with the wage-impact literature, these studies offer a cornucopia of strikingly different findings, with some studies finding strong effects (Filer 1992; Frey 1995), and other studies reporting little connection (Card 2001; Kritz and Gurak 2001).[3]

This chapter can be viewed as an attempt to reconcile two related, but so far unconnected, strands in the immigration literature. I present a theoretical framework that jointly models wage determination in local labor markets and the native migration decision. The theory yields estimable equations that explicitly link the parameters measuring the wage impact of immigration at the national level, the spatial correlation between wages and immigration in local labor markets, and the native migration response. The model clearly shows that the larger the native migration response, the greater will be the difference between the estimates of the national wage effect and the spatial correlation. The model also implies that it is possible to use the spatial correlations to calculate the "true" national impact of immigration as long as one has information on the migration response of native workers.

I use data drawn from all the census cross sections between 1960 and 2000 to estimate the key parameters of the model. The data indicate that the measured wage impact of immigration depends intimately on the geographic definition of the labor market, and is larger as one expands the size of the market – from the metropolitan area, to the state, to the census division, and ultimately to the nation. In contrast, although the measured impact of immigration on native migration rates also depends on the geographic definition of the labor market, these effects become smaller as one expands the size of the market. These mirror-image patterns suggest that the wage effects of immigration on local labor markets are more attenuated the easier that natives find it to "vote with their feet." In fact, the native migration response can account for between 40 to 60 percent of the difference in the measured wage impact of immigration between the national and local labor market levels, depending on whether the local labor market is defined by a state or by a metropolitan area.

19.2.   Theory

I use a simple model of the joint determination of the regional wage structure and the internal migration decision of native workers to show the types of parameters that spatial correlations identify, and to determine if these parameters can be used to measure the national labor market impact of immigration.[4] Suppose that the labor demand function for workers in skill group i residing in geographic area j at time t can be written as:

$$(1) \qquad\qquad w_{ijt} = X_{ijt}L_{ijt}^{\eta},$$

where w_{ijt} is the wage of workers in cell (i, j, t); X_{ijt} is a demand shifter; L_{ijt} gives the total number of workers (both immigrants, M_{ijt}, and natives, N_{ijt}); and η is the factor price elasticity (with $\eta < 0$). It is convenient to interpret the elasticity η as the "true" impact that an immigrant influx would have in a closed labor market in the short run, a labor market where neither capital nor native-born labor responds to the increased supply.

Suppose the demand shifter is both time-invariant and region-invariant $(X_{ijt} = X_i)$. This simplification implies that wages for skill group i differ across regions only because the stock of workers is not evenly distributed geographically.[5] I assume that the total number of native workers in a particular skill group in the national economy is fixed at $\overline{N}_i$. It would not be difficult to extend the model to allow for differential rates of growth (across region-skill groups) in the size of the native workforce.

Suppose that $N_{ij,-1}$ native workers in skill group i reside in region j in the pre-immigration period $(t = -1)$. This geographic sorting of native workers does not represent a long-run equilibrium; some regions have too many workers and other regions too few. The regional wage differentials induce a migration response by native workers even prior to the immigrant influx. In particular, region j experiences a net migration of

ΔN_{ij0} natives belonging to skill group i between $t = -1$ and $t = 0$.
Beginning at time 0, the local labor market (as defined by a particular skill-region cell) receives an influx of M_{ijt} immigrants. The immigrant influx continues in all subsequent periods. A convenient (but restrictive) assumption is that region j receives the same number of immigrants in each year. The annual immigrant influx for a particular skill-region cell can then be represented by M_{ij}.[6]

For simplicity, I assume that immigrants do not migrate internally within the United States – they enter region j and remain there.[7] Natives continue to make relocation decisions, and region j experiences a net migration of ΔN_{ij1} natives in period 1, ΔN_{ij2} natives in period 2, and so on. The labor demand function in Equation (1) implies that the wage for skill group i in region j at time t is given by:[8]

$$(2) \qquad \log w_{ijt} = \log X_i + \eta \log \big[N_{ij,-1} + (t + 1)M_{ij} + \Delta N_{ij0} + \Delta N_{ij1} \\ + \ldots + \Delta N_{ijt} \big],$$

which can be rewritten as:

$$(3) \qquad \log w_{ijt} \approx \log w_{ij,-1} + \eta \big[(t + 1)\, m_{ij} + v_{ij0} + v_{ij1} + \ldots + v_{ijt} \big], \\ \text{for } t \geq 0,$$

where $m_{ij} = M_{ij}/N_{ij,-1}$, the flow of immigrants in a particular skill group entering region j relative to the initial native stock; and $v_{ijt} = \Delta N_{ijt}/N_{ij,-1}$, the net migration rate of natives. Note that $w_{ij,-1}$ gives the wage offered to workers in group (i, j) in the pre-immigration period.

I assume that the internal migration response of native workers occurs with a lag. For example, immigrants begin to arrive at $t = 0$. The demand function in Equation (3) implies that the wage response to immigration is immediate, so that wages fall in the immigrant-penetrated regions. The immigrant-induced migration decisions of natives, however, are not observed until the next period. The lagged supply response that describes the native migration decisions is given by:

$$(4) \qquad v_{ijt} = \sigma(\log w_{ij,t-1} - \log \overline{w}_{i,t-1}),$$

where σ is the supply elasticity, and log $\log w_{i,t-1}$ is the equilibrium wage (for skill group i) that will be observed throughout the national economy once all migration responses to the immigrant influx that has occurred up to time $t - 1$ have been made.[9] Income-maximizing behavior on the part of native workers implies that the elasticity σ is positive. If σ is sufficiently "small," the migration response of natives may not be completed within one period.[10] Note that the migration decision is made by forward-looking native workers who compare the current wage in region j to the wage that region j will eventually attain. Therefore, natives have perfect information about the eventual outcome that results from immigration. Workers are not making decisions based on erroneous information (as in the typical cobweb model). Instead, the lags arise because it is difficult to change locations immediately.[11]

As noted earlier, the existence of regional wage differentials at time $t = -1$ implies that native internal migration was taking place even prior to the beginning of immigration. It is useful to describe the determinants of the net migration flow v_{ij0}. In the pre-immigration period, the equilibrium wage that would be eventually attained in the economy is:

$$(5) \qquad \log \overline{w}_{i,-1} = X_i + \eta \log N_i^*,$$

where N_i^* represent the number of native workers in skill group i that would live in each region once long-run equilibrium is attained.[12] The preexisting net migration rate of native workers is then given by:

$$(6) \qquad v_{ij0} = \sigma(\log w_{ij,-1} - \log \overline{w}_{i,-1}) = \eta \sigma \lambda_{ij},$$

where $\lambda_{ij} = \log(N_{ij,-1}/N_i^*)$. By definition, the variable λ_{ij} is negative when the initial wage in region j is higher than the long-run equilibrium wage (in other words, there are fewer workers in region j than there will be after all internal migration takes place). Equation (6) then implies that the net migration rate in region j is positive (since $\eta < 0$).

Native net migration continues concurrently with the immigrant influx. The mathematical appendix shows that the native net-migration rate can be written as:

$$(7) \qquad v_{ijt} = \eta \sigma (1 + \eta \sigma)^t \lambda_{ij} + \left[1 - (1 + \eta \sigma)^t m_i - 1 - (1 + \eta \sigma)^t m_{ij} \right],$$

where $m_i = M_i/\overline{N}_i$, and M_i gives the per-period flow of immigrants in skill group i. I assume that the restriction $0 < (1 + \eta \sigma) < 1$ holds throughout the analysis.

The total number of native workers in cell (i, j, t) is then given by the sum of the initial stock $(N_{ij,-1})$ and the net migration flows defined by Equation (7), or:

$$(8) \qquad \log N_{ijt} = \log N_{ij,-1} + \left[(1 + \eta \sigma)^{t+1} - 1 \right] \lambda_{ij}$$
$$+ \left[\frac{t}{t+1} + \frac{(1 + \eta \sigma)}{\eta \sigma} \frac{[1 - (1 + \eta \sigma)^t]}{(t+1)} \right] \widetilde{m}_{it}$$

$$- \left[\frac{t}{t+1} + \frac{(1 + \eta\sigma)}{\eta\sigma} \frac{[1 - (1 + \eta\sigma)^t]}{(t+1)} \right] \tilde{m}_{ijt},$$

where $\tilde{m}_{it} = (t + 1)m_i$ gives the *stock* of immigrants with skill i who have migrated as of time t relative to the number of natives with comparable skills; and $\tilde{m}_{ijt} = (t + 1)m_{ij}$ gives the relative *stock* of immigrants with skill i who have migrated to region j as of time t.[13] The wage for workers in cell (i, j, t) is then given by:

$$(9) \qquad \log w_{ijt} = \log w_{ij,-1} + \left[(1 + \eta\sigma)^{t+1} - 1 \right] \lambda_{ij}$$

$$+ \eta \left[\frac{t}{t+1} + \frac{(1 + \eta\sigma)}{\eta\sigma} \frac{[1 - (1 + \eta\sigma)^t]}{(t+1)} \right] \tilde{m}_{it}$$

$$+ \eta \left[\frac{1}{t+1} - \frac{(1 + \eta\sigma)}{\eta\sigma} \frac{[1 - (1 + \eta\sigma)^t]}{(t+1)} \right] \tilde{m}_{ijt}.$$

Equations (8) and (9) describe the evolution of N_{ijt} and w_{ijt} for a particular skill group in a local labor market. The first two terms in each equation indicate that the (current) stock of native workers and the (current) wage level depend on preexisting conditions. The equations also show how the size of the native workforce and wages adjust to the immigrant-induced shifts in supply. In particular, consider the behavior of the coefficients of the region-specific immigration stock variable ($\tilde{m}_{ijt}$) in each of these equations. As t grows large, the coefficient in the native workforce regression (which should be negative) converges to -1, while the coefficient in the wage regression (which also should be negative) converges to zero. Put differently, the longer the time elapsed between the beginning of the immigrant influx and the measurement of the dependent variables, the more likely that native migration behavior has completely neutralized the immigrant-induced local supply shifts and the less likely that the spatial correlation approach will uncover any wage effect on local labor markets.

Equally important, the two coefficients of the region-specific immigrant stock variable provide an intuitive interpretation of how the spatial correlation – that is, the impact of immigration on wages that can be estimated by comparing local labor markets – relates to the factor price elasticity η that gives the national wage impact of immigration. In particular, let γ_{Nt} be the coefficient of the immigrant stock variable in the native workforce equation, and let γ_{Wt} be the respective coefficient in the wage equation. Equations (8) and (9) then imply that:

$$(10) \qquad \gamma_{Wt} = \eta(1 + \gamma_{Nt}).$$

The coefficient γ_{Nt} approximately gives the number of natives who migrate out of a particular labor market for every immigrant who settles there $(\gamma_{Nt} \approx \partial N / \partial \widetilde{M}_t)$.[14] The factor price elasticity η can be estimated by "blowing up" the spatial correlation, where the division factor is the number of natives who do *not* move per immigrant who enters the country. To illustrate, suppose that the coefficient γ_{Nt} is –0.5, indicating that five fewer natives choose to reside in the local labor market for every ten immigrants entering that market. Equation (10) then implies that the spatial correlation that can be estimated by comparing native wages across local labor markets is only half the size of the true factor price elasticity.[15]

19.2.1. Empirical Specification

In the next section, I use data drawn from the 1960–2000 Censuses to estimate the key parameters of the model. These data provide five observations for N_{ijt}, w_{ijt}, and $\widetilde{M}_{ijt}$ (one for each census cross section) for labor markets defined by skill groups and geographic regions. The available data, therefore, are not sufficiently detailed to allow me to estimate the dynamic evolution of the native workforce and wage structure as summarized by Equations (8) and (9). These equations, after all, have time-varying coefficients for the variable measuring the region-specific immigrant influx, and these coefficients are highly nonlinear in time. I instead simplify the framework by applying the approximation $(1 + x)^t \approx (1 + xt)$. Equations (8) and (9) can then be rewritten as:[16]

$$(11) \qquad \log N_{ijt} = \log N_{ij,-1} + \eta\sigma\lambda_{ij} + \eta\sigma(t\lambda_{ij}) - \eta\sigma\widetilde{m}_{it} + \eta\sigma\widetilde{m}_{ijt},$$

$$(12) \qquad \log w_{ijt} = \log w_{ij,-1} + \eta^2\sigma\lambda_{ij} + \eta^2\sigma(t\lambda_{ij}) - \eta^2\sigma\widetilde{m}_{it}$$

$$+ \eta(1 + \eta\sigma)\,\widetilde{m}_{ijt}.$$

Equations (11) and (12) can be estimated by stacking the available data on the size of the native workforce, wages, and immigrant stock across skill groups, regions, and time. Many of the regressors in Equations (11) and (12) are absorbed by including appropriately defined vectors of fixed effects in the regressions. For example, the inclusion of fixed effects for the various skill-region cells absorbs the vector of variables $(N_{ij,-1}, \lambda_{ij})$ in Equation (11) and the vector $(w_{ij,-1}, \lambda_{ij})$ in Equation (12). Similarly, interactions between skill and time fixed effects absorb the variable $\widetilde{m}_{it}$ in both equations.

In addition to these fixed effects, the regression models in Equation (11) and (12) suggest the presence of two regressors that vary by skill, region, and time. The first, of course, is the region-specific measure of the immigrant stock $(\widetilde{m}_{ijt})$, the main independent variable in any empirical study that attempts to estimate spatial correlations. The second is the variable $(t\lambda_{ij})$, which is related to the (cumulative) net migration of natives that would have been observed as of time $(t - 1)$ had there been no immigration, and also introduces the initial conditions in the labor market into the regression analysis. This variable is not observable. In the empirical work reported later, I proxy for this variable by including regressors giving either a lagged measure of the number of natives in the workforce or the lagged growth rate of the native workforce in the particular labor market.

The regression models in Equation (11) and (12) provide some insight into why there is so much confusion in the empirical literature regarding the link between native internal migration and immigration or between wages and immigration. Even abstracting from the interpretation of the coefficient of the immigrant stock variable (which represents an amalgam of various structural parameters), this coefficient is estimated properly only if local labor market conditions are properly accounted for in the regression specification.

Suppose, for instance, that immigrants enter those parts of the country that pay high wages. If the initial wage is left out of the wage regression, the observed impact of immigration on wages will be too positive, as the immigrant supply variable is capturing unobserved preexisting characteristics of high-wage areas. Similarly, suppose that immigrants tend to enter those parts of the country that also attract native migrants. If the regression equation does not control for the preexisting migration flow, Equation (11) indicates that the impact of immigration on the size of the native workforce also will be too positive. In fact, Borjas, Freeman, and Katz (1997: 30) provide a good example of how controlling for preexisting conditions can actually change the sign of the correlation between net migration and immigration. In particular, they show that the rate of change in the number of natives living in a state is positively correlated with a measure of concurrent immigrant penetration in the cross section. But this positive correlation turns negative when they add a lagged measure of native population growth into the regression.

The regression models also suggest that the geographic definition of a labor market is likely to influence the magnitude of the measured spatial correlations. In both regressions, the coefficient of the region-specific immigrant stock variable depends on the value of the parameter σ, the elasticity measuring the native migration response. The spatial correlation estimated in the native workforce regression depends negatively on σ, while the spatial correlation estimated in the wage regression depends positively on σ. The supply elasticity will probably be larger when migration is less costly, implying that σ will be greater when the labor market is geographically small.[17] Equations (11) and (12) then imply that the spatial correlation between the size of the native workforce and the immigrant stock variable will be more negative when the model is estimated using geographically *smaller* labor markets, and that the spatial correlation between the wage and the immigrant stock variable will be more negative for *larger* labor markets. I will show in what follows that the data indeed confirm this mirror-image implication of the theory.

Finally, it is worth stressing that the coefficients of the immigrant stock variable in this linearized version of the two-equation model satisfy the multiplicative property given by Equation (10). In sum, the theory provides a useful foundation for linking the results of very different conceptual and econometric frameworks in the study of the economic impact of immigration.

19.3.   Data and Descriptive Statistics

The empirical analysis uses data drawn from the 1960, 1970, 1980, 1990, and 2000 Integrated Public Use Microdata Series (IPUMS) of the U.S. Census. The 1960 and 1970 samples represent a 1 percent sample of the population, while the 1980, 1990, and 2000 samples represent a 5 percent sample.[18] The analysis is initially restricted to the subsample of men aged 18–64, who do not reside in group quarters, are not enrolled in school, and worked in the civilian sector in the calendar year prior to the census.[19] A person is defined as an immigrant if he was born abroad and is either a noncitizen or a naturalized citizen; all other persons are classified as natives.

As in my earlier work (Borjas 2003), I use both educational attainment and work experience to sort workers into particular skill groups. The key idea underlying this classification is that similarly educated workers with very different levels of work experience are unlikely to be perfect substitutes (Welch 1979; Card and Lemieux 2001). I classify the men into four distinct education groups: workers who are high school dropouts (they have less than 12 years of completed schooling), high school graduates (they have exactly 12 years of schooling), persons who have some college (they have between 13 and 15 years of schooling), and college graduates (they have at least 16 years of schooling).

The classification of workers into experience groups is imprecise because the census does not provide any measure of labor market experience or of the age at which a worker first enters the labor market. I assume that the age of entry (A_T) into the labor market is 17 for the typical high school dropout, 19 for the typical high school graduate, 21 for the typical person with some college, and 23 for the typical college graduate. The measure of work experience is then given by (Age $- A_T$).[20] I restrict the analysis to persons who have between one and 40 years of experience. Welch (1979) suggests that workers in adjacent experience cells are more likely to influence each other's labor market opportunities than workers in cells that are further apart. I capture the similarity among workers with roughly similar years of experience by aggregating the data into five-year experience intervals, indicating if the worker has between one and five years of experience, between six and ten years, and so on. There are eight experience groups.

A skill group i then contains workers who have a particular level of schooling and a particular level of experience. There are 32 such skill groups in the analysis (four education groups and eight experience groups). Consider a group of workers who have skills i, live in region j, and are observed in calendar year t. The (i, j, t) cell defines a particular labor market at a point in time. The immigrant share in this labor market is defined by:

$$(13) \qquad p_{ijt} = \frac{\tilde{M}_{ijt}}{\tilde{M}_{ijt} + N_{ijt}},$$

where $\tilde{M}_{ijt}$ gives the stock of foreign-born workers in skill group i who have entered region j as of time t, and N_{ijt} gives the number of native workers in that cell. The variable p_{ijt} thus measures the fraction of the workforce that is foreign born in a particular labor market at a particular point in time.

I begin the empirical analysis by describing how immigration affected different labor markets in the past few decades. As indicated earlier, most of the immigrants who entered the United States in the past 40 years have clustered in a relatively small number of states.

Figure 19.1 shows the trends in the immigrant share, by educational attainment, for three groups of states: California, the other main immigrant-receiving states (Florida, Illinois, New Jersey, New York, and Texas), and the rest of the country. Not surprisingly, the largest immigrant-induced supply increase occurred in California for the least-educated workers. By 2000, almost 80 percent of high school dropouts in California were foreign born, as compared to only 50 percent in the other immigrant-receiving states, and 20 percent in the rest of the country. Although the scale of the immigrant influx is smaller for high-skill groups, there is still a large disparity in the size of the supply increase across the three areas. In 2000, for example, more than a quarter of college graduates in California were foreign born, as compared to 18 percent in the other immigrant-receiving states, and 8 percent in the rest of the country.

Figure 19.1

The Immigrant Share of the Male Workforce, by Education and Area of Country

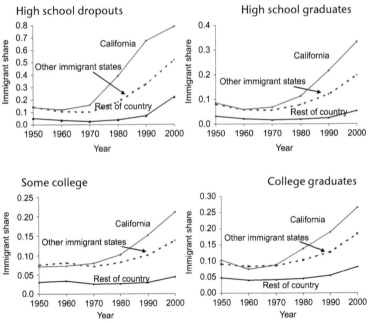

Note: The "other immigrant states" include Florida, Illinois, New Jersey, New York, and Texas.

Figures 19.2 and 19.3 continue the descriptive analysis by showing the trends in the immigrant share for some of the specific schooling-experience groups used in the analysis. To conserve space, I only illustrate these profiles for the two education groups most affected by immigration: high school dropouts (Figure 19.2) and college graduates (Figure 19.3).

Figure 19.2

Immigrant Share for High School Dropouts, by Years of Work Experience

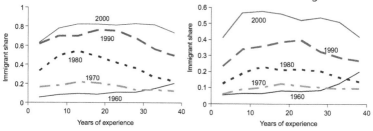

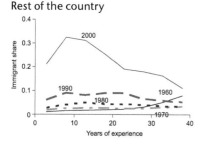

Note: The "other immigrant states" include Florida, Illinois, New Jersey, New York, and Texas.

Figure 19.3

Immigrant Share for College Graduates, by Years of Work Experience

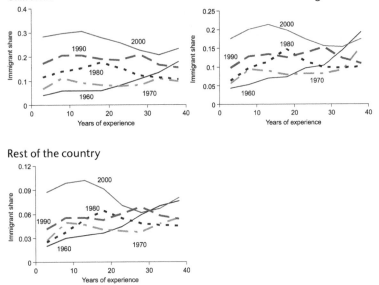

California   Other immigrant states

Rest of the country

Note: The "other immigrant states" include Florida, Illinois, New Jersey, New York, and Texas.

These figures show that there is significant dispersion in the relative size of the immigrant population over time and across experience groups, even when looking at a particular level of education and a particular part of the country. In 1980, for example, the immigration of high school dropouts in California was particularly likely to affect the labor market opportunities faced by workers with around 15 years of experience, where around half of the relevant population was foreign born. In contrast, only 30 percent of the workers with more than 30 years of experience were foreign born. By 2000, however, more than 80 percent of all high school dropouts with between ten and 35 years of experience were foreign born. These patterns differed in other parts of the country. In the relatively nonimmigrant rest of the country, immigration of high school dropouts was relatively rare prior to 1990, accounting for less than 10 percent of the workers in the relevant labor market. By 2000, however, immigrants made up more than 30 percent of the high school dropouts with between five and 15 years of experience.

The data summarized in these figures, therefore, suggest that there has been a great deal of dispersion in how immigration affects the various skill groups in different regional labor markets. In some years, it affects workers in certain parts of the region-education-experience spectrum. In other years, it affects other workers. This chapter exploits this variation to measure how wages and native worker migration decisions respond to immigration.

Before proceeding to a formal analysis, it is instructive to document that the raw data reveals equally strong differences in the way that natives have chosen to sort themselves geographically across the United States. More important, these location choices seem to be correlated with the immigrant-induced supply shifts. Figure 19.4 illustrates the aggregate trend. As first reported by Borjas, Freeman, and Katz (1997), the share of the native-born population that chose to live in California stopped growing around 1970, at the same time that the immigrant influx began. This important trend is illustrated in the top panel of Figure 19.4. The data clearly show the relative numbers of native workers living in California first stalling, and eventually declining, as the scale of the immigrant influx increased rapidly.[21]

The middle panel of Figure 19.4 illustrates a roughly similar trend in the other immigrant states. As immigration increased in these states (the immigrant share rose from about 8 percent in 1970 to 22 percent in 2000), the fraction of natives who chose to live in those states declined slightly, from 26 to 24.5 percent.

Finally, the bottom panel of the figure illustrates the trend in the relatively nonimmigrant areas that form the rest of the country. Although immigration also increased over time in this region, the increase has been relatively small (the immigrant share rose from 2.5 percent in 1970 to 7.5 percent in 2000). At the same time, the share of natives living in this region experienced an upward drift, from 64.5 percent in 1970 to 66.5 percent in 2000. The evidence summarized in Figure 19.4, therefore, tends to suggest a link between native location decisions and immigration.

Figure 19.4

Geographic Sorting of Native Workforce and Immigration

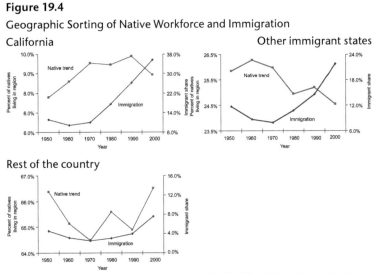

Note: The "other immigrant states" include Florida, Illinois, New Jersey, New York, and Texas.

This link is also evident at more disaggregated levels of geography and skills. I used all of the census data available between 1960 and 2000 to calculate for each (i, j) cell the growth rate of the native workforce during each decade (defined as the log of the ratio of the native workforce at the decade's two endpoints) and the corresponding decadal change in the immigrant share. The top panel of Figure 19.5 presents the scatter diagram relating these decadal changes at the state level after removing decade effects. The plot clearly suggests a negative relation between the growth rate of a particular class of native workers in a particular state and immigration. The bottom panel of the figure illustrates an even stronger pattern when the decadal changes are calculated at the metropolitan area level. In sum, the raw data clearly reveal that the native workforce grew fastest in those labor markets that were least affected by immigration.

Figure 19.5

Scatter Diagram Relating the Growth Rate of the Native Workforce and Immigration

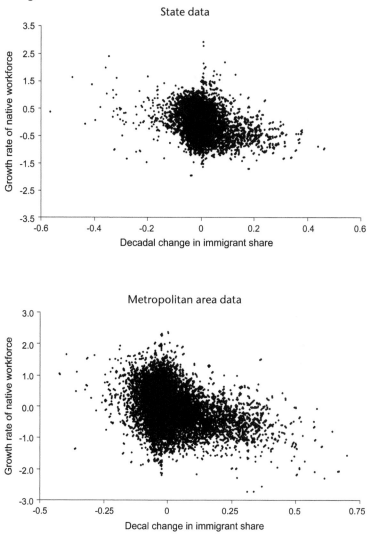

State data

Metropolitan area data

Notes: Each data point represents the decadal change (for the 1960–2000 period in the top panel and the 1980–2000 period in the bottom panel) in the log size of the native workforce and in the immigrant share for a particular skill group in a particular geographic area. Both plots remove decade effects from the data.

Finally, Table 19.1 provides an alternative way of looking at the data that also links native migration decisions and immigration. Beginning in 1970, the census contains information not only on the person's state of residence as of the census date, but also on the state of residence five years prior to the survey. These data can be used to construct net-migration rates for each of the skill groups in each geographic market, as well as in-migration and out-migration rates. (The construction of these rates will be described in detail later in the chapter.) To easily summarize the basic trends linking migration rates and immigration, I again break up the United States into three regions: California, the other immigrant-receiving states, and the rest of the country. A native worker is then defined to be an internal migrant if he moves across these three regions in the five-year period prior to the census.

Table 19.1

Trends in Inter-Area Migration Rates of Native Workers

Area		Year			
		1970	1980	1990	2000
Net migration rates					
High school dropouts	California	-0.2%	-2.2%	-2.3%	-5.4%
	Other immigrant states	0.3	-0.2	-1.6	-1.4
	Rest of country	-0.1	0.3	0.8	1.0
High school graduates	California	0.3	-1.4	-0.8	-4.5
	Other immigrant states	0.0	-0.1	-0.8	-0.9
	Rest of country	0.0	0.2	0.4	0.7
Some college	California	1.3	-1.0	0.3	-3.4
	Other immigrant states	-0.4	-0.3	-0.9	-0.8
	Rest of country	-0.2	0.4	0.3	0.9
College graduates	California	4.4	3.3	4.5	1.9
	Other immigrant states	0.3	-0.3	-0.8	-0.4
	Rest of country	-1.0	-0.4	-0.5	-0.1
In-migration rates					
High school dropouts	California	7.6	6.9	6.2	4.0
	Other immigrant states	3.8	4.7	4.5	4.2
	Rest of country	1.8	2.3	2.6	2.5
High school graduates	California	8.7	8.3	7.7	4.9
	Other immigrant states	5.4	6.0	5.2	4.6
	Rest of country	2.7	2.8	2.6	2.5
Some college	California	8.6	8.8	7.8	5.3
	Other immigrant states	7.0	8.1	6.7	6.2
	Rest of country	4.4	4.8	4.0	3.6
College graduates	California	14.3	14.1	13.0	11.1
	Other immigrant states	11.9	11.9	10.0	9.4
	Rest of country	6.2	6.3	5.4	4.8
Out-migration rates					
High school dropouts	California	7.8	9.1	8.5	9.5
	Other immigrant states	3.6	4.9	6.1	5.6
	Rest of country	1.8	2.0	1.9	1.6
High school graduates	California	8.3	9.7	8.5	9.5
	Other immigrant states	5.4	6.1	6.0	5.5
	Rest of country	2.7	2.6	2.3	1.7
Some college	California	7.3	9.8	7.5	8.7
	Other immigrant states	7.4	8.4	7.6	7.0
	Rest of country	4.6	4.4	3.7	2.8
College graduates	California	9.9	10.8	8.4	9.2
	Other immigrant states	11.7	12.1	10.8	9.8
	Rest of country	7.2	6.7	5.9	4.9

Notes: This table breaks up the country into three distinct areas: California, the other immigrant states, and the rest of the country. The "other immigrant states" include Florida, Illinois, New Jersey, New York, and Texas. A native worker is defined to migrate if he moves from one of these areas to another in the five-year period prior to the census.

The differential trends in the net-migration rate across the three regions are revealing. Within each education group, there is usually a steep decline in the net migration rate into California, a slower decline in the net migration rate into the other immigrant states, and a slight increase in the net migration rate into the rest of the country. In other words, the net migration of natives fell most in those parts of the country most heavily hit by immigration.

The other panels of Table 19.1 show that the relative decline in net migration rates in the immigrant-targeted states arises because of both a relative decline in the in-migration rate and a relative increase in the out-migration rate. For example, the in-migration rate of native high school dropouts into California fell from 7.6 to 4.0 percent between 1970 and 2000, as compared to a respective increase from 1.8 to 2.5 percent in the rest of the country. Similarly, the out-migration rates of high school dropouts rose from 7.8 to 9.5 percent in California and from 3.6 to 5.6 percent in the other immigrant states, but fell from 1.8 to 1.6 percent in those states least hit by immigration.

19.4.   Immigration and Wages

In earlier work (Borjas 2003), I showed that the labor market impact of immigration at the national level can be estimated by examining the wage evolution of skill groups defined in terms of educational attainment and experience. This section of the chapter reestimates some of the models presented in my earlier paper, and documents the sensitivity of the wage impact of immigration to the geographic definition of the labor market.

I measure the wage impact of immigration using four alternative definitions for the geographic area covered by the labor market. In particular, I assume that the labor market facing a particular skill group is: (1) a national labor market, so that the wage impact of immigration estimated at this level of geography presumably measures the factor price elasticity η in the model; (2) a labor market defined by the geographic boundaries of the nine census divisions; (3) a labor market that operates at the state level; or (4) a labor market bounded by the metropolitan area.[22]

Let $\log w_{ijt}$ denote the mean log weekly wage of native men who have skills i, work in region j, and are observed at time t.[23] I stack these data across skill groups, geographic areas, and census cross sections and estimate the model:

$$(14) \qquad \log w_{ijt} = \theta_W p_{ijt} + s_i + r_j + \pi_t + (s_i \times r_j) + (s_i \times \pi_t)$$
$$+ (r_j \times \pi_t) + \varphi_{ijt},$$

where s_i is a vector of fixed effects indicating the group's skill level; r_j is a vector of fixed effects indicating the geographic area of residence; and π_t is a vector of fixed effects indicating the time period of the observation. The linear fixed effects in Equation (14) control for differences in labor market outcomes across skill groups and regions, and over time. The interactions $(s_i \times \pi_t)$ and $(s_j \times \pi_t)$ control for secular changes in the returns to skills and in the regional wage structure during the 1960–2000 period. Finally, the inclusion of the interactions $(s_i \times r_j)$ implies that the coefficient θ_W is being identified from changes in wages and immigration that occur within skill-region cells.

Note that the various vectors of fixed effects included in Equation (14) correspond to the vectors of fixed effects implied by the estimating equation derived from the model (Equation (12)). The only exception is that Equation (14) also includes interactions between region and census year. These interactions would clearly enter the theory if demand shocks were allowed to differentially affect regions over time.

The regression coefficients reported in this section come from weighted regressions, where the weight is the sample size used to calculate the mean log weekly wage in the (i, j, t) cell.[24] The standard errors are clustered by skill-region cells to adjust for the possible serial correlation that may exist within cells.

Finally, the specification I use in the empirical analysis uses the immigrant share, p, rather than the relative number of immigrants as of time t, $\widetilde{m} = \widetilde{M}/N$, as the measure of the immigrant-induced supply increase. It turns out that the relation between the various dependent variables and the relative number of immigrants is highly nonlinear, and is not captured correctly by a linear term in $\widetilde{m}$. The immigrant share approximates $\log\widetilde{m}$, so that using the immigrant share introduces some nonlinearity into the regression model. In fact, the wage effects (appropriately calculated) are similar when including either $\log\widetilde{m}$ or a second-order polynomial in $\widetilde{m}$ as the measure of the immigrant supply shift.[25]

Consider initially the first three columns of Table 19.2, which present the basic estimates of the adjustment coefficient θ_W obtained from the sample of working men. The first row summarizes the regression results when the geographic reach of the labor market is assumed to encompass the entire nation.[26] The estimated coefficient is –0.533, with a standard error of 0.203. It is easier to interpret this coefficient by converting it to an elasticity that gives the percent change in wages associated with a percent change in labor supply. In particular, define the wage elasticity as:

$$(15) \qquad \frac{\partial \log w}{\partial \widetilde{m}} = \frac{\theta_w}{(1 + \widetilde{m})^2}.$$

By 2000, immigration had increased the size of the workforce by 17.2 percent. Equation (15) implies that the wage elasticity – evaluated at the mean value of the relative number of immigrants – can be obtained by multiplying θ_W by 0.73. The wage elasticity for weekly earnings is then –0.39 (or –0.532 × 0.73). Put differently, a 10 percent immigrant-induced supply increase – that is, an immigrant flow that increases the number of workers in a skill group by 10 percent – reduces weekly earnings in that group by almost 4 percent.

Suppose now that the worker's state of residence defines the geographic area encompassed by the labor market. The data then consists of stacked observations on the immigrant share and the mean log weekly wage for cell (i, j, t). The first row of Panel III in Table 19.2 reports the estimated coefficient of the immigrant share variable when Equation (14) is estimated at the state level. The adjustment coefficient is –0.217, with a standard error of 0.033. At the mean immigrant-induced supply shift, the state-level regression implies that a 10 percent increase in supply reduces the native wage by only 1.6 percent, roughly 40 percent of the estimated impact at the national level. Note that the derivative in Equation (15) is precisely the wage impact of immigration captured by the region-specific immigrant stock variable in Equation (12). In terms of the parameters of the theoretical model, this derivative estimates the product of elasticities $\eta(1 + \sigma\eta)$.

As discussed earlier, the model suggests that the log wage regression – when estimated at the local labor market level – should include a variable that approximately measures the lagged relative number of natives who would have migrated in the absence of immigration. The second row of the panel adds a variable giving the log of the size of the native workforce ten years prior to the census date.[27] The inclusion of lagged employment does not alter the quantitative nature of the evidence. The adjustment coefficient is –0.220 (0.033). Finally, the third row of the panel introduces an alternative variable to control for the counterfactual native migration flow, namely the rate of growth in the size of the native workforce in the ten-year period prior to the census date. Again, the estimated wage effects are quite similar.

Table 19.2

Impact of Immigration on Log Weekly Earnings, by Geographic Definition of the Labor Market

Regression model	Men			Men and women		
	Immigrant share	Lagged native employment	Lagged native employment growth	Immigrant share	Lagged native employment	Lagged native employment growth
I. National						
(1)	-0.533	–	–	-0.532	–	–
	(0.203)			(0.189)		
II. Census division						
(1)	-0.274	–	–	-0.352	–	–
	(0.053)			(0.061)		
(2)	-0.273	-0.043	–	-0.350	-0.040	–
	(0.053)	(0.019)		(0.061)	(0.017)	
(3)	-0.274	–	0.048	-0.351	–	0.048
	(0.052)		(0.014)	(0.062)	–	(0.015)
III. State						
(1)	-0.217	–	–	-0.266	–	–
	(0.033)			(0.037)		
(2)	-0.220	-0.027	–	-0.271	-0.033	–
	(0.033)	(0.007)		(0.037)	(0.007)	
(3)	-0.215	–	0.033	-0.265	–	0.035
	(0.033)		(0.005)	(0.037)	–	(0.006)
IV. Metropolitan area						
(1)	-0.043	–	–	-0.057	–	–
	(0.025)			(0.024)		
(2)	0.021	-0.016	–	-0.001	-0.010	–
	(0.048)	(0.012)		(0.051)	(0.012)	
(3)	0.048	–	0.030	0.024	–	0.030
	(0.047)		(0.008)	(0.050)	–	(0.008)

Notes: Standard errors are reported in parentheses and are clustered at the region-skill group level. All regressions are weighted by the size of the sample used to calculate the mean of weekly earnings in the specific region-skill-year cell. The regressions estimated at the national level have 160 observations; the regressions estimated at the region level have 1,440 observations; the regressions estimated at the state level have 8,160 observations (8,083 observations when lagged native employment is included); and the regressions estimated at the metropolitan area level have 25,184 (14,848) observations. The regressors in the national-level regression include a vector of skill fixed effects, a vector of time fixed effects, and all possible two-way interactions between a vector of education fixed effects, a vector of experience fixed effects, and a vector of time fixed effects. The regressions presented in the bottom three panels include a vector of skill fixed effects, a vector of (appropriately defined) region fixed effects, a vector of time fixed effects, and all possible two-way interactions among these vectors.

The remaining panels in Table 19.2 document the behavior of the coefficient θ_W as the geographic boundary of the labor market is either expanded (to the census division level) or narrowed (to the metropolitan area level). The key result implied by the comparison of the various panels is that the adjustment coefficient grows numerically larger as the geographic reach of the labor market expands. Using the simplest specification in Row 1 in each of the panels, for example, the adjustment coefficient is −0.043 (0.025) at the metropolitan area level, increases to −0.217 (0.033) at the state level, increases further to −0.274 (0.053) at the division level, and jumps to −0.533 (0.203) at the national level.

Up to this point, I have excluded working women from the analysis because of the inherent difficulty in measuring their labor market experience and classifying them correctly into the various skill groups. Nevertheless, the last three columns of Table 19.2 replicate the entire analysis using both working men and women in the regression models. The national-level coefficient is almost identical to that obtained when the regression analysis used only working men. Equally important, the regressions reveal the same clear pattern of a numerically smaller adjustment coefficient as the labor market becomes geographically smaller: from −0.352 (0.061) in the division-level regression to −0.266 (0.037) in the state-level regression to −0.057 (0.024) in the regressions estimates at the level of the metropolitan area. The results, therefore, are quite robust to the inclusion of working women.

The theoretical model presented earlier suggests an interesting interpretation for this correlation between the geographic size of the labor market and the measured wage effect of immigration. As the geographic region becomes smaller, there is more spatial arbitrage – due to interregional flows of labor – that tends to equalize opportunities for workers of given skills across regions.

An alternative explanation for the pattern is that the smaller wage effects measured in smaller geographic units may be due to attenuation bias. The variable measuring the immigrant stock will likely contain more measurement errors when it is calculated at more disaggregated levels of geography. As I show in the next section, it is unlikely that attenuation bias can completely explain the monotonic relation between the adjustment coefficient and the geographic reach of the labor market.

Overall, the evidence seems to indicate that even though immigration has a sizable adverse effect on the wage of competing workers at the national level, the analysis of wage differentials across regional labor markets conceals much of that impact. The remainder of this chapter examines whether these disparate findings can be attributed to native internal migration decisions.

19.5.   Immigration and Internal Migration

I now estimate a variety of models – closely linked to the theoretical discussion in Section 19.2 – to determine if the evolution of the native workforce or the internal migration behavior of natives is related to immigrant-induced supply increases in the respective labor markets.

19.5.1.   The Size of the Native Workforce

Consider the following regression model:

$$(16) \qquad \log N_{ijt} = X_{ijt}\beta + \theta_N P_{ijt} + s_i + r_j + \pi_t + (s_i \times \pi_t) + (r_j \times \pi_t)$$
$$+ (s_i \times r_j) + \varepsilon_{ijt},$$

where X is a vector of control variables discussed later. As with the wage regression specified earlier, the various vectors of fixed effects absorb any region-specific, skill-specific, and time-specific factors that affect the evolution of the native workforce in a particular labor market. Similarly, the interactions allow for decade-specific changes in the number of workers in particular skill groups or in particular states caused by shifts in aggregate demand. Finally, the interaction between the skill and region fixed effects implies that the coefficient of the immigrant supply variable is being identified from changes that occur within a specific skill-region grouping. As before, all standard errors are adjusted for any clustering that may occur at the skill-region level.[28] I again estimate the model using three alternative definitions for the geographic area encompassed by the labor market: a census division, a state, and a metropolitan area. Table 19.3 presents alternative sets of regression specifications that show how the immigrant-induced supply shift affects the evolution of the size of the native workforce.

Table 19.3

Impact of Immigration on the Size of the Native Workforce (Dependent variable = log of number of natives in workforce)

Geographic area and sample	Independent variables				
	Immigrant share	Lagged native employment	Lagged native employment growth	Mean log wage	Unemployment rate
I. Census divisions					
1. Men	-0.023	–	–	–	–
	(0.158)				
2. Men	0.055	0.243	–	0.172	-1,327
	(0.121)	(0.042)		(0.116)	(0.437)
3. Men	0.139	–	0.094	0.264	-1485
	(0.147)		(0.031)	(0.158)	(0.529)
4. Men and women	0.106	0.306	–	0.072	-1282
	(0.107)	(0.048)		(0.124)	(0.402)
5. Men and women	0.243	–	0.085	0.071	-1816
	(0.133)		(0.034)	(0.167)	(0.483)
II. State					
1. Men	-0.381	–	–	–	–
	(0.094)				
2. Men	-0.281	0.056	–	0.020	-0.376
	(0.081)	(0.015)		(0.048)	(0.194)
3. Men	-0.273	–	0.037	0.117	-0.635
	(0.085)		(0.011)	(0.056)	(0.208)
4. Men and women	-0.300	0.106	–	-0.002	-0.597
	(0.082)	(0.015)		(0.047)	(0.176)
5. Men and women	-0.218	–	0.043	0.075	-0.611
	(0.083)		(0.011)	(0.054)	(0.184)
III. Metropolitan area					
1. Men	-0.785	–	–	–	–
	(0.060)				
2. Men	-0.839	-0.402	–	0.072	-0.307
	(0.091)	(0.022)		(0.044)	(0.151)
3. Men and women	-0.712	-0.365	–	0.057	-0.237
	(0.087)	(0.021)		(0.044)	(0.125)

Notes: Standard errors are reported in parentheses and are clustered at the region-skill group level. The regressions estimated at the region level have 1,440 observations (1,152 observations when the lagged native employment growth is included); the regressions estimated at the state level have 8,160 (6,451) observations; and the regressions estimated at the metropolitan area level have 25,183 (14,848) observations. All regressions include a vector of skill fixed effects, a vector of (appropriately defined) region fixed effects, a vector of time fixed effects, and all possible two-way interactions among these vectors.

Consider initially the regressions estimated at the state level, reported in the middle panel of the table. The specification in Row 1 uses the sample of working men and does not include any variables in the vector X. The estimated coefficient of the immigrant share variable is −0.381, with a standard error of 0.094. This regression model, therefore, confirms that there is a numerically important and statistically significant negative relation between immigration and the rate of growth of the native workforce at the state level. The coefficient is easier to interpret by calculating the derivative $\partial N/\partial \tilde{M}$, which gives the change in the size of the native workforce when the stock of immigrant workers increases by one. It is easy to show that the derivative of interest is:

$$(17) \qquad \frac{\partial N}{\partial \tilde{M}} = \frac{\theta_N}{(1 + \tilde{m})^2}.$$

As before, the derivative in Equation (17) can be evaluated at the mean value of the immigrant supply increase by multiplying the regression coefficient θ_N by 0.73. The simplest specification reported in Panel II of Table 19.3 implies that 2.8 fewer native workers chose to live in a particular state for every ten additional immigrants entering that state. In terms of the theoretical model, Equation (11) implies that the derivative reported in Equation (17) estimates the product of elasticities $\eta\sigma$.

The next two rows of the middle panel of Table 19.3 estimate more general specifications of the regression model. As noted earlier, I adjust for preexisting migration flows by including either the lagged log of the number of native workers or the lagged rate of growth in the size of the native workforce.[29] I also include variables measuring the mean log weekly wage and the unemployment rate in the labor market (again measured at the state level).[30] These additional variables control for factors that, in addition to immigration, motivate income-maximizing native workers to move from one market to another.

Rows 2 and 3 yield very similar results, so the evidence is not sensitive to which variable is chosen to proxy for the lagged size of native net migration in the absence of immigration. Not surprisingly, lagged measures of the size of the native workforce or its growth rate have a positive impact on the current number of native workers. Similarly, the mean log wage has a positive (sometimes insignificant) coefficient, while the unemployment rate has a negative effect. The coefficient of the immigrant share variable falls to around −0.27 in the most general specification.[31] This estimate implies that around two fewer native workers choose to reside in a particular state for every ten additional immigrants who enter that state.

The final two rows of the middle panel add the population of working women to the regression analysis. These regressions, in effect, examine the evolution of the entire workforce for a particular labor market defined by skills and region. The inclusion of women in this type of regression model could be problematic because of the possibility that many women may be tied-movers or tied-stayers, so that their location decisions may crucially depend on factors (such as family composition and the distribution of skills within the family) that are ignored in the study. Nevertheless, the state-level regressions suggest that, at least qualitatively, the inclusion of women barely alters the results. The coefficients of the immigrant share variable are not only negative and statistically significant, but are also roughly similar to the ones estimated in the sample of working men.

The other panels of Table 19.3 reestimate the regression models at the census division and metropolitan area levels. The estimated impact of the immigrant supply variable typically has the wrong sign at the division level, but with large standard errors. In contrast, the adjustment coefficient is very negative (and statistically significant) at the metropolitan area level. The obvious conclusion to draw by comparing the three panels of the table is that the negative impact of the immigrant share variable gets numerically stronger the smaller the geographic boundaries of the labor market. In the general specification reported in Row 2 for working men, for example, the estimated coefficient of the immigrant share variable is 0.055 (0.121) at the census division level, −0.281 (0.081) at the state level, and −0.839 (0.091) at the metropolitan area level.[32] The coefficient of the metropolitan area regression, in fact, implies that 6.1 fewer native workers choose to reside in a particular metropolitan area for every ten additional immigrants who enter that locality.

It is worth noting that the geographic variation in the observed spatial correlation between the size of the native workforce and immigration is an exact mirror image of the geographic variation in the spatial correlation between wages and immigration reported in Table 19.2. As implied by the model, the wage effects are larger when the impact of immigration on the size of the native workforce is weakest (at the census division level); and the wage effects are weakest when the impact of immigration on the size of the native workforce is largest (at the metropolitan area level).

It would seem as if this mirror-image pattern is not consistent with an attenuation hypothesis: more measurement error for data estimated at smaller geographic units would lead to smaller coefficient estimates at the metropolitan area level in both Tables 19.2 and 19.3. There is, however, one possible source of measurement error that could potentially explain the mirror-image pattern. In particular, note that the adjustment coefficient θ_N estimated by Equation (16) may suffer from division bias. The dependent variable appears (in transformed form) as part of the denominator in the immigrant share variable. If the size of the native workforce were measured with error, the division bias would lead to downward-biased estimates of the adjustment coefficient. One could argue that such measurement error would be more severe at the metropolitan area level than in larger geographic regions.

I show in what follows, however, that division bias does not play a central role in generating the mirror-image pattern of coefficients in Tables 19.2 and 19.3. Instead, the mirror-image pattern revealed by the two tables provides some support for the hypothesis that there is indeed a behavioral response by the native population that is contaminating the measured wage impact of immigration on local labor markets.

19.5.2. Migration Rates

Since 1970 the census contains detailed information on the person's state of residence five years prior to the census, and since 1980 there is similar information for the metropolitan area of residence. These data, combined with the information on geographic location at the time of the census, can be used to compute in-, out-, and net-migration rates for native workers in the various skill-region groups. I now examine how these native migration rates respond to the immigrant influx. Therefore, the results presented in this section, which examine the flows of *actual* native movers, can be interpreted as providing independent confirmation of the findings presented above that link the evolution of the size of the native workforce to the immigrant influx.

To illustrate the calculation of the net migration rate, consider the data available at the state level in a particular census. The worker is an out-migrant from the "original" state of residence (that is, the state of residence five years prior to the survey) if he lives in a different state by the time of the census. The worker is an in-migrant into the current state of residence if he lived in a different state five years prior to the census. I define the in-migration and out-migration rates by dividing the total number of in-migrants or out-migrants in a particular skill-state-time cell by the relevant workforce in the baseline state.[33]

The net migration rate is then defined as the difference between the in-migration and the out-migration rate. To make the results in this section comparable to those reported in Table 19.3, I multiply all the migration rates by two – this adjustment converts the various rates into decadal changes (which was the unit of change implicitly used in the native workforce regressions).

I concluded the presentation of the theoretical model in Section 19.2 by deriving estimable equations that related the size of the native workforce and the native wage to the immigrant supply shift. This section uses a variation of the model with a different dependent variable. Equation (7) gives the expression for the net migration rate for cell (i, j, t). By using the approximation that $(1 + x)^t \approx 1 + x_t$, the equation determining the net-migration rate, v_{ijt}, can be rewritten as:

$$(18) \qquad v_{ijt} = \eta\sigma\lambda_{ij} + (\eta\sigma)^2(t\lambda_{ij}) - \eta\sigma\,\widetilde{m}_{it} + \eta\sigma\widetilde{m}_{ijt}.$$

As before, the regression model that I actually use to analyze how migration rates respond to immigration is:

$$(19) \qquad y_{ijt} = X_{ijt}\beta + \theta_N P_{ijt} + s_i + r_j + \pi_t + (s_i \times \pi_t) + (r_j \times \pi_t)$$
$$+ (s_i \times r_j) + \varepsilon_{ijt},$$

where y_{ijt} represents the net-migration, in-migration, or out-migration rate for cell (i, j, t). Note that the coefficient of the region-specific immigrant share variable θ_N identifies the product of elasticities $\eta\sigma$.

Table 19.4 summarizes the evidence. To conserve space, I only report the general specification that includes all of the variables in the vector X. Consider initially the regression results reported for the sample of working men in Panel II, where the dependent variable is the net migration rate estimated at the state level. Because the dependent variable in this regression model measures a change in the native population, I use the lagged native employment growth rate as a preferred way of controlling for preexisting conditions.[34] The estimated coefficient of the immigrant share variable in the net migration regression is -0.284, with a standard error of 0.064. As before, this coefficient is more easily interpretable by multiplying it by 0.73, indicating that 2.1 fewer native workers (on net) move to a particular state for every ten immigrants who enter that state. It is worth noting that the estimated product of elasticities $\eta\sigma$ is very similar to the corresponding estimate reported in Table 19.3, when the dependent variable was the log of the size of the native workforce.

Rows 2 and 3 of the middle panel show that the effect of immigration on net migration rates arises both because immigration induces fewer natives to move into the immigrant-penetrated labor markets, and because immigration induces more natives to move out of those markets. The coefficient of the immigrant share variable in the in-migration regression is –0.151 (0.042), while the respective coefficient in the outmigration regression is 0.133 (0.049). In rough terms, an influx of ten immigrants into a state's workforce induces one fewer native worker to migrate there and encourages one native worker already living there to move out.

Finally, the last row in the middle panel replicates the net migration rate regression in the sample of workers that includes both men and women. The adjustment coefficient is negative and significant (–0.232, with a standard error of 0.057). As before, the inclusion of women into the analysis does not fundamentally change the results.

The top and bottom panels of Table 19.4 reproduce the earlier finding that the negative impact of immigration on native migration rates is numerically larger as the geographic area that encompasses the labor market becomes smaller. In the sample of working men, the estimated coefficient of the immigrant share variable on the net migration rate is –0.076 (0.046) at the division level, –0.284 (0.064) at the state level, and –0.396 (0.086) at the metropolitan area level.[35] The evidence, therefore, again suggests that natives find it much easier to respond to immigration by voting with their feet when the geographic area is relatively small, and that this response is attributable to both fewer in-migrants and more out-migrants.

More importantly, this mirror image pattern – relative to the respective pattern in the spatial correlations between wages and immigration – *cannot* be attributed to measurement error or division bias. After all, both the dependent variable (the net migration rate) and the independent variable (the immigrant share) have a measure of the year t native workforce in the denominator. If the size of the native workforce were measured with error, the division bias would now induce a *positive* bias in the adjustment coefficient θ_N. It seems plausible to argue that this bias would be most severe at the metropolitan area level – where the adjustment coefficient (although not as negative as the respective coefficient in Table 19.3) is still negative and numerically large. In short, the mirror-image pattern in the spatial correlations that is evident when comparing Tables 19.2 and 19.4, cannot be solely attributed to measurement error. It seems to be the result of a systematic behavioral response by native workers that helps to attenuate the wage impact of immigration on local labor markets.

Table 19.4

Impact of Immigration on Migration Rate of Native Workers

Geographic area and specification	Independent variables			
	Immigrant share	Lagged native employment growth	Mean log wage	Unemployment rate
I. Census divisions				
1. Net migration rate, men	-0.076	0.060	0.147	-0.048
	(0.046)	(0.023)	(0.056)	(0.206)
2. In-migration rate, men	-0.103	-0.016	0.110	0.151
	(0.034)	(0.010)	(0.040)	(0.143)
3. Out-migration rate, men	-0.027	-0.076	-0.037	0.200
	(0.033)	(0.018)	(0.040)	(0.165)
4. Net migration rate, men and women	-0.082	0.066	0.071	0.059
	(0.042)	(0.019)	(0.051)	(0.189)
II. State				
1. Net migration rate, men	-0.284	-0.019	0.012	0.242
	(0.064)	(0.014)	(0.070)	(0.216)
2. In-migration rate, men	-0.151	-0.055	0.018	0.026
	(0.042)	(0.009)	(0.035)	(0.127)
3. Out-migration rate, men	0.133	-0.036	0.007	-0.216
	(0.049)	(0.012)	(0.052)	(0.171)
4. Net migration rate, men and women	-0.232	-0.005	0.051	-0.125
	(0.057)	(0.015)	(0.058)	(0.187)
III. Metropolitan area				
1. Net migration rate, men	-0.396	-0.084	-0.046	0.094
	(0.086)	(0.015)	(0.042)	(0.137)
2. In-migration rate, men	-0.114	-0.077	-0.018	0.054
	(0.057)	(0.009)	(0.027)	(0.092)
3. Out-migration rate, men	0.282	0.007	0.028	-0.041
	(0.062)	(0.010)	(0.028)	(0.095)
4. Net migration rate, men and women	-0.336	-0.093	-0.057	0.029
	(0.073)	(0.015)	(0.037)	(0.104)

Notes: Standard errors are reported in parentheses and are clustered at the region-skill group level. The regressions estimated at the region level have 1,152 observations; the regressions estimated at the state level have 6,528 observations; and the regressions estimated at the metropolitan area level have 14,848 observations. All regressions include a vector of skill fixed effects, a vector of (appropriately defined) region fixed effects, a vector of time fixed effects, and all possible two-way interactions among these vectors.

19.5.3. Sensitivity Results

As suggested by the descriptive evidence summarized earlier, the regression results reported in Tables 19.3 and 19.4 consistently reveal a numerically sizable and statistically significant relation between native migration decisions and immigration. I have already shown that the results are unchanged when women are included in the analysis. I now examine whether the results are also robust to other major specification changes.

Table 19.5 summarizes the sensitivity experiments that I conducted on the various regression models. To conserve space, the table reports the coefficients of the immigrant share variables estimated at the state level from the size-of-workforce and net migration regressions. For convenience, the top row of the table reproduces the "baseline" results obtained in the sample of working men that has been the focus of the discussion up to this point.

Table 19.5

Sensitivity of Migration Results at State Level (Coefficient of immigrant share variable)

Geographic area and specification	Dependent Variable			
	Log size of workforce	Net migration rate	In-migration rate	Out-migration rate
1. Baseline (men)	-0.281	-0.284	-0.151	0.133
	(0.081)	(0.064)	(0.042)	(0.049)
2. Uses ten-year experience groups	-0.331	-0.244	-0.105	0.139
	(0.194)	(0.076)	(0.045)	(0.058)
3. Excludes workers with less than five or more than 35 years of experience	-0.224	-0.227	-0.116	0.112
	(0.085)	(0.065)	(0.044)	(0.050)
4. Excludes California	-0.293	-0.262	-0.140	0.122
	(0.087)	(0.071)	(0.047)	(0.049)
5. Excludes high school dropouts	-0.966	-0.283	-0.251	0.032
	(0.164)	(0.218)	(0.123)	(0.158)
6. Excludes workers with 8 or fewer years of schooling	-0.896	-0.303	-0.175	0.129
	(0.119)	(0.121)	(0.085)	(0.082)

Notes: Standard errors reported in parentheses; all standard errors are clustered by skill and region. The baseline male regressions on the log of the native workforce have 8,160 observations (6,528 observations in the migration rate regressions); the regressions using the ten-year experience groupings have 4,045 (3,264) observations; the regressions excluding workers with fewer than five or more than 35 years of experience have 6,058 (4,896) observations; the non-California regressions have 7,906 (6,398) observations; the regressions for workers with at least a high school education have 6,039 (4,892) observations; and the regressions estimated in the sample of workers with at least nine years of education has 8,043 (6,522) observations. All regressions include a vector of skill fixed effects, a vector of (appropriately defined) region fixed effects, a vector of time fixed effects, all possible two-way interactions among these vectors, and the mean log weekly wage and unemployment rate in the labor market. In addition, the regressions on the log size of the native workforce include the lagged value of the log of the native workforce, while the migration rate regressions include the lagged value of the growth rate of the native workforce.

I have used a five-year experience aggregation to define the various skill groups. Although this classification attempts to capture the insight that workers with roughly the same level of experience are more likely to be perfect substitutes, the choice of the aggregation interval is arbitrary. The results, however, are robust to different classification schemes. Row 2 of Table 19.5 reports the estimated coefficients when experience groups are defined in terms of ten-year groupings (one to ten years of experience, 11–20 years, and so on). The table clearly indicates that the coefficient of the immigrant share in all of the regressions is quite similar to that reported in the baseline specification.

Similarly, the very different nature of the migration behavior of native workers who have just completed their schooling or who are about to retire might be confounding the underlying correlations. Row 3 of the table reestimates the basic model (once again returning to the five-year experience classification), but excludes workers who have fewer than five or more than 35 years of work experience. This specification of the model leads to regression coefficients that are quite similar to those reported in the baseline specification (though somewhat smaller in magnitude).

As I showed earlier, the state of California has played a central role in the resurgence of large-scale immigration in the past few decades. California has atypical labor market characteristics; it is a very large state with historically high native net-migration rates, a relatively high-skill workforce, and a huge immigrant influx. These characteristics could contaminate many of the results presented earlier. It is important, therefore, to determine if the sign or magnitude of the estimated coefficients are driven by the outlying observations that describe the outcomes for specific skill groups in California. Row 4 of Table 19.5 reestimates the baseline regression models in the subsample of skill-state-year cells that excludes all the California observations. Remarkably, despite the demographic importance of California, there is very little change in the regression coefficients: The adjustment coefficient in either the size-of-workforce or the net migration rate regressions still hovers around −0.3.

As I showed earlier, many of the outlying skill-region (in terms of the size of the immigrant influx) likely contain workers who are high school dropouts, and the determinants of the migration behavior of native high school dropouts may differ substantially from that of native workers with higher levels of educational attainment.[36] It is important, therefore, to assess the sensitivity of the results to the presence of these outlying observations. Row 5 reestimates the model using the subsample of workers who have at least 12 years of schooling (so there are now only three education groups in the analysis). The coefficient of the immigrant share variable in the native workforce regression becomes even *more* negative (–0.97, with a standard error of 0.18) when the high school dropouts are excluded from the sample, but the coefficient in the net migration regression is stable at around –0.28.

Finally, Row 6 reports an equally interesting exercise when we redefine the high school dropout category to include only those workers who have between nine and 11 years of schooling. In 2000, 22.1 percent of immigrants had eight or fewer years of schooling. It is doubtful that these very low-skill immigrants are competing in the same labor market as the native high school dropouts, 80 percent of whom have between nine and 11 years of schooling. To analyze the sensitivity of the results to this potential mismatch within the high school dropout category, I simply omitted from the study any workers who have eight or fewer years of schooling. The high school dropout category, therefore, now is composed entirely of workers who have nine to 11 years of schooling. The last row of Table 19.5 shows that the coefficient of the immigrant share variable in the size-of-workforce regression is large and negative, while the coefficient in the net-migration rate regression still hovers at –0.3.

In sum, the sensitivity experiments summarized in this section show that major changes in the specification of the regression models do not alter the qualitative (and often quantitative) nature of the evidence. Immigrant-induced increases in labor supply are associated with lower native net migration rates, lower in-migration rates, higher out-migration rates, and a smaller growth rate in the size of the native workforce in the affected labor markets.

It is important to emphasize that there is a striking contrast between the robustness of the evidence summarized here and the evidence reported in prior studies. The nature of the link between native internal migration and immigration has attracted a great deal of attention in both the economics and geography literatures. A number of studies, led by Filer (1992), Frey (1994, 1995), Frey et al. (1996), and White and Hunter (1993), reported evidence consistent with a "demographic balkanization" of natives and immigrants. Natives respond to immigration by moving to areas that had not been affected by immigration. Subsequent studies, including those of Wright, Ellis, and Reibel (1997), White and Imai (1994), Card and DiNardo (2000), Card (2001), and Kritz and Gurak (2001), presented opposing evidence that questioned the demographic importance of this presumed relation. It should be noted, however, that the studies differ greatly in the time periods analyzed, in sample design, in definitions of the geographic region, and in the methodological framework (see the survey-like discussion in Kritz and Gurak 2001: 133–5). As a result, it is difficult to determine exactly why there is so much dispersion in the evidence across studies.

The empirical analysis presented in this chapter differs from the existing literature in three distinct ways. First, the study is strongly embedded in a theoretical framework that emphasizes the importance of netting out preexisting conditions when attempting to measure the nature of the link between native migration and immigration. As I noted earlier, there is evidence that the sign of the correlation between native migration and immigration can easily switch depending on how a particular study controls for preexisting conditions (Borjas, Freeman, and Katz 1997). To illustrate, some states have been long-time recipients of native internal migrants. These states also may have become important gateways for new immigrants, thus introducing a spurious positive correlation between native net migration and immigration. The correct measure of the impact of immigration on native migration would then depend on how the net migration rate of natives into these states changed *relative* to what it was in the pre-immigration regime.

The current study uses a far longer panel of data than other studies in the literature, many of which have used a single census cross section to uncover what is undoubtedly a relation that has a crucial time dimension. Card (2001) and Kritz and Gurak (2001), for example, estimate correlations using data exclusively from the 1990 Census. Although it is unclear what such cross-section correlations actually measure, it is evident that they do *not* measure the parameters of interest in the context of a dynamic model of native location decisions. The use of a 40-year panel that includes repeated observations on the location decision of native workers and immigrant-induced supply increases experienced by specific groups allows the empirical analysis to net out the long-run trends that undoubtedly characterize internal migration flows for particular groups or particular regions, and thus helps to isolate the impact of immigration.

Second, I emphasize the common-sense (though obviously restrictive) notion that income-maximizing natives will respond to immigration only if their economic opportunities are affected. The immigration of one particular skill group will likely affect the earnings of that skill group more than the earnings of other groups, and one would expect a corresponding differential effect on native migration rates. The empirical study presented here defined skill groups in terms of years of education and work experience – and it is partly this narrower focus on the composition of the skill groups affected by large-scale immigration that allows me to measure a consistent correlation that seems to have been missed by some of the earlier studies.

Finally, my analysis builds on the strong theoretical implication that there exists a systematic relation between the wage structure, native migration decisions, and immigration – and that the nature of this relation is closely linked to the geographic reach of the labor market. The empirical confusion on the nature of the correlation between native migration decisions and immigration is not unique in the immigration literature. As noted earlier, there is an equally confusing set of results contained in the studies that attempt to estimate the labor market impact of immigration by correlating wages in the local labor market and measures of immigrant penetration. The analysis presented here argues that the empirical confusion in these two seemingly unrelated literatures is, in fact, intimately linked. In an important sense, this chapter attempts to reconcile the diverse set of findings in two literatures that have not been closely linked before: the impact of immigration on wages and the impact of immigration on native location decisions.

19.5.4. Synthesis

The theoretical model presented in Section 19.2 suggests that the national wage effect of migration and the spatial correlations estimated between wages and immigration across local labor markets are linked through a parameter that measures the native migration response. I now examine whether the large difference actually estimated in Section 19.3 in the wage impacts for different geographic definitions of the labor market can be "explained" by the impact of immigration on native location decisions.

Table 19.6 summarizes the key results of the study. The first row of the table reports that the wage effect at the national level was estimated to be -0.389 (or the coefficient of -0.533 in Table 19.2 times 0.73). I assume that the national labor market approximates the concept of a closed economy, so that this coefficient estimates the factor price elasticity η.[37] The theoretical model presented in this chapter implies that the estimated wage effect of immigration will not equal this factor price elasticity whenever the corresponding wage regression is estimated using observations on local labor markets where natives can respond to immigration by moving across markets. The spatial correlation will be numerically smaller, and the gap between the spatial correlation and the true factor price elasticity should reflect the native migration effect.

Table 19.6

Synthesis of Wage and Migration Effects

	Census division	State	Metropolitan area
1. Estimate of factor price elasticity (in national labor market)	-0.389	-0.389	-0.389
2. Estimate of migration effect:			
Simple specification: native workforce	-0.017	-0.278	-0.573
Complete specification: native workforce	0.040	-0.205	-0.612
Complete specification: net migration	-0.055	-0.207	-0.289
3. Predicted estimate of wage elasticity at local level:			
Simple specification: native workforce	-0.382	-0.281	-0.166
Complete specification: native workforce	–	-0.309	-0.151
Complete specification: net migration dropouts	-0.368	-0.308	-0.277
4. Wage elasticity actually estimated at local level:			
Simple specification	-0.200	-0.158	-0.031
Complete specification	-0.199	-0.161	0.015

Notes: The synthesis is based on the theory-based interpretation of the coefficients reported in Tables 19.2, 19.3, and 19.4. See the text for details.

Row 2 of Table 19.6 summarizes the estimated migration effects reported earlier (again multiplied by 0.73).[38] This row, therefore, reports the value of the derivative $\gamma_N = \partial N/\partial \tilde{M}$. These migration responses allow me to predict what the spatial correlations should be by using the multiplicative property of the model summarized in Equation (10). In particular, let $\gamma_W = \partial \log w/\partial \tilde{m}$, the wage effect of immigration at a particular geographic level. The theory then predicts that the spatial correlation between wages and immigration, $\hat{\gamma}_W$, is given by:

$$(20) \qquad \hat{\gamma}_W = \eta(1 + \gamma_N).$$

Row 3 of Table 19.6 uses this equation to mechanically predict the spatial correlations that *should* be observed if the only adjustment mechanism contaminating the estimation procedure was the internal migration of native workers. To illustrate, consider the migration response revealed by the simplest specification of the size-of-workforce regression at the state level. This regression implies that $\gamma_N = -0.278$. The theory then implies that the wage elasticity estimated by relating native wages across states and immigration should be –0.28 [or $-0.389 \times (1 - 0.278)$], roughly a cut of one-quarter in the estimated national wage effect. At the metropolitan area level, the migration response is quite large, implying that the spatial correlation between wages and immigration measurable at the metropolitan area level should be –0.17. If I instead use the migration responses estimated in the net migration regressions, the predicted spatial correlations are –0.31 and –0.28 at the state and metropolitan area levels, respectively.

Finally, Row 4 of Table 19.6 reports the *actual* spatial correlations estimated in the data (and first reported in Table 19.2). At the state level, the wage impact of immigration is around –0.16. The evidence summarized in Table 19.6, therefore, indicates that the internal migration response of native workers accounts for about 40 percent of the gap between the wage effects estimated at the state level and at the national level. At the metropolitan area level, the data indicate that the native internal migration response may account for as much as 60 percent of the difference.

This synthesis fails to explain the difference between the national wage effect and the spatial correlation between wages and immigration estimated at the census division level. It may well be that census divisions are not an economically meaningful analogue to a labor market. It is also the case that much of the migration that takes place in the United States is within divisions. Between 1995 and 2000, for example, 11.6 percent of the working-age population migrated across metropolitan areas; 9.4 percent migrated across states; and only 6.8 percent migrated across divisions. The use of division-level data, therefore, is probably masking a great deal of the native migration response to immigrant-induced supply shifts.

19.6. Summary

The empirical literature that attempts to estimate the labor market impact of immigration faces an important puzzle. Studies that examine how immigration alters economic opportunities across local labor markets tend to find that immigration has a negligible impact on the wage of competing native workers, while studies that examine how immigration alters economic opportunities at the national level tend to find substantial wage effects. This chapter presented a theoretical and empirical analysis of one possible adjustment mechanism that can explain the disparate findings: the internal migration decisions made by native workers.

The theoretical model presented in this chapter illustrates how native migration flows diffuse the impact of immigration across the entire economy, making it difficult to measure the "true" wage impact of immigration by comparing conditions across local labor markets. More importantly, the theory provides a framework that explicitly links the parameters measuring the national wage effect of immigration, the spatial correlation estimated across local labor markets, and the impact of immigration on native migration decisions.

The empirical analysis used data drawn from the 1960–2000 decennial censuses. The evidence indicates that native internal migration decisions are sensitive to immigrant-induced increases in labor supply. The native population in a particular skill group grew slowest in those parts of the country that experienced the largest immigrant influx. This native supply response is evident both in terms of a decline in native in-migration and an increase in native out-migration. The net native migration response is sizable: For every ten immigrants who enter a particular state two fewer natives choose to live in that state. The response is even larger at the metropolitan area level: For every ten immigrants who choose to enter a particular metropolitan area between three and six natives will choose not to live in that locality.

These migration responses are sufficiently large to explain an important part of the disparate findings obtained in studies that estimate the wage effects of immigration at the national and local labor market levels. At the state level, the native migration response explains about 40 percent of the gap in wage effects. At the metropolitan area level, the migration response may explain as much as 60 percent of the gap.

Naturally, labor markets adjust to immigration in many other ways. Although native migration can explain a good part of the adjustment mechanism, it is likely that flows of goods or capital are also important ingredients in the story. The magnitude, economic significance, and labor market consequences of those flows are yet to be determined.

Appendix: Mathematical Appendix

To simplify the mathematical derivations, it is useful to start with a simpler version of the immigrant influx, a one-time supply increase. In particular, M_{ij0} immigrants enter region j at time 0. Native migration will then occur for two reasons: a response to the initial disequilibrium, and a response to the impact of immigrants on the wage structure. It is useful to consider these two responses separately. As a result of the initial disequilibrium, Equation (6) in the text shows that $v_{ij0} = \eta\sigma\lambda_{ij}$. By solving the model recursively, it follows that $v_{ijt} = \eta\sigma(1 + \eta\sigma)^t\lambda_{ij}$.

The native response to the one-time immigrant supply increase will depend on the geographic sorting of immigrants relative to the geographic sorting of the native population. Suppose region j has (in the pre-immigration regime) a fraction q_{ij} of the native population in skill group i and receives a fraction ρ_{ij} of the immigrants in that skill group. The region-specific supply increase is then given by:

$$(A1) \qquad m_{ij0} = \frac{M_{ij0}}{N_{ij0}} = \frac{\rho_{ij}M_i}{q_{ij}N_i} = k_{ij}m_i,$$

where $k_{ij} = \rho_{ij}/q_{ij}$, a measure of the penetration of immigrants into region j relative to the region's pre-immigration size (for a particular skill group). Immigration is distributed neutrally if $k_{ij} = 1$.

The impact of the one-time immigrant supply on native migration can be solved recursively. In particular, the supply increase induces $\eta\sigma(k_{ij} - 1)m_i$ natives to move in Period 1, $\eta\sigma(1 + \eta\sigma)(k_{ij} - 1)m_i$ in Period 2, and $\eta\sigma(1 + \eta\sigma)^t(k_{ij} - 1)m_i$ in period t. Combining both sources of native migration flows, the native net migration rate in year t is then given by:

$$(A2) \qquad v_{ijt} = \eta\sigma(1 + \eta\sigma)^t\lambda_{ij} - \eta\sigma(1 + \eta\sigma)^{t-1}(1 - k_{ij})m_i.$$

I assume that $0 < (1 + \eta\sigma) < 1$.

The total (or cumulative) net migration rate of natives at time t is then given by:

$$(A3) \qquad V_{ijt} = \sum_{\tau=0}^{t}\eta\sigma(1 + \eta\sigma)^\tau\lambda_{ij} - \sum_{\tau=1}^{t}\eta\sigma(1 + \eta\sigma)^{\tau-1}(1 - k_{ij})m_i$$

$$= \left[(1 + \eta\sigma)^t - 1\right]\lambda_{ij} + \left[1 - (1 + \eta\sigma)^t\right](1 - k_{ij})m_i.$$

The model can now be more easily extended to the case where the immigrant influx continues indefinitely. The last term of Equation (A3), call it Y_{ijt}, gives the (cumulative) net migration rate of natives as of time t induced by a Period 0 immigrant supply increase. Consider now what the native response would be to a similarly sized supply increase occurring at $t = 1$. The net migration rate of natives induced by the Period 1 migration flow would be $Y_{ij,t-1}$. The total net migration of natives in period t attributable to a supply increase of $k_{ij}m_i$ in region j between periods 0 and $t - 1$ is then given by:

(A4) $\qquad V_{ijt}^* = \left[(1 + \eta\sigma)^t - 1\right]\lambda_{ij} + \sum_{\tau=0}^{t-1} Y_{ijt} = \left[(1 + \eta\sigma)^t - 1\right]\lambda_{ij}$

$\qquad\qquad + \left[t + \dfrac{(1 + \eta\sigma)}{\eta\sigma}\left[1 - (1 + \eta\sigma)^t\right]\right](1 - k_{ij})m_i.$

Equation (7) in the text can be obtained by differencing Equation (A4). In particular:

(A5) $\qquad\qquad\qquad v_{ijt} = V_{ijt}^* - V_{ij,t-1}^* = \eta\sigma(1 + \eta\sigma)^t\lambda_{ij} +$

$\qquad\qquad\qquad \left[1 - (1 + \eta\sigma)^t\right](1 - k_{ij})m_i.$

Equation (7) follows directly by noting that $k_{ij}m_i = m_{ij}$. Equations (8) and (9) can be derived by substituting Equation (A4) in both the equation that determines the current size of the workforce in a particular labor market and in the labor demand function.

Part VI
Our Views on Migration

Reflections on Immigration Economics

George J. Borjas

It has been most rewarding to witness the explosive growth in the amount of effort and attention that economists pay to immigration-related issues over the past 30 years. In the early 1980s, few economists seemed interested in these topics; the debate over immigration issues in the United States and Europe did not raise fundamental questions about social policy; and there were few technical or conceptual issues that cried out for an unambiguous resolution. The intellectual landscape has changed dramatically. Thirty years later, immigration-related issues attract an ever-increasing number of economists to examine the many questions that are raised by the policy debate; by the role that migration flows – and international migration flows, in particular – play in determining labor market outcomes in both sending and receiving countries; and by the ambiguities and difficult identification problems that permeate the models and econometric methods that are used to measure these outcomes.

Given the emotional and controversial policy issues raised by the implications of economic studies of immigration, it should not be surprising that there is a great deal of disagreement about basic questions in immigration economics: How fast do immigrants assimilate? Do immigrants improve or hurt the employment opportunities of the native-born workforce? Do receiving countries benefit, on net, from immigration? Does the melting pot work across generations?

Regardless of these disagreements, the continued application of the economic approach to the study of immigration suggests one lesson that is indisputable: the economic impact of immigration on receiving countries depends on how the skill composition of the immigrant population compares with that of the native born. It is the difference in these skill distributions – and the substitution or complementarities implied by the absence or presence of these differences – that ultimately determines the costs of and benefits from immigration.

My own work in immigration economics can be broadly categorized as contributing to three specific questions in the field: (1) the factors that determine the skills of immigrants; (2) the distributional and efficiency consequences of international labor flows; and (3) the factors that determine the rate of intergenerational mobility in the immigrant population. This collection of essays presents an excellent opportunity to review where I think the literature stands in each of these areas, and to summarize what I believe are the most fruitful avenues for further research in the future.

In terms of the factors that determine the skills of immigrants, it is important to distinguish between two sets of skills: the premigration skills of immigrants, which depend on the selection process that separates the movers from the stayers in the source country, and the skills that immigrants acquire in their new homes after migration occurs. Economic analysis has taught us a great deal about the selection process that determines the subsample of movers. The income-maximization hypothesis can generate either positive or negative selection – i.e., the immigrant flow can be composed of the most or the least skilled workers in the population of any given source country. The model also implies that the type of selection observed depends on how easy it is to transfer skills across countries and on international differences in the rate of return to skills.

I have long believed that the selection models that now permeate the literature miss an important aspect of the problem. The existing models have helped us understand the nature of the selection algorithm in a partial equilibrium framework, where potential migrants take the international distribution of income and employment opportunities as given and make decisions based on the pre-existing cross-country differences. Although this framework seems sensible when the number of immigrants is relatively small, the approach is unlikely to yield useful insights when the migration flows are large and affect earnings and employment opportunities in both sending and receiving regions. It is not an exaggeration to state that we simply do not understand conceptually how the selection algorithm would work in a general equilibrium context, where the migrant flows themselves affect the international distribution of opportunities, nor do our current empirical methods provide any hint as to how one would go about testing the implications of a general equilibrium selection model.

The nature of the selection mechanism determines the "pre-existing" skill composition of immigrants, but immigrants continue to invest in human capital even after the migration takes place. It is these postmigration investments that are the driving force behind the assimilation process. Immigrants arrive in the receiving countries lacking many of the skills that employers in the receiving country find desirable (e.g., language and other forms of host-country-specific human capital). Over time, immigrants acquire some of these skills, helping to narrow down the skills *and* wage gap between themselves and the native-born workforce. The measurement of the rate of "economic assimilation," in fact, was the key question that sparked the birth of the modern literature in immigration economics.

By now, it is widely accepted that the cross-section correlation between the economic performance of immigrants and the length of time that immigrants have lived in the receiving country does not provide any valuable information about the assimilation process. After all, this correlation will be contaminated by difference in the intrinsic "quality" of the various immigrant cohorts – i.e., there may be inherent skill differences among cohorts that arrived in the receiving country at different times. In the U.S. context, for instance, it seems that there was a substantial decline in the relative "quality" of the cohorts that entered the country between 1950 and 1990, so that much of what the positive cross-section correlation between earnings and year-since-migration identified as "assimilation" was, in fact, measuring a decline in the inherent skills of successive immigrant cohorts.

In my view, the assimilation literature has focused far too narrowly on the process of wage convergence. If we take the underlying theory of human capital accumulation seriously, the wage convergence resulting from economic assimilation occurs only because immigrants are investing in "host-country-specific human capital." Remarkably, there has been little analysis of the rate at which the relative human capital stock of a specific immigrant cohort is changing over time.

A refocusing of the literature away from the measurement of wage convergence to the measurement of changes in the human capital stock would also help us address a major problem with the wage-based studies. It is well known that period effects – the impact of macroeconomics shocks on wages – influence the rate of wage growth of both immigrants and natives. If the magnitude of these period effects differs between the two groups, the relative wage gap between any immigrant cohort and the native population will change over time for reasons that have nothing to do with assimilation.

In fact, differential period effects implies that it is impossible to disentangle all three forces that change the relative earnings of immigrants over time (i.e., assimilation, cohort, and period effects), *unless* an assumption is made about one of these three forces. Much of the literature, in fact, assumes that the period effects (or, more precisely, the impact of macroeconomic shocks on the log wage) are the same for immigrants as for some well-defined subset of the native-born workforce. This assumption then allows us to infer trends in assimilation and the earnings potential of different immigrant cohorts from the observed wage trends. Some of the inherent ambiguity in the interpretation of the observed wage data could be resolved by directly observing the differential rate of human capital accumulation in the immigrant and native populations. Unfortunately, the existing literature has not devoted much effort to documenting the rate of assimilation in direct measures of human capital, such as the rate at which English language is acquired, or the rate at which immigrants switch locations, jobs, occupations, and industries.

I believe that one important lesson of the existing research is that there is no universal law guiding the economic assimilation of immigrants. The extent to which immigrants assimilate in any receiving country will obviously depend on the economic benefits from doing so. If immigrants find it profitable to invest in human capital in the postmigration period, they will do so, and assimilation will take place. If immigrants find that the costs of such investments exceed the benefits, then assimilation will not occur.

This simple fact has important implications for the rate of assimilation that may characterize future waves of immigrants. It is evident that the rapidly increasing number of immigrants from specific sending countries choosing to settle in specific receiving countries changes the calculus of the assimilation decision. The incentives to invest in particular types of human capital (e.g., language) are likely to be higher when there are just a few ethnic or linguistic compatriots in the host country than when there are numerous compatriots, and particularly when the ethnic group tends to settle in economically thriving and tightly knit ethnic enclaves.

A second central long-term concern in my work has been the distributional and efficiency impact of immigration on receiving countries. Neoclassical factor demand theory suggests that the immediate impact of an immigration-induced increase in supply is to lower the wage of competing workers, relative to what they otherwise would have earned in the pre-immigration regime. Over time, the labor market adjusts, and this effect is attenuated. Under some conditions, in fact, the theory predicts that the long-run *average* wage effect should be zero. Even if the average wage effect is fully attenuated, however, immigration has a distribution impact and this is a central theoretical insight: native-born skill groups that have the largest supply shocks will inevitably experience a decline in relative wages.

A voluminous literature attempts to test empirically this common-sense theoretical insight. Nevertheless, it has proven surprisingly difficult to document empirically that "the labor demand curve is downward sloping" – the notion that an increase in supply should lower wages. In the 1980s and 1990s, the generic study in the literature addressed this question by comparing native wages in labor markets heavily penetrated by immigrants with native wages in labor markets barely touched by immigration. These studies typically found only a very weak correlation between immigration and wages.

Beginning with my 2003 Quarterly Journal of Economics article, the literature has begun to estimate the wage effect of immigration by noting that the impact can perhaps best be measured by observing the secular evolution of national wages for narrowly defined skill groups, as some of these groups are affected by large immigration-induced supply shocks and others are not. This type of approach suggests that those groups that have large supply shocks do indeed suffer a decline in relative wages, as suggested by factor demand theory.

Although we now know much more about how to approach the question of measuring the labor market impact of immigration than we did even a decade ago, the sensitivity of the results to the choice of empirical strategy and econometric methodology is extremely worrisome and suggests that we should be very cautious when interpreting the evidence. I strongly believe, in fact, that no definite inference is possible until we fully understand why the different approaches lead to radically different results. In particular, why do different aggregations of the *same* data (e.g., aggregating the data into different levels of geographic regions) lead to different conclusions about the wage impact of immigration?

It is likely that many of the puzzles in our current perception will only be resolved when we have a fuller accounting of how labor markets adjust to international migration flows. It is obvious that immigration changes economic opportunities differently for different agents, and the different agents have an incentive to react and adjust differentially.

With few exceptions, the literature has focused on only one particular source of adjustment – the possibility that native workers react to an immigration-induced supply shock in a local labor market by moving to other cities unaffected by immigration. This myopia, however, has masked the fact that there is a vast array of possible adjustments that natives (and immigrants) will undertake. In fact, there are likely to be a large number of margins along which native workers can respond so as to mitigate the adverse effects of supply shocks. The types of adjustments that economists can measure (or even imagine) are but a small subset of the wide array of possibilities available to the agents whose well being is most affected by the supply shocks. All of these adjustments imply that the long-run impact of immigration differs from the short-run impact. In fact, the adjustments suggest that it is unclear that the impact on the most affected "markets" (whether defined in terms of geography or skills) will differ from the impact on the least affected markets. Any type of adjustment will diffuse the impact of immigration from markets most directly penetrated by immigrants into markets that, at least superficially, seemed untouched by the supply shock.

An important insight of the economic framework is that the same structural parameters that determine the distributional impact of immigration on the wage structure also determine the economic benefits from immigration. In fact, the greater the wage loss suffered by competing workers, the greater the net gains for the receiving country's economy.

My work on the economic benefits from immigration, I believe, teaches an important lesson: it is impossible to manipulate the "textbook" model of a competitive labor market in a way that would suggest that the net benefits are sizable in the context of an economy as large as that of the United States. In fact, the model indicates that even a 15 percent immigration-induced supply shock would increase the net income accruing to the native population by less than three-tenths of one percentage point.

It is important to emphasize, however, that everything we know about the economic benefits from immigration follows from simulations of the textbook model of a competitive labor market, regardless of whether the simulation is conducted in the short run or the long run (time frames which are themselves theoretical abstractions) or whether labor is assumed to be homogeneous or heterogeneous. The calibration of an economic model is obviously a standard and useful exercise, but is important to emphasize that we do not have any evidence showing that the actual gains from immigration – as opposed to the theoretically implied gains – are positive. In fact, the literature has not yet even tried to *estimate* these gains in an empirical framework.

It is also notable that there has been no attempt at synthesizing the insights from the studies that portend to show the trends in immigrant skills resulting from the assimilation process and the insights from the studies that measure the distributional and efficiency impacts of immigration. This synthesis is likely to be important. After all, the textbook model of a competitive labor market shows that the net benefits from immigration arise from the complementarities that exist between immigrant labor and native-owned resources (whether labor or capital). The assimilation process presumably attenuates skill differences between immigrants and natives over time, suggesting that the complementarities that generated the initial gains from immigration actually begin to *disappear* as the assimilation process takes hold. It seems obvious that it is important to ascertain the dynamic interaction between the assimilation process and the distributional and efficiency impacts of immigration.

Finally, the ultimate effect of immigration on a receiving country depends not only on the economic, political, and cultural shifts that take place during the life cycle of the immigrant population, but also on the adjustment process experienced by the immigrant household across generations. I have long been interested in examining the impact of immigration in the long, long run: how does the process neatly encapsulated by the melting pot metaphor work, and how long does it take to melt the ethnic differences? It is important to emphasize that, because of data constraints, much of the existing analysis on the intergenerational mobility of immigrants focuses on the U.S. experience, and particularly the U.S. experience in the 20th century. This fact, as I note later, is not sufficiently emphasized or appreciated in policy discussions of the melting pot.

An important empirical finding in the literature is that there is a strong correlation between the mean skills of national origin groups in the immigrant generation and the mean skills of the corresponding ethnic groups in the second generation. It is well known that there is a great deal of heterogeneity in wages among national origin groups when they first arrive in a receiving country. The data suggests that a large part of these wage differentials are transmitted to the second (and third) generation. In fact, the correlation between the mean earnings of ethnic groups across generations is stronger than the correlation we typically observe between the earnings of parents and children.

To explain the surprising strength of the intergenerational correlation in the mean earnings of ethnic groups, my 1992 Quarterly Journal of Economics article proposed that perhaps ethnicity could act as a human capital externality, so that children who grew up in advantageous ethnic environments, where "ethnic capital" is abundant and profitable, do better after they enter the labor market than children who grow up in disadvantaged ethnic neighborhoods. The data, in fact, suggest that the labor market outcomes experienced by the children of immigrants depend not only on parental skills, but also on the average skills of the ethnic group in the parental generation. As a result, ethnicity introduces a "stickiness" in the intergenerational mobility process; even after holding parental skills constant, the children of immigrants in economically successful immigrant groups will themselves tend to be more successful. The strong intergenerational link in the economic performance of ethnic groups suggests that the large-scale migration flows that already entered the developed countries in the past few decades have already set in motion a set of economic and labor market adjustments that are bound to affect these countries throughout the next century.

As mentioned earlier, much of what we know about the intergenerational mobility process comes from the U.S. experience. Although this experience is often used as the "poster child" of successful intergenerational assimilation, it is worth noting that it is far from clear that the U.S. experience may be replicable either in other places or even in the same place at other times.

After all, the immigrants who entered the United States in the early 1900s faced dramatically different economic conditions than the immigrant workforce today. In the early 1900s, the low-skill immigrant workforce helped build the manufacturing sector. Similarly, the political reaction to the social and economic dislocations associated with the First Great Migration was swift and severe. By 1924, the United States had adopted strict limitations on the number and types of persons who could enter the country. Finally, societal attitudes towards what it means to "assimilate" are clearly different now than they were back then. The ideological climate that boosted social pressures for assimilation and acculturation has all but disappeared. In short, the intergenerational mobility of the immigrants who arrived in the United States a century ago may not necessarily be a good predictor of the assimilation prospects of current immigrants in the United States, or of immigrants in other countries.

As I noted earlier, it has been personally rewarding to observe and interact with the increasing number of mainstream economists who are conducting economic research in immigration-related issues. I have long believed that the study of how labor markets adjust to supply shocks can provide fundamental insights about inherently interesting economic questions. However, I would be less than honest if I did not conclude these reflections on a somewhat less upbeat note.

Obviously, much of the increasing interest by mainstream economists is motivated by the ever-larger role that immigration plays in the social policy debate, and by the many controversial questions that this debate engenders. As with everything in life, however, there is no free lunch. The magnetic appeal of these contentious policy issues itself creates a number of problems. Specifically, I have slowly and reluctantly become more appreciative of the fact that the increasing policy scrutiny placed on immigration-related research implies that the newer studies, instead of being judged on the value of the underlying intellectual contribution, are sometimes interpreted through a normative filter. Given the political stakes in the immigration policy debate and the emotional reactions that it evokes in practically all immigrant-receiving countries, it is not surprising that some observers quickly divide the economic studies into "right" and "wrong" based entirely on whether the particular study reached a conclusion that is compatible with the observer's objectives. As we forge ahead, it is important to remember that immigration economics addresses questions that, even putting aside the policy context, are of fundamental importance to our understanding of how labor markets work and that, sometimes, the insights from our research need not coincide with the *du jour* policy proposals.

Managing Immigration in the 21st Century

Barry R. Chiswick

Introduction

In this chapter, written explicitly for this volume, I share my thoughts on immigration policy. As a social scientist it is appropriate to assess the consequences, the costs and benefits, of alternative immigration policies. The policies that a country adopts regarding immigration, however, should be the outcome of a political process which should be informed by, but not dictated by, social science research.

What follows is a non-technical discussion of what I see as some of the key issues regarding immigration policies currently facing the United States and other technologically advanced economies.

Alternative Immigration Policies

Nation-states became deeply involved in regulating immigration in the late 19th and early 20th centuries. The regulations that were adopted, by laws and policies, evolved over the course of the long 20th century and continue to evolve today in the early decades of the 21st century.

If countries want to admit fewer immigrants than the number wanting to enter, or if they want to be selective among potential applicants (e.g., based on health or criminal history), they need an immigration policy that both rations entry visas and selects immigrants. In

Helpful comments from Carmel U. Chiswick are very much appreciated.

a market economy the rationing of goods and services, jobs and dwelling places is accomplished by a price mechanism. In the rationing of immigration visas this could be done by the government through the auctioning of immigration visas or by setting a "visa fee" high enough to clear the market. Some countries, including the United States, have a small proportion of their visas available for "purchase" through a program that grants visas to individuals who will invest funds that create new jobs. There appears to be a consensus, however, in the U.S. and other immigrant-receiving countries, against the explicit selling of visas by the government. The selling of visas does arise in the illicit market, through the prices charged by smugglers of illegal aliens and through fraudulent marriages to U.S. citizens.

Countries differ in the primary focus of their immigration policies. These differences arise from a range of different national histories, philosophies, and socioeconomic objectives. Some countries, such as the United States, place a primary emphasis on "family reunification," so that permanent visas are issued primarily to immediate or close relatives of those who are already citizens or permanent residents. In 2011, of the over one million permanent resident alien visas issued by the United States, 43 percent went to relatives of U.S. citizens and 22 percent to relatives of permanent resident aliens.

Other countries have extended the family reunification concept by granting immigration rights to co-ethnics living abroad. "Reunification or Repatriation of the Diaspora" policies have been adopted by Israel (Jews living elsewhere), Germany (German ethnic minorities living in Eastern Europe and Russia), and Japan (overseas Japanese communities, particularly in Latin America), among other countries.

For some countries the primary focus of immigration policy is humanitarian – providing refuge for those in danger because of civil wars, political tensions, or discrimination based on ethnicity, race, religion, or political ideology. Sweden is a primary example of a refugee-oriented immigration policy.

Yet, for some countries the primary focus is on what the applicant can contribute to the host's economy. In the current economic environment these economic-contribution policies are "skill based." Sometimes skills are evaluated by occupational credentials and "employer petitions," sometimes by a "points system" where measurable skill characteristics (e.g., age, schooling, language fluency) are assigned points and visas are allocated to people with more than a threshold point value, and sometimes a combination of these two methods. Canada, Australia, and New Zealand are important immigrant-receiving countries with skill-based policies that focus on the likely economic contribution of prospective immigrants.

It should be noted that the immigration policies of all immigrant-receiving countries include some combination of reunification, refugee relief, and economic considerations, but the relative emphasis differs across countries.

It should also be noted that while all countries have regulated in-migration to a greater or lesser extent over the past two centuries, the regulation of out-migration has been rare and limited to totalitarian regimes (e.g., the former Soviet Union, East Germany, North Korea). Indeed, there is a nearly universal consensus that while there should be a right of individuals to leave their country of origin, the immigrant-receiving country has a right to select among applicants those who are allowed to enter legally.

The United States and Canada Compared

A comparison of immigrant flows into the United States and Canada is instructive. Table 1 presents data for 2011 on the visa category for entry as a Permanent Resident in the U.S. or Landed Immigrant in Canada. In that year there were over 1.0 million immigrants to the U.S. and nearly 250,000 to Canada, constituting 0.3 percent and 0.7 percent of their respective populations. The different focus of immigration policy is demonstrated by the proportions entering under the family-based and economic skill-based visa categories. For the U.S., nearly two-thirds (65 percent) entered under family visas, whereas for Canada it was less than one quarter (23 percent). In contrast, about one-eighth (13 percent) of the U.S. visas were based on their likely economic contributions (primarily skill but also investments), whereas it was nearly two-thirds (63 percent) for Canada. The refugee proportions were quite similar, 16 percent for the U.S. and 11 percent for Canada. A variety of other immigration programs accounted for an additional 6 percent of the U.S. visas and 3 percent of the Canadian visas.

One of the objections raised by some regarding proposals for the U.S. to reduce family-based visas and increase the economic-based visas is that such a change would advantage European and Canadian applicants and disadvantage non-white immigrants from other parts of the world. The concern is that this would be a way of returning to the pernicious national-origins quota system in effect from 1921 to

1965. A comparison of the regions of origin of immigrants to the U.S. and to Canada is instructive (Table 2). Asia and Africa provided 52 percent of immigrants to the U.S. in 2011, but 69 percent for Canada. Europe provided only 8 percent for the U.S. and 16 percent for Canada. A big difference is the share of immigrants from Latin America, 38 percent for the U.S. and 11 percent for Canada. A skill-based focus of immigration policy disadvantages low-skilled potential immigrants, but it does not necessarily disadvantage immigrants from less developed or non-European countries.

Is Current Immigration Too Large?

Immigration to the United States as a share of the population was highest in the early part of the 20th century when about one million persons entered per year from 1905 to 1914. In recent years about one million immigration visas have been issued annually. The population today is four times greater than a century ago, so the rate of immigration (immigrants per thousand population) is one quarter of the rate a century ago. Immigration to the U.S. has increased in each decade since World War II. The relative number of foreign born reached a low point of 4.7 percent of the population (about one in 20) in the 1970 Census and has grown to over 13 percent (about one in eight) today.

Some ask the following questions: Is one million immigrants per year too high or too low? What is the absorptive capacity of the U.S. economy? Those who argue that the current rate is too high point to crowding and environmental concerns, and that the annual intake has reached the 1905–1914 peak in U.S. history. Those who argue the opposite point to the flexibility and adjustment of the economy and that the current rate relative to the population is only a quarter of that for the peak decade. The economics profession has largely avoided addressing this important, but methodologically and empirically difficult issue.

There are two fundamental differences between the U.S. in the early 20th century (1905–1914) and the U.S. today (2015). Then the industrial (manufacturing) and mining sectors were expanding rapidly, generating what seemed to be an unlimited demand for low-skilled workers that could be satisfied by low-skilled immigrants from Europe, especially Southern and Eastern Europe including the Russian Empire. There was also little public concern about the consequences of immigration for income distribution, for the low-skilled population, or for poverty among immigrants and the native born alike. Immigrants in dire economic circumstances, whose numbers inevitably grew during an economic downturn, could not rely on a largely non-existent public support system. They could seek assistance instead from their relatives, from co-ethnics, or from religious organizations, or – as many did – they could return to their country of origin. Poverty in those days was considered a private (individual) matter rather than a public concern.

This is very different than the U.S. political economy of the early 21st century. The economy and public policies toward the low-income population differ sharply today than a century ago. The United States and the other advanced economies are experiencing a decline in employment opportunities for lower-skilled workers in manufacturing, mining, and agriculture. This is due to a variety of factors, including increases in the use of capital (physical and human) as substitutes for low-skilled labor and the increasing industrialization of the less-developed countries. Manufactured goods previously made in the U.S. by lower-skilled workers are now increasingly imported from the less-developed countries where they are made. The expanding job opportunities in the U.S. are primarily in the high-education STEM (science, technology, engineering, and mathematics) fields. The change in the demand for high- relative to low-skilled workers has widened wage differentials, raising the rate of return on human capital and increasing income inequality. This downward pressure on low-skilled wages has been intensified by the large increase over the past few decades in low-skilled immigration (legal and illegal) from less-developed countries.

The other dramatic difference is the growth of income transfer programs to assist the low-income population, whether immigrant or native born. These programs provide benefits in cash as well as subsidized food, medical care, and housing. Because of a recognition of the negative externalities from poverty, and a wealthier society willing to spend more on the less fortunate, poverty today is considered a public as well as a private concern.

The combination of the change in relative employment opportunities, public policies toward income distribution, a family-oriented immigration program, and an increasing illegal migration has resulted in a growing low-income population that benefits from public support.

There are, however, some parts of the service sector of the economy with expanding employment opportunities for less-skilled workers, in particular in elder care and in child care. With the post-World War II baby boomers reaching elder status, and with increased longevity, an increasing number and population share is in need of caregivers. The demand for companions, physical care, and light nursing for the elderly is increasingly provided by immigrant workers with low educational attainment.

There has been a continuing increase in the labor force participation of native-born women due to their higher levels of education, expanded occupational opportunities, and the consequent greater earnings potential. They have also increased the demand for elder care workers as a substitute for care by adult children. While these labor force developments have had a negative impact on fertility, they have increased the labor demand for child care workers as substitutes for parental (primarily mothers') time in child care. These expanding service sector jobs tend to be urban and filled by low-skilled immigrants, disproportionately female.

There has been an increased recognition in immigration policy of the many positive benefits from high-skilled or STEM immigrant workers. Their skills augment the human capital stock of the destination countries. This tends to decrease (or at least slow the increase in) the earnings of high-skilled workers in general, and it raises the relative earnings of those lower-skilled workers who are their complements in production. The narrowing of wage differentials due to high-skilled immigration has the effect of reducing income inequality. Unlike low-skilled immigrant workers, STEM immigrant workers are likely to pay more in taxes than the benefits they receive from government sources. A characteristic of immigrants in general, but especially STEM workers, is that they typically have a higher level of decision-making (entrepreneurial and innovative) skills. With these skills they can create new products or use existing products in new and different ways. Finally, many of these STEM immigrant workers maintain contacts with STEM workers who remained in their country of origin or emigrated to a third country. This enhances opportunities for international exchange, including the exchange of ideas, as well as the trade of goods and services.

Employer Petitions vs. Points System

There is no clear consensus on the optimal way of implementing a skill-based immigration policy. Some countries, such as the United States in its employment-based permanent and temporary (e.g., H1-B visas) worker programs, rely on "employer petitions." While certain industries or occupations might be favored by this system, the administrative process requires employers to submit a petition explaining why the immigrant applicant is the only person available and suited for the specific job opening. This process encourages the use of political pressure by employers to have their industry or occupations treated favorably, and by employee associations to have these industries or occupations denied special favorable treatment.

Another mechanism for issuing high-skilled employment-based visas is through the "point system" used by Canada and Australia. Visa applicants are awarded points for measurable skills deemed relevant for the labor market, such as being in a preferred age group, having formal schooling, occupational job training, language skills, and being prepared to live in certain regions of the country. Any applicant receiving more than a threshold number of points receives a visa. In this system the number of new immigrants can be regulated by changing the threshold number of points. A disadvantage compared to employer petitions is that the applicant may have difficulty finding a job once he or she arrives in the destination.

It may well be that a synthesis of these two mechanisms for rationing STEM visas would be optimal. For example, using a "point system" but requiring that the occupation-specific training be in fields experiencing a high demand for immigrant workers or that the application be accompanied by a bona fide job offer.

STEM Workers are Highly Mobile

STEM workers are potentially highly mobile internationally.

Increasingly, STEM workers across the globe read and study the same technical books, monographs, and articles. As a result, they have a similar knowledge base in their respective fields.

English has become the *lingua franca* of STEM workers. STEM students across the globe are learning English. Technical books written in a local language get translated into English to reach a wider market. Many journals that were once published in local languages have switched, at least partially, to being published in the international language, English. International conferences and the international exchange of scholars and STEM workers have become important avenues for the sharing and dissemination of knowledge in the STEM fields.

In the past, countries expected their citizens to have only one nationality and to live within that country's borders. Dual citizenship was frequently prohibited or at least discouraged by law. With the growth of the international movement of people and the sharing of knowledge and of workers across countries, there has been an expansion in areas of free or unrestricted mobility of workers, such as among the Nordic countries and the countries in the European Union. Other countries, such as the U.S., have reduced the legal barriers to dual citizenship. These changes facilitate the international mobility of all workers.

The increased international transferability of STEM-worker skills, the reduced barriers to dual or even multiple citizenships, and the reduced barriers in immigration law regarding permanent and temporary visas for STEM workers all combine to increase the mobility of high-skilled workers. This increased international mobility is a two-way street. These developments make it easier for advanced immigrant-receiving economies to attract foreign high-skilled workers, but they also make it easier for their own high-skilled workers, whether native or foreign born, to be recruited for jobs in other countries.

The lines between permanent resident visas and temporary work visas have become blurred. In the past, temporary work visas were used primarily to attract workers for seasonal industries, such as agriculture and construction. The seasonality in these industries has generally declined. The newer temporary worker programs, as in the U.S. and Australia, are not intended for seasonal jobs. They are targeted at high-skilled STEM workers and cover a period of several years. They facilitate a sort of probationary period, testing whether a permanent visa is warranted or appropriate for a particular worker. These newer temporary worker visas are much easier than the seasonal temporary worker visas to convert into permanent visas.

As a result, countries need to think more broadly regarding their immigration and emigration policies. Policies are needed not only to attract foreign-born or foreign-trained STEM workers, but also to retain the country's STEM workers, both native and foreign born.

Policy Issues for the 21st Century

Low-Skilled Immigration
Employment opportunities in the 21st century for low-skilled immigrant workers will be primarily in the service sectors with job opportunities continuing to decline in manufacturing and agriculture. These declines will be a result of the increased use of both human and physical capital in the production of goods in the U.S. and other ad-

vanced economies, and the increased importation of manufactured goods and agricultural products (especially fruits and vegetables) from less-developed countries with a comparative advantage for making these products.

The service sector will increase in importance as both a share of GDP and in employment. For low-skilled foreign-born workers the expanded opportunities will be primarily in the personal care sectors, especially child care and elder care. The supply of low-skilled immigrant workers will likely continue to exceed the number of available visas, thereby encouraging illegal immigration.

The current political discussions of "securing the border" to prevent the illegal immigration of EWI (Entry Without Inspection) workers misses the point. Currently, only about half of the illegal immigrants working in the United States entered by "running" across the border with Mexico. Building a secure fence and adding more border patrol agents would be costly, with an uncertain effect on diminishing the number of people working illegally in the United States. The more costly it is for illegal migrants to go back and forth across the border, the more likely they are to reduce their number of trips home (border crossings) and to remain in the U.S. for longer periods. Moreover, the more costly it is to cross the border on their own, the greater will be their willingness to hire *"coyotes"* (people smugglers) and use other techniques for entering the U.S.

The other half of the illegal immigrants in the U.S. are "visa abusers." These are people who entered with a fraudulent visa or, more likely, with a valid Tourist or Student visa but who have violated one or more of its conditions. Having a job in violation of a visa that prohibits working or staying in the country after the visa has expired is sufficient to put such persons in an illegal status.

Current political debates on illegal migrants have largely ignored "interior enforcement" of immigration law, enforcement away from the country's borders. Illegal immigrants are primarily attracted to the United States by the prospect of jobs. These jobs may offer low wages by the standards of American workers, but these wages tend to be higher than what the migrants could receive in their home countries. Under the 1986 Immigration Reform and Control Act (IRCA) it is illegal for an employer to knowingly hire a person who does not have a legal right to work in the U.S. The effectiveness of this provision is limited, however, because few government resources are devoted to its enforcement, because penalties on employers for violations are minimal, and because there is no easily accessible official clearing house to find out who has a legal right to work. "E-Verify" is a program for establishing such a national up-to-date clearing house. A mandated nation-wide use of an updated electronic E-Verify system is likely to be the most effective tool for interior enforcement of U.S. immigration law.

Three objections have been raised against the nationwide use of an employment verification system. One is that when first implemented there will be many errors in the system. Persons with a legal right to work may be flagged as not qualified, and some not eligible for work will be approved. Experience with the system, however, should diminish such errors over time. A second concern is regarding the cost of implementation and whether it is paid for by the employer, the job applicant, or the government. The third concern is with the implications of an employment verification system for civil liberties, especially for U.S. citizens. The creation of a national data base of who is eligible to work and the establishment of a national identification system to implement the program raises civil liberties issues.

A second major feature of the 1986 IRCA was the granting of amnesty for certain illegal immigrants – and nearly 3 million people received permanent resident status under its provisions. The lax enforcement of employer sanctions and the prospect that the 1986 amnesty foreshadowed future amnesties (a view reinforced by subsequent small amnesties) are in part responsible for the growth of the illegal alien population in the United States to an estimated 11 million people today. The growth in illegal immigration slowed during the Great Recession, but it can be expected to resume as the economy continues to recover.

Public policy is at a stalemate. Promises that granting legal status to millions of illegal immigrants will be accompanied or followed by more stringent enforcement of immigration law falls flat based on the experience with IRCA. The public attitude is one of skepticism – "Fool me once, shame on you; fool me twice, shame on me." The detection, apprehension, and deportation of millions of illegal migrants, many of whom are in families with citizens or legal migrants, is not a feasible solution for practical and political reasons. Yet, the problems become more entrenched with each passing year – "It may already be too late, but it will never be sooner."

High-Skilled Immigration

In recent years, many countries have altered their permanent visa and temporary visa programs to attract high-skilled or STEM workers. The United States, for example, has implemented and expanded an H1-B visa program based on employer petitions to attract high-skilled workers for a period of three years, renewable once for another three years. This is a try-out period for both employers and the foreign-born workers. During the course of this six-year period many are able to obtain a visa that allows them to stay permanently. Other countries have expanded the size of their skill-based permanent visa programs.

With the relative increase in labor market demand for high-skilled workers in the U.S. and other advanced economies, and the increased rate of return from technical higher education, the world-wide supply has increased. Perhaps more important than the increased demand for these workers within countries is the effect on the supply of high-skilled workers through immigration opportunities. One of the benefits from acquiring high levels of skills is the increased opportunity for international migration. This is the "option value" from acquiring STEM skills, the increased probability of obtaining a visa to enter and work in an advanced economy. This mobility substantially raises the rate of return from investing in STEM skills for workers born in lower-income countries.

One issue for both potential STEM migrants and their countries of destination is the optimal timing of the training and migration. Should migration occur after or before the schooling process is completed? It appears that many choose to earn an undergraduate degree in their country of origin and complete their advanced STEM schooling in graduate or professional schools in their destination. It is much easier to enter an advanced economy on a student visa than on a temporary or permanent worker visa. Moreover, being in a preferred destination on a student visa gives the potential migrant an opportunity to test living there, to obtain destination-specific skills, and to gain the experience and make the network contacts that facilitate having a potential employer petition on one's behalf for a permanent visa.

The employment aspects of immigration policy should be thought of in a broader context. It should be one component in an overall skill/educational development policy. How much of a nation's resources should be devoted to enhancing the skills of its population? To what extent should students be encouraged to complete part of their schooling abroad? This runs the risk that the "best and the brightest" may not return home, but it has the benefit that returnees would come back with the latest ideas and technological skills.

A related policy issue in a world where STEM workers are potentially highly mobile across countries is the emigration of native-born as well as immigrant STEM workers. This issue has been discussed in terms of the "brain drain" from less-developed countries, but in the context of international migration it is also relevant for advanced economies. How does Canada discourage its STEM-trained workers from migrating to the U.S., or New Zealand discourage them from migrating to Australia, or in a world where English is their lingua franca how does France discourage them from leaving for Germany?

STEM workers are clearly interested in jobs that keep them at the forefront of their fields through educational opportunities and opportunities on their job. They also, however, are concerned with educational opportunities for their children. Facilitating the cultural, social, and educational adjustment of immigrant STEM workers and their families, including their spouse and children, is clearly part of the solution. So too is maintaining the stability of their employment in STEM jobs. Tax systems that place heavy marginal tax rates on the high earnings of STEM workers gives them an incentive to look elsewhere for more favorable treatment of high-skilled workers.

Policy Conclusion
An immigration policy that effectively limits low-skilled illegal migration, through border enforcement but especially through workplace interior enforcement, and that facilitates high-skilled immigration would have more favorable impacts on the U.S. economy than the present lax enforcement and kinship-based permanent visa policies. With the recognition of these more favorable impacts there would be greater public support for an increase in the annual immigration intake. There would also be more widespread public support for practical solutions to the large illegal immigrant population currently living in the United States. Immigration policy should be thought of as one component of, and in the context of, a nation's overall educational and labor market policies.

Table VI.1

Visa Category, Permanent Resident Status, Canada and the United States, 2011

Visa	Canada		United States	
Category	Number[a]	Percent	Number[a]	Percent
Family	56.4	22.7	688.1	64.8[b]
Economic	156.1	62.8	139.3	13.1
Refugee	27.9	11.2	169.5	16.0
Diversity	—	—	50.1	4.7
Other	8.3	3.3	14.9	1.4
TOTAL	248.7	100.0	1,062.0	100.0
(% of population)	(0.7%)		(0.3%)	

Notes: [a] Number in thousands
   [b] Immediate relatives of citizens, 42.7%. Other family-sponsored, 22.1%.
Sources: US Department of Homeland Security; Citizenship and Immigration Canada.

Table VI.2

Legal Immigrants in Canada and the United States, By Region of Origin, 2011 (percent distribution)

Visa	Canada	United States
Africa	12.5	9.5
Asia	56.7	42.5
Europe	15.6	7.9
Canada/US	3.6	1.2
Other America	10.8	38.3
Oceania	0.7	0.5
Other and Unknown	0.2	0.2
Total	100.0	100.0

Source: US Department of Homeland Security; Citizenship and Immigration Canada.

Notes

Chapter 1

1 Although the skills and earnings of the foreign born were once a subject of lively debate among economists (see, e.g., the 1919 article by Paul H. Douglas), they are now primarily of interest to sociologists and historians (see, e.g., Thernstrom 1973; Greeley 1976; Featherman 1978). For a longitudinal analysis of the occupational mobility of immigrants and an analysis of the earnings of the sons of immigrants, see Chiswick (1977; 1978a). For a brief history of U.S. immigration policy, see Chiswick (1978c).

2 In 1970, 91 percent of the foreign born were white. Eighteen percent of the foreign born were of Spanish heritage, of whom about 93 percent are white (U.S. Bureau of the Census 1973b, Table 1). The analysis is restricted to whites so as to avoid a confounding of the effects of race and foreign origin on earnings, and to men because the problem of estimating labor market experience for women in the data under study requires a separate analysis.

3 The difference in earnings attributable to schooling may be even greater to the extent that some aspects of schooling acquired in the country of origin provide country-specific human capital. For the same number of years of schooling, the foreign born may have less schooling relevant to U.S. labor markets. For example, a Cuban émigré lawyer may have the same number of years of schooling as a U.S.-trained lawyer but may not be able to practice his occupation in the United States.

4 To economize on the number of tables, the relevant partial regression coefficients, rather than the full equations, are reported in some instances. The full regression equations are reported in Appendix A. Little is known about foreign-born persons who subsequently emigrate. Appendix B presents some indirect information on the number and characteristics of foreign-born emigrants to determine whether the self-selection in out-migration from the United States would bias the regression coefficients estimated from cross-sectional data. It appears that because of their relatively small number and fairly similar characteristics to the foreign born in the United States in 1970, they would not substantially bias the findings reported here. I am indebted to Victor Fuchs for having raised this issue.

5 For an analysis of the effect of job change on the earnings of adult male workers, see Bartel and Borjas (1977).

6 The earnings gap would not close if a relevant knowledge deficiency persisted or if there were discrimination against the foreign born in wages, employment, union membership, or occupational licensing. On the other hand, in some jobs there may be discrimination in favor of the foreign born (e.g., the French chef).

7 For an analysis of the greater occupational mobility of immigrants during their first ten years in the United States, see Chiswick (1978a).

8 There is, however, an incentive for some firms to "specialize" in hiring immigrants from particular countries or ethnic groups. Such firms are likely to be small with

Notes

either the owner, manager, or a few senior workers who are bilingual. These firms are effectively "halfway" houses for recent immigrants, with the workers moving on to more "American" firms as they acquire the rudimentary U.S.-specific skills (e.g., knowledge of basic English) and develop a record of job success in the United States.

9 Let r_i be the rate of return from migration for the ith person and $W_{0,i}$ and $W_{d,i}$ be the annual earnings the ith person would receive in the place of origin and destination, respectively. Migration involves opportunity costs (C_0), the forgone earnings while migrating and establishing one's self in the place of destination. The opportunity cost may be thought of as a proportion of the earnings in the place of origin ($C_0 = pW_0$). Migration also involves direct costs (C_d), i.e., the out-of-pocket expenditures incurred in migrating and reestablishing oneself and the psychic costs of leaving family, friends, and familiar surroundings. In a simple model in which wages are constant over time and one's life after migration is very long (infinite), the ith person's rate of return from migration is $r_i = (W_{d,i} - W_{0,i})/(pW_{0,i} + C_d)$. Let us assume that the jth person has greater labor market ability and motivation, which raises his earnings by $100l$ percent ($l > 0$) in both the place of origin and destination, as compared with the ith person, but that this does not reduce the time involved in migration or direct costs. Then, $r_j = (W_{d,j} - W_{0,j})/(pW_{0,j} + C_d) = (W_{d,i} - W_{0,i})/[pW_{0,i} + (C_d/1 + l)] > r_i$. That is, if greater labor market ability and motivation raise earnings relatively more than they raise the cost of migration, the rate of return from migration is greater for the more able and motivated, and they will have a higher propensity to migrate. For analyses suggesting higher rates of migration for those with more schooling, see Sjaastad (1962), O'Neill (1970), and Yezer and Thurston (1976).

10 In his study of immigration in the century prior to World War I, Marcus Lee Hansen (1940a) wrote: "Countries of origin were dismayed by their loss when they saw their ports thronged with the sturdiest of their peasantry. Efforts to stem the movement were attempted" (p. 212).

11 In part because of Civil Service regulations and English language examinations, the foreign born are underrepresented in government employment, especially in the federal and local governments (U.S. Bureau of the Census 1973b, Table 8). Smith (1976) shows that compared with the private sector, other things the same, hourly wages for men are higher in federal employment, lower in local government employment, and about the same in state government employment.

12 Using the functional form in equation (3), controlling for the human capital and demographic variables and including a nonlinear effect of S, for variable TT_a, the coefficient is $-.00003$, and the t-ratio is -0.11; for variable S_a, the coefficient is $-.00534$, and the t-ratio is -1.04.

13 The percentages of foreign-born adult white men for the country-of-origin groupings used in this study, based on 1,924 observations, are: British Isles, 9.70; Western Europe, 16.22; Southern Europe, 12.84; Central Europe, 9.98; the Balkans, 6.34; Russia, 4.68; Canada, Australia, and New Zealand, 13.10; Mexico, 10.97; Cuba, 6.24; other Latin American countries, 4.94; the Middle East and Africa, 2.75; southern Asia (Indian subcontinent), 1.04; and eastern Asia, 1.20 (U.S. Bureau of the Census 1972).

14 Although country of birth has been asked in every decennial census since 1850, year of immigration was asked from 1890 to 1930 and then not until the 1970 Census 5 percent questionnaire. In the 1970 Census, parents' country of birth and mother tongue (language other than or in addition to English spoken in the home when the respondent was a child) were asked only in the nonoverlapping 15 percent questionnaire (U.S. Bureau of the Census 1973c: 7).

15 The question on race in the *1970* Census of Population included the following categories: white, Negro or black, American Indian, Japanese, Chinese, Filipino, Hawaiian, Korean, other (with an identification of the race requested). Only those who indicated white, or whose response to "other" led the Census Bureau to classify them as white, are included in this study. Native residents of North Africa, the

598

Middle East, or southern Asia are generally white, while white persons in eastern Asia or Sub-Saharan Africa are generally descendants of Europeans, Arabs, and Indians.

16 Although the findings here are for all foreign-born men, similar conclusions emerge when the data are limited to men who migrated at age 18 or later.

17 Compare the observed F-ratios (for the inclusion of the foreign variables) with the critical F-ratios at the 1 percent level of significance for 1,000 observations.

Table 1.2	Added Variables (N)	F-Ratios	
		Observed	Critical
Col. 2	1	3.1	6.66
Col. 3	3	15.0	3.80
Col. 4	4	15.3	3.34

18 The rise in the earnings of migrants with time in the place of destination has been found for immigrants to Israel (for men, Hovne 1961: 45, and Hanoch 1961, chaps. 3–4; and, for women Gronau 1976), Canada (Tandon 1977), and U.S. blacks born in the South who moved to the North (Masters 1972). Masters also found that southern-born blacks living in the North eventually had higher earnings than blacks born in the North, both overall and when other variables are held constant.

19 From table 1.2, column 3, e.g., $\partial \ln E / \partial FOR = -0.1636 + 0.0146\ (YSM) -0.00016\ (YSM)^2$, and the partial effect is a maximum at YSM equal to 44 years. The predicted percent difference in earnings between the native and foreign born ($\partial \ln E / \partial FOR$) for different durations since migration are: one year, -14.9; five years, -9.5; ten years, -3.4; 13 years, -0.1; 20 years, 6.4; and 30 years, 13.0. When the native born are compared with foreign-born persons who came to the United States at age 18 or later, the earnings crossover occurs at 11 years since migration.

20 Earnings were evaluated at the mean value of the explanatory variables in the pooled sample, YSM was assumed equal to T, and the postschool earnings stream was assumed to be 40 years long.

21 If immigrants have higher earnings because they are more able or more highly motivated (or for some other unmeasured reason), and if this is, in part, transmitted from one generation to the next, the native-born sons of immigrants would be expected to have higher earnings than the native-born sons of native-born parents. Empirically, other things the same, the native-born sons of immigrants (one or both parents foreign born) have earnings that are 5 percent higher than the sons of native-born parents, and the difference is highly significant ($t = 4.7$). If the mother is native born, a foreign-born father is associated with 8 percent ($t = 4.1$) higher earnings (see Chiswick 1977).

22 For a given level of training, however, it is presumably those whose training is the least country specific who have the highest rates of migration. Thus, lawyers have a lower rate of international migration than physicians or mathematicians.

23 Controlling for $EDUC$, T, $T2$, $LN\ WW$, $RURALEQ1$, $SOUTHEQ1$, and $NOTMSP$, the R^2 is .307 for the native born and .331 for the foreign born.

24 The partial effect of years of schooling in a regression analysis for foreign-born adult white men:

	Regression[a]		
	1	2	3
EDUC	.05740 [b]		.03343
	(12.93)		(2.28)
EDUCPRE	[b]	.05839	[b]
		(13.01)	
EDUCPOST	[b]	.04975	-.01041
		(7.34)	(-1.78)
EDUCSQ[c]	[b]	[b]	.00118
			(1.78)
R^2	.339	.339	.341

Note: t-ratio in parentheses; sample size is 1,924.
[a] Controlling for T, $T2$, $LN\ WW$, $RURALEQ1$, $SOUTHEQ1$, $NOTMSP$, YSM, and $YSM2$.
[b] Variable not entered.
[c] $EDUCSQ$ is the square of $EDUC$.

25 If years of postschool training in the United States is held constant, instead of the total number of years since migration, the difference between the coefficients of pre- and post-immigration schooling is even smaller and is not significant.

26 The partial effect of being an alien in a regression analysis for foreign-born adult white men:

	Regression[a]		
	1	2[b]	3
ALIEN	.14865	-.06787	-.00278
	(-4.01)	(-1.48)	(-.04)
(ALIEN) (YSM)	c	c	-.00512
			(-1.34)
R^2	.3364	.3394	.3400

Note: t-ratios in parentheses; sample size, 1.924.
[a] Controlling for $EDUC, T, T2, LN\ WW, RURALEQ1, SOUTHEQ1$, and $NOTMSP$.
[b] Also controlling for YSM and $YSM2$.
[c] Variable not entered.

When $ALIEN$ and $(ALIEN)\ (YSM)$ are added to the regression equation in Table 1.2, column 5, the R^2 increases from .33866 to .34003, an increase which is not statistically significant.

27 Partial effect on the natural logarithms of earnings of country-of-origin dichotomous variables[a]

Immigrants	All Countries[b]	Non-English-speaking Countries[c]
Western Europe	-.015	d
	(-.23)	
Southern Europe	-.030	-.022
	(-.42)	(-.34)
Central Europe	-.035	-.011
	(-.47)	(-.16)
Balkans	-.107	-.086
	(-1.28)	1.08)
Russia	-.098	-.082
	(-1.07)	(-.92)
Canada	.013	d
	(.19)	
Cuba	-.258	-.195
	(-2.92)	(-2.17)
Mexico	-.345	-.340
	(-4.46)	(-4.58)
Other Latin American countries	-.067	-.034
	(-.73)	(-.38)
Asia, Africa[e]	-.196	-.172
	(-2.15)	(-1.91)
R^2	.352	.336
N	1.924	1.485

Note: t-ratios in parentheses.
[a] Controlling for $EDUC, T, T2, LN\ WW, RURALEQ1, SOUTHEQ1, NOTMSP, YSM$, and $YSM2$.
[b] Excluded country group: British Isles.
[c] Men born in the English-speaking developed countries (Great Britain, Ireland, Canada, Australia, and New Zealand) were excluded from the data. Excluded country group: Western Europe.
[d] Variable not entered.
[e] Includes Australia and New Zealand.

28 The coefficient of the Mexican-origin dichotomous variable is −.34 in an analysis of white male immigrants (compared with immigrants from the British Isles), −.18 in an analysis of native-born sons of Mexican immigrants (compared with those from the British Isles), and −.27 in an analysis of native-born, Spanish surname sons of native-born parents (compared with native-parentage, non-Spanish surname white men). The first and "third" generation coefficients do not differ significantly (see Chiswick 1977).

29 For a detailed analysis, compare the earnings pattern among first, second, and third-generation white male Americans in this chapter and Chiswick (1977) with the pattern among Mexican-origin men in Chiswick (1978c).

30 The partial effect of Cuban birth on earnings in a regression analysis for Cuban- and U.S.-born adult white men:

| | Regression[a] | | | |
| | Urban Florida | | All Urban Areas[b] | |
	(1)	(2)	(3)	(4)
CUBA	-.26914	c		c
	(-2.50)			
YM 1965-69	c	-.45338	c	-.37494
		(-2.30)		(-2.22)
YM 1960-64	c	-.22535	c	-.15483
		(-1.55)		(-1.14)
YM 1955-59	c	.06022	c	.15558
		(.19)		(.73)
YM PRE1955	c	-.33930	c	-.54123
		(-.90)		(-2.14)
(FL) (CUBA)	c	c	c	-.07598
				(-.48)
(NY) (CUBA)	c	c	c	.00136
				(-.00)
R^2	.29589	.29766	.32117	.32333
Native born (N)	789	789	23,890	23,890
Cuban born (N)	57	57	117	117

Note: $CUBA$ = dichotomous variable equal to unity if born in Cuba; YM = year of immigration intervals; FL = dichotomous variable equal to unity if living in Florida; NY = dichotomous variable equal to unity if living in an SMSA in New York or New Jersey; t-ratios in parentheses.
[a] Holding constant $EDUC, T, T2, LN WW$, and $NOTMSP$.
[b] Also holding constant FL and NY.
[c] Variable not entered.

31 Among immigrants from Canada, it is not possible to identify French Canadians in the sample from the 5 percent questionnaire.

32 In their analysis of job mobility among white men in the United States, Bartel and Borjas (1977) found that voluntary job change resulted in an initial increase in earnings, other things the same, but that this increment decreased as time passed. If persons with high levels of schooling from English-speaking countries have no knowledge deficiency compared with native-born men, their migration may be no different than voluntary job change for native-born men in the United States. Combining the findings of Bartel and Borjas with the findings in this study suggests a very high degree of international transferability of the skills of highly educated persons from the developed English-speaking countries.

Chapter 2

1 This argument can also be made for the so-called noneconomic immigrants (e.g., political refugees) (see Borjas 1982).

2 Although the cohort analysis of earnings conducted in this chapter is not available in the literature, a few previous studies have addressed issues related to those discussed later. For example, Chiswick (1980a, Appendix D) has analyzed the earnings growth of the small sample of immigrants available in the Mature Men National Longitudinal Survey. Similarly, both Chiswick (1980a, chapter 10) and DeFreitas (1981) have used the 1965 and 1970 occupation variables available in the 1970 Census to study the extent of occupational mobility in immigrant samples. The results of these studies, however, do not provide a consensus on whether longitudinal data lead to different results from cross-section data. In the

studies of occupational mobility, e.g., Chiswick finds relatively higher rates of upward mobility as immigrants assimilate in the labor market, while DeFreitas, in his analysis of black men, finds either no difference between the native and the foreign born or slower rates of upward mobility for the foreign born. In addition, the study of the longitudinal National Chicano Survey by Snipp and Tienda (1984) finds no evidence that Mexican immigrants experience relatively more upward occupational mobility than Mexican Americans born in this country.

3   In some studies, t_i is defined as a vector of variables indicating the time period in which the immigrant arrived rather than a continuous variable measuring years since migration. The simpler specification is used in the discussion to focus attention on the substantive problems introduced by cross-section data.

4   A simple calculation of the magnitude of the bias could, in principle, be based on the fact that some immigrants (e.g., political refugees) have no possibility of return migration, while other immigrants (e.g., Mexicans) face low return costs due to geographic circumstances. This kind of solution, however, would have to take into account the differences in observable (and unobservable) quality indices among the national groups.

5   Of course, there are many reasons why the cohorts in the 1970 and 1980 Census data may not be perfectly matched. For instance, as noted earlier, the presence of emigration will lead to secular trends in the size (and quality) of a specific immigrant cohort. Similarly, institutional changes in the census enumeration procedures may lead to different counts of immigrants (and native persons) in particular cohorts across censuses. Finally, there may be age- or cohort-related differences in labor supply, self-employment propensities, and mortality rates, which generate additional differences in the cohort samples included in the regressions over time. Note, however, that all these problems will impart biases on *both* cross-section and cohort analyses. Hence the cohort study presented here simply nets out one of the many sources of bias, that due to violations of the assumption of stationarity in the immigrant human capital stock at the time of entry.

6   Equation (7) defines the cross-section growth exactly for all but one of the cohorts in the data. In particular, consider the cohort that arrived in 1950–59. Since the 1960 cohorts are partitioned into two groups, the definition for cross-section growth used for this sample is given by

$$\hat{\gamma}_{80,50} - \hat{\gamma}_{80,60} = \hat{\beta}_{50} - \frac{\hat{\beta}_{60} + \hat{\beta}_{65}}{2},$$

so that a simple average is used to pool the two coefficients from the 1960s.

7   The decomposition of the cross-section growth into its components can also be made by pooling the 1970 and 1980 observations for a specific cohort, and including a dummy variable in the earnings function indicating the census from which the observation is drawn. It is easy to show that this methodology is identical to that given by Equation (8) as long as the γ-coefficient vector is allowed to vary across censuses but is fixed for all cohorts within a census.

8   Of course, this result follows directly from the fact that all the predicted earnings terms are evaluated at a given level of socioeconomic characteristics, $\overline{X}_k$, so that the decompositions in this section are net of any pure aging effects. The empirical analysis which follows will present separate estimates of the earnings differentials created by the aging process.

9   The sampling fractions for 1970 are native white (.001 of the population), all other groups (.01). The 1980 sampling fractions are black natives (.00245), black immigrants (.01651), Mexicans born in the United States (.01652), Mexican immigrants (.01638), white natives (.00042), white immigrants (.00249), all other groups (.05).

10 As was noted earlier, there are many reasons why in actual census data the 1970 and 1980 cohorts of immigrant (and native) men are not exactly matched. In fact, the ratio of the number of immigrants in the 1980 sample to that of the 1970 sample is 1.11. The value of the same ratio for native men is 1.06. Thus the restriction of the

sample to salaried men in the labor force – along with the age restrictions imposed on the two samples – leads to an increase in sample size over the decade. The increase in sample size, however, is relatively neutral for immigrants and native men, since in the 1970 data 4.4 percent of the sample is foreign born, while the same statistic in the 1980 data is 4.6 percent.

11 Two points should be made about this ethnic/racial breakdown. First, the Asian sample aggregates over a wide variety of countries and cultures; hence the results for the Asian sample should be interpreted cautiously. Second, the Hispanic samples do not include the group of Puerto Rican men, since Puerto Ricans born in Puerto Rico are not asked the year they migrated to the United States by the census.

12 Since most immigrants reside within an SMSA, the analysis was also conducted on the subsample of metropolitan residents. This estimation led to only minor changes in the results.

13 The calculation of the 1969 wage rate uses the weekly hours worked reported for the census week, while the estimated 1979 wage rate uses the usual hours worked per week in 1979.

14 The cohort arriving prior to 1950 can also be matched in the two census data files. The open-ended lower interval, however, leads to the aggregation of immigrants from many different cohorts and thus confuses the basic issues.

15 More precisely, using the notation in Sec. II, the statistics presented in Table 2.4 are given by $\hat{\gamma}_{80,k} - \hat{\gamma}_{80,n}$.

16 It has been suggested that a more relevant base group would be the sample of native young men. Since immigrants are new entrants to the labor market, their experiences are likely to resemble those encountered by native youths. This comparison, however, ignores the fact that, e.g., the 1960–64 cohort of white immigrants has been in the United States for 17 years and is, on the average, 43.5 years old. Thus the comparison of this group with teenage workers would be quite misleading.

17 An important implication of the hypothesis that there has been a secular decline in the quality of immigrants is that overtaking will occur at a later point in the life cycle in the 1980 Census than in the 1970 Census. The result in Table 2.4 that white immigrants in 1980 overtake the native cohort after 10–15 years seems to contradict this implication, since Chiswick (1978d) dates overtaking at the same point using the 1970 Census. However, the definitions of "white" men vary significantly across the two studies; in this chapter a distinction is made between Hispanic whites and non-Hispanic whites. In fact, given that the samples are defined identically in the two censuses, the results do show that overtaking occurs at a later point in the 1980 Census. For example, a regression estimated in the 1970 Census using a pooled sample of white native and immigrant men yields

$$\ln w = X\gamma - .0468D65 + .0626D60 + .0603D50 + .0479D40, \qquad R2 = .205,$$
$$\{-1.18\} \qquad \{1.38\} \qquad \{2.11\} \qquad \{1.49\}$$

where the omitted dummy variable indicates native-born status. This 1970 regression implies that among white men overtaking occurs within five to ten years after arrival in the United States, while the 1980 results in Table 2.4 reveal that overtaking (in the same racial-ethnic sample) occurs within 10–15 years after immigration. Thus over a ten-year period the overtaking age increased by five years, a movement consistent with the hypothesis that the quality of white immigrants has declined over time.

18 The astute reader will realize that the cross-section rates of convergence implicit in Table 2.4 are not identical to those given by Equation (13). The reason is that in Table 2.4 the comparison between each immigrant cohort and the native-born population is calculated at the mean level of X for each immigrant cohort, whereas the conceptually correct cross-section growth in Equation (13) holds constant the values of the socioeconomic characteristics across cohorts. The reader can verify that the differences between the two experiments are minimal.

Notes

Chapter 3

1 There is no simple mapping of INS data on past flows to Census Bureau data on the stock of the foreign-born population. Differences by country of origin in mortality and especially in reemigration rates, and in the extent to which illegal aliens are enumerated in the census, serve as a wedge between the flow and the stock data (Warren and Peck 1980; Passel and Woodrow 1984). The divergent pattern for Cubans in Tables 3.1 and 3.2 also reflects a difference between year of entry in census data and year of receipt of a resident alien visa for Cuban refugees "paroled" into the United States. A similar difference between INS flow data and census stock data can arise from persons entering the United States with student or other nonresident alien visas.

2 For estimates of the size of the illegal alien population by country of origin and duration in the United States and the extent of enumeration of illegal aliens in the 1980 Census, see Passel and Woodrow (1984), Siegel, Passel, and Robinson (1981) and Warren and Passel (1983).

3 See, e.g., Borcherding and Silberberg (1978), Chiswick (1978d, 1979, 1984), DaVanzo (1976), Goldfarb (1982), Katz and Stark (1984), Kwok and Leland (1982), Schwartz (1976), and Tidwick (1971).

4 The data are from U.S. Bureau of the Census, 1980 Census of Population, Public Use Sample, C File, 1/100 Sample; U.S. Bureau of the Census, 1970 Census of Population, Public Use Sample, 5% Questionnaire; and U.S. Bureau of the Census, Survey of Income and Education (1976), Public Use Sample.

5 Let W_{ij} be earnings, where $i = 0$ in the origin, $i = d$ in the destination, $j = h$ for high-skilled workers, and $j = l$ for low-skilled workers. The equation $C_j = pW_{oj} + D$ represents the total cost of migration, where p is the proportion of the year devoted to migration and D is the out-of-pocket cost. If high-ability workers earn $100k$ percent more than low-ability workers in both the origin and the destination, then

$$r_l = \frac{W_{dl} - W_{ol}}{pW_{ol} + D},$$

and

$$r_h = \frac{W_{dh} - W_{oh}}{pW_{oh} + D} = \frac{(1 + k)(W_{dl} - W_{ol})}{(1 + k)pW_{ol} + D} = \frac{W_{dl} - W_{ol}}{pW_{ol} + D/(1 + k)},$$

where r_l and r_h are the rates of return to migration for low-ability and high-ability workers, respectively. Under the conditions specified, $r_h > r_l$ as long as $D > 0$. The difference between r_h and r_l is smaller the lower is D relative to W_{ol} and p.

6 The restrictions on Asian immigration began in the 1870s against the Chinese, became general when the Asiatic Barred Zone was created in 1917, and was incorporated into the national origins quota system enacted in the 1920s. A quota for China, a wartime ally, was introduced during World War II. Japan and some other parts of Asia were given small quotas when the immigration law was recodified in 1952.

7 "Surplus" visas arise if the occupational and kinship preferences do not exhaust the hemispheric (now worldwide) ceiling on visas subject to numerical limitation.

8 The data are computed from U.S. Department of Justice (1970, table 7a), U.S. Department of Justice (1975, table 7a), and U.S. Department of Justice (1984, table 5).

9 Among European immigrants subject to numerical limitation, the absolute number of occupational preference principals also declined over the period (from 6,100 in 1970 to 4,600 in 1981), although their relative proportion in European immigration increased. The preference system was extended to the Western Hemisphere under 1977 Amendments, replacing the first-come, first-serve system under the 1965 Amendments. If the Asian experience is a guide, any bulge in the skill level of Western Hemisphere immigration created by extending the coverage in the preference system may be temporary.

Notes

10   Even when other variables are the same, immigrants who enter the United States as relatives of U.S. citizens or resident aliens earn less than those who enter with an occupational or nonpreference (investor) visa (see North 1979; Chiswick 1980a, chapter 9).

11   The decline in migration costs relative to wages may be more important for stimulating illegal rather than legal migration because illegal migrants are more likely to require more than one attempted entry into the United States. Similarly, the smaller the transportation costs from a country to the United States, the greater the extent of illegal migration, other things the same. For data on the low level and relative decline in enforcement resources, see North and Wagner (1980) and Harwood (1983).

12   Included in the pool of unsuccessful visa applicants are "discouraged applicants," i.e., those who wish to migrate but did not apply for a visa because they realized they could not obtain a visa.

13   This is a modification of the usual argument that migrants tend to be self-selected for high skill and ability.

14   The same patterns emerge when the analysis is done for earnings, whether overall or other things the same, in the 1970 Census.

15   The natural logarithm of earnings is regressed on a set of country-of-birth dichotomous variables with immigrants from the United Kingdom serving as the benchmark. For small differences the country regression coefficient approximates the percentage difference in earnings, but not for large differences. The country coefficients in Table 3.3 have been converted to relative differences by computing one minus the antilog of the regression coefficient. When multiplied by 100, it is the percentage difference in earnings.

16   The significant earnings gap disappears for Canadian immigrants when the analysis is done by period of immigration and for South Asians when the analysis is limited to the 1965–69 immigrant cohort (Table 3.3, columns 3–5). This is not due merely to a rise in the standard error of the estimated coefficient with the decline in sample size since the coefficients are close to zero. There is a larger earnings gap in the more recent immigrant cohort for groups that are disproportionately refugees (e.g., Vietnamese) and economic migrants with less transferability of skills to the U.S. labor market (e.g., Africans, Asians, and other Americans). This should not be interpreted as a deterioration in immigrant quality from these countries. These groups would be expected to show a steeper rise in earnings with duration of U.S. residence than would immigrants from the United Kingdom.

17   Similar patterns emerge when earnings differentials in 1970 are correlated with the distribution of the foreign born.

18   This may reflect the increase in illegal immigration in recent decades. It may also reflect a greater reemigration rate among low-schooled Mexican nationals (Chiswick 1980a, Appendix B).

19   The very steep decline for the post-1975 Southeast Asians is presumably due to the Indo-Chinese refugees.

20   This procedure has been used by Chiswick (1978d, 1979), Simon and Sullivan (1982), and Borjas (1985), among others.

21   The SIE analysis is limited to white and Mexican-origin men because the samples for other groups are too small for meaningful comparative analyses. The SIE analysis differs from the census analyses in the statistical control for size of place. Tests with the 1980 Census suggest that controlling for standard metropolitan statistical area residence as in the SIE analysis, rather than urban residence as in the census analyses, lowers the relative earnings of white immigrants by about 2 percentage points but raises it for Mexican immigrants by 2–3 percentage points.

22   What might appear to be "statistical cohorts" drawn from the same population at different points in time may, in fact, be sampling from different populations because of changes in the population under study (e.g., due to changes in the self-identification of race or ethnicity and the reemigration of some of the foreign born) or the intensity with which components of the population are enumerated (e.g., the degree of census undercount). It is believed that there is considerable

born) or the intensity with which components of the population are enumerated (e.g., the degree of census undercount). It is believed that there is considerable reemigration of the foreign born and that it varies by country of origin (see Warren and Peck 1980). Less is known, however, about the degree of favorable self-selection of return migrants (DaVanzo 1976; Chiswick 1980a, Appendix B). As a consequence of the apparent reduction in the census undercount, the 1980 Census may have enumerated a greater proportion of the (presumably larger) illegal alien population than the 1970 Census (Passel and Woodrow 1984; Warren and Passel 1983). The data refer to different phases of the business cycle. The unemployment rate for adult men (age 20 and over) in the reference year (the prior year) was 2.1 percent for the 1970 Census, 6.8 percent for the SIE, and 4.2 percent for the 1980 Census (Council of Economic Advisers 1984, table B-33, p. 259). Employment and earnings are more cyclically sensitive among immigrants, particularly recent immigrants and refugees, than among the native born (Chiswick 1982b).

23 The change in earnings with additional experience in the United States rather than in the origin becomes very small after about 15 years. As a result, the number of years at which the earnings catch-up occurs is very sensitive to small changes in relative earnings when the catch-up involves more than 15 years.

24 The 8 percentage point cohort improvement in earnings over the decade for foreign-born white men relative to the native born in the census is similar to the improvement found in longitudinal data. Among adult white men in the National Longitudinal Survey (NLS), the relative earnings of the foreign born increased by 9 percentage points during the eight years 1965–73 (see Chiswick 1980a, Appendix D). The data on occupational status in 1965 and in 1970, as reported in the 1970 Census, has been used in a longitudinal analysis of the occupational mobility of white immigrants (Chiswick 1978a). Occupational status increases with duration of residence in the longitudinal data, but the partial effect is smaller the longer the duration of residence in the United States.

25 Several studies indicate that the growth in the proportion of youths in the labor force during the 1970s steepened experience earnings profiles (see, e.g., Welch 1979; Berger 1983).

26 It is striking that the relative earnings of the white foreign born in the 1970s is very similar to the relative wage profile in 1909 data collected by the Dillingham Commission. Other things the same, immigrants from English Canada and Northern and Western Europe (excluding Ireland) had earnings 0.4 percent less than native-born white men at ten years after migration and 10.3 percent greater than the native born at 20 years. The earnings crossover occurred at 11 years after immigration. The earnings profile was lower for other white immigrants (French Canada, Mexico, Ireland, Southern and Eastern Europe, and the Middle East). They had earnings that were 6.0 percent lower than the native-born white men at ten years and 4.7 percent greater at 20 years since migration. The earnings crossover was at 16 years (Blau 1980). This suggests that, relative to the native born, the quality of foreign-born workers was the same at the turn of the century as in the 1970s.

27 Cuban immigrants are compared to native-born white men because there are too few Cuban-origin adult men born in the United States for a meaningful statistical analysis.

28 Borjas (1982), e.g., has shown that, other things the same, Cuban refugees acquire more schooling while in the United States than do other Hispanic immigrants.

29 The Korean, South Asian, and Indo-Chinese groups are not shown separately because of their relatively small numbers, particularly among the native born and for the foreign born in the 1970 Census.

Chapter 4

1 For a recent discussion of this identification problem, see Heckman and Robb (1983).

Notes

2　The model is formally identical to that presented in A. D. Roy's (1951) study of the impact of self-selection in occupational choice on the income distribution. The wealth-maximization hypothesis is also the cornerstone of the human capital model by Sjaastad (1962). However, both Sjaastad's work and the literature it engendered pay little attention to the selection biases that are at the core of the Roy model.

3　Two important problems are ignored by the two-country setup. First, it is likely that potential movers from any country j will have more than one possible country of destination. Second, the probability that U.S. native-born persons emigrate to other countries may not be negligible. These possibilities are ignored in order to focus on the essential aspects of the selection problem.

4　The Roy model has been recently used by Willis and Rosen (1979) to analyze the types of selection biases created by the college attendance decision. Heckman and Sedlacek (1985) present a generalization of the Roy model and apply it to the probleof estimating market wage functions.

5　It is possible, of course, that the average person in country 0 has ethnic or racial characteristics which are favored or penalized by the U.S. labor market. Hence the mean income of (equally skilled) natives may not equal μ_1. This possibility is ignored in the discussion that follows, but it can be easily incorporated into the model.

6　A fourth case where $Q_0 > 0$ and $Q_1 < 0$ is theoretically impossible since it requires $\rho > 1$.

7　The generalization of the model to allow for variable mobility costs (π) shows that the necessary conditions for negative (positive) selection remain unchanged as long as mobility costs and earnings do not have an "excessive" negative (positive) correlation. In addition, the impact of variable mobility costs on the results of the analysis is negligible if the variance in mobility costs is small relative to the variance in the income distributions.

8　It must be noted, however, that these data on income inequality do not correspond exactly to the variances that are the primitive parameters of the Roy model. In particular, σ_0^2 and σ_1^2 describe the dispersion in "opportunities" (for a given socioeconomic characteristic).

9　This follows trivially from the fact that λ is defined as $E(x \mid x > z)$, where x is a standard normal random variable.

10　This discussion illustrates how differences in skill characteristics can enter the Roy model. More generally, the earnings distributions in the two countries can be written as

$$\ln w_0 = X\delta_0 + \varepsilon_0, \quad \ln w_1 = X\delta_1 + \varepsilon_1,$$

and the emigration rate (for given characteristics X) is given by

$$P = Pr\{(\varepsilon_1 - \varepsilon_0) > - [X(\delta_1 - \delta_0) - \pi]\}.$$

Selection will occur not only on the basis of unobserved characteristics (ε), but also in terms of the socioeconomic variables X as long as the two countries value these skills differently. Although the empirical analysis below (by holding X constant) focuses on the selections in ε, it would be very interesting to also investigate the types of selections generated in X.

11　In addition, the 1965 Act changed the emphasis in the allocation of visas toward family reunification and away from occupational preferences. This shift may well lead to an even steeper decline in the quality of immigrants admitted to the United States.

12　The parameters β_1 and β_2 capture two kinds of cohort effects: (1) differences in the skill composition of cohorts due to a secular trend in the quality of immigrants; and (2) differences due to selective emigration of foreign-born persons in the

United States. Little is known, however, about the selection biases associated with return migration even though the Roy model can be generalized to account for the possibility that individuals make "mistakes." Unfortunately, U.S. data on the return migration of foreign-born persons is basically nonexistent, and hence this problem is ignored in what follows.

13　Except perhaps for the coefficient of the immigrant dummy. This coefficient gives the wage differential between the most recent cohort of immigrants and the native-born population.

14　Provided that period effects on the immigrant-native wage differential are negligible. This assumption is far from innocuous. Unfortunately, since only two cross sections are available, little can be done to test its validity.

15　The two 1970 samples that are pooled are essentially independent of each other. The only substantive difference between them – in the context of this study – is that the set of persons for whom SMSA residence is defined differs in the two samples. However, the coefficients of the SMSA dummy in earnings functions estimated separately in the two samples are not statistically different from each other.

16　The native-born extract is a .001 sample in the 1970 Census and a .00042 sample in the 1980 Census.

17　The analysis is restricted to men aged 25–64 in either census year. This differs from the more common methodology of tracking the "same" men over time. It can be shown (Heckman and Robb) that if the underlying parameters are constant over time, it is unnecessary to track specific cohorts across censuses in order to identify the structure. In addition, the samples exclude men who are self-employed. This restriction creates its own set of selection biases. However, an equally serious problem would arise if self-employed men were included in the study and their incomes were analyzed jointly with the wages of salaried men. Finally, the data exclude men who had annual earnings under $1,000 in either of the census years.

18　Only two of the countries in the analysis have between 80 to 100 observations in the 1970 Census, an additional 11 countries have between 101 and 200 observations, eight have between 201 and 300 observations, and 20 have more than 300 observations. Of course, the sample sizes in the 1980 Census are significantly larger.

19　The CNTSA was created by Arthur Banks and is available through the Inter-University Consortium for Political and Social Research, Ann Arbor, MI 48106.

20　There is also the possibility that a country gained its freedom during the 1950–73 period. Only one country, however, falls in this category (the Dominican Republic). To reduce the number of exogenous variables, this country was pooled with the countries that were "free" throughout the entire period.

21　The dependent variables in the "second-stage" regressions presented in this section are themselves estimated regression coefficients (or linear combinations thereof). Hence the disturbances in these regressions are heteroskedastic. Let y_i be the true value of the dependent variable (for country i) in the second-stage regressions. The "true" model is given by $y_i = Z_i\beta + \varepsilon_i$, where $E(\varepsilon_i) = 0$ and $E(\varepsilon_i^2) = \sigma_\varepsilon^2$. The variable $\hat{y}_i$ is unobserved, but $\hat{y}_i$ is estimated from the regressions in Section 4.3, where $\hat{y}_i = y_i + v_i$, $E(v_i) = 0$, $E(v_i^2) = \sigma_i^2$, and ε_i and v_i are assumed to be independent. The heteroskedasticity arises because the estimated regressions are given by

$$\hat{y}_i = Z_i\beta + (\varepsilon_i - v_i) = Z_i\beta + \mu_i,$$

where $E(\mu_i) = 0$ and $E(\mu_i^2) = \sigma_\varepsilon^2 + \sigma_i^2$. The OLS regression of the second stage provides an estimate of $\hat{\mu}_i$, and combined with the estimates of σ_i^2 available from the first-stage regressions, the parameter σ_ε^2 can be estimated by

$$\hat{\sigma}_\varepsilon^2 = (SSE - \sum\hat{\sigma}_i^2)/(N - K),$$

where SSE is the error sum of squares from the OLS second-stage regression and $N - K$ is the number of degrees of freedom. The calculated $\hat{\sigma}_\varepsilon^2$ is then used to reestimate the second-stage regression using generalized least squares.

22 These results are consistent with the estimated gains to English language proficiency reported in McManus et al. (1983).

23 To further test the sensitivity of the results, two additional variables were introduced into the regression: the percent of the country's labor force that is in agriculture, and the per capita school enrollment rate. Both of these variables were highly correlated with GNP per capita, and in fact became insignificant once GNP was controlled for. Their impact on the other variables in the regression was negligible.

24 The probits were estimated using generalized least squares. The estimator, therefore, is minimum *chi*-squared and efficient.

25 The regressions in Table 4.8 exclude the age at migration from the list of regressors since this variable was calculated in the subsample of immigrants and may have little relationship to the age distribution of the population in the country of origin.

Chapter 5

1 See Chiswick 1978a, 1978d, 1979, 1980a, 1982b for the theoretical development for the different measures of economic status.

2 For additional empirical studies of immigrant adjustment, see Amir (1981); Blau (1980; 1984); Borjas (1982); Carliner (1980); Chiswick (1980b; 1983b; 1986b); Chiswick and Miller (1985); DeFreitas (1979); Featherman (1978); Martin and Poston (1977); North (1979); North and Houstoun (1976); Portes (1982); Portes and Bach (1980); Reimers (1982); Schultz (1984); Stein (1979); Sullivan and Pedraza-Bailey (1980); Tandon (1978).

3 This section presents a thumbnail sketch of the models. For detailed developments with specific reference to occupational status, earnings, and employment see Chiswick (1978a; 1978d; 1979; 1980a; 1982b).

4 For analyses of differences in labor market outcomes between tied and other female migrants in the United States, see Mincer (1978) for internal migrants and Chiswick (1980a; chapter 9) for international migrants.

5 Perhaps the primary examples of ideological migration in recent decades have been the migration of North American and West European Jews to Israel and the migration of U.S. males to Canada during the 1960s to avoid the draft. For an international comparison of the progress of immigrants in Israel and several other countries, see Chiswick (1979).

6 Tidwick (1971), for example, provides evidence of a greater intention to emigrate from Jamaica among university students who are more able. On the other hand, recent research on asymmetric information suggests that there may be negative self-selection in migration (Katz and Stark 1984). Suppose the migrants and employers in the origin know the migrant's true ability level, but employers in the destination cannot discern an individual migrant's ability and assume it is the average for all migrants. Then less-able workers have a greater economic incentive to migrate. The smaller the differences in the costs to employers of identifying worker ability in the origin and destination, the smaller is the effect. It is not likely that these cost differences will be large or will persist over many years. In addition, since employers will learn that migrants are less-favorably self-selected and hence have lower ability than natives, this model implies lower earnings for immigrants, and if ability is transmitted from one generation to the next, it implies lower earnings for their children than for the native-origin population.

7 For example, it is generally assumed that black males make much smaller investments in on-the-job training than do white males because of their flatter experience-earnings profile. Blacks do have a flatter experience-earnings profile in cross-sectional data. Longitudinal profiles indicate a roughly similar percentage increase in earnings with labor market experience, implying that as a percentage of full-year earnings, black and white males make similar investments and receive

similar rates of return. What seems to be a paradox is explained by the higher black-white earnings ratio among younger age cohorts. See Chiswick and O'Neill (1977: 20–3).

8   See, for example, Cross and Sandos (1981); Jasso and Rosensweig (1982); Warren (1979).

9   Controlling for schooling, total labor market experience, weeks worked, marital status, and place of residence in the United States.

10 This section is based on Chiswick (1978a).

11 North (1979) also finds a rise in occupational status with duration of residence in longitudinal data.

12 Borjas (1982) notes the higher rate of school enrollment among recent immigrants from Cuba than from Mexico.

13 See Vroman (1977) for an analysis of the over-reporting of schooling by age cohorts.

14 Finifter (1976) suggests that among the native born, those with higher levels of schooling expressed a greater willingness to live permanently in another country. However, the emigration rate of persons born in the United States is very low.

15 If there were adverse selection of immigrants, as implied by the asymmetric information model, the second generation would earn less than the third generation, and so forth.

16 The data discussed below are reported in detail in Chiswick (1980a, chapter 4).

17 In Penalosa's (1969) study of family income among United States-born Spanish-surname males in the Southwest, using the 1960 Census of Population, he found that the second generation had higher income in spite of a slightly lower level of schooling.

18 Under the NLS procedures, parents and grandparents born in Canada were given the same code as those born in the United States. Given the extremely high transferability of skills between the United States and Canada and the small costs of this migration, one would expect very small or no differences in ability and earnings. If so, the NLS estimate of the earnings advantage of second-generation Americans would be larger than the advantage found in the 1970 Census analysis.

19 Jewish immigrants to Israel in the 20th century have been predominantly refugees and ideological immigrants. This implies a less-intense favorable self-selection for labor market success and a smaller earnings advantage of second-generation Israeli Jews compared with those with both parents born in the country. In fact, other things the same, second-generation men of Asian-African origin have significantly lower earnings than the native-parentage while those of European-American origin show no earnings differential (Chiswick 1980a, chapter 12).

Chapter 6

1   I am reminded of the bumper sticker that read: "The real world is just a special case."

2   It has come to be widely accepted that sovereign states have the legal right to regulate who may enter their country, under what circumstances and conditions, and for how long. Some, however, contest this proposition and argue for unrestricted rights to immigrate. It has also come to be widely accepted that sovereign states do not have the right to prevent individuals, whether citizens or not, from freely emigrating. Thus, individuals are not considered "bound to the land" as they were under serfdom or as property of their country of residence.

3   Under reasonable discount rates, increases in earnings received far into the future, say starting in 20 years, have a small present value. The length of the effective life can be considered infinite if the decision maker takes into account the higher earnings their descendants would receive if raised in the destination rather than in the origin. The sharp fall off of migration, and other human capital investments, with age among adults has less to do with the finiteness of the working life than with

the rise in the opportunity cost of time with human capital investment, including on-the-job training or labor market experience, location-specific investments, and the incentive to make the most productive human capital investments (for which the internal rate of return is greater than the discount rate) sooner rather than later.

4   An analysis of the adjustment process is beyond the scope of this chapter. The adjustments relevant for the labor market include investments in schooling, on the-job training, information, language, and friendship and social networks, among other factors. See, for example, Chiswick (1978d), Chiswick and Miller (1992), and Khan (1997).

5   The interest cost of funds (or the discount rate) would be the person's borrowing rate if at the margin the person is a borrower, and is the lending rate if this is what the person does at the margin. The rate depends on the person's wealth and rate of time preference for consumption in the present relative to the future. Discount rates may therefore vary across individuals and by age for the same individual (see Hirshleifer 1958). For a model of the supply and demand for funds for investments in human capital, see Becker and Chiswick (1966).

6   Although for simplicity of exposition the discussion will be in terms of labor market earnings and ability, it can easily be extended to include efficiency in consumption. For the same nominal earnings, greater efficiency in consumption enhances real earnings.

7   A high-ability (high earnings) migrant from New York to California may fly, while a low-ability (low earnings) migrant is more likely to drive or take a bus or train. This constitutes a substitution away from a relatively more expensive means of migrating. Out-of-pocket costs are frequently measured by distance. See, for example, Schwartz (1973).

8   For a comment and reply on issues other than those raised here, see Jasso and Rosenzweig (1990) and Borjas (1990).

9   Cobb-Clark (1993), however, does find a marginally significant negative relationship between income inequality in the origin and the earnings of immigrants in some of her equations in her study of immigrant selectivity among women in the United States. The effect is more pronounced for women than for men, perhaps because the women are more likely to be tied-movers. Since the inequality measure is household income inequality, it is unclear whether female labor supply effects in the origin and destination are determining this relationship.

10   For the classic study of tied-movers and tied-stayers, see Mincer (1978). It is sometimes difficult to distinguish between ideological migrants and refugees. Many of the earliest settlers in the United States came for a fuller expression of their religious beliefs, and not necessarily because of persecution, and hence would be ideological migrants. For a study of ideology and emigration from the United States in the post-World War II period, see Finifter (1976). Americans who went to the Soviet Union in the interwar period to build the new Soviet state were ideological migrants. North American Jewish immigrants in Israel would also be an example of ideological migrants (Beenstock 1996). While the latter earn more than other immigrants in Israel, overall and other variables the same, their real earnings are lower than they would have received in the United States (Chiswick 1998).

11   See, for example, DaVanzo (1983), DaVanzo and Morrison (1986), Herzog and Schlottmann (1983), Long and Hansen (1977), Shumway and Hall (1996), Vandercamp (1972), and Yezer and Thurston (1976).

12   Borjas (1985) argues that the appearance of a rise in earnings with duration of residence in cross-sectional data is due to a decline in the quality of more recent cohorts of immigrants. He does not deny the higher ability of earlier cohorts. Using a variety of methodologies, Chiswick (1980a; 1986b), Duleep and Regets (1996, 1997a, 1997b), and LaLonde and Topel (1992) show that Borjas (1985) misinterpreted the data, and that there is no evidence of a decline in the earnings of immigrants relative to natives over successive cohorts during the post-World War II period, other variables being the same. By focusing on immigrant earnings at arrival, Borjas (1985) confused the steepening of human capital earnings profiles

for immigrants and natives (a higher return to various types of skill) due to a rise in the rate of return on human capital and a reduction in the transferability of the skills of immigrants due to a shift in source countries of origin (from Canada and Europe to Latin America and Asia) with a decline in immigrant quality (ability). For a similar earnings catch-up at the turn of the century, see Blau (1980). For an analysis of the catch-up in terms of employment and unemployment, see Chiswick and Hurst (1998). Lindstrom and Massey (1994) how that the emigration of the foreign born does not distort the assimilation of immigrants observed in the U.S. Census.

13   Among native-born men, those who speak a language other than or in addition to English at home, and who are disproportionately second-generation Americans, have lower earnings, other measured variables the same, than the native born who speak only English at home (Chiswick and Miller 1998b). This may be due to their being more closely tied to their immigrant/ethnic enclave and labor market.

Chapter 7

1   The search process may involve a temporary or short-duration sojourn in country Y.

2   Even if nominal wages in a particular job do not decline, even in a recession, the nominal earnings a worker receives may decline because of reduced hours worked or following unemployment the worker accepts a new job offer at a lower nominal wage.

3   Presumably, native-born workers in these sectors also experience an increase in relative earnings to be followed by a regression to the mean. As the costs of international migration exceed the costs of intra-national migration, immigrants will be more likely than the native born to be located in relative high-wage regions. Hence, the negative assimilation will be a more intense phenomenon for them than for their native-born counterparts.

4   Two-way international migration does occur. According to their local censuses, in 1996 about 226,000 people born in the United States lived in Canada, 30,000 Americans and Canadians lived in the Irish Republic and 94,000 Americans and Canadians lived in Australia, respectively (Sources: 1996 Censuses of Irish Republic, Australia, and Canada). See also Dumont and Lemaitre (2005).

5   An alternative test would be migration among the states of the United States with similar levels of income. The U.S. Census provides information on state of birth, state of residence five years ago, and current state of residence, but this offers too little detail on the timing of interstate migration.

6   The language variable is included in large part because of French Canadians. It is not possible to distinguish immigrants from Quebec from other Canadian immigrants in the U.S. Census, other than through their speaking French at home.

7   Note, however, that this information is self-reported, and there is bunching in the data around the years ending in zero or five.

8   The mean of the natural logarithm of earnings (the geometric mean) increased by 0.994 log points, from 9.731 in 1980 to 10.725 in 2000. This increase implies more than a doubling of nominal earnings (e^{**} 0.994 = 2.702). The Consumer Price Index increased from 100.0 in 1980 to 208.5 in 2000, implying that the log of prices increased by 0.735 (ln 2.0850 = 0.735). The log of real earnings, therefore, increased over the 20-year period by a difference of 0.259, or at an annual rate of about 1.3 percent (0.259/20 = 0.01295 and e^{**} 0.01295 = 1.013).

9   There is little research on the earnings of immigrants among the English-speaking developed countries. Lindner (1989) developed a joint emigration-earnings model for emigrants from the United States to Canada. Card (2003) considered Canadian emigrants in the United States, focusing on their educational attainment. Both studies found favorable selectivity among the migrants. Neither study reported on

the effect of duration in the destination on the earnings of the immigrants or on the selectivity of return migrants.

10 When dichotomous variables are included in the immigrant and the pooled immigrant and native-born equations for persons who are black, the changes in the relevant coefficients are trivial. There is no effect on the interpretation of negative assimilation.

11 The significant negative assimilation effect is essentially unchanged if these language variables are deleted from the equation.

12 This does not imply a decrease in real earnings. The change in real earnings will be given by the sum of the impacts of labor market experience and years since migration.

13 In an analysis of annual hours of work among immigrants using the 1980, 1990, and 2000 Censuses, Blau, Kahn, and Papps (2011) found hours worked by immigrants from English-speaking countries or those for which English is an official language was flatter with duration of residence in the United States compared to other immigrants. This is consistent with the negative assimilation hypothesis.

14 The 2000 Census year of immigration data were also recoded to six categories analogous to those available for the 1980 data, and a similar analysis that was undertaken. The estimate of the negative assimilation effect was -0.006 (t-ratio = -12.58).

15 Among adult native-born males, the schooling coefficient is about 10.6 percent and for the foreign-born males as a whole it is about 5.2 percent in the 2000 Census (Chiswick and Miller 2008b).

16 The means and standard deviations of the variables for the separate ESDC immigrants are presented in Appendix Tables A7.2 to A7.5.

17 In the analysis for Australia, the ESDC include the United States, Canada, the United Kingdom, Ireland, and New Zealand.

18 The Finnish language is of central Asian origin, as is Hungarian, and is quite different from the other Scandinavian languages.

19 The results from Pedersen et al. (2008) discussed here are reproduced in Appendix B, which is available from the authors on request.

20 The findings based on only the 1990 and 2000 data are reasonably robust to imposing restrictions on these coefficients across time and between birthplaces. The results following the addition of the 1980 data are, however, sensitive to most restrictions imposed. Thus, we present only the findings from the more complex specification.

21 Funkhouser and Trejo (1995) also reported that the pre-1960 cohort fares the worst in their analysis.

22 We performed a test for the cohort analysis in which the data were separated into adult and child immigrants. The findings for adult and child immigrants reported here persist when cohort analysis is performed.

Chapter 8

1 See Carliner (1980), Chiswick (1978d), DeFreitas (1980), and Long (1980).

2 Lazear and Moore (1984) and Wolpin (1977) have found smaller wage differentials (by skill) among the self-employed than among salaried workers. Studies by Fuchs (1968, 1982a) provide a descriptive analysis of the extent of self-employment among older workers and in the service economy.

3 In addition, nonrandom emigration of the immigrant population biases the impact of t_i on both market wage rates and self-employment incomes. See Borjas (1985) for a discussion of the biases introduced by the high emigration rates of the foreign born.

4 Of course, there are many reasons why, in actuality, the cohorts in the 1970 and 1980 Census data may not be perfectly matched. For instance, the presence

of emigration will lead to secular trends in the size (and quality) of a specific immigrant cohort. Similarly, institutional changes in the census enumeration procedures may lead to different counts of immigrants (and native-born persons) in particular cohorts across censuses. Finally, there may be age (and/or cohort) related differences in labor supply and mortality rates which generate additional differences in the size of the cohort samples included in the regressions over time. Note, however, that all these problems will impart biases on both cross-section and cohort analyses so that, in a sense, the cohort study presented here nets out only one of the many sources of bias, that due to violations of the assumption of stationarity in the quality of immigrants at the time of entry.

5   The sampling fractions for 1970 are: white native born (.001 of the population), all other groups (.01). The 1980 sampling fractions are: black natives (.00245), black immigrants (.01651), Mexican natives (.01652), Mexican immigrants (.01638), white natives (.00042), white immigrants (.00249), all other groups (.05).

6   The Hispanic samples do not include the group of Puerto Rican men since the census does not ask Puerto Ricans born in Puerto Rico for the year they migrated to the U.S.

7   The t-ratios in Table 8.4 refer to the relevant transformations of the logit coefficients and are estimated from the covariance matrix of the regression coefficients.

8   Note that since the constraints $\gamma_{70} = \gamma_{80} = \gamma$ and $\delta_{70} = \delta_{80} = \delta$ have been imposed on the estimates, the cross-section regressions in Table 8.3 are not directly comparable to the cross-section estimates in Table 8.4. In particular, Table 8.3 constrains the socioeconomic variables to have the same impact for the foreign and native born in the 1980 Census year, while Table 8.4 allows a differential impact between the two groups but assumes this difference is invariant to calendar year.

9   See Jasso and Rosenzweig (1986) for an interesting discussion and empirical study of some of the implications of the family reunification emphasis in the current law.

10   The analysis was also conducted with alternative definitions for the variable q_h. These specifications included such variables as percent Mexican, percent Cuban, etc. The model in Equation (15) does as good a job in describing the enclave effect as the more detailed specification.

11   It would be of interest, of course, to analyze – along similar lines – the relative levels of salaried and self-employment incomes. Unfortunately, this extension of the work introduces the problem of correcting for sample selection biases both within and across immigrant cohorts. In addition, self-employment incomes, as reported in the census, are an amalgam of returns to human and physical capital. A complete study of the income levels, therefore, will require much more detailed data on the source and types of incomes of the self-employed.

Chapter 9

1   Much of the data for early analyses (1950s to 1970s) was in terms of a white-nonwhite dichotomy, but blacks comprised about 90 percent of nonwhites in these data.

2   The data are limited to the native born because the analysis is concerned with the socioeconomic adjustment in the United States of racial and ethnic groups and seeks to avoid confounding these patterns with the selection criteria of recent U. S. immigration policy. In addition, analyses of earnings for women are far more complex than for men because of the effects on interrupted work histories of child care activities, marital stability, and spouse's income. For the purpose of this analysis the 1970 Census is superior to the 1980 Census. Because the 1980 Census did not ask parental nativity or mother tongue, Jews and foreign-parentage blacks cannot be separately identified. Moreover, there is some evidence of a recent rise in rates of return from schooling for blacks as a result of affirmative action programs temporarily increasing the labor market demand for high-skilled relative to low-

skilled blacks (see Smith and Welch 1986: 85–95). In addition, the 72 percent increase in the number of persons classified as American Indians from the 1970 to the 1980 Census suggests a lack of comparability across these censuses. This change in the self-reporting of race has a small impact on the number of whites but a large impact on the number and characteristics of American Indians.

3 Jews are defined as second-generation Americans raised in a home in which Yiddish, Hebrew, or Ladino was spoken either in addition to or instead of English (see Chiswick 1983c; Kobin 1983). Similar patterns emerge in other data in which Jews can be identified by a question on religion (Chiswick 1985).

4 It is particularly noteworthy that American Jews have a substantially (and significantly) higher coefficient of schooling than white non-Jews. The Jewish coefficient is larger even when there is a statistical control for occupation, including separate variables for high paying professional occupations (Chiswick 1983c). Tomes (1983) found a similar pattern for Canadian Jews. The ranking persists even when schooling is treated as a nonlinear variable. See, for example, Chiswick (1985).

5 This framework first appeared in Becker and Chiswick (1966) and was developed more fully in Becker (1967).

6 For two recent attempts at estimating individual rates of time preference, an important determinant of the supply curve, see Fuchs (1982b) and Viscusi and Moore (1989).

7 It should be noted that many types of human capital have little transferability. For a more detailed discussion of the diaspora hypothesis with regard to American Jews, see Chiswick (1985).

8 It is assumed that the rankings of average and marginal rates of return are the same across groups.

9 This arises so long as the private direct (out-of-pocket) costs of schooling do not decline with discrimination.

10 Skill need not be viewed as homogeneous. A useful distinction (see Schultz 1975) is between "worker skills" – efficiency in performing a task – and "allocative skills" – efficiency in decision making. Groups may differ in the worker-allocative composition of their skills. If so, since allocative skills command a higher payoff during periods of greater disequilibrium in the economy (e.g., when there is a more rapid rate of economic change), group differences in rates of return from schooling could be a function of the state of the economy.

11 The economic approach to the analysis of the quantity and quality of children is most richly developed in Becker (1981), especially chapters 5 and 6.

12 Group differences in the value of time of women may arise from differences in schooling or in location. Cardwell and Rosenzweig (1980), for example, show that the earnings of women relative to men vary systematically with the industrial structure of the metropolitan area. The earnings ratio is lower in metropolitan areas that have more male-intensive industrial structures. A higher cost of fertility control implies more children per family, which in turn implies a greater cost of raising average child quality. Hence, the cost of fertility control affects the relative price of quantity and quality of children.

13 Among other effects, a larger number of siblings imply greater intrafamily time spent interacting with other children rather than with adults (parents). This apparently has adverse effects on average child quality. See Zajonc (1976) for an interesting theoretical time allocation model. See Blake (1987) for both a survey of the literature and a statistical analysis of the inverse relation between performance on standardized tests and the number of siblings. Blake finds the inverse relation is much stronger for verbal ability, which is more dependent on child-parent interaction, than on nonverbal ability. Blake also found that relatively few of the most able children were from large families, despite the obvious fact that large families produce a disproportionate share of children.

If the greater number of children in Group B were to arise from fewer couples remaining childless (i.e., there are more one-child families), it is possible for average child quality in Group B to exceed that in Group A. For an analysis of the relation between fertility rates and the average number of siblings per child, see Preston (1976).

14   The complementarity of types of human capital does not detract from the observation that at the margin they are also substitutes. That is, at the margin more of one type of human capital (e.g., higher quality home-produced human capital) can offset deficiencies in other types of human capital (e.g., low quality of formal schooling).

15   If the relative price difference in Generation I arose from the higher value of time of the mothers in Group A due to a higher schooling level, the quantity-quality fertility decisions will result in their daughters also having a higher value of time. Other determinants of relative prices, such as geographic location and psychic costs of fertility control, may change only slowly from generation to generation.

16   There does not appear to be a literature on the distribution among children in the family of parental child care time or direct expenditures. Research on bequests, however, suggests that parents try to equalize their children's wealth by making larger bequests to their children with less income. See Tomes (1988).

17   An appendix to a published report from the 1930 Census provides comparative statistics on the value of owner-occupied homes and monthly rent for four "racial" minorities. The ranking of value of homes and rental payments were the same. In increasing order of value the groups were the Mexican-Americans, American Indians, Japanese, and Chinese, with a wide gap between the first two and the last two (U.S. Bureau of the Census 1933: 5-6 and Table 29: 201).

18   This is consistent with the finding among whites of an inverse relation between parental ability and the number of children born. The negative effect is stronger (i.e., larger and more highly statistically significant) for the measures of mother's ability than it is for father's ability. For a recent study see Rutherford and Sewell (1988) and the references therein.
     Solon (1989) shows that the small intergenerational correlation coefficients usually observed using microdata arise from measurement error and the homogeneity of the populations under study. By implication, larger correlation coefficients would be observed across heterogeneous groups.

19   Using data from the National Longitudinal Survey Youth Sample, Michael and Tuma (1985) find that among white, black, and Hispanic young women, a later age of entry into motherhood is associated with having been raised in an intact family (i.e., with both parents) and with fewer siblings. The implication is that greater investment in a daughter results in later age for the start of her own childbearing.

20   There is a debate in the literature as to whether race and ethnic differences in fertility can be explained solely by differences in characteristics or whether there is an independent effect of minority group status. The advocates of the latter approach have various hypotheses, some of which imply a positive minority status differential and some of which imply a negative differential. See Bean and Marcum (1978), and the exchange by Rindfuss (1980), Johnson (1980), Johnson and Nishida (1980), Marcum (1980), and Lopez and Sabagh (1980), and the references therein. For a recent discussion of these issues focusing on Mexican-Americans and blacks, see Bean and Swicegood (1985, ch. 7).

21   For the period 1957-1959, the ratios of the group fertility rate to the white fertility rate were as follows:

Chinese	0.89	Mexican-American	1.37
Japanese	0.76	American Indian	1.30
		Black	1.15

These data are from Rindfuss and Sweet (1977: 93). In addition, using census data Chamnivickorn (1988) found that Filipino women had fertility rates higher than white women.

22   In the late 19th and early 20th centuries Japan and China had very different fertility rates. Nakamura and Miyamoto (1982) show that the Japanese attained a high degree of fertility control in the "premodern" period, while the Chinese

maintained high fertility rates. They attribute the divergent pattern, in part, to differences in the family systems, a hierarchical feudal system based on nonpartible inheritance in Japan and a more egalitarian system based on partible inheritance in China. In the United States, however, the Chinese and Japanese are both low-fertility populations.

23 Becker (1981: 110), citing different studies, reports that "the Jewish birth rate was 47 percent below the average birth rate in Florence at the beginning of the 19th century; Jewish marital fertility was 20 percent below Catholic fertility in Munich in 1875."

24 The number of children ever born per 1,000 women, 1957

Religion	Age 15-44 years[a]		Age 45 years and older
	All	Ever married	
Jewish	1,184	1,598	2,218
All women	1,677	2,188	2,798
All women-urban	1,504	2,009	

[a] Standardized by age.

25 Imperfect substitutes for parental time can, to some extent, be purchased in the marketplace.

26 For analyses of time inputs in child care by mothers and the effects of home investments on the children's achievements, see Leibowitz (1974a; 1974b), Gronau (1976), Hill and Stafford (1974; 1980), Hunt and Kiker (1981), and Datcher-Loury (1988). These studies find that time devoted to child care, particularly educational care such as playing, reading, and talking, rises with the level of parental education. The increase is greater for the mother's schooling than for the father's schooling. Studies have also found that greater parental time inputs (measured by mother's labor supply, marital status as a proxy for one- or two-parent households, and number of siblings), raise the performance on standardized tests, school enrollment, school attainment, and earnings of the child. See, for example, Blake (1987), Datcher-Loury (1988), Fleisher (1977), Krein (1986), and Stafford (1985). Unfortunately, time budget surveys and longitudinal data files have sample sizes that are far too small for studies of racial and ethnic group differences in the determinants of child quality.

Chapter 10

1 Classic expositions of the assimilation hypothesis are contained in Park (1950) and Gordon (1964). A more recent study of ethnic differentials within this paradigm is given by Sowell (1981).

2 See Lieberson and Waters (1988) for a systematic documentation of the evidence on the social and economic differences among ethnic groups in the 1980 Census.

3 Theoretical discussions of the process of intergenerational income mobility are given by Becker (1981), Becker and Tomes (1986), Conlisk (1974), and Goldberger (1989). Empirical evidence is reported in Behrman and Taubman (1985); Borjas (1993); Hauser, Sewell, and Lutterman (1975); Solon (1992); and Zimmerman (1992a).

4 The specification of the utility function in (1) ignores the dynastic approach suggested by the work of Becker and Barro (1988). Although the introduction of dynastic households provides a much richer description of the long-run relationship between human capital and fertility (Becker, Murphy, and Tamura 1990), the simpler model presented here captures the key insights that are useful for the empirical study of intergenerational skill transmissions.

5 Conlisk (1977) provides an early application of this technology to the study of income distributions. See also Azariadis and Drazen (1990); Barro (1991); Becker, Murphy, and Tamura (1990); and Romer (1986).

6 Wilson's (1987) influential study of the underclass also hinges on human capital

externalities. He argues that the economic situation of young blacks in poor neighborhoods is worsened because they are not exposed to "mainstream role models that help keep alive the perception that education is meaningful, that steady employment is a viable alternative to welfare, and that family stability is the norm" (Wilson 1987: 56).

7   Even though the model focuses on the comparison of skill levels across two generations, it should be evident that its implications can be easily extended to models with longer time horizons. Also note that although Equation (9) describes the evolution of relative skill differentials among ethnic groups, there are a large number of growth paths for the *level* of the human capital stock that are possible outcomes of the maximization process.

8   See Becker and Tomes (1986) for a survey of the empirical evidence on intergenerational mobility.

9   The relationship between the regression coefficients in Equation (13) and the parameters of the model is easily ascertained. Suppose that the supply function for time allocated to children (Equation (4)) can be approximated by $s_t = \alpha_0 \bar{k}_t^{\alpha 1} \bar{k}_t^{\alpha 2}$. Substituting this expression into the reduced-form equation giving the human capital of children (Equation (6)) yields

$$\log k_{t+1} = \psi + \beta_1(1 + \alpha_1) \log k_t + (\beta_2 + \alpha_2\beta_1) \log \bar{k}_t.$$

Note that the coefficients γ_1 and γ_2 in Equation (13) do not identify the parameters β_1 and β_2 unless the utility function is Cobb-Douglas. As noted in Section 10.2, this functional form implies that the fraction of time devoted by parents to human capital investments in their children is constant across households ($\alpha_1 = \alpha_2 = 0$). In general, the regression coefficients estimate the elasticities in Equations (7a) and (7b), which allow for the impact of parental and ethnic capital on the time devoted to investments in children.

10 The content and sampling frame of the General Social Surveys is described in Davis and Smith (1989).

11 This estimate is obtained from a regression of the income data available in the GSS on the occupational prestige score. I should note, however, that the GSS income data are of much lower quality than are the income data usually used by economists. The intervals used by the GSS to report income are relatively wide, and all incomes above $50,000 in the earlier waves are truncated at that point (the truncation point for the more recent waves is $60,000).

12 To determine the sensitivity of the results reported in what follows to the use of the self-reported ethnicity variable, I estimated a number of alternative specifications of the basic model. For instance, the empirical analysis was conducted on the subsample of workers who named only one ethnic group in their response (and whose ethnicity can presumably be exactly determined). The substance of the results was not affected by this sample selection. I think it would be worthwhile, however, to conduct additional research to help determine how the definition of ethnic capital should be altered in order to accommodate the fact that some workers are exposed to the social, cultural, and economic characteristics of more than one ethnic group.

13 I used the 1970 Census because the NLSY reports the 1970 Census code for the father's occupation, and the occupation codes changed substantially between the 1970 and 1980 Censuses.

14 Persons who give multiple answers to the ethnicity question are asked to report the ethnic background they most identify with. It is this single response that is used in the empirical analysis which follows.

15 I also estimated specifications of the regression models that linked the respondent's skills to those of the mother (or to an average of the skills of both parents), with little change in the substance of the results.

16 Obviously, there are many alternative approaches to operationally defining the concept of ethnic capital. In this chapter I chose the simplest specification. It would

be of interest to determine whether other dimensions of the ethnic environment (such as the labor force participation rate of the ethnic group) provide additional information about the intergenerational mobility process.

17 These restrictions alter the samples available for analysis as follows. There are 14,102 persons aged 18–64 interviewed in the GSS since 1977. Of these persons, 872 are either immigrants or do not report birthplace; 2,346 are blacks or American Indians; 35 do not report parental birthplace; and 2,478 do not report ethnicity. From this base I then delete either 1,615 observations in the education analysis (due to missing own or father's education), or 1,305 observations in the occupation analysis. The 1987 wave of the NLSY contains 10,485 respondents. Of these persons, 279 are deleted because they do not report either their own or their parent's birthplace; 3,019 are blacks or American Indians; 410 do not report their ethnic background; and 607 are immigrants. I then delete either 551 observations in the education analysis or 2,436 in the wage analysis. As a result of these sample selection rules, the data used later tend to contain fewer persons in the less-skilled ethnic groups. For instance, about 2.5 percent of the sample used in the GSS education analysis are of Mexican origin, but 4.8 percent of persons who do not report education (or their father's education) are Mexicans. Similarly, 11.3 percent of the observations in the NLSY education sample are Mexican, but 21.8 percent of those who do not report the education data are Mexican. I show below that my main conclusions are unaffected when the sample is further altered to exclude less-skilled ethnic groups (such as Mexicans and Puerto Ricans).

18 The NLSY data contain a relatively large group of persons who classify their ethnic background as "American." Presumably this group contains well-assimilated persons who no longer identify with any national origin. Although the empirical analysis below treats these persons as an additional ethnic group, deleting this subsample has little effect on the results.

19 Borjas (1993) presents a detailed analysis of the factors underlying these ethnic differentials. The study suggests that the differentials partially arise because of the huge dispersion in skills that characterized the original immigrant flows.

20 The regressions use a minimal set of controls. All regressions include gender, a dummy indicating if either parent was an immigrant (to isolate the possibility that second-generation Americans experience a different type of intergenerational mobility), a dummy indicating if the respondent is enrolled in school (in the NLSY), and dummies indicating the year of the survey (in the GSS). The regressions in column (4) also include age and region. The exclusion of any of these controls does not generally alter the results of the analysis.

21 Although I do not report these test statistics, the data generally rejected the hypothesis that the sum of the parental and ethnic capital coefficients was equal to one.

22 The aggregation of Equation (13) within ethnic groups implies that the parameter $\gamma_1 + \gamma_2$ can also be estimated by regressing the average skills of children in the ethnic group on the average skills of their parents. In earlier work (Borjas 1993) I used the 1940 Census to calculate the average earnings of immigrant groups (by national origin group), and the 1970 Census to calculate the average earnings of second-generation workers (by birthplace of the parents). This intercensal comparison approximates the relationship between the earnings of fathers and children. Interestingly, the census estimate of $\gamma_1 + \gamma_2$ was 0.45, which is quite close to the intergenerational transmission parameters reported in Table 10.3.

23 Note that the wage regressions reported for the NLSY data mix individual data (i.e., the respondent's wage rate) with aggregate data (i.e., the mean wage in the occupation for the father). An alternative specification would also assign the NLSY respondent the mean wage in his occupation. The estimated coefficients (and standard errors) are 0.121 (0.05) for parental capital, and 0.214 (0.19) for ethnic capital (using the model that does not include the vector of socioeconomic characteristics). It is apparent that this type of aggregation, perhaps because the NLSY samples young men and women at a time when they are "shopping" for an

occupation, leads to an imprecise estimate of the ethnic capital effect.

24 I am assuming that measurement errors in parental capital are independent of ethnicity and that there are sufficiently large numbers of observations for each ethnic group so that measurement errors are "washed out" by averaging parental skills within the group. The random variable v_2 then measures only how the skills of an individual parent deviate from the true group-specific mean. I am grateful to Gary Chamberlain for pointing out an error in a previous formulation of this model.

25 This comparison ignores the fact that Tables 10.3 and 10.4 use a random effects estimator, even though Equations (18a) and (18b) are the probability limits of the least-squares estimator.

26 An alternative way of assessing the importance of measurement error is to use an instrument, such as mother's education, for father's education. This exercise reinforces the conclusion that measurement error is not generating a spurious correlation between children's education and ethnic capital. For instance, in the GSS education regression (which does not control for X), the instrumental variables estimate for the coefficient of father's education is 0.368 (0.011), and for the coefficient of ethnic capital is 0.224 (0.027), where the standard errors have not been corrected for the random effects stochastic structure.

27 Given the stochastic nature of the disturbance in Equation (13), it is not surprising to find that the random effects estimator leads to much larger standard errors for the coefficient of ethnic capital than the corresponding OLS estimator. The standard errors estimated by the random effects model behaved more erratically the smaller the sample size.

28 I also conducted the simulations using the regressions presented in Table 10.3, with qualitatively similar results.

Chapter 11

1 The importance of human-capital externalities in intergenerational mobility was stressed in the early work of Conlisk (1977) and Loury (1977), who uses the concept of "social capital" to analyze how racial discrimination influences the social mobility of blacks. Lundberg and Startz (1998) investigate how human-capital externalities may alter the impact of antidiscrimination programs on social mobility.

2 The role played by neighborhood effects in determining socioeconomic outcomes is currently the subject of intensive research; see, for instance, the survey of Christopher Jencks and Susan E. Meyer (1990) and the critical appraisal by Manski (1993). Empirical evidence linking neighborhood effects to teenage pregnancy, criminal behavior, educational attainment, and human-capital accumulation is given by Case and Katz (1991), Crane (1991), Corcoran et al. (1992), and Rauch (1993).

3 A large literature documents the extent of residential segregation among blacks and Hispanics; see Bean and Tienda (1987), Massey and Denton (1989), McKinney and Schnare (1989) and Hughes and Madden (1991).

4 In particular, I take the Census Bureau estimate of the proportion of persons in the neighborhood who are first or second generation to be the population proportion. I then multiply this number by the sample estimate of the proportion of the first- and second-generation individuals in the neighborhood who are foreign born.

5 Calculations from the General Social Surveys indicate that over 90 percent of persons who classify themselves as Hispanic are foreign born, have parents who are foreign born, or have grandparents who are foreign born.

6 Although the residential segregation found among these ethnic groups is substantial, it is not nearly as striking as that found among blacks. Table 11.1 reports that the average black lives in a neighborhood that is 54.7 percent black.

Notes

7　This methodology does not entirely solve the problem, because extended-family members are also likely to be type-j ethnics and to live in the same neighborhood (but as part of a different household unit).

8　The numbering system used to identify zip codes in the NLSY file differs from that used by the Postal Service. Although the data indicate subsets of NLSY respondents who live in the same postal area, it is impossible to locate the zip code within a particular metropolitan area. Because the zip code refers to the 1979 residence, many of the respondents were still living in the parental household. As a result, the residential-segregation measures in the NLSY tend to reflect the ethnic environment in which the respondents were raised.

9　To reduce costs, the NLSY also sampled households which resided geographically close to each other. This sampling strategy suggests that the measures of residential segregation calculated in these data probably overstate the true extent of segregation.

10　Of the 12,686 observations in the 1979 wave of the NLSY, I deleted two persons because they had invalid zip codes, and 939 persons because they had invalid ethnic classifications.

11　As with the census data, the NLSY residential-segregation measures should be interpreted with caution. There are fewer than 100 observations for 11 of the 25 ethnic groups.

12　Barro and Sala-i-Martin (1992) provide a discussion of alternative concepts of convergence in the context of growth models.

13　Alba's (1990) study of social contacts among U.S.-born white ethnics indicates that half of all nonrelated childhood friends belong to the same ethnic group. Holzer (1988) has shown that friends are a key source of information about job opportunities, so that intragroup referrals play a major role in the job-search process and might explain the concentration of some ethnic groups in narrowly defined occupations.

14　It would be interesting to analyze how parents choose the type and intensity of "ethnicity" that they wish to expose to their children. Evans et al. (1992) show that endogenizing the "peer group" effects greatly weakens the relationship between outcomes and neighborhood characteristics.

15　It is easy to determine how the coefficients of parental skills and ethnic capital change when neighborhood effects are introduced into the model and the skill invariance assumption does not hold. Suppose that highly skilled type-j workers move into wealthy neighborhoods, and unskilled type-j workers move into poor neighborhoods. This implies that $E(x_{ij}|e) > E(\overline{x}_j|e)$ in wealthy neighborhoods (e) and that $E(x_{ij}|k) < E(\overline{x}_j|k)$ in low-income neighborhoods (k). It follows from Equation (6) that $E(\hat{\beta}_1) = \delta_1 + \varphi$, where $\varphi > 0$. Thus the nonrandom sorting of skilled workers into "good" neighborhoods magnifies the impact of the parental contribution to the children's skills. As a result, the inclusion of neighborhood effects will reduce the coefficient of parental skills in the intergenerational-transmission equation. It is also easy to show that this type of nonrandom sorting leads to a smaller ethnic capital coefficient in models that omit the neighborhood fixed effects.

16　Borjas (1993) discusses the methodology of intercensal comparisons that underlie the empirical analysis using the census data. The intercensal linkage between parents and children can be improved by focusing on workers in specific age groups. For example, the children of immigrants aged 25–44 in 1940 are likely to be relatively young in 1970. I experimented with a number of alternative age breakdowns and obtained similar results.

17　In particular, the residual $\varepsilon_{ij} = \nu_j + u_{ij}$, where ν_j is the group component. It is well known that ignoring the group component in the error term seriously underestimates the standard error of the ethnic capital coefficient.

18　The coefficient of the neighborhood wage level was typically in the 0.4–0.5 range.

19　There are 53,703 observations in the sample of second-generation working men and 23,415 neighborhoods. There are 9,522 neighborhoods with only one

621

observation; 5,895 neighborhoods with two; 3,616 neighborhoods with three; 2,162 neighborhoods with four; and 1,161 neighborhoods with five. The remaining 5 percent of the neighborhoods have between 6 and 12 observations. Despite the fact that a sizable number of neighborhoods have only one observation, the estimated rate of mean convergence is consistent. I use a two-stage procedure to estimate the random-effects model which includes the vector of neighborhood fixed effects. The first-stage regression includes age, age squared, and a vector of ethnic fixed effects. This regression is estimated on a data set in which all variables are differenced from the respective neighborhood means. This procedure is numerically equivalent to introducing the neighborhood fixed effects. The second stage then uses a generalized least-squares estimator to estimate the relationship between the coefficients of the first-stage ethnic dummy variables and the ethnic capital variable.

20 The discussion assumes that the neighborhood of current residence is the same as the neighborhood where the individual was raised. Because of the misdefinition of the neighborhood, the results confound the ethnic externalities that influenced the human-capital accumulation process with externalities that arise from living in an ethnic neighborhood at the present time. This problem, however, does not seem to be very important. The results are very similar for two alternative skill variables, log wages and educational attainment (which presumably was completed at an early age). Moreover, the transmission coefficients are roughly the same regardless of how long the person has lived in his current residence. The estimated transmission parameter is 0.43 for persons who moved to the house prior to 1960, and it is 0.46 for persons who moved to the house after 1967.

21 A regression of education (or log wages) on a vector of county-group dummies has an R^2 of about 0.09, so that 91 percent of the variance in education and log wages is attributable to within-county variation. In contrast, only about 45 percent of the variance in these variables is attributable to within-neighborhood variation.

22 Because education differences across neighborhoods almost entirely reflect true differences in skill levels, I did not attempt an analogous construction of a "skill-adjusted" neighborhood education level.

23 Although I do not report or discuss the estimated coefficients of the neighborhood characteristics, it would be interesting to study how (and why) these various characteristics influence the intergenerational transmission process.

24 The test excludes the 9,522 neighborhoods that have only one second-generation working man.

25 A related way of assessing the importance of the skill-invariance assumption uses the concept of the intracluster correlation (Kish 1965; Cochran 1977). This correlation is positive if the characteristics of persons within a cluster are more closely related than those of persons randomly chosen from the population. When the cluster is defined to be the ethnic group, the intracluster correlation is about 0.1 (for both education and log wages). This correlation increases to 0.2 when the cluster is defined to be type-j ethnics living in neighborhood k. Put differently, the neighborhood provides additional information about the skill distribution of persons in a particular ethnic group.

26 The ethnic characteristics are calculated using a 20 percent random sample of the 5/100 A File of the 1980 Public Use Sample. I also constructed comparable ethnic characteristics from within the NLSY itself. Although the findings do not depend on which measure of ethnic capital is used, I only report the regressions that use the census measure (which are calculated over much larger samples and contain less sampling error).

27 Of the 1,937 zip-code fixed effects included in the educational-attainment regressions, there are 900 zip codes with one observation, 256 with two, 168 with three, and 123 with four; the remainder have five or more observations. Of the 1,453 zip-code fixed effects included in the log-wage regressions, there are 733 zip codes with one observation, 223 with two, 140 with three, and 80 with four; the remainder have five or more observations. A regression of educational attainment

(or log wages) of the NLSY respondents on a vector of zip-code dummies has an R^2 value of about 0.4, so that about 60 percent of the variance in educational attainment and log wages can be attributed to within-zip-code variation. Over 80 percent of the variance in these variables, however, can be attributed to within-county variation.

28 It is also possible to estimate census-type semi-aggregate regressions on the NLSY data, so that the regressions omit the worker's parental background. Using educational attainment as the dependent variable, the coefficient of the ethnic capital variable (and standard error) is 0.438 (0.047) in the model that does not include either county or neighborhood dummies; 0.329 (0.030) in the model that includes county dummies; and 0.173 (0.029) in the model that includes zip-code dummies. This pattern of coefficients closely mirrors the results documented in the census data. A similar pattern is obtained in the log-wage regressions.

29 In particular, highly skilled type-j ethnics tend to cluster in wealthier neighborhoods, while less-skilled type-j ethnics cluster in poorer neighborhoods.

30 It is of interest to note that the results do not change substantially when the model is estimated on the subsample of NLSY respondents who were 14–18 years old at the time of the initial interview in 1979. The residential location decision for these young persons was probably made by their parents, so that the neighborhood fixed effects are less likely to be endogenous. In the educational-attainment regressions which do not include neighborhood fixed effects, the parental coefficient (and standard error) was 0.235 (0.009), and the ethnic capital coefficient was 0.097 (0.026). The inclusion of neighborhood fixed effects changed the coefficients to 0.170 (0.007) and 0.017 (0.032), respectively. In the log-wage regressions which do not include neighborhood fixed effects, the parental and ethnic capital coefficients were 0.343 (0.048) and 0.498 (0.111). Including neighborhood fixed effects changed these coefficients to 0.202 (0.043) and 0.054 (0.160).

31 I did not interact the neighborhood effects with the dummy variables describing the proportion of persons in the neighborhood who have the same ethnic background as the worker. This restriction helps to isolate the impact of ethnic capital among persons who live in the same neighborhood (and hence who were exposed to the same overall neighborhood characteristics). I also estimated the models by simply interacting the fraction of persons in a neighborhood who have the same ethnicity with the relevant variables and obtained qualitatively similar results. Table 11.9 indicates, however, that there are strong nonlinearities in the relationship between the ethnic-capital coefficient and the extent of residential segregation. Moreover, there is a great deal of sampling error in the residential-segregation statistics. As a result, I prefer the specification that clusters persons into a small number of neighborhood types.

32 The results are not sensitive to the particular definition of residential segregation. This particular breakdown, as well as the breakdown of neighborhoods in the NLSY data, was chosen because it provided a reasonable number of observations for each type of neighborhood. In the census data, there were 27,006 persons who lived in the most integrated neighborhoods, 18,676 who lived in the "mixed" neighborhoods, and 8,021 who lived in the most segregated neighborhoods. In the NLSY education regressions, the respective numbers of observations are 1,999, 2,506, and 3,064, while in the NLSY log-wage regressions, they are 1,189, 1,428, and 1,644.

33 Ashenfelter and Krueger (1994) use this methodology to analyze the impact of measurement error in educational attainment on estimates of the rate of return to schooling. Their analysis suggests that measurement error imparts a sizable downward bias on estimates of the rate of return to schooling.

34 I created a vector of dummy variables indicating the ethnic group reported by each sibling in the data. The instrument is formed by averaging this vector over all other siblings, so that it can be interpreted as the probability that the other siblings report a particular ethnic background.

35 The model is estimated in two stages. In the first stage, the children's skills are

regressed on the father's skills, other explanatory variables (age, gender, etc.), and a vector of dummy variables indicating the self-reported ethnic background. The first-stage model is estimated using instrumental variables. The second stage consists of a generalized least-squares regression in which the estimated coefficients of the ethnic dummy variables are regressed on the ethnic capital variable. The regressions that control for neighborhood effects use a data set which has been differenced from the within-zip-code means in the first stage.

36   Although the evidence is not consistent with an explanation that stresses classical measurement error in parental skills or ethnic background, there are other measurement problems which may account for some of the results. I have focused on a one-factor model in which one particular type of skills (either educational attainment or the log wage) is transmitted across generations. There is evidence that this one-factor approach does not provide a satisfactory explanation of the process of intergenerational mobility. Altonji and Dunn (1991) report that the correlation in earnings among siblings is larger than would be expected given the size of the correlation between parents and children. This result suggests that perhaps a vector of traits is being transmitted, so that the ethnic capital variable could be proxying for an aggregate measure of these traits.

Chapter 13

1   Other works on the determinants of immigrant or ethnic concentrations include Bartel (1989), Brettell (2008), Cutler and Glaeser (1977), Lazear (1999), Bauer, Epstein, and Gang (2005), and Sierminska (2002). Lazear (1999: 99) describes concentrations as forming "in large part because doing so enhances trade" in market and nonmarket goods and services.

2   Epstein (2010) distinguishes theoretically between "herd behavior" and "network externalities" in the choice of destination among those from the same origin. Herd behavior refers to following those from the same origin, even if they are few in number, under the belief that they have better information, while "network externalities" implies a larger group and a lower cost of settlement in a specific destination because of linguistic and information networks.

3   Ross (2003) develops a model in which preferences for social interaction by the majority or a minority (whether negative as in prejudice or positive as in cultural affinity) result in social segregation of neighborhoods.

4   For research on network externalities see Economides (1996) and Katz and Shapiro (1985).

5   Distinctiveness is important as the ethnic goods of English immigrants to the United States would be much less distinctive than would those of, say, Chinese immigrants. To some extent the cost of ethnic goods can be reduced if the host society "adopts" the ethnic good, as, for example, often happens for certain foods, such as in Chinese restaurants. The "Americanized" version of the ethnic good may well differ from the version consumed in the origin or by members of the ethnic group in the destination.

6   For a study of consumer network markets and group size, see Etziony and Weiss (2002).

7   For a discussion of Chinese schools, see Zhou and Li (2003).

8   Workers of a given level of skill can be thought of as randomly drawing wage offers from a given distribution of wage offers available in the high-concentration and the low-concentration areas. If ethnic goods are an important part of their market basket, the ethnic immigrants will move to or stay in a low-concentration area only if their wage offer in this area exceeds by a sufficient margin the wage offer from the high-concentration area to compensate for the higher cost of living. Once settled in a specific area explicit and implicit location-specific investments in human capital, relevant for consumption and the labor market, tend to reduce

subsequent migrations. Thus, those who leave a high-concentration enclave for a low- or zero-concentration area will tend to be those who receive a high wage offer in the latter location and those for whom ethnic goods (including ties to the ethnic community) are least important.

9   The "ethnic goods" concept and its implications for concentrations and wage differentials can be applied to other affinity groups, for example, the gay population.

10   In the data under study for earnings, Mexican immigrants are 29 percent of the sample and have a mean schooling level of 7.9 years, in contrast to 13.3 years for the other immigrants.

11   The definition of the population under study and the variables used in the analysis are described in more detail in Appendix B.

12   Bertrand, Luttmer, and Mullainathan (2000) also use language as the basis for their "networks" (concentrations) in an analysis of welfare participation.

13   The finding that a higher level of secular schooling is associated with greater proficiency in Hebrew among immigrants in Israel suggests that exposure to English in school prior to immigration is not the primary mechanism for the positive effect of schooling on English language skills in the United States (Chiswick and Repetto 2001).

14   On the other hand, the effect of having been in the U.S. Armed Forces differs sharply between these two groups. Veteran status is associated with about 8 percent higher earnings for Mexican immigrants but 10 percent lower earnings for non-Mexican immigrants.

15   Clark and Drinkwater (2002) find that unemployment rates for racial and ethnic minorities are higher among those living in ethnically concentrated areas of England and Wales.

16   The labor supply or "crowding" hypothesis would imply a larger coefficient on the concentration measure for Mexican immigrants than for the much more heterogeneous group of immigrants from other countries. That the opposite is found suggests that the negative relation between concentration and earnings is not a consequence of ethnic crowding in the labor market.

17   Partial effects of education and the concentration ratio on earnings:

	Table A13 Column iv	Table A13, Column (iv), Plus Interaction
Education	0.045	0.056
	(82.9)	(78.3)
Minority Language Concentration	−0.0056	0.0062
	(15.3)	(10.9)
Education-Concentration Interaction	—	−0.0012
		(26.9)

18   For a similar finding for Sweden, see Edin, Fredriksson, and Åslund (2003).

19   The regression coefficient is $\ln(1 + X) = 0.59$, where X is the percentage increase in earnings. X is then 0.80 or 80 percent. $\ln(1 + X)$ is approximately equal to X when X is a small number. When $\ln(1 + X) = 0.15$, X is approximately 16 percent.

20   See Chiswick and Miller (1995), and the references therein, for the United States, Canada, Australia, and Israel, and Dustmann and van Soest (2001) for Germany. The difference between the OLS and IV effects on earnings is much smaller in the United Kingdom (Dustmann and Fabbri 2003).

Chapter 14

1   The importance of dominant-language skills, even for low-skilled workers, has been explicitly recognized in the amnesty program in the 1986 Immigration

Notes

Reform and Control Act. To change their status from "temporary resident alien" to "permanent resident alien" within the one-year grace period, those granted amnesty need to demonstrate a minimal command of English or enroll in at least 40 hours of English language instruction in an approved program (see Chiswick 1988a).

2 The person's "mother tongue," the language other than or in addition to English spoken in the home when the person was a child, was asked in the 1970 Census questionnaire administered to 15 percent of the population, but a key variable, duration in the United States, was asked only on the questionnaire administered to a nonoverlapping 5 percent of the population.

3 The SIE also included a question on reading: "How often does (the respondent) read an English language newspaper?" with "most days," "occasionally," and "(almost) never" as the acceptable responses. While it is not clear what the reading question does measure, it is clearly not a satisfactory measure of English reading fluency.

4 The longitudinal data on a skill relevant in the labor market can be used to address the critique of Borjas (1985) that the improvement in earnings with duration in the destination observed in cross-sectional data is due to declining cohort quality, with no change in the skills relevant for the U.S. labor market as duration of residence increases. Although reestimations using the Borjas data and technique do find "assimilation" effects (see, e.g., Chiswick 1986b; and LaLonde and Topel 1992), the logitudinal data in this study provide a more direct test.

5 McManus et al. (1983) used a two-step procedure (p. 121). First, standard earnings functions were computed "to identify important interactions and to identify important questions." Three language questions that had the highest explanatory power for earnings were retained. They then write: "Using interactive responses to these questions we identified seven groups that captured most of the information about wages in the SIE language questionnaire and that, at the same time, are arguably well ordered in terms of proficiency in English. By design, they are ordered in terms of wage predictions after the common variables [e.g., region, marital status, schooling, and experience] are taken into account." Thus, the seven English language proficiency groups used in the McManus et al. earnings analysis are proxies for earnings intervals or categories. Predictable results emerge. They find that their seven dichotomous English fluency variables are very highly statistically significant – far more so than in other studies. They also find that the effects of other determinants of earnings are reduced and that Hispanic ethnicity loses its statistical significance. The statistical methodology has ensured that the partial effects of the variables other than language are biased downward. McManus et al. also analyze the determinants of their English language proficiency variable (pp. 119–20). They combine the seven categories into a single index to serve as a dependent variable. Weights are obtained from the earnings function with the dichotomous language variables on the right-hand side. They find that U.S. schooling and U.S. experience raise English language proficiency, but that foreign schooling and foreign experience lower it. What is less clear, however, is whether the analysis is reflecting the effects of the explanatory variables on the language categories or on the earnings weights.

6 For the United States, these studies include Reimers (1983), Grenier (1984), Chiswick (1987), Kossoudji (1988), Tainer (1988), Rivera-Batiz (1996), and Chiswick and Miller (1992). For studies of the determinants of language fluency and the impact of language fluency on earnings in Canada, where promoting English-French bilingualism is official policy, see, e.g., Carliner (1981), Grenier and Vaillancourt (1983), and Chiswick and Miller (1988). One of the few studies of language proficiency among women is in Boyd (1992).

7 A detailed discussion of the survey procedures, an analysis of the survey methodology, and discussion of the randomness of the sample and the characteristics of the population can be found in Chiswick (1989, Appendix A). Chiswick (1989) also provides an extensive analysis of these data.

8 For an analysis of the provisions of the 1986 Act and its implications for the

characteristics of aliens not eligible for legalization, see Chiswick (1988a).

9   Chiswick and Miller (1992) show that in the United States and in Canada residence in an area in which many others speak the same minority language has a significant negative effect on the acquisition of the dominant language. It is not possible to explicitly test the minority-language concentration effect on language fluency in the survey under study that is limited to the Los Angeles area.

10 The means and standard deviations of the variables are reported in Chiswick (1989).

11 Tests indicate this is the most efficacious dichotomization of the four-category language variable for analyses of spoken language fluency.

12 Essentially the same results emerge from the OLS and logit analyses.

13 There is also a large and highly significant difference in the effect of duration on English speaking fluency between Mexican and other Latin American men when the equations are computed separately by origin, where the effect is larger for the latter group.

14 The statistical control for fluency at arrival may also control for individual differences in self-assessment of the same "objective" level of fluency.

15 Tests indicate this is the most efficacious dichotomization of the four-category variable. Similar results emerge when "not at all" is compared to all other reading categories.

16 The average usual weekly earnings during the current stay for the 398 adult men who responded to this question was $174. The earnings were lower for the Mexican men ($172) than for the men from other Latin America ($182) or other countries $180).

17 For previous applications to illegal aliens, see Chiswick (1984 or 1988b), Kossoudji and Ranney (1986), and Massey (1987).

18 The only exception is the large and marginally significant effect (coefficient = -0.23, t = 1.8) when hours are not held constant. Mexican men have a longer workweek, 40.7 hours, in contrast to the 37.7 hours for the Canadian and Eastern Hemisphere men.

19 The coefficient for Canada/Eastern Hemisphere (OTHER) is -0.40 (t = -2.5) but declines to -0.26 (t = -2.0) when hours worked per week are held constant. These represent earnings that are lower by 33 percent and 23 percent, respectively. When the hourly wage is the dependent variable, the coefficient of OTHER becomes more negative but remains insignificant when the language variables are added to the equation. Many of the Eastern Hemisphere illegal aliens were students in the United States who had violated a condition of their visa, usually by working. Their low hourly wage may reflect the adverse effects on job opportunities of dovetailing work with schooling (Lazear 1977).

Chapter 15

1   For a study of high-skilled immigrants to the United States in the 19th and early 20th centuries, see Ferrie (2010).

2   The employment-preference categories include: (i) priority workers; (ii) professionals with advanced degrees or aliens with exceptional ability; (iii) skilled workers, professionals without advanced degrees, and needed unskilled workers; (iv) special immigrants, such as religious workers; and (v) employment-creation immigrants (that is, investors). The data include the immediate family members (spouse and minor children) of the principal applicant as recipients of employment visas. Family members typically constitute about one-half of the category.

3   In the immigration literature this is frequently referred to as the nonrecognition of foreign educational credentials.

4   For a more robust review, see Chiswick and Miller (2008b).

5   For example, Remennick (2002) found that primary- and secondary-school

teachers from the former Soviet Union who immigrated to Israel generally could not make the adjustment from the rigid, highly disciplined, highly structured Soviet classroom to the informal, flexible, less-structured Israeli classroom. These teachers may have been able to overcome differences in subject matter or language issues, but the school and classroom cultural gap was too great for their teaching skills to be transferable.

6   The issue of the nonrecognition of the skills of immigrant physicians in the United States and Canada is the theme of Lesky (2010) and McDonald, Warman, and Worswick (2010). For a study of the adjustment of high-skilled immigrants in Israel, see Cohen-Goldner and Weiss (2010).

7   See Appendix 15.4A for definitions of the various educational categories. Sensitivity tests were performed for alternate measures of years of schooling for those with master's, professional, and doctorate degrees as their highest level of schooling. The findings are essentially invariant with respect to these alternative values.

8   See Ferrie (2010) for a discussion of why the definition of skilled immigration is time and place specific.

9   The standard equation, $\ln Y_i = \beta_0 + \beta_1 \text{Actual Educ}_i + \dots + v_i$, forces $\alpha_1 = \alpha_2 = |\alpha_3|$. As this condition does not hold, the ORU specification results in a higher R-squared and $\alpha_2 > \beta_1$.

10   Two other options are the worker self-assessment (WSA) and the job analyst technique, where the latter is based on experts' "objective" evaluations. For a comparative analysis of the WSA and RM techniques, see the methodological analysis in Chiswick and Miller (2010a). That analysis shows a strong correlation between the WSA and RM data series in which the simple correlation coefficient between these measures is around 0.8 for all skill-nativity groups considered in that study. Under each of the three assessment methods, the "typical" or "required" level of education is related to the technology employed, the relative factor prices, and the educational distribution of the population under study. There is no fixed or unique required level of education in an occupation across either time or space.

11   Conventionally, a 64-year upper threshold has been used to minimize any selection bias associated with retirement from the paid labor force. Using a lower threshold of 54 years has no material effect on the regression estimates presented in Tables 4.4 and 4.5.

12   Chiswick and Miller (2008b) report that tests of robustness with respect to alternative definitions of the population for defining the modal education showed virtually no substantive differences.

13   These numbers are based on imputed years of schooling where a bachelor's degree is assumed to require 16 years, a master's degree 17.5 years, a professional degree 18.5 years, and a doctorate 20 years.

14   Chiswick and Miller (2008b) report estimated effects of the required level of education on earnings of 0.154 for all native-born workers and 0.153 for all foreign-born workers. Their estimates of the effects of surplus years of schooling on earnings were 0.056 for the native born and 0.044 for the foreign born.

15   The mean earnings in 1999 for bachelor's, master's, professional, and doctorate degrees are $72,067; $88,168; $111,730; and $82,521, respectively, for the adult, male, native-born population, and $65,163; $78,393; $92,011; and $78,650, respectively, for the adult, male, foreign-born population. Especially for the native born, earnings are very high for those with a professional degree.

16   The payoff to origin-country labor market experience (evaluated at ten years) is 1.88 percent in the Table 15.5 estimates for foreign-born workers, compared to 1.62 percent in the Table 15.4 estimates. The payoff to labor market experience (evaluated at ten years) acquired in the United States is 1.26 percent in the Table 15.5 results, compared to 0.80 in the Table 15.4 results.

17   There are 22 major nonmilitary occupations listed in the 2000 U.S. population census data. Due to the absence of variation in the usual level of schooling within two of these occupations, the analyses in this subsection are performed on 20 occupations.

18 All means in this section are weighted by the number of workers in the occupation.
19 In this presentation, doctorates are ranked above professional qualifications based on the typical years of formal schooling. If postqualification training, such as residencies for physicians, is considered formal schooling rather than on-the-job training, professional qualifications might be ranked above doctorates. This alternative ranking would reduce or remove the anomaly associated with the comparison of points E and F in the figures.
20 To ascertain if the relatively poor earnings outcome for doctorates was simply linked to either low salaries in the education sector or misreporting of weeks worked in that sector, a dichotomous variable for employment in the education industry was included in the model. This variable was associated with coefficients of -0.154 among the native born, and -0.192 among the foreign born. This change in the specification was associated with a 4 (native born) to 8 (foreign born) percentage-point improvement in the *ceteris paribus* earnings of workers holding doctorates compared to workers who hold bachelor's degrees, but there is little change in the relative standing of workers with professional qualifications and doctorates.
21 The points test used in Australia at present, for example, allocates points for "specific employment," defined as employment in an occupation listed as a government-determined "skilled occupation" for at least three of the four years immediately preceding application for a visa. Further points are allocated for "occupation in demand (and job offer)," for which visa applicants earn points if they have been offered a job in an occupation listed as a government-determined "migration occupation in demand."
22 For a study of the effect of school quality in the country of origin on the payoff to schooling for immigrants in the United States that uses PISA scores to index school quality, see Chiswick and Miller (2010b).

Chapter 16

1 A number of theoretical models in the international trade literature explore how immigrants affect the welfare of natives; see, for example, Bhagwati and Srinivasan (1983) and Ethier (1985). A rare empirical analysis is given by Svorny (1991), who estimates the gains to American consumers from the immigration of physicians.
2 It is easy to relax the assumption of inelastic supply curves. However, the calculation of the gains from immigration would be more cumbersome because we would have to account for the change in utility experienced by native workers as they move between the market and nonmarket sectors.
3 In particular, note that if we let $(w_1 - w_0) \approx (\Delta w/\Delta L) \times M$, the immigration surplus can be rewritten as

$$\frac{\Delta Q_N}{Q} = -\frac{1}{2} \cdot \left(\frac{\Delta w}{\Delta L} \cdot M \right) \frac{M}{Q} = -\frac{1}{2} \cdot \frac{wL}{Q} \cdot \left(\frac{\Delta w}{\Delta L} \frac{L}{w} \right) \cdot \frac{M}{L} \cdot \frac{M}{L}.$$

4 If there are only two factors of production, the elasticity of factor price for labor must equal $(1 - s)^2/\eta$, where η is the output-constant elasticity of labor demand (Hamermesh 1993: 26–9). There is some consensus that η is about -.3. Because the share of labor income is .7, the elasticity of factor price is also -.3.
5 It is easy to see this point with a CES production function, so that $Q = [\delta_1 K^\rho + \delta_2 L^\rho]^{1/\rho}$. The immigration surplus is then given by:

$$\frac{\Delta Q_N}{Q} = \frac{1}{2} \frac{s(1 - s)m^2}{\sigma},$$

where σ is the elasticity of substitution between labor and capital. Natives have less to gain from immigration when the elasticity of substitution is large.
6 To calculate the total losses accruing to native workers, again let $(w_1 - w_0) \approx (\Delta w/\Delta L) \times M$. The reduction in total labor income, as a fraction of GDP, can then be

written as:

$$\frac{(w_1 - w_0)N}{Q} = \left(\frac{\Delta w}{\Delta L} \cdot M\right) \cdot \frac{N}{Q} = \frac{wL}{Q}\left(\frac{\Delta w}{\Delta L}\frac{L}{w}\right) \cdot \frac{M}{L} \cdot \frac{N}{L}.$$

The gains accruing to capitalists are calculated by adding the absolute value of this expression to the immigration surplus (that is, to the area of the triangle).

7   This implication is analogous to the result from international trade theory, which shows that cheap foreign imports, typically seen as having harmful and disruptive effects, often benefit the importing country.

8   The immigration surplus, as a fraction of GDP, is given by:

$$\frac{\Delta Q_N}{Q} = -\frac{1}{2}\frac{s_s e_{ss}(\beta - b)^2}{p_s^2(1 - p_s)^2}(1 - m)^2 m^2,$$

where s_s is the share of national income accruing to skilled workers; e_{ss} is the elasticity of factor price for skilled workers (that is, the percentage change in the skilled wage with respect to a 1 percent change in the number of skilled workers); and p_s is the fraction of the labor force that is composed of skilled workers. Figure 16.3 is obtained by differentiating the immigration surplus with respect to β and assuming that immigration is "small" so that the fraction of the workforce that is skilled is not affected by immigration (that is, $\partial p_s/\partial \beta = 0$).

9   This conclusion is closely related to the result from international trade theory that the benefits from trade are larger when the trading countries differ greatly in their factor endowments.

10   The reader will note that this formulation is closely related to the original calculation of the immigration surplus in the model that had only an aggregate labor input and capital. Instead of depending on the share of income going to all workers, the immigration surplus now depends on the share of income going to skilled labor. Similarly, instead of depending on the elasticity of factor price for all labor, the formula now depends on the elasticity of factor price for skilled workers (as well as on the fraction of the workforce that is skilled).

11   Because $p_S = 1/2$, the share of income accruing to skilled workers s_S exceeds the share of income accruing to unskilled workers s_U.

12   The empirical evidence supporting the capital-skill complementarity hypothesis reflects an important property of technology in the postwar era. Because the production function is not stable over time, the technology available in earlier time periods may reflect different relationships among the various inputs. For instance, it seems plausible that unskilled workers and some fixed factors of production (such as land) were complements in the U.S. economy at the end of the 19th century. In fact, there is some empirical evidence (James and Skinner 1985) suggesting that, around 1850, skilled labor and capital were better substitutes than unskilled labor and capital. As a result, the theoretical implication that the immigration surplus is maximized by admitting a skilled immigrant flow might not have applied to the United States in earlier time periods.

13   If skilled workers and unskilled workers are sufficiently "strong" substitutes (in the sense that an increase in the quantity of one of the inputs reduces the wage of the other), it is possible for the minimum point to occur at the corner where the immigrant flow is exclusively unskilled.

14   See Borjas (1987b) for an analysis of the immigration decision.

Chapter 17

1   The historical context of Samuelson's (1964: 552) assertion is interesting. He was writing just before the enactment of the 1965 Amendments to the Immigration and Nationality Act, the major policy shift that initiated the resurgence of large-

scale immigration.

2   Representative studies include Altonji and Card (1991), Borjas (1987a), LaLonde and Topel (1991), Pischke and Velling (1997), and Schoeni (1997). Friedberg (2001) presents a rare study that uses the supply shock in an occupation to identify the labor market impact of immigration in the Israeli labor market. Although the raw Israeli data suggest a substantial negative impact, correcting for the endogeneity of occupational choice leads to the usual result that immigration has little impact on the wage structure. Card (2001) uses data on occupation and metropolitan area to define skill groups and finds that immigration has a slight negative effect.

3   Angrist and Krueger (1999) replicate Card's study using an alternative time period, and find that a "phantom" influx of immigrants (in the sense that had it not been for a policy intervention, many immigrants would likely have arrived) had a sizable adverse effect on Miami's labor market. This result suggests that many other factors influence labor market conditions in Miami and comparison cities. At the least, one should be cautious when interpreting the spatial correlations estimated from comparisons of specific localities.

4   Borjas (2001) presents evidence indicating that new immigrants belonging to a particular schooling group tend to settle in those regions that offer the highest return for their skills.

5   Borjas, Freeman, and Katz (1997) and Card (2001) provide the first attempts to jointly analyze labor market outcomes and native migration decisions. The two studies reach different conclusions. Card reports a slight positive correlation between the 1985–1990 rate of growth in the native population and the immigrant supply shock by metropolitan area, while Borjas, Freeman, and Katz report a negative correlation between native net migration in 1970–1990 and immigration by state – once one standardizes for the preexisting migration trends.

6   The generic regression of wages on some measure of immigrant penetration is used frequently in the literature. Suppose that the labor demand function in the pre-immigration period is $\log w_{kt} = D_{kt} + \varepsilon \log N_{kt} + \varphi$, where k is a skill group. The wage change resulting from an exogenous influx of immigrants is

$$\Delta \log w_{kt} = \Delta D_{kt} + \varepsilon \log \left[(N_{kt}(l + n_{kt}) + M_{kt})/N_{kt} \right] + \xi \approx \Delta D_{kt} + \varepsilon(n_{kt} + m_{kt}) + \xi,$$

where n_{kt} gives the percent change in the number of natives, and $m_{kt} = M_{kt}/N_{kt}$. The rate of change n_{kt} is determined by the native labor supply function, $n_{kt} = S_{kt} + \sigma\Delta\log w_{kt} + \mu$. The reduced-form wage equation is

$$\Delta\log w_{kt} = X_{kt} + \varepsilon^* m_{kt} + \xi^*,$$

where $X_{kt} = (\Delta D_{kt} + \varepsilon S_{kt})/(1 - \varepsilon\sigma)$ and $\varepsilon^* = \varepsilon(1 - \varepsilon\sigma)$. Equation (3) is a transformation of this reduced-form equation that approximately uses $\log m_{kt}$, rather than m_{kt}, as the measure of immigrant penetration. In particular, $\log m \approx (M - N)/(0.5(M + N)) = 2(2p - 1)$. I opted for the immigrant share specification because the relation between wages and m is nonlinear and m has a large variance both over time and across groups.

7   As already noted, the immigrant share approximates $\log m$. Because there are no cells with zero immigrants in the data used in Table 17.3, the results are virtually identical (once properly interpreted) if $\log m$ is used as the regressor. In the next section, however, where I categorize workers by state of residence, education, and experience, 15.7 percent of the cells have no immigrants, and using $\log m$ would create a serious selection problem.

8   The variable p_{ijt} gives the immigrant share among labor force participants. The labor force participation decision may introduce some endogeneity in this variable. The problem can be addressed by using an instrument given by the immigrant share in the population of all men in cell (i, j, t). The IV estimates of θ (and standard errors) are -0.803 (0.586) for log annual earnings, -0.541 (0.153) for log weekly earnings, and -0.493 (0.125) for the fraction of time worked. These coefficients are similar

to those reported in the first row of Table 17.3. The immigrant share may also be endogenous in a different sense. Suppose that the labor market attracts foreign workers mainly in those skill cells where wages are relatively high. There would be a spurious positive correlation between p_{ijt} and the wage. The results in Table 17.3 should then be interpreted as lower bounds of the true impact of immigration. Finally, the 2000 Census was released while the original version of this chapter was in press. I reestimated the basic models to determine the sensitivity of the results when the 2000 CPS cross section was replaced with the 2000 Census. The coefficients for the key specification reported in the first row are quite similar: -0.924 (0.462) for log annual earnings, -0.514 (0.203) for log weekly earnings, and -0.468 (0.077) for the fraction of time worked.

9   The results would be roughly similar if the regressions were estimated separately using each set of two adjacent cross sections, so that the regression models would be differencing the data over a decade. The adjustment coefficients (and standard errors) for log weekly earnings are -1.042 (0.484) in 1960–1970, -0.427 (0.561) in 1970–1980, -0.277 (0.480) in 1980–1990, and -0.285 (0.270) in 1990–2000. This rough similarity contrasts with the inability of the spatial correlation approach to generate parameter estimates that even have the same sign over time; see Borjas, Freeman, and Katz (1997) and Schoeni (1997).

10 I also estimated the regression model within experience groups. The adjustment coefficients (and standard errors) for log weekly earnings were 1–5 years of experience, -0.403 (0.470); 6–10 years, -0.358 (0.286); 11–15 years, -0.475 (0.285); 16–20 years, -0.555 (0.244); 21–25 years, -0.568 (0.244); 26–30 years, -0.634 (0.193); 31–35 years, -0.495 (0.288); and 36–40 years, -0.147 (0.228). Although these regressions only have 20 observations, the point estimate of θ is negative and significant for many groups.

11 It is of interest to use the labor market outcomes of immigrants as the dependent variable. I used the sample of immigrants with fewer than 30 years of experience because there are relatively few observations in the cells for older workers in 1970 and 2000, and did not use data from the 1960 Census because that survey does not provide information on the immigrant's year of entry into the United States. The estimates are imprecise, but the results resemble those found for native workers once I control for cohort and assimilation effects. If the regression is estimated on the sample of immigrants who have been in the United States for fewer than ten years, the adjustment coefficients (and standard errors) are -0.506 (0.398) for log annual earnings, -0.290 (0.350) for log weekly earnings, and -0.192 (0.105) for the fraction of time worked.

12 I use states to define the geographic boundary of the labor market because a worker's state of residence is the only geographic variable that is consistently coded across the entire 1960–2000 span. The 1960 Census does not report the person's metropolitan area of residence, and the metropolitan area identifiers for the 1970 Census differ substantially from those reported in later surveys.

13 The smaller wage effects estimated at the state level could also be due to attenuation bias from the measurement error that arises when I calculate the immigrant supply shock at such a detailed level of disaggregation. I reestimated the model using the nine census regions (rather than states) as the geographic unit. The region-level regression coefficients corresponding to the last column of Table 17.5 are -0.346 (.096) in the log annual earnings regression, -0.289 (.070) in the log weekly earnings regression, and -0.057 (.023) in the fraction of time worked regression. Even though the coefficients in the annual and weekly earnings regressions are numerically larger than those obtained in the state-level analysis, the coefficient in the log weekly earnings regression is still only half the size of the one reported in Table 17.3. Moreover, it is unclear if the relatively larger effects estimated at the region level result from the partial elimination of attenuation bias or from the possibility that some of the native flows induced by immigration are intraregional, and hence the region is a slightly better conceptual representation of the "closed market" required for measuring the local impact of immigration; see Borjas,

Freeman, and Katz (1996) for related evidence.

14 Neither the census nor the CPS reports the exact year in which immigrants entered the United States, but instead reports the year of entry within particular intervals (e.g., 1980–1984). I used a uniform distribution to randomly assign workers in each interval to each year in the interval. Because the immigrant's year of arrival is not reported in the 1960 Census, the analysis is restricted to data drawn from the 1970 through 2000 cross sections.

15 The fraction of time worked variable used in the regression reported in the second row of Table 17.7 has a different definition than elsewhere in this chapter. To simplify the sorting of persons into the quantiles of the wage distribution, I restricted the analysis to working men. One could classify nonworkers into the various quantiles by using a first-stage regression that predicts earnings based on a person's educational attainment, experience, and other variables. For native men this approach leads to results that are similar to those reported in the text.

16 Early empirical studies of the labor market impact of immigration (Grossman 1982; Borjas 1987a) actually imposed a structure on the technology of the local labor market, such as the translog or the Generalized Leontief, and used the resulting estimates to calculate the various substitution elasticities. Although this approach fell out of favor in the early 1990s, the evidence reported by Card (2001) and the results presented in this section suggest that the structural approach may be due for a timely comeback.

17 The three-level CES technology slightly generalizes the two-level approach used in the labor demand context by Bowles (1970) and Card and Lemieux (2001).

18 If $\log \hat{\alpha}_{ij}$ is an estimated fixed effect coefficient, then $\hat{\alpha}_{ij} = \exp(\log \hat{\alpha}_{ij})/\sum_j \exp(\log \hat{\alpha}_{ij})$.

19 Consider the regression model given by $\log w = \beta \log L + u$. The IV estimate of β has the property:

$$\text{plim } \hat{\beta} = \beta + \frac{\text{cov}(\log M, u)}{\text{cov}(\log M, \log L)},$$

where $\log M$ is the instrument. The total number of workers in a skill group is, in fact, positively correlated with the number of immigrants in that group, so that $\text{cov}(\log M, \log L) > 0$. Further, $\text{cov}(\log M, u) > 0$ because skill cells with favorable demand shocks will probably attract larger numbers of income-maximizing immigrants. The IV regression coefficient then provides a lower bound for the wage reduction resulting from a supply increase.

20 In principle, the elasticity σ_{KL} could be estimated even without direct information on the aggregate capital stock by going up an additional level in the CES hierarchy. This exercise yields the marginal productivity condition for the average worker at time t. This marginal productivity condition depends on a time fixed effect and on L_t, the CES-weighted aggregate of the workforce. The coefficient of L_t identifies $-1/\sigma_{KL}$. However, this regression would only have five observations in my data, and I would need to find a variable that could proxy for the movements in the period fixed effects.

21 The instrument is $\log M_{ijt}$ and the standard errors are clustered by education-experience group. To avoid introducing errors due to composition effects, the regressions reported in this section use the mean log weekly wage of native workers as the dependent variable. The results would be very similar if the mean log wage was calculated in the pooled sample of natives and immigrants. The relevant coefficients (and standard errors) in Equations (16), (17), and (17′) would be -0.281 (0.059), -0.676 (0.518), and -0.680 (0.462), respectively. The regressions estimated in this section are weighted by the size of the sample used to calculate the cell mean on the left-hand side.

22 The "linear trend interacted with education fixed effects" vector includes the linear trend and education fixed effects, as well as the interactions. The instrument in (17) is $\log M_{it}$, where

$$M_{it} = \left[\sum_j \alpha_{ij} M_{ijt}^{\eta} \right]^{1/\eta}.$$

The alternative specification in (17′) uses the instrument $\log M_{it}^*$ where $M_{it}^* = \sum_j M_{ijt}$.

23   Card and Lemieux (2001) estimate the elasticity of substitution between high school and college equivalents to be between 1.1 and 3.1, depending on the sample composition.

24   The factor price elasticity holds marginal cost and the quantities of other factors constant.

25   My calculation of the cell's income share uses all men and women who reported annual earnings in 1989. The estimated shares for the eight experience groups within each education group are high school dropouts (0.003, 0.004, 0.006, 0.005, 0.005, 0.007, 0.007, 0.007); high school graduates (0.018, 0.030, 0.034, 0.030, 0.028, 0.026, 0.022, 0.017); some college (0.018, 0.030, 0.036, 0.036, 0.030, 0.022, 0.016, 0.011); and college graduates (0.025, 0.039, 0.044, 0.049, 0.037, 0.025, 0.019, 0.013). These income shares, when aggregated to the level of the education group, are similar to the shares reported by Autor, Katz, and Krueger (1998: 1209). The share of income accruing to high school dropouts is 4.5 percent; high school graduates, 20.5 percent; workers with some college, 19.9 percent; and college graduates, 25.1 percent.

26   The own elasticities reported in Table 17.8 are not directly comparable to the "wage elasticities" reported earlier. As noted in endnote 6, the regression model estimated in previous sections identifies the reduced-fonn effect of immigration on wages. This reduced-form effect is $\varepsilon/(1 - \varepsilon\sigma)$, where ε is the factor price elasticity and σ is the labor supply elasticity. If $\varepsilon = 0.33$ and $\sigma = 0.4$, for example, the implied reduced-form effect estimated in this section is 0.29, which is somewhat smaller than the estimates that do not use a structural approach.

27   Murphy and Welch (1992) report elasticities of complementarity (defined as $Q_{yz}Q/Q_y Q_z$) for a number of education-experience groups. In the Murphy-Welch exercise, the cross elasticities between high school graduates and college graduates tend to be positive, but the within-branch elasticities for a given education group are not always negative.

28   The assumption of a constant capital stock implies that the resulting wage consequences should be interpreted as short-run impacts. Over time, the changes in factor prices will fuel adjustments in the capital stock that attenuate the wage effects.

Chapter 18

1   Borjas (1999b), Friedberg and Hunt (1995), and LaLonde and Topel (1993) survey this voluminous literature. Recent studies of the impact of immigration on native labor market opportunities include Borjas, Freeman, and Katz (1997), Card (2001), and Schoeni (1997); recent studies of the fiscal impact of immigration include Borjas and Hilton (1996), Smith and Edmonston (1997), and Storesletten (2000).

2   Barro and Sala-i-Martin (1991, 1992); Blanchard and Katz (1992).

3   The analysis is similar in spirit to Card and Hyslop's (1997) investigation of the hypothesis that inflation greases the wheels of the labor market by making it easier for employers to adjust real wages downward; see also Tobin (1972).

4   Borjas (1999a) first developed some of the implications of this argument in the context of immigrant and native responses to interstate differences in welfare benefits.

5   Karoly and Klerman (1994) investigate the contribution of regional wage differentials to overall trends in U.S. wage inequality.

6   Equation (1) implicitly assumes that the national labor market is in disequilibrium, in the sense that different regions offer different opportunities to the same worker. However, regional wage differences may partly reflect compensating factors that penalize or reward workers for various amenities or disamenities in the region

where they live (Roback 1982; Topel 1986). Even though a particular worker might face different wages in different labor markets, that worker's utility would then be constant across labor markets. The wage differentials that determine the migration decision summarized by Equation (1) are those that persist after the analysis has controlled for regional differences in the value of amenities and disamenities.

7   Of course, the provisions of immigration policy allow the United States to pick and choose among the many persons who demand entry. But these policy restrictions are binding only on the subsample of foreign-born persons who find it optimal to move to the United States in the first place.

8   Borjas (1995b) and Johnson (1998) provide extended discussions of the economic benefits from immigration in a one-sector framework.

9   Suro (1998) describes how the migration of a single person from the Guatemalan region of Totonicapan to Houston developed into a flow over the subsequent years, with many of the workers in this immigrant flow ending up in related jobs.

10 Borjas (1995b: 7).

11 I am grateful to Robert Topel for raising a number of questions that helped to clarify some of the conceptual issues that arise in this type of framework.

12 Note that this "neutrality" result hinges crucially on the assumed linearity of the labor demand curves. With constant-elasticity demand curves (as implied by a Cobb-Douglas production function), the convexity of the demand curve would imply that the gains accruing to natives are larger when $\theta = 1$ than when $\theta = 0$.

13 This discussion implicitly assumes that expenditure on migration vanishes from the economy rather than being transferred to other persons. This is likely to be the case if the main component of migration costs is the disutility associated with leaving a familiar environment and starting over again in a different and unfamiliar area.

14 A numerical example also helps to illustrate this point. Suppose there are 100 million native workers in the economy and that immigration increases the supply of workers by 10 percent, so that there are 10 million immigrants. Suppose further that $\lambda = 0.4$ and $k = 0.5$. In this example, 5 million natives would have to move to equalize wages when immigrants cluster in the high-wage region, and 15 million would have to move when immigrants cluster in the low-wage region. Even if the annualized migration cost were as low as \$1,000, the additional migration cost incurred by natives because of the "inefficient" immigrant clustering would be \$10 billion, easily swamping most available estimates of the gains from immigration.

15 This analysis is closely related to the study of the benefits from trade when there is an intersectoral difference in marginal products; see Hagen (1958) and Magee (1972; 1973).

16 The notion of an equilibrium where immigrants are clustered in the low-wage area is not as far-fetched as it sounds. During the late 1980s, for example, Sweden routinely placed refugees in regions outside Stockholm, which are coincidentally the country's low-wage regions. See Edin, Fredriksson, and Åslund (2003).

17 Although the discussion has focused on determining how the gains from improved efficiency are distributed between immigrants and natives, there are equally interesting distributional consequences within the native population. As with the immigration surplus in the one-sector model, the gains from immigration defined in Equation (14) – abstracting from the savings in migration costs – accrue to native capitalists. In contrast, the gains attributable to the savings in migration costs accrue to native workers.

18 This extension of the model raises a number of very interesting and policy-relevant questions. For example, an inelastic labor demand curve in a particular region may reflect a relatively low volume of physical capital in that region. Immigration policy could then be used to build up the capital stock in the low-capital region by granting entry to persons willing to invest in those regions (and, perhaps not coincidentally, also increase the short-run gains that accrue to the native population). This argument can be used to justify the employment creation program in current U.S. immigration policy, where visas are "sold" at lower prices

to those persons willing to invest in regions that have relatively poor economic prospects.

19   I also conducted the analysis with the skill groups defined in terms of occupation. The results were qualitatively similar to those reported.

20   Ideally, one would want to use the sample of immigrant workers to predict the wage that a foreign-born worker could expect to earn in each of the states. Because immigrants are highly clustered in a very small number of states, however, there are many empty (j, k) cells, preventing the calculation of a complete series of the log wage index. Moreover, Jaeger's (1996) analysis of the 1980 and 1990 Censuses indicates that changes in relative supplies of immigrants and natives within a sex-education group have little effect on the wage gap between immigrants and natives for that group. This evidence suggests that immigrants and natives may be nearly perfect substitutes in production within broad education categories, further justifying the use of the log wage index estimated in the native population to approximate the regional wage dispersion faced by potential migrants. The regression for the 1960 Census has 434,195 observations, that for the 1970 Census has 567,620, and that for the 1980 Census has 860,365.

21   Topel (1986).

22   The remaining correlations between college graduates and other workers are as follows: 0.73 for workers with nine to 11 years of schooling, 0.82 for workers with 12 years, and 0.90 for workers with 13 to 15 years.

23   The supplies of immigrants and natives are calculated using the sample of all persons who are not living in group quarters and who are 18 to 59 years old at the middle of the decade.

24   I also calculated the statistics reported in Table 18.2 using alternative breakdowns of the "best" and "worst" states, such as the ten (rather than five) states offering the highest and the ten offering the lowest wages. The qualitative conclusions were very similar.

25   For example, the group of earlier immigrants defined in the 1970 Census would include immigrants who arrived in the United States before 1955 (since the relevant log wage index is measured as of 1960).

26   Note, however, that there is little evidence that the new immigrants in the 1960s (that is, the 1960–64 arrivals) cluster in very different places than the earlier immigrants (the pre-1955 arrivals). All of these immigrants, however, arrived before the resurgence of immigration to the United States, and a relatively large fraction were refugees. It is unclear that income maximization plays an important role in determining where these types of immigrants settle when they first enter the country.

27   The generic first-difference regression model in Equation (18) can also be estimated in terms of a level specification. With the data pooled over all three decades, the following regression model can be estimated:

$$Z_{jk}(t) = \theta v_{jk}(t) + (\eta_j \times \varphi_t) + (\gamma_k \times \varphi_t) + (\gamma_k \times \varphi_j) + \varepsilon_{jk}(t),$$

where $(\eta_j \times \varphi_t)$ represents a vector of fixed effects that fully interact the cell's state of residence and the period fixed effect; $(\gamma_k \times \varphi_t)$ gives a vector of fixed effects interacting the cell's education and the period fixed effect; and $(\gamma_k \times \eta_j)$ gives a vector of fixed effects interacting the cell's education and the state of residence. If the level regression is weighted by the sample size of the (j, k) cell, the numerical value of the coefficient θ is the same in this level specification as in Equation (18).

28   To see how the state fixed effects in a first-difference regression control for differences in the cost of living, consider a generic regression model $\Delta y_j = a + b$ $\Delta \log(w_j/p_j) + e$, where $\Delta \log w_j$ is the change in the logarithm of the wage in state j over some time period, and $\Delta \log p_j$ is the change in the logarithm of the price index. Note that this regression is equivalent to $\Delta y_j = a + b \Delta \ln w_j - b \Delta \ln p_j + e$. This regression can be estimated either by including a measure of the cost-of-living index (which is not available before the 1970s) or, more generally, by including a

vector of state fixed effects.

29 The mean of the relative supply index for new immigrants relative to earlier immigrants is 0.9.

30 Borjas, Freeman, and Katz (1997); Schoeni (1997).

31 The mean of the relative supply index for new male immigrants relative to male natives is 1.5, so that the relative supply elasticity in the male sample is 1.3. The mean of the relative supply index for new female immigrants relative to female natives is 1.4, and the relative supply elasticity in the female sample is 1.1.

32 Mincer (1978).

33 One possible source of endogeneity bias could be reverse causation between the relative supply index and the log wage index. For example, the sample of earlier immigrants (who arrived at least five years before the observation of the log wage index) could have themselves affected the wage in the local labor market.

34 The empirical analysis uses the "sample line" observations from the 1950 Public Use Microdata Sample, since these are the only observations that contain information on educational attainment (the sample-line observations from a 1/330th sample). The regressions estimated in the 1950 Census use the sample weights provided in the data file. The log wage regression in the 1950 Census has 90,363 observations. Note further that the 1950 Public Use Microdata Sample does not contain any information on wages for workers in Alaska and Hawaii, which became states after 1950. As a result, the second-stage relative supply regressions that use the instrumental variables procedure have 500 observations.

35 The correlation is +0.14 between 1950–60 and 1960–70, and −0.22 between 1960–70 and 1970–80. Borjas, Freeman, and Katz (1997) show that the correlation between wage growth in 1970–80 and that in 1980–90 became much more negative than over previous decades. It would be difficult to justify the use of the previous decade's wage growth as an instrument for the current decade's growth unless one can first understand why the regional wage structure changed in such a dramatic fashion during that period.

36 In addition, the predicted last period's wage growth is highly collinear with the vector of education and state fixed effects included in the first-difference regression model.

37 U.S. Department of State (2000).

38 Thirteen countries accounted for 90 percent of refugees awarded permanent residence status during the 1970s and 1980s: Afghanistan, Bulgaria, Cambodia, Cuba, Czechoslovakia, Ethiopia, Hungary, Laos, Poland, Romania, Thailand, the Soviet Union, and Vietnam.

39 This alternative test of the theory could help strengthen the argument that the results reported in Tables 18.3 and 18.4 *cannot* be attributed to a spurious correlation created by the possibility that immigrants tend to move to a few states, which just happen to offer relatively high wages. Native movers, after all, do not typically move to the same six immigrant-receiving states. Only 34.1 percent of natives who moved between 1985 and 1990 moved to one of those states, compared with 74 percent of the new immigrant arrivals.

40 The 1980 Census data contain information on place of residence in 1975 for only half of the sample, randomly selected. The analysis summarized in what follows, therefore, uses a 0.5 percent random sample of native workers in 1980.

41 Greenwood (1993) surveys the extensive internal migration literature.

42 Bartel (1989), in a study of the internal migration decisions of immigrants, concludes that immigrants enter the United States through a limited number of gateway cities and that their subsequent internal migration within the United States is not very sensitive to regional wage differentials.

43 See, for example, Barro and Sala-i-Martin (1991; 1992); Blanchard and Katz (1992).

44 To derive the steady-state level of income in the national economy, we can write the difference Equation (19) in terms of the initial wage in the state. Ignoring the subscript j, the wage at time t is

$$\ln w(t) = \alpha\left[1 + (1 + \beta) + (1 + \beta)^2 + \ldots + (1 + \beta)^{t-1}\right] + (1 + \beta)^t \ln w(0),$$

where $\ln w(0)$ is the logarithm of the initial wage. The steady-state wage is obtained by letting $t \to \infty$. It is given by $\ln w^* = -\alpha/\beta$. One can then write the current period wage as

$$\ln w(t) = \left[1 - (1 + \beta)^t\right] \ln w^* + (1 + \beta)^t \ln w(0).$$

The initial log wage gap has been cut by half when $\ln w(t)$ is the simple average of $\ln w^*$ and $\ln w(0)$. This implies that the half-life can be calculated from the equation $(1 + \beta)^t = 0.5$. The time required to cut the initial wage gap in half is then given by $t^* \approx -\ln 2/\beta$.

45   The framework is a special case of the multisector migration model presented in Borjas (1999b).

46   The quadratic cost function implies that it is very expensive for all natives to move at the same time. The increasing marginal cost of migration can be justified if there are limited resources to facilitate the geographic move, and if rising demand for internal migration leads to more congestion and hence higher costs for the marginal internal migrant.

47   Note that $\ln(L_2/L_1) \approx (L_2 - L_1)/0.5(L_1 + L_2)$. Equation (32) follows from applying this approximation to the lagged adjustment function in Equation (28).

48   Gould (1968); Hamermesh (1993). The rate of change of employment in the dynamic model of labor demand with quadratic adjustment costs is $dE_t/dt = \kappa(E^* - E_t)$, where E^* gives steady-state employment and E_t gives employment at time t. The alternative definition of R_t given in Equation (32) implies that $R_t - R_{t-1} = -\delta\sigma R_{t-1}$. This relationship is identical to that implied by the dynamic model of labor demand because the steady-state value of R^* is zero.

49   This comparison is related to the discussion in the trade literature that analyzes the optimal timing of trade liberalizations; see Lapan (1976) and Mussa (1986).

50   The algebraic structure of the model does not lead to a closed-form solution for the maximization problem in Equation (34). The simulation conducts the maximization by calculating the efficiency gain under each regime for many alternative values of σ, and then choosing the value of the elasticity that maximizes the net gain.

51   The assumption that $\delta = 0.3$ is consistent with the evidence summarized in Hamermesh's (1993) survey of the labor demand literature.

52   The assumption that $\beta = 0.7$ implies that 70 percent of the $10 trillion in national income accrues to workers. Since there are 100 million workers, income per worker equals $70,000. Equation (31) implies that the average cost of migration equals ϕR. I obtain the value of ϕ by evaluating the expression for average costs at the point that would be observed if 1 percent of native workers (or 1 million workers) migrated in any particular year.

53   Equations (25) and (30) indicate that the regional wage gap has been cut in half when $(1 - \delta\sigma)^t = 0.5$. The implied half-life is then given by $t^* = \ln 0.5/\ln (1 - \delta\sigma)$.

54   It is also possible that native migration is inefficient because it fails to maximize native income net of migration costs.

55   Fitzpatrick (1971) gives a comprehensive history of the population flow between Puerto Rico and the United States.

56   Ramos (1992).

57   World Bank, World Development Indicators, 1998.

58   Fröhlich (1997: 6).

Chapter 19

1   See also Altonji and Card (1991), Borjas (1987a), Card (1990, 2001), LaLonde and Topel (1991), and Schoeni (1997). Friedberg and Hunt (1995) survey the literature.

2 Borjas (2001) argues that income-maximizing immigrants would want to cluster in high-wage regions, helping to move the labor market toward a long-run equilibrium. The evidence indeed suggests that, within education groups, new immigrants tend to locate in those states that offer the highest rate of return for their skills.

3 See also Borjas, Freeman, and Katz (1997); Card and DiNardo (2000); Walker, Ellis, and Barff (1992); White and Hunter (1993); White and Liang (1998); and Wright, Ellis, and Reibel (1997).

4 The model is an application of the Blanchard and Katz (1992) framework that analyzes how local labor market conditions respond to demand shocks. It builds on a framework developed by Borjas, Freeman, and Katz (1997, unpublished appendix), and further elaborated in Borjas (1999b). The current presentation differs from the earlier iterations in several ways, particularly by incorporating the presence of internal migration flows before the immigrant influx begins and by deriving estimable equations that can be used to identify the key theoretical parameters.

5 The extension of the model to incorporate differences in the level of the demand curve would be very cumbersome unless the determinants of the regional differences in demand are well specified. The assumption that the demand shifter is time-invariant implies that the immigrant influx will necessarily lower the average wage in the economy. This adverse wage effect could be dampened by allowing for endogenous capital growth (or for capital flows from abroad).

6 The model can incorporate a time-varying immigrant influx to each region as long as the growth rate of the immigrant stock in group (i, j) is constant. It is worth noting, however, that the location decisions of new immigrants may shift over time. In the 1990s, for example, the traditional immigrant gateways of New York and Los Angeles attracted relatively fewer immigrants as the new immigrants began to settle in areas that did not have sizable foreign-born populations; see Funkhouser (2000) and Zavodny (1999).

7 The initial evidence reported in Bartel (1989) and Bartel and Koch (1991) suggested that immigrants had lower rates of internal migration than natives and that the internal migration decisions of immigrants were not as sensitive to regional wage differences, but instead were heavily influenced by the location decisions of earlier immigrant waves. However, more recent evidence reported in Gurak and Kritz (2000) indicates that the interstate migration rate of immigrants is almost as high as that of natives and that immigrant migration decisions are becoming more sensitive to economic conditions in the state of origin; see also Belanger and Rogers (1992) and Kritz and Nogle (1994).

8 Note that the model assumes the market clears and ignores the participation decision of native workers. However, part of the adjustment mechanism to the immigrant-induced supply shifts may occur through a decline in labor force participation or an increase in unemployment in the native population. The corresponding decline in the number of working natives would attenuate the wage response and reduce the need for native internal migration; see Rowthorn and Glyn (2006) for a related discussion.

9 More precisely, $\log \overline{w}_{i,t-1} = \log \overline{w}_{i,-1} + \eta(tm_i)$, where m_i gives the flow of immigrants in skill group i relative to the total number of natives in that skill group. The model implicitly assumes that the native population is large enough (relative to the immigrant stock) to be able to equalize the number of workers across labor markets through internal migration.

10 The migration behavior underlying Equation (4) is analogous to the firm's behavior in the presence of adjustment costs (Hamermesh 1993). The staggered native response can be justified a number of ways. The labor market is in continual flux, with persons entering and leaving the market. Because migration is costly, workers may find it optimal to time the lumpy migration decision concurrently with these transitions. Workers also may face constraints that prevent them from taking immediate advantage of regional wage differentials, including various forms of "job-lock" or short-term liquidity constraints.

Notes

11   It may seem preferable to specify the supply function so that natives take into account the expected impact of continued future immigration. In a sense, however, the flow of immigrants (m_{ij}) is a "sufficient statistic" because I have assumed that the region receives the same number of immigrants in every period.

12   This number equals the total number of natives in a skill group divided by the number of regions.

13   A tilde above a variable indicates that the variable refers to the stock of immigrants at a particular point in time (rather than the flow). The multiplicative factor used to define the stocks is $(t + 1)$ rather than t because the immigrant influx began in period 0.

14   In particular, note that $\gamma_{Nt} = \partial \log N_{ijt}/\partial \tilde{m}_{ijt}$ and that $\tilde{m}_{ijt} = \tilde{M}_{ijt}/N$, where N is a (fixed) native baseline.

15   It is important to emphasize that the model presented here, although useful from an empirical perspective, is very restrictive. For instance, the model assumes that native workers anticipate the future impact of immigration, but ignores the fact that firms have similar expectations and that the capital stock will adjust in an optimal fashion to the immigrant-induced increase in labor supply, likely dampening the adverse wage effects of immigration and the need for native internal migration to equilibrate the labor market. Similarly, the asymptotic properties of the model result from restrictive assumptions about how the native workforce is distributed across skill groups, the nature of the immigrant inflows, the absence of capital flows, and the shape of the production function. It would be important to determine how these factors alter the interpretation of spatial correlations. Finally, a more complete analysis would explicitly incorporate the assumption that all agents – native workers, immigrants, and firms – have rational expectations about future immigration.

16   I also use the approximation that t is relatively large so that the ratio $t/(t + 1) \approx 1$ and $1/t \approx 0$; in other words, the wage convergence process has been going on for some time before we observe the data points.

17   Put differently, it is cheaper to migrate across metropolitan areas to escape the adverse affects of immigration than it is to migrate across states or census divisions.

18   The person weights provided in the public use files are used in the calculations.

19   The analysis uses the information provided by the variable giving the person's labor force status in the survey week to exclude persons in the military.

20   This definition of work experience is reasonably accurate for native men, but surely contains measurement errors when applied to working women, particularly in the earlier cross sections when the female labor force participation rate was much lower. The definition also does not capture correctly the level of "effective" experience – the number of years of work experience that are valued by an American employer – in the sample of immigrants. Borjas (2003) finds that correcting for this problem does not greatly affect the measured wage impact of immigration.

21   Undoubtedly, other factors also account for California's demographic trends in the past 20 years, including the impact of the defense cutbacks of the late 1980s and the high-tech boom of the late 1990s.

22   The metropolitan area is defined in a roughly consistent manner across censuses beginning in 1980. The analysis conducted at the metropolitan area level, therefore, uses only the 1980–2000 cross sections and excludes all workers residing outside the identifiable metropolitan areas.

23   The mean log weekly wage for each cell is calculated in the sample of salaried workers who do not reside in group quarters, are not enrolled in school, are in the civilian workforce, and report a positive value for annual earnings, weeks worked, and usual hours worked in the calendar year prior to the census.

24   The coefficients of the immigrant share variable are quite similar when the regressions are not weighted.

25   To illustrate, a regression of the log weekly wage on the relative number of immigrants variable $\tilde{m}$ (and all the fixed effects) has a coefficient of –0.160 (with a standard error of 0.082). The same regression on the log of the relative number

variable has a coefficient of −0.071 (.027). Evaluated at the mean value of $\widetilde{m}$ in 2000 (0.172), the implied wage elasticity is −0.41. A regression specification that includes a second-order polynomial in the relative number variable yields coefficients of −0.558 (0.214) and 0.298 (0.124), implying a wage elasticity of −0.45. The wage elasticity obtained from the immigrant share specification reported in Table 19.2 is −0.39. It is evident that the linear specification greatly understates the wage impact of immigration.

26 The specification of the national level regression differs slightly from the generic model presented in Equation (14). In particular, the regression equation includes the immigrant share variable, fixed effects indicating the skill group, and fixed effects indicating the time period. Because it is impossible to introduce interactions between the skill group and the time period, I instead introduce all two-way interactions between the following three vectors: fixed effects indicating the group's educational attainment, fixed effects indicating the group's labor market experience, and fixed effects indicating the time period.

27 I used the 1950 Census to calculate the lagged workforce variable pertaining to the skill-region cells drawn from the 1960 cross section.

28 The regressions presented in this section are not weighted by the size of the sample used to calculate the dependent variable in a particular skill-region-time cell, as the weight is proportionately identical to the unlogged value of the dependent variable in some of the cross sections, and differs only slightly in others (due to the presence of sampling weights in the 1990 and 2000 Censuses). A weighted regression is problematic because it introduces a strong positive correlation between the weight and the dependent variable (observations with large values of the dependent variable would mechanically count more in the regression analysis), and errors in the measurement of the dependent variable would be amplified by the weighting scheme. This type of nonclassical measurement error, which has not been appreciated sufficiently in previous studies, imparts a positive bias on the adjustment coefficient in Equation (16). In fact, a weighted regression of the state-level specification reported in Row 1 of Table 19.3 leads to an adjustment coefficient of −0.135 (0.094).

29 To avoid reintroducing the dependent variable on the right-hand-side, the regressions presented in this section use the lagged growth rate of the native workforce ten to 20 years prior to the census date. For example, the lagged growth rate for the observation referring to high school graduates in Iowa in 1980 would be the growth rate in the number of high school graduates in Iowa between 1960 and 1970. This definition of the lagged growth rate implies that the regression models using this specification do not include any cells drawn from the 1960 Census.

30 The mean log weekly wage and unemployment rate for each cell are calculated from the data available in each census cross section.

31 The coefficient would be virtually identical if both the lagged level and growth rate of the native workforce were included in the regression.

32 The metropolitan area regressions cannot be estimated with the lagged growth rate because that would then leave only one cross section with sufficient data to estimate the model.

33 The baseline state is the original state of residence when calculating out-migration rates and the current state of residence when calculating in-migration rates. Let N_a be the number of native workers in the baseline state (in a particular skill group) five years prior to the census, and let N_b be the number of workers in the same state at the time of the census. The denominator of the in- and out-migration rates is then given by $(N_a + N_b)/2$.

34 The use of the lagged native employment variable (instead of the lagged employment growth rate) would lead to very similar coefficients. In the state-level regressions, the analogous specification to that reported in Row 1 of the middle panel yields a coefficient of −0.291 (0.064).

35 The inclusion of the lagged native workforce variable in the metropolitan area regressions implies that the regressions can only include the 1990 and 2000 cross-

sections, as the 1970 Census does not contain the required information.

36   Many studies, including some of the classic articles in the economics of internal migration, analyze the strong positive correlation between migration propensities and education; see Sjaastad (1962); Ladinksy (1967); and the survey by Greenwood (1993). The analysis in this chapter assumes that the elasticity measuring the marginal response of immigrant-induced supply increases to native migration propensities is the same for all skill groups. The inclusion of skill-specific fixed effects throughout the regression analysis, however, allows the various groups to differ in their migration propensities.

37   Put differently, I assume that the supply elasticity $\sigma = 0$ at the national level.

38   The estimated effects for the size of the native workforce are drawn from Rows 1 and 2 of Table 19.3, and Row 1 of Table 19.4.

References

Introduction by the Editors

Akgüc, M., Giulietti, C., Zimmermann, K. F. (2014). The RUMiC Longitudinal Survey: Fostering Research on Labor Markets in China, in: IZA Journal of Labor and Development, 3(5).

Arni, P., Caliendo, M., Künn, S. (2014). The IZA Evaluation Dataset Survey: A Scientific Usefile, in: IZA Journal of European Labor Studies, 3(6).

Ashraf, Q., Galor, O. (2013). The "Out of Africa" Hypothesis, Human Genetic Diversity, and Comparative Economic Development, in: The American Economic Review, 103(1): 1–46.

Barbone, L., Kahanec, M., Kureková, L. M., Zimmermann, K. F. (2013). Migration from the Eastern Partnership Countries to the European Union – Options for a Better Future, IZA Research Report No. 55.

Bauer, T., Zimmermann, K. F. (1997). Integrating the East: The Labor Market Effects of Immigration, in: Black, S. W. (ed.), Europe's Economy Looks East: Implications for Germany and the European Union, Cambridge, UK: Cambridge University Press, 269–306.

Bauer, T., Zimmermann, K. F. (1999). Assessment of Possible Migration Pressure and its Labour Market Impact Follwing EU Enlargment to Central and Eastern Europe, IZA Research Report No. 3.

Bonin, H., Eichhorst, W., Florman, C., Hansen, M. O., Skiöld, L., Stuhler, J., Tatsiramos, K., Thomasen, H., Zimmermann, K. F. (2008). Geographic Mobility in the European Union: Optimising its Economic and Social Benefits, IZA Research Report No. 19.

Borjas, G. J. (1999). Heaven's Door. Immigration Policy and the American Economy, Princeton, NJ: Princeton University Press.

Borjas, G. J. (2014). Immigration Economics, Cambridge, MA: Harvard University Press.

Chiswick, B. R. (2005). The Economics of Immigration, Cheltenham, UK: Edward Elgar.

Constant, A. F. (1998). The Earnings of Male and Female Guestworkers and their Assimilation into the German Labor Market: A Panel Study 1984–1993, Dissertation, Vanderbilt University.

Constant, A. F. (2014a). Do Migrants take the Jobs of Native Workers?, in: IZA World of Labor, 10.

Constant, A. F. (2014b). Ethnic Identity and Work, in: Wright, J. D. (ed.), International Encyclopedia of the Social and Behavioral Sciences, 2nd edition, Amsterdam: Elsevier, 106–112.

Constant, A. F., Gataullina, L., Zimmermann, K. F. (2009). Ethnosizing Immigrants, in: Journal of Economic and Behavioral Organization, 69(3): 274–287.

Constant, A. F., Kahanec, M., Zimmermann, K. F. (2011). The Russian-Ukrainian Political Divide, in: Eastern European Economics, 49(6): 103–115.

Constant, A. F., Kahanec, M., Zimmermann, K. F. (2012). The Russian-Ukrainian Earnings Divide, in: Economics of Transition, 20(1), 1–35.

References

Constant, A. F., Nottmeyer, O., Zimmermann, K. F. (2013). The Economics of Circular Migration, in: Constant, A.F., Zimmermann, K.F. (eds.), International Handbook on the Economics of Migration, Cheltenham, UK: Edward Elgar Publishing, 55–74.

Constant, A. F., Tatsiramos, K., Zimmermann, K. F. (eds.) (2009). Ethnicity and Labor Market Outcomes: Research in Labor Economics, 29.

Constant, A. F., Zimmermann, K. F. (eds.) (2004). How Labor Migrants Fare, Berlin et al: Springer-Verlag.

Constant, A. F., Zimmermann, K. F. (2008). Measuring Ethnic Identity and Its Impact on Economic Behavior, in: Journal of the European Economic Association, 6(2–3): 424–433.

Constant, A. F., Zimmermann, K. F. (2009). Work and Money: Payoffs by Ethnic Identity and Gender, in: Research in Labor Economics, 29, 3–30.

Constant, A. F., Zimmermann, K. F. (eds.) (2013a). International Handbook on the Economics of Migration, Cheltenham, UK: Edward Elgar Publishing.

Constant, A. F., Zimmermann, K. F. (2013b). Frontier Issues in Migration Research, in: Constant, A. F., Zimmermann, K. F. (eds.), International Handbook on the Economics of Migration, Cheltenham, UK: Edward Elgar Publishing, 1–9.

Constant, A F., Zimmermann, L., Zimmermann, K. F. (2007). Ethnic Self-identification of First-Generation Immigrants, in: International Migration Review, 41(3): 769–781.

Eichhorst, W., Giulietti, C., Guzi, M., Kendzia, M. J., Monti, P., Frattini, T., Nowotny, K., Huber, P., Vandeweghe, B. (2011). The Integration of Migrants and its Effects on the Labour Market, IZA Research Report No. 40.

Giulietti, C., Guzi, M., Kahanec, M., Zimmermann, K. F. (2013). Unemployed Benefits and Immigration: Evidence from the EU, in: International Journal of Manpower, 34(1): 24–38.

Kahanec, M., Zimmermann, K. F., Kureková, L. M., Biavaschi, C. (2013). Labour Migration from EaP Countries to the EU – Assessment of Costs and Benefits and Proposals for Better Labour Market Matching, IZA Research Report No. 56.

Kahanec, M., Zimmermann, K. F. (eds.) (2009). EU Labor Markets After Post-Enlargement Migration, Berlin et al: Springer.

Kahanec, M., Zimmermann, K. F. (2010). Migration in an Enlarged EU: A Challenging Solution?, in: Keereman, F., Szekely, I. (eds.), Five Years of an Enlarged EU – A Positive Sum Game, Berlin et al.: Springer, 63–94.

Kahanec, M., Zimmermann, K. F. (eds.) (2011). Ethnic Diversity in European Labor Markets: Challenges and Solutions, Cheltenham, UK: Edward Elgar.

Kahanec, M., Zimmermann, K. F. (eds.) (2016). Labor Migration, EU Enlargement, and the Great Recession, Berlin et al: Springer.

Lehmann, H., Muravyev, A., Zimmermann, K. F. (2012). The Ukrainian Longitudinal Monitoring Survey: Towards a Better Understanding of Labor Markets in Transition, in: IZA Journal of Labor and Development, 1(9).

Teixeira, P. N. (2007). Jacob Mincer. A Founding Father of Modern Labor Economics, New York: Oxford University Press.

Tranaes, T., Zimmermann, K. F. (2004). Migrants, Work, and the Welfare State, Odense: University Press of Southern Denmark.

Zimmermann, K. F. (1992). Migration and Economic Development, Berlin et al: Springer.

Zimmermann, K. F. (1994). Some General Lessons for Europe's Migration Problem, in: Giersch, H. (ed.), Economic Aspects of International Migration, Heidelberg et al: Springer, 249–273.

Zimmermann, K. F. (2005). European Migration. What Do We Know?, Oxford: Oxford University Press.

Zimmermann, K. F. (2014a). Circular Migration, in: IZA World of Labor, 1.

Zimmermann, K. F. (2014b). Migration, Jobs and Integration in Europe, in: Migration Policy Practice, 6(4): 4–16.

Zimmermann, K. F., Bauer, T. K. (eds.) (2002). The Economics of Migration, Cheltenham, UK: Edward Elgar.

Zimmermann, K. F., Bonin, H., Fahr, R., Hinte, H. (2007). Immigration Policy and the Labor Market: The German Experience and Lessons for Europe, Berlin et al: Springer.

Zimmermann, K. F., Hinte, H. (2005). Zuwanderung und Arbeitsmarkt. Deutschland und Dänemark im Vergleich, Berlin et al: Springer.

References

Zimmermann, K. F., Kahanec, M., Giulietti, C., Guzi, M., Barrett, A., Maitre, B. (2012). Study on Active Inclusion of Migrants, IZA Research Report No. 43.

Bibliography

Ahmed, B., Robinson, J. G. (1994). Estimates of Emigration of the Foreign-Born Population, 1980-1990, U.S. Bureau of the Census Population Division Working Paper No. 9.

Alba, R. D. (1990). Ethnic Identity: The Transformation of White America, New Haven, CT: Yale University Press.

Alexander, K. L., Reilly, T. W. (1981). Estimating the Effects of Marriage Timing on Educational Attainment: Some Procedural Issues and Substantive Clarifications, in: American Journal of Sociology, 87(1): 143-156.

Altonji, J. G., Card, D. (1991). The Effects of Immigration on the Labor Market Outcomes of Less-Skilled Natives, in: Abowd, J. M., Freeman, R. B. (eds.), Immigration, Trade, and the Labor Market, Chicago, IL: University of Chicago Press, 201-234.

Altonji, J. G., Dunn, T. A. (1991). Relationships Among the Family Incomes and Labor Market Outcomes of Relatives, in: Research in Labor Economics, 12: 269-310.

Amir, S. (1981). Changes in the Wage Function for Israeli Jewish Male Employees between 1968/69 and 1975/1976, in: Bank of Israel Economic Review, 52: 5-29.

Angrist, J. D., Krueger, A. B. (1999). Empirical Strategies in Labor Economics, in: Ashenfelter, O. C., Card, D. (eds.), Handbook of Labor Economics, Vol 3A, Amsterdam: Elsevier, 1277-1366.

Ashenfelter, O., Krueger, A. B. (1994). Estimates of the Economic Return to Schooling from a New Sample of Twins, in: The American Economic Review, 84(5): 1157-1173.

Autor, D. H., Katz, L. F., Krueger, A. B. (1998). Computing Inequality: Have Computers Changed the Labor Market?, in: Quarterly Journal of Economics, 113(4), 1169-1214.

Axelrod, B. (1972). Historical Studies of Emigration from the United States, in: International Migration Review, 6(1): 32-49.

Azariadis, C., Drazen, A. (1990). Threshold Externalities in Economic Development, in: The Quarterly Journal of Economics, 105(2): 501-526.

Bailey, A. (1993). A Migration History, Migration Behavior and Selectivity, in: Annals of Regional Science, 27(4): 315-326.

Barro, R. J. (1991). Economic Growth in a Cross Section of Countries, in: The Quarterly Journal of Economics, 106(2): 407-443.

Barro, R. J., Sala-i-Martin, X. (1991). Convergence across States and Regions, in: Brookings Papers on Economic Activity, 22(1): 107-158.

Barro, R. J., Sala-i-Martin, X. (1992). Convergence, in: Journal of Political Economy, 100(2): 223-251.

Bartel, A. (1989). Where Do the New U.S. Immigrants Live?, in: Journal of Labor Economics, 7(4): 371-391.

Bartel, A. P., Borjas, G. (1977). Middle-Age Job Mobility: Its Determinants and Consequences, in: Wolfbein, S. (ed.), Men in Pre-Retirement Rears, Philadelphia, PA: Temple University Press, 39-97.

Bartel, A. P., Koch, M. J. (1991). Internal Migration of U.S. Immigrants, in: Abowd, J. M., Freeman, R. B. (eds.), Immigration, Trade, and the Labor Market, Chicago, IL: University of Chicago Press, 121-134.

Bauer, T., Epstein, G. S., Gang, I. N. (2005). Enclaves, Language, and the Location Choice of Migrants, in: Journal of Population Economics, 18(4): 649-662.

Beach, C., Green, A., Worswick, C. (2007). Impacts of the Point System and Immigrant Policy Levers on Skill Characteristics of Canadian Immigrants, in: Research in Labor Economics, 27: 349-401.

Bean, F. D., Marcum, J. P. (1978). Differential Fertility and the Minority Group Status Hypothesis: An Assessment and Review, in: Bean, F. D., Frisbie, W. P. (eds.), The Demography of Racial and Ethnic Groups, New York: Academic Press, 189-211.

References

Bean, F. D., Swicegood, G. (1985). Mexican American Fertility Patterns, Austin: University of Texas Press.

Bean, F. D., Tienda, M. (1987). The Hispanic Population of the United States, New York: Russell Sage Foundation.

Becker, G. S. (1964). Human Capital, New York: Columbia University Press.

Becker, G. S. (1967). Human Capital and the Personal Distribution of Income, Woytinsky Lecture No.1, Ann Arbor, MI: University of Michigan Press.

Becker, G. S. (1975). Human Capital, 2nd edition, New York: Columbia University Press.

Becker, G. S. (1981). A Treatise on the Family, Cambridge, MA: Harvard University Press.

Becker, G. S., Barro, R. J. (1988). A Reformulation of the Economic Theory of Fertility, in: The Quarterly Journal of Economics, 103(1): 1–25.

Becker, G. S., Chiswick, B. R. (1966). Education and the Distribution of Earnings, in: The American Economic Review, 56(1/2): 358–369.

Becker, G. S., Lewis, H. G. (1973). On the Interaction Between the Quantity and Quality of Children, in: Journal of Political Economy, 81(2): S279-S288.

Becker, G. S., Murphy, K. M., Tamura, R. (1990). Human Capital, Fertility, and Economic Growth, in: Journal of Political Economy, 98(5): S12-S37.

Becker, G. S., Tomes, N. (1986). Human Capital and the Rise and Fall of Families, in: Journal of Labor Economics, 4(3): S1-S39.

Beenstock, M. (1993). Learning Hebrew and Finding a Job. Econometric Analysis of Immigrant Absorption in Israel, Paper presented at the Conference on the Economics of International Migration: Econometric Evidence, February, Konstanz, Germany.

Beenstock, M. (1996). Failure to Absorb: Remigration by Immigrants into Israel, in: International Migration Review, 30(4): 950–978.

Beenstock, M., Chiswick, B. R., Paltiel, A. (2010). Testing the Immigrant Assimilation Hypothesis with Longitudinal Data, in: Review of Economics of the Household, 8(1): 7–27.

Behrman, J., Taubman, P. (1985). Intergenerational Earnings and Mobility in the United States: Some Estimates and a Test of Becker's Intergenerational Endowments Model, in: The Review of Economics and Statistics, 67(1): 144–151.

Belanger, A., Rogers, A. (1992). The Internal Migration and Spatial Redistribution of the Foreign-Born Population in the United States: 1965-70 and 1975-80, in: International Migration Review, 26(4): 1342–1369.

Bell, D. (1974). Why Participation Rates of Black and White Wives Differ, in: The Journal of Human Resources, 9(4): 465–479.

Ben-Porath, Y. (1967). The Production of Human Capital and the Life Cycle of Earnings, in: The Journal of Political Economy, 75(4): 352–365.

Berger, M. C. (1983). Changes in Labor Force Composition and Male Earnings: A Production Approach, in: The Journal of Human Resources, 18(2): 177–196.

Bertrand, M., Luttmer, E. F. P., Mullainathan, S. (2000). Network Effects and Welfare Cultures, in: The Quarterly Journal of Economics, 115(3): 1019–1055.

Bhagwati, J. N., Srinivasan, T. N. (1983). Lectures on International Trade, Cambridge, MA: MIT Press.

Blake, J. (1987). Differential Parental Investment: Its Effects on Child Quality and Status Attainment, in: Lancaster, J. B., Altmann, J. , Rossi, A. S., Sherrod, L. R. (eds.), Parentage Across the Life Span: Biosocial Dimensions, New York: Aldine de Gruyter, 351–385.

Blanchard, O. J., Katz, L. F. (1992). Regional Evolutions, in: Brookings Papers on Economic Activity, 23(1), 1–76.

Blau, F. (1980). Immigration and Labor Earnings in Early Twentieth Century America, in: Simon, J., DaVanzo, J. (eds.), Research in Population Economics, vol. 2, Greenwich, CT: JAI, 21–41.

Blau, F. D. (1984). The Use of Transfers by Immigrants, in: Industrial and Labor Relations Review, 37(2): 222–239.

Blau, F. D., Kahn, L. M., Papps, K. L. (2011). Gender, Source Country Characteristics and Labor Market Assimilation Among Immigrants: 1980-2000, in: Review of Economics and Statistics, 93(1): 43–58.

References

Bonacich, E., Modell, J. (1980). The Economic Basis of Ethnic Solidarity: Small Business in the Japanese American Community, Berkeley and Los Angeles, CA: University of California Press.

Borcherding, T., Silberberg, E. (1978). Shipping the Good Apples Out: The Alchian and Allen Theorem Reconsidered, in: Journal of Political Economy, 86(1): 131–138.

Borjas, G. J. (1982). The Earnings of Male Hispanic Immigrants in the United States, in: Industrial and Labor Relations Review, 35(3): 343–353.

Borjas, G. J. (1985). Assimilation, Changes in Cohort Quality, and the Earnings of Immigrants, in: Journal of Labor Economics, 3(4): 463–89. [Chapter 2 in this volume]

Borjas, G. J. (1987a). Immigrants, Minorities, and Labor Market Competition, in: Industrial and Labor Relations Review, 40(3): 382–392.

Borjas, G. J. (1987b). Self-Selection and the Earnings of Immigrants, in: The American Economic Review, 77(4): 531–553.

Borjas, G. J. (1990). Self-Selection and the Earnings of Immigrants: Reply, in: American Economic Review, 80(1): 305–308.

Borjas, G. J. (1991). Immigration and Self-Selection, in: Abowd, J., Freeman, R. (eds.), Immigration, Trade and the Labor Market, Cambridge, MA: NBER, 29–76.

Borjas, G. J. (1992). Ethnic Capital and Intergenerational Mobility, in: Quarterly Journal of Economics, 107(1): 123–150.

Borjas, G. J. (1993). The Intergenerational Mobility of Immigrants, in: Journal of Labor Economics, 11(1): 113–135.

Borjas, G. J. (1994a). Long-Run Convergence of Ethnic Skill Differentials: The Children and Grandchildren of the Great Migration, in: Industrial and Labor Relations Review, 47(4): 553–573.

Borjas, G. J. (1994b). The Economics of Immigration, in: Journal of Economic Literature, 32(4): 1667–1717.

Borjas, G. J. (1995a). Assimilation and Changes in Cohort Quality Revisited: What Happened to Immigrant Earnings in the 1980s?, in: Journal of Labor Economics, 13(2): 201–245.

Borjas, G. J. (1995b). The Economic Benefits from Immigration, in: The Journal of Economic Perspectives, 9(2): 3–22.

Borjas, G. J. (1999a). Immigration and Welfare Magnets, in: Journal of Labor Economics, 17(4): 607–637.

Borjas, G. J. (1999b). The Economic Analysis of Immigration, in: Ashenfelter, O., Card, D. (eds.), Handbook of Labor Economics, Vol 3A, Amsterdam: North-Holland, 1697–1760.

Borjas, G. J. (2001). Does Immigration Grease the Wheels of the Labor Market?, in: Brookings Papers on Economic Activity, 32(1): 69–134.

Borjas, G. J. (2003). The Labor Demand Curve is Downward Sloping: Reexamining the Impact of Immigration on the Labor Market, in: The Quarterly Journal of Economics, 118(4): 1335–1374.

Borjas, G. J., Freeman, R. B., Katz, L. F. (1992). On the Labor Market Effects of Immigration and Trade, in: Borjas, G. J., Freeman, R. B. (eds.), Immigration and the Workforce: Economic Consequences for the United States and Source Areas, Chicago, IL: NBER, 213–244.

Borjas, G. J., Freeman, R. B., Katz, L. F. (1996). Searching for the Effect of Immigration on the Labor Market, in: The American Economic Review, 86(2): 246–251.

Borjas, G. J., Freeman, R. B., Katz, L. F. (1997). How Much Do Immigration and Trade Affect Labor Market Outcomes?, in: Brookings Papers on Economic Activity, 28(1): 1–90.

Borjas, G. J., Hilton, L. (1996). Immigration and the Welfare State: Immigrant Participation in Means-Tested Entitlement Programs, in: The Quarterly Journal of Economics, 111(2): 575–604.

Borjas, G. J., Tienda, M. (eds.) (1985). Hispanics in the U.S. Economy, New York: Academic Press.

Bowles, S. (1970). Aggregation of Labor Inputs in the Economics of Growth and Planning: Experiments with a Two-Level CES Function, in: Journal of Political Economy, 78(1): 68–81.

References

Boyd, M. (1992). Gender Issues in Immigration Trends and Language Fluency: Canada and the United States, in: Chiswick, B. R. (ed.), Immigration, Language and Ethnicity: Canada and the United States, Washington, DC: American Enterprise Institute, 305–372.

Breton, A. (1978a). Bilingualism. An Economic Approach, Montreal: CD Howe Research Institute.

Breton, A. (1978b). Nationalism and Language Policies, in: The Canadian Journal of Economics, 11(4): 656–668.

Brettell, C. (2008), Meet Me at the Chat/Chaat Corner: The Embeddedness of Immigrant Entrepreneurs, in: Barkan, E., Diner, H., Kraut, A. M. (eds.), From Arrival to Incorporation: Migrants to the U.S. in a Global Era, New York: New York University Press, 121–142.

Bronfenbrenner, M. (1982). Hyphenated Americans-Economic Aspects, in: Law and Contemporary Problems, 45(2): 9–27.

Caplovitz, D. (1963). The Poor Pay More: Consumer Practices of Low-income Families, New York: Free Press.

Card, D. (1990). The Impact of the Mariel Boatlift on the Miami Labor Market, in: Industrial and Labor Relations Review, 43(2): 245–257.

Card, D. (2001). Immigrant Inflows, Native Outflows, and the Local Labor Market Impacts of Higher Immigration, in: Journal of Labor Economics, 19(1): 22–64.

Card, D. (2003). Canadian Emigration to the United States, in: Beach, C. (ed.), Canadian Immigration Policy for the 21st Century, Kingston, ON: John Deutsch Institute for the Study of Economic Policy, 295–313.

Card, D., DiNardo, J. (2000). Do Immigrant Inflows Lead to Native Outflows?, in: The American Economic Review, 90(2): 360–367.

Card, D., Hyslop, D. (1997). Does Inflation "Grease the Wheels of the Labor Market"?, in: Romer, C. D., Romer, D. H. (eds.), Reducing Inflation: Motivation and Strategy, Chicago, IL: University of Chicago Press, 71–122.

Card, D., Lemieux, T. (2001). Can Falling Supply Explain the Rising Return to College for Younger Men? A Cohort-Based Analysis, in: The Quarterly Journal of Economics, 116(2): 705–746.

Cardwell, L. A., Rosenzweig, M. R. (1980). Economic Mobility, Monopsonistic Discrimination and Sex Differences in Wages, in: Southern Economic Journal, 46(4): 1102–1117.

Carliner, G. (1980). Wages, Earnings and Hours of First, Second, and Third Generation American Males, in: Economic Inquiry, 18(1): 87–102.

Carliner, G. (1981). Wage Differences by Language Group and the Market for Language Skills in Canada, in: The Journal of Human Resources, 16(3): 384–399.

Carpenter, N. (1927). Immigrants and Their Children, 1920, Washington, DC: U.S. Bureau of the Census.

Case, A. C., Katz, L. F. (1991). The Company You Keep: The Effects of Family and Neighborhood on Disadvantaged Youths, NBER Working Paper No. 3705.

Catsiapis, G., Robinson, C. (1981). The Theory of the Family and Intergenerational Mobility: An Empirical Test, in: The Journal of Human Resources, 16(3): 313–336.

Chamnivickorn, S. (1988). Fertility, Labor Supply and Investment in Child Quality Among Asian-American Women, Dissertation, University of Illinois at Chicago.

Chapman, B. J., Iredale, R. R. (1993). Immigrant Qualifications: Recognition and Relative Wage Outcomes, in: International Migartion Review, 27(2): 359–387.

Chiswick, B. R. (1967). Human Capital and the Distribution of Personal Income, Dissertation, Columbia University.

Chiswick, B. R. (1974). Income Inequality: Regional Analyses Within a Human Capital Framework, New York: National Bureau of Economic Research.

Chiswick, B. R. (1976). Domestic Impact of Illegal Aliens – The Issues of Employment and Earnings, Preliminary Report, Domestic Council Committee on Illegal Aliens, Domestic Council, Office of the White House.

Chiswick, B. R. (1977). Sons of Immigrants: Are They at an Earnings Disadvantage?, in: The American Economic Review, 67(1): 376–380.

References

Chiswick, B. R. (1978a). A Longitudinal Analysis of the Occupational Mobility of Immigrants, in: Dennis, B. (ed.), Proceedings of the 30th Annual Winter Meeting, Madison, WI: Industrial Relations Research Association, 20–27.

Chiswick, B. R. (1978b). An Analysis of the Earnings of Mexican-Origin Men, in: American Statistical Association (ed.), Proceedings of the Business and Economics Statistics Section, Washington: American Statistical Association 222–231.

Chiswick, B. R. (1978c). Immigrants and Immigration Policy, in: Fellner, W. (ed.), Contemporary Economic Problems, Washington: American Enterprise Institute.

Chiswick, B. R. (1978d). The Effect of Americanization on the Earnings of Foreign-born Men, in: Journal of Political Economy, 86(5): 897–921. [Chapter 1 in this volume]

Chiswick, B. R. (1979). The Economic Progress of Immigrants: Some Apparently Universal Patterns, in: Fellner, W. (ed.), Contemporary Economics Problems, Washington, DC: American Enterprise Institute, 357–399.

Chiswick, B. R. (1980a). An Analysis of the Economic Progress and Impact of Immigrants. Report submitted to U.S. Department of Labor, Employment and Training Administration. N.T.I.S. no. PB80–200454, Washington, DC: National Technical Information Service.

Chiswick, B. R. (1980b). The Earnings of White and Coloured Immigrants in Britain, in: Economica, 47(185): 81–87.

Chiswick, B. R. (1982a). Tables on the Earnings of American Indians, University of Illinois at Chicago, mimeo.

Chiswick, B. R. (1982b). The Employment of Immigrants in the United States, Washington, DC: American Enterprise Institute.

Chiswick, B. R. (1982c). The Impact of Immigration on the Level and Distribution of Economic Well-Being, in Chiswick, B. R. (ed.), The Gateway: U.S. Immigration Issues and Policies, Washington, DC: American Enterprise Institute, 289–313.

Chiswick, B. R. (1983a) An Analysis of the Earnings and Employment of Asian-American Men, in: Journal of Labor Economics, 1(2): 197–214.

Chiswick, B. R. (1983b). Illegal Aliens in the United States Labor Market, in: Weisbrod, B., Hughes, H. (eds.), Human Resources, Employment and Development, Vol. 3, The Problems of Developed Countries and the International Economy, London: Macmillan, 346–367.

Chiswick, B. R. (1983c). The Earnings and Human Capital of American Jews, in: The Journal of Human Resources, 18(3): 313–336.

Chiswick, B. R. (1984). Illegal Aliens in the United States Labor Market: Analysis of Occupational Attainment and Earnings, in: International Migration Review, 18(3): 714–732.

Chiswick, B. R. (1985). The Labor Market Status of American Jews: Patterns and Determinants, in: The American Jewish Year Book, 85: 131–153.

Chiswick, B. R. (1986a). Human Capital and the Labor Market Adjustment of Immigrants: Testing Alternative Hypothesis, in: Research in Human Capital and Development, 4: 1–26.

Chiswick, B. R. (1986b). Is the New Immigration Less Skilled than the Old?, in: Journal of Labor Economics, 4(2): 168–192.

Chiswick, B. R. (1986c). Labor Supply and Investment in Child Quality: A Study of Jewish and Non-Jewish Women, in: The Review of Economics and Statistics, 68(4): 700–703.

Chiswick, B. R. (1987). The Labor Market Status of Hispanic Men, in: Journal of American Ethnic History, 7(1): 30–58.

Chiswick, B. R. (1988a). Illegal Immigration and Immigration Control, in: The Journal of Economic Perspectives, 2(3): 101–115.

Chiswick, B. R. (1988b). Illegal Aliens: Their Employment and Employers, Kalamazoo, MI: Upjohn.

Chiswick, B. R. (1989). Unlegalized Aliens: A Survey and Analysis of Aliens Not Eligible for Legalization, Report prepared for the Immigration and Naturalization Service, U.S. Department of Justice.

Chiswick, B. R. (1991). Speaking, Reading and Earnings Among Low-skilled Immigrants, in: Journal of Labor Economics, 9(2): 149–170.

References

Chiswick, B. R. (1998). Hebrew Language Usage: Determinants and Effects on Earnings Among Immigrants in Israel, in: Journal of Population Economics, 11(2): 253–271.

Chiswick, B. R. (1999). Are Immigrants Favorably Self-Selected?, in: The American Economic Review, 89(2): 181–185.

Chiswick, B. R. (2008). Are Immigrants Favorably Self-Selected? An Economic Analysis, in: Brettell, C. B., Hollifield, J. F. (eds.), Migration Theory: Talking across Disciplines, New York: Routledge, 63–82.

Chiswick, B. R. (ed.) (2011). High-Skilled Immigration in a Global Labor Market, Washington, DC: American Enterprise Institute.

Chiswick, B. R., Chiswick, C. U. (1984). Race and Public Policy: The Statistical Connection, in: Challenge, 27(4): 51–55.

Chiswick, B. R., Cox, D. (1988). Racial and Ethnic Differences in Inter Vivos Transfers and Human Capital Investments, University of Illinois at Chicago, mimeo.

Chiswick, B. R., Hatton, T. (2003). International Migration and the Integration of Labor Markets, in: Bordo, M. D., Taylor, A. M., Williamson, J. G. (eds.), Globalization in Historical Perspective, Cambridge, MA: National Bureau of Economic Research, 65–120.

Chiswick, B. R., Hurst, M. (1998). The Labor Market Status of Immigrants: A Synthesis, in: Kurthen, H. et al. (eds.), Immigration, Citizenship and the Welfare State in Germany and the United States: Immigrant Incorporation, Greenwich, CT: JAI Press, 73–94.

Chiswick, B. R., Liang Lee, Y., Miller, P. W. (2006). Immigrant Selection Systems and Immigrant Health, in: Contemporary Economic Policy, 26(4): 555–578.

Chiswick, B. R., Miller, P. W. (1985). Immigrant Generation and Income in Australia, in: Economic Record, 61(2): 540–553.

Chiswick, B. R., Miller, P. W. (1988). Earnings in Canada: The Roles of Immigrant Generation, French Ethnicity and Language, in: Research in Population Economics, 6: 183–224.

Chiswick, B. R., Miller, P. W. (1992). Language in the Immigrant Labor Market, in: Chiswick, B. R. (ed.), Immigration, Language, and Ethnicity: Canada and the United States, Washington, DC: American Enterprise Institute, 229–296.

Chiswick, B. R., Miller, P. W. (1994a). Language and Labor Supply. The Role of Gender Among Immigrants in Australia, in: Slottje, D. (ed), Research on Economic Inequality, Vol. 5., Greenwich, CT: JAI Press, 153–190.

Chiswick, B. R., Miller, P. W. (1994b). Language Choice Among Immigrants in a Multilingual Destination, 7(2): 119–131.

Chiswick, B. R., Miller, P. W. (1995). The Endogeneity between Language and Earnings: International Analyses, in: Journal of Labor Economics, 13(2): 246–288.

Chiswick, B. R., Miller, P. W. (1998a). English Language Fluency Among Immigrants in the United States, in: Research in Labor Economics, 17: 151–200.

Chiswick, B. R., Miller, P. W. (1998b). The Economic Cost to Native-Born Americans of Limited English Language Proficiency, report prepared for the Center for Equal Opportunity.

Chiswick, B. R., Miller, P. W. (2003). The Complementarity of Language and Other Human Capital: Immigrant Earnings in Canada, in: Economics of Education Review, 22(5): 469–480.

Chiswick, B. R., Miller, P. W. (2006). Language Skills and Immigrant Adjustment: The Role of Immigration Policy, in: Cobb-Clark, D., Khoo, S.-E. (eds.), Public Policy and Immigrant Settlement, Cheltenham: Edward Elgar, 121–148.

Chiswick, B. R., Miller, P. W. (2008a). Occupational Attainment and Immigrant Economic Progress in Australia, in: Economic Record, 1(9): S45-S56.

Chiswick, B. R., Miller, P. W. (2008b). Why is the Payoff to Schooling Smaller for Immigrants?, in: Labour Economics, 15(6): 1317–1340.

Chiswick, B. R., Miller, P. W. (2009). The International Transferability of Immigrants' Human Capital Skills, in: Economics of Education Review, 28(2): 162–169.

Chiswick, B. R, Miller, P. W. (2010a). Does the Choice of Reference Levels of Education in the ORU Earnings Equation Matter?, in: Economics of Education Review, 29(6): 1076–1085.

Chiswick, B. R, Miller, P. W. (2010b). The Effects of School Quality in the Origin on the Payoff to Schooling for Immigrants, in: Epstein, G. S., Gang, I. N. (eds.), Migration and Culture (Frontiers of Economics and Globalization, Vol. 8), Bingley, UK: Emerald, 67–103.

References

Chiswick, B. R., O'Neill, J. A. (1977). Human Resources and Income Distribution: Issues and Policies, New York: W. W. Norton.

Chiswick, B. R., Repetto, G. (2001). Immigrant Adjustment in Israel: Literacy and Fluency in Hebrew and Earnings, in: Djajic, S. (ed.), International Migration: Trends, Policy and Economic Impact, New York: Routledge, 207–231.

Chiswick, C. U., Chiswick, B. R., Karras G. (1992). The Impact of Immigrants on the Macroeconomy, in: Carnegie-Rochester Conferences Series on Public Policy, 37(1): 279–316.

Ciccone, A., Hall, R. E. (1996). Productivity and the Density of Economic Activity, in: The American Economic Review, 86(1): 54–70.

Clark, K., Drinkwater, S. (2002). Enclaves, Neighbourhood Effects and Employment. Outcomes: Ethnic Minorities in England and Wales, in: Journal of Population Economics, 15(1): 5–29.

Clyne, M. (1991). Community Languages. The Australian Experience, Cambridge: Cambridge University Press.

Cobb-Clark, D. A. (1993). Immigrant Selectivity and Wages: The Evidence for Women, in: American Economic Review, 83(4): 986–993.

Cochran, W. G. (1977). Sampling Techniques, New York: Wiley.

Cohen-Goldner, S., Weiss, Y. (2010). High-Skilled Russian Immigrants in the Israeli Labor Market: Adjustment and Impact, in: Chiswick, B. R. (ed.), High-Skilled Immigration in a Global Labor Market, Washington DC: American Enterprise Institute Press, 231–263.

Cohn, E., Khan, S. P. (1995). The Wage Effects of Overschooling Revisited, in: Labour Economics, 2(1): 67–76.

Coleman, J. S. (1988). Social Capital in the Creation of Human Capital, in: American Journal of Sociology, 94: S95-S120.

Coleman, J. S. (1990). Foundations of Social Theory, Cambridge, MA: Harvard University Press.

Conlisk, J. (1974). Can Equalization of Opportunity Reduce Social Mobility?, in: The American Economic Review, 64(1): 80–90.

Conlisk, J. (1977). An Exploratory Model of the Size Distribution of Income, in: Economic Inquiry, 15(3): 345–366.

Corcoran, M., Gordon, R., Laren, D., Solon, G. (1992). The Association Between Men's Economic Status and Their Family and Community Origins, in: The Journal of Human Resources, 27(4): 575–601.

Council of Economic Advisers (1984). Economic Report of the President, 1984. Washington, DC: U.S. Government Printing Office.

Crane, J. (1991). The Epidemic Theory of Ghettos and Neighborhood Effects on Dropping Out and Teenage Childbearing, in: American Journal of Sociology, 96(5): 1226–1259.

Cross, H. E., Sandos, J. A. (1981). Across the Border: Rural Development on Mexico and Recent Migration to the United States, Berkeley, CA: University of California Press.

Cummings, S. (ed.) (1980). Self-Help in Urban America: Patterns of Minority Business Enterprise, New York: Kenikart Press.

Cutler, D. M., Glaeser, E. L. (1997). Are Ghettos Good or Bad?, in: The Quarterly Journal of Economics, 112(3): 827–672.

Datcher-Loury, L. (1988). Effects of Mother's Home Time on Children's Schooling, in: The Review of Economics and Statistics, 70(3): 367–373.

DaVanzo, J. (1976). Differences between Return and Nonreturn Migration: An Econometric Analysis, in: International Migration Review, 10(1): 13–27.

DaVanzo, J. (1983). Repeat Migration in the United States: Who Moves Back and Who Moves On?, in: Review of Economics and Statistics, 65(4): 552–559.

DaVanzo, J., Morrison, P. (1986). The Prism of Migration: Dissimilarities between Return and Onward Movers, in: Social Science Quarterly, 67(3): 504–516.

Davis, J. A., Smith, T. W. (1989). General Social Surveys, 1972-1989. Cumulative Codebook, Chicago, IL: National Opinion Research Center.

DeFreitas, G. (1980). The Earnings of Immigrants in the American Labor Market, Dissertation, Columbia University.

References

DeFreitas, G. (1981). Occupational Mobility among Recent Black Immigrants. Proceedings of the Thirty-third Annual Winter Meetings, Industrial Relations Research Association, 41–47.

Dekle, R., Eaton, J. (1999). Agglomeration and Land Rents: Evidence from the Prefectures, in: Journal of Urban Economics, 46(2): 200–214.

Diamond, P. A. (1982). Aggregate Demand Management in Search Equilibrium, in: Journal of Political Economy, 90(5): 881–894.

Douglas, P. H. (1919). Is the New Immigration More Unskilled Than the Old?, in: Journal of the American Statistical Association, 16(126): 393–403.

Duleep, H. O., Regets, M. C. (1996). The Elusive Concept of Immigrant Quality: Evidence from 1970–1990, Urban Institute Discussion Paper PRIP-UI-41, Program for Research on Immigration Policy.

Duleep, H. O., Regets, M. C. (1997a). Measuring Immigrant Wage Growth Using Matched CPS Files, in: Demography, 34(2): 239–249.

Duleep, H. O., Regets, M. C. (1997b). The Decline in Immigrant Entry Earnings: Less Transferable Skills or Lower Ability?, in: Quarterly Review of Economics and Finance, 37(1): 189–208.

Dumont, J.-C., Lemaître, G. (2005). Counting Immigrants and Expatriates in OECD Countries: A New Perspective, in: OECD Economic Studies, 1: 49–83.

Duncan, G. J., Hoffman, S. D. (1981). The Incidence and Wage Effects of Overeducation, in: Economics of Education Review, 1(1): 75–86.

Dustmann, C. (1994). Speaking Fluency, Writing Fluency and Earnings of Migrants in Germany, in: Journal of Population Economics, 7(2): 133–156.

Dustmann, C., Fabbri, F. (2003). Language Proficiency and Labor Market Performance in the UK, in: The Economic Journal, 113(489): 695–717.

Dustmann, C., van Soest, A. (2001). Language Fluency and Earnings: Estimation with Misclassified Language Indicators, in: The Review of Economics and Statistics, 83(4): 663–674.

Economides, N. (1996). The Economics of Networks, in: International Journal of Industrial Organization, 14(2): 673–699.

Edin, P. A., Fredriksson, P., Åslund, O. (2003). Ethnic Enclaves and the Economic Success of Immigrants. Evidence from a Natural Experiment, in: The Quarterly Journal of Economics, 118(1): 329–357.

Epstein, G. S. (2010). Informational Cascades and Decision to Migrate, in: Epstein, G. S., Gang, I. N. (eds.), Migration and Culture, Bingley, UK: Emerald Publishing, 25–44.

Ethier, W. J. (1985). International Trade and Labor Migration, in: The American Economic Review, 75(4): 691–707.

Etziony, A., Weiss, A. (2002). Coordination and Critical Mass in a Network Market: An Experimental Evaluation, Bar-Ilan University Department of Economics Working Paper No 2002–05.

Evans, M. D. R. (1986). Sources of Immigrants' Language Proficiency. Australian Results with Comparisons to the Federal Republic of Germany and the United States of America, in: European Sociological Review, 2(3): 226–236.

Evans, W. N., Oates, W. E., Schwab, R. M. (1992). Measuring Peer Group Effects: A Study of Teenage Behavior, in: Journal of Political Economy, 100(5): 966–991.

Farley, R. (1990). Blacks, Hispanics, and White Ethnic Groups: Are Blacks Uniquely Disadvantaged?, in: The American Economic Review, 80(2): 237–241.

Featherman, D. C. (1978). Nativity. Heritage and Achievement, in: Featherman, D. C., Hauser, R. M. (eds.), Opportunity and Change, New York: Academic Press, 429–479.

Ferrie, J. P. (2010). A Historical Perspective on High-Skilled Immigrants to the United States, 1820–1920, in: Chiswick, B. R. (ed.), High-Skilled Immigration in a Global Labor Market, Washington DC: American Enterprise Institute Press, 15–49.

Filer, R. K. (1992). The Effect of Immigrant Arrivals on Migratory Patterns of Native Workers, in: Borjas, G. J., Freeman, R. B. (eds.), Immigration and the Workforce: Economic Consequences for the United States and Source Areas, Chicago, IL: University of Chicago Press, 245–270.

Finifter, A. W. (1976). American Emigration, in: Society, 13(5): 30–36.

References

Fitzpatrick, G. L., Modlin, M. J. (1986). Direct-Line Distances: United States Edition, Metuchen, NJ: The Scarecrow Press.

Fitzpatrick, J. P. (1971). Puerto Rican Americans: The Meaning of Migration to the Mainland, Englewood Cliffs, NJ: Prentice-Hall.

Fleisher, B. M. (1977). Mother's Home Time and the Production of Child Quality, in: Demography, 14(2): 197–212.

Frey, W. H. (1994). The New White Flight, in: American Demographics, 16: 40–48.

Frey, W. H. (1995). Immigration and Internal Migration "Flight" from U.S. Metro Areas: Toward a New Demographic Balkanization, in: Urban Studies, 32(4–5): 733–757.

Frey, W. H., Liaw, K.-L., Xie, Y., Carlson, M. J. (1996). Interstate Migration of the U.S. Poverty Population: Immigration "Pushes" and White Magnet "Pulls", in: Population and Environment, 17(6): 491–533.

Friedberg, R. M. (2001). The Impact of Mass Migration on the Israeli Labor Market, in: The Quarterly Journal of Economics, 116(4): 1373–1408.

Friedberg, R. M., Hunt, J. (1995). The Impact of Immigration on Host Country Wages, Employment and Growth, in: The Journal of Economic Perspectives, 9(2): 23–44.

Fröhlich, B. (1997). SOPEMI Report for Germany, in: Trends in International Migration, Annual Report 1997, Paris: OECD.

Fuchs, V. R. (1968). The Service Economy, New York: National Bureau of Economic Research.

Fuchs, V. R. (1982a). Self-Employment and Labor Force Participation of Older Males, in: Journal of Human Resources, 17(3): 339–357.

Fuchs, V. R. (1982b). Time Preference and Health: An Exploratory Study, in: Fuchs, V. R. (ed.), Economic Aspects of Health, Chicago, IL: University of Chicago Press, 93–120.

Funkhouser, E. (2000). Changes in the Geographic Concentration and Location of Residence of Immigrants, in: International Migration Review, 34(2): 489–510.

Funkhouser, E., Trejo, S. J. (1995). The Labor Market Skills of Recent Male Immigrants: Evidence from the Current Population Survey, in: Industrial and Labor Relations Review, 48(4): 792–811.

Gabriel, P. E., Schmitz, S. (1995). Favorable Self-Selection and the Internal Migration of Young White Males in the United States, in: Journal of Human Resources, 30(3): 460–471.

Glazer, N., Moynihan, D. P. (1963), Beyond the Melting Pot: The Negroes, Puerto Ricans, Jews, Italians, and Irish of New York City, Cambridge, MA: MIT Press.

Goldberger, A. S. (1989). Economic and Mechanical Models of Intergenerational Transmission, in: American Economic Review, 79(3): 504–513.

Goldfarb, R. (1982). Occupational Preferences in the U.S. Immigration Law: An Economic Analysis, in: Chiswick, B. R. (ed.), The Gateway: U.S. Immigration Issues and Policies, Washington, DC: American Enterprise Institute, 412–448.

Goldscheider, C. (1967). Fertility of the Jews, in: Demography, 4(1): 196–209.

Gordon, M. (1964). Assimilation and American Life, New York: Oxford University Press.

Gould, J. P. (1968). Adjustment Costs and the Theory of Investment of the Firm, in: The Review of Economic Studies, 35(1): 47–55.

Greeley, A. (1976). Ethnicity, Denomination and Inequality, Beverly Hills, CA: Sage.

Greenwood, M. (1993). Internal Migration in Developed Countries, in: Rosenzweig, M. R., Stark, O. (eds.), Handbook of Population and Family Economics, Vol 1B, Amsterdam: Elsevier, 647–720.

Grenier, G. (1984). The Effects of Language Characteristics on the Wages of Hispanic-American Males, in: The Journal of Human Resources, 19(1): 35–52.

Grenier, G., and Vaillancourt, F. (1983). An Economic Perspective on Learning a Second Language, in: Journal of Multicultural and Multilingual Development, 4(6): 471–483.

Grimes, J. E., Grimes, B. F. (1993). Ethnologue: Languages of the World, 13th edition, Dallas, TX: Summer Institute of Linguistics.

Gronau, R. (1976). The Allocation of Time of Israeli Women, in: Journal of Political Economy, 84(4): S201-S220.

Grossman, J. B. (1982). The Substitutability of Natives and Immigrants in Production, in: The Review of Economics and Statistics, 54(4): 596–603

References

Gurak, D. T., Kritz, M. M. (2000). The Interstate Migration of U.S. Immigrants: Individual and Contextual Determinants, in: Social Forces, 78(3): 1017–1039.

Hagen, E. E. (1958). An Economic Justification of Protectionism, in: The Quarterly Journal of Economics, 72(4): 496–514.

Hamermesh, D. S. (1993). Labor Demand, Princeton, NJ: Princeton University Press.

Hanoch, G. (1961). Income Differentials in Israel, in: Fifth Report, 1959 and 1960, Jerusalem: Falk Project for Economic Research in Israel.

Hansen, M. L. (1940a). The Immigrant in American History, Cambridge, MA: Harvard University Press, 1940.

Hansen, M. L. (1940b). The Mingling of the Canadian and American Peoples, New Haven, CT: Yale University Press.

Hart-Gonzalez, L., Lindermann, S. (1993). Expected Achievement in Speaking Proficiency, U.S. Department of State, mimeo.

Hartog, J. (2000). Over-Education and Earnings: Where Are We, Where Should We Go?, in: Economics of Education Review, 19(2): 131–147.

Harwood, E. (1983). Can Immigration Laws Be Enforced?, in: Public Interest: 108–23.

Hauser, R. M., Sewell, W. H., Lutterman, K. G. (1975). Socioeconomic Background, Ability, and Achievement, in: Sewell, W. H., Hauser, R. M. (eds.), Education, Occupation, and Earnings: Achievment in the Early Career, New York: Academic Press, 43–88.

Hausman, J. A., Taylor, W. E. (1981). Panel Data and Unobservable Individual Effects, in: Econometrica, 49(6): 1377–1398.

Heckman, J. J. (1979). Sample Selection Bias as a Specification Error, in: Econometrica, 47(1): 153–161.

Heckman, J. J., Robb, R. (1983). Using Longitudinal Data to Estimate Age, Period, and Cohort Effects in Earnings Equations, in: Winsborough, H., Duncan, O. (eds.), Analyzing Longitudinal Data for Age, Period, and Cohort Effects, New York: Academic Press, 137–150.

Heckman, J. J., Sedlacek, G. (1985). Heterogeneity, Aggregation, and Market Wage Functions: An Empirical Model of Self-Selection in the Labor Market, in: Journal of Political Economy, 93(6): 1077–1125.

Helpman, E., Krugman, P. R. (1985). Market Structure and Foreign Trade, Cambridge, MA: MIT Press.

Herzog, H. W., Schlottmann, A. M. (1983). Migrant Information, Job Search and the Remigration Decision, in: Southern Economic Journal, 50(1): 43–51.

Higgs, R. (1971). Race, Skills and Earnings: American Immigrants in 1909, in The Journal of Economic History, 31(2): 420–428.

Hill, C. R., Stafford, F. P. (1974). Allocation of Time to Preschool Children and Educational Opportunity, in: The Journal of Human Resources, 9(3): 323–343.

Hill, C. R., Stafford, F. P. (1980). Parental Care of Children: Time Diary Estimates of Quantity, Predictability and Variety, in: The Journal of Human Resources, 15(2): 220–239.

Hirshleifer, J. (1958). On the Theory of Optimal Investment Decisions, in: Journal of Political Economy, 66(4): 329–352.

Holzer, H. J. (1988). Search Method Use by Unemployed Youth, in: Journal of Labor Economics, 6(1): 1–20.

Hovne, A. (1961). The Labor Force in Israel, Jerusalem: Falk Project for Economic Research in Israel.

Huddle, D. (1993). The Net National Costs of Immigration: Fiscal Effects of Welfare Restorations to Legal Immigrants, Washington, DC.

Hughes, M. A., Madden, J. F. (1991). Residential Segregation and the Economic Status of Black Workers: New Evidence for an Old Debate, in: Journal of Urban Economics, 29(1): 28–49.

Humphrey, L. G. (1978). To Understand Regression from Parent to Offspring. Think Statistically, in: Psychological Bulletin, 85(6): 1317–1322.

Hunt, J. C., Kiker, B. F. (1981). The Effect of Fertility on the Time Use of Working Wives, in: Journal of Consumer Research, 7(4): 380–387.

Iannaccone, L. R. (1988). A Formal Model of Church and State, in: American Journal of Sociology, 94: S241-S268.

References

Islam, M. N., Choudhury, S. A. (1990). Self-Selection and Interprovincial Migration in Canada, in: Regional Science and Urban Economics, 20(4): 459–472.

Jaeger, D. A. (1996). Skill Differences and the Effect of Immigrants on the Wages of Natives, U.S. Bureau of Labor Statistics Working Paper No. 273.

Jaeger, D. A. (1997). Reconciling the Old and New Census Bureau Education Questions: Recommendations for Researchers, in: Journal of Business & Economic Statistics, 15(3): 300–309.

James, J. A., Skinner, J. S. (1985). The Resolution of the Labor-Scarcity Paradox, in: The Journal of Economic History, 45(3): 513–540.

Jasso, G., Rosensweig, M. R. (1982). Estimating the Emigration Rates of Legal Immigrants Using Administrative and Survey Data: The 1971 Cohort of Immigrants to the United States, in: Demography, 19(3): 279–290.

Jasso, G., Rosenzweig, M. R. (1986). Family Reunification and the Immigration Multiplier: U.S. Immigration Law, Origin-Country Conditions, and the Reproduction of Immigrants, in: Demography, 23(3): 291–311.

Jasso, G., Rosenzweig, M. R. (1988). How Well Do US Immigrants Do? Vintage Effects, Emigration Selectivity, and Occupational Mobility of Immigrants, in: Schultz, P. T. (ed.), Reasearch of Population Economics 6, A Research Annual, Greenwich, CT: JAI Press, 229–253.

Jasso, G., Rosenzweig, M. R. (1990). Self-Selection and the Earnings of Immigrants: Comment, in: The American Economic Review, 80(1): 298–304.

Jencks, C., Meyer, S. E. (1990). The Social Consequences of Growing Up in a Poor Neighborhood: A Review, in: Lynn, L. E., McGeary, M. G. H. (eds.), Inner City Poverty in the United States, Washington, DC: National Academy Press, 111–186.

Johnson, G. (1998). The Impact of Immigration on Income Distribution among Minorities, in: Hamermesh, D. S., Bean, F. D. (eds.), Help or Hindrance? The Economic Implications of Immigration for African Americans, New York: Russell Sage Foundation, 17–50.

Johnson, G., Solon, G. (1986). Estimates of the Direct Effects of Comparable Worth Policy, in: The American Economic Review, 76(5): 1117–1125.

Johnson, N. E. (1980). A Response to Rindfuss, in: American Journal of Sociology, 86(2): 375–377.

Johnson, N. E., Nishida, R. (1980). Minority-Group Status and Fertility: A Study of Japanese and Chinese in Hawaii and California, in: American Journal of Sociology, 86(3): 496–511.

Juhn, C., Murphy, K. M., Topel, R. H. (1991). Why Has the Natural Rate of Unemployment Increased over Time?, in: Brookings Papers on Economic Activity, 22(2): 75–126.

Kahan, A. (1978). Economic Opportunities and Some Pilgrim's Progress: Jewish Immigrants from Eastern Europe in the U.S., 1890–1914, in: The Journal of Economic History, 38(1): 235–251.

Karoly, L. A., Klerman, J. A. (1994). Using Regional Data to Reexamine the Contribution of Demographic and Sectoral Changes to Increasing U.S. Wage Inequality, in: Bergstrand, J. H., Cosimano, T. F., Houck, J. W., Sheehan, R. G. (eds.), The Changing Distribution of Income in an Open U.S. Economy, edited by Jeffrey H. Bergstrand and others. Amsterdam: North-Holland, 183–216.

Katz, E., Stark, O. (1984). Migration and Asymmetric Information: Comment, in: The American Economic Review, 74(3): 533–534.

Katz, E., Stark, O. (1987). International Migration under Asymmetric Information, in: The Economic Journal, 97(387): 718–726.

Katz, L. F., Murphy, K. M. (1992). Changes in the Wage Structure, 1963–1987: Supply and Demand Factors, in: The Quarterly Journal of Economics, 107(1): 35–78.

Katz, M. L., Shapiro, C. (1985). Network Externalities, Competition and Compatibility, in: The American Economic Review, 75(3): 424–440.

Kee, P.-K. (1990). The Language Dimensions. Issues in Multicultural Australia, Canberra: Office of Multicultural Affairs, Department of Prime Minister and Cabinet.

Khan, A. H. (1997). Post-Migration Investments in Education by Immigrants in the United States, in: The Quarterly Review of Economics and Finance, 37(1): 285–313.

References

Kish, L. (1965). Survey Sampling, New York: Wiley.

Kobin, F. E. (1983). National Data on American Jewry, 1970–71: A Comparative Evaluation of the Census Yiddish Mother Tongue Subpopulation and the National Jewish Population Survey, in: Papers in Jewish Demography, 1981: 129–143.

Kossoudji, S. A. (1988). English Language Ability and the Labor Market Opportunities of Hispanic and East-Asian Immigrant Men, in: Journal of Labor Economics, 6(2): 205–228.

Kossoudji, S. A., Cobb-Clark, D. A. (2002). Coming Out of the Shadows: Learning About Legal Status and Wages from the Legalized Population, in: Journal of Labor Economics, 20(3): 598–628.

Kossoudji, S. A., Ranney, S. I. (1986). Wage Rates of Temporary Mexican Migrants to the U.S.: The Role of Legal Status, University of Michigan Population Studies Center Discussion Paper.

Krein, S. F. (1986). Growing Up in a Single Parent Family: The Effect on the Education and Earnings of Young Men, in: Family Relations, 35(1): 161–168.

Kritz, M. M., Gurak, D. T. (2001). The Impact of Immigration on the Internal Migration of Natives and Immigrants, in: Demography, 38(1): 133–145.

Kritz, M. M., Nogle, J. M. (1994). Nativity Concentration and Internal Migration among the Foreign-Born, in: Demography, 31(3): 509–524.

Kruger, J., Dunning, D. (1999). Unskilled and Unaware of it: How Difficulties in Recognizing One's Own Competence Lead to Inflated Self-Assessments, in: Journal of Personality and Social Psychology, 77(6): 1121–1134.

Kwok, V., Leland, H. (1982). An Economic Model of the Brain Drain, in: American Economic Review, 72(1): 91–100.

Ladinsky, J. (1967). The Geographic Mobility of Professional and Technical Manpower, in: The Journal of Human Resources, 2(4): 475–494.

LaLonde, R. J., Topel, R. H. (1991). Labor Market Adjustments to Increased Immigration, in: Abowd, J. M., Freeman, R. B. (eds.), Immigration, Trade, and the Labor Market, Chicago, IL: University of Chicago Press, 167–199.

LaLonde, R. J., Topel, R. H. (1992). The Assimilation of Immigrants in the U.S. Labor Market, in: Borjas, G. J., Freeman, R. B. (eds.), Immigration and the Work Force: Economic Consequences for the United States and Source Areas, Chicago, IL: University of Chicago Press, 67–92.

LaLonde, R. J., Topel, R. H. (1993). Economic Impact of International Migration and the Economic Performance of Migrants: Rosenzweig, M. R., Stark, O. (eds.), Handbook of Population and Family Economics, Vol 1B, Amsterdam: North-Holland, 799–850.

Lapan, H. E. (1976). International Trade, Factor Market Distortions, and the Optimal Dynamic Subsidy, in: The American Economic Review, 66(3): 335–346.

Lazear, E. (1977). Schooling as a Wage Depressant, in: The Journal of Human Resources, 12(2): 164–176.

Lazear, E. P. (1999). Culture and Language, in: Journal of Political Economics, 107(6): S95-S126.

Lazear, E., Moore, J. (1984). Incentives, Productivity, and Labor Contracts, in: The Quarterly Journal of Economics, 99(2): 275–296.

Lehrer, E., Nerlove, M. (1981). The Impact of Female Work on Family Income Distribution in the United States: Black-White Differentials, in: Review of Income and Wealth, 27(4): 423–431.

Leibowitz, A. (1974a). Education and Home Production, in: The American Economic Review, 64(2): 243–250.

Leibowitz, A. (1974b). Home Investments in Children, in: Journal of Political Economy, 82(2): S111-S131.

Lesky, L. G. (2010). Physician Migration to the United States and Canada: Criteria for Admission, in: Chiswick, B. R. (ed.), High-Skilled Immigration in a Global Labor Market, Washington DC: American Enterprise Institute Press, 155–164.

Lieberson, S., Waters, M. C. (1988). From Many Strands: Ethnic and Racial Groups in Contemporary America, New York: Russell Sage.

Lindner, D. J. (1989). The Determinants of Emigration and Earnings: Evidence from Canadian and U.S. Data, Dissertation, University of Wisconsin-Madison.

References

Lindstrom, D., Massey, D. (1994). Selective Emigration, Cohort Quality and Models of Immigrant Assimilation, in: Social Science Research, 23(4): 315-349.

Long, J. E. (1980). The Effect of Americanization on Earnings: Some Evidence for Women, in: Journal of Political Economy, 88(3): 620-629.

Long, L. H. (1974). Poverty Status and Receipt of Welfare among Migrants and Nonmigrants in Larger Cities, in: American Sociological Review, 39(1): 46-56.

Long, L. H., Hansen, K. A. (1977). Selectivity of Black Return Migration to the South, in: Rural Sociology, 42(3): 317-331.

Long, L. H., Heitman, L. R. (1975). Migration and Income Differences between Black and White Men in the North, in: American Journal of Sociology, 80(6): 1391-1409.

Lopez, D. E., Sabagh, G. (1980). Reply to Marcum, in: American Journal of Sociology, 86(2): 382-385.

Loury, G. C. (1977). A Dynamic Theory of Racial Income Differences, in: Wallace, P. A., LaMond, A. A. (eds.), Women, Minorities, and Employment Discrimination, Lexington, MA: Lexington Books, 153-186.

Lubotsky, D. (2007). Chutes or Ladders: A Longitudinal Analysis of Immigrant Earnings, in: Journal of Political Economy, 115(5): 820-67.

Lucas, R. E. (1988). On the Mechanics of Economic Development, in: Journal of Monetary Economics, 22(1): 3-42.

Lundberg, S., Startz, R. (1998). On the Persistence of Racial Inequality, in: Journal of Labor Economics, 16(2): 292-323.

Magee, S. P. (1972). The Welfare Effects of Restrictions on U.S. Trade, in: Brookings Papers on Economic Activity, 3(3): 645-708.

Magee, S. P. (1973). Factor Market Distortions, Production, and Trade: A Survey, in: Oxford Economic Papers, 25(1): 1-43.

Manski, C. F. (1993). Identification of Endogenous Social Effects: The Reflection Problem, in: The Review of Economic Studies, 60(3): 531-542.

Marcum, J. P. (1980). Comment on "Untangling Structural and Normative Aspects of the Minority Status-Fertility Hypothesis" by Lopez and Sabagh, in: American Journal of Sociology, 86(2): 377-381.

Mare, R. D., Winship, C. (1988). Ethnic and Racial Patterns of Educational Attainment and School Enrollment, in: Sandefur, G., Tienda, M. (eds.), Divided Opportunities: Minorities, Poverty, and Social Policy, New York: Plenum Press, 173-203.

Martin, W. T., Poston. D. L. Jr. (1977). Differentials in the Ability to Convert Education into Income: The Case of the European Ethnics, in: International Migration Review, 11(2): 215-231.

Massey, D. S. (1987) Do Undocumented Migrants Earn Lower Wages than Legal Immigrants? New Evidence from Mexico, in: International Migration Review, 21(2): 236-274.

Massey, D. S., Denton, N. A. (1989). Hypersegregation in U.S. Metropolitan Areas: Black and Hispanic Segregation Along Five Dimensions, in: Demography, 26(3): 373-391.

Masters, S. H. (1972). Are Black Migrants from the South to the Northern Cities Worse off Than Blacks Already There?, in: The Journal of Human Resources, 7(4): 411-423.

McDonald, J. T., Warman, C., Worswick, C. (2010). Earnings, Occupations, and Schooling Decisions of Immigrants with Medical Degrees: Evidence for Canada and the United States, in: Chiswick, B. R. (ed.), High-Skilled Immigration in a Global Labor Market, Washington DC: American Enterprise Institute Press, 165-198.

McDonald, J. T., Worswick, C. (1998). The Earnings of Immigrant Men in Canada: Job Tenure, Cohort, and Macroeconomic Conditions, in: Industrial and Labor Relations Review, 51(3): 465-482.

McKinney, S., Schnare, A. B. (1989). Trends in Residential Segregation by Race: 1960-1980, in: Journal of Urban Economics, 26(3): 269-280.

McManus, W., Gould, W., Welch, F. (1983). Earnings of Hispanic Men: The Role of English Language Proficiency, in: Journal of Labor Economics, 1(2): 101-130.

Michael, R. T., Tuma, N. B. (1985). Entry into Marriage and Parenthood by Young Men and Women: The Influence of Family Background, in: Demography, 22(4): 515-544.

Mincer, J. (1974). Schooling, Experience, and Earnings, New York: Columbia University Press.

References

Mincer, J. (1978). Family Migration Decisions, in: Journal of Political Economy, 86(5): 749–773.

Murphy, K. M., Welch, F. (1992). The Structure of Wages, in: The Quarterly Journal of Economics, 107(1): 285–326.

Mussa, M. (1986). The Adjustment Process and the Timing of Trade Liberalization, in: Choksi, A. M., Papageorgiou, D. (eds.), Economic Liberalization in Developing Countries, Oxford, UK: Basil Blackwell.

Nakamura, J. I., Miyamoto, M. (1982). Social Structure and Population Change: A Comparative Study of Tokugawa Japan and Ch'ing China, in: Economic Development and Cultural Change, 30(2): 229–269.

Newport, F. (1979). The Religious Switcher in the United States, in: American Sociological Review, 44(4): 528–552.

North, D. (1979). Seven Years Later: The Experiences of the 1970 Cohort of Immigrants in the United States, R&D Monograph no. 71, Washington, DC: US Department of Labor.

North, D., Wagner, J. R. (1980). Enforcing the Immigration Law: A Review of the Options, Washington, DC: New TransCentury Foundation.

North, D. S., Houstoun, M. F. (1976). The Characteristics and Role of Illegal Aliens in the U.S. Labor Market: An Exploratory Study, Washington, DC: Linton and Co.

O'Neill, J. (1970). The Effect of Income and Education on Inter-Regional Migration, Dissertation, Columbia University.

Park, R. (1950). Race and Culture, Glencoe, IL: Free Press.

Passel, J. S., Clark, R. L. (1994). How Much Do Immigrants Really Cost? A Reappraisal of Huddle's "The Costs of Immigration", Washington, DC.

Pedersen, P. J., Roed, M., Wadensjo, E. (2008). The Common Nordic Labour Market at 50, Copenhagen: Nordic Council of Ministers.

Penalosa, F. (1969). Education-Income Disparities between Second Generation and Later Generation Mexican-Americans in the Southwest, in: Sociology and Social Research, 43: 448–454.

Perlmann, J. (1988). Ethnic Differences: Schooling and Social Structure Among the Irish, Italians, Jews, and Blacks in an American City, 1880–1935, New York: Cambridge University Press.

Piore, M. (1979). Birds of Passage: Migrant Labor and Industrial Societies, New York: Cambridge University Press.

Pischke, J.-S., Velling, J. (1997). Employment Effects of Immigration to Germany: An Analysis Based on Local Labor Markets, in: Review of Economics and Statistics, 79(4): 594–604.

Portes, A. (1982). Immigrants Attainment: An Analysis of Occupation and Earnings among Cuban Exiles in the United States, in: Hauser, R. M., Mechanic, F., Haller, A. O, Hauser, T. S. (eds.), Social Structure and Behavior: Essays in Honor of William Hamilton Sewell, New York: Academic Press, 91–111.

Portes, A., Bach, R. L. (1980). Immigrant Earnings: Cuban and Mexican Immigrants in the United States, in: International Migration Review, 14(3): 315–340.

Preston, S. H. (1976). Family Sizes of Children and Family Sizes of Women, in: Demography, 13(1): 105–114.

Ramos, F. A. (1992). Out-Migration and Return Migration of Puerto Ricans, in: Borjas, G. J., Freeman, R. B. (eds.), Immigration and the Work Force: Economic Consequences for the United States and Source Areas, Chicago, IL: University of Chicago Press, 49–66.

Rauch, J. E. (1993). Productivity Gains from Geographic Concentration of Human Capital: Evidence from the Cities, in: Journal of Urban Economics, 34(3): 380–400.

Reimers, C. (1982). Why Some Immigrants Earn More Than Others, Princeton, NJ: Princeton University.

Reimers, C. (1985). A Comparative Analysis of the Wages of Hispanics, Blacks and Non-Hispanic Whites, in: Borjas, G. J., Tienda, M. (eds.), Hispanics in the U.S. Economy, New York: Academic Press, 27–75.

Reimers, C. R. (1983). Labor Market Discrimination against Hispanic and Black Men, in:

References

The Review of Economics and Statistics, 65(4): 570–579.

Remennick, L. (2002). Survival of the Fittest: Russian Immigrant Teachers in Israeli Schools, in: International Migration, 40(1): 99–121.

Rutherford, R. D., Sewell, W. H. (1988). Intelligence and Family Size Reconsidered, in: Social Biology, 35(1–2): 1–40.

Rindfuss, R. R. (1980). Minority Status and Fertility Revisited-Again: A Comment on Johnson, in: American Journal of Sociology, 86(2): 372–375.

Rindfuss, R. R., Sweet, J. A. (1977). Postwar Fertility Trends and Differentials in the United States, New York: Academic Press.

Rivera-Batiz, F. (1996). English Language Proficiency, Quantitative Skills, and the Conomic Progress of Immigrants, in: Duleep, H. O., Wunnava, P. V. (eds.), Immigrants and Immigration Policy: Individual Skills, Family Ties, and Group Identities, Greenwich, CT: JAI Press, 57–77.

Rivera-Batiz, F. L. (1999). Undocumented Workers in the Labor Market: An Analysis of the Earnings of Legal and Illegal Mexican Immigrants in the United States, in: Journal of Population Economics, 12(1): 91–116.

Roback, J. (1982). Wages, Rents, and the Quality of Life, in: Journal of Political Economy, 90(6): 1257–1278.

Robinson, C., Tomes, N. (1982). Self-Selection and Interprovincial Migration in Canada, in: The Canadian Journal of Economics, 15(3): 474–502.

Rogers, R. (1984). Return Migration in Comparative Perspective, in: Kubat, D. (ed.), The Politics of Return. International Return Migration in Europe. Proceedings of the First European Conference on International Return Migration, Rome and New York: Center for Migration Studies, 277–299.

Romer, P. M. (1986). Increasing Returns and Long-Run Growth, in: Journal of Political Economy, 94(5): 1002–1037.

Ross, S. (2003). Segregation and Racial Preferences: New Theoretical and Empirical Approaches, University of Conneticut Department of Economics Working Paper No. 200204.

Rowthorn, R., Glyn, A. (2006). Convergence and Stability in U.S. Regional Employment, in: The B.E. Journal of Macroeconomics, 6(1): 1–43.

Roy, A. D. (1951). Some Thoughts in the Distribution of Earnings, in: Oxford Economic Papers, 3(2): 135–146.

Rubb, S. (2003). Post-College Schooling, Overeducation, and Hourly Earnings in the United States, in: Education Economics, 11(1): 53–72.

Rumberger, R. W. (1987). The Impact of Surplus Schooling on Productivity and Earnings, in: The Journal of Human Resources, 22(1): 24–50.

Samuelson, P. A. (1964). Economics, 6th edition, New York: McGraw-Hill.

Schoeni, R. F. (1997). The Effect of Immigrants on the Employment and Wages of Native Workers: Evidence from the 1970s and 1980s, RAND Corporation.

Schultz, T. P. (1984). The Schooling and Health of Children of U.S. Immigrants and Natives, in: Research in Population Economics, 5: 251–288.

Schultz, T. W. (1975). The Value of the Ability to Deal with Disequilibrium, in: Journal of Economic Literature, 13(3): 827–846.

Schwartz, A. (1973). Interpreting the Effect of Distance on Migration, in: Journal of Political Economy, 81(5): 1153–1169.

Schwartz, A. (1976). Migration, Age, and Education, in: Journal of Political Economy, 84(4): 701–720.

Shumway, J. M., Hall, G. (1996). Self-Selection, Earnings and Chicano Migration: Differences between Return and Onward Migrants, in: International Migration Review, 30(4): 979–994.

Siegel, P. S. (1971). Prestige in the American Occupational Structure, Dissertation, University of Chicago.

Sierminska, E. (2002). Immigrants and State Clustering: The Effect of Welfare Benefits, Johns Hopkins University Department of Economics, mimeo.

Sjaastad, L. A. (1962). The Costs and Returns of Human Migration, in: Journal of Political Economy, 70(5): 80–93.

References

Smith, J. P., Edmonston, B. (eds.) (1997), The New Americans: Economy, Demographic, and Fiscal Effects of Immigration, Washington, DC: National Academy Press.

Smith, J. P., Welch, F. R. (1986). Closing the Gap: Forty Years of Economic Progress for Blacks, Santa Monica, CA: Rand Corporation.

Smith, J. P., Welch, F. R. (1989). Black Economic Progress After Myrdal, in: Journal of Economic Literature, 27(2): 519–564.

Smith, S. P. (1976). Government Wage Differentials by Sex, in: The Journal of Human Resources, 11(2): 185–199.

Snipp, C. M., Tienda, M. (1984). Chicano Occupational Mobility, in: Social Science Quarterly, 65(2): 364–380.

Solon, G. (1989). Biases in the Estimation of Intergenerational Earnings Correlations, in: The Review of Economics and Statistics, 71(1): 172–174.

Solon, G. R. (1992). Intergenerational Income Mobility in the United States, in: The American Economic Review, 82(3): 393–408.

Sowell, T. (1981). Ethnic America, New York: Basic Books.

Stafford, F. P. (1985). Cognitive Skills of Gradeschoolers: Does Parental Care Really Matter?, University of Michigan, mimeo.

Stein, B. N. (1979). Occupational Adjustment of Refugees: The Vietnamese in the United States, in: International Migration Review, 13(1): 25–45.

Steinberg, S., (1989). The Ethnic Myth: Race, Ethnicity, and Class in America, Boston, MA: Beacon Press.

Storesletten, K. (2000). Sustaining Fiscal Policy through Immigration, in: Journal of Political Economy, 108(2): 300–323.

Sullivan, T. A., Pedraza-Bailey, S. (1980). Differential Success among Cuban-American and Mexican-American Immigrants: The Role of Policy and Community. Report submitted to the Employment and Training Administration, U.S. Department of Labor.

Suro, R. (1998). Strangers among Us: How Latino Immigration Is Transforming America, New York: Alfred A. Knopf.

Svorny, S. (1991). Consumer Gains from Physician Immigration to the U.S.: 1966–1971, in: Applied Economics, 23(2): 331–337.

Sweet, J. A. (1973). Women in the Labor Force, New York: Seminar Press.

Tainer, E. (1988). English Language Proficiency and the Determination of Earnings among Foreign-Born Men, in: The Journal of Human Resources, 23(1): 108–122.

Tandon, B. B. (1977). An Empirical Analysis of the Earnings of Foreign-Born and Native-Born Canadians, Dissertation, Queen's University.

Tandon, B. B. (1978). Earnings Differentials among Native Born and Foreign Born Residents of Canada, in: International Migration Review, 12(3): 406–410.

Thernstrom, S. (1973). The Other Bostonians: Poverty and Progress in the American Metropolis, 1880–1970, Cambridge, MA: Harvard University Press.

Tidwick, K. (1971). Need for Achievement, Social Class and Intention to Emigrate in Jamaican Students, in: Social and Economic Studies, 20(1): 52–60.

Tobin, J. (1972). Inflation and Unemployment, in: The American Economic Review, 62(1): 1–18.

Tomes, N. (1983). Religion and the Rate of Return on Human Capital: Evidence from Canada, in: The Canadian Journal of Economics, 16(1): 122–138.

Tomes, N. (1988). Inheritance and Inequality Within the Family: Equal Division Among Unequals, or Do the Poor Get More?, in: Kessler, D., Masson, A. (eds.), Modelling the Accumulation and Distribution of Wealth, Oxford: Clarendon Press, 79–104.

Topel, R. H. (1986). Local Labor Markets, in: Journal of Political Economy, 94(3): S111–S143.

Topel, R. H. (1994). Regional Trends in Wage Inequality, in: The American Economic Review, 84(2): 17–22.

U.S. Arms Control and Disarmament Agency (1975). World Military Expenditures and Arms Trade, 1963–1973, Washington, DC: U.S. Government Printing Office.

U.S. Arms Control and Disarmament Agency (1984). World Military Expenditures and Arms Transfers, 1972–1982, Washington, DC: U.S. Government Printing Office.

U. S. Bureau of the Census (1933). Fifteenth Census of the United States: 1930, Popula-

References

tion, Special Report, Foreign-Born White Families by Country of Birth of Head with an Appendix Giving Statistics for Mexican, Indian, Chinese, and Japanese Families, Washington, DC: U.S. Government Printing Office.

U. S. Bureau of the Census (1943a). Sixteenth Census of the United States, Population, Characteristics of the Non-White Population by Race, Washington, DC: U.S. Government Printing Office.

U. S. Bureau of the Census (1943b), Sixteenth Census of the United States: 1940, Population, Parentage and Nativity, General Characteristics, Washington, DC: U.S. Government Printing Office, 1943b.

U. S. Bureau of the Census (1958a). Religion Reported by the Civilian Population of the United States: March 1957, Current Population Reports-Population Characteristics, Series P. 20, No. 79, February 2.

U. S. Bureau of the Census (1958b). Statistical Abstract of the United States: 1958, Washington, DC: U.S. Government Printing Office.

U.S. Bureau of the Census (1960). Historical Statistics of the United States. Colonial Times to 1957, Washington, DC.

U. S. Bureau of the Census (1968). Tabulations of Data on the Social and Economic Characteristics of the Major Religious Groups, March 1957, Washington, DC: U.S. Government Printing Office.

U.S. Bureau of the Census (1972). 1970 Census of Population. 1/1,000 Sample, 5 Percent Questionnaire. Data tape.

U.S. Bureau of the Census (1973a). 1970 Census of Population, Subject Report, Age at First Marriage, Washington, DC: U.S. Government Printing Office.

U.S. Bureau of the Census (1973b). 1970 Census of Population. Subject Reports, National Origin and Language. Report no. PC(2)-1A, Washington: Government Printing Office.

U.S. Bureau of the Census (1973c). Population and Housing Inquiries in U.S. Decennial Census, 1790–1970, Washington, DC: U.S. Government Printing Office.

U.S. Bureau of the Census (1973d). Supplement No. 1 to Public Use Samples of Basic Records from the 1970 Census: Description and Technical Documentation, Washington, DC: U.S. Government Printing Office.

U.S. Bureau of the Census (various issues). Statistical Abstract of the United States, Washington, DC: U.S. Government Printing Office.

U.S. Census Bureau (2005). Public Use Microdata Sample: 5 Percent Sample of the Population, in: 2000 US Census of Population and Housing, Washington, DC.

U.S. Department of Homeland Security (2006). 2004 Yearbook of Immigration Statistics, Washington, DC.

U.S. Department of Homeland Security (2008). 2007 Yearbook of Immigration Statistics, Washington, DC.

U.S. Department of Labor. Bureau of Labor Statistics (1999). Current Population Survey, Washington, DC.

U.S. Department of State (2000). U.S. Refugee Admissions and Resettlement Program., Washington: U.S. Department of State, Bureau of Population, Refugees and Migration.

U.S. Immigration and Naturalization Service (1965). Annual Report of the Immigration and Naturalization Service, Washington, DC: U.S. Government Printing Office.

United Nations (1977). Compendium of Social Statistics, New York: UN.

Vahey, S. P. (2000). The Great Canadian Training Robbery: Evidence on the Returns to·Educational Mismatch, in: Economics of Education Review, 19(2): 219–227.

Vanderkamp, J. (1972). Return Migration: Its Significance and Behavior, in: Economic Inquiry, 10(1): 460–465.

Veltman, C. (1983). Language Shift in the United States, Berlin: Mouton Publishers.

Veltman, C. (1988). Modelling the Language Shift Process of Hispanic Immigrants, in: International Migration Review, 22(4): 545–562.

Verdugo, R. R., Verdugo, N. T. (1989). The Impact of Surplus Schooling on Earnings: Some Additional Findings, in: The Journal of Human Resources, 26(4): 629–643.

Viscusi, W. K., Moore, M. J. (1989). Rates of Time Preference and Valuation of the Duration of Life, in: Journal of Public Economics, 38(2): 297–317.

References

Vroman, W. (1977). Changes in Cohort Educational Attainment-Exploring Alternative Explanations, University of Maryland, mimeo.

Walker, R., Ellis, M., Barff, R. (1992). Linked Migration Systems: Immigration and Internal Labor Flows in the United States, in: Economic Geography, 68(3): 234-338.

Warren, R. (1979). Alien Emigration from the United States: 1961 to 1974, Paper Presented at Annual Meeting. Population Association of America, Philadelphia, PA.

Warren, R, Marks Peck, J. (1980). Foreign-Born Emigration from the United States: 1960 to 1970, in: Demography, 17(1): 71-84.

Warren, R., Peck, J. M. (1980) Foreign-born Emigration from the United States: 1960 to 1970, in: Demography, 17(1): 71-84.

Welch, F. (1979). Effects of Cohort Size on Earnings: The Baby Boom Babies' Financial Bust, in: Journal of Political Economy, 87(5): 865-897.

Welch, F. (1999). In Defense of Inequality, in: The American Economic Review, 89(2): 1-17.

White, H. (1980). A Heteroskedasticity-Consistent Covariance Matrix Estimator and a Direct Test for Heteroskedasticity, in: Econometrica, 48(4): 817-838.

White, M. J., Hunter, L. (1993). The Migratory Response of Native-Born Workers to the Presence of Immigrants in the Labor Market, Providence, RI: Brown University.

White, M. J., Liang, Z. (1998). The Effect of Immigration on the Internal Migration of the Native-Born Population, 1981-1990, in: Population Research and Policy Review, 17(2): 141-166.

Willard, K. A. (1994). Broadcasting and Cable Yearbook, 1994, New Providence, NJ: R.R. Bowker Publishers.

Willis, R. J., Rosen, S. (1979). Education and Self-Selection, in: Journal of Political Economy, 87(5): S7-S36.

Wilson, W. J. (1987). The Truly Disadvantaged: The Inner City, the Underclass, and Public Policy, Chicago, IL: University of Chicago Press.

Wolpin, K. (1977). Education and Screening, in: The American Economics Review, 67(5): 949-958.

World Bank (various issues). World Development Report, New York: Oxford University Press.

Wright, R. A., Ellis, M., Reibel, M. (1997). The Linkage between Immigration and Internal Migration in Large Metropolitan Areas in the United States, in: Economic Geography, 73(2): 234-254.

Yezer, A. M. J., Thurston, L. (1976). Migration Patterns and Income Change: Implications for the Human Capital Approach to Migration, in: Southern Economic Journal, 42(4): 693-702.

Zajonc, R. B. (1976). Family Configuration and Intelligence: Variations in Scholastic Aptitude Scores Parallel Trends in Family Size and the Spacing of Children, in: Science, 192(4236): 226-236.

Zavodny, M. (1999). Determinants of Recent Immigrants' Locational Choices, in: International Migration Review, 33(4): 1014-1030.

Zhou, M., Li, Y.-Y. (2003). Ethnic Language Schools and the Development of Supplementary Education in the Immigrant Chinese Community in the United States, in: New Directions for Youth Development: Understanding the Social Worlds of Immigrant Youth, 100: 57-73.

Zimmerman, D. J. (1992a). Intergenerational Mobility and the Transmission of Inequality: An Empirical Study Using Longitudinal Data, Disseration, Princeton University.

Zimmerman, D. J. (1992b). Regression Toward Mediocrity in Economic Stature, in: The American Economic Review, 82(3): 409-429.

Index

About the Authors...

George J. Borjas is the Pforzheimer Professor of Public Policy at the John F. Kennedy School of Government, Harvard University. He is also a Research Associate at the National Bureau of Economic Research and an IZA Research Fellow since March 2000. Professor Borjas received his Ph.D. in economics from Columbia University in 1975. Prior to moving to Harvard in 1995, he was a Professor of Economics at the University of California at San Diego. Borjas has written extensively on labor market issues. He is the author of several books, including *Wage Policy in the Federal Bureaucracy* (1980), *Friends or Strangers: The Impact of Immigrants on the U.S. Economy* (1990), *Labor Economics* (1996; 2000), and *Heaven's Door: Immigration Policy and the American Economy* (1999). He has published over 100 articles in books and scholarly journals, including the American Economic Review, the Journal of Political Economy, and the Quarterly Journal of Economics. Borjas is an editor of the Review of Economics and Statistics, and has been on the editorial boards of the Quarterly Journal of Economics and the International Migration Review. He was a member of Governor Pete Wilson's Council of Economic Advisors (1993–1998), of the National Academy of Sciences Panel on the Demographic and Economic Impact of Immigration (1995–97), and chaired the National Science Foundations Committee of Visitors for the Economics Program (1996). Borjas has also been a consultant to the Office of the Attorney General of the State of California, to the World Bank, and to law firms engaged in employment discrimination litigation. Professor Borjas' research on the economic impact of immigration is widely perceived as playing a central role in the debate over immigration policy in the United States and abroad.

Barry R. Chiswick is Professor and Chair of the Department of Economics at the Columbian College of Arts and Sciences (CCAS), George Washington University (since 2011). Until 2010 he was UIC Distinguished Professor (since 2002) and Research Professor (since 1978) of the Department of Economics, University of Illinois at Chicago (UIC). He was Research Professor in the Department of Sociology and in the Survey Research Laboratory at UIC and Founding Director of the UIC Center for Economic Education (2000). From 2004 until 2011 he was Program Director for Migration Studies at IZA. Chiswick received his Ph.D. with Distinction in Economics from Columbia University (1967) and has held permanent and visiting appointments at UCLA, Columbia University, CUNY, Stanford University, Princeton University, Hebrew University (Jerusalem), Tel Aviv University, University of Haifa, and the University of Chicago. From 1973 to 1977 he was Senior Staff Economist at the President's Council of Economic Advisers. He has been a consultant to numerous U.S. government agencies, as well as to the World Bank and other international organizations. He is currently Associate Editor of the Journal of Population Economics and Research in Economics of the Household, and on the editorial boards of four additional academic journals. Chiswick has an international reputation for his research in Labor Economics, Human Resources, the Economics of Immigration, the Economics of Minorities, the Economics of Language, Economics of Religion, and Income Distribution. He continues to be a leader in the field, whose research has been published in 14 books and monographs and in over 140 scholarly journal articles and chapters in books. His latest book is *The Economics of Language* (with Paul W. Miller, 2007). Chiswick has received numerous awards for his research.

George J. Borjas and **Barry R. Chiswick** received the 2011 IZA Prize in Labor Economics.

...and the Editor

Benjamin Elsner is an Assistant Professor of Economics at University College Dublin. His main research lies at the intersection of labor economics, public economics, and microeconometrics. While in his earlier work he mainly studied the economic impacts of migration, his current research agenda focuses on the determinants of people's investment in human capital and the impact of these investments on life outcomes such as health, educational attainment, and success in the labor market. Before joining UCD, Elsner acted as a Senior Research Associate at IZA in Bonn, where he focused on migration and integration topics. He continues to serve as IZA Deputy Program Co-ordinator of the "Labor Mobility" program area. He is also a research fellow at the Centre for Research and Analysis of Migration (CReAM) and the Geary Institute for Public Policy.